D1789306

# Financial Management and Business Accounting

# Financial Management and Business Accounting

Edited by Terry Ness

LANRYE
INTERNATIONAL
www.clanryeinternational.com

Clanrye International,
750 Third Avenue, 9th Floor,
New York, NY 10017, USA

Copyright © 2018 Clanrye International

This book contains information obtained from authentic and highly regarded sources. Copyright for all individual chapters remain with the respective authors as indicated. All chapters are published with permission under the Creative Commons Attribution License or equivalent. A wide variety of references are listed. Permission and sources are indicated; for detailed attributions, please refer to the permissions page and list of contributors. Reasonable efforts have been made to publish reliable data and information, but the authors, editors and publisher cannot assume any responsibility for the validity of all materials or the consequences of their use.

**Trademark Notice:** Registered trademark of products or corporate names are used only for explanation and identification without intent to infringe.

ISBN: 978-1-63240-688-0


**Cataloging-in-Publication Data**

Financial management and business accounting / edited by Terry Ness.
   p. cm.
Includes bibliographical references and index.
978-1-63240-688-0
1. Business enterprises--Finance. 2. Accounting. 3. Finance--Management. I. Ness, Terry.
HG4026 .F56 2018
658.15--dc23

For information on all Clanrye International publications
visit our website at www.clanryeinternational.com

# Contents

# Preface

Financial study is a vital part of economics. It refers to the study of the assets and liabilities to determine risk and profit of any company or organization. It is further divided into three parts namely personal finance, public finance, and corporate finance. It compliments business accounting by providing figures and analysis of any company's profit and loss and helps in determining the market scenario of the organization. The objective of this book is to give a general view of the different areas of finance management and business accounting, and their applications. Different approaches, evaluations, methodologies and advanced studies have been included in it. This book is a vital tool for all researching and studying this field.

This book is a comprehensive compilation of works of different researchers from varied parts of the world. It includes valuable experiences of the researchers with the sole objective of providing the readers (learners) with a proper knowledge of the concerned field. This book will be beneficial in evoking inspiration and enhancing the knowledge of the interested readers.

In the end, I would like to extend my heartiest thanks to the authors who worked with great determination on their chapters. I also appreciate the publisher's support in the course of the book. I would also like to deeply acknowledge my family who stood by me as a source of inspiration during the project.

**Editor**

# Rand volatility and inflation in South Africa

Azwifaneli Innocentia (Mulaudzi) Nemushungwa [a*]

[a] Department of Economics, University of Venda, South Africa.
[*]Corresponding author's email address: azwifaneli.nemushungwa@univen.ac.za

ARTICLE INFO

ABSTRACT

Keywords:
Consumer prices;
ERPT;
Granger (non-) causality test;
South Africa;
VAR model.

The floating exchange rate regime, coupled with a more open trade policy and the growth in imports, leaves South Africa vulnerable to the effects of exchange rate behaviour on import, producer and consumer prices, which all contribute to inflation. Given the central role that inflation targeting occupies in South Africa's monetary policy, this paper examines the effect of exchange rate shocks on consumer prices using monthly data covering the period January 1994 to December 2013. Consistent with developing countries story, results show a modest exchange rate pass-through to inflation, although inflation is mainly driven by own shocks. The variance decompositions also reveal that foreign exchange rate shocks (REER) contribute relatively more to inflation than money supply shocks (M3). This suggests that South African inflation process is not basically influenced by money supply changes. The practical implication is that that the volatility of the rand is not a serious threat to inflation. The SARB should therefore focus on price stability and not be unduly worried about the volatility of the rand.

## 1.0    Introduction

Since 1980, South Africa has experienced three distinct monetary policy regimes. During the first period (1980 to 1989), monetary policy was not successful in containing inflation. The second period (1990 to 2000) saw a significant improvement in the pursuit of a lower inflation rate. The third period (2000 till present), also sees the South African Reserve Bank (SARB) in pursuit of low inflation. However, unlike during the second period, the SARB is now pursuing an official and explicit inflation target (Burger and Marinkov, 2008).

In February 2000, the South African Reserve Bank announced its aim to adopt an explicit inflation targeting monetary policy as an official target regime. Under this approach, the CPIX (the overall consumer price index, excluding the mortgage interest cost) basket was introduced as the targeted inflation measure, as this excludes the direct impact of monetary policy, namely interest rates. The inflation target aims to achieve a rate of increase in the CPIX of between 3 and 6 percent per year (van der Merwe, 2004).

Unlike in the period of implicit inflation targeting, where the SARB protected both the internal and external value of the rand, with explicit inflation targeting, only the internal value of the rand is protected. This was done with the view that low and stable inflation will, without the need for policy intervention, translate into a stable exchange rate.  In the inflation targeting era, the SARB abandoned its pre-commitment of protecting both the internal value (interest rate parity) and external value of the rand(exchange rate parity).It was only protecting the internal value of the rand, thus the exchange rate was left to be determined by  market forces, making it more volatile (Ncube and Ndou, 2011). The floating exchange rate regime, coupled with a more open trade policy and the growth in imports, leaves South Africa vulnerable to the effects of exchange rate behaviour on import, producer and consumer prices, which all contribute to inflation (SARB, 2001; Karoro, 2008). The transmission of exchange rate fluctuations to import prices, producer prices and finally to consumer prices, is referred to as exchange rate pass-through (Karoro, 2008).

Though there is a large and growing body of empirical literature on the extent and magnitude of ERPT, much focus is on industrialized nations such as the USA, the UK and other members of the European (Woo, 1984; Feinberg, 1989; Goldberg and Knetter 1997; Kim, 1998; Gagnon and Ihrig, 2001; Campa and Goldberg, 2002; Yang et al., 2004 and Campa et al., 2005). Menon (1995) conducted a comprehensive survey of some 43 empirical studies on exchange rate pass-through in both industrialized and developing countries. However, the majority of the surveyed studies focus on the USA. This study will therefore help to deepen literature on developing countries and also to indirectly contribute to the current strong debate on the usefulness of inflation targeting monetary policy framework in South Africa. To this end, this paper analyses the impact of an exchange rate shocks on consumer prices in South Africa, using the Granger (non-) Causality Test, Impulse response functions and Variance decompositions within the Toda and Yamamoto's (1995) VAR procedure. Furthermore, it examines the extent and the speed of the pass through to different prices (and the key drivers thereof) and also determines the causal relationship among variables under review (inflation, real exchange rate, nominal exchange rate, real prime lending rate and money supply).

The rest of the paper is organized as follows: section 2 reviews theoretical and empirical literature. Section 3 present theoretical framework and model specification. In section 4 data sources and time domain are presented. Estimation techniques and empirical results are given in sections 5 and 6. Section 7 contains conclusions. In section 8, policy recommendations are made from conclusion drawn in section 7.

## 2.0    Literature review

### 2.1    Theoretical literature review

There are several possible channels through which exchange rate changes may affect prices (Tandrayen-Ragoobur and Chicooree, 2012). The two main channels of exchange rate pass through are direct channel and indirect channel.

The direct channel stresses that a depreciated exchange rate will imply that imported inputs have become more expensive; consequently there will be a rise in production costs. The higher production costs will then be pushed to local consumers in the form of higher prices. Alternatively, a depreciated exchange rate may also imply that imports of finished goods have become more expensive. Consumers will then have to pay higher prices on imported goods.

The direct channel arises mainly because of the "law of one price" and the purchasing power parity (PPP) in its aggregation. The relative version of PPP claims that, starting from a base of an equilibrium exchange rate between two currencies, the future of the exchange rate between the two currencies will be determined by the relative movements in the price levels in the two countries. For a given import price, changes in the exchange rate will translate directly into higher domestic prices. Therefore,

$$P = E . P^* P$$

Where E is the exchange rate in terms of domestic currency per unit of foreign currency; P* represents the foreign currency price of the imported good and P is the domestic currency price of the imported good. The pass-through is only complete (=100 percent) if:
(a) Markups of prices over costs are constant and
(b) Marginal costs are constant

The indirect channel, on the other hand, stresses that a depreciated exchange rate will result in an increase in local demand for import substitutes, consequently substitute goods will become more expensive and in turn, the general (consumer) price level will increase. A depreciated exchange rate also implies that export prices have become cheaper and as a result there will be an increase in demand for exports. There will therefore be an increase in demand for labour to expand production and in turn the price of labour (wages) will increase. Producers will then be forced to push these higher costs to consumers by charging higher prices to final products.

The indirect channel of exchange rate pass-through arises because of the impact on aggregate demand. A depreciation of the exchange rate makes domestic products relatively cheaper for foreign consumers, and hence, exports and aggregate demand will rise relative to potential output, inducing an increase in the domestic price level. Since nominal wage contracts are fixed in the short run, real wages will decrease and output will eventually increase. However, when real wages return to their original level over time, production costs then increases, the overall price level increases and; output falls. Thus, in the end the exchange rate depreciation leaves a permanent increase in the price level with only a temporary increase in output (Laflèche, 1996).

## 2.2      Empirical literature review

Results on studies conducted for developed countries are conclusive on the idea that low exchange rate pass-through occurs during periods of low inflation.

McCarthy (2000) presents a comprehensive study of exchange rate pass-through on the aggregate level for a number of industrialized countries. Using vector autoregressive (VAR) model and data from 1976 up until 1998, he estimates ERPT to import, producer and consumer-price. In most of the countries analyzed, the exchange rate pass-through to consumer prices is found to be modest. The rate of pass-through is, furthermore, shown to be positively correlated with the openness of the country and with the persistence of and exchange rate change, and negatively correlated with the volatility of the exchange rate. Goldfajn and Werlang (2000) estimate ERPT to consumer prices for 71 countries (both developed and emerging), using panel estimation methods on data from 1980 to 1998. They report that the pass-through effects on consumer prices increase over time and reach a maximum after 12 months. The degree of pass-through is, furthermore, found to be substantially higher in emerging market economies than in developed economies.

Studies conducted on developing countries show contradicting results. Adeyemi and Samuel (2013) using the Variance Decomposition analyses within the framework a structural Vector autoregressive, estimate the pass-through effect of exchange rate changes to consumer prices in Nigeria for the period 1970 to 2008. The results show a substantial large ERPT, although it is incomplete. The findings by Tandrayen-Ragoobur and Chicooree (2012) also show that ERPT to consumer is highest, followed by producer prices, while the ERPT to import prices is lowest. Bwire et al. (2013) examines the degree of exchange rate pass through to inflation in Uganda for the period 1999Q3 to 2012Q2 using vector error correction method (VECM) and structural VAR (SVAR) models. The findings show a modest pass-through to domestic inflation, although incomplete. Ocran (2010), using impulse response functions and variance decompositions within the framework of unrestricted VAR that incorporates a distribution chain, examines the degree of ERPT to import, producer and consumer prices in South Africa for the period 2001:1 to 2009:5. The results show that ERPT to producer prices is modest (at 19 percent) and very modest to consumer prices (at 13 percent).

## 3.0      Estimation techniques

### 3.1      Theoretical framework

The model by Macfarlane (2002) is one of the earliest theories that examine the link between exchange rate volatility and consumer price inflation. It focuses on the influence of the *direct* channel of pass-through. In this context the pass-through relation can be expressed simply by the PPP relation in logs i.e.

$$p = \beta p^* + \lambda e \dots\dots\dots\dots\dots\dots\dots\dots\dots\dots\dots\dots\dots\dots\dots\dots\dots \quad (1)$$

Where $p$ *is the* log *of* the general (consumer) price level, $p*$ is the log of the foreign price and; $e$ is the log of exchange rate.
The "law of one price" implies that $\beta = \lambda = 1$ in which case changes in the exchange rate completely pass through to the domestic price of the traded good.

### 3.2      Model specification

This study uses a modified version of Parsely and Popper (1998) and Macfarlane (2002) models, which embrace the Central Bank's behaviour, by including base money and interest rates. The present study uses M3 money supply as a proxy of base money. The model is presented as follows:

$$p = \beta p^* + \lambda_1 e_t + \lambda_2 m3_t + \lambda_3 r_t \dots\dots\dots\dots\dots\dots\dots\dots\dots\dots\dots\dots\dots \quad (2)$$

Where $m3_t$ is the broad money supply and; $r_t$ is the rate of interest.

Central banks that target consumer price inflation will try to insulate prices from exchange rate movements. Neglecting the behaviour of policy variables may distort the true consequences of exchange rate variations on consumer prices. By including policy variables, the observed relationship between prices and exchange rates would take into account the central bank's behaviour rather than the direct influence of exchange rates on prices (McFarlane, 2002).

## 4.0    Data sources and time domain

The data consists of 240 monthly observations, covering the period from 1994m1 to 2013m12. The sample period is long enough to enable one to carry out proper cointegration analysis. The sample span is chosen so as to include both the period of single managed floating (1995 to January 2000) and an independently floating exchange rate regime (February 2000 till present).The beginning of the sample corresponds with the launch of the first South African Democratic government in 1994.

The data used are obtainable from the South African Reserve Bank (SARB) online database. The variables include foreign price (p*) is proxied by foreign exchange rate (REER), that is the real value of the rand against its 15 major trading partners. The real exchange rate is used to absorb external (foreign) shocks. Nominal effective exchange rate (NEER) is the proxy for the exchange rate. It is calculated as the trade weighted average of the country's exchange rate against other currencies and it was chosen as a measure of the exchange rate rather than the bilateral exchange rate, because countries engage in trade with more than one country, implying that one should consider not only how changes in the bilateral rate affects prices, but how changes in the currency against the currencies of its major trade partners affect consumer prices. The index therefore represents the ratio of the rand's period average exchange rate to a weighted geometric average of exchange rates of the currencies of South Africa's fifteen main trading partners. The NEER series is measured in foreign currency terms, thus an increase in this variable indicates an appreciation of the rand, while a decrease indicates depreciation thereof. The consumer price Index (CPI) is the core inflation. It is also expressed as an index. It excludes certain items that face volatile price movements. It therefore, eliminates products that can have temporary price shocks as these shocks can diverge from the overall inflation trend and give a false measure of inflation. The real prime lending rate (RPRIMRATE) is used as a proxy for the short-term interest rate. The choice of the prime rate is based on the assumption that, the series for the Central Banks repurchase rate only started in the eleventh month of 1999. The real prime lending rate is used as it is closely linked with the policy rate. Money supply (M3) is used as a proxy for base money supply. It is simply the broadly defined money supply. The seasonally adjusted time series for M3 money supply were used. Money supply and real prime lending rate are used to absorb monetary shocks.

## 5.0    Estimation techniques

### 5.1    Toda and Yamamoto (1995)'s VAR procedure

It is an improved Granger causality procedure. Unlike Johansen (1990) cointegration procedure, Toda and Yamamoto's (1995) VAR procedure or simply T-Y VAR, is a methodology of statistical inference, which makes parameter estimation valid even when the VAR system is not co-integrated.

#### 5.1.1    Stationarity test

The first step in conducting Toda and Yamamoto (1995) procedure is testing each of the time-series to determine their order of integration, using stationarity test. The theory behind autoregressive moving average (ARMA) estimation is based on stationary time series. A series is said to be stationary if the mean and auto-covariance of the series do not depend on time.

A common example of a non-stationary series is the *random walk*:

$$y_t = y_{t-1} + \varepsilon_t \dots\dots\dots\dots\dots\dots\dots\dots\dots\dots\dots\dots\dots\dots\dots\dots \quad (3)$$

where, $\varepsilon_t$ is a stationary random disturbance term. The series $y$ has a constant forecast value, conditional on $t$, and the variance is increasing over time. The random walk is a difference stationary series since the first difference of $y$ is stationary:

$$y_t - y_{t-1} = (1 = L)_{yt} = \varepsilon_t \dots\dots\dots\dots\dots\dots\dots\dots\dots\dots\dots\dots\dots \quad (4)$$

A difference stationary series is said to be *integrated* and is denoted as I ($d$) where $d$ is the order of integration. The order of integration is the number of unit roots contained in the series, or the number of differencing operations it takes to make the series stationary. For the random walk above, there is one unit root, so it is an $I(1)$ series. Similarly, a stationary series is $I(0)$.

Standard inference procedures do not apply to regressions which contain an integrated dependent variable or integrated regressors. Therefore, it is important to check whether a series is stationary or not before using it in a regression. The formal method to test the stationarity of a series is the unit root test.

There is a variety of tests used to test for the presence of unit root. Amongst them are the Augmented Dickey-Fuller (1979) and Phillips-Perron (1988), the GLS-detrended Dickey-Fuller (Elliot, Rothenberg, and Stock, 1996), Kwiatkowski, Phillips, Schmidt, and Shin (KPSS, 1992), Elliott, Rothenberg, and Stock Point Optimal (ERS, 1996), and Ng and Perron (NP, 2001) unit root tests. This study uses the Augmented Dickey-Fuller (ADF) and Phillips-Perron (PP) test.

## A. The Augmented Dickey-Fuller (ADF) test

The standard Dickey Fuller test is carried out by estimating the following equation:

$$\Delta Y_t = \propto Y_{t-1} + X_t' \delta + e_t \dots\dots\dots (5)$$

Where,

$$\propto = p - 1.$$

The null and alternative hypotheses may be written as,

$$H_0 : \propto = 0 \ \text{(null hypothesis)} \dots\dots\dots (6)$$

$$H_1 = \propto = 1 \ \text{(alternative hypothesis)} \dots\dots\dots (7)$$

The simple Dickey-Fuller unit root test described above is valid only if the series is an AR (1) process. If the series is correlated at higher order lags, the assumption of white noise disturbances $\varepsilon_t$ is violated. The Augmented Dickey-Fuller (ADF) test therefore constructs a parametric correction for higher-order correlation by assuming that the $y$ series follows a AR($p$) process and adding $p$ lagged difference terms of the dependent variable $y$ to the right-hand side of the test regression. This is presented as follows:

$$\Delta y_t = \propto y_{t-1} + x_t' \delta + \beta \Delta y_{t-1} + \beta_1 \Delta y_{t-1} + \beta_2 \Delta y_{t-2} + \beta_p \Delta y_{t-p} + V_t \dots\dots\dots (8)$$

There are two practical issues in performing an ADF test. Firstly, one should choose whether to include exogenous variables in the test regression. Therefore, one has the choice of including a constant, a constant and a linear time trend, or neither in the test regression. One approach would be to run the test with both a constant and a linear trend since the other two cases are just special cases of this more general specification. However, including irrelevant regressors in the regression will reduce the power of the test to reject the null of a unit root.
Secondly, one will have to specify the number of lagged difference terms (the lag length) to be added to the test regression (0 yields the standard DF test, whereas integers greater than 0 correspond to ADF tests). The usual (though not particularly useful) advice is to include a number of lags sufficient to remove serial correlation in the residuals.

## B. The Phillips-Perron (PP) test

Phillips and Perron (1988) developed a number of unit root tests that have become popular in the analysis of financial time series. The Phillips-Perron (PP) unit root tests differ from the ADF tests mainly in how they deal with serial correlation and heteroskedasticity in the errors. In particular, where the ADF tests use a parametric autoregression to approximate the ARMA structure of the errors in the test regression, the PP tests ignore any serial correlation in the test regression.It is therefore, an alternative (nonparametric) method of controlling for serial correlation when testing for a unit root.

When performing the PP test, one should also choose whether to include a constant, a constant and a linear time trend, or neither, in the test regression.

The test regression for the PP tests is: It is therefore

$$\Delta Y_t = \beta^1 D_t + \pi Y_{t-1} + \mu_t \dots\dots\dots (9)$$

The Augmented Dickey-Fuller (ADF) test and the Phillips-Perron test have a null hypothesis of a unit root process of the form:

$$y_t = y_{t-1} + c + \delta t + \varepsilon_t, \dots\dots\dots\dots\dots\dots\dots\dots\dots\dots\dots\dots\dots\dots \quad (10)$$

which the functions test against an alternative model

$$y_t = \gamma y_{t-1} + c + \delta t + \varepsilon_t, \dots\dots\dots\dots\dots\dots\dots\dots\dots\dots\dots\dots \quad (11)$$

where $\gamma < 1$. The null and alternative models for a Dickey-Fuller test are like those for a Phillips-Perron test. The ADF extends the model with extra parameters accounting for serial correlation among the innovations:

$$y_t = c + \delta t + \gamma y_{t-1} + \phi_1 \Delta y_{t-1} + \phi_2 \Delta y_{t-2} + \dots + \phi_p \Delta y_{t-p} + \varepsilon_t, \dots\dots\dots \quad (12)$$

where
- $L$ is the lag operator: $Ly_t = y_{t-1}$.
- $\Delta = 1 - L$, so $\Delta y_t = y_t - y_{t-1}$.
- $\varepsilon_t$ is the innovations process, whereas, Phillips-Perron adjusts the test statistics to account for serial correlation.

  There are three alternatives of both ADF test and PP test, corresponding to the following values of the 'model' parameter:
- 'AR' assumes $c$ and $\delta$, which appear in the preceding equations, are both 0; the 'AR' alternative has mean 0.
- 'ARD' assumes $\delta$ is 0. The 'ARD' alternative has mean $c/(1-\gamma)$.
- 'TS' makes no assumption about $c$ and $\delta$.

## C.  KPSS test

The KPSS test is an inverse of the Phillips-Perron test: it reverses the null and alternative hypotheses. The KPSS test uses the model:

$$y_t = c_t + \delta t + u_t, \text{ with}$$

$$c_t = c_{t-1} + v_t.$$

Here $u_t$ is a stationary process, and $v_t$ is an i.i.d. process with mean 0 and variance $\sigma^2$. The null hypothesis is that $\sigma^2 = 0$, so that the random walk term $c_t$ becomes a constant intercept. The alternative is $\sigma^2 > 0$, which introduces the unit root in the random walk, where:

$\mu_t$ is I (0) and may be heteroskedastic.

The PP tests correct for any serial correlation and heteroskedasticity in the errors $u_t$ of the test regression by directly modifying the test statistics:
$t_\pi = 0$ and $t_\pi^{\wedge}$ .

### 5.1.2   Selection of lag-length criteria

The next step is determining the appropriate maximum lag length for the variables in the VAR. According to Brooks (2002: 335) financial theory has little to say on what an appropriate lag length used for a VAR model should be and how long changes in the variables should persist to work through the system. However, the optimal lag length selected should produce the number and form of co-integration relations that conform to all the *a priori* knowledge associated with economic theory (Seddighi *et al.* 2000: 309).

Three most popular information criteria (ICs) used to determine optimal lag length are the Akaike (1974) information criterion (AIC), Schwarz's (1978) Bayesian information criterion (SBIC) and the Hannan-Quinn information criterion (HQIC). However, these information criteria sometimes produce conflicting vector autoregressive (VAR) order selections.

The VAR model is illustrated in the following manner:

$$y_t = \beta_0 + \beta_1 t^1 + \dots \beta_q t^q + \eta^q \dots\dots\dots\dots\dots\dots\dots\dots\dots\dots \quad (13)$$

Where $\{\eta_t\}$ sequence is a vector autoregression with k lag length and it can be presented as:

$$\eta_t = J_1 \eta_{t-1} + \dots J_k \eta_{t-k} + \varepsilon_t \dots\dots\dots\dots\dots\dots\dots\dots\dots \quad (14)$$

It is assumed that k is the optimal lag length and $\varepsilon_t$ is random vector.

Accordingly, the null hypothesis is to jointly test vector J:

$$H_0: J_1 = J_2 = \ldots J_k = 0 \ldots\ldots\ldots\ldots\ldots\ldots\ldots\ldots\ldots\ldots\ldots\ldots\ldots\ldots\ldots \quad (15)$$

### 5.1.3 Diagnostic tests

The next step is making sure that the VAR is well-specified. This is done by conducting diagnostic tests. Diagnostic checks for serial correlation, normality and heteroskedasticity are then performed on the residuals from the VAR. These tests are most often used to detect model misspecification and as a guide for model improvement (Norat, 2005) and aid in the validation of the parameter estimation outcomes achieved by the model (Karoro, 2007).The tests include serial correlation test, heteroskedasticity test and normality test.

### A. Testing for serial correlation

Testing for serial correlation helps to identify any relationships that may exist between the current values of the regression residuals ($\mu_t$) and any of its lagged values (Brooks, 2002). Such tests can be done via graphical exploration or by using formal statistical tests such as the Durbin-Watson test or the Lagrange Multiplier (LM) test. Although the first step in testing for autocorrelation would be to plot the residuals and look for any patterns, graphical methods may not be easy to interpret (Brooks, 2002). In this study, the LM test is used to investigate residual serial correlation. According to Harris (1995), the lag order for the LM test should be the same as lag order chosen for the VAR. The null hypothesis of the LM test is that the residuals are not serially correlated, while the alternative is that the residuals are serially correlated.

### B. Testing for heteroskedasticity

According to Brooks, (2002: 445), heteroskedasticity describes a scenario where the variance of the errors in a model is not constant. Thus a problem arises when errors are heteroscedastic but are assumed to be homoscedastic (constant variance). The result of such an assumption would be that the standard error estimates might be wrong (Brooks, 2002: 445). In this study, the test for heteroscedasticity is done using an extension of White's (1980) test to systems of equations. The null hypothesis of the test is that the errors are homoscedastic and independent of the regressors, and that there is no problem of misspecification. In performing the test, each of the cross products of the residuals is regressed on the cross products of the regressors, testing for the joint significance of the regression. If the test statistic produced from this process is significant, the null hypothesis of homoscedasticity (no heteroscedasticity) and no misspecification will be rejected.

### C. Testing for normality

In this study, the Jarque-Bera normality test is used to ascertain whether the regression errors are normally distributed. Under the null hypothesis of normally distributed errors, the test statistic has a Chi-Square distribution with two degrees of freedom (Brooks, 2002: 181). Thus, if the Jarque-Bera statistic is not significant, that is, the p-value is greater than 0.05, then the null of normality is not rejected at the 5 percent level of significance (Brooks, 2002: 181).

### 5.1.4 Granger (non-) causality test

According to the concept of Granger's causality test (Granger, 1969; 1988), a time series $x_t$ Granger-causes another time series $y_t$ if series $y_t$ can be predicted with better accuracy by using past values of $x_t$ rather than by not doing so, other information is being identical.

We can test for the absence of Granger causality by estimating the following VAR model:

In the case of two time-series variables, $X$ and $Y$:

$$Y_t = a_0 + a_1 Y_{t-1} + \ldots a_p Y_{t-p} + b_1 X_{t-1} + \ldots b_p X_{t-p} + \mu_1 \ldots\ldots\ldots\ldots\ldots\ldots (16)$$

$$X_t = c_0 + c_1 X_{t-1} + \ldots c_p X_{t-p} + d_1 Y_{t-1} + \ldots d_p Y_{t-p} + \mu_2 \ldots\ldots\ldots\ldots\ldots (17)$$

Then, testing $H_0 : b_1 = b_2 = \cdots . b_p$ against the alternative hypothesis:

$H_A:' Not\ H_0'$ is a test that $X$ does not Granger-cause $Y$.

Similarly, testing $H_0 : d_1 = d_2 = \cdots . d_p$ against the alternative hypothesis:

$H_A$:' Not $H_0$' is a test that Y *does not* Granger-cause X.

In each case, a *rejection* of the null implies there is Granger causality (Giles, 2011).

## 5.2    Impulse response and variance decomposition

The second-stage of ERPT is analyzed by estimating the impulse responses and variance decompositions of consumer prices to shocks from exchange rate changes. These tests are important in determining whether changes in the exchange rate has a positive or negative effect on the consumer prices, determining how long it would take for that effect to work through the system, as well as establishing the variables in the model that have a significant impact on the future values of each of the other variables in the system (Brooks, 2002).

### 5.2.1    Impulse response function

An impulse response can be described as a shock to the *i-th* variable that not only affects the *i-th* variable directly, but is also transmitted to all the other endogenous variables through the dynamic (lag) structure of the VAR. Impulse responses determine the responsiveness of the dependent variables in the VAR to fluctuations of each of the other variables (Brooks, 2002; Elder, 2003:1). Thus, for each variable from each equation, a unit shock to the error is analyzed in order to determine the effects upon the VAR system over time (Brooks 2002). In the case of this study, the impulse response function will be able to reveal the sign, size and persistence of shocks from the exchange rate to consumer prices. Two approaches are commonly used in econometrics literature to estimate impulse responses. These are the generalized impulse response and the Cholesky decomposition. The main advantage of the generalized impulse response is that it does not require orthogonalization of innovations and is invariant of the ordering of the variables in VAR (Pesaran and Shin, 1998: 17 in Aziakpono, 2006: 8).

However, similar to Kiptui *et al.* (2005), this study uses the Cholesky decomposition because, unlike other approaches, it incorporates a small sample degrees of freedom adjustment when estimating the residual covariance matrix used to derive the Cholesky factor (Lutkepohl, 1991).

### 5.2.2    Variance decomposition

Variance decompositions highlight the proportion of the movements in the dependent variables which are a result of their own shocks, versus shocks from the other variables. Brooks (2002: 342) notes that in practice, self or own series shocks explain most of the (forecast) error variance of the series in a VAR.

## 6.0    Empirical tests results

### 6.1    Unit root tests

We use the traditional Augmented Dickey-Fuller test, supplemented by the Phillips-Peron (PP) tests which are structured under the null hypothesis of a unit root against stationarity alternative to check for the unit root in each variable and thereby determine the order of integration. Both tests indicate that some the variables are stationary at levels, that is, they are integrated of order 0 or *I (0)*, whereas others are stationary after first differencing, which I (1) is.

In this chapter, assumption 1 was selected, which presupposes that there is no deterministic trend but intercept in the data. Therefore, unit root tests shows the results of the variables with intercept only.

Table 1: Augmented Dickey Fuller test

| Variable | 5% calculated t-statistic(at level) | t*value (at level) | 5% calculated t-statistic I (1) | t*value $I$(1) |
|---|---|---|---|---|
| CPI | -2.874 | -4.958*I(0)* | -2.874 | -6.460*I(1)* |
| NEER | -1.339 | -2.873*I(0)* | -2.873 | -15.296*I(1)* |
| M3 | -2.874 | 1.927 | -2.874 | -10.621*I(1)* |
| Rprimrate | -2.873 | -1.339 | -2.874 | -9.819*I(1)* |
| FOIL | -2.461 | -2.874*I(0)* | -6.460 | -2.874 |

Table 2: Phillips-Perron test

| Variable | 5% calculated t-statistic (at level) | t*value (at level) | 5% calculated t-statistic I (1) | t*value $I$(1) |
|---|---|---|---|---|
| CPI | -2.873 | -13.428 I(0) | -2.873 | -8.621I(1) |

| NEER | -2.873 | -13.691 I(0) | -2.873 | -23.756I(1) |
|------|--------|--------------|--------|-------------|
| M3 | -2.873 | -1.117 | -2.873 | -29.6701(1) |
| rprimrate | -2.873 | -3.249 I(0) | -2.873 | -8.621 I(1) |
| FOIL | -2.873 | -103.469 *I(0)* | -2.873 | -13.691 I(1) |

## 6.2 Selection of lag order criterion

The LR, FPE and AIC indicate lag order selection at level 4, whereas SC and HQ selects lag 2, which is lower. The Akaike Information Criterion (AIC) and Schwarz Information Criterion (SC) are the two commonly used criteria as they give appropriate lag order. Lag 2 is therefore selected in this study, as it is selected by the Schwarz criteria (SC) and is the lowest selected lag order.

Table 3: VAR lag order selection criteria

| Lag | LogL | LR | FPE | AIC | SC | HQ |
|-----|------|-----|-----|-----|-----|-----|
| 0 | -5503.693 | NA | 2.90e+14 | 47.48873 | 47.56301 | 47.51869 |
| 1 | -4330.572 | 2285.564 | 1.46e+10 | 37.59113 | 38.03683 | 37.77088 |
| 2 | -4204.737 | 239.7360 | 6.11e+09 | 36.72187 | 37.53899* | 37.05141* |
| 3 | -4175.756 | 53.96581 | 5.91e+09 | 36.68755 | 37.87608 | 37.16687 |
| 4 | -4148.979 | 48.70576* | 5.82e+09* | 36.67223* | 38.23218 | 37.30134 |
| 5 | -4132.596 | 29.09360 | 6.29e+09 | 36.74652 | 38.67788 | 37.52542 |
| 6 | -4111.432 | 36.67226 | 6.52e+09 | 36.77959 | 39.08236 | 37.70827 |
| 7 | -4095.074 | 27.64007 | 7.06e+09 | 36.85408 | 39.52828 | 37.93256 |
| 8 | -4087.581 | 12.33665 | 8.26e+09 | 37.00501 | 40.05062 | 38.23327 |

* indicates lag order selected by the criterion
LR: sequential modified LR test statistic (each test at 5% level); FPE: Final prediction error; AIC: Akaike information criterion; SC: Schwarz information criterion; HQ: Hannan-Quinn information criterion.

## 6.3 Diagnostic tests

### a. AR Roots

The reported inverse roots of the AR polynomial have roots with modulus less than one and lie inside the unit circle, indicating that the estimated VAR is stable (stationary). This is a very favorable result because if the VAR were not stable, certain results, such as impulse response standard errors, would not be valid making the model results and conclusions questionable.

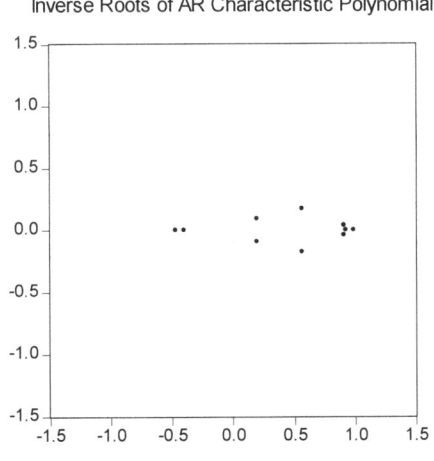

Inverse Roots of AR Characteristic Polynomial

Figure 1: AR Roots

### b. Serial Autocorrelation test and normality test

Most of the p-values are greater than 0.05 at the 5% level of significance, therefore we cannot reject the null hypothesis that the residuals are not serial correlated. Thus, we conclude that misspecification does not exist, that is the model is well specified. In case of normality test as the p-value of the Jacque-Bera test is less than 0.05, we therefore reject the null hypothesis that normal distribution does not occur. Therefore, there is normal distribution.

Table 4: Serial Autocorrelation LM test and normality test

| Panel A: Autocorrelation LM test | | | Panel B: Jarque-Bera test | | | |
|---|---|---|---|---|---|---|
| Ho: No serial correlation at lag order. | | | | | | |
| Lags | LM-Stat | Prob | Component | Jarque-Bera | df | Prob. |
| | | | 1 | 47.47232 | 2 | 0.0000 |
| 1 | 62.88407 | 0.0000 | 2 | 30883.61 | 2 | 0.0000 |
| 2 | 55.52037 | 0.0004 | 3 | 28.58675 | 2 | 0.0000 |
| 3 | 33.47199 | 0.1197 | 4 | 337.2948 | 2 | 0.0000 |
| 4 | 20.23011 | 0.7347 | 5 | 192.5373 | 2 | 0.0000 |
| 5 | 38.86774 | 0.0380 | Joint | 31489.50 | 10 | 0.0000 |
| 6 | 25.45159 | 0.4373 | | | | |
| 7 | 28.54878 | 0.2832 | | | | |
| 8 | 32.84909 | 0.1349 | | | | |
| Probs from chi-square with 25 df. | | | | | | |

## 6.4   Granger (non-) causality test

The results from table 9 show a unidirectional causality, running from M3 to CPI, from NEER to CPI and from REER and CPI. The causal relationship between NEER and CPI and between REER and CPI reflects the presence of exchange rate pass through to consumer inflation.

Table 5: Results of Granger causality between CPI and selected variables (M3, RPRIMRATE AND REER)

| Direction of Causality | Chi-sq | (df) | Prob. |
|---|---|---|---|
| NEER does not Granger cause CPI | 5.130914 | 2 | 0.0769 |
| CPI does not Granger cause NEER | 0.900986 | 2 | 0.6373 |
| M3 does not Granger cause CPI | 5.526629 | 2 | 0.0631 |
| CPI does not Granger cause M3 | 1.199259 | 2 | 0.5490 |
| RPRIMRATE does not Granger cause CPI | 0.907484 | 2 | 0.6352 |
| CPI does not Granger cause RPRIMRATE | 49.39967 | 2 | 0.0000 |
| REER does not Granger cause CPI | 5.734570 | 2 | 0.0569 |
| CPI does not Granger cause REER | 0.289661 | 2 | 0.8652 |

## 6.5   Impulse response function (IRF) and variance decomposition

The Table below shows the response of price to a *structural* one standard deviation shock to each of the variables. According to the table, the immediate effect of a shock to money supply (M3) at month 8 is about 19 percent increase in the price level. . The results are consistent with that of Ocran (2010), which also reveal that ERPT to consumer prices was about 13 percent for the period 1998m1 to 2009m5. However, the effect of exchange rate shock (REER) is modest, at about 22 percent. The results show low average pass-through for nominal than for real shocks.

Consistent with the IRFs discussed above, the results of variance decomposition show that  foreign exchange rate (REER) contribute relatively more to inflation (about 44 percent) than money supply shocks (M3), at about 38 percent. This suggests that South African inflation is not basically influenced by money supply changes. Specifically, while money supply shocks account for only 0.6 to 42 percent of the variations of the price level, exchange rate changes and interest rate account for about 0.8 to 54 percent at the same horizon respectively.

Table 6: Impulse response function

| Period | CPI | NEER | M3 | RPRIMRATE | REER |
|---|---|---|---|---|---|
| 1 | 0.545741 | 0.000000 | 0.000000 | 0.000000 | 0.000000 |
| 2 | 0.810116 | 0.003656 | 0.021787 | 0.013868 | -0.056549 |
| 3 | 0.901487 | -0.000165 | 0.108580 | 0.021752 | -0.111143 |
| 4 | 0.900674 | 0.003637 | 0.161794 | 0.024088 | -0.164740 |
| 5 | 0.850391 | 0.008225 | 0.195271 | 0.019897 | -0.198049 |
| 6 | 0.779533 | 0.017751 | 0.206049 | 0.011330 | -0.217822 |
| 7 | 0.702714 | 0.027840 | 0.203268 | 0.000380 | -0.224779 |
| 8 | 0.628129 | 0.038646 | 0.192083 | -0.011118 | -0.224311 |
| 9 | 0.559018 | 0.048434 | 0.176891 | -0.021955 | -0.218808 |
| 10 | 0.496515 | 0.057078 | 0.160355 | -0.031442 | -0.210781 |

Table 7: Variance decomposition

| Period | S.E. | CPI | NEER | M3 | RPRIMRATE | REER |
|---|---|---|---|---|---|---|
| 1 | 0.545741 | 100.0000 | 0.000000 | 0.000000 | 0.000000 | 0.000000 |
| 2 | 0.978774 | 99.59518 | 0.001395 | 0.049548 | 0.020074 | 0.333799 |
| 3 | 1.339886 | 98.41287 | 0.000746 | 0.683129 | 0.037066 | 0.866184 |
| 4 | 1.631079 | 96.90261 | 0.001001 | 1.444947 | 0.046822 | 1.604625 |
| 5 | 1.860484 | 95.37120 | 0.002723 | 2.212180 | 0.047425 | 2.366471 |
| 6 | 2.039465 | 93.97591 | 0.009842 | 2.861663 | 0.042552 | 3.110037 |
| 7 | 2.178496 | 92.76871 | 0.024956 | 3.378667 | 0.037297 | 3.790374 |
| 8 | 2.286748 | 91.73845 | 0.051211 | 3.771921 | 0.036213 | 4.402203 |
| 9 | 2.371437 | 90.85996 | 0.089332 | 4.063728 | 0.042245 | 4.944736 |
| 10 | 2.438161 | 90.10202 | 0.139314 | 4.276904 | 0.056595 | 5.425170 |

## 7.0 Conclusion

This chapter analyzed the impact of exchange rate volatility on inflation (exchange rate pass-through to prices) in South Africa for the period 1994m1 to 2013m12, using Granger (non-) causality test within the framework of Toda-Yamamoto (1995) VAR procedure. Impulse response functions and variance decomposition of consumer prices to shocks from exchange rate changes are also estimated.

The results from Granger causality test show a unidirectional causality, running from M3 to CPI, from NEER to CPI and from REER and CPI. The causal relationship between NEER and CPI and between REER and CPI reflects the presence of exchange rate pass through to consumer inflation. The IRFs results show that ERPT to consumer prices was modest during the period under review. The immediate effect of a shock to the exchange rate (REER) at month 8 is about 0.22 (22 percent) increase in the price level. This is consistent with literature on developed countries, which suggest that exchange rate pass-through (ERPT) in an environment of low inflation is more subdued. Since the implementation of inflation targeting monetary policy in February 2000, the South African Reserve Bank was able to contain inflation within the target range most of the times.

Consistent with other studies for developing countries, the variance decomposition results show a modest exchange rate pass-through to inflation, although inflation is mainly driven by own shocks. This is consistent with Bwire *et, al.* (2013). The variance decompositions also reveal that foreign exchange rate shocks (REER) contribute relatively more to inflation than money supply shocks (M3).This suggests that South African inflation process is not basically influenced by money supply changes.

## 8.0 Policy recommendations

Low pass-through into consumer prices has important policy implication for the adoption of inflation targeting by the South African Reserve Bank. Floating exchange rate system is the requirement for a well- functioning inflation targeting regime because in a world of capital mobility, independent monetary policy cannot coexist with a pegged exchange rate regime.

The adoption of flexible exchange rate regime in mid-1990's, in conjunction with inflation targeting monetary policy in 2000 has raised question of exchange rate volatility and resulting fear of exchange rate pass-through into consumer price inflation. Therefore, the evidence of low inflation regime since 2000 and the associated low ERPT for the period under review support the adoption of an inflation targeting regime in South Africa. This implies that the volatility of the rand does not pose any serious threat to inflation. It is therefore suggested that the SARB focus on its commitment to protect he internal value of the rand (price stability) and allow the rand to float freely. As foreign exchange rate shocks contribute relatively more to inflation than money supply shocks, this implies that money supply changes have insignificant impact on inflation in South Africa. There is therefore no need for monetary surveillance in South Africa.

The present study only focuses on ERPT to consumer prices and ignores other types of inflation (import and producer prices).From the third quarter of 2012 to early 2014, the country witnessed a significant decline in exports due to the ongoing labour unrest, which led to production stoppage in mines. Consequently, many mines were forced to shut down, consequently, a sharp drop in exports occurred. A decline in exports implied that the country had to depend on imports. Consequently, import prices surged relative to export prices. The present framework that we proposed can be extended to incorporate import and producer prices. Another interesting avenue of future research would be to conduct a model of two disaggregated periods (pre-2000 and post-2000).

## References

An, L, (2006). Exchange rate pass-through: Evidence based on Vector Auto regression with sign restrictions. Munich Personal RePEc Archive. [Online]. Available:

Aron et al.(2012). 'Exchange Rate Pass-through to Import Prices, and Monetary Policy in South Africa,' South African Reserve Bank, WP/12/08.South African Reserve Bank Working Paper, Research Department .September 2012.

Bhundia, A. (2002). "An Empirical Investigation of Exchange Rate Pass-through in South Africa." IMF Working Paper 165.

Bwire, T et al.(2013).Exchange rate Pass-through to Domestic Prices Research Department Bank of Uganda .March 2013 Working Paper Series .Working Paper No. 05/2013

Campa, J. M. and L. S. Goldberg (2005). "Exchange Rate Pass-through into Import Prices." The Review of Economics and Statistics 87(4).

Campa, J., and L. Goldberg, 2002, "Exchange Rate Pass-through into Import Prices: Macro or Micro Phenomenon?" IESE Business School University of Navarra Research Paper No. 475(Barcelona: Centro Internacional de Investigación Financiera).

Campa, J., and L. Goldberg, 2006, "Distribution Margins, Imported Inputs, and the Sensitivity of the CPI to Exchange Rates," NBER working paper no. 12121.

Chaoudhri, E. and D. Hakura (2001). "Exchange Rate Pass-through to Domestic Price: Does Inflation Environment Matter." IMF Working Paper 01/194.

Cheikh, B  and Louhichi, W. (2013).The Exchange Rate Pass-Through in a Cointegrated VAR Model, ESSCA School of Management, PRES UNAM. October 2013

Choudhri, E and Hakura, D.(2006). Exchange Rate Pass-Through to Domestic Prices:\Does the Inflationary Environment Matter? Journal of International Money and Finance,25: 614-639.

Coricelli, F, et al. (2006). Exchange rate pass-through in EMU acceding countries: Empirical analysis and policy implications. Journal of Banking & Finance, 30: 1375 - 1391.

Corsetti, G. and Dedola, L. (2005), "The Macroeconomics of International Price Discrimination." *Journal of International Economics*, Vol. 67, pp. 129-155.

Devereux, Engel and Tille (1999) Exchange Rate Pass-Through and the Welfare Effects of the Euro," NBER Working Papers 7382.

Devereux, M. B and J. Yetman, (2003) Price Setting and Exchange Rate Pass-Through: Theory and Evidence. Hong Kong, School of Economics & Finance the University of Hong Kong.

Devereux, M. B. and C. Engel (2001). "Endogenous Currency of Price Setting in a Dynamic Open Economy Model." NBER Working Paper w8559. ---(2003). "Monetary Policy in the Open Economy Revisited: Price Setting and Exchange-Rate Flexibility." The Review of Economic Studies 70: 765-783.

Dornbush, R. (1987), Exchange rates and prices, *American Economic Review* 77, 93-106.

Gagnon, J. and Ihrig, J. (2004), "Monetary Policy and Exchange Rate Pass-Through."*International Journal of Finance and Economics*, Vol. 9, pp. 315-338.

Gagnon, J. E. and  Ihrig, J. (2001). 'Monetary Policy and Exchange Rate Pass-Through.' Federal Reserve System, International Finance Discussion Paper No.704.

Goldberg, P. K. and M. M. Knetter (1997). "Goods Prices and Exchange Rates: What Have We Learned?" Journal of Economic Literature 35(3): 1243.Government of Ghana (1998) Ghana — Enhanced Structural Adjustment Facility Economic and Financial Policy Framework Paper, 1998–2000,

Goldfajn, I and S. R. C.Werlang (2000), "The Pass Through from Depreciation to Inflation: A Panel Study",Working Paper No. 423 (Rio de Janeiro: Department of Economics, Pacifica UniversiadadeCatolica)

Gueorguiev, N. 2003, "Exchange Rate Pass Through in Romania", IMF Working Paper No. 03/130 (Washington: International Monetary Fund).

Hahn, E. (2003), "Pass-Through of External Shocks to Euro Area Inflation." ECB Working Paper 243

http://mpra.ub.uni-muenchen.de/527/. [Accessed 10 October 2009].

http://mpra.uh.uni-muenchen.de/21115/. [Accessed 24 March 2010].

http://www. imf.org/external/pubs/ft/wp/2006/wp061S0.pdf. [Accessed 24 April 2010].

http://www.imf.org/external/np/pfp/ghana/ghana0.htm, IMF.

Ihing J. Marnass, M. and Rothenberg A., 2006. *Exchange Rate Pass-through in the G. 7 countries. International finance discussion paper NO. 851*, Federal Reserve Board of Governors

Jaffri, A.A. (2010).Exchange Rate Pass-through to Consumer Prices in Pakistan: Does Misalignment Matter? The Pakistan Development Review, 49: 1 (Spring 2010) pp. 19–35

Karoro, T. D. et al. (2009). "Exchange Rate Pass-through to Import Prices in South Africa: Is There Asymmetry?" *South African Journal of Economics* 773:380–398.

Karoro, T.A (2007). An analysis of exchange rate pass-through to prices in South Africa, Department of Economics and Economic History, Rhodes University, Graham's town, July 2007.

Kim, K.H. (1998), US inflation and the dollar exchange rate: A vector error correction model, *Applied Economics* 30 (5), 613-619.

Krugman (1987). "Pricing to Market when the Exchange Rate Changes", in Sven W. Arndt, and J. David

Krugman, P. (1986). "Pricing to Market When the Exchange Rate Changes." NBER Working Paper No. w1926.

Laflèche, T., 1996. The impact of exchange rate movements on consumer prices. *Bank of Canada Review*, winter 1996-1997, 21-32.

Mann, C.L., 1986. Prices, Profits Margins, and Exchange Rates. *Federal Reserve Bulletin*, 72 (6), 366-79.

Marazzi, M. et al. (2006), "Exchange Rate Pass-Through to U.S. Import Prices: Some New Evidence." International Finance Discussion Papers 833 (Washington, D.C.: Board of Governors of the Federal Reserve System).

Masha, I., and Park, C. (2012).Exchange Rate Pass Through to Prices in Maldives. May 2012 IMF Working Paper,Asia and Pacific Department

McCarthy, J. (2000), "Pass-Through of Exchange Rates and Import Prices to Domestic Inflation in Some Industrialized Economies." Working Paper No. 79, Bank for International Settlements, Basel.

McCarthy, J., 2006. Pass through of exchange rates and import prices to domestic inflation in some industrialized economies. *Federal Reserve Bank of New York*.

McCarthy, Jonathan (1999). "Pass-Through of Exchange Rates and Import Prices to Domestic Inflation in Some Industrialized Economies", in *Bank for International Settlements,* Working Paper, No. 79, Basel.

McFarlane, L. (2002). Consumer Price Inflation and Exchange Rate Pass-Through in Jamaica. Research Services Department, Research and Economic Programming Division, Bank of Jamaica. October 2002.

Menon, J. (1995a), "Exchange Rate Pass-Through", *Journal of Economic Surveys*, 69. Monetary Policy Review, 2008

Menon, J., 1996. The Degree and Determinants of Exchange Rate Pass-Through: Market Structure, Non-Tariff Barriers and Multinational Corporations. *The Economic Journal*, 106 (435), 434-444.

Mihaljek, D and Klau, M. (2007).Exchange rate pass-through in emerging market economies: What has changed and why? BIS Papers No 35.

Mwase, N, (2006). An Empirical Investigation of Exchange Rate Pass-through to Inflation in Tanzania. IMF Working Paper WP/06I1S. [Online]. Available :

Ocran, M.K (2010). 'Exchange Rate Pass-Through to Domestic Prices: The case of South Africa'. Prague Economic Papers, 4, 2010.

Ogundipe, A. and Egbetokun, S. (2013).Exchange Rate Pass-Through to Consumer Prices in Nigeria. volume II Issue 4, July 2013 Scientific Papers (www.scientificpapers.org) Journal of Business Management and Applied Economics.

Parsley, D, 2010. Exchange Rate Pass-through in South Africa: Panel Evidence from Individual Goods and Services. MPRA Paper No. 21115. [Online]. Available:

Parsley, D. C., Popper, H. A. (1998), "Exchange Rates, Domestic Prices, and Central Bank Actions: Recent U.S. Experience." *Southern Economic Journal*, Vol. 64, pp. 957–972.Review of Economics and Statistics. 87, 4: 679-690.

Rowland, P., (2003). "Uncovered Interest Parity and the USD/COP Exchange Rate", in Borradores de Economía, *Banco de la República*, No. 227, Bogotá

Sanusi, .A.R. (2010). Exchange rate pass-through to consumer prices in Ghana: Evidence from structural Vector Auto-regression.' Department of Economics, Ahmadu Bello University, Zaria, Nigeria, June 2010.

Sanusi, A.R. (2010), ''Exchange Rate Pass-Through to Consumer Prices in Ghana: Evidence from Structural Vector Auto-Regression'', Journal of Monetary and Economic Integration 10(1): 25-54.

Soto, C. and Selaive, J., 2003. Openness and imperfect pass-through: Implications for the Monetary Policy. *Central Bank of Chile Working Papers* No.216 Devereux *et al.* (2004)

South African Reserve Bank (2002): "Exchange rate pass-through and South African import prices", *Monetary Policy Review*, April, 14–15. © 2012 International Monetary Fund. WP/12/126.

South African Reserve Bank (2008). "Monetary Policy Review. © South African Reserve Bank. November, 2008. South African Reserve Bank South African Reserve Bank South African Reserve Bank South African Reserve Bank.

Tandrayen-Ragoobur and Chicooree, (2012) .Exchange Rate Pass Through to Domestic Prices: Evidence from Mauritius, *Department of Economics and Statistics, University of Mauritius* ICITI 2012 ISSN: 16941225.

Taylor, J. B. (2000), "Low Inflation, Pass-Through, and the Pricing Power of Firms." *European Economic Review*, Vol. 44, No. 7, pp. 1389-1404.

van der Merwe, E. 2004. "Inflation Targeting in South Africa". Occasional Paper No. 19, .July. Pretoria: South African Reserve Bank.

# 2

# Macroeconomic conditions and unemployment in Nigeria

Augustine C. Osigwe [a*], Kenneth O. Ahamba[b]

[a] Department of Economics and Development Studies, Federal University, Ikwo, Nigeria.
[b] Department of Economics and Development Studies, Federal University, Ikwo, Nigeria. E-mail: kendrys4jesus@yahoo.com
[*] Corresponding author's email address: onyi2amaka@yahoo.com

| ARTICLE INFO | ABSTRACT |
|---|---|
| Keywords:<br>Macroeconomic variables;<br>Nigeria;<br>Unemployment. | We examine the effect of selected macroeconomic variables on unemployment rate in Nigeria using a battery cointegration tests. Results reveals a long run relation between unemployment rate (UNER) and chosen macroeconomic variables. The results of the vector error correction model (VECM) show that real GDP at lag 2 and current exchange rate (EXR) positively affect UNER. Moreover, UNER at lag 1, money supply (M2) at lag 2, EXR at lag 2, current lending rate (LR) and its first lag negatively affects UNER. These results are robust to the satisfaction of various diagnostic tests including residual normality assumption, correction for autocorrelation and white heteroskedasticity. |

## 1.0    Introduction

Unemployment is one of the most critical problems facing Nigeria. The years of corruption, civil war, military rule, and mismanagement have hindered economic growth of the country. Nigeria is endowed with diverse and infinite resources, both human and material. However, years of negligence and adverse policies have led to the under-utilization of these resources. This is one of the primary causes of unemployment in Nigeria (EconomyWatch, 2010). Unemployment in Nigeria is a key problem both from economic and social view point. It contributes to low purchasing power which dovetails into less consumption and in turn to lower production and economic growth. Unemployment also has social consequences as it increases the rate of crime in the society. For instance, Asaju et al (2014) revealed that widespread poverty, youth restiveness, high rate of social vices and criminal activities are prevalent because of joblessness, and warned that if not controlled, apathy, cynicism and revolution might become the consequence. World Bank (2009) reports that 40 million (28.57%) of Nigeria's employable people are unemployed. EconomyWatch (2010) documented that secondary-school graduates consist of the principal fraction of the unemployed in Nigeria, accounting for nearly 35% to 50%. The rate of unemployment within the age group of 20 to 24 years is 40 % and between 15 to 19 years it is 31 %.

The Nigeria's population pyramid captured in the CIA World Factbook (2014) indicated the following age structure 0-14 years: 43.2% (male 39,151,304/female 37,353,737), 15-24 years: 19.3% (male 17,486,117/ female 16,732,533), 25-54 years: 30.5% (male 27,697,644/female 26,285,816), 55-64 years: 3.9% (male 3,393,631/female 3,571,301) and 65 years and over: 3.1% (male 2,621,845/female 2,861,826). The massage deduced from these statistics is that the Nigerian population is children and youths dominating. A further implication of this is that a lot of youths who are able, ready and willing to work cannot find work in Nigeria.

WDI (2014) put Nigeria youth unemployment at 13.7% (% of total labour force ages 15-24). The Coordinating Minister for the Economy and Minister of Finance, Dr. Ngozi Okonjo-Iweala while quoting official statistics from the National Bureau of Statistics (NBS) stated that no fewer than 5.3 million youths are jobless in Nigeria, while 1.8 million graduates enter the labour market every year (The Sun Newspaper of 24th November, 2014). However, this figure Minister of Finance seem somewhat a conservative estimate of the actual number of unemployed youths in the country, going by the previous statistics released by the NBS, which put the number of jobless Nigerians at 20.3 million. Despite repeated claims by the Federal Government that it has been able to create 1.6 million jobs this year, there is no demonstrable evidence that that figure has done much to reduce the rate of unemployment and poverty level in the country. Instead, the contrary appears to be the case.

Macroeconomic variables and unemployment rate nexus has been explored in different studies from various perspectives. The macroeconomic variables that enter any unemployment model are predicated by the combination of economic theory and the peculiarity of the economy the modeller is interested in. Early in the literature, Okun (1962) documented that economic growth and unemployment has negative relationship. The relationship between economic growth, unemployment and inflation based on traditional macro model is derived by the combination of Okun's law and Philips curve. Perman and Tavera (2007) noted that such relationship is a significant indicator of interdependence of output and labour movement in long run to capture the effect of higher unemployment.

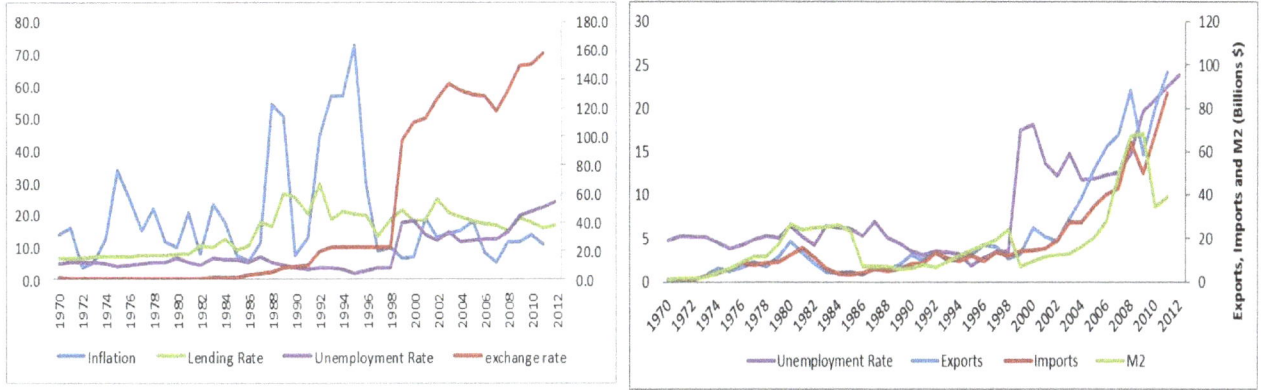

Source: Authors initiative with underlying data obtained from CBN (2014)
Figure 1: Trends in some selected macroeconomic variables and unemployment rates Nigeria

The remainder of this paper is structured in the following way. Section 2 presents the trends in some selected macroeconomic variables and unemployment rates Nigeria. Section 3 centres on literature review whereas section 4 briefly describes the theoretical framework and Methodology adopted. Section five presents and discusses the empirical results while section six concludes the study.

## 2.0    Literature review

Numerous empirical studies such as Cascio (2001) for 11 European countries, Orphanides and Williams (2002), Djivre and Ribon (2003) for Israel, and Ravn and Simonelli (2006) for the US, have investigated the relationship between monetary policy shocks and total unemployment. On the whole, these studies found that tight monetary policy increased unemployment. On the other hand, Agenor and Aizenman (1999) theoretically examined the effects of fiscal policies on output, wages and employment within a small open economy using the general equilibrium framework. They argued that expansionary fiscal policies increased unemployment. Alexius and Holmlund (2007) discovered that monetary policy had more persistent effects on unemployment than the fiscal policy and foreign demand in Sweden. Their results indicated that 30 per cent of the fluctuations in unemployment were caused by shocks to monetary policy during 1980 to 2005.

Lynch and Hyclak (1984) and Ewing, Levernier and Malikin (2002) evaluated the effect of output deviations on unemployment rate for different age, gender and race groups of the United States. They discovered that the effects of output deviations are different on each of the different subgroups age, gender and race. Further, Blackley (1991), Freeman (2000), Izraeli and Murphy (2003) and Bisping and Patron (2005) showed that output and unemployment relationship differs among demographic groups within and between regions in the United States. Paci, Pigliaru and Pugno (2001) also analyzed the existing patterns of unemployment across western European regions. Within a three-sector model framework (agriculture, industry and services) they assessed whether sectoral dynamics help explaining the observed heterogeneity in growth and employment. But failed to consider the relationship between policy shocks and the type of unemployment.

Zavodny and Zha (2000) scrutinised the relationship between monetary policy and the race-specific unemployment rates in the US. They found that the black unemployment rate does respond slightly differently than the overall unemployment rate to macroeconomic variable shocks. Carlino and DeFina (1998) study the possibility that the monetary policy has different effects across regions in the US since the timing and the magnitude of cycles in economic activity vary across regions. They concluded that different regions are affected differently by monetary policy. Algan (2002) found that a positive demand shock decreases the unemployment rate permanently in France and USA.

Berument et al (2008) investigated how macroeconomic policy shocks in Turkey affect the total unemployment and provides evidence on the differential responses of the unemployment by sectors of economic activity. The study made two remarkable contributions to knowledge. First, it considered not only the response of total unemployment but also the response of unemployment by sectors of economic activity. Second, it considered not only the effect of monetary policy shocks, but also the effects of several other macroeconomic shocks. Quarterly data that covered the period 1988:01 to 2004:04 was used. A VAR model with a recursive order was employed to estimate the effects of shocks in real GDP, price, exchange rate, interbank interest rate, money supply and own sectoral unemployment on unemployment by sectors of economic activity. The results of the study indicated that positive income shock is followed by a decrease in unemployment in all economic activity groups during the initial periods except the unemployment in the *Electricity* sector and the *Community Services* sector. The study, therefore, concluded that unemployment in different sectors of economic activity respond differently to various macroeconomic policy shocks.

Zawojska (2010) focused on overall unemployment in Poland and went ahead to highlight the agriculture connections with the national economy and particularly with labour market that might govern individual choices between employment in the farm and non-farm sectors. The study aimed first to complement the literature on unemployment in Poland, and second to examine the relationship between macroeconomic indicators and unemployment rate. It consisted of two major parts. The first part presented an overview of the relevant literature concerning the above-mentioned relations. The next part, laid out the results of the study. Correlation analysis and simple linear models were applied to explain the relationship of unemployment rate with individual macroeconomic indicators. The results showed that during the years included in this study (2002-2008), unemployment rate in Poland was statistically significant and negatively impacted by the economic growth, Gross Domestic Product per capita, exports and imports, foreign direct investments, final consumption expenditures, gross capital formation, and central government expenditures. At the same time, the real interest rates of the central bank were positively related to the unemployment rate. No statistically significant linear relationship was found between the current and past unemployment rates in Poland.

Dogan (2012) investigated the response of unemployment to selective macroeconomics shocks for the period of 2000: Q1-2010:Q1. He found that positive shocks to growth, growth in export and inflation reduced unemployment. On the other hand, shocks to exchange rate, interbank interest rate and money supply increased unemployment. The results, according to the author, were consistent with Phillips curve and Okun's Law suggestion. Namely, negative relationship between output and unemployment and positive relationship between unemployment and inflation were found.

The Bankole and Fatai (2013) estimated the Okun's coefficient, and checked the validity of Okun's law in Nigeria, using the time series annual data that spanned the period 1980 to 2008. The Engle granger co-integration test and Fully Modified OLS were employed. The empirical evidence from the study showed that there is positive coefficient in the regression, implying that Okun's law interpretation is not applicable to Nigeria. They, thus, recommended that government and policy makers should adopt economic policies that are more oriented to structural changes and reform in labour market.

## 3.0    Theoretical framework and methodology

### 3.1    Theoretical framework

A number of studies (Cascio, 2001; Orphanides and Williams, 2002; Djivre and Ribon, 2003; Berument et al, 2008; Bankole and Fatai, 2013; among others) have examined the relationship between Unemployment and other macroeconomic variables. In this study, we re-examined the Okun's law for Nigeria, using the vector error correction model (VECM). The model has the capacity to produce parameters that are consistent with theory and of good fit. Unlike most existing studies, Bankole and Fatai, 2013 inclusive, the present study carried out several diagnostic tests of model adequacy to check how "good" the fitted model is and gauge the error process of the would-be determinants of unemployment in Nigeria.

## 3.2    Methodology

The model presents unemployment rate as the dependent variable and introduces some selected macroeconomic variables as explanatory variables that attempt to capture the variations in unemployment rate in Nigerian economy. The model is expressed as:

UNER = f(UNER$_{t-1}$, INF, RGDP, M2, EXR, LR, GEX, OPEN)                                                 (1)

Where, UNER = unemployment rate, UNER$_{t-1}$ = is the immediate past value of unemployment rate, INF = Inflation Rate, RGDP = Real Gross Domestic Product, M2 = Money Supply, EXR= Exchange Rate, LR = Lending Rate, GEX = Government Expenditure, and OPEN = Openness of the economy. The parameterized version of equation the unemployment model is presented as follows:

$$UNER_t = \lambda_0 + \lambda_1 UNER_{t-1} + \lambda_2 INF_t + \lambda_3 RGDP_t + \lambda_4 M2_t + \lambda_5 EXR_t + \lambda_6 LR_t + \lambda_7 GEX_t + \lambda_8 OPEN_t + \varepsilon_{1t} \qquad (2)$$

## 3.3    Estimation technique

Time series data are often assumed to be non-stationary and thus, it is necessary to perform unit root test to ensure that there is stationarity of data. The test would be employed to avoid the problem of spurious regression. In conducting this test, the Augmented Dickey-Fuller (ADF) and the Philip-Perron (PP) unit root tests would be employed to determine the stationarity of data. The ADF approach addresses the serial correlation of the first differences of a series in a parametric fashion by estimating additional nuisance parameters whereas the PP test follows non-parametric statistical methods to account for the autocorrelation in the error terms without adding lagged difference terms (Gujarati, 2009).The decision rule is that Augmented Dickey-Fuller (ADF) and Philip-Perron tests statistics must be greater than Mackinnon Critical Value at either 1%, 5%, or 10% and at absolute term i.e. ignoring the negative sign of the ADF and PP tests statistics and Mackinnon critical value, before the variable can be adjudged to be stationary.

We proceed to test for co-integration among the variables. The concept of co-integration is relevant to the problem of determination of long-run equilibrium relationship. Co-integration is the statistical implication of the existence of a long-run equilibrium relationship between variables. The condition for a long run co-integrating vector is that the trace statistics (likelihood ratio) must be greater than 5% critical value. According to Granger (1986), a test for cointegration can be believed to be a pre-test to avoid 'spurious regression' situations. In this study, we adopt the Johansen and Juselius (1990, 1992, and 1994) approach for cointegration test because of its advantages over the Engle Granger static procedure.

Next, we specify the short-run dynamic equation. The existence of cointegration necessitates the construction of error correction model in order to model dynamic relationships. The error correction mechanism is the speed or degree of adjustment from the short run equilibrium to the long run equilibrium state. Precisely, it shows the rate at which unemployment rate adjusts to changes in the explanatory variables. Therefore, the greater the co-efficient of the parameter, the higher the speed of adjustment of the model from short run to the long run and vice-versa. The result of the ECM is specified in an over parameterized form. However, the parsimonious encompassing model depicts the best fitted result for the dynamic specifications. The acceptable rule is that the coefficient of the ECM term must be negatively signed and significant to ensure convergence of the dynamics to the long-run equilibrium.

Finally, we carry out several diagnostic tests of model adequacy. Specifically, we adopt the Jarque-Bera (JB) Test of Normality, the Breusch-Godfrey (BG) test for serial correlation, White heteroskedasticity and Ramsey Reset Test.

## 4.0    Empirical analysis

### 4.1    Unit roots results

The results of the ADF and the PP tests of stationarity are reported in Table 5.1. All the variables (UNER, INF, RGDP, M2, EXR, LR, GEX and OPEN) were stationary at first difference. This is because their respective ADF and PP tests statistics value is greater than Mackinnon critical value at 1%(5%) and at absolute term after first difference. The results of two techniques reveal that all the variables are integrated of order one, I(1). Thus, the null hypothesis of non-stationarity is rejected at both 1% and 5% levels of significance.

## 4.2    Johansen cointegration test results

Table 5.2 presents the results of the Johansen cointegration test. Lag length of three (3) was selected as suggested by FPE, AIC and HQ. The results show that long-run relationship or co-integration exists among unemployment rate (UNER), inflation rate (INF), real gross domestic product (RGDP), money supply (M2), exchange rate (EXR), lending rate (LR), government expenditure (GEX) and openness of the economy (OPEN). This is because the critical value at 5% is less than both trace statistic and maxi-eigen statistic. Therefore, the hypothesis of no co-integration has been rejected at 5% significance level. Thus, there is evidence of a long run relationship among the macroeconomic variables. Specifically, Trace test indicates three cointegrating equations at 5% critical level while Maxi-Eigen test indicates two cointegrating equations at 5% critical level. This implies that there is a stable long-run relationship among the eight macro-variables and so we can avoid both the spurious and inconsistent regression problems which otherwise would occur with regression of non-stationary data series.

Table 1: ADF and PP unit root results

| Variable | ADF Statistic | Order of Integration | PP Statistic | Order of Integration |
|----------|---------------|----------------------|--------------|----------------------|
| UNER | -6.12** | I(1) | -6.11** | I(1) |
| INF | -6.75* | I(1) | -12.68* | I(1) |
| RGDP | -6.11** | I(1) | -6.12** | I(1) |
| M2 | -12.02* | I(1) | -14.64* | I(1) |
| EXR | -5.78* | I(1) | -5.77* | I(1) |
| LR | -10.42* | I(1) | -10.51* | I(1) |
| GEX | -7.63* | I(1) | -7.58* | I(1) |
| OPEN | -7.69* | I(1) | -7.63* | I(1) |

**(*) denotes rejection of the null hypothesis at 1%(5%) significance level.

## 4.3    Johansen cointegration test results

Table 5.2 presents the results of the Johansen cointegration test. Lag length of three (3) was selected as suggested by FPE, AIC and HQ. The results show that long-run relationship or co-integration exists among unemployment rate (UNER), inflation rate (INF), real gross domestic product (RGDP), money supply (M2), exchange rate (EXR), lending rate (LR), government expenditure (GEX) and openness of the economy (OPEN). This is because the critical value at 5% is less than both trace statistic and maxi-eigen statistic. Therefore, the hypothesis of no co-integration has been rejected at 5% significance level. Thus, there is evidence of a long run relationship among the macroeconomic variables. Specifically, Trace test indicates three cointegrating equations at 5% critical level while Maxi-Eigen test indicates two cointegrating equations at 5% critical level. This implies that there is a stable long-run relationship among the eight macro-variables and so we can avoid both the spurious and inconsistent regression problems which otherwise would occur with regression of non-stationary data series.

Table 2: Johansen cointegration test results

| $H_0$ | $H_1$ | Trace Statistic | 0.05 Critical Value | Max-eigen Statistic | 0.05 Critical Value |
|-------|-------|-----------------|---------------------|---------------------|---------------------|
| $r = 0$ | $r > 0$ | 611.99* | 159.53 | 287.94* | 52.36 |
| $r \leq 1$ | $r > 1$ | 324.05* | 125.61 | 134.02* | 46.23 |
| $r \leq 2$ | $r > 2$ | 190.03* | 95.75 | 83.05 | 40.07 |
| $r \leq 3$ | $r > 3$ | 106.98 | 69.81 | 40.45 | 33.87 |
| $r \leq 4$ | $r > 4$ | 66.52 | 47.85 | 31.11 | 27.58 |
| $r \leq 5$ | $r > 5$ | 35.41 | 29.79 | 20.53 | 21.13 |
| $r \leq 6$ | $r > 6$ | 14.87 | 15.49 | 14.86 | 14.26 |
| $r \leq 7$ | $r > 7$ | 0.00 | 3.84 | 0.00 | 3.84 |

* denotes rejection of the null hypothesis ($H_0$) at 5% significance level. The Trace test indicates 3 cointegrating eqn(s) at the 0.05 level while max-eigen value test indicates 2 cointegrating equations at 5% level.

## 4.4    Vector error correction model

Having established that the variables are stationary and integrated of order I(1) with a long run relationship, we then employed the vector error correction model (VECM) to capture the short run deviations that might have occurred in estimating the long run cointegration equation. The final parsimonious vector error correction model results are presented in table 5.3 below. The model which specifically assumed a linear trend and no intercept in the co-integrating equations was adopted based on data coherence, parameter consistency with theory, and goodness of fit.

From table 5.3(below), RGDP made positive and significant impact on unemployment (UNER) at lag 2. Specifically, a 1% increase in RGDP at the second lag generates about 1.14% increase in unemployment. This result lends credence to the empirical findings of Dogan (2012) but contradicts Zawojska (2010). The result also reveals that current exchange rate (EXR) impacted positively and significantly on UNER whereas its impact at lag 2 was negative. Basically, a 1% increase in current EXR leads to a 0.15% increase in UNER while a 1% increase in EXR at the second lag period depresses UNER by 0.13%. Government expenditure (GEX) positively affects UNER both at its current and second lag periods although it impacts are not significant.

Table 3: Parsimonious vector error correction model results

Dependent Variable: D(UNER)

Method: Least Squares

| Variable | Coefficient | Std. Error | t-Statistic |
|---|---|---|---|
| C | 0.033313 | 0.263759 | 0.126301 |
| D(UNER(-1)) | -0.186119 | 0.087298 | -2.131998 |
| D(LRGDP(-2)) | 1.148458 | 0.486337 | 2.361443 |
| D(LM2) | -1.411482 | 0.631282 | -2.235896 |
| D(EXR) | 0.159795 | 0.014445 | 11.06199 |
| D(EXR(-2)) | -0.067915 | 0.012691 | -5.351476 |
| D(LR) | -0.123149 | 0.049095 | -2.508380 |
| D(LR(-1)) | -0.133719 | 0.049456 | -2.703804 |
| D(LGEX) | 1.100684 | 0.763974 | 1.440735 |
| D(LGEX(-2)) | 0.790856 | 0.659686 | 1.198836 |
| D(OPEN(-1)) | -2.983301 | 2.014983 | -1.480559 |
| D(OPEN(-2)) | -4.076973 | 2.134180 | -1.910323 |
| ECM | -0.394427 | 0.112555 | 3.504302 |
| R-square | 0.909952 | Mean dependent var | 0.511905 |
| Adjusted R-square | 0.872690 | Akaike info criterion | 2.960129 |
| S.E. of regression | 0.938746 | Durbin-Watson stat | 1.953533 |
| F-statistic | 24.42080 | Prob(F-statistic) | 0.000000 |

As the result indicates, a 1% increase in GEX leads to 1.10% and 0.79% increases in UNER at current and second lag periods respectively. This result does not support a priori expectation as increase in government expenditure is expected to reduce unemployment. A possible reason for this contradictory result is that huge government spending goes into non-employment generating sectors/ventures and looting of public treasuries by corrupt public office holders which reflects in government account as economic spending. The results further indicate a negative and significant relationship between money supply (M2) at lag 2 and UNER; current lending rate (LR) and UNER; LR at lag 1 and UNER whereas openness (OPEN) of the economy at both first and second lag periods impacted negatively and insignificantly on UNER. It is evident from the result that previous UNER at lag 1 impacted negatively and significantly on current UNER within the period under study. The impact of M2 and OPEN of the economy on unemployment aligns with theoretical expectations as both are expected to dampen UNER.

A striking finding from the result is that inflation (INF) is not make it to the parsimonious result. Thus, suggesting that it does not determine UNER in Nigeria, at least in the short-run. This result deviates from empirical regularity as captured in the Philips curve. This empirical finding may be due to the fact that INF has become inherent in the Nigerian economy and UNER might have become immune to its shocks.

The coefficient of the error correction term which measures the speed of adjustment of UNER towards long-run equilibrium is well-behaved as it is negatively signed and significant at 5% level. This implies that the rate at which variation of UNER at time t, adjusts to the single long-run co-integrating relationship is different from zero. Specifically, the coefficient of the ECM revealed that the speed with which UNER adjusts the regressors is about 39% in the short run. The coefficient of determination (R-squared) shows that about 90% of the variation in UNER is jointly explained by the explanatory variables in the model. Implicitly, the remaining 10% may be attributed to the stochastic variables. The overall model is significant as revealed by the F-statistic and its corresponding probabilistic value.

## 4.5    Diagnostic test

Having presented and analyzed the parsimonious vector error correction results, we further carried out several diagnostic tests of model adequacy to check how "good" the fitted model is. Specifically, we employed the Jarque-Bera (JB) Test of Normality, the Breusch-Godfrey (BG) test for serial correlation, White heteroskedasticity and the Ramsey Reset Test. The JB test of normality which is an large-sample (or *asymptotic*) test is based on the OLS residuals while the Breusch-Godfrey test, which is also known as the Lagrange Multiplier (LM) test, is used to test for autocorrelation. It has been generally adduced to be more robust in empirical diagnostic tests than the Durbin Watson test statistics because it is amenable to use for: (i) simple or higher-order moving averages of white noise error terms; (ii) non-stochastic regressors such as lagged values of the dependent variable and (iii) higher-order schemes. According to White (1980), White Heteroskedasticity Test is a test of heteroskedasticity in the residuals from a least square regression. OLS estimates are consistent in the presence of heteroskedasticity, but the conventional computed errors are no longer valid. White's test is a test of the null hypothesis of no heteroskedasticity against heteroskedasticity of some unknown general form. The Ramsey Reset Test is a general test of specification error. If the *F* value is highly significant, it suggests that the initial model might have been wrongly specified.

Table 4: Summary of diagnostic tests for the model

| Tests | Results |
| --- | --- |
| Jarque-Bera Normality | 8.14(0.01) |
| Breusch-Godfrey (B-G) | 0.50(0.31) |
| Heteroskedasticity | 0.47(0.42) |
| Ramsey Reset | 0.01(0.00) |

Source: Authors' computation using Eviews6
*Note:* The probability is given in parenthesis while figures outside the parenthesis are the F-statistics.

The outcome of the diagnostic tests as reported in Table 5.4 is satisfactory. Under the null hypothesis that the residuals are normally distributed, the JB test for residual normality assumption is not violated. The table also shows that the error process could be described as normal for the determinants. The B-G test which is noted to have stronger statistical power revealed the absence of autocorrelation. Also, the absence of white heteroskedasticity and specification error was indicated. The results of the tests suggest that the model is well specified, and hence the obtained empirical results are plausible.

## 5.0　　Conclusion and recommendation

This paper empirically examined the effects of selected macroeconomic variables on unemployment rate in Nigeria. Review of related literature was robust. The unit root tests results using ADF and the PP test of stationary implicated all the variables as being integrated of order one, I(1). The Johansen cointegration test results revealed a long run relationship among the chosen variables which necessitated the use of the Vector Error Correction Model (VECM). The results revealed that while RGDP at lag 2 and current EXR positively and significantly affect UNER within the period under study whereas UNER at lag 1, M2 at lag 2, EXR at lag 2, current LR and its first lag negatively and significantly affected it. Current GEX and its lag 2 positively and insignificantly influenced UNER while OPEN at lags 1 and 2 negatively and insignificantly affected unemployment. The outcome of all the diagnostic tests validates the acceptability of the model's results as plausible.

Based on our empirical findings, we recommend as follows. *First,* the corrupt government officials should abstain from looting of public treasuries and channel spending to greater employment sectors/ventures. *Second,* the government should keep tab on the variables implicated by the model of this study as significant determinants of unemployment in Nigeria to ensure that they move in the desired direction with a view to alleviating unemployment and its associated menace.

## References

Agenor Pierre R. and J. Aizenman, (1999). Macroeconomic Adjustment with Segmented Labor Markets, *Journal of Development Economics*, 58, 277-296.

Alexius A. and B. Holmlund, (2007). Monetary Policy and Swedish Unemployment Fluctuations. *IZA Discussion Paper*, No. 2933, Bonn.

Algan, Yann (2002). How Well Does the Aggregate Demand-Aggregate Supply Framework Explain Unemployment Fluctuations? A France-United States Comparison. *Economic Modelling*, 19, 153-177.

Asaju K., Arome S. and Anyio F. (2014). The rising rate of unemployment in Nigeria: the socio-economic and political implications, Global business and Economic Research, Vol. 3, No 2.

Bankole A. S. and Fatai B. O. (2013). Empirical Test of Okun's Law in Nigeria, International Journal of Economic Practices and Theories, Vol. 3, No. 3.

Berument H., Dogan N. and Tansel A. (2008). Macroeconomic Policy and Unemployment by Economic Activity: Evidence from Turkey, Economic Research Center, Middle East Technical University, Ankara, Turkey.

Bisping T. and H. Patron, (2005). Output Shocks and Unemployment: New Evidence on Regional Disparities, *International Journal of Applied Economics*, 2(1), 79-89.

Blackley, P.R., (1991). The Measurement and Determination of State Equilibrium Unemployment Rates, *Journal of Macroeconomics*, 13(4), 641-656.

Carlino, G and R. DeFina, (1998). The Different Regional Effects of Monetary Shocks. The Review of Economics and Statistics, 80(4), 572-587.

Cascio Lo I., (2001). Do Labor Markets Really Matter? University of Essex, Department of Economics, Colchester, Essex.

CBN (2014). Statistical Bulletin, Central Bank of Nigeria, Abuja, Nigeria.

Djivre J. and S. Ribon, (2003). Inflation, Unemployment, the Exchange Rate, and Monetary Policy in Israel, 1990-99: a SVAR Approach, *Israel Economic Review*, 2, 71-99.

Doğan T. (2010). Macroeconomic Variables and Unemployment: The Case of Turkey. International Journal of Economics and Financial Issues, Vol. 2, No. 1, 2012, pp.71-78.

EconomyWatch. (2010). Nigeria Unemployment, Retrieved fromhttp://www.economywatch.com/unemployment/countries/nigeria.html on 21/11/14.

Ewing B. T., W. Levernier and F. Malik, (2002). The Differential Effects of Output Shocks on Unemployment Rates by Race and Gender, *Southern Economic Journal*, 68(3), 584-599.

Freeman D. G., (2000). Regional Tests of Okun's Law, *International Advances in Economic Research*, 6(3), 557-570.

Izraeli O. and K. J. Murphy, (2003). The Effect of Industrial Diversity on State Unemployment Rate and Per Capita Income, *The Annals of Regional Science*, 37(1), 1-14.

Lynch G.J. and T. Hyclak, (1984). Cyclical and Noncyclical Unemployment Differences among Demographic Groups, *Growth and Change*, 15(1), 9-17.

Okun, A. (1962). Potential GNP: Its measurement and significance. In American Statistical Association, Proceedings of the Business and Economic Statistics Section (pp. 98-104).

Orphanides A. and J. C. Williams, (2002). Robust monetary policy rules with unknown natural rates", *Board of Governors of the Federal Reserve System*, Finance and Economics Discussion Series: 2003-11, US.

Paci R., F. Pigliaru and M. Pugno, (2001). Disparities in Economic Growth and Unemployment across the European Regions: A Sectoral Perspective, *North South Economic Research*, Working Paper CRENOS: 200103, University of Cagliari and Sassari, Sardinia.

Perman, R., and Tavera, C. (2007). Testing for convergence of the Okun's law coefficient in Europe. Empirica, 34(1), 45-61.

Ravn, M and S Simonelli, (2006). Labor Market Dynamics and the Business Cycle: Structural Evidence for the United States, *Center for Studies in Economics and Finance, Working Paper,* no 182.

The Sun Newspaper. (2014). Nigeria's grim unemployment statistics, Retrieved from http://sunnewsonline.com/new/?p=59179 on 24th November, 2014.

Zavodny M. and T. Zha, (2000). Monetary Policy and Racial Unemployment Rates, Federal Reserve Bank of Atlanta, Economic Review, 85(4), 1-16.

Zavodny M. and T. Zha, (2000). Monetary Policy and Racial Unemployment Rates, Federal

Zawojska A. (2010). Effect of Macroeconomic Variables on Unemployment Rate in Poland, Economic Science for Rural Development Conference Proceedings; Issue 22, p48.

# 3

# Effect of different price indices on linkage between real GDP growth and real minimum wage growth in Turkey

Onur Sunal[a*], Özge Sezgin Alp[b]

[a] Başkent University, Department of Banking and Finance, Bağlıca Kampüsü, Ankara-Turkey
[b] Başkent University, Department of Accounting and Financial Management, Bağlıca Kampüsü, Ankara-Turkey
[*] Corresponding author's email address: osunal@baskent.edu.tr

| ARTICLE INFO | ABSTRACT |
|---|---|
| Keywords:<br>Economic growth;<br>minimum wages;<br>price indices;<br>Turkey. | The accuracy of Turkish CPI as a price deflator is questionable especially when it comes to calculating real minimum wages. In this study we investigate the effect of different price indices on the relation between real GDP growth rates and real minimum wage growth rates by using a Granger causality analysis framework using VAR based granger causality tests. Result reveals that there is no causality between real minimu wage growth rates and real GDP growth rates in both directions. We also find a biderectional Granger causality between nominal minimum wage growth rates and COLI (an alternative price indice) growth rates. The results also showed that in line with our assumptions when an alternative deflator is used, the causality relations significantly differes. |

## 1.0 Introduction

Minimum wages are important not only because their current or future expected values have impact on equilibrium market employment rates, price (nominal wage) inflation rates or growth rates. In a country like Turkey, minimum wage earners represent 41% of formal sector employees according to Turkish Social Security Agency statistics (2012). Moreover when employees who have earnings very close to minimum wage rates (within the range of maximum 10% more of minimum wages) are taken into account this ratio increases to 58%. This roughly means that, more than 50% of the formal sector workers live on minimum wages as the numbers reveal. In our previous study (Sunal and Sezgin Alp, 2015) using Granger causality framework we found a one-way causality from real GDP growth rates to real minimum wage growth rates. Nevertheless the calculations made and the results obtained heavily depend on the deflator selected. In our previous study we used TUIK's (Turkish National Statistics Agency) price deflators to calculate real minimum wages. Therefore we assume that if other deflators were to be used the outcomes might have been significantly different. Besides we also assume that TUIK's deflators are underestimating the true change in price levels as a result of basket selection and item weighing. In that manner it can be observed that the accuracy of price deflators has long been debated internationally after The Stigler Committee Report (1961) and The Boskin Report (1996). In line with these debates in many studies (Costa, 2000; Hamilton, 1998; Barrett and Brzozowski, 2010; Beatty and Larsen, 2005) the official CPIs were found to be overestimating the true change in prices. Nevertheless in some other studies (Murphy and Garvey, 2004; Murphy and Garvey, 2005; Heineke, 1979; Moosa, 1997) it has been revealed that the official CPIs were an underestimate of the real change in price levels.

In that respect the accuracy of Turkish CPI constructed by TUIK (Turkish National Statistics Agency) as a measure of change in the cost of living especially for minimum wage earners seems questionable. The main reason is that TUIK constructs the CPI basket and determines the weight of items in this basket by taking a representative household into account. As declared by TUIK, CPI basket is constructed so as to represent all the individuals in Turkey. Therefore the representative household or the individual is merely a weighted average of the rich and the poor households. Though according to Engel's law households are considered to be equally well-off if their food expenditure/budget ratios are equal to each other. In other words as income falls the share of expenditure devoted to food rises. Therefore COLI calculated by Istanbul Chamber of Commerce (ITO) seems an important alternative to CPI. Although the same representative household approach is taken into account the share of food and housing expenditures are substantially higher in COLI basket.

We assume that the use of such a different price index (ITO's Cost of Living Index) might have some important implications. When the change in real GDPs (155%) and real minimum wages (%167) during 1988-2012 period are calculated and compared by using CPI (1994=100) deflators a one way causality (Turkish GDPs → Turkish Real Minimum Wages) was observed in our previous study (Sunal and Sezgin Alp, 2015). In fact when CPI is used as a price deflator the overall rise in real minimum wages is even higher than the overall rise in real GDP levels during 1988-2012 period and moreover GDP growths cause real minimum wage growths. Nevertheless contrasting with this finding if real minimum wages were to be deflated by ITO's COLI the overall rise in real minimum wage rates (76%) is not even half of the overall rise in real GDP growth rates (%155) for the same period. Therefore the main objective of this study is to determine whether real GDPs still granger cause real wages if real wages were to be calculated by using COLI deflators. This objective is important as the outlined relationship above seems to create a legitimate ground for the governments to justify their minimum wage determination policy when the official TUIK CPIs are used. In fact in the presence of a different price index if the outcomes will be different (no causality and a lower minimum wage growth rate) then the minimum wage determination policy and the process might somehow be altered. Also another important fact is that when the current real minimum wage rate is taken as a steady state level only the inflationary concerns and expectations shape the nominal minimum wage rate determination process which is practically controlled by the government although the workers are represented by the biggest labor union confederation during the process where a collective bargaining procedure is used as a tool for progression. Moreover, we also aim to reveal the relationship between nominal minimum wage rate growths and COLI growth rates (COLI price inflation rates). Hence a two way Granger causality between these variables would indicate that the minimum wage determination process is inflation driven rather than welfare oriented.

We also aim to contribute to the relevant international and national literature in a few ways. It can be observed that the relationship between minimum wages and employment has been investigated in numerous studies (Stigler, 1946; Deere, Murphy, and Welch 1995; Prasch, 1996; Dickens, Machin and Manning, 1999; Rama, 2001; Irmen and Wigger, 2002; Neumark and Wascher, 2006; Kaufman, 2010) when international literature is reviewed. In these studies regardless of the sign of the effect –whether minimum wages have a positive or a negative effect on employment or growth rates– the direction of the relationship investigated has always been from minimum wages to employment or growth rates. In other words the effects of economic growth on minimum wages were not principally studied as the employment effects of minimum wages were considered to be at the center of the debate. Also the minimum wage earners consist of only a small minority of the employed in highly industrialized western economies. Therefore the effect of economic growth on minimum wages might not be considered as a primary issue. Although for a country like Turkey the relationship is very important as 41% of employed are receiving minimum wages. Moreover these minimum wage earners claim to have a fair share from the rises in national income growths. As a result we also would like to make a contribution to the relevant field by emphasizing the effect of economic growth on real minimum wages.

## 2.0    Data

The annual growth rates of Turkish Real GDP, Turkish Real Minimum Wages, COLI and Turkish Nominal Minimum Wages during 1988-2012 period are used in this study. Annual Real GDP growth rates are measured by using TUIK's data (1987 reference base year series are used for calculating real GDP growths for 1988-2006 period and 1998 reference base year series are used for calculating 2007-2012 period). COLI price deflators are calculated by using ITO's COLI data (1968=100). Then real minimum wages are obtained by using COLI price deflators and their annual growth rates are calculated respectively.

| Table 1: Annual Inflation Rates in Turkey calculated by using COLI and CPI (1998-2012)[1] | | |
|---|---|---|
| | COLI Inflation Rates % (1968=100) | CPI Inflation Rates % (1994=100) |
| 1988 | 66,22 | 61,57 |
| 1989 | 73,31 | 64,28 |
| 1990 | 63,22 | 60,41 |
| 1991 | 67,86 | 71,14 |
| 1992 | 75,18 | 65,97 |
| 1993 | 85,83 | 71,08 |
| 1994 | 135,74 | 125,49 |
| 1995 | 74,75 | 76,05 |
| 1996 | 87,95 | 79,76 |
| 1997 | 108,03 | 99,09 |
| 1998 | 71,26 | 69,73 |
| 1999 | 59,87 | 68,79 |
| 2000 | 41,69 | 39,03 |
| 2001 | 55,26 | 68,53 |
| 2002 | 29,41 | 29,75 |
| 2003 | 21,75 | 12,71 |
| 2004 | 7,44 | 9,35 |
| 2005 | 11,59 | 7,72 |
| 2006 | 10,37 | 9,65 |
| 2007 | 12,01 | 8,39 |
| 2008 | 12,73 | 10,06 |
| 2009 | 6,92 | 6,53 |
| 2010 | 8,87 | 6,40 |
| 2011 | 8,19 | 10,45 |
| 2012 | 7,98 | 6,16 |

Consistent with our expectations, Table 1 reveals that inflation rates calculated by COLI and CPI largely differ from each other. When the period in this study (1988-2012) is taken into consideration the prices rose 8922 and 5907 times respectively with COLI and CPI indexes. Turkey has experienced very high levels of chronic inflation rates for a very long period. Moreover the aggregate effect in the last 25 year period is so high that it can only be stated with numbers in thousands. And as a matter of fact even the difference in between the change in general price levels in between COLI and CPI is 0.338 fold during the 1988-2012 period. In other words the CPI underestimates the rise in prices by 33.8% when compared to COLI during 1988-2012. This number might lead to an important misperception as it sounds small though the effect it creates when calculating real wages are enormous.

During 1988-2012 period when real wages are calculated by COLI deflators, real wages rose by 76.9%. Alternatively when real wages are calculated by CPI deflators, real wages rose by 167.2%. The purchasing power or the welfare of minimum wage earners not even doubles (the rise is only 0.76 fold) when determined by COLI and not surprisingly it nearly triples (the rise is 1.67 fold) when determined by CPI during the same period.

| Table 2: Consumer Baskets Used in calculating CPI and COLI in Turkey (2014) | | | |
|---|---|---|---|
| Cost of Living Index (COLI) 1968=100 | | CPI (Consumer Price Index) 1994=100 | |
| COLI Basket | Weights (%) | CPI Basket | Weights (%) |
| Food Expenditures | 42,49 | Food Expenditures | 29,74 |
| Housing Expenditures | 20,72 | Housing Expenditures | 16,41 |
| Furniture and Household Goods | 8 | Furniture and Household Goods | 7,52 |
| Clothing Expenditures | 12,78 | Clothing Expenditures | 7,17 |
| Health and Personal Care Expenditures | 2,82 | Health and Personal Care Expenditures | 2,44 |
| Transportation Expenditures | 5,95 | Transportation and Communication Exp. | 20,24 |
| Education, Culture and Entertainment | 4,44 | Education, Culture and Entertainment | 5,62 |
| Other | 2,80 | Other | 10,86 |

As presented in Table 2, Food and Housing Expenditures consist of 63.21% of consumer basket in COLI and 46.15% of consumer basket in CPI. There is a very high significant difference in between these two price index series when it comes to weighing food and housing expenditures. Yet alone the difference in between the weights assigned to only food expenditures is 12.75% (42.49% and 29.74%). Hence as a result the annual inflation rates differ from each other as can be seen from Table 1. Also consistent with our expectations when a basket with a higher food expenditure ratio is used CPI tends to underestimate the rises in cost of living conditions by 33.8%.

---

[1] The data used for constructing monthly CPI values represent prices of items obtained from 26 different regions from all over Turkey where the monthly reference price of the specific item is a population weighed average price. The data used for constructing COLI values represent prices of items obtained from 15 different districts of İstanbul (Though the population of İstanbul is officially 18.50% of the whole national population). Moreover, the prices of 432 and 242 items are collected for CPI and COLI respectively. Both indexes are calculated by using the same Laspeyres' formula.

## 3.0　Methodology

In this paper, we used causality analysis proposed by Granger (1969) to investigate the relationships between real GDP growth rates and real minimum wage growth rates and between COLI growth rates and nominal minimum wage growth rates. In Granger causality framework the definition of the relation is based on the stationarity hypothesis of the series. Therefore stationarity tests are the first step analysis of Granger causality framework. In relevant literature there are different types of stationarity tests also known as unit root tests. In this study, Augmented Dickey Fuller (ADF) test, a unit root test which is introduced by Dickey and Fuller (1979) is used. In general if the series are stationary after determining the optimal lag lengths, VAR model based Granger causality tests might be conducted. Conversely, if the series are non-stationary the second step involves co-integration analysis which displays the long run co-movement of variables. In this study, a Vector Autoregressive (VAR) based co-integration test introduced by Johansen and Jeselius (1990) is used. This test is also known as Johansen and Jeselius co-integration test. As it is well known VAR model includes lagged terms of all variables and moreover lag length plays a crucial role for correct modeling. In addition, Johansen and Jeselius co-integration test is sensitive to lag lengths. The determination of the optimal leg lengths requires the use of different information criteria. The further step involves the application of the co-integration tests. If no co-integration relations are observed then Granger causality tests can be applied directly. However, if there is co-integration; Vector Error Correction Model (VECM) will be more appropriate to use as VECM not only includes the lagged terms of the variables but also includes the first differences of the variables in separate equations. VECM shows both short-run and long-run relationships at the same time. Finally VECM based Granger Causality Tests might be conducted to find out both the presence and the direction of the causality relationships in between relevant series or variables. This explained methodological procedure was used step by step in this paper to investigate the relationships in between the relevant variables discussed earlier.

### 3.01　ADF Unit Root Test

As mentioned above, the first step in Granger causality analysis is the verification of the stationarity of the time series used in the study. In time series modelling, stationarity is a very important concept as this is an essential condition for both obtaining valid inferences and for determining the orders of integration for co-integration analysis.

In ADF approach to test the stationary of time series variable x the following regression equation is used,

$$\Delta x_t = \beta_0 + \lambda t + \psi x_{t-1} + \sum_{i=1}^{p} \alpha_i \Delta x_{t-i} + \varepsilon_t \qquad (1)$$

In equation 1, $\Delta$ is the difference operator, $\beta_0$ is the constant and $t$ is the trend term. If the estimated coefficient $\psi$ is equal to zero, the equation is said to be in the form of first differences $I(1)$ and contains a unit root. If the calculated ADF statistic is higher than McKinnon's critical value then the null hypothesis cannot be rejected and it may be concluded that the considered variable is non-stationary.

### 3.02　Johansen-Jeselius co-integration test

When time series are non-stationary the second step of causality analysis involves co-integration analysis. Co-integration analysis is needed to identify the long-run relationships between two or more variables and to overcome the risk of obtaining invalid inferences. A set of variables are defined as co-integrated if a linear combination of them is stationary after the series are differenced.

Johansen-Jeselius co-integration test is a Vector Autoregressive (VAR) based co-integration test. The separate equations of each variable in VAR include the lagged terms of all variables. For a k variable VAR model with p-lags, the specification is:

$$x_t = A_0 + B_1 x_{t-1} + B_2 x_{t-2} + \ldots + B_p x_{t-p} + E_t \qquad (2)$$

Where, $A_0$ is the $k{x}1$ vector of constants, $B_j$ is the $k{x}k$ matrix of coefficients and $E_t$ is the $k{x}1$ vector of residuals.

The transformation of equation 2 into a VECM model as below is needed if Johansen and Jeselius co-integration test is going to be used:

$$\Delta x_t = A_0 + \Gamma_1 \Delta x_{t-1} + \Gamma_2 \Delta x_{t-2} + ... + \Gamma_{p-1} \Delta x_{t-p+1} + \Pi x_{t-k} + E_t \qquad (3)$$

Here, $\Pi = \sum_{j=1}^{p} B_j - I_k$ and $\Gamma_i = \sum_{j=1}^{i} B_j - I_k$, $I_k$ is the $k{\times}k$ identity matrix, $\Gamma_i$ represents the coefficient vector of short-run dynamics, $\Pi$ is the long-run impact matrix.

The Johansen and Jeselius co-integration test has two statistics obtained from the Eigen values of $\Pi$ matrix. The first one is the Trace Test statistic.

$$\lambda_{trace}(r) = -T \sum_{i=r+1}^{k} \ln(1 - \hat{\lambda}_i) \qquad (4)$$

The second one is the Maximum Eigen Value test statistic.

$$\lambda_{max}(r, r+1) = -T \ln(1 - \hat{\lambda}_{r+1}) \qquad (5)$$

Where, $r$ is the number of co integrated vectors ranges from 0 to n-1, $\hat{\lambda}_i$ is the estimated value for i[th] ordered Eigen value of $\Pi$ matrix and $T$ is the number of usable observations.

The trace test is equal to the maximum likelihood ratio test for r co-integrated vectors against the alternative n vectors. It is a joint test where the null hypothesis is that the number of co - integrated vectors are less than or equal to r.

The maximum eigenvalue test is based on the null hypothesis that the number of co-integrating vectors is r against the alternative of r+1 vectors. It is conducted as separate tests on Eigen values.

## 3.03    Granger causality test

Granger causality test is developed by Granger (1969) to find out whether the values of one particular time series are useful in predicting another one. If $x_t$ and $y_t$ are two stationary time series. The causal model between them is:

$$x_t = \alpha_1 + \sum_{j=1}^{p} a_j x_{t-j} + \sum_{j=1}^{p} b_j y_{t-j} + \varepsilon_{1t}$$

$$\qquad (6)$$

$$y_t = \alpha_2 + \sum_{j=1}^{p} c_j x_{t-j} + \sum_{j=1}^{p} d_j y_{t-j} + \varepsilon_{2t}$$

In Granger causality framework the null hypothesis includes the non-causality and can be tested with F statistics. Here, if $b_j$ is not equal to zero $y_t$ is causing $x_t$ and if $c_j$ is not equal to zero than $x_t$ is causing $y_t$.

In Granger causality the series are assumed to be stationary but in reality some macroeconomic series are non-stationary. Nevertheless Engle and Granger (1987) provided a new method to overcome this problem. They revealed that if independent series $x_t$ and $y_t$ are non-stationary and are integrated of the same order d then the linear combination $z_t = x_t - ay_t$ is integrated of order d-b. When this is the case the series are said to be co-integrated of order (d,b). The Granger Representation Theorem given in their paper states that if a set of variables are co-integrated, a valid error correction representation of these series exist. Hence there is no need to take the differences of these series. One known implication of this result is that if $x_t$ and $y_t$ is co-integrated of order (1,1) then there exists a Granger causality relationship at least in one direction. The causality model for the co-integrated series is as follows:

$$\Delta x_t = \alpha_1 + \beta_1 \pi_{t-1} + \sum_{j=1}^{p-1} a_j \Delta x_{t-j} + \sum_{j=1}^{p-1} b_j \Delta y_{t-j} + \varepsilon_{1t}$$

$$\qquad (7)$$

$$\Delta y_t = \alpha_2 + \beta_2 \pi_{t-1} + \sum_{j=1}^{p-1} c_j \Delta x_{t-j} + \sum_{j=1}^{p-1} d_j \Delta y_{t-j} + \varepsilon_{2t}$$

**Table 3:** ADF Stationarity Test Results of Real GDP Growth Rate Series and Real Minimum Wage Growth Series on Their Own Levels

| | Δ GDP | | | Δ Real Wage | | |
| --- | --- | --- | --- | --- | --- | --- |
| | none | int. | int./trend | none | int. | int./trend |
| ADF Test Statistics | -5.898 | -5.774 | -3.701 | -4.797 | -4.689 | -4.641 |
| P-Value | 0.0001 | 0.0005 | 0.0007 | 0.0008 | 0.0053 | 0.0001 |

Δ GDP: Annual Rate of change of Real GDP
Δ Real Wage: Annual Rate of change of Real Minimum Wages

**Table 4:** ADF Stationarity Test Results of COLI Growth Rate Series and Nominal Minimum Wage Growth Series on Their Own Level

| | Δ COLI | | | Δ Nominal Minimum Wage | | |
| --- | --- | --- | --- | --- | --- | --- |
| | none | int. | int./trend | none | int. | int./trend |
| ADF Test Statistics | -1.191 | -2.786 | -1.179 | -1.426 | -3.232 | -1.062 |
| P-Value | 0.6609 | 0.2153 | 0.2109 | 0.5527 | 0.1021 | 0.2516 |

Δ COLI: Annual Rate of change of COLI (COST of Living Index)
Δ Nominal Wage: Annual Rate of Change of Nominal Minimum Wages

## 4.0    Results and discussion

As explained above initally the stationarity of the series were investigated by using ADF tests. Table 3 and 4 shows the ADF test results for all of the variables including the intercept, intercept and trend and none of the components. It can be seen that the null hypothesis that the series are non-stationary was rejected for real GDP growth rate series and real minimum wage growth rate series. However it can be concluded that both COLI growth rates and nominal minimum wage growth rate series were non-stationary at 5% significance levels.

As COLI growth rate series and nominal minimum wage growth rate series were found to be non-stationary, as a conventional next step the stationarity of these series on their first difference levels were examined. Therefore, ADF test was applied to COLI growth rate and nominal minimum wage growth rate series on their first difference levels. Table 5 shows the ADF stationary test results for COLI growth rate and nominal minimum wage growth rate variables on their first differences.  The results showed that these series were stationary at their first difference levels. Then it was concluded that these series' integrating order was 1. These results indicated co-integration between these variables and therefore co-integration order of the model should be selected as 1.

**Table 5:** ADF stationarity test results for COLI and nominal minimum wage variables on first differences

| | Δ COLI | | | Δ Nominal Wage | | |
| --- | --- | --- | --- | --- | --- | --- |
| | none | int. | int./trend | None | int. | int./trend |
| ADF Test Statistics | -4.4849 | -1.1242 | -6.7806 | -7.0257 | -6.9263 | -7.0528 |
| P-Value | 0.0020 | 0.8974 | 0.0000 | 0.0000 | 0.0000 | 0.0000 |

As real minimum wage growth rate series and real GDP growth rate series were stationary on their own levels VAR model based causality tests were conducted after determining the optimal lag lenghts. The information criteria results for the optimal lag lengths to analyze the relationships between real GDP growth rates and real minimum wage growth rates are given in Table 6. As seen from Table 6 the optimal lag length for this model was one.

**Table 6: Optimal Lag Length Criteria for Real GDP Growth Rates and Real Minimum Wage Growth Rates Model**

| Lag | LogL | LR | FPE | AIC | SC | HQ |
| --- | --- | --- | --- | --- | --- | --- |
| 0 | -1.408.704 | NA | 5494.238 | 14.28704 | 14.38662 | 14.30648 |
| 1 | -1.385.376 | 3.965744* | 6519.617* | 14.45376* | 14.75248* | 14.51208* |
| 2 | -1.378.324 | 1.057867 | 9220.051 | 14.78324 | 15.28110 | 14.88043 |
| 3 | -1.367.002 | 1.471873 | 12785.14 | 15.07002 | 15.76703 | 15.20608 |
| 4 | -1.352.271 | 1.620428 | 17778.64 | 15.32271 | 16.21887 | 15.49765 |
| 5 | -1.283.218 | 6.214716 | 15213.73 | 15.03218 | 16.12749 | 15.24600 |

* indicates lag order selected by the criterion
LR: sequential modified LR test statistic (each test at 5%level);
FPE: Final prediction error
AIC: Akaike information criterion
SC: Schwarz information criterion

HQ: Hannan-Quinn information criterion

**Table 7**: Granger causality test results between real GDP growth rates and real minimum wage growth rates

| Null Hypothesis: | Obs | F-Statistic | Prob. |
|---|---|---|---|
| RWAGES does not Granger Cause GDP | 24 | 2.55386 | 0.1250 |
| GDP does not Granger Cause RWAGES | | 1.22437 | 0.2810 |

As the optimal lag lenght of the real minimum wage growth rate and real GDP growth rate series model was calculated as one VAR based Granger causality tests were conducted. Table 7 shows Granger causality relations between real GDP growth rates and real minimum wage growth rates. It can be seen from Table 7 that neither variable granger caused the other one. In other words there was not a significant causal relationship between real GDP growth rate series and real minimum wage growth rate series in both directions.

**Table 8**: Optimal Lag Length Criteria for COLI growth rates and nominal minimum wage growth rates model

| Lag | LogL | LR | FPE | AIC | SC | HQ |
|---|---|---|---|---|---|---|
| 0 | -1.908.706 | NA | 815432.2 | 19.28706 | 19.38663 | 19.30650 |
| 1 | -1.740.314 | 28.62667 | 226827.9 | 18.00314 | 18.30186 | 18.06145 |
| 2 | -1.674.560 | 9.863073* | 178349.1 | 17.74560 | 18.24347 | 17.84279 |
| 3 | -1.643.747 | 4.005723 | 203513.8 | 17.83747 | 18.53448 | 17.97353 |
| 4 | -1.560.530 | 9.153880 | 142677.8 | 17.40530 | 18.30146 | 17.58024 |
| 5 | -1.478.755 | 7.359715 | 107508.2* | 16.98755* | 18.08286* | 17.20137* |

\* indicates lag order selected by the criterion
LR: sequential modified LR test statistic (each test at 5% level)
FPE: Final prediction error
AIC: Akaike information criterion
SC: Schwarz information criterion

Nominanl minimum wage growth rate and COLI growth rate series were found to be stationary on their first differences. Prior to Johansen and Jeselius co-integration tests, optimal lag lenghts were determined. The information criteria results for optimal lag lengths to analyze the relationship between COLI growth rates and nominal minimum wage growth rates are given in Table 8. As seen from Table 8 the optimal lag length for this model was five according to four information criteria.

**Table 9**: Co-Integration Test Results to Analyze The Relationship Between COLI Growth Rates and Nominal Minimum Wage Growth Rates

| | Unrestricted Co-Integration Rank Test (Trace) | | | |
|---|---|---|---|---|
| No. of CE(s) | Eigenvalue | Trace Statistic | 0.05 Critical Value | Prob.** |
| None * | 0.864956 | 45.05508 | 15.49471 | 0.0000 |
| At most 1 * | 0.308688 | 7.014112 | 3.841466 | 0.0081 |

Trace test indicates 2 co-integrating eqn(s) at the 0.05 level
\* denotes rejection of the hypothesis at the 0.05 level
\*\*MacKinnon-Haug-Michelis (1999) p-values

| | Unrestricted Co-Integration Rank Test (Maximum Eigenvalue) | | | |
|---|---|---|---|---|
| No. of CE(s) | Eigenvalue | Max-Eigen Statistic | 0.05 Critical Value | Prob.** |
| None * | 0.864956 | 38.04097 | 14.26460 | 0.0000 |
| At most 1 * | 0.308688 | 7.014112 | 3.841466 | 0.0081 |

Max-eigenvalue test indicates 2 cointegrating eqn(s) at the 0.05 level
* denotes rejection of the hypothesis at the 0.05 level
**MacKinnon-Haug-Michelis (1999) p-values

After determining the optimal lag lengths and orders of co-integration, Johansen and Jeselius co-integration tests can be applied. Table 9 shows the results of the co-integration tests for the models respectively. It can be seen that for each model there was a long-run relationship in between variables. The tables also reveal that there were two co-integration equations for our models.

Table 10: VECM Granger Causality/Block Exogeneity Wald Tests Between COLI Growth Rates and Nominal Minimum Wage Growth Rates

| D(INF) Excluded | Chi-sq | df | Prob. |
|---|---|---|---|
| D(NWAGE) | 24.84592 | 5 | 0.0001 |
| All | 24.84592 | 5 | 0.0001 |

| D(NWAGE) Excluded | Chi-sq | df | Prob. |
|---|---|---|---|
| D(INF) | 123.4934 | 5 | 0.0000 |
| All | 123.4934 | 5 | 0.0000 |

VECM based Granger causality relationships between COLI growth rates and nominal minimum wage growth rates were calculated in the last step. It can be concluded from Table 10 that a two way causality was present in between COLI growth rates and nominal minimum wage growth rates.

## 5.0    Conclusion and policy implication

The evaluation of the changes in real minimum wages and hence the relationship between real minimum wage growth rates and real GDP growth rates depend on the type of price deflator selected. In this study we assumed that the Turkish CPI (1994=100) underestimates the changes in the cost of living conditions of the minimum wage earners during 1988-2012 period. Moreover our hypothesis was that if minimum wages were to be deflated by using a different price index – Istanbul Chamber of Commerce's cost of living index (COLI) where the assigned weights of food and housing are higher– rather than the CPI (1994=100) the granger causality outcomes we observed in our earlier study (Sunal and Sezgin Alp, 2015) would have been significantly different. The findings obtained from our analysis were consistent with our expectations. No causality between real minimum wage growth rates and real GDP growth rates (in both directions) were observed in this study. In our previous paper a one way causality (Turkish GDPs → Turkish Real Minimum Wages) was prevalent when real minimum wages were deflated by using CPI (1994=100). Besides bidirectional causality between nominal minimum wage growth rates and COLI inflation rates were observed in this study.

In a similar way in line with our expectations official Turkish CPI in this study was found to underestimate the changes in price levels by 33.8% when compared to a different price index COLI (1968=199) constructed by Istanbul Chamber of Commerce where food expenditures have a substantially higher (+12,75%) weight. Therefore when real minimum wages are calculated by using COLI deflators the rise in real wages between 1988-2012 period is 76%. Though the same ratio is 167% when official CPI deflators are used. Also Yükseler (2014) revealed in his study by using TUİK's and Eurostat's data that the lowest 20% income group spent 34.1% on food in 2013 while the share of food in CPI (2013) was 29.16%. Also the housing expenditures of the same income group were 33.3% and the share of housing expenditures in CPI (2013) was 16.68%. Also between 2005-2013 period the cumulative rise in general prices according to CPI was 0.88 fold while the rises in food and housing were way higher than that respectively 1.05 fold and 1.19 fold. Therefore there is a strong evidence that The Turkish CPI underestimates especially the cost of living for low income households in Turkey.

We believe that these findings might have some very important policy implications. The miscalculation of changes in prices either as an underestimation or an overestimation of the real cost of living changes poses a major threat for the economy as a whole. Likewise in this manner the accuracy of the calculations have long been argued internationaly as well. In our case when calculated by using COLI deflators the rise in real minimum wage rates are slightly higher than a third of the rise in real GDP growth rates during 1988-2012 period. Moreover no Granger causality is present. In that respect asserting that the minimum wage earners took their fair shares from national income growths seems highly doubtful since the determination of minimum wage levels has been a source of debate for a long time in Turkey.

The employers are concerned with higher operational costs in an era of tight competition conditions both domestically and internationally. The governments feel responsible for controlling fast rising highly volatile general price levels as it poses a major threat for the economy as a whole. And on the other hand the welfare and the purchasing power of millions of families in Turkey (41% of formal workers were receiving minimum wages as of year 2012) depend on minimum wages. Under these tight constraints minimum wage rates are being determined every year. The more important issue is that the minimum wages represent the welfare of more than half of the workforce in Turkey. As of year 2014 according to TÜRK-İŞ (The largest Trade Union Confederation in Turkey) the minimum wages were 77% below the poverty line for a typical 4 member household. Moreover at least 4 household members had to be working and bringing minimum wages to the household so as to surpass the poverty threshold in Turkey by year 2014. Therfore, the non-causality and the underestimation findings of this study might have a crucial role in the correction of the negative minimum wage bias. As an important suggestion for the policy makers first of all at least a price index which will reveal the true change in the cost of living of minimum wage dependent households might be used. More specifically an index should be constructed where the CPI basket items and their weights will be determined from the data that will be gathered only from the expenditures of minimum wage dependent households. Moreover rather than an inflation oriented minimum wage determination a welfare driven process might be implemented. Therefore as an alternative policy suggestion a better price deflator should be constructed and the rises in real national income growths and productivity growths should also be reflected directly when determining minimum wages to provide a just and a better distribution.

## References

Barrett, G.F., Brzozowski, M. (2010). "Using Engel Curves to Estimate The Bias in The Australian CPI", The Economic Record, 68 (272), 1-14. http://dx.doi.org/10.1111/j.1475-4932.2009.00594.x

Beatty, K.M., Larsen, E.R. (2005). "Using Engel Curve to Estimate Bias in The Canadian CPI As a Cost of Living Index", Canadian Journal of Economics, 38(2), 482-99. http://dx.doi.org/10.1111/j.0008-4085.2005.00289.x

Boskin (Chair), M. J., E. R. Dulberger, R. J. Gordon, Z. Griliches, D. W. Jorgenson. 1996. Final report of the Commission to Study the Consumer Price Index. U.S. Senate, Committee on Finance, Washington DC: GPO.

Costa, D.L. (2000). "American Living Standards 1888-1994: Evidence From Consumer Expenditures", NBER Working Papers, No: 7650, 1-29.

Deere, D., Murphy, K. and Welch, F. (1995). "Employment and the 1990-1991 Minimum Wage Hike." American Economic Review, 85(2), 232-37.

Dickens, R., Manning,S. ve Machin, A. (1999). "The Effects of Minimum Wages on Employment: Theory and Evidence from Britain", Journal of Labor Economics,17(1), 1-22. http://dx.doi.org/10.1086/209911

Dickey, D. A., Fuller, W. A. (1979). "Distribution of the Estimators for Autoregressive Time Series with a Unit Root", Journal of the American Statistical Association, 74 (366), 427-431 http://dx.doi.org/10.2307/2286348

Engle, R. F., Granger, C. W. J. (1987). "Cointegration and Error Correction: Representation, Estimation and Testing," Econometrica, 55(2), 251-276. http://dx.doi.org/10.2307/1913236

Granger, C. W. J. (1969). "Investigating Causal Relations by Econometric Models and Cross- Spectral Methods", Econometrica, 37, 424-438. http://dx.doi.org/10.2307/1912791

Hamilton, B.W. (1998). "The True Cost of Living: 1974-1991", J. Hopkins University Working Paper Archive. http://krieger2.jhu.edu/economics/wpcontent/uploads/pdf/papers/wp395Hamilton.pdf (15.04.2015)

Heineke, J.M. (1979). "Exact Aggregation and Estimation", Economics Letters, 4, 157-62. http://dx.doi.org/10.1016/0165-1765(79)90227-1

Irmen, A. and Wigger, B. (2002). "National Minimum Wages, Capital Mobility and Global Economic Growth," CEPR Discussion Papers 3286..

Johansen, S. and Juselius, K. (1990), "Maximum Likelihood Estimation and Inference on Co-integration With Applications for the Demand for Money", Oxford Bulletin of Economics and Statistics, 52 (2), 169-210. http://dx.doi.org/10.1111/j.1468-0084.1990.mp52002003.x

Kaufman, B.E. (2010). "Institutional Economics and The Minimum Wage: Broadening The Theoretical and Policy Debate", Industrial and Labor Relations Review, 63(3), 427-453. http://dx.doi.org/10.1177/001979391006300304

Moosa, I.A. (1997). "Does The Chinese Official CPI Underestimate Inflation?", Applied Economics Letters, 4, 301-4. http://dx.doi.org/10.1080/758532597

Murphy, E., Garvey, E. (2005). "Cost of Living Indices and Flexible Consumption Behaviour: A Partial Critique", National University of Ireland Working Paper, No:103, 1-13.

Murphy, E., Garvey, E. (2004). "A Consumer Price Index For Low Income Households in Ireland (1989-2001)", Combat Poverty Agency Working Paper Series, No: 04/03, 1-34.

Neumark, D., Wascher, W. (2006). "Minimum Wages and Emplyment:A Review of Evidence from The New Minimum Wage Research", NBER Working Paper Series, Working Paper 12663, Cambridge:USA.

Prasch, E. (1996). "In Defence of The Minimum Wage", Journal of Economic Issues, 30(2), 391- 397. http://dx.doi.org/10.1080/00213624.1996.11505802

Rama, M. (2001). "Teh Consequences of Doubling The Minimum Wage: The Case of Indonesia", Industrial and Labour Relations Review, 54(4), 864-881. http://dx.doi.org/10.2307/2696117

SGK İstatistik Yıllıkları (2012). 5510 Sayılı Kanunun 4-1/a Maddesi Kapsamındaki Zorunlu Sigortalıların ve Prim Ödeme Gün Sayılarının Kazanç Aralıklarına, Sektörlere ve Cinsiyete Göre Dağılımı, http://www.sgk.gov.tr/wps/portal/tr/kurumsal/istatistikler/sgk_istatistik_yilliklari (15.03.2014)

Stigler, G. (1946). "The Economics of Minimum Wage Legislation" American Economic Review, 36(3), 358–65.

Stigler, G. (1961). The Price Statistics of The Federal Government. New York: National Bureau of Economic Research.

Sunal, O., Sezgin Alp, Ö. (2015). "Türkiye'de Reel Asgari Ücretler ve Reel GSYİH Değişmeleri Arasındaki Nedensellik İlişkisi: Enflasyon Oranına Endekslenmiş Bir Nominal Asgari Ücret Politikası", Ankara Üniversitesi SBF Dergisi, 70(1), 111-29. http://dx.doi.org/10.16987/ausbf.80017

TÜİK Hanehalkı İşgücü Anketi Sonuçları, İstihdam Edilenlerin Yıllara Göre İşteki Durumu, http://www.tuik.gov.tr/PreTablo.do?alt_id=1007 (15.03.2104)

TÜRK-İŞ Haber Bülteni, Şubat 2014 Açlık ve Yoksulluk Sınırı, http://www.turkis.org.tr/source.cms.docs/turkis.org.tr.ce/docs/file/acliksubat14.pdf (15.03.2014)

Yükseler, Z. (2014). "Türkiye'de Tüketim Harcamalarının Yapısı ve Gıda Harcamaları". http://www.researchgate.net/publication/258808662_YATIRIMTASARRUF_DENGES_TRKYE_UYGULAMASI. (21.03.2015)

# 4

# Linkage between emigration and export flows: The case of Bangladesh

Muhammad Shariat Ullah[a]*, Mohammad Thoufiqul Islam[b]

[a] Associate Professor, Department of Management, University of Dhaka, Dhaka 1000, Bangladesh.
[b] Associate Professor, Department of Management, University of Dhaka, Dhaka 1000, Bangladesh.
*Corresponding author's email address: shariat@du.ac.bd

| ARTICLE INFO | ABSTRACT |
| --- | --- |
| Keywords:<br>Emigration; Export;<br>Complementary;<br>Gravity model;<br>Substitution. | This paper applies the well-known gravity model to empirically assess the linkage between emigration and export flows of a developing country. Econometric analysis of panel data unveils a significant substituting relationship between export flows from the source country and stock of emigrants to the destination country. This result not only contradicts with existing literature but also justifies manifold relationship between goods and manpower exports. Economic policy as well as foreign policy in Bangladesh must address this inherent relationship between export of goods and labor since emigration of unskilled labor largely depends on bilateral diplomatic relations whereas export patterns depend on comparative cost advantage. |

## 1.0    Introduction

Bangladesh is one of the leading exporters of manpower and it consistently strives to promote labor emigration since the country's balance of payments heavily relies on inward remittances. The World Bank (2011) estimated that there were 5.4 million Bangladeshi emigrants in the world that placed it as the second largest South Asian country of international labor supply and the sixth largest source of global immigration. Besides, Bangladesh has long been liberalizing its trade and investment policies with the aim of achieving export-led growth. Since the country aspires to stimulate growth of both labor and goods export; the key question is how these two flows are inter-related. In other words, it is imperative to ascertain the impact of labor emigration on the export of manufactures. Hence, we intend to investigate whether labor export promotes or hurts export of goods. Although such notion has been investigated from the perspective of export and immigration; research evidence is by far very rare on the relationship between export and emigration.

Wong (1995) notes that factor movements beyond borders are significant and can exert profound effects not only on countries' bilateral trade in goods but also on their economic welfare. Though not unanimous, it is apparent that there are significant interactions between trade and factor mobility. However, international trade theories lack consensus, as to whether the goods and labor flows are substitutes or complements (Mundra, 2005). Standard neo-classical trade theory treats trade and migration as substitutes. Mundell (1957) postulates that international trade in goods and factor mobility is substitutes because more of one leads to less of the other. Growth in international trade lowers the potential mobility of factors, while a rise in international mobility of factors reduces the volume of trade between countries.

The assertions that international trade and factor mobility are substitutes derive from Paul Samuelson's advancement of the Factor-Price-Equalization theorem which states that international trade brings about equalization in earnings for homogenous factors across nations which is corollary to Heckscher-Ohlin trade theory. The logic behind this idea is that as long as relative factor prices differ between countries, same happens to commodity prices, and trade continues to rise. Therefore, international trade continues to expand until relative commodity prices and relative factor prices are exactly equal between countries. This intuition is corollary to the H-O theorem of trade and is commonly referred to as H-O-S theorem which holds only of assumptions of the H-O theorem, as such perfect competition in all commodity and factor markets and constant returns to scale. The essence of the H-O-S theorem is that trade acts as substitutes for the international mobility of factors of production in its effect on factor prices. With perfect mobility, labor would migrate from low wage nation to the high wage nation and capital would move from the low-return to the high-return nation (Salvatore, 2010). Hence, from the Heckscher-Ohlin perspective, trade and factor flows are substitutes when the countries involved possess dissimilar factor endowments. On the contrary, trade and factor flows between countries with similar factor endowments but dissimilar technologies are complements.

Thus, international migration is driven by differences in both factor endowments and technologies across countries, and trade theory does not provide unanimous picture of whether trade and immigration act as substitutes or complements (Mundra, 2005). In order overcome theoretical contradictions, empirical researches were relied on. Nonetheless, empirical research mostly evidenced the relationship between immigration and trade of host countries. Considering lack of literature on linkage between emigration and trade, we devised this study that employs the gravity model of trade to empirically examine the impact of emigrants' stock on the export flows from Bangladesh. It is worth mentioning that Bangladesh not only constitutes a major source of international labor supply; the country profoundly relies on inward remittances for dealing with macroeconomic shocks. Thus, this research aims to minimize the gap of existing literature by incorporating the supply side perspective; and deliver important policy implications for the developing countries that appear to be major sources of manpower supply.

The rest of the paper is structured as follows: Section 2 reviews empirical literature; Section 3 provides empirical model of this research along with operational definition of the underlying variables; Section 4 explains data and methodology; Section 5 reports results and discussion; and the last section gives conclusion and policy implications.

## 2.0    Literature review and research hypothesis

The realm of globalization consists of a number of pillars, including international trade, international migration, and international investment (Roy and Berg, 2006) and, these three components are growing much more rapidly than output (Kugler and Rapoport, 2011). As a result of the rapid rise in international labor flows, research on migration related aspects drew immense attention. Empirics on international migration can be grouped into three streams of analyses: (1) determinants of international labor migration (Borjas, 1987; Clark et al. 2007; Karemera et al. 2000; Kim and Cohen, 2010; Lewer and Berg, 2008; Mayda, 2007; Pedersen et al. 2008; Zavodny, 1999); (2) relationship between international trade and immigration (Gould, 1994; Co et al. 2004; Dunlevy and Hutchinson, 1999; Girma and Yu, 2002; Hatzigeorgiou, 2010; Lewer and Berg, 2009; Mundra, 2005); and (3) migration and development linkage (Emmanuel et al. 2009; Olesen, 2002).

Wong (1995) argues that international labor migration is a very special type of factor movement because it involves not just the movement of the factor but also the movement of the factor of owners. Flows of labor internationally cause a change in the quantity and quality composition of factor supplies in the source and destination countries. Thus, movement of labor augments production and demand in the receiving country, while creates the opposite impact on the sending country. Immigrants also influence international trade flows across countries because they bring a preference for their home country products that foster bilateral trade between home and host economies. Furthermore, immigrants form a network in the host country and lower the transaction cost with host country, thereby, facilitates bilateral trade. But the very fundamental question of whether labor migration and trade acts as complements or substitutes remains unsettled in the theoretical domain. The empirical evidences in this regard are provided in the following.

Pioneering studies by Gould (1994) and Dunlevy and Hutchinson (1999) indicate a positive link between trade flows and immigration in the USA. In recent studies, Co et al. (2004) and Mundra (2005) also document a strong pro-trade effect of immigration in the USA, with state level data and country level data, respectively. Co et al.

(2004) explore the export effect of immigration using state level exports to 28 immigrant source countries for a single year, while Mundra (2005) examines the effects of immigration on both components of international trade—export and imports. The later study undertakes a semi-parametric approach with the dynamic fixed effects estimation technique which shows that inbound labor migration and US's trade flows act as complements. Immigration effect on imports is positive for all goods (finished and intermediate) but the effect on exports is positive only for finished goods. 'The findings supports the hypothesis that for finished goods where country specific information is crucial for trading, immigrants have a pro-trade effect for both US imports and US exports'(Mundra 2005, p.65).

Head and Ries (1998) examine the trade and migration link in the case of Canada using the host country's trade with 136 partners from year 1980 to 1992. The same study uncovers a positive relationship between Canadian trade flows and international migration to this country. The gravity type analysis reveals that a 10 percent rise in immigrants contributes to one percent increase in export flows from Canada to the immigrants' home country and three percent increase in imports to the former from the latter.

Girma and Yu (2002) explore the relationship between immigration and trade using UK data and show that the impact on trade differ depending on whether immigrants come from commonwealth or non-commonwealth countries. Specifically, it finds that immigration from non-commonwealth countries have a positive significant effect on exports from and imports to the UK. While looking on the commonwealth countries, it finds no significant export impact and a reduction of imports. Thus, immigrants from the commonwealth countries appear to substitute imports to the UK.

Lewer and Berg (2009) present the findings on trade and immigration link from the group of OECD countries. They study 10 year panel data of bilateral trade among 16 OECD countries and a large set of immigrant source countries and find a result supportive to the hypothesis that trade and immigration link in the OECD countries is complementary. Their findings establish that immigration influences trade positively through a number of channels as such creating trade networks between immigrants' sending and receiving countries, and raising income in the home countries.

The available empirical literature mostly unveils a pro-trade link between trade and migration from the perspective of advanced countries that receive immigrants and thus clearly signal a dearth of literature from the home country perspective. Under this backdrop, we develop the following hypothesis for empirical testing:
**Hypothesis:** Export of manufactures from Bangladesh stimulates export of manpower and thus these two flows act as complements.

## 3.0    Model specification

In order to assess the link between emigration and export flows, a gravity type specification with panel data is employed. Many authors including Head and Ries (1998), Dunlevy and Hutchinson (1999), Rauch and Trindade (2002), Co et al. (2004), Lewer and Berg (2009) applied the gravity model of trade for exploring linkage between trade and immigration. In line with the gravity model of trade, we specify the equation.

$$\ln(EX_{ijt}) = \beta_0 + \beta_1 \ln(GDP_{it}) + \beta_2 \ln(GDP_{jt}) + \beta_3 \ln(RGDPPC_{ijt})$$
$$+ \beta_4 \ln(DIST_{ij}) + \beta_5 \ln(RER_{ijt}) + \beta_6 \ln(MSTOCK_{ijt}) + \varepsilon_{ijt}$$
$$j = 1,\dots,n \quad t = 1,\dots,T$$

In equation, $ln$ denotes natural logarithm, $i$ indicates the exporting country which is Bangladesh in the current analysis, $j = 1,\dots,n$ stands for the cross-section and $t = 1,\dots,T$ implies the time period. The dependent variable $EX_{ijt}$ stands for export flows from Bangladesh to country $j$ at time $t$.

▪    $GDP_{it}$ and $GDP_{jt}$ (Gross domestic product of exporter and importer): The GDP of the exporter ($GDP_{it}$) is the measure of supply of exports, while the importer's GDP ($GDP_{jt}$) is the measure of demand for imports. Exports from a country increase with its own GDP growth and imports to a country increase with the growth of its own GDP. Therefore, $\beta_1$ and $\beta_2$ are expected to have positive effects on bilateral trade flows. In this study, GDP data is measured at nominal US $.

▪    $RGDPC_{ijt}$ (Country $j$'s GDP per capita relative to $i$'s GDP per capita): This variable can have a positive or negative sign. A positive sign indicates that export from Bangladesh mainly flows to the countries having high income difference with the former and export pattern falls with inter-industry type, while a negative sign implies that export patterns fits with intra-industry type.

- DIST$_{ij}$ (Distance): In the gravity model, distance is commonly used as the proxy of transportation costs. Transportation costs have both direct and indirect effects on international trade flows. The direct effects of transportation costs on trade flows come in the form a change in the price of the traded commodity between nations, while indirect influence is exerted through the firm's international location decision. The higher the costs of transportation including freight charges, insurance charges, cost of loading and unloading; the lower will be the volume of bilateral trade. That means, a homogeneous good will be traded internationally only if the pre-trade price difference between two countries exceeds the costs of transporting the good from one nation to the other (Salvatore, 2010). Since transportation costs are inversely related to trade flows, the distance variable should have a negative sign.

- RER$_{ijt}$ (Bilateral real exchange rates): Bilateral nominal exchange rate can be defined as unit(s) of home currency (currency of the exporting country) to a unit of foreign currency (currency of the importing country). When nominal exchange rate is adjusted with the foreign to domestic price ratio, it becomes the bilateral real exchange rate. The process of finding the bilateral real exchange rates is as follows:

$$RER_{ij} = NER_{ij/\$}\frac{CPI_j}{CPI_i}$$

where RER denotes real exchange rate; NER stands for nominal exchange rates in US $; CPI indicates consumer price index; $i$ and $j$ means exporter and importer, respectively. A rise (fall) in the bilateral exchange rate indicates depreciation (appreciation) of exporter's currency. Depreciation of an exporter's currency stimulates export flows due to decline in relative price levels. Hence, it should have a positive sign.

- $MSTOCK_{ijt}$ measures the export effects of the stock of Bangladesh's emigrants in country $j$. A positive sign of $\beta_6$ indicates complementarity between export and emigration, while a negative sign implies that these flows act as substitutes. Stock data were not available for the GCC countries for some years and are generated by the authors. In doing so, emigration stock in year $t$ have been calculated by summing the annual number of emigrants to country $j$ during five consecutive years in the past and deducting the number of emigrants entering into the same destination in year $t_{-6}$. The assumption of this calculation process was that the workers emigrate to the GCC countries for contract job and have to return to home after certain period of time, five years in this case, since the host countries do not allow life time settlement.

## 4.0 Data and methodology

### 4.01 Data sources

Empirical analysis deals with export flows both labor and goods from Bangladesh to 20 destinations[1] during the period of 1995-2010. The destination countries have been limited to those that are the major recipients of immigrants from Bangladesh. Ironically, these sample countries also constitute Bangladesh's major export partners and they shared over 67 percent of Bangladesh's total export of goods in the year 2010. We obtained bilateral exports data in current US ($) from the IMF's Direction of Trade Statistics (CD-ROM). Consumer price index, GDP and GDP per capita data came from WDI (CD-ROM) while bilateral nominal exchange rates in US$ were collected from the UNCTAD. Distance data were generated from the CEPII's distance data set. Data on labor emigration were accumulated from numerous sources as such Citizenship and Immigration Statistics of Canada, Australian Department of Immigration and Citizenship, International Labor Organization (ILO), Migration Information Organization, National Statistical Institute of Italy, World Bank's Global Migration Database.

### 4.02 Methodology

As empirical tools, we employ random effects (RE) and fixed effects (FE). Post estimation tests indicate the presence of serial correlation as well as cross-sectional dependence.

    (i) Wooldridge test of autocorrelation:
    H$_0$: No first order autocorrelation.
    F = 10.32, P > F = 0.00. Hence, the null of no autocorrelation in the panel is rejected.
    (ii) Pesaran's test of cross-sectional dependence:
    H$_0$: There is no cross-sectional dependence (CD).
    CD = 29.81, P = 0.00. Thus, the null of cross-sectional independence is rejected.

Due to the presence of serial correlation and cross-sectional dependence in the series, RE and FE with AR(1) is

---

[1] The export partners of Bangladesh included Australia, Bahrain, Brunei Darussalam, Canada, Germany, Italy, Republic of Korea, Kuwait, Malaysia, Netherlands, Norway, Oman, Qatar, Saudi Arabia, Singapore, Spain, Sweden, United Arab Emirates, United Kingdom, and United States.

applied and estimation results are reported in Table 1. Both estimation techniques show proper sign and significance at the same level, *i.e.*, at a 1% level of significance. As usual, the fixed effects model reports slightly lower magnitude of coefficients due to the control of unobserved fixed effects. Although, both RE and FE report closely similar findings, Hausman test has been conducted in order to select the appropriate one. The Hausman test shows a value of Chi = 3.16 with P = 0.68 and thus, RE model is appropriate over the FE. However, this choice causes no difference in the analysis of linkage between emigration and export since both regressions reveal exactly the same level of coefficient with the same level of significance. One reason for no variation in the two alternative estimation methods is that all the variables included in the regression are in the bilateral (*i* and *j*) form. In the presence of variables that are unilaterally related to either *i* or *j*, FE shows more consistent result as suggested by Feenstra (2002).

## 5.0    Results and discussion

This study finds theoretically and empirically consistent results relating to the conventional determinants of goods exports as such GDP, difference between GDP per capita of export and import country, geographic distance, and real exchange rate. More specifically, $\beta_1$ and $\beta_2$ indicate that GDP of the export and import country have significant positive effects on export flows. Thus, capacity expansion of the exporter and income growth of the importer are important determinants of bilateral trade. RGDPC reports a positive sign indicating that export from Bangladesh mainly flows to those countries that have high income difference with the former and export pattern fits with inter-industry type. Geographic distance between countries also constitutes an important determinant of export. Higher distance exerts negative effect on export since transportation cost rises with a distant trade partner. Real exchange rate was found to have positive impact on export which means depreciation of the exporter's currency stimulates export flows due to a decline in relative price levels.

| Table 1: RE and FE with AR (1) correction | | |
|---|---|---|
| VARIABLES | RE | FE |
| GDPj | 1.38*** | 1.34*** |
|  | (0.000) | (0.000) |
| GDPi | 1.13*** | — |
|  | (0.000) |  |
| RGDPPC | 0.40*** | 0.37*** |
|  | (0.000) | (0.000) |
| DIST | -0.99*** | -0.70*** |
|  | (0.000) | (0.000) |
| RER | 0.29*** | 0.28*** |
|  | (0.000) | (0.000) |
| MSTOCK | -0.14*** | -0.14*** |
|  | (0.000) | (0.000) |
| CONSTANT | -39.46*** | -12.69*** |
|  | (0.000) | (0.000) |
| $R^2$ | 0.91 | 0.92 |
| Wald Chi | 2941 | — |
| F | — | 616 |
| Observations | 318 | 302 |
| Number of year | 16 | 16 |
| Number of cross section | 20 | 20 |

*Notes:* All variables are in natural logarithms. *P*-values are in parenthesis. *** indicate significance at a 1 % level. It fails to reject the null hypothesis that the error term is normally distributed at any level of significance since the probability of skewness of residual was 0.72.

They key finding of the empirical exercise here is that stock of emigrants significantly lower exports from Bangladesh. In other words, a higher stock of manpower substitutes Bangladesh's exports in the immigrants receiving countries. The estimated coefficient of emigrant stock variable (MSTOCK) indicates that a one percent increase in the stock of emigrants reduces exports by 0.14 percent. That means, export falls about one percent by a 10 percent rise in emigrants stock in the destination country. Thus, we reject the hypothesis of complementary relationship between goods and manpower exports from Bangladesh to the rest of the world. Our results contradict with Co et al. (2004), Dunlevy and Hutchinson (1999), Gould, 1994, Head and Ries (1998), Lewer and Berg (2009) and Mundra, 2005 who investigated linkage between export of goods from and migration to advanced countries. Such contrasted results signify that effects of labor migration on goods export from home and host countries are different. The cause of such variation can also be attributed to the type of manufacturing exports. In essence, manpower exports from a country will substitute its export of labor intensive manufactures. Our findings further document that both labor and goods export from Bangladesh do not flow to the same high income economies even though high income of destination countries have positive effect on both of these flows. In fact, Bangladesh's major export partners are the high income OECD countries, whereas the GCC countries are the prime locations for labor emigration.

## 6.0    Conclusion and policy implications

The gravity model analysis of relationship between export of goods and labor from Bangladesh to 20 major trade partners demonstrates that these two flows function as substitutes to one another. As a result of substituting relationship, higher growth of one will reduce the growth of the other in the same location. Our results sharply contradict with empirical literature. Such dissimilar empirics carry a number of connotations as such (i) impact of labor migration on the home and host country's export of goods may be different; (ii) the nature of relationship between manpower and goods export depends on the skill level of manpower and labor vs. capital intensity of goods; (iii) labor and goods from Bangladesh move to two distinct types of destinations. Thus, economic policy to stimulate export of goods and manpower must give cognizance to this intrinsic relationship between them.

The policy implications of this finding is that high income countries in the West will continue to serve as export markets for Bangladesh's manufactured goods, while the Gulf countries will remain as the key locations for emigration, at least under the current pattern of labor intensive manufactures and export of unskilled manpower. Economic policy as well as foreign policy in Bangladesh must address this inherent relationship between export and labor flows since emigration of unskilled labor largely depends on bilateral diplomatic relations whereas export patterns depend on comparative cost advantage. Furthermore, expansion of domestic production capacity and employment generation must be facilitated in the country to foster pro-trade oriented long-run economic development. This objective can be put in action by proper channeling of remittances in the short to midterm. However, a long term tendency of high growth in labor outflows and growing dependence of Bangladesh's economy on remittance receipts will depress role of export as an engine of growth. Apart from minimizing the gap in existing literature and making policy related contributions, the authors generated emigration stock data for Bangladesh by accessing to numerous sources.

## References

Borjas, J.G. (1987) Self-selection and the Earnings of Immigrants, American Economic Review, 77(4), 531-553.

Clark, X., Timothy, J., J.G. Williamson (2007) Explaining U.S. Immigration, 1971-1998, The Review of Economics and Statistics, 89(2):359-373. http://dx.doi.org/10.1162/rest.89.2.359

Co, C.Y., Euzent, P., Martin, T. (2004) The Export Effect of Immigration into the US. Applied Economics, 36(6): 573-583. http://dx.doi.org/10.1080/0003684042000217616

Dunlevy, J.A., Hutchinson, W.K. (1999) The Impact of Immigration on American Import Trade in the Late Nineteenth Centuries. Journal of Economic History, 59(4):1043-1062. http://dx.doi.org/10.1017/S002205070002413X

Emmanuel, L., Mark, P., Francisco, R., Mathew, C. (2009) Revisiting the Migration-Development Nexus: A Gravity Model Approach, Human Development Research Paper 2009/44, UNDP. http://mpra.ub.uni-muenchen.de/19227/ (Accessed: 10 January 2012).

Feenstra, R.C. (2002) Border Effects and the Gravity Equation: Consistent Methods for Estimation, Scottish Journal of Political Economy, 49(5):491-506. http://dx.doi.org/10.1111/1467-9485.00244

Girma, S., Yu, Z. (2002) The Link between Immigration and Trade: Evidence from the United Kingdom. Review of World Economics, 138(1): 115-130. http://dx.doi.org/10.1007/bf02707326

Girma, S., Yu, Z. (2002) The Link between Immigration and Trade: Evidence from the United Kingdom. Review of World Economics, 138(1): 115-130. http://dx.doi.org/10.1007/bf02707326

Gould, D. (1994) Immigration Links to the Home Country: Empirical Implications for US Bilateral Trade Flow. The Review of Economics and Statistics, 76(2):302-316. http://dx.doi.org/10.2307/2109884

Hatzigeorgiou, A. (2010) Migration as Trade Facilitation: Assessing the Links between International Trade and Migration. The B.E. Journal of Economic Analysis & Policy, 10(1): 1-33. http://dx.doi.org/10.2202/1935-1682.2100

Hatzigeorgiou, A. (2010) Migration as Trade Facilitation: Assessing the Links between International Trade and Migration. The B.E. Journal of Economic Analysis & Policy, 10(1): 1-33. http://dx.doi.org/10.2202/1935-1682.2100

Head, K., Ries, J. (1998) Immigration and Trade Creation: Econometric Evidence from Canada. Canadian Journal of Economics, 31(1): 47-62. http://dx.doi.org/10.2307/136376

Karemera, D., Oguledo, V.I., Davis, B. (2000) A Gravity Model Analysis of International Migration to North America, Applied Economics, 32(13):1745-1755. http://dx.doi.org/10.1080/000368400421093

Kim, K., Cohen, J.E. (2010) Determinants of International Migration Flows to and from Industrialized Countries: A panel Data Approach beyond Gravity, International Migration Review, 44(4):899-932. http://dx.doi.org/10.1111/j.1747-7379.2010.00830.x

Kugler, M., Rapoport, H. (2011) Migration, FDI, and the Margins of Trade. Center for International Development at Harvard University, Working Paper No. 222.

Lewer J.J. and Berg, H. Van den (2008) A Gravity Model of Immigration, Economic Letters, 99(1):164-167. http://dx.doi.org/10.1016/j.econlet.2007.06.019

Mayda, A.M. (2007) International Migration: A Panel Data Analysis of the Determinants of Bilateral Flows, Center for Research and Analysis of Migration, Discussion Paper No. 07/07. http://eprints.ucl.ac.uk/14276/1/14276.pdf (Accessed: 4 May 2012).

Mundell, R.A. (1957) International Trade and Factor Mobility. The American Economic Review, 47(3):321-335.

Mundra, K. (2005) Immigration and International Trade: A Semiparametric Empirical Investigation. Journal of International Trade and Economic Development, 14(1):65-91. http://dx.doi.org/10.1080/0963819042000333252

Olesen, H. (2002) Migration, Return and Development: An Institutional Perspective. International Migration, 40(5):125-150. http://dx.doi.org/10.1111/1468-2435.00214

Pedersen, P.J., Pytlikova, M., Smith, N. (2008) Selection and Network Effects-Migration flows into OECD Countries, European Economic Review, 52(7):1160-1186. http://dx.doi.org/10.1016/j.euroecorev.2007.12.002

Rauch, J.E., Trindade, V. (2002) Ethnic Chinese Networks in International Trade. The Review of Economics and Statistics, 84 (1):116–130. http://dx.doi.org/10.1162/003465302317331955

Roy, A.G., Berg, H. (2006) Foreign Direct Investment and Economic Growth: A Time Series Approach. Global Economy Journal, 6(1):1-19.

Salvatore, D. (2010) Introduction to International Economics. Second Edition, USA: John Wiley and Sons.

Wong, K. (1995) International Trade in Goods and Factor Mobility. The MIT Press: Massachusetts, USA.

World Bank (2011) Migration and Remittances Fact Book 2011, 2nd Edition, Washington: USA.

Zavodny, M. (1999) Determinants of Recent Immigrants' Locational Choices, The International Migration Review, 33(4):1014-1030. http://dx.doi.org/10.2307/2547361

# 5

# Banking access for the poor: Adoption and strategies in rural areas of Bangladesh

Mohammad Anisur Rahman [a*], Xu Qi[b], Md. Tariqul Islam[b]

[a] Department of Logistics Management and e-Commerce, Glorious Sun School of Business and Management Donghua University, Shanghai, China.
[a] Department of Management Information Systems, University of Dhaka, Bangladesh.
[b] Department of Logistics Management and e-Commerce, Glorious Sun School of Business and Management, Donghua University, Shanghai, China. E-mail: xuqi@dhu.edu.cn
[c] Department of Business Administration, BGMEA University of Fashion & Technology(BUFT), Dhaka, Bangladesh. E-mail: tareq.islam.du@gmail.com
*Corresponding author's email address: anisur@du.ac.bd

| ARTICLE INFO | ABSTRACT |
|---|---|
| Keywords:<br>Adoption; Bangladesh;<br>Mobile banking; Rural;<br>Strategies. | The progress of Mobile Banking (M-banking) is unsatisfactory in terms of achieving a key objective, i.e. to reach the inaccessible unbanked customers at an affordable cost for financial inclusion. We identify the causes to this problem through the investigating the factors affecting the adoption of m-banking in remote areas of Bangladesh using a 236 primary sample of m-bank customers from seven geographical locations and across professions. We document a positive effect of perceived ease of use, trusts, and perceived usefulness, and a negative effect of user interface on adopting m-banking in rural Bangladesh. our findings provides significant policy implications for policy planners and the bank managers to enrich their policies and strategies for promoting financial inclusion as well as successful banking business in rural of Bangladesh. |

## 1.0    Introduction

Financial inclusion (FI) and development are closely related. Sarma and Pais (2011) defined financial inclusion as *a process that ensures availability, the ease of access, and usage of the formal financial system for all members of an economy.* It facilitates efficient allocation of resources and financial management; increasing formal savings and credits; reduction of poverty and improving equality (Chibba, 2009; Sarma & Pais, 2011). Different countries especially lower and the middle-income group set FI as their policy priority to achieve SDGs by capitalizing the use of ICT to embrace the marginal people financially.

Mobile phone, a blessing of ICT, has shown promising outcome in both economic empowerment and social development in different countries (Rashid & Elder, 2009). Citizen around the world can access information related to health, education, weather, news, jobs, finance and market through mobile phones. People in developing countries are enjoying financial systems, government services, and citizen feedback mechanisms with the increased mobile penetration (Canuto, 2013). These economic and social benefits of a cell phone, however, evidently found to be the highest in rural areas (Sarma and Pais 2011), where the marginal, hard to reach and unbanked people live. These people have access to mobile but financially excluded, which is evident from the world development indicators.

The World Bank data (2014) shows that in the high-income group countries 73% of the population (age 15+) has bank account, and 126% of the population (age 15+) has mobile phone subscription; whereas in low to middle income countries about 53% of the population (age 15+) has bank account while 90% of the population (age 15+) has mobile access. In Bangladesh, 29% of the population (age 15+) has a bank account while 76% of the population (age 15+) has mobile access. The data reveals that people in the high-income group have higher banking and mobile access than that of lower and middle-income nations. Mobile banking is one of the best ways to reach these unbanked population for financial inclusion.

The term mobile banking simply means the banking services delivered and received using cell phones. The adoption of ICT in the banking and financial sector opened this new, innovative and affordable channel of delivering banking and financial services. Mobile banking, is using same technology like e-banking (Welch, 1999), enabled the banking industry to perform fastest wireless and Internet commercial transactions (Greenacre & Buckley, 2014). However, the core advantage of mobile banking is that banks can serve its customers even where the internet is absent and with minimum technological knowledge of customers. As a result, the modern means of sitting in front of computers for getting any services is no more required to obtain the defined services (Ahmed, Rayhan, Islam, & Mahjabin, 2012).

Taking the advantage of the mobility (Suoranta, 2003) and internet independent technology, mobile banking in different countries were launched to access the unbanked population for financial inclusion (Nabi et al., 2012). The assumption behind the financial inclusion of the unbanked population is facilitating them to access the economic benefits, such as increased savings, credits, increased income and protection from financial shocks (Donner & Tellez, 2008). The government can reap the benefits of increased capital from the untapped portion of the population, transparency in the transactions, increased tax potentiality and greater circulation of money that were currently not in the account. For example, M-Pesa, mobile banking service in Kenya is a blockbuster success story for the world. It was introduced in 2007 to make and receive payments. The household that adopted M-Pesa seemed to have increased in income by 5-30% (The Economist, 2013). Through mobile banking, the Kenya have been able to drop its financially excluded population to 3% (The Daily Prothom Alo, 2015). M-Pesa today operates in 10 countries. M-Pesa, the mobile banking model, has been replicated in other parts of the world including Bangladesh.

Mobile banking in Bangladesh, started in the year 2011, is playing a significant role in the rural economy of Bangladesh. The most popular services they enjoy from mobile banking are deposit and withdrawal of money, payment of gas, electricity and water bill. According to Bangladesh Bank (till May 2016), 29 banks are authorized for providing mobile banking services, of which 19 have already started their functions; about Tk. 6.2 billion transacted daily over mobile banking platform through 592 thousand agents.

However, the effect of mobile banking on the financial inclusion of the poorest 40% of the adult population, who reside in the rural areas in Bangladesh, is scanty. In the year 2011, while the mobile banking was introduced, the financial inclusion of the poorest 40% adult in Bangladesh was 21.2% and in the year 2014, that grew to 21.5% (The World Bank, 2014a). Clearly, the policy makers both the government and the banks are missing something, which is deterring the poorest 40% of the adult population to adopt mobile banking although they are the subscribers of cell phones.

Till date, most of the research on mobile banking adoption (Aderonke, 2010; Akturan & Tezcan, 2012; Al-Jabri & Sohail, 2012; AlSoufi & Ali, 2014; Crabbe, Standing, Standing, & Karjaluoto, 2009; DiVanna, 2003; Goi, 2006; Gu, Lee, & Suh, 2009; Haig, 2002; Hanafizadeh, Behboudi, Abedini Koshksaray, & Jalilvand Shirkhani Tabar, 2014; Hassan, Rahman, Afrin, & Rabbany, 2014; Kabir, 2013; Karjaluoto, Koenig-Lewis, Palmer, & Moll, 2010; Karjaluoto, Riquelme, & Rios, 2010; Kazi & Mannan, 2013; Khraim, Al Shoubaki, & Khraim, 2011; Laforet & Li, 2005; Lee, Lee, & Kim, 2015; Luarn & Lin, 2005; Mattila, 2003; Mbiti & Weil, 2011; Medhi, Ratan, & Toyama, 2009; Nayak, Nath, & Goel; Oshunloye, 2009; Suoranta, 2003; Yu, 2012; Zhou, Lu, & Wang, 2010) either focus on developed countries or on developing countries from a narrow or urban scope. Most of the previous research is lagging behind in identifying the factors contributing to the adoption of mobile banking in rural areas. Reaching the unbanked inaccessible population of the countryside remain a challenge for any developing as well as developed nations. This study tried to fill this research gap by identifying the determinants of mobile banking adoption in rural areas.

## 2.0    Literature review

Mobile banking has given the opportunity to the customer to perform banking operations irrespective of time, place and the Internet (Chitungo & Munongo, 2013; Suoranta, 2003). It has opened the possibility of financial inclusion of millions of people remotely located and unbanked to share the economic development. However, compared to the overall banking transactions, the market for mobile has remained subtle in Bangladesh. It seems that the widespread adoption of cell phones does not reflect the high level of mobile banking adoption(Yu, 2012). Customers of Iran, Guatemala and Mexico, can obtain banking services through the local mobile network. Pakistan has also launched mobile banking services with limited facilities, but India provides services in wider areas. The scenario in China, Brazil and Kenya is quite different regarding the number of users. Here the number of users soared over 100 %. In UK, USA, Singapore, South Korea and Sweden, banks provide new services to their customers via mobile handset (Khraim, et al., 2011).

In 2011, Zimbabwe started mobile banking services which were the panacea for the unbanked rural areas of the country. Now it has become the most popular financial channel for all in Zimbabwe (Aboelmaged & Gebba, 2013). Applications of mobile banking in Bahrain has been growing up rapidly and expected to increase in the coming year; most of the banks of Bahrain now operate mobile banking due to the popularity of this service (AlSoufi & Ali, 2014). However, the economy where banking access is comparatively higher, adoption of mobile banking seems to lower (Cudjoe, Anim, & Nyanyofio, 2015).

Direct marketing of mobile banking is very crucial for the penetration of mobile banking on a grand scale. The service providers sometimes think that promotion of mobile banking may occur within the branch, but the scenario has changed (Bankole, Bankole, & Brown, 2011). Customer's recognition or understanding of the potential value of mobile banking is very urgent for increasing the number of users. Creating awareness for the value of mobile banking can be a useful tool for this purpose (Nayak et al.).

Medhi et al. (2009) undertook a qualitative study in four countries (India, Kenya, Philippines and South Africa) on 90 respondents to identify the barriers to mobile banking adoption. They found that household type, services, usage frequency, ease of use and uptake deter the use of mobile banking adoption of the financially excluded group. On the contrary, Kazi and Mannan (2013) identified innovative promotional and pricing strategies should adopt by the service providers to increase the number of acceptance. Findings of the researchers on the mobile banking adoption have been summarized in Table 1.

| Table 1: Determinants of mobile banking adoption identified in different research / countries | | |
|---|---|---|
| **Researchers** | **Determinants Identified** | **Location / Context** |
| Suoranta (2003) | relative advantage, compatibility, communication and trialability | Finland |
| Laforet and Li (2005) | security, perception of risks, technological skills, and awareness | China |
| Crabbe et al. (2009) | perceived credibility, facilitating conditions, perceived elitisation, and demographic factors | Ghana |
| Medhi et al. (2009) | household type, key service adopted pace of uptake, frequency of usage, and ease of use. | India, Kenya, Philippines and South Africa (rural / poor) |
| Karjaluoto, Koenig-Lewis, et al. (2010) | compatibility, perceived usefulness, and risk | Germany |
| Bankole et al. (2011) | culture, utility expectancy, effort expectancy, and behavioral intention | Nigeria |
| Khraim et al. (2011) | self-efficacy, trialability, compatibility, complexity, risk and relative advantage | Jordan |
| Al-Jabri and Sohail (2012) | relative advantage, compatibility, received risk and observability | Saudi Arabia |
| Akturan and Tezcan (2012) | attitude, perceived usefulness, perceived social risk, perceived performance risk and perceived benefit | Turkey |
| Kazi and Mannan (2013) | perceived risk, ease of use, usefulness and social influence | Pakistan |
| Aboelmaged and Gebba (2013) | Attitude, subjective norm, perceived ease of use and perceived usefulness | Dubai |
| Kabir (2013) | perceived risks (except social risk), trust, convenience, and comparative advantages | Bangladesh |
| Chitungo and Munongo (2013) | perceived ease of use, relative advantages, social norms, personal innovativeness, perceived risks, perceived usefulness, and costs | Zimbabwe |
| AlSoufi and Ali (2014) | perceived Usefulness and Ease of Use | Bahrain |
| Ndumba and Muturi (2014) | perceived risk, perceived convenience, perceived usefulness and trust | Kenya |

**Table 1: Determinants of mobile banking adoption identified in different research / countries**

| Researchers | Determinants Identified | Location / Context |
|---|---|---|
| Blumenstock, Callen, and Ghani (2014) | violence, intention | Afghanistan |
| (Nayak, Nath, & Goel, 2014) | awareness, perceived usefulness, perceived ease of use, trust | India |
| K. S. Lee et al. (2015) | perceived risk, trust, and perceived usefulness | South Korea |
| (Cudjoe et al., 2015) | perceived credibility, perceived financial cost, perceived usefulness and perceived ease of use | Ghana |

## 3.0    Theoretical framework and hypotheses development

Our study aimed at finding out the determinants of mobile banking adoption by the rural people. Previously, researchers have used many models available to identify the adoption of new technology; such as the technology acceptance model (Davis, Bagozzi, & Warshaw, 1989), the Unified Theory of Acceptance and Use of Technology (Venkatesh, Thong, Chan, Hu, & Brown, 2011), Theory of Planned Behavior (Venkatesh et al., 2011), Theory of Reasoned Action (Albarracin, Johnson, Fishbein, & Muellerleile, 2001), and the Innovation Diffusion Theory (Moore & Benbasat, 1996), etc. Among these, Technology acceptance model (TAM) is the most dominant model used for the study of the adoption of information technology and thus TAM has been used for this study. The theoretical framework has been shown in Figure 1.

### 3.1    Perceived ease of use and m-banking adoption

Perceived ease of use has significant influences on technology adoption (Iqbal & Bhatti, 2015). In mobile banking, it means a degree to which a person is free of difficulty with the usage of mobile banking technology (Aderonke, 2010). The relationship between perceived ease of use and mobile banking efficacy is positive because it indicates the hands on experience of the users (Luo, Li, Zhang, & Shim, 2010). We hypothesized that:
H1: PEU has significant positive influences on mobile banking adoption.

### 3.2    User interface and m-banking adoption

The user interface requires an in-depth understanding of user need (Thakur & Srivastava, 2014). The best interface is that a user will have all types of access regarding usability and understanding. It enhances the relationship between users and the system (Ha, Canedoli, Baur, & Bick, 2012). So we hypothesized that:
H2: User interface has positive influences on mobile banking adoption.

### 3.3    Trust and m-banking adoption

When the user chooses a particular system, (s)he must consider the overall trust on that technology (Slade, Williams, & Dwivedi, 2013). Trust on using a technology fosters the adoption of technology (Lee, Kim, & Ahn, 2011) and the degree of confidence heading towards the adoption of new technology (Shareef, Kumar, Kumar, & Dwivedi, 2011). Based on above discussion, we hypothesized that:
H3: Trust has positive influences on mobile banking adoption.

### 3.4    Perceived usefulness and m-banking adoption

Perceived usefulness is a critical construct in our proposed model which means that to what extent the person believes that using the technology will enhance his/ her performance (Hoque, Bao, & Sorwar, 2016). In mobile banking, it means obtaining services as desired by the user (Karjaluoto, Koenig-Lewis, et al., 2010). Accordingly, we hypothesized that:
H4: Perceived usefulness has positive influences on mobile banking adoption.

## 4.0    Research design and methods

### 4.1    Research setting

Due to the limited research on the adoption of mobile banking in rural areas of Bangladesh, we undertook an exploratory research in rural parts of Bangladesh with a structured questionnaire. Sample frame included Gazipur (40), Tongi (30), Norsingdi (25), Faedabad (33), Savar (35), Narayanganj (42) and Comilla (31) regions of Bangladesh. Due to the cost effectiveness, a convenience sampling method was used. The participants were informed about the purpose of the study.

**Figure 1:** Research model

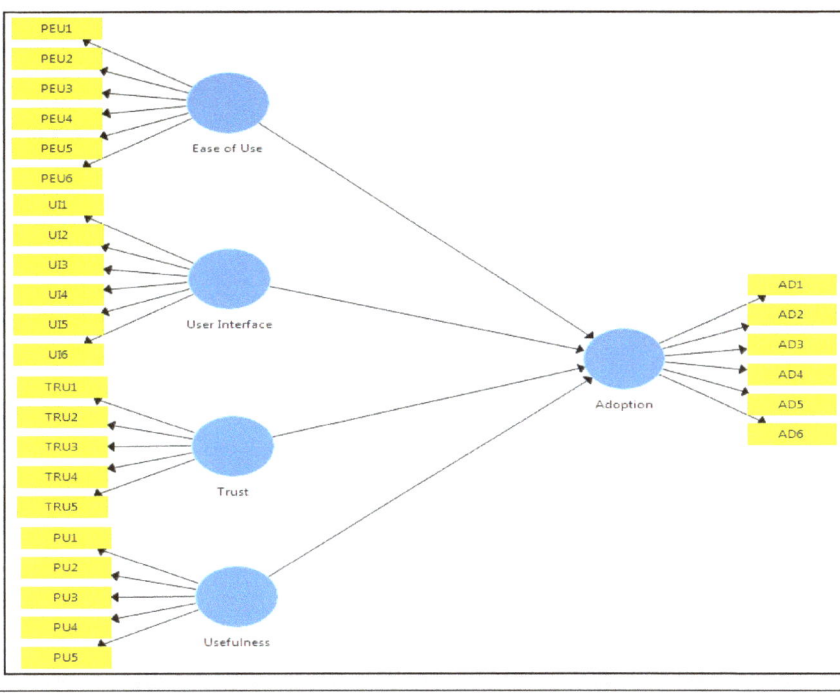

## 4.2    Questionnaire design and data collection

To collect the relevant data for measuring the latent constructs in the research hypotheses, we adopt the structured questionnaire survey method. There were two parts in the questionnaire. Part A contains the demographic information that was used to have the descriptive characteristics of the sample.

In part B, there were some questions regarding the different constructs in the research model on a 5 point Likert scale. A face-to-face meeting was conducted to obtain the response of the participants for this study. We distributed 300 questionnaires, and 243 were returned. We used 236 questionnaires for further analysis, and seven incomplete questionnaires were excluded from the survey. We used statistical analysis technique, based on structural equation modeling (SEM) called the partial least squares (PLS) method to test and validate the proposed model and the relationships among the hypothesized constructs. Smart PLS 3.0 (Ringle, Wende, & Becker, 2015) software has been used to analyze the data.

## 5.0    Findings

### 5.1    Measurement model evaluation

The measurement model has been assessed through the internal reliability, convergent validity, and discriminant validity. The internal reliability was examined through the Cronbach's alpha and Composite Reliability (CR). For both of the measurement, the constructs had more than recommended value, i.e., greater than 0.7. So all the constructs or latent variables used in this study were found reliable. The average variance extracted (AVE) and item loading for all the elements or observed variables are above the threshold value of 0.50. The items used in this study thus have the convergent validity. Table 2 shows the Measurement model results.

The discriminant validity has been assessed by the square root of the AVE and crosses loading matrix. For discriminant validity, the diagonal elements must be larger than the entries in corresponding columns and rows.

From the results of Table 3, it can be seen that all the diagonal values are greater than the values of corresponding columns and rows, indicating the discriminant validity of the constructs.

| Table 2: The measurement model | | | | | |
|---|---|---|---|---|---|
| Constructs | Items | Loadings | C.R | Cronbach's Alpha | AVE |
| | AD1 | 0.845 | | | |
| | AD2 | 0.853 | 0.94 | 0.92 | 0.71 |
| Adoption | AD3 | 0.809 | | | |

**Table 2:** The measurement model

| Constructs | Items | Loadings | C.R | Cronbach's Alpha | AVE |
|---|---|---|---|---|---|
| | AD4 | 0.834 | | | |
| | AD5 | 0.845 | | | |
| | AD6 | 0.863 | | | |
| | PEU1 | 0.740 | | | |
| | PEU2 | 0.702 | | | |
| Perceived Ease of Use | PEU3 | 0.658 | 0.86 | 0.81 | 0.51 |
| | PEU4 | 0.725 | | | |
| | PEU5 | 0.761 | | | |
| | PEU6 | 0.692 | | | |
| | PU1 | 0.822 | | | |
| Perceived Usefulness | PU2 | 0.843 | | | |
| | PU3 | 0.766 | 0.90 | 0.87 | 0.70 |
| | PU4 | 0.787 | | | |
| | PU5 | 0.819 | | | |
| | TRU1 | 0.867 | | | |
| | TRU2 | 0.805 | | | |
| Trust | TRU3 | 0.820 | 0.91 | 0.88 | 0.70 |
| | TRU4 | 0.788 | | | |
| | TRU5 | 0.820 | | | |
| | UI1 | 0.931 | | | |
| | UI2 | 0.920 | | | |
| User Interface | UI3 | 0.952 | | | |
| | UI4 | 0.930 | 0.98 | 0.97 | 0.87 |
| | UI5 | 0.924 | | | |
| | UI6 | 0.932 | | | |

AVE=Average Variance Extracted, CR=Composite Reliability

**Table 3:** Correlation matrix and square root of the AVE (Latent Variable Correlations)

| | Adoption | Ease of Use | Trust | Usefulness | User Interface |
|---|---|---|---|---|---|
| Adoption | 0.714 | | | | |
| Ease of Use | 0.712 | 0.841 | | | |
| Trust | 0.650 | 0.816 | 0.820 | | |
| Usefulness | 0.663 | 0.835 | 0.818 | 0.848 | |
| User Interface | -0.682 | -0.839 | -0.718 | -0.732 | 0.932 |

## 5.2   Hypotheses Testing

To identify the relationships among the constructs in the research model, we develop the structural model. By the path coefficient ($\beta$) and t-statistics, we evaluate the relationship between dependent and independent variables. Table 4 shows the PLS results of the structural model for this study. The results indicate the relationships between PEU and AD (t = 2.813, $\beta$=0.111, p<0.05), UI and AD (t = 7.999, $\beta$= -0.403, p <0.05), TRU and AD (t = 3.790, $\beta$=0.206, p <0.05), PU and AD (t = 4.673, $\beta$=0.290, p <0.05). So H1, H2, H3, and H4 were significant and accepted in the current study. Overall the constructs in this model explain about 83% of the variations in the adoption of mobile banking, which is greater than recommended level of 20-25%.

**Table 4:** Structural model

| Hypothesis | Path | ($\beta$) | t-statistics | Comments | $R^2$ |
|---|---|---|---|---|---|
| H1 | PEU -> AD | 0.111 | 2.813 | Accepted | 0.828 |
| H2 | UI -> AD | -0.403 | 7.999 | Accepted | |
| H3 | TRU -> AD | 0.206 | 3.790 | Accepted | |
| H4 | PU -> AD | 0.290 | 4.673 | Accepted | |

## 6.0   Discussion

We tried to identify the factors determining the adoption of mobile banking in rural Bangladesh using TAM model. Through analyzing the survey data of 236 respondents, we found that all the constructs have a strong relationship with the adoption of mobile banking. The results revealed the significant influences of PEU, UI, TRU and PU on the adoption of mobile banking.

The unique finding of this study is the User Interface, which is exceptional from the results of the previous studies (see Table 1). UI seems to work as a deterrent for the adoption of mobile banking in Bangladesh. The plausible cause may the language used in mobile banking. The language in the mobile banking is English, which is not understood by many rural users. Using the Bengali language might help here. Akturan and Tezcan (2012) has found that the user interface is more crucial when users have the lacking of experience in using technology. The rural adults are using mobile technology, which is relatively new to this section of the population. Using this technology for money transaction might make them nervous. We believe the use of local language and more experience over time will help the users to overcome UI related nervousness.

The second most influencing factor is the Perceived Usefulness (PU); which confirms most of the previous findings (see Table 1). Currently, the users of mobile banking are mostly using money transfer facility of the mobile banking services. Because a large number of people such as garments workers, factory workers, and rickshaw pullers are working remotely from their home. They constantly need to send money to their family members back at home safely. Mobile banking has become a safe tool for them to send and receive money. However, the transaction is mainly done through agents rather than opening an own mobile banking account. After PU, the user needs to trust the mobile banking system to adopt it.

Like the previous research (Kabir 2013, Ndumba and Muturi 2014, Lee et al. 2015; Nayak et al., 2014, Wu and Wang 2005), our research also found trust as an influencing factor for adoption of mobile banking. Mobile banking is more sensitive unlike any other technology because it relates to the money.

Lastly, Perceived Ease of Use (PEU) found to be a statistically significant factor for mobile banking adoption like previous studies (see Table 1). Complex and hard to use issues increase the barrier to learning new technology. For the rural people, this factor is more crucial because their exposure to new technology and their educational level do not allow them to accept new technology as easily as the rich group. For this reason, in Bangladesh the popular mobile banking service providers such as BKash, DBBL uses push and pull services which are easy to use and work even in feature phones.

## 7.0 Conclusion and implications

Financial inclusion is one of the vital indicators of development. It also indicates the financial strength of a nation. Mobile banking in different parts of the world found to be an effective tool to embrace financially the marginal people who do not have any banking access.

Mobile banking introduced in Bangladesh for about six years. However, its effect on the financial inclusion is found to be ineffective unlike other parts of the world. Our research tried to find the answer for this situation by identifying the determinants of mobile banking adoption by the rural people of Bangladesh.

We discovered that user interface (UI), perceived ease of use (PEU), trust, and perceived usefulness (PU) are statistically significant factor for the adoption of mobile banking in the rural parts of Bangladesh. However, the user interface has significant negative impact on the mobile banking adoption.

### 7.1 Theoretical Implications

This study contributes to IS research by providing a conceptual framework for using and accepting mobile banking in rural areas. Our study uniquely identified the user interface as the major influencing factor for mobile banking adoption by the marginal people. The research is conducted in only some specific rural areas of Bangladesh, so the results may not provide an accurate reflection towards the adoption of mobile banking in Bangladesh. A potential future research might be to focus on the wider areas of Bangladesh to identify and include some other possible factors for making a more widely applicable model.

### 7.2 Managerial implications

The managers of the mobile banking operations may use this finding to design their products and services more customer friendly and technologically superior for the adoption by the marginal rural population. They should especially concentrate on the user interface and perceived usefulness. Managers can design the push-pull services in local Bengali language so that the rural people can understand. Introduction of interactive voice response (IVR) service in addition to push-pull message interface may help the less educated and senior citizen to use the system. The more benefits relating to product and services the managers can offer, the more they can penetrate the market.

## 7.3 Policy implications for government

Policy makers as such the government should introduce different services that motivate the marginal people to adopt mobile banking to accelerate the adoption rate. For example, the government can disburse social security benefits and receive payment of tax, tariff, fees through personal mobile banking account. In this way, people can be benefited by micros savings, interest income, micro-credits, and payments; that will result in an equitable share of development.

## References

Aboelmaged, M., & Gebba, T. R. (2013). Mobile banking adoption: an examination of technology acceptance model and theory of planned behavior. *International Journal of Business Research and Development (IJBRD), 2*(1).

Aderonke, A. A. (2010). An empirical investigation of the level of users' acceptance of e-banking in Nigeria. *Journal of Internet Banking and Commerce, 15*(1), 1.

Ahmed, S. S., Rayhan, S. J., Islam, A., & Mahjabin, S. (2012). Problems and prospects of mobile banking in Bangladesh. *Researchers World, 3*(1), 47.

Akturan, U., & Tezcan, N. (2012). Mobile banking adoption of the youth market: Perceptions and intentions. *Marketing Intelligence & Planning, 30*(4), 444-459.

Al-Jabri, I. M., & Sohail, M. S. (2012). Mobile Banking Adoption: Application Of Diffusion Of Innovation Theory. *Journal of Electronic Commerce Research 13*(4), 379-391.

Albarracin, D., Johnson, B. T., e Fishbein, M., & Muellerleile, P. A. (2001). Theories of reasoned action and planned behavior as models of condom use: a meta-analysis. *Psychological bulletin, 127*(1), 142.

AlSoufi, A., & Ali, H. (2014). Customers perception of mbanking adoption in Kingdom of Bahrain: an empirical assessment of an extended tam model. *arXiv preprint arXiv:1403.2828*.

Bank, T. B. (2016). Mobile Financial Services (MFS) Data. *Mobile Financial Services (MFS) comparative summary statement of April, 2016 and May, 2016.* Retrieved 29 June 2016, 2016, from https://www.bb.org.bd/fnansys/paymentsys/mfsdata.php

Bankole, F. O., Bankole, O. O., & Brown, I. (2011). Mobile banking adoption in Nigeria. *The Electronic Journal of Information Systems in Developing Countries, 47*.

Blumenstock, J., Callen, M., & Ghani, T. (2014). Violence and Financial Decisions: Evidence from Mobile Money in Afghanistan. *University of Washington*.

Canuto, O. (2013). Mobilizing Development via Mobile Phones. *Growth and Crisis.* Retrieved 27 June 2016, 2016, from http://blogs.worldbank.org/growth/mobilizing-development-mobile-phones

Chibba, M. (2009). Financial Inclusion, Poverty Reduction and the Millennium Development Goals. *The European Journal of Development Research, 21*(2), 213-230. doi: 10.1057/ejdr.2008.17

Chitungo, S. K., & Munongo, S. (2013). Extending the technology acceptance model to mobile banking adoption in rural Zimbabwe. *Journal of Business Administration and Education, 3*(1), 51.

Crabbe, M., Standing, C., Standing, S., & Karjaluoto, H. (2009). An adoption model for mobile banking in Ghana. *International Journal of Mobile Communications, 7*(5), 515-543.

Cudjoe, A. G., Anim, P. A., & Nyanyofio, J. G. N. T. (2015). Determinants of mobile banking adoption in the Ghanaian banking industry: a case of access bank Ghana limited. *Journal of Computer and Communications, 3*(02), 1.

Davis, F. D., Bagozzi, R. P., & Warshaw, P. R. (1989). User acceptance of computer technology: a comparison of two theoretical models. *Management science, 35*(8), 982-1003.

DiVanna, J. A. (2003). *The future of retail banking*: Springer.

Donner, J., & Tellez, C. A. (2008). Mobile banking and economic development: Linking adoption, impact, and use *Asian journal of communication, 18*(4), 318-332.

Goi, C. L. (2006). Factors influence development of e-banking in Malaysia. *Journal of Internet Banking and Commerce, 11*(2), 1-21.

Greenacre, J., & Buckley, R. P. (2014). Using trusts to protect mobile money customers. *Sing. J. Legal Stud.,* 59.

Gu, J.-C., Lee, S.-C., & Suh, Y.-H. (2009). Determinants of behavioral intention to mobile banking. *Expert Systems with Applications, 36*(9), 11605-11616. doi: 10.1016/j.eswa.2009.03.024

Ha, K.-H., Canedoli, A., Baur, A. W., & Bick, M. (2012). Mobile banking—insights on its increasing relevance and most common drivers of adoption. *Electronic Markets, 22*(4), 217-227.

Haig, M. (2002). *Mobile marketing: The message revolution*: Kogan Page Publishers.

Hanafizadeh, P., Behboudi, M., Abedini Koshksaray, A., & Jalilvand Shirkhani Tabar, M. (2014). Mobile-banking adoption by Iranian bank clients. *Telematics and Informatics, 31*(1), 62-78. doi: 10.1016/j.tele.2012.11.001

Hassan, M. M., Rahman, A., Afrin, S., & Rabbany, G. (2014). Factors Influencing the Adoption of Mobile Banking Services in Bangladesh: An Empirical Analysis. *International Research Journal of Marketing, 2*(1), 9. doi: 10.12966/irjm.02.02.2014

Hoque, M. R., Bao, Y., & Sorwar, G. (2016). Investigating factors influencing the adoption of e-Health in developing countries: A patient's perspective. *Informatics for Health and Social Care*, 1-17.

Iqbal, S., & Bhatti, Z. A. (2015). An Investigation of University Student Readiness towards M-learning using Technology Acceptance Model. *The International Review of Research in Open and Distributed Learning, 16*(4).

Kabir, M. R. (2013). Factors influencing the usage of mobile banking: Incident from a developing country. *World Review of Business Research, 3*(3), 96-114.

Karjaluoto, H., Koenig-Lewis, N., Palmer, A., & Moll, A. (2010). Predicting young consumers' take up of mobile banking services. *International journal of bank marketing, 28*(5), 410-432.

Karjaluoto, H., Riquelme, H. E., & Rios, R. E. (2010). The moderating effect of gender in the adoption of mobile banking. *International Journal of Bank Marketing, 28*(5), 328-341.

Kazi, A. K., & Mannan, M. A. (2013). Factors affecting adoption of mobile banking in Pakistan: Empirical Evidence. *International Journal of Research in Business and Social Science, 2*(3), 54.

Khraim, H. S., Al Shoubaki, Y. E., & Khraim, A. S. (2011). Factors affecting Jordanian consumers' adoption of mobile banking services. *International Journal of Business and Social Science, 2*(20).

Laforet, S., & Li, X. (2005). Consumers' attitudes towards online and mobile banking in China. *International journal of bank marketing, 23*(5), 362-380.

Lee, J., Kim, H. J., & Ahn, M. J. (2011). The willingness of e-Government service adoption by business users: The role of offline service quality and trust in technology. *Government Information Quarterly, 28*(2), 222-230.

Lee, K. S., Lee, H. S., & Kim, S. Y. (2015). Factors influencing the adoption behavior of mobile banking: a South Korean perspective , 2007. *The Journal of Internet Banking and Commerce, 2007*.

Luarn, P., & Lin, H.-H. (2005). Toward an understanding of the behavioral intention to use mobile banking. *Computers in Human Behavior, 21*(6), 873-891. doi: 10.1016/j.chb.2004.03.003

Luo, X., Li, H., Zhang, J., & Shim, J. (2010). Examining multi-dimensional trust and multi-faceted risk in initial acceptance of emerging technologies: An empirical study of mobile banking services. *Decision support systems, 49*(2), 222-234.

Mattila, M. (2003). Factors affecting the adoption of mobile banking services. *Journal of Internet Banking and Commerce, 8*(1), 0306-0304.

Mbiti, I., & Weil, D. N. (2011). *MOBILE BANKING: THE IMPACT OF M-PESA IN KENYA*. NATIONAL BUREAU OF ECONOMIC RESEARCH. Retrieved from http://www.nber.org/papers/w17129

Medhi, I., Ratan, A., & Toyama, K. (2009). *Mobile-banking adoption and usage by low-litcrate, low-income users in the developing world.* Paper presented at the International Conference on Internationalization, Design and Global Development Berlin Heidelberg.

Moore, G. C., & Benbasat, I. (1996). Integrating diffusion of innovations and theory of reasoned action models to predict utilization of information technology by end-users *Diffusion and adoption of information technology* (pp. 132-146): Springer.

Nabi, M. G., Talukder, M. S., Saha, P. P., Sutradhar, R. R., Fahmida, A., Chen, G., & Banerjee, B. (2012). *Mobile Financial Services in Bangladesh: An Overview of Market Development*. Bangladeh Bank Retrieved from https://www.bb.org.bd/pub/research/policypaper/pp072012.pdf.

Nayak, N., Nath, V., & Goel, N. A Study Of Adoption Behaviour Of Mobile Banking Services By Indian Consumers.

Nayak, N., Nath, V., & Goel, N. (2014). A Study Of Adoption Behaviour Of Mobile Banking Services By Indian Consumers. *International Journal of Research in Engineering & Technology, 2*(3), 2347-4599

Ndumba, H. W., & Muturi, W. (2014). Factors Affecting Adoption Of Mobile Banking In Kenya; Case Study Of Kenya Commercial Bank Limuru. *International Journal of Social Sciences Management and Entrepreneurship, 1*(3), 92-112.

Oshunloye, A. O. (2009). ICT in Marketing: A Study of The Use of Internet and Mobile Phones in. *Journal of Business Venturing, 18*(6), 789-814.

Rashid, A. T., & Elder, L. (2009). Mobile phones and development: An analysis of IDRC-supported projects. *The Electronic Journal of Information Systems in Developing Countries, 36*(2), 1-6.

Ringle, C. M., Wende, S., & Becker, J.-M. (2015). Bönningstedt: SmartPLS (Version 3.0). Retrieved from http://www.smartpls.com

Sarma, M., & Pais, J. (2011). Financial Inclusion and Development. *Journal of International Development, 23*(5), 613-628. doi: 10.1002/jid.1698

Shareef, M. A., Kumar, V., Kumar, U., & Dwivedi, Y. K. (2011). e-Government Adoption Model (GAM): Differing service maturity levels. *Government Information Quarterly, 28*(1), 17-35.

Slade, E. L., Williams, M. D., & Dwivedi, Y. K. (2013). Mobile payment adoption: Classification and review of the extant literature. *The Marketing Review, 13*(2), 167-190.

Suoranta, M. (2003). Adoption of mobile banking in Finland. . *Jyväskylän yliopisto*.

Thakur, R., & Srivastava, M. (2014). Adoption readiness, personal innovativeness, perceived risk and usage intention across customer groups for mobile payment services in India. *Internet Research, 24*(3), 369-392.

The Daily Prothom Alo. (2015, 26 Aug 2015). Mobile banking is increasing financial inclusion, *The Daily Prothom Alo*. Retrieved from http://www.prothom-alo.com/economy/article/612703

The Economist. (2013). Why does Kenya lead the world in mobile money?  Retrieved 27 June 2016, 2016, from http://www.economist.com/blogs/economist-explains/2013/05/economist-explains-18

The World Bank, World Development Indicator. (2014a). Account at Financial Institutions (% age 15+). Retrieved 27                     June                     2016,                     from http://databank.worldbank.org/data/reports.aspx?source=2&country=&series=WP_time_01.3&period=

The World Bank, World Development Indicator. (2014b). Mobile cellular subscriptions (per 100 people). Retrieved                     27                     June                     2016,                     from http://databank.worldbank.org/data/reports.aspx?source=2&country=&series=WP_time_01.3&period=

Venkatesh, V., Thong, J. Y., Chan, F. K., Hu, P. J. H., & Brown, S. A. (2011). Extending the two-stage information systems continuance model: Incorporating UTAUT predictors and the role of context. *Information Systems Journal, 21*(6), 527-555.

Welch, B. (1999). *Electronic banking and treasury security*. Woodhead Publishing.

Wu, J.-H., & Wang, S.-C. (2005). What drives mobile commerce?: An empirical evaluation of the revised technology acceptance model. *Information & management, 42*(5), 719-729.

Yu, C.-S. (2012). Factors affecting individuals to adopt mobile banking: Empirical evidence from the UTAUT model. *Journal of Electronic Commerce Research, 13*(2), 104.

Zhou, T., Lu, Y., & Wang, B. (2010). Integrating TTF and UTAUT to explain mobile banking user adoption. *Computers in Human Behavior, 26*(4), 760-767. doi: 10.1016/j.chb.2010.01.013

# 6

# Budget deficits, money supply and price level in West Africa

Yaya Keho [a*]

[a] Ecole Nationale Supérieure de Statistique et d'Economie Appliquée (ENSEA) Abidjan.
[*] Corresponding author's email address: yayakeho@yahoo.fr

ARTICLE INFO

Keywords:
ARDL bounds test;
Budget deficit;
Money supply;
WAEMU.

ABSTRACT

Using West African Economic and Monetary Union (WAEMU) dataset for 1970 to 2013, and Pesaran et al. (2001) methodology, this study examines the effect of budget deficit and money supply on inflation. Evidence shows that there is a long run relation among the variables in all countries except Mali. Price and budget deficit are positively related in Niger and Togo, and negatively related in Benin and Senegal. Further, money supply and price are positively related in Burkina Faso, Cote d'Ivoire and Senegal. Results from the Granger causality tests indicate that deficits cause money growth in Cote d'Ivoire, Mali and Togo, and cause the price level in Senegal. There is no causality from money supply to inflation in the short-run. Results suggest that idea that budget deficits are not inflationary in WAEMU countries. Hence, the policy of reducing inflation should focus on other macroeconomic and structural determinants of inflation across WAEMU.

## 1.0    Introduction

Inflation is an undesirable factor due to its adverse effects on consumption, investment and economic growth. For this reason, price stability is the primary goal of monetary policy for almost all central banks. Understanding the sources of inflation is therefore a subject of interest of policymakers as well as monetary authorities. Among the possible sources of inflation, budget deficits and money supply are those whose importance has grown over years. Theoretically, there are several competing views explaining the impacts of budget deficits and money growth on inflation. The conventional wisdom of monetarist view opines that inflation is always and everywhere a monetary phenomenon, and monetary authorities can maintain a sustainable inflation rate by the control of the money supply. In this framework, budget deficits are inflationary only to the extent that they are monetized. The Keynesian view suggests that budget deficit leads to inflation by stimulating aggregate demand and driving up the real interest rate. The Ricardian equivalence proposition contends that increases in budget deficits do not alter aggregate demand, interest rates and the price level because economic agents anticipate that current tax cuts by the government will be financed by future tax hikes (Barro, 1989). Contrary to these views, the fiscal theory of price level contends that inflation rate is dependent upon the coordination between monetary and fiscal authorities. Under the monetary dominant regime, monetary policy determines the price level and fiscal policy remains reactive (Sargent and Wallace, 1981). In the fiscal dominant regime, however, the price level is determined by the government's inter-temporal budget constraint and monetary policy is reactive. In the strong version of the theory, the price level is determined merely by fiscal variables and monetary factors play no role in price determination (Leeper, 1991; Sims, 1994; Woodford, 1994).

Empirical studies examining the relationship between budget deficits, money supply and inflation have also produced conflicting results. While some studies (see Metin, 1998; Darrat, 2000; Neyapti, 2003; Nguyen, 2015) provided evidence showing that budget deficits contribute to inflation, others (see Karras, 1994; Brown and Yousefi, 1996; Hondroyiannis and Papapetrou, 1997) failed to find any direct impact of budget deficit on inflation. Furthermore, most existing studies focus either on the nexus of money-inflation or deficit-inflation. But little effort has been made to test these two links in the same framework. In addition, despite the burgeoning literature on the relationship between deficit, money and inflation, very few studies have been conducted for Sub-Saharan African countries. This study therefore attempts to investigate the topic for the member countries of the West African Economic and Monetary Union (WAEMU). Budget is the core instrument in the hand of these countries for attainment of sustainable economic growth target. They experienced persistent deficits over the period from 1980 to 1990. Faced with the vicious circle of these deficits, WAEMU embarks on economic and fiscal reform programs aiming at raising tax revenues and restructuring tax systems. Thus, since 1994 the WAEMU member countries have adopted convergence criteria aiming at explicit targets for deficits and inflation rate. To meet the convergence criteria, the member countries should, among others, keep public deficit at a minimum of zero percent of GDP and keep inflation rate under 3%. To the best of our knowledge, there has not been empirical analysis investigating the relationship between money, deficits and the price level in the context of the WAEMU member countries. This study seeks to fill the gap by addressing the following questions: what are the impacts of budget deficits and money supply on the price levels in WAEMU countries? What is the effect of budget deficit on money supply? How do budget deficit, money supply and price interact with each other? To address these questions, we apply the bounds test to cointegration developed by Pesaran et al. (2001). The variables under study are the consumer price index, the money supply ratio to GDP and budget deficit as share of GDP. The results reveal a positive relationship between price and deficit in Niger and Togo, and a negative relationship between the two variables in Benin and Senegal. On the contrary, budget deficits have no significant impact on price in Burkina Faso and Cote d'Ivoire. Furthermore, money growth increases price in Burkina Faso, Cote d'Ivoire and Senegal. We also find that in the short run budget deficits cause money growth in Cote d'Ivoire, Mali and Togo, and prices in Senegal. These findings suggest that deficits are not inflationary in the WAEMU member countries. Therefore, the policy of reducing prices should focus on other macroeconomic and structural determinants of inflation.

The rest of the study is organized as follows. Section 2 reviews the literature on the relationship between deficit, money and inflation. Section 3 outlines the econometric methodology. Section 4 analyses the empirical results. Finally, Section 5 provides summary and gives some policy implications.

## 2.0    Literature review

The relationship between deficit, money supply and inflation has long been the subject of debate among economists. This is because a clear understanding of the link between these variables is of crucial importance in ensuring that effective stabilization policies can be implemented effectively. Over the years, a number of theories have been developed to explore the relationship between budget deficit, money supply and inflation. The quantity theory of money predicts that increases in money supply give rise to inflation, provided that the velocity of money is constant (Fisher, 1911). The monetary approach assumes that money supply and inflation are positively related through the assumption of neutrality of money (Friedman, 1968). The neutrality of money refers to the hypothesis that changes in the quantity of money affect the nominal but not the real variables of the economy. In the monetary framework, money supply is exogenously determined and controlled by the monetary authorities. Inflation occurs when money supply expands more rapidly than money demand. Budget deficits are inflationary only if it is monetized to increase the monetary base of the economy (Hamburger and Zwick, 1981). The Keynesian view argues that money is important but is not responsible for changes in price levels. Instead, structural factors play important role suggesting that money supply is not an effective instrument to control price changes. The Keynesian view suggests that government budget deficit leads to inflation by stimulating aggregate demand and driving up the real interest rate. The Ricardian equivalence proposition contends that increases in budget deficits do not alter aggregate demand, interest rate and the price level because economic agents anticipate that current tax cuts by the government will be financed by future tax hikes (Barro, 1989). In anticipation of future taxes, they will not consider themselves wealthier and therefore will not increase their consumption. The proponents of the fiscal theory of price level emphasize the role of fiscal policy in price determination. They highlight the importance of fiscal and monetary policy coordination while ensuring price stability (Sargent and Wallace, 1981). According to them, monetary policy cannot permanently control inflation. Under the so-called "monetary dominant" regime, monetary policy determines the price level, and fiscal policy remains reactive. The government balances its inter temporal constraint taking the inflation as given. Sargent and Wallace (1981) argue that, in this coordination scheme, inflation is completely under the control of the monetary authority. In the "fiscal dominant" regime, however, the price level is determined by the government's inter-temporal budget constraint, and monetary policy is reactive that is money supply reacts to price level changes to bring the money demand equation in balance (Carlstrom and Fuerst, 2000). In the strong version of the fiscal theory of price level, introduced by Leeper, (1991); Sims, (1994); Woodford, (1994), the price level is determined merely by fiscal variables, and monetary factors play no role in price determination. Price levels adjust to ensure the government's inter-temporal budget constraint and the adjustment is driven by individuals' wealth effect which raises aggregate demand thereby creating inflation and leaving no role for the monetary authority. The fiscal theory of price suggests a direct correlation between inflation and budget deficits.

Some attempts have been made to test the validity of these theories. Giannaros and Kolluri (1986) examine the relationship between government deficits, money growth and inflation for ten industrialized countries during the period 1950 to 1981. The results show that fiscal deficits do not increase the money supply and the inflation rate. Using the VAR methodology, De Haan and Zelhorst (1990) investigate the budget deficit, money growth and inflation relationship for 17 developing countries from 1960 to 1985. They find that in the majority of countries budget deficits do not cause monetary expansion. The studies by Chang (1994) for Taiwan, Cottarelli *et al.* (1998) for 47 industrial and transition countries, Metin (1998) for Turkey, Catão and Terrones (2003) for emerging market countries, Neyapti (2003) for 54 developed and less developed countries, and Jalil *et al.* (2014) for Pakistan, also provide evidence showing that budget deficits contribute to inflation. However, the studies by Barnhart and Darrat (1989) for the US, Karras (1994) for 32 countries, Brown and Yousefi (1996) for developing countries, and Hondroyiannis and Papapetrou (1997) for Greece fail to find any direct impact of budget deficit on inflation. Hondroyiannis and Papapetrou (1994) support the hypothesis of bidirectional causality between deficit and price level in Greece. Darrat (2000) tests whether high budget deficits have any inflationary consequences in Greece over the period 1957-1993. The empirical results show that besides money growth, budget deficits have also played a significant and direct role in the Greek inflationary process. Tekin-Koru and Özmen (2003) investigate the long-run relationship between budget deficits, inflation and money growth in Turkey. Their results reject the validity of both the monetarist view and the pure fiscal theory of price. Using causality tests, Ashra *et al.* (2004) find bidirectional relationship between money and price, but not between deficit and inflation in India for the period from 1950 to 2001. Narayan *et al.* (2006) analyze the case of Fiji and find that money supply and deficit have statistically significant positive impacts on inflation. They also find that in the short-run there is unidirectional causality running from money supply to inflation and bidirectional causality between money and deficit, and in the long-run both deficits and money supply cause inflation. Nguyen (2015) examines the effects of fiscal deficit and money supply on inflation in nine Asian countries over the period of 1985-2012. Using the pooled mean group estimator and the panel differenced GMM estimator, He find evidence that money supply increases inflation only in the pooled mean group estimation whereas fiscal deficit has a positive impact on inflation in both methods of estimation.

Regarding the African countries, the empirical evidence is also mixed. Using an error-correction model, Sowa (1994) estimates an inflation equation for Ghana over the period 1963-1990. The study find that inflation in Ghana is influenced more by output volatility than by monetary factors, both in the long run and in the short run. He also reports a positive relationship between government budget deficits and inflation, and strongly recommends control of inflation-targeting policies to keep the budget deficit as low as possible. Durevall and Ndung'u (2001) use a dynamic error correction model of inflation for Kenya and find that money supply affects prices only in the short-run. Anoruo (2003) uses the Johansen cointegration procedure and Granger causality tests to show that money supply causes both budget deficits and inflation rate in South Africa. He also finds bidirectional causal relationship between deficits and inflation. Solomon and De Wet (2004) find a positive relationship between budget deficit and inflation in Tanzania due to massive monetization of deficits by monetary authorities. Dembo Toe and Hounkpatin (2007) examine the relationship between money growth and inflation in the WAEMU using the VAR methodology. They find that price of imported goods, nominal exchange rate and money growth are among the drivers of inflation rate in the WAEMU zone. Diop *et al.* (2008) examine the determinants of long-run inflation in the WAEMU countries over the period 1970-2005. Using the ARDL approach they find that money supply, foreign prices of imported goods, supply constraints in the agricultural sector and nominal exchange rate are the significant determinants of long-run consumer price index in the WAEMU countries. Zonon (2003) also confirms the role of money supply and price of imported goods in explaining inflation in Burkina Faso. Wolde-Rufael (2008) investigates the causal link among inflation, money and budget deficit in Ethiopia over the period 1964 to 2003 using the bounds test approach and Granger causality tests. He finds evidence of a long-run relationship among the variables with money supply and budget deficit causing inflation. But, deficit has no impact on money growth. In the case of Nigeria, Nyong and Odubekun (2002) examine the effects of monetary financing of budget deficit on macroeconomic instability. They find that monetary financing of fiscal deficit in Nigeria is partly responsible for liquidity in the money market and inflation. Chimobi and Igwe (2010) find bilateral causality between budget deficit and inflation in Nigeria, whereas Awe and Shina (2012) report a causal relationship running from budget deficit to inflation, and Ogunmuyiwa (2008) supports the reverse causality from inflation to budget deficit. Further, Olusoji and Oderinde (2011) and Dockery *et al.* (2012) find no significant causation between fiscal deficits and inflation in Nigeria over the period 1970 to 2006. Recently, Chukwu (2013) finds a long-run relationship between budget deficits, money growth and price level in Nigeria over the period 1971 to 2008 with unidirectional causality running from budget deficit to money growth and then from money supply growth to price level. Raji *et al.* (2014) applies the bounds test to Nigerian data covering the period 1970 to 2010. They find a short-run causality running money supply and budget deficit to price level while the long-run results indicate bidirectional causality between money supply and price level. As we can see, empirical studies on African countries are very limited. Nigeria is the country that has been extensively examined. This study contributes to the empirical literature by investigating the case of seven African countries that have not previously examined.

## 3.0    Data and methodology

### 3.1    Model

This study examines the existence and direction of the relation between budget deficit, money supply and price level. To that end, the model that consists of budget deficit and money supply as determinants of inflation is defined as follows:

$$P_t = \theta_0 + \theta_1 D_t + \theta_2 M_t + \mu_t \tag{1}$$

where P indicates the price level, D is budget deficit and M is broadly defined money supply. The $\theta_1$ and $\theta_2$ coefficients are the parameters which show respectively the effects of budget deficit and money supply on price level.

### 3.2    ARDL bounds test to cointegration

The study uses the autoregressive distributed lag (ARDL) bounds test developed by Pesaran *et al.* (2001) to depict the long run relationship between the variables. The advantages of ARDL bounds testing method over other alternative methods are as follows: first, the technique allows the use of variables which differ from order integration (I (0) and I (1)). Second, the ARDL bounds test solves the endogeneity problem of explanatory variables and the inability to test hypotheses on the estimated coefficients in the long-run. Third, the technique estimates both long-run and short-run parameters simultaneously. Fourth, it provides better results for small sample data (Haug, 2002). The bounds testing procedure is based on the following ARDL-ECM equation:

$$\Delta P_t = \phi_0 + \phi_1 P_{t-1} + \phi_2 D_{t-1} + \phi_3 M_{t-1} + \sum_{i=1}^{m} \gamma_{1i} \Delta P_{t-i} + \sum_{i=0}^{n} \gamma_{2i} \Delta D_{t-i} + \sum_{i=0}^{p} \gamma_{3i} \Delta M_{t-i} + \mu_t \tag{2}$$

The presence of cointegration is tested by restricting all estimated coefficients of lagged level variables equal to zero. That is, the null hypothesis of no cointegration is: $\phi_1 = \phi_2 = \phi_3 = 0$. This hypothesis is tested by the mean of an *F*-test. The asymptotic critical values are provided by Pesaran *et al.* (2001). An important issue in applying the bounds testing procedure is the selection of the lag structure (*m, n, p*). In this study, lag length on each variable was selected using the general-to-specific approach with maximum lag set to five. As cointegration indicates only whether or not a long-run relationship exists between the variables, we provide information on the direction of causal relationships through Granger causality tests.

### 3.3    Granger causality test

To examine the causal relationship between the variables we use the Granger causality framework. In the presence of a long-run relationship, Granger-causality test requires the inclusion of a lagged error correction term within a vector error correction model (VECM). Accordingly, Granger-causality analysis involves estimating the following equations:

$$(1-L)\begin{bmatrix} P_t \\ D_t \\ M_t \end{bmatrix} = \begin{bmatrix} \alpha_1 \\ \alpha_2 \\ \alpha_3 \end{bmatrix} + \sum_{i=1}^{p}(1-L)\begin{bmatrix} \beta_{1i} & \gamma_{1i} & \phi_{1i} \\ \beta_{2i} & \gamma_{2i} & \phi_{2i} \\ \beta_{3i} & \gamma_{3i} & \phi_{3i} \end{bmatrix} \times \begin{bmatrix} P_{t-i} \\ D_{t-i} \\ M_{t-i} \end{bmatrix} + \begin{bmatrix} \lambda_1 \\ \lambda_2 \\ \lambda_3 \end{bmatrix} ECT_{t-1} + \begin{bmatrix} e_{1t} \\ e_{2t} \\ e_{3t} \end{bmatrix} \tag{3}$$

where (1-L) stands for the difference operator and $ECT_{t-1}$ denotes the lagged residuals of the long-run relationship. The lag length *p* is determined using the Akaike Information Criterion (AIC). The significance of the differenced explanatory variables indicates the existence of short-run causality, whereas the significance of $ECT_{t-1}$ indicates the existence of long-run causality. For instance, $\gamma_{1i} \neq 0$ shows that deficit Granger-causes price whereas the reverse causality is indicated by $\beta_{2i} \neq 0$.

The empirical analysis is carried out for seven member countries of the West African Economic and Monetary Union (WAEMU), namely: Benin, Burkina Faso, Côte d'Ivoire, Mali, Niger, Senegal and Togo. The variables under study are the logarithm of the consumer price index as the price level, the money supply ratio to GDP and budget deficit as share of GDP. All variables were obtained from Central Bank of West African States and World Development Indicators of World Bank. All data cover the time period of 1970/1972 to 2013.

## 4.0    Empirical results and discussion

Before starting estimation, we test for the order of integration of the series by means of unit root tests. This step is important in order to ensure that variables are not integrated of order two or higher. Moreover, the bounds test requires the dependent variable to be a I(1) series. To this end, we perform the well-known unit root test of Phillips and Perron (1988). This test has been performed under the model with constant and trend for the level series and with constant for series in first difference. The results displayed in Table 1 show that all the variables are non-stationary in their level but are stationary after taking the first difference, with the exception of budget deficit variable which is stationary in Benin, Burkina Faso and Mali. This result shows that there may be a long-term relation between budget deficits, money supply and price level and indicates the possibility of cointegration analysis.

| Table 1: Unit root tests | | | | | | |
|---|---|---|---|---|---|---|
| Country | P | D | M | $\Delta$P | $\Delta$D | $\Delta$M |
| Benin | -2.018 | -3.865 | -2.391 | -4.353 | -11.434 | -7.312 |
| Burkina Faso | -1.469 | -4.307 | -3.236 | -6.682 | -12.381 | -7.623 |
| Cote d'Ivoire | -0.954 | -2.559 | -1.646 | -3.761 | -5.321 | -7.414 |
| Mali | -2.228 | -6.481 | -3.604 | -4.482 | -25.873 | -7.549 |
| Niger | -2.247 | -3.197 | -1.672 | -4.046 | -10.344 | -5.572 |
| Senegal | -2.010 | -3.042 | -1.411 | -4.382 | -10.167 | -6.625 |
| Togo | -2.111 | -3.506 | -1.580 | -4.865 | -10.373 | -7.058 |

*Notes:* Critical values at the 5% level are -3.518 (level) and -2.933 (difference).

The second step of our empirical analysis consists in testing cointegration among the variables using the bounds testing approach. The results of the bounds F-test statistics along with long-run coefficients are displayed in Table 2. From the table we can see that the computed F-statistic exceeds the upper critical values at 5% level of significance for all countries except Mali. Accordingly, we reject the null hypothesis of no cointegration among the variables and conclude that there is a long-run relationship among budget deficit, money supply and price level for all countries, except Mali.

The estimates of the long-run parameters show that deficit increases price levels in Niger and Togo. On the contrary, budget deficit reduces price level in Benin and Senegal. Therefore, fiscal policies that reduce budget deficits would be good for households in Niger and Togo. For Burkina Faso and Cote d'Ivoire, fiscal deficit is not a significant driver of price levels. On the other hand, the results provide evidence supporting the monetary view of a positive long run-relationship between money supply and inflation in Burkina Faso, Cote d'Ivoire and Senegal. This implies that a continuous increase in the supply of money relative to GDP leads to an increase in price levels in these three countries.

| Table 2: Results of bounds test for cointegration | | | |
|---|---|---|---|
| | | Long-run relationship | |
| Country | F-Stat. | Deficit | Money |
| Benin | 5.338* | -0.156 (-2.358)* | 0.031 (1.398) |
| Burkina Faso | 5.705* | -0.003 (-0.067) | 0.076 (5.101)* |
| Cote d'Ivoire | 4.354 (1)* | -0.055 (-0.669) | 0.199 (6.675)* |
| Mali | 2.460 | - | - |
| Niger | 5.054* | 0.037 (2.456)* | -0.005 (-0.746) |
| Senegal | 6.242* | -0.131 (-1.994)* | 0.056 (2.254)* |
| Togo | 5.903* | 0.060 (3.046)* | -0.005 (-0.909) |

*Note:* Critical values for F-statistics are taken from Pesaran *et al.* (2001). * indicates that the null hypothesis of no cointegration is rejected at the 5% level.

The results of the Granger-causality tests are reported in Table 3. Starting with the analysis of long-run effects, there is a unidirectional causality running from deficit to price in Benin, Niger, Senegal and Togo and from money supply to price in Burkina Faso, Cote d'Ivoire and Senegal. This result confirms our previous finding that a long-run relationship exists between deficit, money supply and price level. With regard to the short-run causality, the results indicate that budget deficit causes money growth in Cote d'Ivoire, Mali and Togo, and price level in Senegal. This supports the proposition of monetarists that increase of deficits induces higher money supply. There is however no causality from money supply to deficit and inflation in the short-run. Contrary to the monetary view, inflation is not everywhere a monetary phenomenon in the long-run. Money growth has significant impact on price only in Burkina Faso, Cote d'Ivoire and Senegal. Overall, our results for Niger, Togo, Burkina Faso, Cote d'Ivoire and Senegal accord with those of Dembo Toe and Hounkpatin (2007), Diop *et al.* (2008) and Zonon (2003), but contradict with Olusoji and Oderinde (2011) and Dockery *et al.* (2012) who found no significant causation between fiscal deficits and inflation. Mali is the only country where we fail to find significant impact of money and deficit on price. In this country, indeed, variations in consumer price index are largely driven by changes in food prices and therefore by the agricultural sector production.

**Table 3:** Results of Granger causality tests

| Country | Dep. var | Short-run causal variable | | | $ECT_{t-1}$ |
| | | Price | Deficit | Money | |
|---|---|---|---|---|---|
| Benin | Price | - | 0.138 (0.710) | 0.633 (0.426) | -0.056 (-3.305)* |
| | Deficit | 1.404 (0.236) | - | 0.467 (0.494) | 1.276 (1.423) |
| | Money | 1.387 (0.238) | 0.125 (0.723) | - | -0.774 (-0.880) |
| Burkina Faso | Price | - | 2.479 (0.115) | 0.218 (0.640) | -0.110 (-2.704)* |
| | Deficit | 0.030 (0.861) | - | 2.197 (0.138) | 0.946 (0.459) |
| | Money | 0.129 (0.718) | 0.051 (0.821) | - | 1.466 (1.043) |
| Cote d'Ivoire | Price | - | 0.028 (0.865) | 0.677 (0.410) | -0.019 (-2.444)* |
| | Deficit | 1.362 (0.243) | - | 2.104 (0.146) | 0.401 (0.776) |
| | Money | 0.928 (0.335) | 2.866 (0.090)** | - | -0.075 (-0.187) |
| Mali | Price | - | 3.538 (0.170) | 1.608 (0.447) | - |
| | Deficit | 2.980 (0.225) | - | 1.020 (0.600) | - |
| | Money | 3.164 (0.205) | 5.476 (0.064)** | - | - |
| Niger | Price | - | 0.001 (0.968) | 0.556 (0.455) | -0.172 (-2.490)* |
| | Deficit | 0.255 (0.613) | - | 0.025 (0.873) | -1.802 (-0.794) |
| | Money | 0.412 (0.520) | 0.136 (0.711) | - | 0.269 (0.143) |
| Senegal | Price | - | 20.464 (0.000)* | 0.000 (0.980) | -0.052 (-2.237)* |
| | Deficit | 3.099 (0.078)** | - | 0.000 (0.995) | 1.814 (2.413)* |
| | Money | 0.735 (0.391) | 0.493 (0.482) | - | -0.345 (-0.407) |
| Togo | Price | - | 0.001 (0.972) | 0.814 (0.366) | -0.176 (-3.547)* |
| | Deficit | 0.001 (0.969) | - | 0.308 (0.578) | -3.630 (-1.399) |
| | Money | 0.986 (0.320) | 7.980 (0.004)* | - | 2.688 (1.058) |

*Note:* Statistics for short-run causality are Chi2-statistics with *p-values* in parentheses. Column $ECT_{t-1}$ shows coefficients on $ECT_{t-1}$ with *t-statistics* in parentheses. The asterisks * and ** denote statistical significance at the 5% and 10% levels, respectively.

## 5.0    Conclusion and policy implications

This study has investigated the causal relationship between budget deficit, money supply and price dynamics in the member countries of the West African Economic and Monetary Union. It made use of the ARDL bounds testing procedure and Granger causality tests. The empirical evidence reveals a positive relationship between price levels and budget deficits in Niger and Togo, implying that an increase in budget deficit lead to an increase in prices.

Hence, for the level of prices to be reduced in these two countries, governments need to cut down the level of expenditure or increase significantly the level of tax revenues. The study finds a negative relationship between deficits and prices in Benin and Senegal, while deficits do not have any significant impact on price in Burkina Faso and Cote d'Ivoire. Furthermore, the results reveal that money expansion increases price levels in Burkina Faso, Cote d'Ivoire and Senegal. Results from the short-run Granger causality tests indicate that budget deficits cause money growth in Cote d'Ivoire, Mali and Togo, and prices in Senegal. There is no causality from money supply to deficit and inflation in the short-run. Thus, the widely accepted belief that deficits are inflationary does not hold in the case of WAEMU member countries. Budget deficits cannot be held responsible for inflation in WAEMU countries. Therefore, the policy of reducing price levels should focus on other macroeconomic and structural determinants of inflation such as agricultural production, economic growth, trade openness and policy regime. The control of budget deficits is, however, essential to achieve sustainable economic growth and the long run macroeconomic stability of the Union.

# References

Anoruo, E. C. (2003). An empirical investigation into budget deficit-inflation nexus in South Africa. *South African Journal of Economics,* 71(2): 146-154. http://dx.doi.org/10.111/j.1813-6982.2003.tb01309.x.

Ashra, S., Chattopadhyay, S. and Chaudhuri, K. (2004). Deficit, Money and Price: the Indian experience. *Journal of Policy Modeling,* 26(3), 289-299. http://dx.doi.org/10.1016/j.jpolmod.2004.03.010.

Awe, A. A. and Shina, O. S. (2012). The Nexus between Budget Deficit and Inflation in the Nigerian Economy (1980 – 2009), *Research Journal of Finance and Accounting,* 3(10), 78-92.

Barnhart, S.W. and Darrat, A. F (1989). Federal Deficits and Money Growth in the United States. *Journal of Banking and Finance,* 13(1), 137-149. http://dx.doi.org/10.1016/0378-4266(89)90024-1.

Barro, R. J. (1989). The Ricardian Approach to Budget Deficits. *Journal of Economic Perspectives,* 3(2), 37-54. http://dx.doi.org/10.1257/jep.3.2.37.

Brown, K. H. and Yousefi, M. (1996). Deficits, Inflation and Central Banks' Independence: Evidence from Developing Nations. *Applied Economics Letters* 3(8), 505-509. http://dx.doi.org/10.1080/135048596356122.

Carlstrom, C.T. and Fuerst, T. S. (2000). The fiscal theory of the price level. *Economic Review,* Federal Reserve Bank of Cleveland: 22–32.

Catão, L. A. and Terrones, M. (2003). Fiscal Deficits and Inflation: A New Look at the Emerging Market Evidence. IMF Working Paper, No. 65, Washigton, DC: International Monetary Fund.

Chang, H. J. (1994). Impact of Inflation, Output, Employment, and Income Effect in Budget Deficits for Taiwan: A Forecast of Regional Input-Output Approach. *Journal of Policy Modeling* 16(3), 345-351. http://dx.doi.org/10.1016/0161-8938(94)900337.

Chimobi, O.P., and Igwe, O.I. (2010). Budget Deficit, Money Supply and Inflation in Nigeria. *European Journal of Economics, Finance and Administrative Sciences,* 1(19), 52-60.

Chukwu, J. O. (2013). Budget Deficits, Money Growth and Price Level in Nigeria. *African Development Review,* 25(4), 468-477. http://dx.doi.org/10.1111/1467-8268.12042.

Cottarelli, C., Griffiths, M.E.L. and Moghadam, R. (1998). The Nonmonetary Determinants of Inflation: A Panel Data Study. IMF Working Paper, 98, 1-29. http://dx.doi.org/10.5089/9781451844016.001.

Darrat, A.F. (2000). Are budget deficits inflationary? A reconsideration of the evidence. *Applied Economics Letters,* 7(10), 633–636. http://dx.doi.org/10.1080/135048500415914.

De Haan, J. and Zelhorst, D. (1990). The Impact of Government Deficits on Money Growth in Developing Countries. *Journal of International Money and Finance,* 9(4), 455-469. http://dx.doi.org/10.1016/0261-5606(90)90022-R.

Dembo Toe. M. and Hounkpatin, M. (2007). *Lien entre la masse monétaire et l'inflation dans les pays de l'UEMOA.* Document d'Etude et de Recherche N°DER/07/02. Banque Centrale des Etats de l'Afrique de l'Ouest (BCEAO). p.43.

Diop, A., Dufrenot, G. and Sanon, G. (2008). Long-run determinants of inflation in WAEMU. In Gulde, A. M. and Tsangarides, C. G. (eds.) *"The CFA Franc Zone: common currency, uncommon challenge".* Washington, International Monetary Fund, Chapter 3, pp.54-76.

Dockery, E., Ezeabasili, V. N. and Herbert, W. E. (2012). On the relationship between fiscal deficits and inflation: Econometric Evidence for Nigeria. *Economics and Finance Review,* 2(7), 17-30.

Durevall, Dick and Ndung'u, N. S. (2001). A Dynamic Inflation Model for Kenya, 1974-1996. *Journal of African Economics,* 10(1), 92-125. http://dx.doi.org/10.1093/jae/10.1.92.

Fisher, I. (1911). *The Purchasing Power of Money.* Macmillan, New York.

Friedman, M. (1968). The Role of Monetary Policy. *American Economic Review,* 58(1), 1-17.

Giannaros, D.S. and Kolluri, B.R. (1986). Deficit Spending, Money, and Inflation: Some International Empirical Evidence. *Journal of Macroeconomics,* 7, 401-417. http://dx.doi.org/10.1016/0164-0704(85)90079-5.

Hamburger, M.J. and Zwick, B. (1981). Deficits, money and inflation. *Journal of Monetary Economics,* 7(1), 141–50.. http://dx.doi.org/10.1016/0304-3932(81)90057-X.

Haug, A. A. (2002). Temporal Aggregation and the Power of Cointegration Tests. A Monte Carlo Study. *Oxford Bulletin of Economics and Statistics* 64(4), 399-412. http://dx.doi.org/10.1111/1468-0084.00025.

Hondroyiannis, G. and Papapetrou, E. (1994). Cointegration, Causality and the Government Budget-Inflation Relationship in Greece. *Applied Economic Letters*, 1(11), 204-206. http://dx.doi.org/10.1080/135048594357880.

Hondroyiannis, G. and Papapetrou, E. (1997). Are Budget Deficits Inflationary? A Cointegration Approach. *Applied Economics Letters*, 4(8), 493–96. http://dx.doi.org/10.1080/758536632.

Jalil, A., Tariq, R. and Bibi, N. (2014). Fiscal Deficit and Inflation: New Evidences from Pakistan Using a Bounds Testing Approach. *Economic Modeling*, 37, 120-126. http://dx.doi.org/10.1016/j.econmod.2013.10.029.

Karras, G. (1994). Macroeconomic effects of budget deficits: further international evidence, *Journal of International Money and Finance*, 13(2), 190-210. http://dx.doi.org/10.1016/0261-5606(94)90015-9.

Leeper, E.M. (1991). Equilibria under "Active" and "Passive" Monetary and Fiscal Policies. *Journal of Monetary Economics*, 27, 129-147. http://dx.doi.org/10.1016/0304-3932(91)90007-B.

Metin, K. (1998). The Relationship between Inflation and the Budget Deficit in Turkey, *Journal of Business and Economic Statistics*, 16 (4), 412-422. http://dx.doi.org/10.2307/1392610.

Narayan, P. K., Narayan, S. and Prasad, A. (2006). Modeling the relationship between budget deficits, money supply and inflation in Fiji. *Pacific Economic Bulletin*, 21(2), 103-116.

Neyapti, B. (2003). Budget Deficits and Inflation: The Roles of Central Bank Independence and Financial Market Development. *Contemporary Economic Policy*, 21, 458-475. http://dx.doi.org/10.1093/cep/byg025.

Nguyen, V. B. (2015). Effects of Fiscal Deficit and Money M2 Supply on Inflation: Evidence from Selected Economies of Asia. *Journal of Economics, Finance and Administrative Science*, 20, 49-53. http://dx.doi.org/10.1016/j.jefas.2015.01.002.

Nyong, M. O. and Odubekun, F. O. (2002). The Macroeconomic Effects of Monetary Financing of Fiscal Deficits in Nigeria. *West African Journal of Monetary and Economic Integration*, 2(2), 129-192.

Ogunmuyiwa, M. S. (2008). Fiscal Deficit-Inflation-Nexus in Nigeria. *Indian Journal of Economics,* 3(10), 580-585.

Olusoji, M. O. and Oderinde, L. O. (2011). Fiscal deficit and inflationary trend in Nigeria: A Cross-causal Analysis. *Journal of Economic Theory*, 5(2), 37-43. http://dx.doi.org/10.3923/jeth.2011.37.43.

Pesaran H., Shin Y., and Smith, R. J. (2001). Bounds Testing Approaches to the Analysis of Level Relationships. *Journal of Applied Econometrics* 16(3), 289-326. http://dx.doi.org/10.1002/jae.616.

Phillips, P. C. B. and Perron, P. (1988). Testing for a Unit Root in a Time Series Regression, *Biometrika*, 75 (2), 335–346. http://dx.doi.org/10.1093/biomet/75.2.335.

Raji, J. O., Jusoh, J. and Jantan, M-D. (2014). Real Money Supply, Price and Fiscal Deficit in Nigeria: Evidence from Multivariate Granger Causality Tests. *Journal of Economic Cooperation and Development,* 35(4), 85-112.

Sargent, T. J. and Wallace, N. (1981). Some Unpleasant Monetarist Arithmetic. *Federal Reserve Bank of Minneapolis Quarterly Review*, 5(3), 1-17.

Sims, C. (1994). A Simple Model for the Study on the Determination of the Price Level and the Interaction of Monetary and Fiscal Policy. *Economic Theory*, 4, 381-399. http://dx.doi.org/10.1007/BF01215378.

Solomon, M. and De Wet, W. A. (2004). The Effect of a Budget Deficit on Inflation: The Case of Tanzania, *South African Journal of Economic and Management Sciences*, 7(1), 100-116.

Sowa, N. K. (1994), Fiscal Deficits, Output Growth and Inflation Targets in Ghana, *World Development Report*, 22(8), 1105-1117. http://dx.doi.org/10.1016/0305-750X(94)90079-5.

Tekin-Koru, A. and Özmen, E. (2003). Budget deficits, money growth and Inflation: The Turkish Evidence. *Applied Economics*, 35(5), 591-596. http://dx.doi.org/10.1080/0003684022000025440.

Wolde-Rufael, Y. (2008). Budget deficits, Money and Inflation: The Case of Ethiopia. The *Journal of Developing Areas*, 42(1), 183-199. http://dx.doi.org/10.1353/jda.0.0028.

Woodford, M. (1994). Monetary Policy and Price Level Determinacy in a Cash-in-Advance Economy. *Economic Theory*, 4, 345-380. http://dx.doi.org/10.1007/BF01215377.

Zonon, A. (2003). *Les déterminants de l'inflation au Burkina Faso*. Document de Travail N°02/2003. Centre d'Analyse des Politiques Economiques et Sociales (CAPES). Burkina Faso, pp.29

# 7

# Has the risk index of Islamic banks and conventional banks in GCC countries changed in response to the 2008 economic crisis?

Talla M Aldeehani [a*]

[a] Department of Finance & Financial Institutions, College of Business Administration, Kuwait University, Safat 13055, Kuwait.
*Corresponding author's email address: talla@cba.edu.kw

| ARTICLE INFO | ABSTRACT |
| --- | --- |
| Keywords:<br>Banking; Capital Structure;<br>Financial Crisis; Islamic Banking;<br>Financial Risk. | In this empirical study, we investigate the effect of the 2008 economic crisis on the level of risks Islamic banks (IB) and conventional banks (CB) are facing and the determinants of their risk indices. We cover 20 banks operating in the Gulf Cooperation Council (GCC) countries during 2001-2014. The results indicate that while the state of the economy had no effect on the risk index (RI) of banks, the type of bank did have an effect. The results suggest that the RI of IB was significantly lower than that of CB before and after the crisis indicating higher risks for IB. While the RI of CB is explained by solvency and liquidity variables, the RI of IB is explained by liquidity and profitability variables. Discussions, interpretations of research results and implications are provided. |

## 1.0    Introduction

The recent economic crisis has raised many questions regarding bank risks. Ever since the start of the 2008 economic downturn, banks were exposed to tremendous pressures from regulators and clients to exercise more control over their risks. Goodhart (2008) listed many policies and regulatory issues commanding serious discussions. These issues are scale and scope of deposit insurance, bank insolvency, central banks roles, liquidity risk management, capital adequacy requirements, the scope of regulation and crisis management. Blundell-Wignall et al. (2008) who discussed how the crisis evolved share the same concern and pointed *to the need for far-reaching reforms* in the banking system to better mitigate risks and avoid a similar crisis. Since then, several researchers have strived to investigate these issues. However, the extent of the effect of the crisis on bank risks has not been fully researched, especially with the existing structural differences between IB and CB.

IB and CB differ in their capital structures (Aldeehani et al., 1999 and Archer et al. 1998). As a result, the level of financial risk assumed by the bank also differs (Arifin et al., 2009). Indeed, Vogel and Hayes, III (1998) argued that for IB, *"The risk assumed by depositors enables the institution to tolerate greater risk on its assets side, as it must if it is to make equity investments in Mudaraba ventures instead of lending on interest."* It follows that one would assume that the Islamic bank's RI is lower than that of a typical conventional bank indicating higher risks. The 2008 economic crisis with its long-lasting effect provides an opportunity to study this issue.

In this paper, the focus is on the concept of risk in conventional and Islamic banking. The RI is the specific variable of concern. Given the presumed tendency of IB to take risks, the key question of this research is; does the RI of IB differ from that of CB before and after the crisis? If it does, then, what are the fundamental determinants of the RI of both types before and after the crisis?

The relevant literature will be reviewed to discuss the various definitions of bank's RI and its determinants. From such a discussion, we should be able to extract the research hypotheses and the factors representing the dependent and explanatory variables.

Our research data covers the period from 2001 to 2014 for 20 banks, within the region of the GCC, classified as Islamic and conventional. Investigating the determinants of the RI for this type of data commands a general panel regression model which will be discussed later.

This paper is organized as follows: in section 2, we discuss the relevant literature and hypotheses development. In section 3, we discuss our research sample, data, and methodology. This is followed by hypotheses testing and model estimation in section 4. The main results of the paper are discussed in section 5 then we the paper concludes in Section 6.

## 2.0    Literature review and hypotheses development

Similar to conventional banking, the main objective of Islamic banking is to maximize the value of shareholders' wealth. This objective is achieved through making profit from borrowing money at a cost rate lower than the rate of return they get from lending the money. The general operation of the two types is the same. They both attract money from savers (depositors) who expect to receive returns on their deposits and provide finances to borrowers who are expected to pay interest (profit) on the money they borrowed. Conventional banking provides finances and facilities to their clients through various contracts of loans. Islamic banking, however, uses profit and loss sharing contracts to provide facilities to the clients. The most popular ones are *murabahah*, *mudarabah*, *musharakah*, *istisna'*, and *ijarah*. Boumediene (2011) provides in-depth definitions and discussions for these contracts. However, the capital structure of IB is unique and differs fundamentally from that of CB. This issue was researched rigorously earlier in the past three decades. That is because IB is not allowed, by the shari'a (Islamic law), to pay or receive interest. They rather attract money in the form of profit sharing and loss bearing investment accounts. The funds in these accounts are mobilized under a contractual agreement called *mudarabah*. The *mudarabah* contract is neither a financial liability instrument nor a shareholder's equity instrument. Unlike lenders, in the case of bankruptcy, Investment account holders are not given priority over shareholders. Theoretical propositions and potential implications regarding profit-sharing risk and returns of IB were provided by pioneering papers (see for example Aldeehani et al., 1999 and Archer et al. 1998). Indeed, Aldeehani et al., (1999) argue that "*the concept of financial risk, on which capital structure theories are based, is not relevant to Islamic banks.*"

Ever since the 2008 economic downturn and its evident effect on global economies, it was important to understand the magnitude of that effect on financial markets and institutions. Because of the fundamental differences between IB and CB, researchers have strived to compare between the two type of banks regarding the effect of that crisis on performance and riskiness. Rashwan (2012), for example, investigated the effect of the 2008 crisis on the efficiency and profitability of IB compared to CB. He found that while IB performed better before the crisis, CB performance was better after the crisis. The same result was concluded by other researchers like Ouerghi (2014) and Al-Deehani et al. (2015). Ouerghi (2014) concluded that CB outperformed IB in terms of profitability, credit risk and efficiency in the post-crisis period. This was also supported by Al-Deehani et al. (2015). Exploring the banking industry in the country of Kuwait (a member of the GCC countries), Alkulaib et al. (2013) argued that while having an issue with systematic risk, IB has outperformed CB regarding liquidity.

### 2.1    Risk Index and development of hypotheses

When discussing Islamic bank risks, researchers are not in absolute agreement on how to define credit, debt or credit risks. One research, for example (see Sadaqat *et al.*, 2011), oddly defined, bank liquidity risk as the ratio of cash to total assets. The concept of risk in IB was thoroughly explained by Arifin et al., (2009). They state that risk in Islamic banking can best be understood when viewed from two dimensions: *gharar* (uncertainty) and freedom of contract. The word "*Gharar*" in the Arabic language is a synonym to cheating (the act of concealing information) in a business transaction. This act is prohibited by the Sharia' (Islamic law) and unlawful in a business transaction. They argue that "*Islam fully recognizes the risk that is generated by financial and commercial factors and elements extrinsic to the formation of the business transaction.*" Given the distinctive nature of their capital structures and the unique contracts they use to provide facilities, IB is bound to deal with credit risks differently. Boumediene

(2011) provides a detailed discussion of the credit risk associated with each contract. Exploring the assertion that Islamic banking exhibits higher credit risk than conventional banking, he found that CB faces higher credit risk. To measure credit risk, Boumediene (2011) used the distance-to-default (DD) measure modeled by Merton (1974) based on Black and Scholes' option pricing formula. The problem with the DD measure is that it is based on the notion that the chance of default leading to bankruptcy -and consequently the transfer of control to debt holders- is determined by the probability that the market value of the bank assets will drop below the value of debt at maturity. Because of the nature of the 'profit and loss' contracts, IB does not treat deposits as debt, therefore, in the case of insolvency, they don't submit to deposit accounts holders (debt holders in the case of CB). As mentioned earlier, the capital structures of IB are fundamentally different from those of CB. Therefore, we believe that the DD method is not applicable to IB.

Investigating the determinants of bank capital ratios in Malaysia during 1995 to 2002, Ahmad et al. (2015) found a strong association between regulatory capital and bank risk taking behavior. Their findings were consistent with how banks all over the world have engaged in risky lending before the 2008 economic downturn. Two risk variables were investigated; the total risk-weighted capital adequacy ratio ($CAR$) as the dependent variable and RI as an independent explanatory variable. Stan and McIntyre (2012) used the accounting measure of risk in the form RI to investigate the riskiness of over 7 thousand banks in the FDIC database for the period from 2001 to 2008. They found that larger banks face higher risks than smaller banks regarding RI measure. Risk variability was found to be explained by ratios like capital to assets and higher variances in return to assets.

An extensive investigation of the RI of Indians banks was conducted by Kantawala (2004). Examining the effect of 21 variables on RI, the author found that the groups of variables groups of profitability, solvency and liquidity do have an impact on RI. Many research attempts were conducted to compare the performance IB to CB in the GCC region. Some authors investigated individual countries (see for example Alkulaib et al. 2013), and others have focused on the region as a whole. Some of the studies were theoretical (see for example Aldeehani et al., 1999 and Archer et al. 1998) and some applied (the latest is Al-Deehani *et al.* 2015). However, none have conducted a comparative study on the effect of the economic crisis on the RI of IB versus CB. This research is intended to bridge this gap. Therefore, and referring to the research questions on the differences in the RI of CB versus IB before and after the crisis, we are proposing two groups of hypotheses. Group 1 tests the significance of means' differences of RI for CB versus IB at times of economic stability and during times of instability. Group 2 test the significance of means' differences of RI of each bank type before and after the economic crisis. The following are detailed statements of the null and alternative hypotheses of the two groups.

**Group 1 hypotheses:**
1. *Ho:* at times of economic stability (before the crisis), the RI for CB is not significantly different from that of IB.
   *H1:* at times of economic stability, the RI for CB is significantly different from that of IB.
2. *Ho:* at times of economic instability (before the crisis), the RI for CB is not significantly different from that of IB.
   *H1:* at times of economic instability, the RI for CB is significantly different from that of IB.

**Group 2 hypotheses:**
1. *Ho:* the RI for CB at times of economic stability is not significantly different from that at times of economic instability.
   *H1:* the RI for CB at times of economic stability is significantly different from that at times of economic instability.
2. *Ho:* the RI for IB at times of economic stability is not significantly different from that at times of economic instability.
   *H1:* the RI for IB at times of economic stability is significantly different from that at times of economic instability.

## 3.0    Sample, data, and methods

Originally, we collected fundamental data for 25 GCC banks. Twelve of which were CB and thirteen were IB covering the period from 2001 to 2014. Unfortunately, some of the IB did not have data for earlier periods. Therefore, and to have a more strongly balanced data, IB with data covering the period from 2001 to 2014 were qualified for inclusion in the sample of this study. The number of IB to be investigated was reduced to 7 banks. The data was collected from specialized reports on GCC countries by the Institute of Banking Studies in Kuwait.

GCC countries have relative similarities in culture, language, religion, economics and characteristics of the financial markets. It is the region in which Islamic banking and finance have originated in the seventies of the past century. According to the IMF (2015), Islamic banking in the GCC accounted for 38.2% of global Islamic banking.

As of 2014, a total of 72 banks are operating in the region, 50 of which are conventional and 22 are IB. According to the Institute of Banking Studies (2015), the size of the banking industry in 2014, regarding total assets, amounts to $1,802,238 million, 22% of which is Islamic. The aggregate return on assets is 1.76% for CB and 1.55% for IB. Return on equity is 13.4% for CB and 11.59% for IB. The size of deposits is $1,083,380 million for CB and $288,582 million for IB. The size of finances is $858,779 million for CB and $294,827 for IB. Table 1 below, summarizes the GCC banking industry as of 2014:

| Table1: Summary of GCC banking industry as of 2014 | Conventional Banks | Islamic Banks |
|---|---|---|
| Total Assets | 1,404,529 | 397,709 |
| Loans | 858,779 | 294,827 |
| Deposits | 1,083,380 | 288,582 |
| Capital | 51,512 | 23,431 |
| Equity | 187,052 | 53,849 |
| Net Profit | 24,782 | 6,150 |
| ROA | 1.76% | 1.55% |
| ROE | 13.25% | 11.42% |
| Loans/Assets | 61.14% | 74.13% |
| Deposits/Assets | 77.13% | 72.56% |
| Loans/Deposits | 79.27% | 102.16% |

The IMF (2015) states that Islamic banking has 25% market share in the GCC market indicating the significant importance of Islamic banking and finance in the region. The list of banks investigated by this study is shown in Table 2 below:

| Table 2: List of banks investigated | | |
|---|---|---|
| Type | No | Name of Banks |
| Conventional | 1 | Bank of Bahrain and Kuwait |
| | 2 | National Bank of Bahrain |
| | 3 | National Bank of Kuwait |
| | 4 | Commercial Bank of Kuwait |
| | 5 | Bank Muscat |
| | 6 | Bank Dhofar |
| | 7 | Qatar National Bank |
| | 8 | Commercial Bank of Qatar |
| | 9 | The National Commercial Bank |
| | 10 | Samba Financial Group |
| | 11 | National Bank of Abu Dhabi |
| | 12 | Commercial Bank of Dubai |
| Islamic | 13 | Al-Rajhi Banking &Inv Co. |
| | 14 | Kuwait Finance House |
| | 15 | Dubai Islamic Bank |
| | 16 | Abu Dhabi Islamic Bank |
| | 17 | Qatar Islamic Bank |
| | 24 | Bahrain Islamic Bank |
| | 25 | ABC Islamic Bank |

From the literature discussed earlier, we elected the *RI*, developed by Hannon and Hanweck (1988), as a measure of the overall riskiness of banks. It is calculated as the bank soundness cushion per one unit of risk. The bank soundness cushion is measured by the combined ratios of return on assets and equity to assets divided. Risk is measured by the standard deviation of the return on assets ($\sigma_{ROA}$). The higher the unit of risk the lower the risk index. Similarly, the higher the soundness cushion the, higher the *RI*, hence, the lower the risk.

Because of the fundamental differences in the capital structures of CB versus IB, we believe that the RI method is suitable for comparing the risk levels facing the two types of banks. That is because most of the measures of bank risks involve the element of debt which is not applicable to IB. The RI is a function of three variables return on assets, equity to assets and the standard deviation of the return on assets. No debt is involved.

We follow the definition of *RI* adopted by Sinkey (1988), Eisenbeis & Kwast (1991), Sinkey & Nash (1993), Nash & Sinkey (1997), Kantawala (2004) and Stan and McIntyre (2012) which can be written as:

$$RI = \left(\frac{ROA + E/A}{\sigma_{ROA}}\right) \quad\text{..........................} (1)$$

Where RI is the risk index, ROA is the return on assets, E/A is the equity to total assets and $\sigma_{ROA}$ is the standard deviation of return on assets. From earlier discussions of the literature review, eight fundamental variables were to be investigated for potential explanatory power. The variables represent four influential areas. Bank liquidity is the most important influential area. It is represented by four variables; loan to total assets (*loa*), deposits to total assets (*doa*), loan to deposits (*lod*) and current assets to current liabilities (*caocl*). The second potential influential area is profitability which is represented by two variables; return on assets (*roa*) and return on equity (*roe*). Equity to total assets (*eoa*) represents solvency and total assets (*ta*) represents size of the bank. The following is a summary of the selected explanatory variables and the areas they represent.

Table 3 below provides a summary of the variables' means for each of the banks under investigation.

**Table 3:** Summary of the variables' means

| | Bank No | eoa | loa | doa | lod | caocl | ta | roa | roe | RI |
|---|---|---|---|---|---|---|---|---|---|---|
| Conventional Banks | 1 | 0.104 | 0.519 | 0.789 | 0.661 | 6.700 | 5667.107 | 0.015 | 0.143 | 49.501 |
| | 2 | 0.128 | 0.433 | 0.842 | 0.514 | 16.340 | 5094.018 | 0.018 | 0.142 | 93.838 |
| | 3 | 0.148 | 0.497 | 0.912 | 0.583 | 7.094 | 36911.785 | 0.023 | 0.162 | 14.848 |
| | 4 | 0.138 | 0.577 | 0.796 | 0.729 | 5.155 | 11048.086 | 0.016 | 0.115 | 11.868 |
| | 5 | 0.123 | 0.698 | 0.739 | 0.946 | 1.663 | 12362.966 | 0.017 | 0.136 | 34.771 |
| | 6 | 0.127 | 0.796 | 0.700 | 1.825 | 3.653 | 3407.588 | 0.020 | 0.154 | 27.627 |
| | 7 | 0.136 | 0.657 | 0.776 | 0.847 | 1.823 | 49524.963 | 0.023 | 0.175 | 44.365 |
| | 8 | 0.162 | 0.592 | 0.627 | 1.531 | 1.930 | 19298.840 | 0.022 | 0.137 | 19.849 |
| | 9 | 0.112 | 0.459 | 0.852 | 0.540 | 3.569 | 60708.715 | 0.020 | 0.192 | 17.045 |
| | 10 | 0.130 | 0.501 | 0.826 | 0.608 | 3.090 | 39679.344 | 0.026 | 0.213 | 24.146 |
| | 11 | 0.098 | 0.612 | 0.793 | 0.774 | 2.794 | 45232.866 | 0.018 | 0.187 | 27.447 |
| | 12 | 0.171 | 0.686 | 0.762 | 0.903 | 5.680 | 7373.918 | 0.027 | 0.156 | 37.106 |
| | 13 | 0.146 | 0.818 | 0.773 | 1.062 | 2.541 | 41547.929 | 0.035 | 0.243 | 13.992 |
| Islamic Banks | 14 | 0.103 | 0.700 | 0.645 | 1.140 | 0.559 | 34506.799 | 0.016 | 0.149 | 13.273 |
| | 15 | 0.103 | 0.779 | 0.772 | 1.012 | 2.287 | 18712.742 | 0.015 | 0.144 | 17.653 |
| | 16 | 0.123 | 0.821 | 0.673 | 1.877 | 2.306 | 13694.827 | 0.013 | 0.113 | 32.533 |
| | 17 | 0.157 | 0.716 | 0.657 | 1.117 | 2.542 | 9684.823 | 0.033 | 0.248 | 10.631 |
| | 24 | 0.163 | 0.699 | 0.772 | 1.467 | 3.270 | 1611.399 | 0.003 | -0.019 | 6.488 |
| | 25 | 0.171 | 0.739 | 0.170 | 34.241 | 0.880 | 872.754 | 0.134 | 1.244 | 0.655 |

Table 4 depicts the means of the variables for CB versus IB before and after the 2008 economic downturn.

**Table 4:** Means of the variables for CB versus IB before and after the 2008 economic downturn

| | | eoa | loa | doa | lod | caocl | ta | roa | roe | RI |
|---|---|---|---|---|---|---|---|---|---|---|
| Before Crisis | Conv | 0.132 | 0.578 | 0.799 | 0.730 | 3.978 | 12742.586 | 0.023 | 0.182 | 34.784 |
| | Islamic | 0.139 | 0.768 | 0.673 | 4.800 | 1.612 | 8295.492 | 0.023 | 0.186 | 14.245 |
| After Crisis | Conv | 0.131 | 0.594 | 0.770 | 1.014 | 5.937 | 36642.447 | 0.017 | 0.136 | 32.284 |
| | Islamic | 0.136 | 0.738 | 0.601 | 7.176 | 2.498 | 26170.586 | 0.048 | 0.420 | 12.962 |

To test the main hypotheses regarding the significance of the RI of conventional versus IB before and after the economic downturn, we adopt a two independent samples t-test to compare the means of the RI. Following Stan and McIntyre (2012), the t-test will then be supported by the Mann-Whitney nonparametric test to check the significance of the results in the lack of normality.

The data will then be arranged in the form of a balanced panel data. A linear regression model will then be estimated to investigate the relationship between the independent explanatory variables and the RI. Our panel has the form

$X_{it}, i = 1, ..., N\ t = 1, ..., T,$

Where *i* is the dimension of banks and *t* is the dimension of time. A general panel regression model is written as

$$y_{it} = \alpha + \beta' X_{it} + u_{it} \quad\text{......................} (2)$$

We select a fixed effect model with robust standard error to overcome the possibility of the existence of heteroskedasticity which may increase the probability of type I error. The fixed effects model is denoted as

$$y_{it} = \alpha + \beta' X_{it} + u_{it}, \dots\dots\dots\dots\dots (3)$$

$$u_{it} = \mu_i + v_{it}. \dots\dots\dots\dots\dots(4)$$

Where $\mu_i$ are the banks specific, time-invariant effects assumed to be fixed over time.

Before testing the research hypotheses and estimate our panel regression model, it would be interesting to have a general idea of how variables are associated. Table 5 illustrated the correlation coefficients between all of the variables.

| | RI | caocl | doa | eoa | ln(ta) | loa | lod | roa | roe | ecnmy | type |
|---|---|---|---|---|---|---|---|---|---|---|---|
| **Table 5:** Correlation coefficient between all of the variables | | | | | | | | | | | |
| RI | | | | | | | | | | | |
| Caocl | 0.500 | | | | | | | | | | |
| doa | 0.265 | 0.211 | | | | | | | | | |
| eoa | -0.005 | -0.007 | -0.142 | | | | | | | | |
| ln(ta) | -0.021 | -0.033 | 0.267 | -0.260 | | | | | | | |
| loa | -0.372 | -0.441 | -0.360 | -0.011 | -0.219 | | | | | | |
| lod | -0.226 | -0.130 | -0.617 | 0.079 | -0.314 | 0.154 | | | | | |
| roa | -0.055 | -0.053 | -0.186 | -0.003 | -0.069 | 0.048 | 0.166 | | | | |
| roe | -0.059 | -0.054 | -0.185 | -0.056 | -0.065 | 0.049 | 0.168 | 0.998 | | | |
| ecnmy | -0.049 | 0.161 | -0.104 | -0.023 | 0.423 | -0.003 | 0.052 | 0.025 | 0.028 | | |
| type | -0.462 | -0.288 | -0.327 | 0.072 | -0.227 | 0.601 | 0.242 | 0.069 | 0.068 | 0.000 | |
| year | -0.026 | 0.156 | -0.094 | 0.019 | 0.472 | -0.026 | 0.039 | -0.016 | -0.018 | 0.868 | 0.000 |

With regard to the dependent variable under investigation, *RI*, five variables are significantly correlated with it. These variables are *caocl*, *doa*, *loa, lod* and *type*. The first four variables represent bank liquidity and the fifth represents bank type. The correlation table affirms the importance of the association between bank liquidity and risk variability. The positive correlation signs of *caocl* and *doa* indicate a movement in the same direction with *RI*. In other word, an increase in deposits (more liquidity) is always associated with higher RI indicating lower risks and that is logical. The negative signs of *loa* and *lod* indicate a movement in the opposite direction with *RI*. The two variables also represent liquidity, but they focus on utilization (use) of that liquidity. Therefore, an association of opposite directions is logical. That is, more loans (lower liquidity) is always associated with less RI indicating higher risks. *Type* is the last variable showing a negative association with the RI. The negative sign is just a reflection of the coding used to classify bank types. The codes are 0 for CB and 1 for IB. The sign is negative because the mean RI of IB is lower indicating higher risks. Therefore, the higher code (1) is associated with low RI (higher risk), hence, the movement in opposite directions.

With regards to the potential explanatory variables, the various significant coefficients between these variables may indicate possible multi-co-linearity problems that may arise when estimating the regression models.

## 4.0     Tests and model estimation

This section consists of two subsections. In the first subsection, we perform tests of the research hypotheses and a discussion of these results. In the second subsection, we estimate our panel data regression model and discuss the resulting outcome on the determinants of RI.

## 4.1     Hypotheses testing and discussion of results

As mentioned earlier, two groups of hypotheses were developed. The results of testing the hypotheses of group 1 should provide solid statistical evidence on the different levels of risks each bank type faces. We use a two independent samples t-test to compare the means of the RI of the two types of banks supported by the Mann-Whitney nonparametric test to check the significance of the results in the lack of normality. To test the first hypothesis, we canceled out the post-crisis observations, hence, the reduction of the sample to 133 observations for the period from 2001 to 2014. To test the second hypothesis, pre-crisis observations were canceled out, and the sample was also reduced to 133 observations. The results of testing the two hypotheses are provided in Table 6 below.

The results of the t-test and the Mann-Whitney test indicate that both null hypotheses of group 1 are rejected which means that the RI of CB is significantly different from that of IB before and after the economic downturn. The results also show that the RI of IB is significantly lower than that of CB before and after the crisis indicating a higher risk for IB. The mean RI for CB is 34.78 at times of stability (before the 2008 crisis) and 32.28 at times of instability (after the crisis). We can notice a slight decrease in the RI of CB after the crisis indicating higher risks but we are not sure whether it is statistically significant different or not. The results also indicate that the mean RI for IB is 14.25 before the crisis and 12.96 after the crisis. Similar to CB, we can also notice a slight decrease in the RI of IB after the crisis indicating higher risks, but we are not sure whether it is statistically significant different or not. This is tested next.

| Banks | Before Downturn | | After Downturn | |
|---|---|---|---|---|
| | N | Mean | N | Mean |
| Conventional | 84 | 34.78 | 84 | 32.28 |
| Islamic | 49 | 14.25 | 49 | 12.96 |
| t-test | 5.729 | | 6.303 | |
| p-value | 0.000 | | 0.000 | |
| Mann-Whitney U | 702.000 | | 646.000 | |
| Z | -6.325 | | -6.586 | |
| Asymp. Sig. | 0.000 | | 0.000 | |

Table 6: Results of testing Group 1 hypotheses

The results of testing the hypotheses of group 2 should also provide statistical evidence of the effect of economy state on each bank type individually. Again the two independent samples t-test to compare the means of the RI of each bank type is performed supported by the Mann-Whitney nonparametric test to check the significance of the results in the lack of normality. The results of testing the two hypotheses are provided in table 7 below.

| Economic Crisis | Conventional Banks | | Islamic Banks | |
|---|---|---|---|---|
| | N | Mean | N | Mean |
| Pre | 84 | 34.78 | 49 | 14.24 |
| Post | 84 | 32.28 | 49 | 12.96 |
| t-test | 0.738 | | 0.617 | |
| p-value | 0.462 | | 0.539 | |
| Mann-Whitney U | 3406.000 | | 1152.000 | |
| Z | -0.387 | | -0.345 | |
| Asymp. Sig. | 0.699 | | 0.730 | |

Table 7: Results of testing Group 2 hypotheses

The *p-values* of the t-test (0.462 for CB and 0.617 for IB) and the Mann-Whitney test (0.699 for CB and 0.730 for IB) indicate that both null hypotheses cannot be rejected. These results mean that, for CB, the RI before the crisis is not significantly different from that after the crisis. Likewise, for CB, the RI before the crisis is not significantly different from that after the crisis. Although statistically insignificant, the results show that the risk indices did decrease indicating higher risks for both bank types at the time of instability. The pattern of the mean RI of CB versus IB is portrayed by figure 1.

**Figure 1.A:** Patterns of RI for CB versus IB

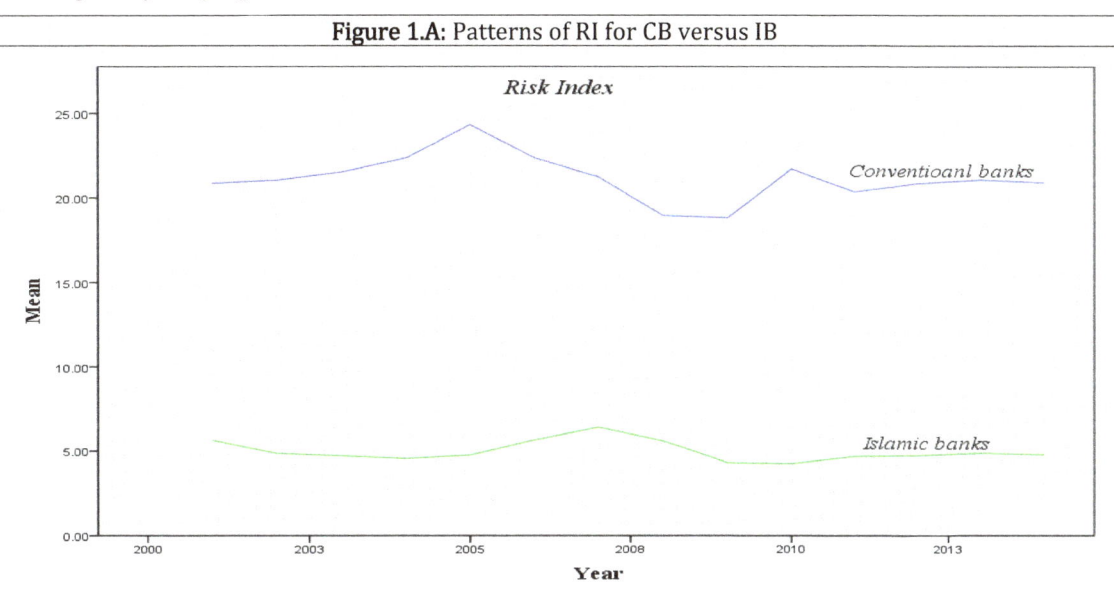

The chart shows the lower and significant RI of IB compared to CB indicating the higher risk IB were facing before and after the 2008 crisis. The trends of the curves also indicate the quicker pickup of CB to increase their RI after the sharp drop in the year 2008. By the end of the year 2010, CB was quicker than IB in lowering and stabilizing their risks. Figure 2 portrays the comparative levels of risk indices of the two bank types before and after the crisis.

The conclusion of the above analysis is that there is conclusive evidence that the RI of CB is significantly different from that of IB before and after the crisis. Referring to our research questions, the logical step now is to provide answers on the determinants of the RI of each bank type before and after the crisis. This is done in the following section.

## 4.2    Estimating the panel data regression model and discussing the results

Before performing the estimation, we check for three important but constraining potential problems; data stationary of all variables, multi-co-linearity of explanatory variables and heteroskedasticity. Autocorrelation shouldn't be a problem with micro panels with few years of time dimension such as the data of this research. Autocorrelation may be of important concern with long time series, typically, over 20 years.

We test data stationary using Levin-Lin-Chu unit-root. Table 8 illustrates the results of this test for all the variables.

| Table 8: Results of stationary test | | | |
|---|---|---|---|
| Series | Statistics | P-Values | Status |
| eoa | -2.5281 | 0.0057 | stationary |
| loa | -5.5832 | 0.0000 | stationary |
| doa | -4.3912 | 0.0000 | stationary |
| lod | -4.4002 | 0.0000 | stationary |
| caocl | -2.3211 | 0.0100 | stationary |
| ta | 4.3571 | 1.0000 | non-stationary |
| roa | -4.1803 | 0.0000 | stationary |
| roe | -2.7477 | 0.0030 | stationary |
| RI | -3.5655 | 0.0003 | stationary |

Table 8 indicates that the total assets variable is the only non-stationary variable, therefore; it was excluded from the list of explanatory variables.

To investigate the variables that explain and determine the RI of conventional and IB before and after the economic downturn, the following panel data regression model is estimated four times.

$$RI_{it} = \alpha + \beta_1 eoa_{it} + \beta_2 loa_{it} + \beta_3 doa_{it} + \beta_4 lod_{it} + \beta_5 caocl_{it} + roa_{it} + u_{it}, \ldots\ldots(5)$$

### 4.2.1    Estimating the model to investigate the determinants of RI for CB at times of economic stability. Table 9 below show the results of the estimated model.

| Table 9: Results of panel data regression for CB before the crisis | | | | | |
|---|---|---|---|---|---|
| Variable | Coef | t | p-value | VIF | 1/VIF |
| Eoa | 217.591 | 2.35 | 0.021 | 1.58 | 0.634 |
| Loa | 95.711 | 0.37 | 0.714 | 154.60 | 0.006 |
| doa | 2.544 | 0.01 | 0.991 | 27.89 | 0.036 |
| lod | -84.882 | -0.40 | 0.689 | 213.01 | 0.005 |
| caocl | 0.928 | 1.11 | 0.269 | 1.13 | 0.882 |
| roa | -688.020 | -1.94 | 0.056 | 1.16 | 0.866 |
| \const | 22.859 | 0.12 | 0.902 | | |
| No of Obs | 84 | | | | |
| F(6,77) | 2.38 | | | | |
| Prob | 0.0365 | | | | |
| Adj R$^2$ | 0.0908 | | | | |
| Breusch-Pagan / Cook-Weisberg test | | | | | $\chi^2(1) =25.85$ |
| for heteroskedasticity | | | | | Prob$> \chi^2$ =0.0000 |
| H$_0$:Constant variance | | | | Hypothesis rejected: heteroskedasticity exists | |

The table indicates that we face two problems. The first is the existence of multi-co-linearity with the variables *lod* and *loa*. The problem is fixed by canceling out one of the two variables and re-estimating the equation. Table 10 shows the results:

Table 10: Results of panel data regression for CB before the crisis after removing a multi-linear variable

| Variable | Coef | t | p-value | VIF | 1/VIF |
|---|---|---|---|---|---|
| eoa | 217.591 | 2.35 | 0.021 | 1.42 | 0.704 |
| doa | 2.544 | 0.01 | 0.991 | 1.70 | 0.588 |
| lod | -84.882 | -0.40 | 0.689 | 1.56 | 0.642 |
| caocl | 0.928 | 1.11 | 0.269 | 1.13 | 0.882 |
| roa | -688.020 | -1.94 | 0.056 | 1.12 | 0.897 |
| \const | 22.859 | 0.12 | 0.902 | | |
| No of Obs | 84 | | | | |
| F(5,78) | 2.86 | | | | |
| Prob | 0.020 | | | | |
| Adj R$^2$ | 0.101 | | | | |

The second problem is heteroskedasticity indicated by the Breusch-Pagan / Cook-Weisberg test for heteroskedasticity rejecting the hypothesis $H_0$: constant variance. The problem is resolved by re-estimating the regression equation with the robust standard error. Table 11 below shows the final results.

Table 11: Results of panel data regression for CB before the crisis after removing a multi-linear variable and fixing heteroskedasticity problem.

| Variable | Coef | t | p-value |
|---|---|---|---|
| eoa | 228.37 | 3.10 | 0.003 |
| doa | 81.18 | 2.60 | 0.011 |
| lod | -7.28 | -0.48 | 0.631 |
| caocl | 0.927 | 1.15 | 0.255 |
| roa | -712.39 | -1.82 | 0.072 |
| \const | -42.13 | -1.30 | 0.198 |
| No of Obs | 84 | | |
| F(5,78) | 2.25 | | |
| Prob | 0.022 | | |
| R$^2$ | 0.155 | | |

The results indicate that the ratio of equity to total assets (*eoa*) and the ratio of deposits to total assets (*doa*) significantly influence the RI of CB at times of stability. Both coefficients are positive and significant at the 5% level. The return to total assets ratio (*roa*) is also an influential variable at the 10% level. Figure 3 depicts the mean level of the variable *doa*.

### 4.2.2    Estimating the model to investigate the determinants of RI for CB at times of economic instability

Table 12 illustrates the results of the estimated regression model along with the Breusch-Pagan / Cook-Weisberg test for heteroskedasticity and the variable inflation factor which test for multi-co-linearity.

Table 12: Results of panel data regression for CB after the crisis

| Variable | Coef | t | p-value | VIF | 1/VIF |
|---|---|---|---|---|---|
| eoa | 36.147 | 1.37 | 0.179 | 1.52 | 0.6583 |
| loa | 96.378 | 4.99 | 0.000 | 1.16 | 0.8606 |
| doa | 0.533 | 0.10 | 0.924 | 1.79 | 0.5588 |
| lod | -0.153 | -1.42 | 0.162 | 1.59 | 0.6289 |
| caocl | -0.451 | -0.35 | 0.728 | 1.31 | 0.7618 |
| roa | 22.428 | 0.28 | 0.781 | 1.10 | 0.9058 |
| \const | -64.285 | -3.88 | 0.000 | | |
| No of Obs | 49 | | | | |
| F(6,42) | 5.49 | | | | |
| Prob | 0.000 | | | | |
| Adj R$^2$ | 0.359 | | | | |
| Breusch-Pagan / Cook-Weisberg test | | | $\chi^2(1) = 12.37$ | | |
| for heteroskedasticity | | | Prob>$\chi^2$ =0.0004 | | |
| $H_0$: Constant variance | | | Hypothesis rejected: heteroskedasticity exists | | |

The results show no multi-co-linearity problem in the explanatory variables. However, the Breusch-Pagan / Cook-Weisberg test for heteroskedasticity rejects the null hypothesis of constant variance indicating that heteroskedasticity problem does exist. Therefore, the fixed effect model was re-estimated with robust standard error to overcome the possibility of the existence of heteroskedasticity. The results of the model estimated are shown in table 13.

**Table 13**: Results of panel data regression for CB after the crisis after fixing the heteroskedasticity problem

| Variable | Coef | t | p-value |
|---|---|---|---|
| eoa | 36.147 | 0.99 | 0.329 |
| loa | 96.378 | 4.14 | 0.000 |
| doa | 0.533 | 0.14 | 0.893 |
| lod | -0.153 | -2.56 | 0.014 |
| caocl | -0.451 | -0.29 | 0.773 |
| roa | 22.418 | 0.27 | 0.785 |
| \const | -64.285 | -3.31 | 0.002 |
| No of Obs | 49 | | |
| F(6,42) | 8.52 | | |
| Prob | 0.000 | | |
| $R^2$ | 0.439 | | |

The results indicate that the ratio of loans to total assets (*loa*) and the ratio of loan to deposits (*lod*) are the only variables explaining the variation in the RI of CB at times of instability. The coefficients of both variables are significant at the 5% level. While *loa* has a positive effect on the RI, *lod*, on the other hand, has a negative effect. The later means that the higher the ratio of *lod*, the lower the RI (i.e. the higher the risk facing the bank). The mean level of the variable *lod* is show in figure 4.

### 4.2.3 Estimating the model to investigate the determinants of RI for IB at times of economic stability. Table 14 shows the result of the estimated model.

**Table 14**: Results of panel the data regression for IB before the crisis

| Variable | Coef | t | p-value | VIF | 1/VIF |
|---|---|---|---|---|---|
| eoa | -53.29 | -1.02 | 0.312 | 1.74 | 0.574 |
| loa | -7.98 | -0.45 | 0.654 | 2.27 | 0.441 |
| doa | -26.64 | -1.64 | 0.105 | 3.34 | 0.300 |
| lod | -2.06 | -1.48 | 0.143 | 2.04 | 0.491 |
| caocl | 1.83 | 7.21 | 0.000 | 1.49 | 0.672 |
| roa | 856.30 | 3.68 | 0.000 | 1.42 | 0.705 |
| \const | 41.14 | 2.05 | 0.044 | | |
| No of Obs | 83 | | | | |
| F(6,76) | 16.23 | | | | |
| Prob | 0.000 | | | | |
| Adj $R^2$ | 0.527 | | | | |
| Breusch-Pagan / Cook-Weisberg test | | | $\chi^2(1) = 8.41$ | | |
| for heteroskedasticity | | | Prob> $\chi^2$ =0.0037 | | |
| $H_0$: Constant variance | | Hypothesis rejected: heteroskedasticity exists | | | |

Multi-co-linearity does not exist between the explanatory variables, but we have a problem of heteroskedasticity. Again this is resolved by re-estimating the regression model and using the robust standard error. Table 15 below shows the results.

**Table 15**: Results of panel the data regression for IB before the crisis after fixing the heteroskedasticity problem

| Variable | Coef | t | p-value |
|---|---|---|---|
| eoa | -53.29 | -1.13 | 0.262 |
| doa | -26.64 | -1.69 | 0.096 |
| lod | -2.06 | -2.19 | 0.032 |
| caocl | 1.83 | 6.51 | 0.000 |
| roa | 856.30 | 4.93 | 0.000 |
| \const | 41.14 | 1.84 | 0.069 |
| No of Obs | 83 | | |
| F(6,76) | 15.22 | | |
| Prob | 0.000 | | |
| $R^2$ | 0.562 | | |

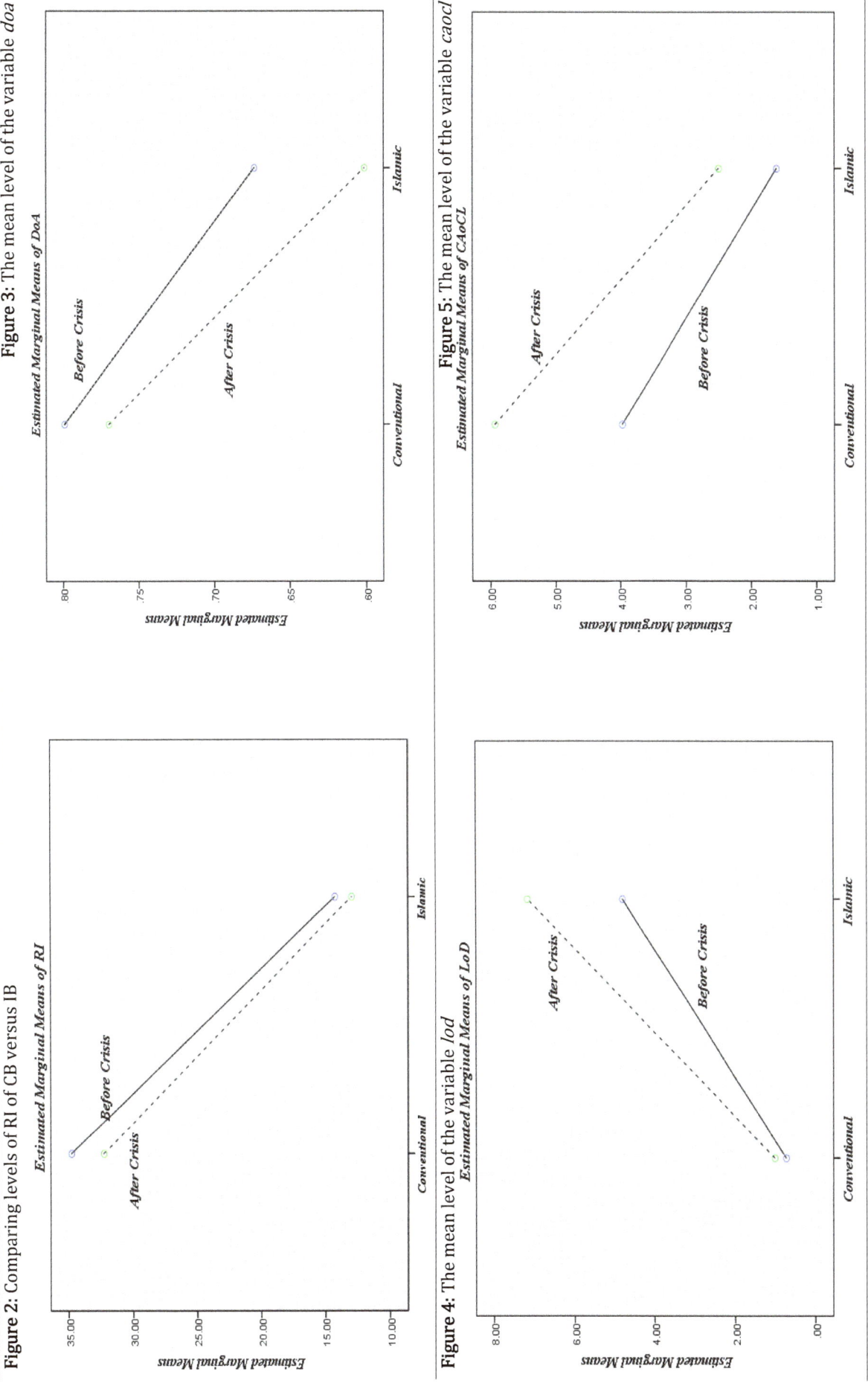

**Figure 2:** Comparing levels of RI of CB versus IB

*Estimated Marginal Means of RI*

**Figure 3:** The mean level of the variable *doa*

*Estimated Marginal Means of DoA*

**Figure 4:** The mean level of the variable *lod*

*Estimated Marginal Means of LoD*

**Figure 5:** The mean level of the variable *caocl*

*Estimated Marginal Means of CAoCL*

The table 15 indicates that the RI of IB at times of stability is determined by three ratios; the loans to deposits (*lod*), and the ratio of current assets to current liabilities (*caocl*) and the returns on assets (*roa*). The coefficients of all these variables are significant at the 5% level. The effects of *doa* and lod on the RI is negative. This means the higher the two ratios the lower the index indicating higher risks facing IB. The effect of *caocl*, however, is positive which means the higher the ratio the higher the RI indicating lower risks for IB. The return to total assets variable (*doa*) ratio also explains the variation in the RI but at the 10% level with positive effect. This means the increase in *doa* will decrease the RI of IB indicating lower risk. The mean level of the variable caocl is depicted in figure 5.

### 4.2.4    Estimating the model to investigate the determinants of RI for IB at times of economic instability

The results in table 16 show that we have no multi-co-linearity problem and the null hypothesis of constant variance is not rejected indicating that heteroskedasticity does not exist. However, the RI of the IB at times of economic instability is not explained by any of the explanatory variables.

**Table 16:** Results of panel data regression for IB after the crisis

| Variable | Coef | t | p-value | VIF | 1/VIF |
|---|---|---|---|---|---|
| eoa | -14.47 | -0.44 | 0.659 | 1.36 | 0.735 |
| loa | 25.00 | 1.35 | 0.186 | 1.11 | 0.903 |
| doa | 7.92 | 0.98 | 0.333 | 3.09 | 0.323 |
| lod | -0.13 | -1.19 | 0.240 | 2.40 | 0.417 |
| caocl | -0.05 | -0.06 | 0.949 | 1.36 | 0.737 |
| roa | -0.06 | -0.10 | 0.918 | 1.18 | 0.848 |
| \const | -7.20 | -0.44 | 0.661 | | |
| No of Obs | 49 | | | | |
| F(6,42) | 2.22 | | | | |
| Prob | 0.060 | | | | |
| Adj R$^2$ | 0.132 | | | | |
| Breusch-Pagan / Cook-Weisberg test for heteroskedasticity | | | | $\chi^2(1) = 2.51$ Prob$> \chi^2 =0.1132$ | |
| H$_0$: Constant variance | | Hypothesis accepted: heteroskedasticity does not exist | | | |

An overall look of the result suggests some outstanding feature. *First*, RI of CB before the crisis is significantly different and higher than that of IB. This indicates that IB were exposed to higher risks compared to CB. The result can be explained by the fact, unlike CB, IB tend to tolerate greater risk when mobilizing the money received from the investment accounts holders. This is a logical outcome of the unique capital structure of an Islamic bank. The result confirms the findings of earlier research discussed in this paper. *Second*, RI of CB after the crisis is also significantly different and higher than that of IB indicating a lower risk for CB. After the crisis, the gap of the mean RI between the two types of banks remained almost constant indicating that the crisis had no effect on significant effect on the level of bank risks. *Third*, although insignificant, the RI of CB has decreased after the crisis indicating higher risks. The same result can be concluded for IB. This result confirms the findings of Nabi and Bourkhis (2013) who concluded that the 2008 crisis did not have a significant effect on the soundness of CB and IB. *Fourth*, Variability of the RI of CB before the crisis was found to be explained by the ratio of equity to total assets and the ratio of deposits to total assets. The results showed positive relationships. This is explained by the fact that equity is a major element of bank solvency (ability to repay and honor liabilities) therefore higher equity amount leads to higher RI and lower levels of risks and vice versa. Although it is classified as a liability in conventional banking, a number of deposits is the main determinant of bank liquidity. More liquidity increases the ability of the bank to repay its liability, hence, the positive effect on the RI. *Fifth*, variability of the RI of CB after the crisis was found to be affected by two ratios; the loans to total assets and the loans to deposits. Again the relationship was positive. This is explained by the fact that the amount of loans is another element that affects the level of bank liquidity. More liquidity leads to lower risks and vice versa, hence the positive effect on the RI of the bank. *Finally*, the RI of IB before the crisis was found to be affected by three variables, loans to deposits, current assets to current liabilities and returns on assets. These variables are different from those affecting CB for the same period. Our interpretation of this result is based on the fact that the capital structure of IB is different. Note that a number of loans in IB represents the profit and loss instruments used to mobilize the funds deposited by the investment accounts holders.

### 5.0    Conclusion

The paper investigates the effect of the 2008 financial crisis on the risk levels of IB compared to CB. We elected the RI as the measure of risk levels. We believe this is a suitable measure as it does not involve the element of debt or credit. Within this context, we had two main objectives. First, we wanted to test whether there is a significant difference between the RI of CB and IB. Second, we wanted to identify the determinants of the RI for each bank type.

Before the crisis, the RI of CB was found to be significantly different (higher) from that of IB indicating higher risk levels for IB. The same result was concluded after the crisis. Moreover, the crisis did have a significant effect on the level of risks of CB. We found the same result for IB. The RI of CB was affected by the ratio of equity to total assets and the ratio of deposits to total assets before the crisis and by the ratios of loans to total assets and loans to deposits. The RI for IB was affected by loans to deposits, current assets to current liabilities and returns on assets.

The results indicated that for CB, liquidity and solvency are important determinants of the risk levels. For IB, the important determinants are liquidity and profitability. Our interpretation of this conclusion is that although important, and given the profit and loss contract, solvency for IB is not a critical issue when compared to CB. Due to the mudaraba, musharakah and murabahah contracts, profit margins of IB exhibit more variability compared to returns made by CB which is of stable nature. We believe the paper has provided two main contributions to the body of knowledge. First, we now know that, although the RI of IB and CB differs significantly, its level was not affected by the crisis. Second, the determinants of the level of RI for IB and CB are not the same. The evidence that IB are lagging in the level of the risks they have been facing before and after the crisis is in line with findings of some earlier research (see for example Hussein, 2010, Hasan and Dridi, 2011, Alkulaib et al. 2013 and Aldeehani et al. 2015). One obvious implication of these findings is that IB still has a long way to improving their management of risk while honoring Shari'a rules. Another implication is that regulators need to put more effort in the development of control policies related to the profitability and liquidity of Islamic banks.

Finally, it is worth noting that this research has focused on banks in the GCC region only. The inclusion of banks in other markets such as the Middle East and the Far East should provide a more profound outcome. Moreover, the paper has elected fundamental explanatory variables. Modeling the panel data with additional external variable may provide a wider understanding of the determinants of the banks' RI levels.

## References

Ahmad, R., Ariff, M. and Skully, M.J. (2015). The determinants of bank capital ratios in a developing economy. Asia-Pacific Financial Markets, 15 (3) 255–272.

Akhtar, M. F., Ali, Kh. and Sadaqat, Sh. (2011). Liquidity risk management: a comparative study between conventional and Islamic banks in Pakistan. Interdisciplinary Journal of Research in Business, 1(1), 35-44.

Al-Deehani, T., EL-Sadi, H. and Al-Deehani, M. (2015). The performance of Islamic banks and conventional banks before and during the economic downturn. Investment Management and Financial Innovation, 12 (2), 238-250.

Aldeehani, T., Karim, R. A. and Murinde, V. (1999). The capital structure of Islamic banks under the contractual obligation of profit sharing. International Journal of Theoretical and Applied Finance, 2 (3), 243-283. http://dx.doi.org/10.1142/S0219024999000157

Alkulaib, Y., Almudhaf, F. and Al-Jassar, S. (2013). The banking industry during an extended financial crisis: an empirical assessment of Kuwait banks, Academy of Banking Studies Journal, 12 (1), 61-73.

Archer, S., Karim, R. A. and Aldeehani, T. (1998). Financial contracting, governance structure and the accounting regulation of Islamic banks: an analysis in terms of agency theory and transaction cost economics. Journal of Management and Governance, 2, 149-170. http://dx.doi.org/10.1023/A:1009985419353

Ariffin Noraini, A., Archer, S. and Abdel Karim, R. A. (2009) Risk in Islamic banks: evidence from empirical research. Journal of Banking Regulations, 10 (2), 153-163. http://dx.doi.org/10.1057/jbr.2008.27

Blundell-Wignall, A., Atkinson, P. and Lee, S. H. (2008). The current financial crisis: causes and policy issues. Financial Market, OECD: ISSN 1995-2864.

Boumediene, A. (2011). Is credit risk really higher in Islamic banks? The Journal of Credit Risk, 7 (3), 97-129. http://dx.doi.org/10.21314/JCR.2011.128

Eisenbeis, R. A. and Kwast, M. L. (1991). Are real estate depositories variables? Evidence from commercial banks. Journal of financial services research, 5, 5-24. http://dx.doi.org/10.1007/BF00127081

Goodhart, C.A. (2008). The regulatory response to the financial crisis. Working paper. http://dx.doi.org/10.1016/j.jfs.2008.09.005

Hasan, M. and Dridi, J. (2011). The effect of the global crisis on Islamic and conventional banks: a comparative study. Journal of International Commerce, Economics and Policy, 2 (2), 163-200. http://dx.doi.org/10.1142/S1793993311000270

Hussein, K. (2010). Bank-level stability factors and consumer confidence – a comparative study of Islamic and conventional banks' product mix. Journal of Financial Services Marketing, 15 (3), 259-270. http://dx.doi.org/10.1057/fsm.2010.21

IMF (2015). Monetary operations and Islamic banking in the GCC: Challenges and options. Working paper: WP/15/234.

Kantawala, A. S. (2004). Apropos the soundness of public sector banks. Finance India, XVIII (4), 1651-1671.

Merton, R. C. (1974). On the pricing of corporate debt: the risk structure of interest rates. Journal of Finance, 29, 449-470. http://dx.doi.org/10.1111/j.1540-6261.1974.tb03058.x

Nabi, M. S. and Bourkhis, Kh. (2013). Islamic and conventional banks' soundness during the 2007–2008 financial crisis. Review of Financial Economics, 22 (2), 68-77. http://dx.doi.org/10.1016/j.rfe.2013.01.001

Nash, R. C., and Sinkey, J. F. (1997). On competition, risk, and hidden assets in the market for bank credit cards. Journal of Banking & Finance, 21, 89-112. http://dx.doi.org/10.1016/S0378-4266(96)00030-1

Ouerghi, F. (2014). Are Islamic banks more resilient to global crisis than conventional banks? Asian Economic and Financial Review, 4 (7), 914-955.

Rashwan, M. H. (2012). How did listed Islamic and Traditional Banks Performed: pre and post the 2008 financial crisis? Journal of Applied Finance & Banking, 2 (2), 149-175.

Sinkey, J. F. (Jr.) (1988). Commercial bank financial management. Prentice Hall India Inc, 80-100.

Sinkey, J. F. and Nash, R. C. (1993). Assessing the riskiness and profitability of credit-card banks. Journal of Financial Services Research, 2, 127-150. http://dx.doi.org/10.1007/BF01046902

Stan, M., and McIntyre, M. (2012). Too big to fail? Size and risk in banking. Academy of Banking Studies Journal, 11(2), 11-21.

Vogel, F. E. and Yayes III, S. L. (1998). Islamic law and finance religion, risk, and return, Kluwer Law International.

# 8

# Threshold effects of fiscal policy on economic growth in developing countries

Slimani Salma [a*], El Abbassi Idriss[a], Tounsi Said[a]

[a,] Department of Economics, Mohammed V Rabat –Agdal University, Faculty of Juridical, Economic and Social Sciences, Morocco.
[*]Corresponding author's email address: slimani.salma11@gmail.com

| ARTICLE INFO | ABSTRACT |
|---|---|
| Keywords:<br>Developing countries;<br>Economic growth;<br>Fiscal deficit;<br>Threshold effects. | We examine the relation between fiscal policy and economic growth for a panel of 40 developing countries over the period of 1990 to 2012 using eight macroeconomic variables: real GDP, budget deficit, current government spending, national saving, inflation rate, total investment, public debt, and current account balance. The study documents a double threshold effect of the fiscal balance. The first one is at a level of the deficit around 4.8% of GDP; the second one is at the fiscal surplus level of 3.2% of GDP meaning that economic growth would be negatively affected when exceeding these two different levels. The result also show that the sign of the relation between budget deficit and economic growth is conditioned by the level of total investment i.e. only for total investment higher than 23%, there exists a positive relation. However, it becomes negative, when investment falls below this threshold. |

## 1.0 Introduction

In both theory and evidence, there are controversial thoughts and debates that focus on the impact of the fiscal deficit on economic growth. Since the nineties, this subject becomes highly debated in the literature. Barro (1990) is considered as one of the most important pioneers in the field. He suggested a simple endogenous growth model and showed that the share of government spending in GDP might have a significant effect on economic growth. Nevertheless, a few empirical and theoretical studies have taken into account the non-linearity that can prevail on the relationship between growth and budget deficit [Minea and Villieu (2005), Adam and Bevan (2005), Tanimoune, Combes and Plane (2008) and Minea and Villieu (2008)]. These authors try to identify anti-Keynesian effects, which would be related to the persistence of high fiscal contractions.

Euro convergence criteria in the Maastricht Treaty (1993) outlined that the ratio of the annual general government deficit about gross domestic product (GDP) at market prices, must not exceed 3% at the end of the preceding fiscal year. Even though it is hardly justified[1]. The European debt crisis in 2010 shook the global economy when some indebted countries in Euro area, which had been maintaining high levels of debt and fiscal deficit, faced the default on payment of the public debt and its interest. Although the crisis mainly pertained to European countries, the concern of a similar public debt crisis is also shared by other countries in the world. This paper provides an empirical analysis to identify the nature of the relationship between budget deficit and

---

[1] It has been argued by many economists that the threshold of 3% was set arbitrarily and has no basis but the circumstances as European fiscal deficits in the early 90s were less than 3%. See Buiter, Corsetti and Roubini (1993, and Buiter (2006) for more details.

economic growth for a panel of 40 developing countries using annual data over the period spanning from 1990 to 2012.

This paper is organized as follows: The next section explores the theoretical literature. Section 3 will briefly return to the empirical studies around this topic. Section 4 outlines the methodological approach, data employed in the study and the finding of the econometric analysis of both linear and non-linear model by considering sequentially, the overall fiscal deficit and total investment as threshold variables. The estimation of the linear model will allow us first to identify the economic variables that affect real GDP growth. For the threshold analysis, we used the threshold estimation technique outlined by Hansen (1999). Section 5 concludes the paper and summarizes its main findings.

## 2.0    Theoretical studies

Before the advent of the Keynesian theory, governments tried to implement every effort to reach the fiscal balance. But with the Keynesian theory, this dogma was questioned. Keynes argued that there is a positive relationship between budget deficit and economic growth. Governments are encouraged to run deficits during the recession as it will help to stabilize the economy. On the other hand, there is the liberal theory that argued the opposite. Their main argument is related to the crowding out phenomenon. More recently, Barro[2] (1990) presented an endogenous growth model which is considered now as a fundamental reference. The model highlights an explicit link between government spending and long-run economic growth in the context of endogenous growth and shows that we can determine an optimal public spending. At this point, any additional expenditure may affect economic growth negatively. Therefore, if public expenditures exceed their optimal level, there will be a negative correlation, and conversely, if public expenditures fall below their optimal level, there will be a positive correlation. However, there are, to our knowledge, only a few theoretical studies that deal with non-linear effects of fiscal deficits in growth models. We cite by way of example reference Perotti's model (1999) where non-linear effects of fiscal policy are identified, but not in a growth context. Their model shows that government expenditure may have positive "Keynesian" effects or reversed effects depending on the initial level of public debt[3]. So, in high-debt contexts, a fiscal consolidation may reduce the risk of defaulting on sovereign debt, thus improving confidence and increasing private consumption. By using Barro's (1990) model, Greiner and Semmler (2000) removed the balanced budget assumption and analyzed different budgetary regimes. They claimed that the impact of deficit-financed increase on growth depends on the budgetary regime the government operates within. Thus, governments can generate positive growth effects of a public deficit on the growth rate only for a given debt/capital ratio and if the deficit is used primarily for public investment. Ghosh & Mourmouras (2004) extended the Greiner and Semmler framework to include welfare analysis. Their main objective is to analyze the growth and welfare implications of the golden rule of public finance. They showed that optimal fiscal policy depends on the particular budgetary regime considered.

In Barro's (1990) model, neither public debt nor public deficits are allowed. Thus, all public expenditures are productive and growth-enhancing. Minea and Villieu (2005) tried to examine the nature of fiscal deficit effects on growth by extending the Barro (1990) endogenous growth model. They introduced productive public spending, public deficit and debt in the model to study the non-linear effect of fiscal policy in the short and long run, and showed in their model how the effect of public deficit shifts from one condition to another depending on the multiplicity of balanced growth paths. In the long run, if public deficits are devoted to public investment, we will be in the presence of a lower balanced growth path. On the other hand, in the short run, the effect of public deficit depends on both the level of growth's steady states and the initial level of public debt.

## 3.0    Empirical studies

Beyond the theoretical debates, the study of the relationship between fiscal policy and economic growth received much attention in the empirical literature. However, it is difficult to provide an unclouded characterization of what the appropriate behavior of fiscal policy should be. Empirical results are quite often inconsistent and sometimes contradictory. This discordance regarding evaluation and finding are mainly due to multifarious factors such as time dimension, types of governments, methods of analysis as well as econometric methods that are used. By not taking into account the non-linear hypothesis, a large body of empirical literature on fiscal policy falls under the Keynesian theory, while other studies claim that having a balanced budget is more desirable as it will help the

---

[2] In Barro's model (1990), all public expenditures are productive and goes for public investment increasing marginal productivity of private capital, as for example infrastructure, schools, sanitation, property rights, etc. Investment public spending is financed through income taxes, complement private investments. Thus, since public investments raise the productivity of private investments, higher taxes can be associated with an increase or a decrease in overall growth.

[3] In contrast with Perotti (1999), Giavazzi, Jappelli & Pagano (2000) found no evidence of a small impact of high or rapidly growing public on non-linear effects of fiscal policy, but found instead that during periods of rapidly growing public debt the impact of taxes and government spending on national savings is significantly different.

economy to grow faster over time. To explain the "productivity slowdown" in the 1970s for the United States, Aschauer (1989) indicates, by using time series, a positive relationship between government expenditure and economic growth: a 1% increase in the ratio of public to private capital stocks raises productivity by 0.39%. However, the study points out the importance of how the public capital is composed. The core infrastructure (streets, highways, airports, mass transit, sewers, water systems, etc.) is the most important component in determining productivity. The almost same conclusion is derived from the research made by Easterly and Rebelo (1993) for the period going from 1970 to 1988. By using panel data for 28 countries and cross-sectional data for 100 countries, they found that the share of public investment in transport and communication is robustly and positively correlated with growth. Public outlays on infrastructure investment raise growth. Contrariwise, agriculture investment is consistently negatively correlated with growth, while Public enterprise investment has no effect on growth. Based on the research made by Benos (2009), the previous result related to infrastructure spending was again proven to be accurate. The author used panel data on 14 EU countries during 1990-2006 and also found that public expenditures on property rights protection enhance growth, while government expenditures on human capital have no effect on growth.

On the opposite side, other studies agreed with the liberal theory thought, in which fiscal deficits have a negative effect on economic growth. A theory that gives support to the budgetary rule assuming that obtaining a balanced budget is considered as the only way to maintain a sustainable growth over time. Within the same framework, Gupta, Clements, Baldacci, Mulas-Granados (2005) found for a panel of 39 low-income countries during the period 1990 - 2000 that a balanced budget stance generally leads to an increase in economic growth in both short and long terms. The study pointed out also the significant importance that holds the composition of public spending: when wages accounts for a big share of public expenditure, growth falls dramatically, while governments which concentrate their spending on capital and nonwage goods and services are more likely to experience a significant increase in growth. With an emphasis on the causal relationship lying between budget deficit and economic growth, keho's study (2010) focused on the member countries of the West African Economic and Monetary Union during the period 1980 - 2005. The results suggest that for three countries there is no causality link between budget deficit and growth, whereas for the remaining four countries deficits exert a negative impact on growth.

Consistent with the Ricardian equivalence hypothesis[4], other studies claimed that there is a neutral relationship between fiscal deficit and growth[5]. From Malaysia's perspective, Abd Rahman's study (2012) gives support to the previous hypothesis. By using an Autoregressive Distributed Lag Modeling, it was found that there is no long-run relationship between fiscal deficit and growth and that only the GDP and productive spending can bring the economy to its equilibrium state in a case where the Malaysian economy undergoes a shock.

Differences regarding results may be due to default in taking into account the non –linearity hypothesis as fiscal deficits may have either traditional Keynesian effects or reversed effects. Nevertheless, more recently, a major importance was given to this hypothesis. For instance, we can find Adam and Bevan's research paper (2005) where the authors try to identify thresholds effects of fiscal deficit on growth for a panel of 45 developing countries for the period 1979 - 1999. The study indicates that fiscal deficits are associated with robust non-linear effects on growth and finds evidence of a threshold effect at a level of the deficit around 1.5% of GDP. When reducing deficits to this level, there appears that governments enjoy faster growth expansion; this effect reverses itself when exceeding the determined threshold. Nearly, the same conclusion was made by Tanimoune, Combes and Plane (2008) on the pattern of public debt with a focus on the member countries of the West African Economic and Monetary Union during the period 1986 - 2002. The study indicates a threshold effect at a debt level of 83%. There appears to be a growth shrinking to exceeding debt at this level. As regards for OECD countries, Minea and Villieu (2008) carried out research to determine if there can be a non-linear effect of fiscal deficit on growth, depending on the public debt to GDP ratio. Results confirm that budget deficits are growth-increasing only for low-indebted economies as long as the debt burden may be absorbed by a cut in government consumption. In contrast, for further high debt values, raising deficits are growth-decreasing since the government can no longer reduce public consumption and the budget adjustment will inevitably rely on decreasing productive spending. Hence above a certain level of public debt, raising deficits becomes growth-reducing. The study indicates a threshold for a debt level standing at around 90%. This is consistent with the Rogoff and Reinhart's (2010) analysis. It was also claimed that exceeding 90% of public debts will result in impeding the process of economic growth. On the basis of a database covering forty-four countries spanning about two hundred years, the study finds evidence that growth for countries above 90% of public debt is -0.1% on average. A result which has been rectified in Herndon, Ash and Pollin's review study (2013) reporting only a 1% drop in growth.

---

[4] See Barro (1974) for more details on Ricardian equivalence.

[5] There is, however, an extensive empirical literature that has found evidence against this hypothesis [Feldstein (1986), Kotlikoff, Razin and Rosenthal (1988), Modigliani and Sterling (1990), Dalamagas (1992), Graham (1995), Evans (1993), Cardia (1997) and Banzhaf and Oates (2012)].

These last studies indicate that fiscal deficits are in general associated with strong non-linear effects on growth. In high debt contexts, growth drops off sharply. And inversely, for low debt values, growth remains high. Hence, we will investigate in this paper fiscal policy from the perspective of a non-linearity by using the panel threshold regression technique proposed by Hansen (1999).

## 4.0    Methodology, data, and econometric estimation

This section empirically evaluates the fiscal policy initially by considering that the relationship between fiscal policy and economic growth is a linear one and then trying to determine the economic variables that affect growth. Secondly, we will consider that this relationship may be non-linear and then conduct a threshold effects analysis by considering sequentially the overall fiscal deficit and total investment as threshold variables.

The study covers a panel of forty[6] developing countries. The sample selection was made a priori depending on data availability. Indeed, Hansen's method (1999) is valid only for a balanced panel. We use annual data for the period 1990 to 2012, the choice of the period being determined by their availability since 1990 and the lack of monthly and quarterly data.

### 4.1    Linear model estimation

Appendix B provides a summary of the statistics of the data and defines the variable mnemonics used later in the paper. We estimate the following empirical growth model:

$$GDP_{it} = \mu_i + \alpha_1\, GE_{it} + \alpha_2\, NS_{it} + \alpha_3\, FD_{it} + \alpha_4\, INV_{it} + \alpha_5\, INF_{it} + \varepsilon_{it}$$

Where (i,t) captures the cross-sectional and temporal dimensions of the panel, $\mu_i$ represents the country-fixed effects and $\varepsilon_{it}$ is a stochastic error term. Our econometric model is a fixed effects model where the relationship between the dependent variable and the explanatory variables are supposed to be identical for the countries in question. Using a fixed effects model will enable us to take into consideration differences regarding economic structure and history for each country. Choosing this specification is backed by the Hausman[7] and the Breusch & Pagan[8] test. As a matter of fact, it was concluded that the choice of "Within" estimator is required. To eliminate the individual effect, we will proceed by removing the individual-specific means.

The expected sign for $\alpha_5$ is negative, while for $\alpha_2$ and $\alpha_4$ it is positive:

$$GDP_{it} = f(GE_{it},\ NS_{it},\ FD_{it},\ INV_{it},\ INF_{it})$$
$$\qquad ? \quad + \quad ? \quad + \quad -$$

As regards, the domestic saving, classical and neoclassical theories show their importance for economic activity. When allowing for investment financing, savings enable for maintaining productivity growth. Aghion, Comin, and Howitt (2006) found that for poor countries, national saving plays an important role in attracting foreign investment and therefore to promote innovations. Thus, local savings matter for economic growth. Hence, we expect a positive sign for this variable. Regarding the fiscal deficit and the government current expenditure, it seems a little equivocal to predict a priori, under the linearity assumption, their impact on economic growth. While Keynesian economies showed their beneficial effect, liberal economies indicated the opposite. Similarly, for empirical literature, findings are mitigated and contradictory. Concerning investment, it is, as is well known, a determining factor of growth and productivity, for both the neoclassical and the Keynesian economies. Furthermore, it may generate, in accordance with the endogenous growth theory, positive externalities. As for inflation, Liberals consider it as highly injurious for economic growth. Besides, a wide range of empirical studies indicates a negative relationship between inflation and growth. Khan and Senhadji (2001) claimed the presence of a threshold effect of inflation on growth. Both industrialized and developing countries caught their interest. For the industrialized ones, when inflation exceeds 1-3% it has a negative impact on growth. Whereas for developing countries, inflation has constantly a negative impact on productivity, and it does widen even more when inflation surpasses 11-12%. Therefore, we expect a negative sign for inflation.

Appendix C reports the estimation results. On the basis of the information criterion[9], the best model would be (3). The p-value of the first Fisher test is below 5% (0.000), which attests to the significance of the explanatory

---

[6] Details of country coverage, data source and descriptions are provided in Appendix (A and B).
[7] The Hausman test probability is less than 10% (P-value = 0.0002% <10%), implying that the fixed effects model is preferred over random effects model.
[8] This test allows examining the significance of the individual specific effects. It is based on the residues obtained by the OLS. The probability of the Breusch & Pagan statistic showed that fixed effects are significant at the 5% level (P-value <0, 05). And therefore, a fixed effects model is preferred.
[9] The AIC (Akaike Information Criterion) outputs for model selection are shown in Appendix C.
 The BIC (Bayesian Information Criterion) outputs for model selection are shown in Appendix C.

variables. The second Fisher test shows the wide heterogeneity of individuals in the form of fixed effect, as the p-value is lower than 5% (0.000). All the variables have the signs that were previously anticipated. The variables FD, INV and INF, are significant at a 1% level. GE variable is significant at the 5% level. And finally, the variable NS is significant at the 10% level. Current government expenditure is negatively correlated with growth, and thus its increase can hinder the process of growth. A high ratio of national savings to GDP should have a favorable impact on economic activity. The fiscal deficit has a negative sign, which means that raising deficit is growth reducing. As for total investment, it has a positive sign and hence a positive effect on GDP growth. And finally, inflation has a negative sign, and thus having high inflation rates would have an adverse economic impact, with harmful consequences for growth.

## 4.2 Threshold effects analysis

We propose, before moving to the more systematic analysis, to explore a simple scatter plot visualizing the relationship between budget deficit and GDP growth. The existence of threshold effects assumes implicitly that this relationship is non-linear. Figure 1 illustrates this relation in the form of a cloud diagram. The non-linear function is plotted, as a locally weighted smoothing[10] (lowess smoother) with a "bandwidth" setting of 0.5, to identify graphically the existence of non-linearities.

It can be drawn from figure 1 that a linear representation may hide important and relevant nonlinearities at many budget deficits' levels. Moreover, it is clear that high budget deficit is associated with a very low GDP growth. However, growth payoffs start as the deficit falls from around 3.5%. The existence of a threshold effect implies not only a variation in the slope of the regression line but also a sign switch in the relationship. For a budget deficit value below a given threshold, there appears to be a favorable effect on economic activity, this effect inverse itself for higher fiscal deficit values.

---

**Figure 1:** Fiscal Deficit and GDP Growth in 40 Developing Countries, 1990-2012

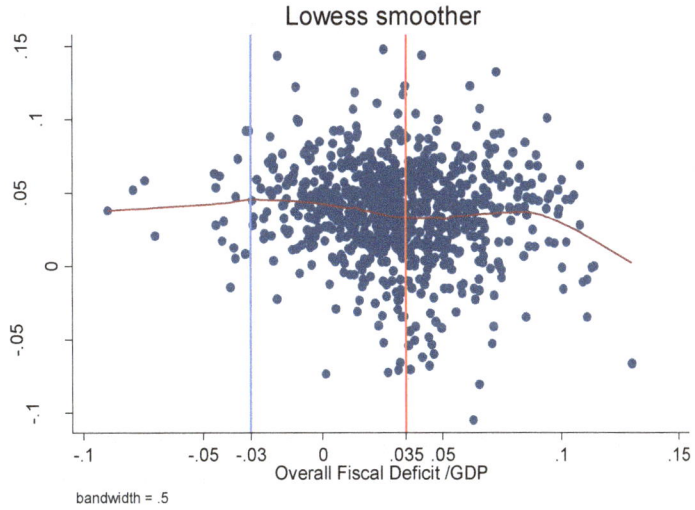

---

Given the high degree of dispersion, as observed in the scatter plot, we should note that this attempt to view the data is just preliminary and that we will submit hereafter the findings to a more systematic analysis using econometric methods.

## 4.3 A brief description of the econometric approach: Hansen (1999)

The panel threshold regression model with individual-specific effects proposed by Hansen (1999) will be used below to characterize the relationship between growth and fiscal policy. Estimating the PTR requires the minimization of the sum of squared errors according to the following equation:

$$y_{it} = \mu_i + \alpha_1 x_{it} I(q_{it} \leq \gamma) + \alpha_2 x_{it} I(q_{it} > \gamma) + \varepsilon_{it}$$

---

[10] It is a smoothing method that tends to follow the data. Basically, the main idea is to create a new variable, so that each observation in the data may correspond to a smoothed value. The smoothed values are obtained from a regression, growth of GDP in the fiscal deficit. This regression is weighted so that each point receives the highest weight.

Where $q_{it}$ is the threshold variable[11], $\gamma$ refers to the threshold, $I(.)$ is an indicator function of the "regimes" transition which equals 1 when the condition in parenthesis is satisfied and 0 otherwise. Although, in this model, we have a single threshold where the observations are divided into two regimes depending on whether the threshold variable $q_{it}$ is smaller or larger than the threshold parameter $\gamma$, we can generalize our model to a more larger specification with r thresholds (i.e. r + 1 regimes) as illustrated below:

$$y_{it} = \mu_i + \alpha_1 x_{it} I(q_{it} \leq \gamma_1) + \alpha_2 x_{it} I(\gamma_1 < q_{it} \leq \gamma_2) + ... \alpha_r x_{it} I(\gamma_{r-1} < q_{it}) + \varepsilon_{it}$$

Estimating this model is carried out by stages. First, the individual fixed effects $\mu_i$ should be removed by eliminating individual specific means, and then we apply the ordinary least squares procedure. Afterwards, we can compute the sum of squared residuals referred to as $S_1(\gamma)$:

$$S_1(\gamma) = \sum_{i=1}^{N} \sum_{t=1}^{T} \hat{\varepsilon}_{it}^2$$

The threshold parameter $\gamma$ is then estimated by minimizing $S_1(\gamma)$.

$$\hat{\gamma} = Arg\ Min_\gamma\ S_1(\hat{\gamma})$$

As Hansen (1999) stresses, the sum of squared error function is a step function with at most $nT$ steps. Thus, the minimization problem can be reduced to a search over values of $\gamma$ equal to the distinct values of $q_{it}$ in the sample. The next step consists of testing whether the identified threshold is statistically significant or not. The null hypothesis describes a linear specification and can be writen as: $H_0 : \alpha_1 = \alpha_2$. We use the likelihood ratio test verify this hypothesis:

$$F_1 = \frac{S_0 - S_1(\gamma)}{\sigma^2}$$

Where $S_0$ indicates the sum of the squared residuals of the linear model, $S_1(\gamma)$ is the sum of the squared residuals of the model with a single threshold, and $\sigma^2 = S_1(\gamma) / n(T-1)$. However, Hansen emphasizes that the distribution of this statistic $F_1$ has a non-standard character since that the PTR model contains unidentified nuisance parameters under $H_0$, and propose, in order to resolve this problem, to simulate by Bootstrap the asymptotic distribution of the statistic $F_1$. When a single threshold effect is attested to be significant, the same procedure can be applied to the general model in order to determine the number of regimes. In this case, the new null hypothesis consists of testing a specification with r regimes versus a specification with r+1 regimes. For determining the number of thresholds, Hansen advocates to start by testing one threshold versus two, then two versus three, and so forth. The procedure stops when the null hypothesis is not rejected.

## 4.4    Fiscal deficit as a threshold variable

Our threshold least square regression model is specified as follows:

$$GDP_{it} = \mu_i + \alpha_1 GE_{it-1} + \alpha_2 FD_{it-1} + \alpha_3 INV_{it-1} + \alpha_4 INF_{it-1} + \beta_1 NS_{it-1} I (FD_{it-1} \leq \gamma_1)$$
$$+ \beta_2 NS_{it-1} I (\gamma_1 < FD_{it-1} \leq \gamma_2) + \beta_3 NS_{it-1} I (\gamma_2 < FD_{it-1}) + \varepsilon_{it}$$

Where $\mu_i$ represents the country-fixed effects, (i,t) captures the cross-sectional and time dimensions of the panel, and $\varepsilon_{it}$ is a stochastic error term.

| **Table 1:** Threshold effects tests for the fiscal deficit | |
| --- | --- |
| Test for a single threshold effect | |
| $F_1$ | 16.001 |
| P-Value | 0.016 |
| (10%, 5%, 1% critical values) | (11.714 ; 13.745 ; 18.262) |
| Test for a double threshold effect | |
| $F_2$ | 18.382 |
| P-Value | 0.006 |
| (10%, 5%, 1% critical values) | (11.599 ; 13.175 ; 17.322) |
| Test for a triple-threshold effect | |
| $F_1$ | 14.160 |
| P-Value | 0.050 |
| (10%, 5%, 1% critical values) | (11.850 ; 14.124 ; 18.805) |

In order to determine the number of threshold effects, the model above has been estimated by the least squares method, sequentially, for one, two and three threshold effects. The test statistics F1, F2 and F3, set out together with their bootstrap p-values[12] are presented in the table 1. The statistic F1 which made a reference to the test for

---

[11] The threshold variable is assumed to be time independent, and it cannot be contemporaneous endogenous variable.
[12] 500 bootstrap replications were used for each test.

a single threshold effect is significant at a 5% level with a bootstrap p-value of 0.016. The test for a double threshold effect F2 is even more significant at a 1% level with a bootstrap p-value of 0.006. Finally, the test for a triple threshold effect F3 may be considered as not statistically significant at the 5% level as the bootstrap p-value is equal to 0.050. These tests allow us to conclude that there are two thresholds effect of fiscal deficit on economic productivity according to our empirical growth regression model. The two thresholds estimated values and their asymptotic confidence intervals 95% are reported in table 2. The point estimates are -0.032 and 0.048. Appendix D, E and F present the likelihood ratio function $LR_1(\gamma)$, $LR_2^r$ $(\gamma)$ and $LR_1^r$ $(\gamma)$, respectively, corresponding to estimates for $\gamma_1$, $\gamma_1^r$ and $\gamma_2^r$. The point estimates are the value of $\gamma$ at which the likelihood ratio reached the zero axis.

**Table 2:** Threshold estimates for the fiscal deficit

|  | Estimate | 95% Confidence Interval |
|---|---|---|
| $\gamma_1^r$ | -0.032 | [-0.032 ; 0.055] |
| $\gamma_2^r$ | 0.048 | [0.017 ; 0.055] |

The point estimates are -0.032 and 0.048. Figures (5, 6 and 7) present the likelihood ratio function $LR_1(\gamma)$, $LR_2^r$ $(\gamma)$ and $LR_1^r$ $(\gamma)$, respectively, corresponding to estimates for $\gamma_1$, $\gamma_1^r$ and $\gamma_2^r$. The point estimates are the value of $\gamma$ at which the likelihood ratio reached the zero axis. In what remains, we will consider a double threshold effect. The regression coefficient estimates and their standard deviations are shown in the table 3.

**Table 3:** Regression Estimates for a double threshold effect of the fiscal deficit

| Explanatory Variables | Coefficient estimate | OLS Standard-errors | White-corrected Standard-errors |
|---|---|---|---|
| $INV_{it-1}$ | 0.003 | 0.028 | 0.028 |
| $GE_{it-1}$ | -0.023 | 0.027 | 0.028 |
| $FD_{it-1}$ | -0.237*** | 0.054 | 0.053 |
| $INF_{it-1}$ | -0.00084 | 0.00078 | 0.00061 |
| $NS_{it-1}$ I $(FD_{it-1} \leq -0.032)$ | -0.115*** | 0.047 | 0.056 |
| $NS_{it-1}$ I $(-0.032 < FD_{it-1} \leq 0.048)$ | 0.056** | 0.030 | 0.033 |
| $NS_{it-1}$ I $(0.048 < FD_{it-1})$ | 0.148*** | 0.035 | 0.037 |
| *** Significant coefficient at the 1% level, ** 5% and * 10%. | | | |

To test the significance of the non-linear regression slope estimates, we used the Student's t-test[13]. We can see that the variables FD and NS are the only significant ones. The ratio of the budget deficit / GDP lagged by one period ($FD_{it-1}$) has a negative impact on GDP growth. Results also indicate that when the ratio of budget deficit / GDP approaches 0.048 starting from the highest deficit value of 0.13, domestic savings $NS_{it-1}$ should then have a positive effect on growth with the coefficient estimate of 0.148. And conversely, domestic saving should have a positive impact on growth, but with a smaller coefficient equal to 0.056, only for countries being close from a balanced budget with a deficit lower than 0,048 and a surplus not exceeding 0.032. And finally, if the surplus exceeds the value of 0.032, then domestic savings should have a negative impact on growth. The percentages of countries belonging to each of the three defined regimes in each year are reported in table 4. This distribution will allow us to see the countries division per year according to the pension deficit.

**Table 4:** Percentage of Countries per year in Each Regime of the Fiscal Deficit

| Regime (Year) | 1991 | 1992 | 1993 | 1994 | 1995 | 1996 | 1997 | 1998 | 1999 | 2000 | 2001 |
|---|---|---|---|---|---|---|---|---|---|---|---|
| 1st $FD_{it-1} \leq -0.032$ | 0 | 3 | 0 | 3 | 0 | 0 | 0 | 3 | 3 | 3 | 0 |
| 2nd $-0.032 < FD_{it-1} \leq 0.048$ | 90 | 75 | 80 | 78 | 73 | 80 | 70 | 78 | 60 | 75 | 80 |
| 3rd $0.048 < FD_{it-1}$ | 10 | 23 | 20 | 20 | 28 | 20 | 30 | 20 | 38 | 23 | 20 |
| Regime (Year) | 2002 | 2003 | 2004 | 2005 | 2006 | 2007 | 2008 | 2009 | 2010 | 2011 | 2012 |
| 1st $FD_{it-1} \leq -0.032$ | 0 | 0 | 0 | 0 | 3 | 10 | 5 | 5 | 0 | 3 | 3 |
| 2nd $-0.032 < FD_{it-1} \leq 0.048$ | 78 | 68 | 73 | 88 | 83 | 80 | 80 | 80 | 68 | 68 | 70 |
| 3rd $0.048 < FD_{it-1}$ | 23 | 33 | 28 | 13 | 15 | 10 | 15 | 15 | 33 | 30 | 28 |

We can see that the percentage of countries which fall into the first regime varies from 0% to 10% over the years. The percentage of countries, in the second regime, ranges from 60% to 90%, and finally, in the third regime, it varies from 10% to 33%. We can also observe that most countries fall into the second regime, and this is valid for all years. It is interesting to note that in 2010, we can perceive the highest number of countries with a budget deficit exceeding the level of 4.8%.

---

[13] When Student's t-test statistic is greater than the value read in the student's table (1.96 at the 5% level and 1.64 at the 10% level), we reject the null hypothesis of the non-significance of the parameters.

## 4.5    Investment as a threshold variable

The following threshold least square regression model will be estimated:

$$GDP_{it} = \mu_i + \alpha_1 GE_{it-1} + \alpha_2 NS_{it-1} + \alpha_3 INV_{it-1} + \alpha_4 INF_{it-1} + \beta_1 FD_{it-1} I (INV_{it-1} \leq \gamma_1)$$
$$+ \beta_2 FD_{it-1} I (\gamma_1 < INV_{it-1}) + \varepsilon_{it}$$

Where $\mu_i$ represents the country-fixed effects, (i,t) captures the cross-sectional and time dimensions of the panel, and $\varepsilon_{it}$ is a stochastic error term.

The same procedure will be adopted. The test statistics F1, F2 and F3, set out together with their bootstrap p-values[14], are presented in table 5. The statistic $F_1$ which refers to the test for a single threshold effect is the only significant statistic at a 1% level with a bootstrap p-value of 0.002. Both tests for a double threshold effect $F_2$ and for a triple-threshold effect $F_3$ are not significant at the 5% level. These Tests allow us to conclude that there is a single threshold effect for investment. The threshold estimates with its asymptotic confidence interval 95% is reported in Table 6.

**Table 5:** Threshold effects tests for investment

| Test for a single threshold effect | |
| --- | --- |
| $F_1$ | 18.687 |
| P-Value | 0.002 |
| (10%, 5%, 1% critical values) | (11.148 ; 12.421 ; 15.649) |
| Test for a double threshold effect | |
| $F_2$ | 3.271 |
| P-Value | 0.876 |
| (10%, 5%, 1% critical values) | (10.446 ; 12.295 ; 16.357) |
| Test for a triple-threshold effect | |
| $F_1$ | 2.086 |
| P-Value | 0.968 |
| (10%, 5%, 1% critical values) | (9.062 ; 10.348 ; 12.884) |

**Table 6:** Threshold estimates for investment

| | Estimate | 95% Confidence Interval |
| --- | --- | --- |
| $\gamma_1$ | 0.236 | [0.212 ; 0.250] |

The point estimate is 0.236. Appendix G presents the likelihood ratio function $LR_1(\gamma)$ corresponding to the estimate for $\gamma_1$. The regression coefficient estimates and their standard deviations are shown in the table 7.

**Table 7:** Regression Estimates for a Single Threshold Effect of Investment

| Explanatory Variables | Coefficient estimate | OLS Standard-errors | White-corrected Standard-errors |
| --- | --- | --- | --- |
| $NS_{it-1}$ | 0.062*** | 0.030 | 0.032 |
| $GE_{it-1}$ | -0.032 | 0.027 | 0.027 |
| $INV_{it-1}$ | -0.024 | 0.029 | 0.034 |
| $INF_{it-1}$ | -0.0008 | 0.0008 | 0.0006 |
| $FD_{it-1} I (INV_{it-1} \leq 0.236)$ | -0.137*** | 0.047 | 0.042 |
| $FD_{it-1} I (0.236 < INV_{it-1})$ | 0.167*** | 0.069 | 0.076 |
| *** Significant coefficient at the 1% level, ** 5% and * 10%. | | | |

Similar to the previous analysis, we will use the Student's t-test[15] to test the significance of the non-linear regression slope estimates. We can see that only the coefficient estimates for the following variables NS, FD and INV are significant and that investment is significant just in the case of regimes switching. Gross national savings lagged by one period $NS_{it-1}$ has a significant positive impact on growth. We can also note that when investment in the previous year is less than or equal to the threshold of 23.6%, then the budget deficit $FD_{it-1}$ should have a negative effect on growth with a coefficient estimate of -0.137. And conversely, it should have a positive impact on growth with a coefficient estimate of 0.167 as the investment exceeds the defined threshold.

---

[14] 500 bootstrap replications were used for each test.

[15] When Student's t-test statistic is greater than the value read in the student's table (1.96 at the 5% level and 1.64 at the 10% level), we reject the null hypothesis of the non-significance of the parameters.

| | Year | | | | | | | | | | |
|---|---|---|---|---|---|---|---|---|---|---|---|
| **Table 8:** Percentage of Countries per Year in Each Regime of Investment | | | | | | | | | | | |
| Regime | 1991 | 1992 | 1993 | 1994 | 1995 | 1996 | 1997 | 1998 | 1999 | 2000 | 2001 |
| 1er  INV $_{it-1}$ ≤ 0.236 | 55 | 75 | 75 | 70 | 65 | 63 | 63 | 65 | 60 | 73 | 70 |
| 2ème  0.236 < INV $_{it-1}$ | 45 | 25 | 25 | 30 | 35 | 38 | 38 | 35 | 40 | 28 | 30 |
| Regime | Year | | | | | | | | | | |
| | 2002 | 2003 | 2004 | 2005 | 2006 | 2007 | 2008 | 2009 | 2010 | 2011 | 2012 |
| 1er  INV $_{it-1}$ ≤ 0.236 | 78 | 75 | 80 | 70 | 65 | 65 | 60 | 55 | 73 | 70 | 63 |
| 2ème  0.236 < INV $_{it-1}$ | 23 | 25 | 20 | 30 | 35 | 35 | 40 | 45 | 28 | 30 | 38 |

Table 8 reports that the percentage of countries belonging to the first regime - where the ratio of total investment / GDP is below the threshold of 23% - varies from 55% to 80%. Whereas the second regime - where investment exceeds the threshold of 23% - the percentage ranges from 20% to 45%. Hence, we can say that most countries fall into the first regime.

## 5.0    Summary and conclusion

This paper contributes to the fiscal policy literature by re-examining the relationship between the fiscal deficit and economic growth. Initially, the study identifies, under a linear hypothesis, the impact of five economic variables, namely the fiscal deficit, government current expenditure, national savings, inflation rate and total investment. In a second step, examining the scatter plot in Figure 1 urged us to call into question the nature of the relation between growth and the fiscal deficit as it shows an apparent non- linearity, hence we consider the existence of threshold effects in the relationship between fiscal policy and growth by using the threshold estimation approach as proposed by Hansen (1999) for non-dynamic panels. The data cover a sample of 40 developing countries for the period 1990 – 2012.

We present, in our analysis, an empirical growth model in which two types of non- linearity emerged, one related to the impact of the fiscal deficit on growth, and the other involving the effects of investment. The empirical results strongly suggest the existence anti-Keynesian effects that would be associated with high budget deficits levels. We find an evidence of a double threshold effect of the fiscal balance which is robust to their inclusion. A fiscal deficit exceeding 4.8% of GDP would exert a negative effect on growth, but also a fiscal surplus exceeding the threshold of 3.2% of GDP would negatively impact economic growth. Results also shows that the sign of the relationship between the budget deficit and growth is conditioned by the level of total investment: when total investment exceeds the threshold of 23% of GDP, then the budget deficit is positively correlated to economic growth with a coefficient estimates of 0.167, whereas it is negatively correlated to growth with a coefficient estimates of -0.137 when total investment falls below this threshold. Our findings also suggest the 4.8% threshold is a deficit level beyond which Domestic savings exert a positive effect on growth with coefficient estimates of 0.148, and with a lower coefficient of 0.056 for countries being close from a balanced budget with a deficit lower than 4.8% and a surplus not exceeding 3.2%. When the surplus exceeds 3.2%, then Domestic savings are negatively related to economic growth. As for inflation, results indicate that increases in inflation rates may have an adverse effect on growth in developing economies. Current government expenditure is also negatively correlated to GDP growth. Within this framework, countries are expected to set priorities for reducing government final consumption expenditure for productive investment. Therefore, a rational public spending management is required.

While the results are instructive, some caveats are important to bear in mind when interpreting these results. First, the asymptotic distribution of the statistic $F_1$ on the threshold variable has a non-standard character and requires bootstrap methods to compute its significance level. Second, the estimated model does not provide the precise channels through which fiscal policy affects growth. There are also some particular issues related to data which may skew the results. Inflation rate and the current account balance show a high degree of dispersion and heterogeneity within the sample of countries. Strong asymmetry in the inflation distribution was detected as it reveals the presence of a few high values.

**Acknowledgments:** I would like to thank EL ABBASSI Idriss[16] and TOUNSI Said[17] for the very helpful comments and suggestions.

---

[16] Professor, Department of economics, Mohammed V Rabat –Agdal University, Faculty of Juridical, Economic and Social Sciences, Morocco. E-mail Address: idriss_elabbassi@yahoo.fr

[17] Professor, Department of economics, Mohammed V Rabat –Agdal University, Faculty of Juridical, Economic and Social Sciences, Morocco. E-mail Address: sadtounsi@gmail.com

## References

Abd Rahman N. H., (2012). How Federal Government's Debt Affect the Level of Economic Growth?. International Journal of Trade, Economics and Finance, Vol. 3, No. 4. http://dx.doi.org/10.7763/ijtef.2012.v3.220

Adam C. S., Bevan D. L., (2005). Non-linear Effects of Fiscal Deficits on Growth in Developing Countries. Journal of Public Economics, P. 571– 597. http://dx.doi.org/10.1016/j.jpubeco.2004.02.006

Aghion P., Comin D., Howitt P., (2006). When Does Domestic Saving Matter for Economic Growth?. NBER Working Papers 12275, National Bureau of Economic Research.

Aschauer D. A., (1989). Is Public Expenditure Productive? Journal of Monetary Economics, P.177-200. http://dx.doi.org/10.1016/0304-3932(89)90047-0

Banzhaf H. S., Oates W. E., (2012). On Fiscal Illusion and Ricardian Equivalence in Local Public Finance. NBER Working Papers 18040, National Bureau of Economic Research. http://dx.doi.org/10.2139/ssrn.2062473

Barro R., (1990). Government Spending in a Simple Model of Endogenous Growth. Journal of Political Economy, P.103-125. http://dx.doi.org/10.1086/261726

Barro R., (1974). Are Government Bonds Net Wealth? Journal of Political Economy 82(6), P. 1095-1117. http://dx.doi.org/10.1086/260266

Benos N., (2009). Fiscal Policy and Economic Growth: Empirical Evidence from EU Countries. MPRA Paper No. 19174, University Library of Munich, Germany.

Buiter, W. H., CorsettiG., Roubini N., (1993). Excessive Deficits: Sense and Nonsense in the Treaty of Maastricht, Economic Policy, Centre for Economic Policy Research, London, United Kingdom, October 15-16, 1992. Revised March 1993. Reprinted in The Political Economy of Monetary Union, Edited by Paul de Grauwe, P. 297-331, Edward Elgar Publishing Ltd, Cheltenham, 2001.

Buiter W. H., (2006). The 'Sense and Nonsense of Maastricht' Revisited: What Have we Learnt about Stabilization in EMU?. Journal of Common Market Studies, vol. 44, P. 687-710. http://dx.doi.org/10.1111/j.1468-5965.2006.00658.x

Cardia E., (1997). Replicating Ricardian Equivalence Tests with Simulated Series. American Economic Review, Vol. 87, P. 65-87.

Dalamagas B.A., (1992). Testing Ricardian Equivalence: A Reconsideration. Applied Economics, Vol. 24, 1, P. 59-69. http://dx.doi.org/10.1080/00036849200000103

Easterly W., Rebelo S., (1993). Fiscal Policy and Economic Growth: An Empirical Investigation. Journal of Monetary Economics, P.417-458. http://dx.doi.org/10.1016/0304-3932(93)90025-B

Evans P., (1993). Consumers are not Ricardian: Evidence from Nineteen Countries. Economic Inquiry, Vol. 31, P. 534-548. http://dx.doi.org/10.1111/j.1465-7295.1993.tb00889.x

Feldstein M., (1986). The Effects of Fiscal Policies When Incomes are Uncertain: A Contradiction to Ricardian Equivalence. NBER Working Papers 2062, National Bureau of Economic Research.

Ghosh S., Mourmouras I. A., (2004). Endogenous Growth, Welfare and Budgetary Regimes. Journal of Macroeconomics, 26, P. 623-635. http://dx.doi.org/10.1016/j.jmacro.2004.09.001

Giavazzi F., Japelli T., Pagano M., (2000). Searching for Non-linear Effects of Fiscal Policy: Evidence from Industrial and Developing Countries. European Economic Review 44, P. 1259-1289. http://dx.doi.org/10.1016/S0014-2921(00)00038-6

Graham, F. C., (1995). Government Debt, Government Spending, and Private Sector Behavior: Comment. American Economic Review, Vol. 85, P.1348-1356.

Greiner A., Semmler W., (2000). Endogenous Growth, Government Debt and Budgetary Regimes. Journal of Macroeconomics, 22, P. 363-384. http://dx.doi.org/10.1016/S0164-0704(00)00136-1

Gupta S., Clements B., Baldacci E., Mulas-Granados C., (2005). Fiscal Policy, Expenditure Composition, and Growth in Low-income Countries. Journal of International Money and Finance, P. 441-463. http://dx.doi.org/10.1016/j.jimonfin.2005.01.004

Hansen B., (1999). Threshold Effects in Non-Dynamic Panels: Estimation, Testing, and Inference. Journal of econometrics, P. 345-368. http://dx.doi.org/10.1016/S0304-4076(99)00025-1

Herndon T., Ash M., Pollin R., (2013). Does High Public Debt Consistently Stifle Economic Growth? A Critique of Reinhart and Rogoff. PERI Working Paper Series, No. 322.

Keho Y., (2010). Budget Deficits and Economic Growth: Causality Evidence and Policy Implications for WAEMU Countries. European Journal of Economics, Finance and Administrative Sciences, P. 1450-2275.

Khan M. S., Senhadji A. S., (2001). Threshold Effects in the Relationship between Inflation and Growth. IMF Staff Papers, vol. 48(1), No. 1.

Kotlikoff L. J., Razin A., Rosenthal R. W., (1988). A Strategic Altruism Model in which Ricardian Equivalence Does Not Hold. NBER Working Papers 2699, National Bureau of Economic Research.

Minea A., Villieu P., (2005). Persistent Deficits, Growth and Indeterminacy: The "Golden Rule" of Public Finance revisited. University of Orléans, LEO Working Paper, No. 4.

Minea A., Villieu P., (2008). Un réexamen de la Relation Non-linéaire entre Déficits Budgétaires et Croissance Économique. Presses de Sciences Po |Revue économique, P. 561- 570. http://dx.doi.org/10.3917/reco.593.0561

Modigliani, F., Sterling A. G., (1990). Government Debt, Government Spending and Private Sector Behavior: A Further Comment. American Economic Review, 80, 3, P. 600-603.

Perotti R., (1999). Fiscal Policy when Things Are Going Badly. Quarterly Journal of Economics 64, P.1399-1436. http://dx.doi.org/10.1162/003355399556304

Reinhart C. M., Rogoff K.S., (2010). Growth in a Time of Debt. American Economic Review, Vol. 100, No. 2, P.573-578. http://dx.doi.org/10.1257/aer.100.2.573

Reinhart C.M., Rogoff K.S., (2013). Errata, Growth in a Time of Debt. Harvard University.

Tanimoune N. A., Combes J.-L., Plane P., (2008). La politique budgétaire et ses effets de seuil sur l'activité en Union Economique et Monétaire Ouest Africaine (UEMOA). La Doc. française| Economie & prévision, P.145-162.

## Appendices

**Appendix A:** Sample Countries

Bahamas, Bangladesh, Barbados, Benin, Bolivia, Brazil, Central African Republic, Chile, Colombia, Comoros, Costa Rica, Djibouti, Dominica, Dominican Republic, Ecuador, El Salvador, Fiji, Ghana , Honduras, Hungary, India, Jamaica, Jordan, Kenya, Malaysia, Mexico, Morocco, Mozambique, Namibia, Pakistan, Poland, South Africa, Sri Lanka, Suriname, Saint Vincent and the Grenadines, Syria, Thailand, Tunisia , Uruguay, Vanuatu.

| Appendix B: Summary Statistics, Data for 40 Developing Countries | | | | | | | | | | |
|---|---|---|---|---|---|---|---|---|---|---|
| Variables | Mnemonic | Obs. | Mean | Standard Deviation | Median | Min. | Max. | Total Variance | Within Variance | Between Variance |
| Real GDP growth | GDP | 915 | 0.036 | 0.034 | 0.040 | -0.119 | 0.148 | 0.001 | 0.001 | 0.000 |
| Ratio of current government expenditure to GDP | GE | 854 | 0.153 | 0.058 | 0.143 | 0.032 | 0.402 | 0.003 | 0.000 | 0.003 |
| Ratio of gross national savings to GDP | NS | 849 | 0.178 | 0.077 | 0.175 | -0.061 | 0.399 | 0.006 | 0.002 | 0.004 |
| Ratio of the overall budget deficit to GDP | FD | 824 | 0.031 | 0.030 | 0.030 | -0.090 | 0.130 | 0.001 | 0.001 | 0.000 |
| Ratio of total investment to GDP | INV | 872 | 0.215 | 0.063 | 0.211 | 0.047 | 0.466 | 0.004 | 0.002 | 0.002 |
| Inflation rate | INF | 911 | 0.113 | 0.311 | 0.056 | -0.074 | 5.858 | 0.097 | 0.085 | 0.012 |
| Ratio of the general government debt to GDP | GD | 670 | 0.547 | 0.304 | 0.482 | 0.039 | 2.197 | 0.092 | 0.031 | 0.061 |
| Ratio of current account balance to GDP | CCB | 917 | -0.039 | 0.065 | -0.032 | -0.331 | 0.171 | 0.004 | 0.002 | 0.002 |

**Sources:**

Data on real GDP growth, gross national savings, overall budget deficit, investment, Inflation, general government debt are taken from the IMF's World Economic Outlook database April 2013.

Data on current government expenditure are taken from the World Bank database.

**Definitions:**

Data on current government expenditure, overall fiscal balance, gross national savings, total investment, current account balance and government's total debt are expressed in current local currency as ratios to nominal GDP. Data on inflation are expressed as annual percentages of the average consumer prices. Data on GDP growth are expressed on constant prices.

General government final consumption expenditure includes all government current expenditures for purchases of goods and services (including compensation of employees). It also includes national defense and security outlays, but excludes government military spending.

Overall fiscal balance expresses a net lending (+) or borrowing (–) and measures the extent to which the government is either putting, in the event of a surplus, financial resources at the disposal of the other economic sectors and the rest of the world, or, in the case of a deficit, utilizing the financial resources generated by the other sectors and the rest of the world.

Gross national saving is calculated as gross disposable income minus final consumption expenditure after taking account of an adjustment for pension funds.

Total investment or gross capital formation is measured by the total value of the gross fixed capital formation – Gross fixed capital formation include land improvements (fences, ditches, drains, and so on), plant, machinery, and equipment purchases; and the construction of roads, railways, etc. including schools, offices, hospitals, private residential dwellings, and commercial and industrial buildings – plus net changes in the level of inventories and acquisitions of valuables.

Current account balance is the sum of net exports of goods and services, net primary income, and net secondary income.

General government debt consists of all liabilities that require payment or payments of interest and/or principal by the debtor to the creditor at a date or dates in the future. It includes domestic and foreign liabilities such as currency and money deposits, securities other than shares, and loans.

Inflation rate and real GDP growth are measured on the basis of year-on-year changes; the base year is country-specific.

| Appendix C: Linear Model Estimation | | | |
|---|---|---|---|
| Dependent Variable: Real GDP Growth | | | |
| | The linear models | | |
| Explanatory Variables | (1) | (2) | (3) |
| GE | -0.159** | -0.159** | -0.119** |
| | (2.29) | (2.30) | (2.23) |
| NS | 0.099 | 0.080** | 0.053* |
| | (0.84) | (2.41) | 1.88 |
| FD | -0.121** | -0.120** | -0.201*** |
| | (2.14) | (2.13) | 4.18 |
| INV | 0.167 | 0.186*** | 0.164*** |
| | (1.36) | (5.68) | 5.75 |
| INF | -0.034 | -0.034 | -0.042*** |
| | (1.42) | (1.43) | 3.01 |
| GD | -0.006 | -0.006 | |
| | (0.95) | (0.95) | |
| CCB | -0.020 | | |
| | (0.17) | | |
| Constant | 0.017 | 0.016 | 0.020** |
| | (1.20) | (1.20) | 2.06 |
| Fisher Test (1) | F (7.517) = 11.76 | F(6.518) = 13.74 | F(5.666) = 21.62 |
| Fisher Test (2) | F (34.517) = 4.11 | F(34.518) = 4.23 | F(36.666) = 5.23 |
| AIC | -2453.441 | -2455.412 | -3092.999 |
| BIC | -2418.832 | -2425.129 | -3065.624 |
| $R^2$ | 0.14 | 0.14 | 0.14 |
| Number of observations | 559 | 559 | 708 |

*** Significant coefficient at the 1% level, ** 5% and * 10%.

Student's t-values are put between brackets.

Fisher Test (1) checks the significance of the explanatory variables.

Fisher Test (2) is used to examine the significance of the fixed effects.

| Appendix D: Likelihood Ratio Function $LR_1(\gamma)$ for a Single Threshold Effect of the Fiscal Deficit |
|---|

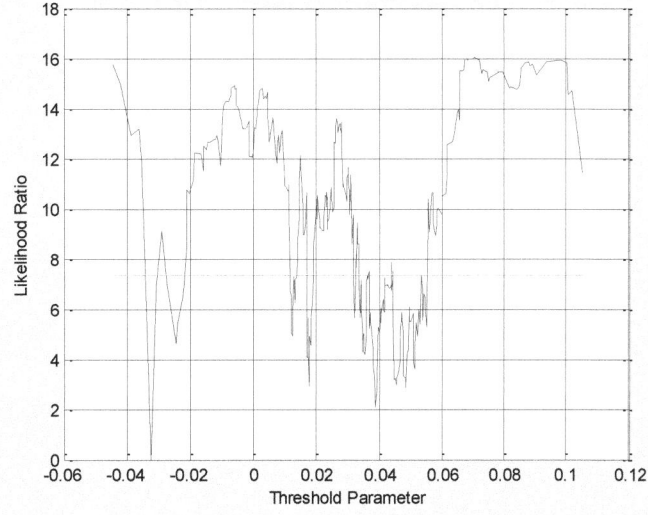

**Appendix E:** Likelihood Ratio Function 〖LR〗_2^r (γ) for a Double Threshold Effect of the Fiscal Deficit

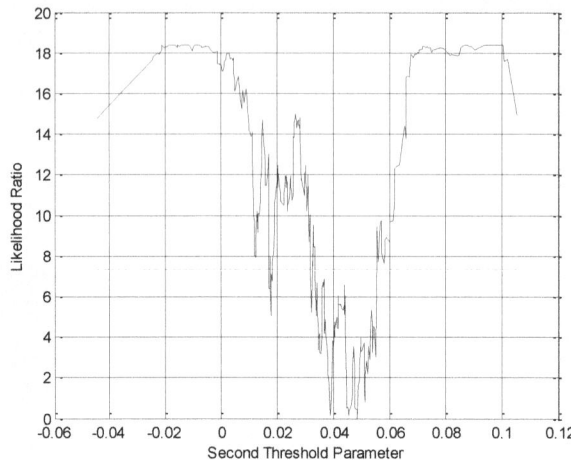

**Appendix F:** Likelihood Ratio Function $LR_1^r$ (γ) for a Double Threshold Effect of the Fiscal Deficit

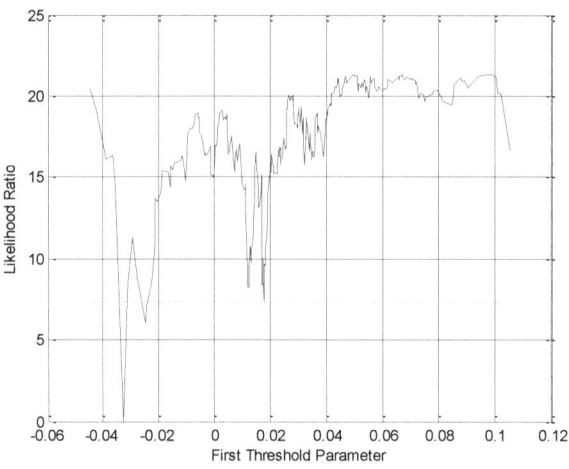

**Appendix G:** Likelihood Ratio Function $LR_1$ (γ) for a Single Threshold Effect of Investment

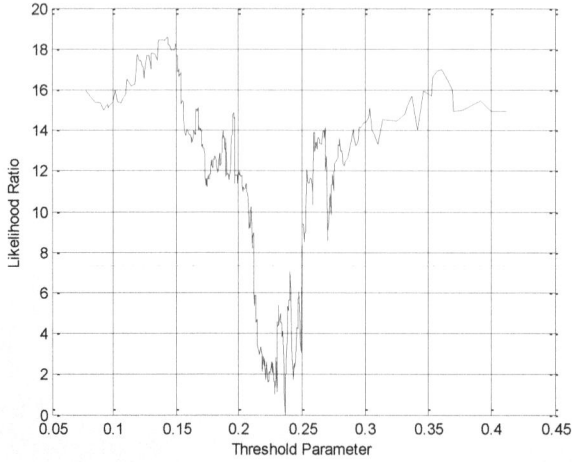

# 9

# Demand for money under low interest rates in Japan

Yutaka Kurihara [a*]

[a] Professor, Department of Economics, Aichi University, Japan.
*Corresponding author's email address: kurihara@vega.aichi-u.ac.jp

| ARTICLE INFO | ABSTRACT |
|---|---|
| Keywords:<br>Demand for Money;<br>Exchange Rate;<br>Japan;<br>Monetary Policy;<br>Volatility. | In both theoretical and empirical fields of economics, demand for money has been received much attention in the past. In Japan, deflation has been prevailed more than 20 years, and there is some possibility that the Bank of Japan's monetary easing policy, which expands money to markets by buying government bonds, has had a significant influence apart from traditional factors. Also, exchange rates for Japanese currency have fluctuated greatly recently because of the introduction of unprecedented monetary policy in the 2010s that may have affected macroeconomic variables and the money demand function in Japan. Using Japanese experience with deflation over last two decades, I provide strong evidence that recent demand for money is affected by real GDP, exchange rates, and economic volatility; however, interest rates and consumer prices have not impacted demand for money. The results also show that introduction of the drastic quantitative easing policy changed the demand function for money. |

## 1.0    Introduction

Demand for money has been discussed continuously and a great deal in the literature both in the theoretical and empirical fields of economics. In Japan, very low or almost zerio interest rate policies designed to overcome deflationary pressure have been in place since the end of 1990s after the bubble economy burst; also, exchange rates against the main foreign currencies and stock prices have fluctuated greatly, especially following the Lehman shock. The Japanese central bank, Bank of Japan (BOJ), bought a huge number of Japanese government bonds as part of its monetary policy, and there has been a strong demand for Japanese government bonds because of low interest rates and because of typical safe assets, so there is some possibility that the money demand function has changed dramatically such that it differs from the traditional money demand function.

The BOJ conducts monetary policy with the goal of maintaining price stability, which is thought to be important because it is considered to be the foundation of economic activity. This goal has been adopted in many countries and Japan is not an exception. However, deflation has seriously damaged the Japanese economy, so starting in 2013, more drastic monetary policy has been conducted and the BOJ set the price rate goal at 2%. The main operating target of the BOJ's monetary policy changed from the uncollateralized overnight call rate (interbank interest rate) to the outstanding balance of the current account held at the BOJ as the interest rates in Japanese financial markets have been almost zero since the beginning of the 2000s.

At the end of 2001, the BOJ raised the outstanding balance of the current account at the BOJ. This objective can be perceived as a change from holding a level of reserves at the BOJ to one that transfers funds into lending to boost the economy and remove deflationary pressures. Under this quantitative easing policy, the BOJ purchased Japanese government bonds to reach its target of current account balances held by financial institutions such as banks. With interest rates were at the lower bound of zero, the BOJ set a goal to purchase government bonds from financial institutions and to raise the level of cash reserves held by private financial institutions. With interest rates at the zero bound, the BOJ lost conventional instruments to stimulate the real economy. This was called *unconventional financial policy,* which was unprecedented in the world at that time. However, only a few studies have examined this policy despite that such examinations are very important. One serious reason for the lack of studies is that only a short time has passed since this unprecedented policy was implemented.

On April 4, 2013, the policy board of the BOJ decided to introduce quantitative and qualitative monetary easing policy, a more aggressive monetary policy. The BOJ decided to attain the price target of 2% in terms of the year-on-year rate of change in consumer prices. It was said that the BOJ imposed a new phase of monetary easing both in terms of quantity and quality. The BOJ doubled the monetary base and the amounts outstanding of Japanese government bonds as well as exchange-traded funds (ETFs) in two years and more than doubled the maturity of Japanese government bond purchases (quality). To achieve quantitative monetary easing, the main target of financial policy instruments was changed from the uncollateralized overnight call (interbank interest) rate to the monetary base as mentioned above.

Anusic (1994) showed that the main determinants of the demand for money are inflation and real economic activity, and interest rates have no impact on money demand in Croatia. Arize (1994) used ECM (error-correction model) and found that Taiwanese demand for money is stable and that interest rates of foreign countries play important roles in determining demand for money. Klacek and Smidkova (1995) showed the expected signs for inflation and interest rates. Bahmani-Oskooee and Bohl (2000) showed that cointegration does not necessarily imply a stable relationship between the variables for Germany. Choi and Oh (2003) showed that economic uncertainty can affect the public's decisions in allocating their wealth among different financial assets. The authors found that output uncertainty had negative effect on money demand and monetary uncertainty had positive effect on demand in the United States. Bahmani-Oskooee and Rehman (2005) showed that in some Asian countries, real M1 and M2 money aggregates are cointegrated and the estimated variables are unstable. Rao and Singh (2005) showed that money demand of M1 has been stable. Hussain (2007) indicated that long-run income elasticity of the demand for narrow money has remained stable. Zouhar and Kacemi (2008) showed that there is a strong link between real narrow money, real GDP, and interest rate. Odularu and Okunrinboye (2009) found that income is positively related to money demand but financial innovation has not affected the money demand in Nigeria. Rao and Kumar (2011) showed that US demand for money has been stable. Singh and Kumar (2010) found that real income, nominal interest rate, and narrow money are cointegrated and demand for money is stable. Avouyi-Dovi, Drumetz, and Sahuc (2012) showed that money demand function is unstable for the Euro area by using vector error correction model.

Dobnik (2013) examined the long-run money demand function for OECD countries and found that impact of income on money demand is positive but negative for interest rate, exchange rate, and stock prices. Dogru and Recepoglu (2013) found that real demand for money in Turkey is positively related to income and negatively related to nominal interest rate. Khan and Hye (2013) demonstrated that GDP and real deposit rates positively impact the demand for money both in long- and short-run periods. Kumar, Chowdhury, and Rao (2013) showed that income elasticity of the demand for money has increased and response to interest rate changes has increased. Paudel and Perera (2013) indicated that liberalization does not have a positive relationship with money demand. Sarwar, Sarwar, and Waqas (2013) showed that demand for money using M1 has been stable, real GDP is positively related, and opportunity cost of money is negatively related. Jiranyakul and Opiela (2014) found that in the short term, only a change in real GDP affects M1 money holdings. Also, in the long term, both real GDP and interest rate determine money demand. As many developed countries are under deflationary pressures and people hold money instead of investing risky assets, demand for money, which has been very traditional in the field of economics, should receive a lot of attention. It is difficult to conclude, however, as most studies confirm the traditional theory for money demand, which includes income and interest rate as explanation variables, although there are exceptions for various time periods, countries, and so on.

Exchange rates have not received attention in the past in analysis of demand for money. Arango and Nadiri (1981) showed that exchange rate depreciation has a positive impact on the demand for money as the domestic currency value of foreign assets, which leads to an increase in the wealth of the country and an increase in the demand for real cash balances. Craig (1982) found that the exchange rate in West Germany relates to demand for money. Bamani-Oskooee and Pourheydarian (1990) showed that when domestic currency depreciates, this can most certainly cause markets. Bahmani-Oskooee and Malixi (1991) found that depreciation of domestic currency promotes a decrease in the demand for domestic currency in many less developed countries. Bahmani-Oskooee, Miquel-Angel, and Niroomand (1998) demonstrated that demand for money, including the effective exchange rate, were stable. Hueng (1998) showed that changes in the foreign interest rate and exchange rate affect the demand for money in Canada. Cuthbertson and Bredin (2001) indicated the degree of dollarization of the economy impacts the demand for money. Gunnar (2001) argued that shocks to the nominal exchange rate impact domestic prices in the short term but have no impact on real output, and shocks to money have a temporary impact on real output before causing inflation. Klos and Wrobel (2001) showed significant effects of exchange rate changes on demand for money. Dreger, Hans-Eggert, and Roffia (2007) showed that for new EU member states, the US exchange rate is significantly related to demand for money. Tang (2007) demonstrated that the real M2 aggregate, real expenditure components, exchange rate, and inflation have a cointegration relationship in Malaysia, Philippines, and Singapore. Yu (2008) showed that the demand for real M1 in Argentina had a positive relationship with real income and peso depreciation in Argentina. Abdullah, Ali, and Matahir (2010) found that depreciation of domestic currency increases the demand for money. Arize and Nam (2012) showed that increases in the exchange rate have a significant and positive effect on money demand and that exchange rate and domestic interest rates have positive and negative impacts respectively on money demand.

Abdulkheir (2013) showed the existence of a long-run cointegration relationship between the demand for money and its explanatory variables (i.e., real GDP, interest rate, inflation rate, and exchange rate). Moreover, along with the changing of economic circumstances, demand for money, which is not necessarily a new topic of economics, has been discussed and examined again recently. Bahmani (2013) showed that exchange rate volatility has short-run effects on the demand for real M2 monetary aggregate in less developed countries; on the other hand, these short-run effects are not sustained. Hussain and Wijeweera (2013) showed that real GDP has a positive impact on the demand for real money and interest rate and exchange rate have a negative impact on money demand for M1. Kjosevski (2013) found that exchange rate and interest rate payable on time deposits up to one month explains the most variations of money demand in the long term, and interest rate is significant only in the short term. It is also difficult to conclude, depending on kinds of exchange rates, time, and so on, but the effects of exchange rates on demand for money is inconclusive.

This paper examines the recent Japanese demand for money function. Demand for money, including the Japanese case, has been discussed a lot; however, exchange rates have not been considered in the empirical analyses in many cases. Also, the recent Japanese economic and financial condition (i.e., drastic monetary policy and almost zero interest rate) may have greatly changed the demand function for money. This situation has not been considered, though it seems very important not only for the business world but also for policymakers. When deciding economic policies, demand for money has and should be examined and considered.

This paper is structured as follows. Section 2 provides theoretical background for the empirical analysis. Section 3 shows the empirical analyses. Section 4 reviews the results and ends with a brief summary.

## 2.0    Theory and hypothesis development

This study examines basically traditional demand for money function in Japan; however, (1) exchange rate and (2) economic uncertainty are considered in the estimations. Few studies have examined the impact of economic uncertainty on the demand for money, including Japanese case. Along with the traditional variables, two nontraditional variables (i.e., exchange rate and economic volatility) are included in the empirical equation, as there seems some possibility that demand for money has changed significantly. This paper examines this equation. Since the 2000s, world economic activity has changed and fluctuated to a large degree. The estimation equation is as shown in (1).

$$\ln M_t = \alpha + \beta_1(\ln RGDP_t) + \beta_2(INTEREST_t) + \beta_3(\ln(P_t/P_{t-1})) + \beta_4(\ln EXC_t) + \beta_5(\ln VOLATILITY_t) + \varepsilon_t \qquad (1)$$

where t means time. M denotes real M1 and real M2 (both are seasonally adjusted real ones). A measure of economic activity is real income (RGDP), which indicates transaction demand for money. $\beta_1$ is an estimate of income elastic and is expected to be positive. The measure of opportunity cost of holding money against financial assets is interest rate (INTEREST). $\beta_2$ should be negative. Interest rates seem to be no longer available as a stimulating instrument; however, the usefulness of money as a policy instrument is still conditional. As an interest rate, money market interest rate is used for estimations. The inflation rate [i.e., ln (Pt/Pt-1)] measures the opportunity cost against real assets. $\beta_3$, is expected to be negative. For the inflation rate, consumer price is used. To explain the degree of each currency substitution between domestic and foreign currency, the exchange rate, EXC, is included in the regression analysis. This variable has been regarded as unimportant or an ineffective variable against money supply. The exchange rate is the effective exchange rate. Hence, a decline reflects depreciation. Because the depreciation of domestic currency promotes domestic currency value of foreign assets held by domestic residents, the demand for money could rise as a result of perceived increase in wealth (Arango and Nadiri, 1981). However, Bahmani-Oskooee and Pourheydarian (1990) demonstrated that if depreciation of domestic currency causes increased expectations for more depreciation, domestic residents have less domestic currency and more foreign currency. Therefore, an estimate of $\beta_4$ could be negative or positive. It would be inconclusive. The measure of economic volatility (i.e., real output volatility) is also estimated. Increased volatility of economic uncertainty makes market participants more pessimistic, and they save money by increasing cash holdings. However, the strong degree of substitution between money and other less volatile assets, such as Japanese government bonds, could have negative effects on the demand for money. So the coefficient of $\beta_5$ is inconclusive.

## 3.0    Empirical analysis

### 3.1    Method

The sample period is from 1990Q1 to the latest 2015Q4. The sample period is divided into two; from 1990Q1 to 2001Q4 and from 2002Q1 to 2015Q4. At the end of 2001, the BOJ raised the outstanding balance of the current account at the BOJ at the beginning of unprecedented financial policy. This policy has been changing gradually and sometimes drastically; however, the basic stance to boost the economy has not been changing. From 2006 to 2012, quantitative easing policy was not performed; in April 2013, a drastic monetary easing policy was implemented and has continued since then. However, the stance is not different (scale and contents are different), so the sample period is set like this. One reason is the number of samples. All of the data are from International Financial Statistics (IMF).

### 3.2    Regression analyses

Empirical methods are OLS (ordinary least squares), GMM (generalized method of moments). One problem in equations that use the OLS method is the existence of unobservable specific effects and also lagged dependent variables. This problem can be overcome with the use of the GMM. GMM requires a decision on which variables to use as instrumental variables. J-test is used for estimation. This test checks whether or not the model's moment contains match the data. In a GMM context, when there are more moment conditions than parameters to be estimated, this chi-square test can be used to test the over-identifying restrictions. In this analysis, the lagged values of the dependent variables are used as instrumental variables.

| Table 1: Demand for money (M1) in Japan | | | |
| --- | --- | --- | --- |
|  | 1990Q1–2015Q4 | 1990Q1–2001Q4 | 2002Q1–2015Q4 |
| C | -2.157*** | 7.668*** | 8.390*** |
|  | (-3.971) | (5.140) | (10.212) |
| RGDP | 8.012*** | 3.358*** | 2.724*** |
|  | (30.120) | (4.513) | (6.654) |
| INTEREST | -0.046*** | -0.091*** | -0.003 |
|  | (-7.021) | (-9.040) | (-0.629) |
| PRICE | 0.019 | 0.012 | 0.011 |
|  | (1.021) | (0.620) | (1.014) |
| EXCHANGE | 0.402*** | -0.008 | 0.151** |
|  | (3.307) | (-0.058) | (2.063) |
| VOLATILITY | -4.461 | 1.623 | 12.995*** |
|  | (-1.062) | (0.441) | (3.877) |
| Adj.R2 | 0.934 | 0.921 | 0.698 |
| F-statistic (Prob) | 291.447 | 101.487 | 23.702 |
|  | (0.000) | (0.000) | (0.000) |
| Durbin-Watson | 0.495 | 0.979 | 0.846 |

*Note.* Figures in parentheses are t-statistic. ***, **, and * denote significance at 1, 5, 10%.

Almost all of the results are clear and some of them are as expected. The coefficients of interest rates are negative as expected for the first half; however, they are not significant for the latter part. The reason is the low or zero interest rates policies enacted in the 2000s. Interest rates have become insensitive by now. Prices also are insensitive; however, they are insensitive for all of the periods. The reason is similar to the case of interest rates and they are quite low (i.e., deflation). The results of exchange rates may explain that the depreciation of domestic currency (plus means depreciation of the yen) promotes domestic currency value of foreign assets held by domestic people, so the demand for money could rise as a result of perceived increase in wealth; however, it is insignificant for the first estimation period. Finally, volatility of economic activity increased for the latter sample period. During the 2000s, large economic shocks occurred and was a huge demand for money for safe assets.

| Table 2: Demand for money (M2) in Japan | | | | |
|---|---|---|---|---|
| | | | OLS | GMM |
| | 1990Q1–2015Q4 | 1990Q1–2001Q4 | 2002Q1–2015Q4 | 2002Q1–2015Q4 |
| C | 9.423*** | 12.477*** | 11.387*** | 10.935*** |
| | (46.323) | (24.660) | (20.428) | (16.198) |
| RGDP | 2.513*** | 1.123*** | 1.500*** | 1.772*** |
| | (25.234) | (4.452) | (4.864) | (5.096) |
| INTEREST | -0.006*** | -0.028*** | -0.0006 | -0.0003 |
| | (-2.811) | (-8.209) | (-0.108) | (-0.068) |
| PRICE | 0.013* | 0.006 | 0.007 | 0.006 |
| | (1.954) | (0.852) | (0.726) | (0.476) |
| EXCHANGE | 0.213*** | 0.035 | 0.198*** | 0.192** |
| | (4.691) | (0.746) | (2.982) | (2.408) |
| VOLATILITY | 4.034** | 1.307 | 14.127*** | 12.718*** |
| | (2.563) | (1.047) | (4.044) | (3.876) |
| Adj.R2 | 0.913 | 0.915 | 0.936 | 0.706 |
| F-statistic (Prob) | 196.847 | 93.748 | 120.292 | |
| | (0.000) | (0.000) | (0.000) | |
| J-statistic(Prob) | | | | 4.07E-37 |
| Durbin-Watson | 0.502 | 0.747 | 0.955 | 0.598 |

*Note.* Figures in parentheses are t-statistics. ***, **, and * denote significance at 1, 5, 10%.

Moreover, the time lag of explanation variables influences the effects of money demand. M2 is regressed by each lagged variable. The results are shown in Table 3.

| Table 3: Effects of lagged variables on the demand for money (M2) in Japan | | | | |
|---|---|---|---|---|
| | One-Time Lag | Two-Time Lag | Three-Time Lag | Four-Time Lag |
| C | 9.461*** | 9.496*** | 9.526*** | 9.538*** |
| | (47.973) | (49.748) | (50.577) | (52.198) |
| RGDP | 2.472*** | 2.433*** | 2.406*** | 2.382*** |
| | (25.362) | (25.553) | (-2.897) | (25.778) |
| INTEREST | -0.007*** | -0.007*** | -0.007*** | -0.006*** |
| | (-2.958) | (-2.995) | (-2.897) | (-2.714) |
| PRICE | 0.019*** | 0.022*** | 0.021** | 0.019*** |
| | (2.749) | (3.209) | (3.068) | (2.883) |
| EXCHANGE | 0.238*** | 0.262*** | 0.276*** | 0.295*** |
| | (5.338) | (6.030) | (6.457) | (7.082) |
| VOLATILITY | 3.887** | 3.666** | 3.717** | 3.122** |
| | (2.535) | (2.462) | (2.547) | (2.164) |
| Adj.R2 | 0.918 | 0.922 | 0.923 | 0.923 |
| F-statistic (Prob) | 205.980 | 215.919 | 217.903 | 225.817 |
| | (0.000) | (0.000) | (0.000) | (0.000) |
| Durbin-Watson | 0.430 | 0.489 | 0.499 | 0.493 |

*Note.* Figures in parentheses are t-statistics. ***, **, and * denote significance at 1, 5, 10%

The results are conclusive; however, the results should be also analyzed with those shown in Tables 1 and 2.

## 3.3    Causality test

Granger causality tests also were performed to check the relationship among the explanation variable and dependent variable. This test is as follows: A time series *X* is said to Granger-cause *Y* if one can show a series of t value and F value on lagged values of $X$ (lagged values of $Y$ included) and those $X$ values give statistically significant for values of $Y$. The estimations of the equation. The results are Table 4.

Table 4: Pairwise Granger causality tests

| Null Hypothesis | F-Statistic | Prob. |
|---|---|---|
| GDP does not Granger Cause M2 | 5.794 | 0.018 |
| M2 does not Granger Cause GDP | 1.942 | 0.167 |
| INTEREST does not Granger Cause M2 | 4.542 | 0.036 |
| M2 does not Granger Cause INTEREST | 0.024 | 0.879 |
| PRICE does not Granger Cause M2 | 0.372 | 0.544 |
| M2 does not Granger Cause PRICE | 0.033 | 0.857 |
| EXCHANGE does not Granger Cause M2 | 3.718 | 0.057 |
| M2 does not Granger Cause EXCHANGE | 0.229 | 0.634 |
| VOLATILITY does not Granger Cause M2 | 27.228 | 1.00E-06 |
| M2 does not Granger Cause VOLATILITY | 0.521 | 0.472 |

The results are almost expected. It can be said safely that demand function of this study is quite stable.

## 4.0    Conclusions

In Japan, low or almost zero interest rates has prevailed, and there has been a strong demand for Japanese government bonds, so there is some possibility that money demand has changed dramatically. The findings are important to consider in deciding on economic policies. This paper examined the recent Japanese case. Despite recent dramatic changes in the economy, money demand function is very stable and accountable mostly according to the traditional money demand function presented by traditional economic theory. Empirical evidence shows that demand for money has recently been affected by real GDP, exchange rates, and economic uncertainty. It may be said that market participants can have faith in the policies because demand for money is stable and predictable. However, the effects of interest rates on demand for money disappeared recently, which can be expected as a result of low or zero interest rate policies. Also, the empirical results show that exchange rate has developed an influence on money demand. Because depreciation of domestic currency promotes domestic currency value of foreign assets held by domestic residents, the demand for money could rise as a result of a perceived increase in national wealth. Moreover, the results show that introduction of the drastic quantitative easing policy changed the demand function for money.

Finally, the Japanese government not only implemented drastic economic policy but also took measures to strengthen competitiveness and economic growth. These measures included possible policy actions to reform the economic structure, such as concentrating resources on innovative research and development, strengthening the foundation for innovation, performing regulatory and institutional reforms, and changing the tax system. Moreover, by strengthening coordination between the BOJ and the government, the Japanese government has implemented measures to achieve a new fiscal structure to ensure the credibility of the fiscal condition since 2013. This approach is called *Abenomics*. Abe is from the name of Japan's current prime minister. So much more time to do research seems necessary as there is some possibility that demand for money function may change.

**Acknowledgements:** I appreciate the editor and the referee for their valuable comments and suggestions. I was supported by JSPS KAKENHI Grant Number 15H03366 for this work.

## References

Abdullah, H., Ali, J., & Matahir, H. (2010). Re-examining the demand for money in Asean-5 countries. Asian Social Science, 6(7), 146–155. http://dx.doi.org/10.5539/ass.v6n7p146

Abdulkheir, A. Y. (2013). An analytical study of the demand for money in Saudi Arabia. International Journal of Economics and Finance, 5(4), 31–38. http://dx.doi.org/10.5539/ijef.v5n4p31

Anusic, Z. (1994). The determinants of money demand in Croatia and simulation of the post-stabilization period. Croatian Economic Survey, 2, 85–120.

Arize, A. C. (1994). An econometric analysis of money demand in Taiwan, 1950–1989. American Economist, 38(1), 27–35. http://dx.doi.org/10.1177/056943459403800104

Arize, A., & Nam, K. (2012). The demand for money in Asia: some further evidence. International Journal of Economics and Finance, 4(8), 59–71. http://dx.doi.org/10.5539/ijef.v4n8p59

Avouyi-Dovi, S., Drumetz, F., & Sahuc, J. G. (2012). The money demand function for the Euro area: Some empirical evidence. Bulletin of Economic Research, 64(3), 377–392. http://dx.doi.org/10.1111/j.1467-8586.2010.00388.x

Bahmani, S. (2013). Exchange rate volatility and demand for money in less developed countries. Journal of Economics and Finance, 37(3), 442–452. http://dx.doi.org/10.1007/s12197-011-9190-y

Bahnami-Oskooee, M. &, Bohl, M. T. (2000). German monetary unification and the stability of the German M3 money demand function. Economics letters, 66(2), 203–208. http://dx.doi.org/10.1016/S0165-1765(99)00223-2

Bahmani-Oskooee, M., & Malixi, M. (1991). Exchange rate sensitivity of the demand for money in developing countries. Applied Economics, 23(8), 1377–1384. http://dx.doi.org/10.1080/00036849100000060

Bahmani-Oskooee, M., Miquel-Angel, M., & Niroeemand, F. (1998). Exchange rate sensitivity of the demand for money in Spain. Applied Economics, 30(5), 607–612. http://dx.doi.org/10.1080/000368498325598

Bahmani-Oskooee, M., & Pourheydarian, M. (1990). Exchange rate sensitivity of the demand for money and effectiveness of fiscal and monetary policies. Applied Economics, 22, 1377–1384. http://dx.doi.org/10.1080/00036849000000029

Bahnami-Oskooee, M., & Rehman, H. (2005). Stability of money demand function in Asian developing countries. Applied Economics, 37(7), 773–792. http://dx.doi.org/10.1080/0003684042000337424

Choi, W. G., & Oh, S. (2003). A demand function with output uncertainty, monetary uncertainty, and financial innovations. Journal of Money, Credit, and Banking, 35(5), 685–709. http://dx.doi.org/10.1353/mcb.2003.0034

Craig, H. (1982). Exchange rate determination and the demand for money. The Review of Economics and Statistics, 64(4), 681–686. http://dx.doi.org/10.2307/1923952

Cuthbertson, K., & Bredin, D. (2001). Money demand in the Czech Republic since transaction. Journal of Policy Reform, 4(4), 271–290. http://dx.doi.org/10.1080/13841280108523422

Dobnik, F. (2013). Long-run money demand in OECD countries: What role do common factors play? Empirical Economics, 45(1), 89–113. http://dx.doi.org/10.1007/s00181-012-0600-6

Dogru, B., & Recepoglu, M. (2013). Dynamic analysis of money demand function in Turkey. International Journal of Economics and Finance, 5(9), 20–27. http://dx.doi.org/10.5539/ijef.v5n9p20

Dreger, C., R. Hans-Eggert, R., & Roffia, B. (2007). Long-run money demand in the new EU member states with exchange rate effects. Eastern European Economics, 45(2), 75–94. http://dx.doi.org/10.2753/EEE0012-8775450204

Gunnar, J. (2001). Inflation, money demand, and purchasing power parity in South Africa. IMF Staff Papers, 48(2), 243–265.

Hueng, C. J. (1998). The demand for money in an open economy: Some evidence for Canada. North American Journal of Economics and Finance, 9(1), 15–31. http://dx.doi.org/10.1016/S1062-9408(99)80078-3

Hussain, A. A. (2007). The narrow money demand behavior in Indonesia, 1970–2005. ASEAN Economic Bulletin, 24(3), 320–338. http://dx.doi.org/10.1355/AE24-3C

Hussain, M. N., & Wijeweera, A. (2013). Estimation of the money demand function in a heterogeneous panel for selected Asian countries. Indian Journal of Economics and Business, 12(1), 23–35.

Jiranyakul, K., & Opiela, T. P. (2014). Instability of money demand: Recent evidence for Thailand. Modern Economy, 5(8), 907–913. http://dx.doi.org/10.4236/me.2014.58083

Khan, R. E. A., & Hve, Q. M. A. (2013). Financial liberalization and demand for money: A case of Pakistan. The Journal of Developing Areas, 47(2), 175–198. http://dx.doi.org/10.1353/jda.2013.0034

Kjosevski, J. (2013). The determinants and stability of money demand in the Republic of Macedonia. Journal of Economics and Business, 31(1), 35–54.

Klacek, J., & Smidkova, K. (1995). The demand for money function: The case of the Czech economy. Working Paper Series 41, Czech National Bank Praha.

Klos, B., & Wrobel, E. (2011). The monetary transmission mechanism and the structural modelling of inflation at the National Bank of Poland. National Bank of Poland.

Kumar, S., Chowdhury, M. B., & Rao, B. B. (2013). Demand for money in the selected OECD countries: A time series panel data approach and structural breaks. Applied Economics, 45, 13–15. http://dx.doi.org/10.1080/00036846.2011.637897

Odularu, G. O., & Okunrinboye, O. A. (2009). Modeling the impact of financial innovation on the demand for money in Nigeria. African Journal of Business Management, 3(2), 39–51.

Paudel, R. C., & Perera, N. (2013). Does financial liberalisation boost money demand? Evidence from Sri Lanka. Indian Journal of Economics and Business, 12(2–4), 223–242.

Rao, B., & Singh, R. (2005). Cointegration and error correction approach to the demand for money in Fiji. Pacific Economic Bulletin, 20(2), 76–82.

Rao, B. B., & Kumar, S. (2011). Is the US demand for money unstable? Applied Financial Economics, 21, 1263–1272. http://dx.doi.org/10.1080/09603107.2011.568395

Sarwar, H., Sarwar, M., & Waqas, M. (2013). Stability of money demand function in Pakistan. Economic and Business Review, 15(3), 197–212.

Singh, R., & Kumar, S. (2010). Some empirical evidence on the demand for money in the Pacific island countries. Studies in Economics and Finance, 27(3), 211–222. http://dx.doi.org/10.1108/10867371011060045

Tang, T. C. (2007). Money demand function for Southeast Asian countries: An empirical view from expenditure components. Journal of Economic Studies, 34(6), 476–496. http://dx.doi.org/10.1108/014435807108309 52

Yu, H. (2008). Impacts of the exchange rate and the foreign interest rate on the Argentine money demand function. Applied Economics Letters, 15(1), 35–39. http://dx.doi.org/10.1080/13504850600706685

Zouhar, Y., & Kacemi, A. (2008). Financial liberalisation and money demand in Morocco. Working Paper, 389, Economic Research Forum.

# 10

# Assessing performance of Morningstar's star rating system for equity investment

Paul J. Bolster[a]*, Emery A. Trahan[b], Pinshuo Wang[c]

[a] CFA, Professor of Finance, D'Amore-McKim School of Business, Northeastern University, Boston, MA 02115.
[b] CFA, Senior Associate Dean, D'Amore-McKim School of Business, Northeastern University, Boston, MA 02115.
[c] Ph.D. Candidate, Department of Economics, College of Social Studies and Humanities, Northeastern University
*Corresponding author's email address: p.bolster@neu.edu

| ARTICLE INFO | ABSTRACT |
|---|---|
| Keywords:<br>Asset pricing,<br>investment decisions,<br>ratings and rating agencies,<br>security analyst. | Both institutional and individual investors have a vast array of advisory and ratings services to assist with security selection. One of the most prominent sources of stock ratings is Morningstar. This is the first large-scale study evaluating the performance of portfolios formed using Morningstar's Star rating system for stocks. We evaluate the performance of portfolios formed using this rating system. Our results provide evidence that the Morningstar stock rating system allows an investor to build a portfolio with superior absolute and risk-adjusted returns over a long period of time. We show that a modest transaction cost will reduce, but not eliminate, these benefits. Overall, our results indicate that Morningstar ratings effectively discriminate between over- and undervalued stocks over the long term. |

## 1.0    Introduction

Individual investors are frequently searching for convenient and inexpensive advice regarding security selection and portfolio construction. One of the most prominent providers of such advice is Morningstar. This firm is best known for its ratings of a very large number of U.S.-based mutual funds. However, Morningstar also provides ratings of individual stocks. In this study, we address the following basic question: Can an investor employ these stock ratings to create a portfolio with superior performance?

There is a rich and varied literature in academic finance indicating that markets are essentially efficient in the semi-strong sense. In other words, once a recommendation or rating becomes public, any information it conveys is immediately incorporated into market prices. By the time the investor reads and reacts to the information, it is too late to exploit it. Numerous studies of national financial publications, independent newsletters and established rating services routinely conclude there is no material benefit in terms of investment returns. However, there are other studies, particularly those focused on analyst ratings of individual stocks that have found positive returns.

In this study, we employ the historical record of all Morningstar stock ratings over a period of approximately eleven years, nearly 140,000 unique ratings. We construct five portfolios, corresponding to the five "star" categories employed by Morningstar's stock rating system. Our analysis shows that the Morningstar stock rating system is able to effectively distinguish between the most overvalued (1-star) and undervalued (5-star) stocks.

Based on risk-adjusted returns, a portfolio of 5-star stocks outperformed a portfolio of 1-star stocks in 8 of 12 years from 2001 to 2012 and by 173.42% in unadjusted cumulative returns over our entire period of analysis.

We employ a Fama-French model to further assess sources of returns for the five portfolios. This analysis shows that the style characteristics of the five portfolios, particularly the 1-star and 5-star portfolios, vary widely during the 11 years of our study. Our results indicate that individual investors could benefit by properly exploiting the information provided in Morningstar's stock ratings. Return differences between the highest and lowest rated stocks are substantial and persist even after adjustment for risk and transaction costs.

The remainder of the study proceeds as follows. Section 2.0 provides an overview of empirical studies assessing the value of published investment advice. Section 3.0 provides a background of investor services provided by Morningstar. This is followed by a detailed discussion of data and methodology in section 4.0. Results of our analysis and conclusions appear in sections 5.0 and 6.0 respectively.

## 2.0    Review of literature

There is an extensive literature assessing the value of investment advice in general and stock ratings systems in particular. Several studies provide examples of the former. Metrick (1999) evaluates the performance of 153 investment newsletters and finds no case for outperformance. Dewally (2003) reports that stock recommendations distributed by major newsgroups through internet discussion forums produce no abnormal performance in the short or long term. Bolster, Trahan and Venkateswaran (2012) evaluate a large sample of stock recommendations made by the popular investment guru, Jim Cramer and conclude that his performance is in line with the risk level of his picks.

There is also considerable prior work examining the value of stock rating systems. Among the earliest studies, Black (1973) found that a portfolio formed from the top rated stocks on Value Line produced significant excess returns over a five year period from 1965 to 1970 even when adjusting for transaction costs. However, a study of Value Line rankings by Hall and Tsay (1988) found that top rated stocks did not provide significant excess returns during the period from 1976 to 1982. The disappearance of a Value Line premium is consistent with the major conclusion of a recent study of 95 pricing anomalies by McLean and Pontiff (2014). They find that returns attributed to most pricing anomalies are significantly reduced after their presence is reported in a publication.

Another common approach among studies of stock ratings exploits the system used by analysts where ratings of 1 to 5 represent strong buy, buy, hold, sell, and strong sell, respectively. Barber, Lehavy, McNichols and Trueman (2001) find that a strategy of shorting the lowest rated stocks generates superior returns. However, they also report that these returns may be eliminated by transaction costs. A more recent study, also by Barber, Lehavy, McNichols and Trueman (2010), shows that a portfolio that is long all buy and strong buy stocks and short all sell and strong sell stocks will produce positive and significant abnormal returns. The abnormal returns would be materially higher if this portfolio was further conditioned to focus on only stocks being upgraded to buy or strong buy or downgraded to sell or strong sell.

There are many studies of Morningstar's mutual fund ratings but there is very little published analysis of Morningstar's stock rating system. Examples of these studies include Blake and Morey (2000) who find predictive power in ratings, especially for the lowest rated funds, and DelGurico and Tkac (2001) who document a strong relationship between fund flows and changes in a fund's Morningstar rating.

Nearly all of the aforementioned studies pose a question similar to the one we pose here: Can an investor employ publically available information provided by an investment advisory firm to create a portfolio with superior performance? While the empirical finance literature generally supports the paradigm of semi-strong form market efficiency, there are a number of studies showing that publically available information can be used to generate positive, risk adjusted returns. Our study, which we believe is the first to comprehensively examine the efficacy of Morningstar's 5-star stock rating system, provides such a test.

## 3.0    About Morningstar

Morningstar was founded in 1984 by Joe Mansueto to provide individual investors with mutual fund analysis and commentary. Its first product was *The Mutual Fund Sourcebook*™, a quarterly publication containing performance data, portfolio holdings, and other information on approximately 400 mutual funds. Today, Morningstar claims to be one of the most recognized and trusted names in the investment industry, serving more than 7.4 million individual investors, 270,000 financial advisors, and 4,300 institutional clients.

On its website Morningstar.com, Morningstar, Inc. touts itself as a "leading provider of independent investment research in North America, Europe, Australia, and Asia; offering an extensive line of products and services for individuals, financial advisors, and institutions." The company provides data on more than 380,000 investments, including stocks, mutual funds and other types of funds, along with real-time global market data on more than eight million equities, indexes, futures, options, commodities, precious metals, foreign exchange, and Treasury markets. Morningstar also offers investment management services, with over of $190 billion assets under management or advisement and operations in 27 countries.

Morningstar offers products and services to advisors, institutions and individual investors. Much of their service is targeted toward providing independent information and advice to individual investors. Their website states that "individuals use Morningstar to make educated investment decisions. These investors want all the pertinent facts, as well as the assurance that their information source is completely independent." The company lists various attributes that relate to its ability to deliver world-class investment research and services. These attributes include, investor focus (maintaining an independent view and designing products to help investors make well-informed investment decisions); depth, breadth, and accuracy of data (employing 270 analysts worldwide and providing information on approximately 330,000 investment offerings); innovative, proprietary investment tools (e.g., Morningstar Rating™, Morningstar Style Box™, Morningstar Ownership Zone™, and a proprietary sector classification system for stocks); and finally, research and technology expertise (striving to rapidly adopt new technology and providing a flexible technology platform allowing products to work together). The primary tool for individual investors is Morningstar.com®, which Morningstar claims consistently ranks among the best investment sites on the web.

In 1985, shortly after its founding, Morningstar released its now famous Morningstar Rating™ for mutual funds, using the familiar rating of from one to five stars. In 1988, the company expanded into analysis of individual stocks, launching its Morningstar® StockInvestor™ newsletter. In 2001, Morningstar launched its Morningstar rating for individual stocks. Similar to its ratings of mutual funds, the Morningstar rating for stocks assigns each stock a rating of from one to five stars. A stock's rating is driven by its level of expected return, with 5-star stocks being those expected to offer investors returns well above a company's cost of capital.

## 4.0    Data and methodology

Morningstar analysts cover over 1800 companies in more than 100 industries, including more than 85% of the market value of the Wilshire 5000 Index. Morningstar evaluates each company as a business and conducts a fundamental analysis valuation considering how much capital a company invests and its return on capital, free cash flow, growth, and sources of competitive advantage and the likely fade in returns as competitive advantages erode over time. It examines each company using a discounted cash flow model and computes the value as the present value of the company's expected future free cash flows discounted at its cost of capital.

Morningstar analysts compare each company's fair value estimate to its market value and assign a rating of from one to five stars. Stocks trading at large discounts to fair value receive higher (4 or 5) star ratings, while those trading at large premiums to fair value estimates receive lower (1 or 2) star ratings. Stocks trading close to fair value receive 3-star ratings. Risk is also factored into the rating so that the greater the uncertainty of the stock, the greater its discount to fair value needs to be to earn a 5-star rating. A 5-star rating can be interpreted as a "consider buying" recommendation, i.e., the price of the stock is below the fair value by a sufficient margin to be purchased. Morningstar also advises individuals to consider their circumstances, including diversification, risk tolerance, and tax considerations.

Ratings are updated daily and therefore may change daily. Ratings can change due to: 1) a movement in the stock's price, 2) a change in the analyst's estimate of the stock's fair value, 3) a change in the analyst's assessment of a company's business risk, or 4) a combination of these factors. It should be noted that the Morningstar stock ratings are fundamentally different than the star ratings for mutual funds. The mutual fund ratings are descriptive, backward-looking, based on historical performance, strictly quantitative, calculated once a month, and rank funds according to a fixed distribution (i.e., only 10% of the funds in each category can receive 5-star ratings). The ratings for stocks are based on forward-looking estimates, adjusted for uncertainty, based on quantitative and qualitative inputs, calculated daily, and do not rank stocks according to a fixed distribution. Dorsey (2008) provides a more complete description of the Morningstar rating system for stocks.

Table 1 shows the number and proportion of stocks in each rating category at the end of each year from 2001 to 2012. We note that the number of stocks rated climbs from a low of 469 in 2001 to a high of 2107 in 2008 before tapering off to 1897 in 2012. But the most interesting element of this table relates to the proportion of stocks in each star category. Three-star stocks comprise the greatest proportion of the sample of rated stocks in every year, ranging from 33.75% to 56.09%. Stocks in this category are considered "fairly valued", a neutral rating. The proportion of 5-star stocks ranges from a low of 3.74% to a high of 24.82%. The high proportion occurs at the end of 2008, a fantastically bad year for the U.S. equity market. Conversely, the proportion of 1-star stocks is at its lowest point, 2.18% in 2008. This suggests that the depressed values for stocks at this time indicated a disproportionate number of bargains and relatively few overvalued securities.

Our main source of data is assembled from daily reports of stock ratings for Morningstar's entire sample of rated stocks. The data begins on June 26, 2001 and ends on October 1, 2012. The number of rated stocks varies over time and is 1897 at the end of our period of analysis. This data set allows us to identify (1) whether a stock is rated, (2) a stock's rating on a particular trading day, and (3) the day of a change in a stock's rating. Using this data we are able to identify 144,083 individual rating changes. After merging this database with CRSP to obtain stock returns, we retained 139,636 useable rating changes.

The CRSP data we employ measures daily total returns for individual stocks using closing prices. We create portfolios comprised of stocks with a specific rating using two different approaches. The first approach derives a simple arithmetic average, or equal weighted (EW) return for stocks assigned to a particular star portfolio for each of the 2,835 trading days in our sample period. Analysis of these returns should give us insight into whether the rating system is an effective discriminator on average.

On the other hand, perhaps all ratings are not equally informative. For example, what if some 5-star stocks perform incredibly well while most perform just a bit better than average? In this scenario, the EW return would underreport the effectiveness of the 5-star rating from an investor's perspective. Alternatively, maybe most 5-star stocks do a bit better than average but a minority perform poorly. In this case, the EW return would exaggerate the return that an investor who maintained a consistent portfolio of 5-star stocks would actually achieve. Furthermore, an EW portfolio would not be investable in any practical way. To adjust for possible asymmetry in performance and to create a more investable portfolio, we create a series of dollar weighted (DW) returns for each of our five portfolios.

**Table 1:** Distribution of Star Ratings by Year

| Year | 1-star | 2-star | 3-star | 4-star | 5-star | Total |
|------|--------|--------|--------|--------|--------|-------|
| 2001 | 78     | 98     | 180    | 85     | 28     | 469   |
|      | 16.63% | 20.90% | 38.38% | 18.12% | 5.97%  |       |
| 2002 | 66     | 88     | 254    | 65     | 86     | 559   |
|      | 11.81% | 15.74% | 45.44% | 11.63% | 15.38% |       |
| 2003 | 150    | 152    | 216    | 59     | 63     | 640   |
|      | 23.44% | 23.75% | 33.75% | 9.22%  | 9.84%  |       |
| 2004 | 386    | 226    | 527    | 111    | 59     | 1309  |
|      | 29.49% | 17.27% | 40.26% | 8.48%  | 4.51%  |       |
| 2005 | 353    | 201    | 684    | 218    | 98     | 1554  |
|      | 22.72% | 12.93% | 44.02% | 14.03% | 6.31%  |       |
| 2006 | 384    | 208    | 826    | 271    | 101    | 1790  |
|      | 21.45% | 11.62% | 46.15% | 15.14% | 5.64%  |       |
| 2007 | 255    | 148    | 765    | 424    | 382    | 1974  |
|      | 12.92% | 7.50%  | 38.75% | 21.48% | 19.35% |       |
| 2008 | 46     | 78     | 792    | 668    | 523    | 2107  |
|      | 2.18%  | 3.70%  | 37.59% | 31.70% | 24.82% |       |
| 2009 | 98     | 407    | 1169   | 319    | 91     | 2084  |
|      | 4.70%  | 19.53% | 56.09% | 15.31% | 4.37%  |       |
| 2010 | 106    | 510    | 1041   | 298    | 76     | 2031  |
|      | 5.22%  | 25.11% | 51.26% | 14.67% | 3.74%  |       |
| 2011 | 100    | 336    | 793    | 565    | 154    | 1948  |
|      | 5.13%  | 17.25% | 40.71% | 29.00% | 7.91%  |       |
| 2012 | 95     | 376    | 877    | 446    | 103    | 1897  |
|      | 5.01%  | 19.82% | 46.23% | 23.51% | 5.43%  |       |

The rightmost column shows the total number of stocks rated by Morningstar at the end of each calendar year. Other columns show the distribution of star ratings by number of stocks and as a proportion of the total of rated stocks.

To create the vector of DW returns, we invest $1 in a stock as it initially enters its designated portfolio at the close of the market on the day Morningstar releases the new information. We believe the closing price incorporates any short-term information effects of the disclosure of the rating change itself and better focuses the analysis on the continued performance of the portfolio. The stock remains in its designated portfolio until Morningstar assigns it a different rating. When a stock is reassigned to a new portfolio, we remove all accumulated value the original $1 investment has produced from the old portfolio and invest $1 in the new portfolio.

Here is a more concrete explanation of the rebalancing process for the DW portfolio. Morningstar announced an upgrade of Comcast from 4-star to 5-star on the morning of April 10, 2008. We invest $1 in Comcast at the market close on that day. We then use CRSP daily returns to revalue our investment in Comcast at the end of each subsequent trading day. On April 30, 2008, Comcast was downgraded from 5-star to 4-star. As of the close of the market on that day, our original $1 investment had grown to $1.0296. At this point, we calculate the aggregate value of all securities in the 5-star portfolio and the daily return for April 30. We then deduct $1.0296 from the aggregate value of the 5-star portfolio and also adjust for any other entries into or exits from the portfolio. The resulting adjusted aggregate value becomes the beginning value used to calculate the May 1, 2008 daily return.

In addition to evaluating raw returns, we also use the 4-factor Fama-French model to create risk-adjusted returns for both EW and DW approaches. This approach allows us to examine differential performance among the five portfolios formed from Morningstar's ratings and also to observe differences in style, or factor exposures across the portfolios and over time.

## 5.0 Results

### 5.01 Portfolio performance

Table 2 provides basic data on average daily returns by star rating for both EW and DW portfolios. For the EW portfolios, shown in Panel A, the 5-star portfolio outperforms the 1-star portfolio in 9 of 12 years. This difference is positive and significant in 2003 and 2010 and negative and significant in 2007. Across all 2835 days in our sample, the 5-star portfolio outperformed the 1-star by an average of 2.05 bps per day. This difference is not statistically significant. Overall, the 5-star portfolio provided the highest daily average return of 7.00 bps. However, the 4 and 1-star portfolios nearly tied for second place with 5.00 and 4.95 bps per day respectively.

Panel B shows returns for the DW portfolios. While the figures are different, the results are quite similar in a relative sense. The 5-star portfolio outperforms the 1-star portfolio in 8 of 12 years. The difference is positive and significant in 2003 and negative and significant in 2007. Over the entire sample, the average difference in daily returns was 1.12 bps higher for the 5-star, again not statistically significant. Again, the overall return for the 5-star portfolio produced the highest average, 4.67 bps per day. The performance of the five portfolios was nearly monotonic overall.

While the annual results provide modest support at best for superior performance of the 5-star portfolio relative to the 1-star portfolio, the cumulative returns over the entire period provide a much stronger result. The cumulative EW return for the 5-star portfolio is 322.26% overall, or 13.66% annualized. The 1-star portfolio returned 148.86% overall, or 8.44% annualized. Comparable returns for the DW portfolios were 127.89% overall (9.09% annualized) for the 5-star and 62.37% overall (5.25% annualized) for the 1-star. It's also worth noting that there was no material difference in cumulative performance between the 5-star portfolio and the 3-star and 4-star portfolios. The differential performance of the five portfolios is illustrated in Figure 1.

### 5.02 Basic risk metrics

Analysis of cumulative returns clearly shows that investors who focused solely on 5-star stocks would outperform those focused solely on 1-star stocks. This could suggest that Morningstar's ranking model is able to effectively discriminate between the best and worst performers, at least on a relative basis. Alternatively the difference could be explained by characteristics of the 5-star and 1-star portfolios.

Equal weighted portfolios are formed by calculating the arithmetic average return for all stocks carrying the specified ranking each day. Dollar weighted portfolios assume $1 is invested in a stock as it enters a portfolio. The accumulated value of this investment is removed from the portfolio when the stock leaves the portfolio. The aggregate end of day value of all stocks in a specified star portfolio is then used to calculate the daily dollar weighted portfolio return. For both equal weighted and dollar weighted portfolios all rebalancing occurs at the end of the trading day. The rightmost column shows the differential return between the highest rated (5-star) and lowest rated (1-star) stock portfolios.

**Table 2:** Average daily returns for portfolios created based on star ratings (in basis points per day, or bps)

| Year | 1-star | 2-star | 3-star | 4-star | 5-star | 5-1 |
|------|--------|--------|--------|--------|--------|------|
| | | | | Panel A: Equal Weighted portfolios | | |
| 2001 | 1.24 | 3.15 | 2.66 | 0.75 | 3.88 | 2.64 |
| 2002 | -19.14 | -14.23 | -7.07 | -5.09 | -16.32 | 2.83 |
| 2003 | 15.55 | 14.63 | 16.29 | 19.41 | 31.22 | 15.67*** |
| 2004 | 5.81 | 7.41 | 6.87 | 8.78 | 9.50 | 3.69 |
| 2005 | 5.02 | 3.03 | 3.64 | 2.58 | 2.32 | -2.70 |

| Year | | | | | | |
|------|------|------|------|------|------|------|
| 2006 | 6.93 | 6.54 | 7.16 | 8.17 | 9.97 | 3.03 |
| 2007 | 4.35 | 3.44 | 2.44 | -1.18 | -4.18 | -8.53* |
| 2008 | -15.42 | -19.78 | -18.51 | -16.53 | -10.65 | 4.77 |
| 2009 | 39.11 | 16.65 | 22.96 | 26.64 | 32.00 | -7.11 |
| 2010 | 9.03 | 11.99 | 10.67 | 10.63 | 17.09 | 8.06** |
| 2011 | -3.67 | 1.24 | -1.43 | -3.44 | -2.14 | 1.53 |
| 2012 | 10.07 | 6.96 | 7.42 | 7.99 | 10.78 | 0.71 |
| Overall | 4.95 | 3.34 | 4.43 | 5.00 | 7.00 | 2.05 |

Panel B:  Dollar Weighted portfolios

| Year | 1-star | 2-star | 3-star | 4-star | 5-star | 5-1 |
|------|--------|--------|--------|--------|--------|-----|
| 2001 | -0.30 | 1.64 | 2.02 | 0.63 | 0.55 | 0.85 |
| 2002 | -20.70 | -13.66 | -8.11 | -6.11 | -23.78 | -3.07 |
| 2003 | 15.89 | 15.57 | 16.28 | 17.57 | 24.37 | 8.49** |
| 2004 | 6.79 | 6.97 | 7.29 | 8.87 | 7.29 | 0.50 |
| 2005 | 5.58 | 3.18 | 3.75 | 3.10 | 3.10 | -2.49 |
| 2006 | 6.47 | 6.38 | 6.97 | 8.43 | 9.32 | 2.84 |
| 2007 | 4.60 | 3.35 | 2.38 | -0.95 | -3.70 | -8.30* |
| 2008 | -19.39 | -16.65 | -20.28 | -17.73 | -10.91 | 8.48 |
| 2009 | 27.26 | 14.68 | 20.59 | 23.12 | 25.75 | -1.51 |
| 2010 | 8.15 | 11.84 | 10.70 | 8.93 | 13.62 | 5.47 |
| 2011 | -1.61 | 1.04 | -0.41 | -2.86 | -0.98 | 0.63 |
| 2012 | 9.56 | 6.74 | 7.38 | 7.12 | 11.06 | 1.50 |
| Overall | 3.55 | 3.42 | 4.05 | 4.26 | 4.67 | 1.12 |

\* significant at 10%, \*\* significant at 5%, \*\*\*significant at 1%

**Figure 1:** Cumulative returns for Star Portfolios

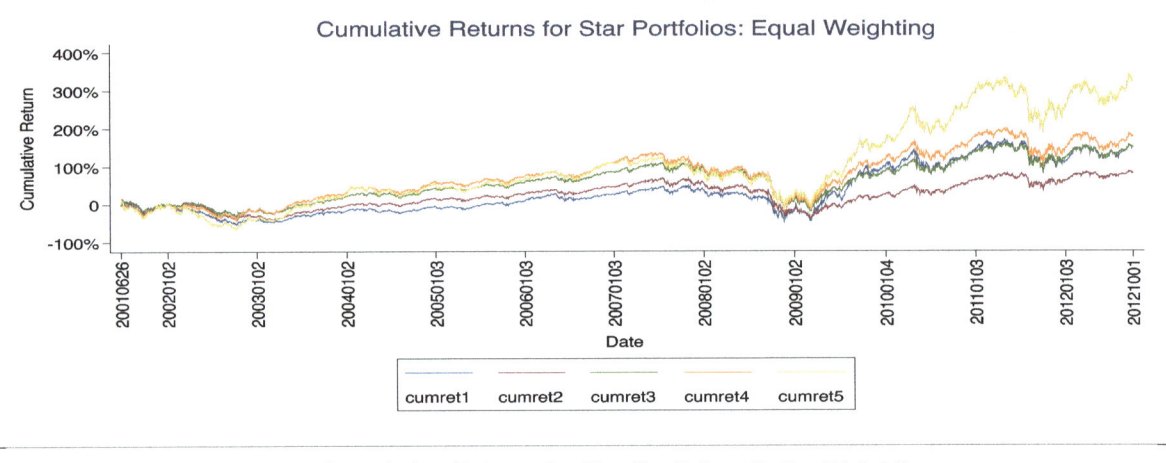

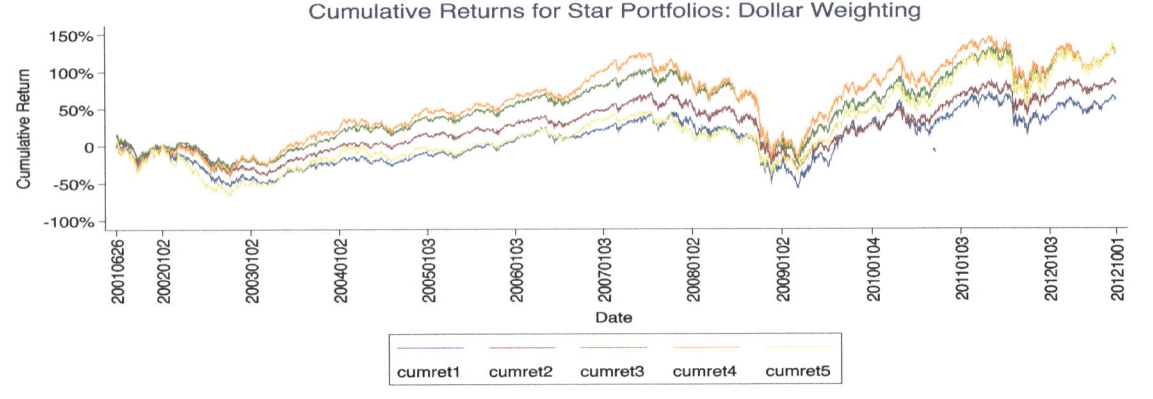

This figure shows the cumulative returns for portfolios formed by star rating for the period June 26, 2001 through October 1, 2012.  Equal weighted portfolios are formed by calculating the arithmetic average return for all stocks carrying the specified ranking each day. Dollar weighted portfolios assume $1 is invested in a stock as it enters a portfolio. The accumulated value of this investment is removed from the portfolio when the stock leaves the portfolio. The aggregate end of day value of all stocks in a specified star portfolio is then used to calculate the daily dollar weighted portfolio return. For both equal weighted and dollar weighted portfolios all rebalancing occurs at the end of the trading day.

We start by examining overall portfolio risk. The annualized standard deviations for equally weighted 5- and 1-star portfolios are 31.07% and 29.51% respectively. An F-test indicates that these risk measures are different at the 1% level. Five-star returns are more volatile than 1-star returns for EW portfolios. However, a similar analysis of dollar weighted portfolios shows no significant difference in standard deviation for 5-star (29.80%) and 1-star (30.42%) portfolios.

What about a long-short portfolio formed by buying the 5-star portfolio and shorting the 1-star portfolio? This strategy would produce a cumulative return of 173.42%, or an annualized return of 9.35%. While these returns are inferior to those produced from a long-only 5-star portfolio, the annualized standard deviation of the long-short portfolio is only 15.07%, materially lower than the 5-star portfolio's risk level. For the DW portfolios, the long-short portfolio provides cumulative returns of 65.51%, 4.58% annually with a standard deviation of 14.61%.

## 5.03    Risk-adjusted returns, equally weighted portfolios

Perhaps there are other systematic differences between the returns generated by 5-star and 1-star stocks. Such style differences in these stocks and their related portfolio returns could explain the differential performance we observe. Fama and French (1993) show that there are other factors effective at explaining return. Their 3-factor model is now considered the standard method for calculating risk-adjusted returns. We also include a fourth factor, identified by Carhart (1997) that detects momentum effects on portfolio returns. The model we estimate appears below:

$$R_{it} - R_{ft} = \alpha_i + \beta_i(RM_t - Rf_t) + s_i SMB_t + h_i HML_t + u_i UMD_t + e_{it}. \qquad (1)$$

In the equation, $R_{it} - Rf_t$ and $RM_t - Rf_t$ represent the day t excess return on the selected portfolio and the market respectively. $SMB_t$ is the difference between returns for small cap and large cap, or "small minus big" securities during day t. The differential return between value stocks (high book-to-market) and growth stocks (low book-to-market) during day t is captured by $HML_t$. Finally, $UMD_t$, represents the difference between the better and worse performing stocks, or "up minus down" for day t. We estimate values for $\alpha_i$, $\beta_i$, $s_i$, $h_i$, and $u_i$ using historical data. The intercept, or $\alpha_i$ term, is interpreted as the risk-adjusted return for the selected portfolio.

Daily return estimates for factors, Rf, SMB, HML, and UMD are obtained from Kenneth French's data library. As we are interested in Morningstar's ability to identify relative winners and losers, our proxy for RM, the market return, is the equally weighted return for all star-rated securities. Table 3 provides the results of this 4-factor regression analysis for EW portfolios.

The results for all years indicate that the 5-star portfolio generated a positive and significant daily alpha of 2 bps (0.02%) per day. Average daily alphas for the remaining portfolios generally decline as we move from 5-star to 1-star. Betas are greater than one for the 1 and 5-star portfolios and less than one for others. This pattern persists for all subperiods examined with the exception of 2007-2009 where betas are much more evenly distributed across portfolios. Both the 1-star and 5-star portfolios exhibit positive and significant SMB coefficients. The strong significance of this coefficient for the 5-1 portfolio suggests that the 1-star portfolio has a more extreme exposure to small caps. Exposure to the remaining two factors is opposite and significant for the 1 and 5-star portfolios. The 1-star portfolio has a significant tilt toward value stocks (positive HML coefficient) while the 5-star portfolio focuses on growth stocks (negative HML coefficient).

**Table 3:** Fama-French 4-Factor Regression Results (Equally Weighted Portfolios)

| 2001-2003 | 1-star | 2-star | 3-star | 4-star | 5-star | 5-1 |
|---|---|---|---|---|---|---|
| Alpha | -0.00047* | -0.00032* | 0.000033 | 0.00028* | 0.00013 | 0.000537 |
| Beta | 1.046662 | 0.92829*** | 0.8882*** | 1.011543 | 1.19608*** | 0.162637* |
| SMB | 0.200014*** | 0.06303** | -0.16945*** | -0.06931*** | 0.311129*** | 0.111699 |
| HML | -0.265*** | -0.07657* | -0.0611** | 0.057881* | 0.215478*** | 0.480697*** |
| UMD | 0.065557 | 0.14124*** | 0.126146*** | -0.00811 | -0.56015*** | -0.62599*** |
| 2004-2006 | 1-star | 2-star | 3-star | 4-star | 5-star | 5-1 |
| Alpha | -0.00006 | -0.000036 | 0.000017 | 0.000067 | 0.000078 | 0.000023 |
| Beta | 1.040769*** | 0.974953** | 0.96561*** | 1.007096 | 1.109133*** | 0.067973** |
| SMB | 0.062662*** | -0.05446*** | -0.07978*** | 0.047405** | 0.23548*** | 0.173116*** |
| HML | -0.04332* | 0.012189 | -0.00389 | 0.01085 | 0.012479 | 0.055026 |
| UMD | 0.29156*** | 0.065294*** | -0.05934*** | -0.20106*** | -0.17481*** | -0.46929*** |
| 2007-2009 | 1-star | 2-star | 3-star | 4-star | 5-star | 5-1 |
| Alpha | 0.000565 | -0.00031* | -0.00012** | -0.000085 | 0.000155 | -0.00049 |
| Beta | 0.993765 | 0.95671*** | 0.971761*** | 0.993913 | 0.999383 | -0.005512 |
| SMB | 0.348388*** | 0.31936*** | 0.040285 | -0.01563 | -0.07994*** | -0.42799*** |

| | 1-star | 2-star | 3-star | 4-star | 5-star | 5-1 |
|---|---|---|---|---|---|---|
| HML | 0.277143*** | 0.161053*** | 0.043614*** | -0.00548*** | -0.12563*** | -0.40336*** |
| UMD | 0.01595 | 0.150437*** | 0.045658*** | -0.03097*** | -0.12702*** | -0.14362*** |
| 2010-2012 | 1-star | 2-star | 3-star | 4-star | 5-star | 5-1 |
| Alpha | -0.00019 | 0.000058 | -0.000012 | -0.000044 | 0.000313** | 0.000494*** |
| Beta | 1.007009 | 0.968147*** | 0.97894*** | 1.025707*** | 1.072872*** | 0.064713*** |
| SMB | 0.252896*** | 0.084157*** | -0.03364*** | -0.05708*** | 0.010113 | -0.24536*** |
| HML | -0.07017** | -0.05082*** | 0.00626 | 0.053983*** | 0.068916*** | 0.139472*** |
| UMD | 0.202739*** | 0.198697*** | 0.019586*** | -0.1409*** | -0.24851*** | -0.45166*** |
| All Years | 1-star | 2-star | 3-star | 4-star | 5-star | 5-1 |
| Alpha | -0.000038 | -0.00016** | -0.000044 | 0.000042 | 0.000205* | 0.000175 |
| Beta | 1.038217*** | 0.946051*** | 0.942662*** | 0.992974 | 1.092388*** | 0.054186*** |
| SMB | 0.257466*** | 0.159907*** | -0.02194*** | -0.02252*** | 0.036795** | -0.22035*** |
| HML | 0.087537*** | 0.066976*** | 0.072549*** | 0.00523 | -0.25647*** | 0.34435*** |
| UMD | 0.020623 | 0.109027*** | 0.04295*** | -0.05327*** | -0.1874*** | -0.2083*** |

*  significant at 10%, ** significant at 5%, ***significant at 1%
Beta is tested versus 1 for the 1 to 5-star portfolios. It is tested versus 0 for the 5-1 portfolio.

This table shows results from a 4-Factor regression of the form: $R_{it} - R_{ft} = \alpha_i + \beta_i(RM_t - Rf_t) + s_i SMB_t + h_i HML_t + u_i UMD_t + e_{it}$. The dependent variable is the daily return for an equally weighted star portfolio minus the risk-free rate.

The UMD factor indicates that the 1-star portfolio has a strong preference for stocks that have done well in the recent past. The 5-star portfolio indicates a contrarian approach, favoring stocks that have not performed well. This result is likely an artifact of the rating process. Recall that stocks are evaluated on the relationship between Morningstar's estimate of fair value and the actual market value.

The 5-star portfolio contains stocks trading at the greatest discount to fair value, the most undervalued stocks. Conversely, 1-star stocks are the most overvalued stocks based on Morningstar's approach. Unlike market prices, the estimate of fair value does not change daily. This means that the majority of stocks upgraded to 5-star status have likely experienced a recent market price decline. Similarly, stocks downgraded to 1-star status have likely experienced a recent increase in market price. This is consistent with the positive UMD factor for the 1-star portfolio and the negative value for the 5-star portfolio.

More careful analysis of results shown in Table 3 indicate that the subperiod from 2007-2009 had a large influence on the overall results. This period captures the global financial crisis and the concurrent decline in U.S. equity markets. During this 3-year period, both 1-star and 5-star stocks produced positive alphas but neither is significant at a meaningful level. The SMB coefficient for the 5-star portfolio was negative in this period indicating a shift in style from small cap to large cap stocks. In 3 of 4 subperiods, the HML coefficients indicate a preference toward value and growth stocks for the 5-star and 1-star portfolios respectively. However, this relationship reversed in the 2007-2009 period. Furthermore, the significance of the reversal was large enough to influence the overall result. To examine these style spikes and transitions, we ran a series of overlapping 252 day Fama-French 4-factor regressions using the daily returns for the 1 through 5-star EW portfolios. The coefficients for these regressions are shown in Figure 2.

The Fama-French alphas for each of the five EW portfolios are shown in the first panel of Figure 2. The 5-star alpha is generally above the 1-star alpha. The major exception occurs from the last half of 2008 through early 2009 when the 1-star alpha exceeds the 5-star alpha. While the 5-star portfolio outperformed the 1-star portfolio in absolute terms in 2008 (see Table 2), it was unable to do so on a risk-adjusted basis during much of that year. This result was not uncommon for quantitative investment strategies during this period of time.

Rolling betas (second panel of Figure 2) generally show a downward drift for the 5-star portfolio before stabilizing between 1.0 and 1.1 in the last half of 2009. While the 1-star beta is generally below the 5-star beta, there are exceptions during 2007 and 2009 when the 1-star beta showed high volatility.

The third panel of Figure 2 shows the SMB coefficient for the rolling Fama-French regressions. This illustration clearly shows the change in style for the 1 and 5-star portfolios. For most of the period from 2001 to 2007, both of these portfolios had a positive SMB coefficient indicating a preference for small cap stock for both portfolios. By mid-2007, both portfolios appear to have an SMB coefficient close to zero. At this point, there is a clear change in strategy for the 5-star portfolio indicated by the change in sign of the SMB coefficient and a simultaneous upward spike in this measure for the 1-star portfolio. From mid-2007 on, the 5-star portfolio generally maintained a negative or neutral SMB coefficient.

**Figure 2:** 252 Day Fama-French 4-Factor Regressions for Equally Weighted Portfolios

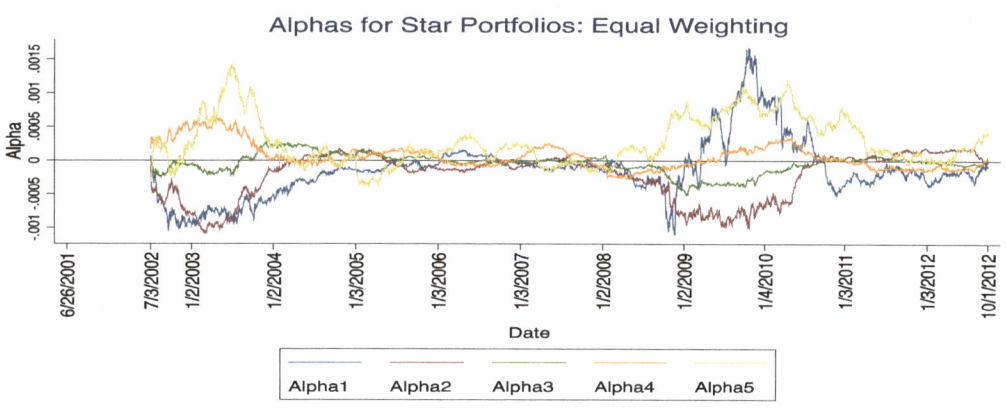

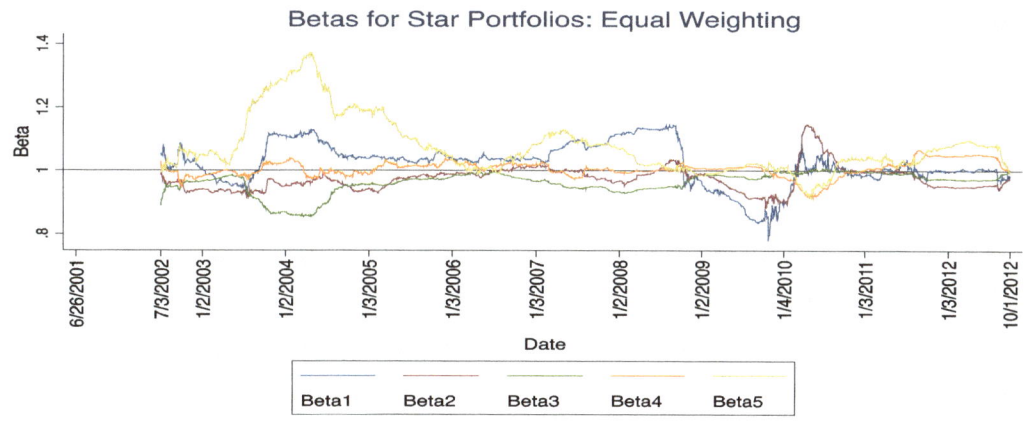

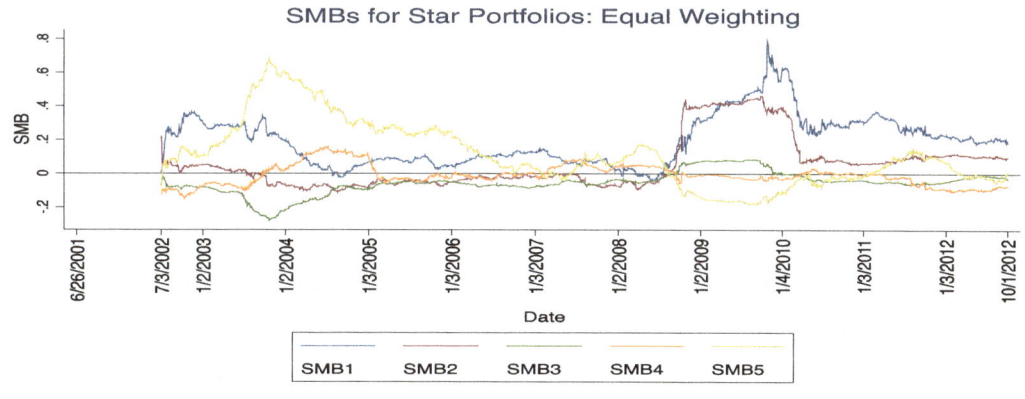

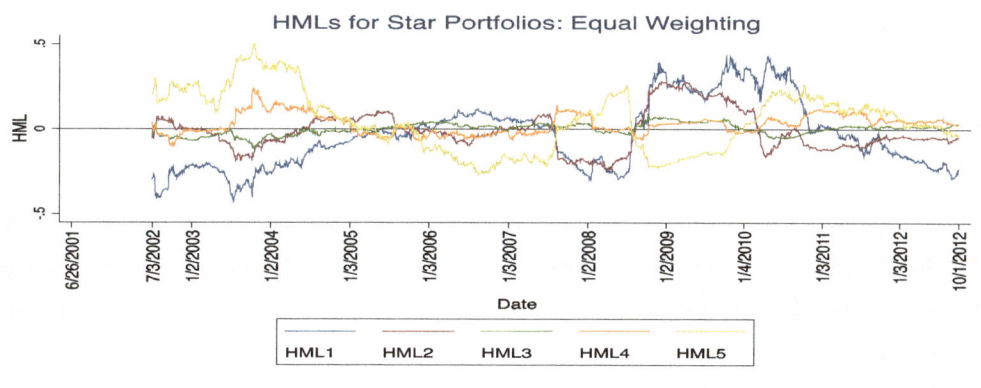

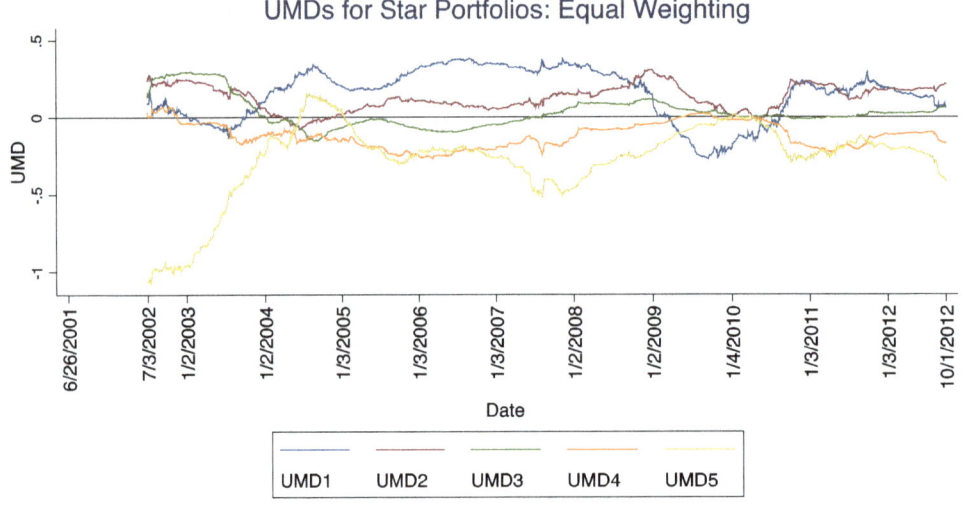

Panels A through E display the coefficients derived from overlapping 252 day 4-factor regressions of the form: $R_{it} - R_{ft} = \alpha_i + \beta_i(RM_t - Rf_t) + s_i SMB_t + h_i HML_t + u_i UMD_t + e_{it}$. The dependent variable is the daily return for an equally weighted star portfolio minus the risk-free rate.

The last two panels of Figure 2 depict the HML and UMD coefficients for each of the five star portfolios. Both the 1-star and 5-star portfolio HML coefficients cross the horizontal axis numerous times and appear to have an inverse relationship. The UMD coefficients are much more consistent, remaining negative for the 5-star portfolio with minor exceptions. The 1-star portfolio displays a similar pattern on the positive side. Again, this is consistent with the rating process described by Morningstar. Stocks with declining values are more likely to be undervalued and rising stocks are more likely to be overvalued.

## 5.04     Risk-adjusted returns, dollar weighted portfolios

The dollar weighted results shown in Table 4, indicate that the 1-star portfolio generated a negative and significant alpha of 2 bps (0.02%) per day over the entire period of analysis.  Unlike the alphas from our analysis of equal weighted returns, which increased monotonically from 1-star to 5-star, there is little variation in alphas for the various dollar weighted portfolios.  Similar to the EW results, betas are greater than 1 for the 1 and 5-star portfolios and less for others.  Other factor exposures are also similar to the analysis of EW portfolios. The 1-star portfolio appears exposed to small value stocks and the 5-star is exposed to large growth stocks. There is still a clear preference for stocks with positive momentum in the 1-star portfolio and negative momentum in the 5-star portfolio.

Similar to the analysis of EW portfolios, the 2007-2009 period has a strong influence on the overall results. The strong preference for large cap stocks (negative SMB) within this period offsets a strong preference for small caps during the period from 2001 to 2006.
A modest distinction between the EW and DW portfolios relates to the behavior of the HML coefficient. This factor is only significant during one sub-period, 2007-2009, when it indicates a preference for growth stocks in that portfolio. The HML coefficient for the 1-star portfolio exhibits the same behavior as in the analysis of EW returns.

| Table 4: Fama-French 4-Factor Regression Results (Dollar Weighted Portfolios) | | | | | | |
|---|---|---|---|---|---|---|
| 2001-2003 | 1-star | 2-star | 3-star | 4-star | 5-star | 5-1 |
| Alpha | -0.0006** | -0.0003 | -0.000031 | 0.00015 | -0.00049 | 0.00004 |
| Beta | 1.063044*** | 0.931564*** | 0.887256*** | 1.019927 | 1.196592*** | 0.133678*** |
| SMB | 0.244108*** | 0.035971 | -0.15458*** | -0.07741*** | 0.254423*** | 0.010899 |
| HML | -0.22343*** | -0.08052* | -0.08008*** | 0.028313 | 0.039883 | 0.263539*** |
| UMD | 0.098655** | 0.200431*** | 0.158049*** | 0.073395*** | -0.35558*** | -0.45452*** |
| 2004-2006 | 1-star | 2-star | 3-star | 4-star | 5-star | 5-1 |
| Alpha | -0.000024 | -0.000045 | 0.000033 | 0.000095 | 0.000002 | -0.00009 |
| Beta | 1.054582*** | 0.964383*** | 0.959741*** | 1.00492 | 1.101732*** | 0.046759* |
| SMB | 0.053742** | -0.05138*** | -0.07761*** | 0.054236*** | 0.217775*** | 0.164331*** |
| HML | -0.09087*** | 0.006633 | -0.02472 | 0.005628 | -0.01557 | 0.074529 |
| UMD | 0.374134*** | 0.074486*** | -0.01935* | -0.18022*** | -0.2677 | -0.40022*** |
| 2007-2009 | 1-star | 2-star | 3-star | 4-star | 5-star | 5-1 |

| | 1-star | 2-star | 3-star | 4-star | 5-star | 5-1 |
|---|---|---|---|---|---|---|
| Alpha | 0.000051 | -0.00026 | -0.00024*** | -0.00022*** | -0.00016 | -0.00015 |
| Beta | 1.062309*** | 0.954757*** | 0.953051*** | 0.984086*** | 0.978386*** | -0.08403*** |
| SMB | 0.313069*** | 0.390897*** | 0.056557*** | -0.01136 | -0.09072*** | -0.40345*** |
| HML | 0.272248*** | 0.231662*** | 0.060667*** | -0.01258 | -0.12837*** | -0.40121*** |
| UMD | 0.084379** | 0.18333*** | 0.07196*** | -0.0066 | -0.05891*** | -0.14394*** |
| 2010-2012 | 1-star | 2-star | 3-star | 4-star | 5-star | 5-1 |
| Alpha | -0.0002 | 0.000023 | -0.000009 | -0.00012** | 0.000211* | 0.000405** |
| Beta | 1.047495*** | 0.969574*** | 0.998718*** | 1.014953*** | 1.081813*** | 0.034319* |
| SMB | 0.288913*** | 0.112666*** | -0.00982 | -0.05127*** | -0.01151 | -0.30047*** |
| HML | -0.00504 | -0.0388** | -0.00717 | 0.046148*** | -0.00226 | 0.002796 |
| UMD | 0.277353*** | 0.246288*** | 0.084469*** | -0.08629*** | -0.19247*** | -0.46982*** |
| All Years | 1-star | 2-star | 3-star | 4-star | 5-star | 5-1 |
| Alpha | -0.00021* | -0.00017** | -0.000082** | -0.000032 | -0.000029 | 0.000108 |
| Beta | 1.088811*** | 0.944657*** | 0.935125*** | 0.987131*** | 1.085408*** | -0.00339* |
| SMB | 0.255151*** | 0.188087*** | -0.00738 | -0.02192*** | 0.025653 | -0.22918*** |
| HML | 0.112998*** | 0.107952*** | 0.06811*** | -0.00205 | -0.27281*** | 0.38614*** |
| UMD | 0.084316*** | 0.133848*** | 0.074487*** | -0.01185** | -0.09494*** | -0.17953*** |

* significant at 10%, ** significant at 5%, ***significant at 1%

Beta is tested versus 1 for the 1 to 5-star portfolios. It is tested versus 0 for the 5-1 portfolio.

This table shows results from a 4-Factor regression of the form: $R_{it} - R_{ft} = \alpha_i + \beta_i(RM_t - Rf_t) + s_i SMB_t + h_i HML_t + u_i UMD_t + e_{it}$. The dependent variable is the daily return for a dollar weighted star portfolio minus the risk-free rate.

## 5.05    Transaction costs

Recall that the 5-star DW portfolio generated an average annual return of 13.66%. But this return does not reflect costs associated with the significant amount of trading necessary to maintain a portfolio of purely 5-star stocks. During the entire period of analysis, the average number of daily trades needed to maintain the 5-star portfolio is 7.6, or approximately 1914 trades per year. To assess the impact of this activity, we use a simple approach to model transaction costs. We assume that a retail investor can execute a $10,000 trade for $10 and then scale that to our $1 trade. This results in a fixed transaction cost of $0.001 that we apply to each purchase and sale. When we account for this cost in the 5-star dollar weighted returns, we end up with an annualized return of 7.02%.

The long-short portfolio designed to capture the return difference between the 5-star and 1-star stocks is even more severely affected by the recognition of this modest transaction cost. This portfolio's annual return declines from 9.35% to 3.02% when transaction costs are included. If the fixed transaction cost is increased to $0.0029 per trade, the net return on this portfolio is reduced to 0.00%.

## 6.0    Conclusion

The objective of this paper has been to examine the portfolio returns earned by investing in portfolios of stocks categorized by Morningstar's 5-star rating system for individual stocks. Morningstar, Inc. is a well-established provider of information and analysis on a wide variety of financial investments. If markets are semi-strong form efficient, then we would not expect to find risk-adjusted outperformance from trading on Morningstar ratings. While the preponderance of evidence shows that markets are semi-strong form efficient, some prior studies do document evidence of abnormal returns from various trading strategies, including some from following the advice of select investment newsletters or information providers. Our results provide some perspective on the overall value of Morningstar's stock ratings service. The results show that the Morningstar ratings are able to effectively able to distinguish between the most overvalued (1-star) and undervalued (5-star) stocks over the period of our study.

Using equally-weighted returns, over the 2001-2012 period, the 5-star portfolio earns a cumulative return of 322.26%, or 13.66%, annualized, compared to 148.86%, or 8.44% annualized for the 1-star portfolio, for a difference of 173.4%, or 5.22% annualized. For a dollar-weighted returns, the 5-star portfolio earns a cumulative return of 127.89%, or 9.09% annualized, compared to 62.37%, or 5.25% annualized for the 1-star portfolio, for a difference of 65.52%, or 3.84% annualized. Using a four-factor model to adjust for risk, and using equally-weighted returns, we find that the 5-star portfolio generated a positive and significant alpha of 2 bps (0.02%), and that alphas decline monotonically for the other portfolios. The 5-star portfolio tilts to large, growth stocks, while the 1-star portfolio tilts to small, value stocks. The 1-star portfolio shows a preference for stocks that have done well in the past, while the 5-star portfolio indicates a contrarian approach, favoring stocks that have not performed well in the recent past. Using dollar-weighted returns in the risk analysis, yields slightly different results.

These results provide evidence that the Morningstar stock rating system does allow an investor to build a portfolio that outperforms the market average over a long period of time. The results are not as strong after adjusting for portfolio risk, but there is still some evidence of outperformance on a risk-adjusted basis. The risk factors also vary across the different portfolios and the results exhibit some variation over time. It should also be noted that the investment strategies examined herein required a significant amount of trading activity and therefore would incur transactions costs. We show that a modest transaction cost will reduce, but not eliminate, the benefits available from a trading strategy based on the ranking system.

Overall, the results are consistent with Morningstar analysts providing valuable analysis. They should be of interest to both institutional and individual investors seeking to develop an active, or alpha-generating, investment strategy, to those interested in an unbiased and scientific analysis of this Morningstar service, and to those interested in studies of the impact of analysts' recommendations.

# References

Barber, B., R. Lehavy, M. McNichols, B. Trueman, (2001). Can Investors Profit from the Prophets? Security Analysts Recommendations and Stock Returns, Journal of Finance, 61(2), 531-563. http://dx.doi.org/10.1111/0022-1082.00336

Barber, B., R. Lehavy, M. McNichols, B. Trueman. (2010). Ratings changes, ratings levels, and the predictive value of analysts' recommendations, Financial Management, 39(2), 533-553. http://dx.doi.org/10.1111/j.1755-053X.2010.01083.x

Black, F. (1973). Yes, Virginia, There Is Hope: Tests of the Value Line Ranking System, Financial Analysts Journal, 29(5), 10-14+.

Blake, C., M. Morey. (2000). Morningstar Ratings and Mutual Fund Performance, Journal of Financial and Quantitative Analysis, 35(3), 451-483. http://dx.doi.org/10.2307/2676213

Bolster, P., E. Trahan, A. Venkateswaran, (2012). How Mad Is Mad Money: Jim Cramer as a Stock Picker and Portfolio Manager, Journal of Investing, 22(2), 27-39. http://dx.doi.org/10.3905/joi.2012.21.2.027

Carhart, M. (1997). On Persistence in Mutual Fund Performance, Journal of Finance, 52(1), 57-82. http://dx.doi.org/10.1111/j.1540-6261.1997.tb03808.x

Del Guericio, D., P. Tkac, (2008) . Star Power: The Effect of Morningstar Ratings on Mutual Fund Flow, Journal of Financial and Quantitative Analysis, 43(4), 907-936. http://dx.doi.org/10.1017/S0022109000014393

Dewally, M., (2003). Internet Investment Advice: Investing with a Rock of Salt, Financial Analysts Journal 59(4), 65-77. http://dx.doi.org/10.2469/faj.v59.n4.2546

Dorsey, P. (2008). FAQ: The Morningstar Rating for Stocks. Retrieved from: http://news.morningstar.com/articlenet/article.aspx?id=4982

Fama, E., K. French. (1993). Common Risk Factors in the Returns on Stocks and Bonds, Journal of Financial Economics, 33(1), 3-56. http://dx.doi.org/10.1016/0304-405X(93)90023-5

Hall, T., J. Tsay. (1988). An evaluation of the performance of portfolios selected from Value Line Rank One stocks: 1976-1982, Journal of Financial Research 11(3), 227-240. http://dx.doi.org/10.1111/j.1475-6803.1988.tb00084.x

McLean, R., J. Pontiff. (2014). Does Academic Research Destroy Stock Return Predictability?. Working paper. Retrieved from: http://ssrn.com/abstract=2156623.

Metrick, A. (1999). Performance evaluation with transactions data: The stock selection of investment newsletters. Journal of Finance 54(5), 1743-1775. http://dx.doi.org/10.1111/0022-1082.00165

# Corporate takeovers in the US oil and gas sector

Alex Ng [a*], Raymond A. K. Cox [b]

[a] Thompson Rivers University, Associate Professor of Finance, British Columbia, Canada.
[b] Thompson Rivers University, Chair and Professor of Finance, Department of Accounting & Finance, British Columbia, Canada.
*Corresponding author's email address: ang@tru.ca

ARTICLE INFO

ABSTRACT

We examine corporate takeovers in the U.S. oil and gas sector from 1990 to 2008. We test the hypotheses that energy prices and reserves influence takeovers in the energy market for corporate control. We employ these methods: 1. capital asset pricing model, 2. regression analysis, and 3. Granger causality test. Our results show that oil reserves cause takeover deals and affect the value of the merger. High oil prices propel management to acquire oil firms as well as affect the target value. However, the reverse cause-effect mechanism occurs for natural gas prices. That is, takeover activity causes gas prices to decrease. Acquirers are motivated to purchase reserves; whereas, targets are disposed to sell based on energy prices. Hence, our findings imply that countries can consider policies, which address the motivations of the oil and gas industries to facilitate well-functioning takeover markets.

Keywords:
Mergers and acquisitions;
Oil and gas;
Reserves energy;
Takeovers.

## 1.0    Introduction

Commodity markets have major impacts on the capital markets and economy. More specifically, the oil and gas (O & G) sector of the energy industry has been the propelling force causing swings in the business cycle from boom to recession and back. In the currency market, numerous foreign-exchange rates move in response to changes in the prices of oil and gas. The operating performance of industries such as airlines is highly dependent on the input costs of fuel derived from oil. Recently Saudi Arabia has driven down the price to retain customers and market share and to drive out competitors. In particular, the previous high oil prices has made it attractive for oil and gas fields' development especially in the US gas shale industry. As a result, the US became a net exporter of oil for the first time in decades. Do events occurring in the O & G sector affect financial decision-making? Our study focuses on the takeover activities of O & G firms in the U.S. from 1990 to 2008. We present evidence that energy reserves and commodity prices modify takeover behavior. Managers can be motivated to purchase (or sell) O & G companies dependent on the level of O & G reserves and prices.

The mergers and acquisitions (M&A) literature has an extremely long tradition [Martynova28] with recurring themes, such as agency costs, merger waves, performance, payment options, market power, synergy effects, stock market driven acquisition, and managerial objectives. The impact of energy markets is fundamental to the world economy and influences inflation, monetary policy, economic growth and wealth.

Weston, et al. (1990) argue that takeover activities have been high in industries undergoing deregulation, experiencing oil price shocks, or facing structural alteration. Jensen (1993) and Mitchell and Mulherin (1996) demonstrate that M & A activities were driven by economic shocks in the industry, including oil shocks. Our motivation to study corporate takeovers in the oil and gas industry is that there could be different motives for takeovers compared to other industries. Donker and Ng (2013) first discover acquiring reserves and commodity price driven motivation for oil and gas takeovers recently in the Canadian market. In our study, we examine these new motivations in the US O & G sector, which remains unexamined. Our study is particularly relevant to the US oil and gas industry, which is experiencing one of its largest expansions in history.

Our contribution to the literature is to demonstrate that the US O & G corporations are: 1. motivated to consummate takeovers to purchase reserves, 2. takeovers are connected to energy prices as well as firm value, 3. acquirer firm stockholder's wealth significantly decreases during the announcement period of takeovers (while target wealth increases significantly) and 4. Commodity price-driven takeovers are different from stock market-driven takeovers.

We find US acquirers incur negative returns when announcing an acquisition, controlled for beta risk and the stock market, as other acquirers do in other sectors. The valuation of M & A deals is negatively (positively) tied to oil (gas) reserves. Further, the level of oil prices positively affects the number of M & A deals. Our findings imply that for countries with an interest in promoting their energy industry, can evaluate and consider policies, which address the motivations of the oil and gas industries to facilitate well-functioning takeover markets.

We organize the rest of the paper as follows. In Section two, we discuss the literature. Section three we develop our hypotheses. Section 4 contains our sample selection and research design. In Section five, we discuss our empirical findings. We conduct robustness tests in Section 6 and we conclude and present policy implications in Section 7.

## 2.0    Literature review

The literature recognizes these motivations for managers to engage in M & A. Bruner's (2002) survey shows managers seek to create synergies to improve firm value and from attaining economies of scale. Jensen and Meckling (1976) articulate that managers engage in takeovers because they benefit themselves as agents at the likely expense of decreasing shareholder value. Jensen (1986) posits that managers of firms with rich cash flows, as with oil and gas firms, are known to expend them on value destroying M & A. Dong et al. (2006), Rhodes-Kropf et al. (2005) and Shliefer et al. (2003) present evidence that agent motivated takeover occurs when managers take advantage of high stock prices of their firms to buy other companies relatively cheaply. Fan et al. (2013) show that for overvalued firms, takeovers profit the manager with higher compensation at the expense of shareholders in which there are no synergy gains for the firm and significant overpayment for the target.

Weston, et al. (1990) examine mergers and restructuring in the global oil industry in the 1990s. There is a high degree of consolidation, and the basic change forces responsible are technological advances, globalization, and deregulation. They conclude that instability in oil prices triggers M&A and restructuring. Ferguson and Popkin (1982) observe that managers of oil firms pay excessive takeover premiums for their targets in their examination of the deal between Conoco and Marathon Oil. In their analysis, they show that when an acquirer can increase tax deductions such as depreciation and depletion, the acquirer can possibly gain at the expense of the government. By purchasing a target for its reserves, it is possible for an oil company to make a risk-free profit. Ng and Donker (2013) find that oil and gas reserves and prices cause and affect takeover activity, value, and performance in the Canadian energy industry. They conclude that acquirers are motivated to purchase reserves using takeovers.

Servaes (1994) finds that oil firms tend to overinvest their capital expenditures in the years leading up to takeovers. Ruback (1983), and Wan et al. (2009) explore case studies on oil takeovers. Reid (1973) examines the capital budgeting consequences arising from O & G takeovers.

## 3.0    Hypotheses development

### 3.01    Stock performance

When acquirers purchase a firm for its reserves, they lower business risk, raise production, and increase assets. This reduction in business risk results in a decline in market risk along with a commensurate trimming in stock return. Boyer and Filion (2007) support this theorizing empirically whereby firms who increased their oil and/or gas production suffered lower stock returns. They explained the cause of this outcome is the exercise of real options to produce more energy that decreased the risk and so too should the return. This leads to hypothesis 1:

   H1: Oil and gas acquirer's stock return declines subsequent to a takeover

### 3.02    Purchasing reserves motivation

Kretzschmar and Kirchner (2009) provide market evidence of the effects of reserves location and oil prices on O & G company returns. O & G firm valuation is dependent on reserves. Reserves are the amount of proven and probable stocks that are profitable to extract using available technology. Proven reserves can change in the long-term because of changes in O & G prices, the advancement of extraction technologies, changes in extraction costs, discoveries of new stocks, and the depletion of current stocks.

Figure 1 clearly shows that energy reserves become more valuable over time. This figure also presents the average firm value of proven O&G reserves worldwide from 2001 to 2009[1].

**Figure 1:** Historical Chart of the Average Firm Value of Proven O&G Reserves

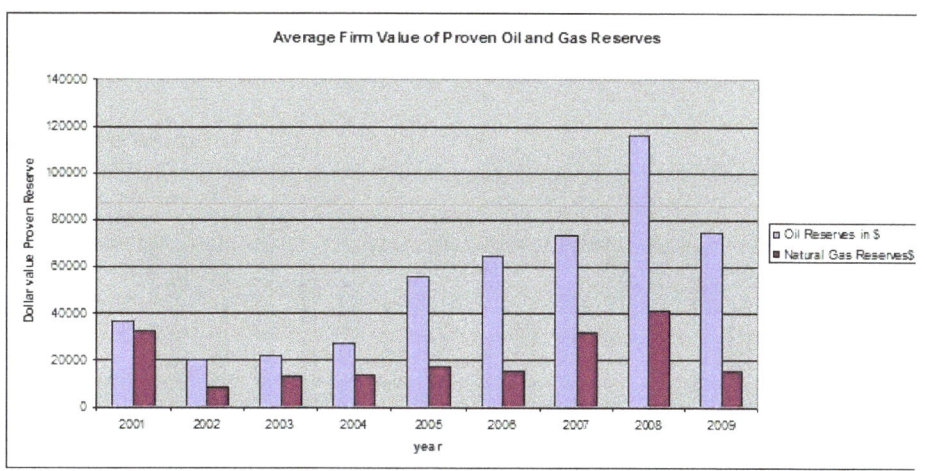

The fact that average proven reserves have increased over time supports our notion that managers have a strong rationale to purchase reserves through M&A because they are an appreciating asset that increases shareholder wealth in the long run.

Figure 2 presents oil and gas takeover deals and energy reserves for oil and gas. As shown, O&G reserves display a negative downward sloping trend, while takeover deals show a positive upward sloping trend. Thus, we suggest that diminishing reserves are related to takeovers. Natural gas reserves appear to trend positively and moves with the number of M&A deals. There appears to be a positive relationship between natural gas reserves and takeovers. Therefore, our second hypothesis is:

H2: Energy reserves relate to takeover activities, value and performance

**Figure 2:** O&G Reserves and Takeover Activity, United States

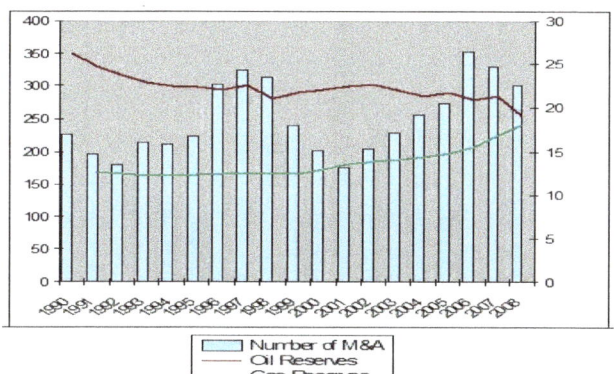

This chart presents takeover activity and industry data on proven O&G reserves for US O&G firms.

3.03 Commodity prices motivation

---

[1] Data are aggregated O&G firms' average proven reserves obtained from Capital IQ. Average firm proven reserves represent a worldwide industry average.

Acquirers may be interested in undertaking a merger when their stock price is high and/or the target stock price is low. Studies supporting this stock market price rationale include Shleifer and Vishny (2003), Rhodes-Kropf et al. (2005), and Dong et al. (2013). Further, Graham and Harvey (2001) surveyed managers who conceded to issuing equity to take advantage of market timing. Baker and Wurgler (2002) give additional evidence endorsing managers employing market timing in selling and buying back their firm's stock. While there are studies supportive of market timing of stock prices in the M&A literature, the notion of managers timing oil and gas commodity prices for takeovers is new and clearly relevant to the energy industry.

Figure 3 illustrates the history of annual takeover activity during this sample period with an overlay of historical crude oil spot prices. We can see a pronounced takeover wave that moves closely with the rise in crude oil prices in 1998 to 2008. While there is an earlier takeover wave between 1995 and 1998, there does not appear to be a corresponding rise in oil prices.

**Figure 3:** Mergers, acquisition deals, and oil prices

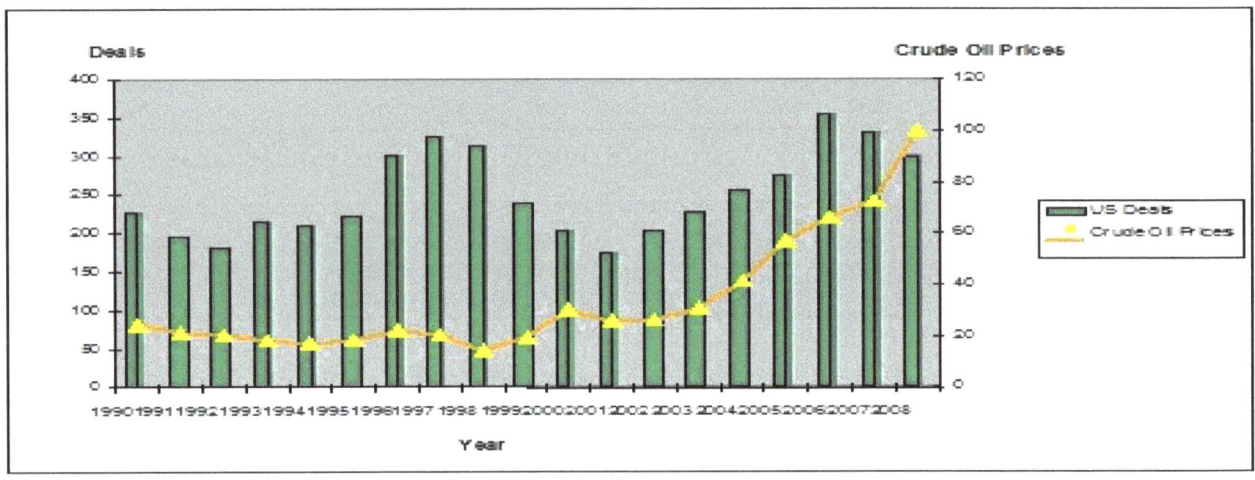

Figure 4 illustrates a history of takeover deal values with historical crude oil spot prices. Examining this figure gives intuition to our hypothesis that energy prices affect deal value and takeover performance. We can clearly see two waves of deal values, 1998 to 2001 and 2003 to 2008. Average deal values move closely with the rise and fall in crude oil prices during these takeover waves.

**Figure 4:** M & A Deal Values and Energy Prices in the United States

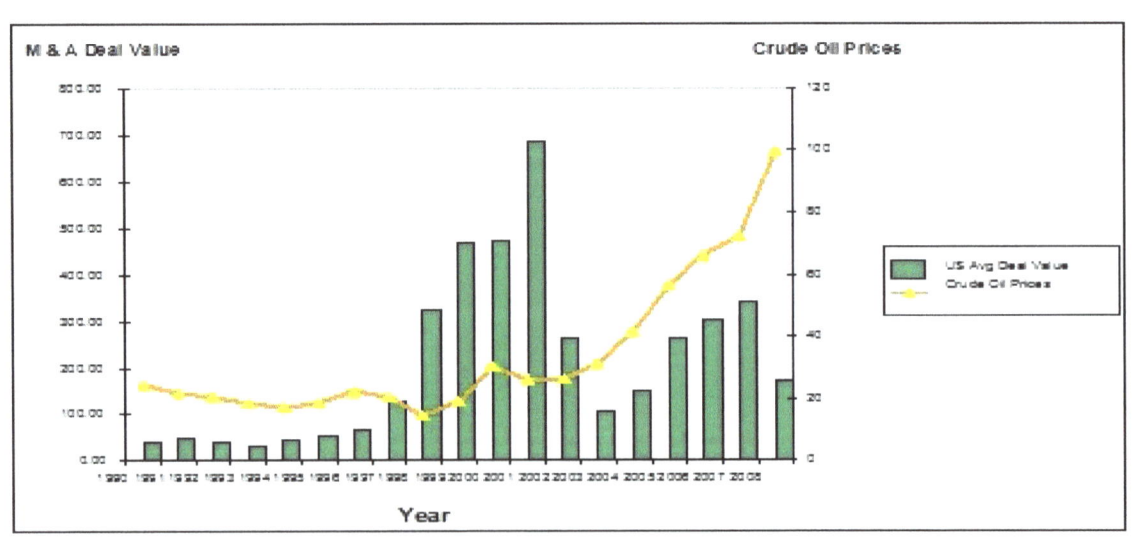

This leads us to hypothesis 3, the commodity prices driven motivation:

       H3: Energy prices relate to takeover activity, value and performance

## 4.0    Sample and methodology

## 4.01    Sample and variables

We began by collecting all M&A deals that occurred in the United States between January 1, 1990 and December 31, 2008 from the Thompson One Banker database excluding the period post-financial crisis. For the energy sector, we include only deals whose acquirer or target have a primary Standard Industrial Classification (SIC) codes corresponding to the energy sector (SIC numbers 1311, 1381, 1382, 1389, 2911, 2990, 4610, 4922, 4923, and 4924).

We eliminate incomplete deals, as well as share repurchases, self-tender offers, and non-controlling stake purchases along with deals in which there were insufficient deal information like discontinuous trading or no stock return. All firms are listed on the New York Stock Exchange (NYSE), NASDAQ, or American Stock Exchange (AMEX). In addition, the sample reduces if the firm stock price fell below $5 per share, or the acquirer return on assets (ROA) is 100% or more (outlier). Stock return data came from Datastream. Our final sample is 183 firms. Table I provides a breakdown of the number of deals and total deal value by year. Appendix 1 provides variable definitions.

**Table 1:** Completed Mergers and Acquisitions by Year US and Foreign Acquirers

| Year | Number | Total Value (USD M) | U.S. | Foreign | Undisclosed |
|------|--------|---------------------|------|---------|-------------|
| 1990 | 226 | 9,002 | 199 | 20 | 9 |
| 1991 | 195 | 9,320 | 187 | 9 | 12 |
| 1992 | 180 | 7,178 | 166 | 5 | 13 |
| 1993 | 214 | 6,700 | 200 | 10 | 7 |
| 1994 | 211 | 9,398 | 197 | 8 | 10 |
| 1995 | 223 | 11,594 | 209 | 11 | 10 |
| 1996 | 302 | 20,711 | 291 | 9 | 16 |
| 1997 | 324 | 41,480 | 295 | 14 | 19 |
| 1998 | 314 | 101,061 | 296 | 15 | 14 |
| 1999 | 239 | 111,825 | 233 | 12 | 4 |
| 2000 | 202 | 95,034 | 194 | 21 | 14 |
| 2001 | 175 | 120,081 | 179 | 16 | 9 |
| 2002 | 204 | 53,205 | 178 | 14 | 23 |
| 2003 | 228 | 24,049 | 206 | 5 | 11 |
| 2004 | 257 | 38,542 | 237 | 13 | 14 |
| 2005 | 274 | 71,784 | 243 | 22 | 14 |
| 2006 | 354 | 107,392 | 310 | 36 | 14 |
| 2007 | 330 | 112,338 | 278 | 38 | 39 |
| 2008 | 100 | 17,005 | 87 | 10 | 14 |
| **Total** | 4552 | 967,697 | 4185 | 288 | 266 |
| **Median** | 226 | 38542 | 206 | 13 | 14 |
| **Mean** | 240 | 50931 | 220 | 15 | 14 |

## 4.02    Estimation techniques

For testing H1, we use a standard event study methodology, market model, from Brown and Warner (1985) to measure the abnormal daily returns around the announcements of a takeover. For the market return benchmark, we use two stock market return indexes, the Russell 1000, and the Standard and Poor's 500. The estimation period is 180 trading days prior to 30 days before the merger announcement day. The event window for abnormal returns is between 15 days before and after the merger announcement.

For testing H2, we determine whether a time series of crude oil and natural gas reserves have a causality effect on takeover activity, value, and performance using the Granger causality test. Historical data (1990–2008) consist of annual crude oil reserves levels and natural gas reported by the US Energy Information Administration. We measure takeover activity as the annual number of M & A deals. We measure takeover value as the average annual deal value calculated as the total value of takeovers divided by the number of completed deals.

For testing H3, we examine the time series of average annual spot price quotes for West Texas Intermediate (WTI) crude oil and Henry Hub Natural Gas from the US Energy Information Administration with lagged values of the yearly number of M & A deals. Specifically, the O & G price changes are relative to the year of the M & A deal; for example, P0-P2 denotes the change in the O&G price between the year of the merger and the price two years before the merger.

We use the Granger causality test to assess whether energy prices positively relate to takeover performance at the industry level. We define takeover performance as the short-term cumulative average abnormal returns CAAR for both acquirers and targets.

Lastly, we use regression analyses to study the effects of reserves and market timing of energy prices on takeover performance. We define a proxy measure for firm-level reserves as the fixed asset ratio (calculated as fixed assets divided by total assets) controlling for size, profit, leverage, deal value, payment, tender or merger, free cash flow, and the market-to-book value ratio.

## 5.0    Results

### 5.01    Takeover performance in the oil industry

Table 2 shows the announcement effect of takeovers on oil and gas stockholder wealth. The cumulative average abnormal returns for US acquirers is significantly negative by one to two percent with CAAR windows of (-1, +1), (0, +1), (0, +3), and (0, +5). Given the insignificant, but still negative sign, CAAR windows of (-1, 0) lends support to no information leakage prior to the M & A event announcement. The insignificant CAAR of 0.03 for the (-10, +10) window suggests the impact of the event is short-lived.

Thus, these results clearly support hypothesis 1; namely, we accept that oil and gas acquirer's stock return declines subsequent to a takeover. In contrast, the US targets greatly benefit from M & A announcements with positive returns with statistical significance (alpha equal to 1%) for all event windows regardless if the acquirer is domestic or foreign. When the acquirer is foreign, it appears that abnormal returns are much lower than when the acquirer is a domestic US company. US target shareholders gain from as much as 8 to 22 percent from takeover announcements.

**Table 2:** Cumulative average abnormal returns for acquirers and targets

| | U.S. ACQUIRERS | | | | U.S. TARGETS | | | |
| | | | | | Acquirer is Domestic | | Acquirer is Foreign | |
| Event Windows | Mean (%) | % + | % - | t-statistic | Mean (%) | t-statistic | Mean (%) | t-statistic |
|---|---|---|---|---|---|---|---|---|
| (-1,+1) | -1.12* | 44 | 56 | -1.642 | 17.53*** | 6.43 | 8.45*** | 3.72 |
| (-1,0) | -0.64 | 47 | 53 | -1.074 | 13.38*** | 5.44 | 8.55*** | 3.82 |
| (0,+1) | -1.54*** | 40 | 60 | -3.132 | 15.02*** | 6.19 | 8.21*** | 3.03 |
| (0,+3) | -1.77*** | 42 | 58 | -2.489 | 15.23*** | 5.52 | 11.64*** | 2.62 |
| (0,+5) | -2.52*** | 39 | 61 | -3.083 | 14.76*** | 5.42 | 11.54*** | 2.61 |
| (-10,+10) | 0.03 | 42 | 58 | 0.010 | 22.36*** | 4.96 | 16.15*** | 3.77 |
| | | | | $n = 125$ | | $N = 150$ | | $n = 17$ |

Table 2 presents short term Cumulative Abnormal Returns (CARS) for US oil and gas acquiring and target firms. We use a standard event study methodology to measure the abnormal returns around the announcements of a takeover deal. We use daily stock returns to estimate the abnormal returns associated with the merger announcement (Brown and Warner, 1985). For each security in our sample, we use the market model. to estimate the abnormal returns $AR_{i,t}$ as follows: $AR_{i,t} = R_{i,t} - (a_i + B R_{m,t})$ where a and B are OLS regression values from the estimation period prior to the event window and $t=0$ is the first trading day after the announcement of the M&A transaction. Specifically, the pre-estimation period is 180 days prior to 30 days before the merger announcement day. *, **, *** indicate estimates are statistically different from zero at the 0.10, 0.05 and 0.01 level of significance respectively.

### 5.02    Energy reserves affect takeovers

Our findings to test hypothesis two, energy reserves are related to takeover activities, value and performance, are shown in Table 3. The conclusions are sensitive to the methodology employed and aspect of the relation. The methods of Spearman correlation and F-statistic indicate that M & A deals are negatively associated with a firm's oil reserves. That is, companies with low oil reserves pursue M & A deals. There appears to be no statistically significant relationship between gas reserves and M & A deals.

Viewing the relation between energy reserves and M & A value, table 3 shows that the correlation technique generates statistical significance. Oil reserves show negative correlation with M & A value; whereas, gas reserves show positive correlation with M & A value. These results endorse hypothesis two on the influence of energy reserves on takeovers.

**Table 3:** Energy reserves effect and relations on takeover activity and value

| Energy Reserves and Takeover Activity | F- Statistic (Probability) | Correlation (Probability) |
|---|---|---|

| | | |
|---|---|---|
| OIL RESERVES does not Granger Cause M&A DEALS | 1.259 (.345) | -.695*** |
| M&A DEALS does not Granger Cause OIL RESERVES | 3.630* (.058) | (.001) |
| GAS RESERVES does not Granger Cause M&A DEALS | 1.178 (.341) | .374 |
| M &A DEALS does not Granger Cause GAS RESERVES | 0.482 (.629) | (.115) |
| **Energy Reserves and Takeover Value** | | |
| OIL RESERVES does not Granger Cause M&A VALUE | 1.272 (.316) | -.654*** |
| M & A VALUE does not Granger Cause OIL RESERVES | 0.077 (.927) | (.002) |
| GAS RESERVES does not Granger Cause M&A VALUE | 0.368 (.553) | .570*** |
| M & A VALUE does not Granger Cause GAS RESERVES | 3.024* (.101) | (.010) |

This table presents results of an analysis of causality direction by Granger Causality test. We test Annual number of takeover deals in Canada, United States and North America against reported proven national oil and gas reserves from 1990 to 2008. This table also presents non-parametric, Spearman's rho correlations between energy reserves and takeover activity and value. The top number is Spearman Rho Correlation, and the bottom number is significance in parenthesis. Source is the United States Energy Information Administration. Takeover deals and reserve variables are made stationary using first order changes, and takeover activity is lagged by two[a] and three[b] years. Test F-statistics and p-values are reported, and significance levels are indicated by * at the 10% level, ** at the 5% level, *** at the 1% level or less.

## 5.03 Energy prices affect takeovers

To analyze hypothesis 3, energy prices relate to takeover activity, value and performance, we present Table 4. Observing the F-statistic for the Granger causality tests for the variable pairings of oil price, oil price change and number of deals we see the reciprocity relationship. That is, oil prices positively relate to number of M & A deals, as well as, oil price changes positively relate to deals. Nevertheless, this outcome does not extend to gas prices to deals nor changes in gas prices to deals.

The far right panel of Table 4 shows the connection between energy prices and mean takeover value. The data establish a statistically significant link between oil prices and M & A value as well as oil price changes and takeover value. Moreover, the investigation of the effect of gas prices to takeover value plus gas price changes to takeover value validates the significant correlation for both pairings.

Table 5 shows our results on the relationship between energy prices and takeover announcement performance. Energy prices, for both acquirers and targets, positively correlate to takeover performance and demonstrate a feedback relationship. The correlations between prices and performance are stronger for targets than for acquirers. This collection of results reinforce acceptance of hypothesis 3 on the effect prices have on takeover performance.

**Table 4:** Causality analysis of energy prices and takeover activity and value

| Energy Prices and Number of Takeover Deals *Null Hypothesis:* | F-statistic (Prob) | Energy Prices and Mean Takeover Value *Null Hypothesis:* | F-Statistic (Prob) |
|---|---|---|---|
| OIL PRICE does not Granger Cause DEALS[a] | 2.852* (.084) | OIL PRICE does not Granger Cause VALUE[a] | 1.722 (0.232) |
| DEALS does not Granger Cause OIL PRICE | 7.289** (.026) | VALUE does not Granger Cause OIL PRICE | 5.283** (0.023) |
| OIL PCHG02 does not Granger Cause DEALS[b] | 5.429** (0.034) | OIL PCHG02 does not Granger Cause VALUE[b] | 3.299* (0.072) |
| DEALS does not Granger Cause OIL PCHG02 | 1.621 (0.284) | VALUE does not Granger Cause OIL PCHG02 | 0.264 (0.772) |
| GAS PRICE does not Granger Cause DEALS[a] | 1.273 (0.315) | GAS PRICE does not Granger Cause VALUE[a] | 1.019 (0.467) |
| DEALS does not Granger Cause GAS PRICE | 0.277 (0.763) | VALUE does not Granger Cause GAS PRICE | 38.477*** (0.000) |
| GAS PCHG02 does not Granger Cause DEALS[b] | 1.094 (0.367) | GAS PCHG02 does not Granger Cause VALUE[b] | 1.161 (0.413) |

| | | | |
|---|---|---|---|
| DEALS does not Granger Cause GAS PCHG02 | 0.989 (0.400) | VALUE does not Granger Cause GAS PCHG02 | 3.578* (0.080) |

This table presents results of an analysis of causality direction by Granger Causality test. Annual number of takeover deals is tested against average annual spot prices for West Texas Intermediate Crude Oil and Henry Hub natural gas. We test Average takeover deal value against average annual spot prices for West Texas Intermediate Crude Oil and Henry Hub natural gas. We make Takeover deals and WTI Crude variables stationary using first order changes, and takeover activity is lagged by two[a] and three[b] years. Test F-statistics and p-values are reported, and significance levels are indicated by  * at the 10% level ** at the 5% level *** at the 1% level, or less

**Table 5:** Causality test of energy prices and m & a performance

| | Panel A: Energy Prices and Acquirer Performance | |
|---|---|---|
| | U.S. (-1,+1) & WTI Crude | U.S. (-10,+10) & WTI Crude |
| Test 1 | 2.906* | 2.703* |
| p value 1 | (0.081) | (0.094) |
| Test 2 | 7.426** | 6.907** |
| p value 2 | (0.024) | (0.032) |
| Result | Feedback Relationship | Feedback Relationship |

| | Panel B: Energy Prices and Target Performance | |
|---|---|---|
| | U.S. (-1,+1) & WTI Crude | U.S. (-10,+10) & WTI Crude |
| Test 1 | 3.676** | 6.389*** |
| p value 1 | (0.046) | (0.008) |
| Test 2 | 9.394*** | 16.327*** |
| p value 2 | (0.009) | (0.000) |
| Result | Feedback Relationship | Feedback Relationship |

This table presents results of an analysis of causality direction by Granger Causality test. Two annualized CAAR windows (-1,+1) and (-10,+10) for targets and acquirers are tested against average annual spot prices for West Texas Intermediate Crude Oil. CAAR windows and WTI Crude variables are made stationary using first order changes, and performance is lagged by one and two years. Test F-statistics and p-values are reported, and significance levels are indicated by  * at the 10% level ** at the 5% level  *** at the 1% level or less

## 5.04    Further analysis on energy prices and performance

We perform further analysis of the link between oil and gas prices versus M & A deals (takeover activity) and CAARs (target performance) for the event window (-3, 0) using the Spearman rho correlation. Table 6 presents these results. Again, we see that M & A deals positively connect with oil prices, oil price changes, gas prices, and the interaction of oil and gas prices. We observe that there is insignificant and close to zero correlation between gas price changes to M & A deals. We explain that a reason for this observation is that the long-term production sales contracts in the gas industry are insensitive to short-term price variations.

**Table 6:** Oil and gas price relations with U.S. M & A deals

| Energy Prices | Takeover Activity, M&A Deals | Acquirer Performance CAR (-2,0) | Target Performance CAR (-3,0) |
|---|---|---|---|
| Oil Price | .315* (.094) | -.028 (.914) | -.687*** (.010) |
| Oil Price Change (P0-P2) | .358* (.066) | -.223 (.390) | -.665** (.013) |
| Oil x Gas Price | .400** (.045) | .007 (.978) | -.676*** (.011) |
| Gas Price | .456** (.025) | .098 (.708) | -.659** (.014) |
| Gas Price Change (P0-P2) | .004 (.989) | .169 (.516) | -.582** (.037) |
| N of years | 19 | 17 | 13 |

This table presents non-parametric, Spearman's rho correlations between energy prices and takeover activity. It also presents same correlations between energy prices and acquirer and target M&A performance. The top number is Spearman Rho Correlation, and the bottom number is (significance). Sample is yearly number of U.S. M&A deals and annual reported spot prices for Oil (WTI Crude) and Gas (Henry Hub) from 1990 to 2008. Sample is yearly average cumulative abnormal returns CAR (-2,0) for acquirers and CAR (-3,0) for targets. ***. Correlation is significant at the 0.01 level or less (2-tailed). **. Correlation is significant at the 0.05 level or less (2-tailed). 1-tailed results are reported for US deals for takeover activity.

Oil and gas prices and their changes appear to have non-significant correlations on acquirer performance (-2, 0) window. However, they negatively correlate to target performance. This would mean that low energy prices are associated with higher target announcement returns. This result appears to be surprising as one would expect higher oil prices to raise the valuation of targets and hence their performance. However, this is in line with the explanation that when energy prices are low, target oil and gas firms are valued lower, and tends to invite more takeover activity from acquirers. With more takeover interest, there is more acquirer competition, bids and higher takeover premiums for target firms, and thus their takeover performance increases.

## 5.05    Commodity price-driven and not stock market price-driven acquisitions

Our conception of the commodity market timing motivation for M&A is very different from stock market-driven acquisitions (Shleifer and Vishny, 2003; Dong et al., 2006; Rhodes-Kropf et al., 2005). In stock market-driven acquisitions, acquirers make takeovers to take advantage of the overpricing of their equity (relative to their targets) and tend to use stock payments. In that theory, acquirers time the market based on stock prices. In the theoretical notion of commodity price-driven acquisitions (Ng and Donker, 2012), acquirers and targets take advantage of changes in energy prices when making takeovers which would *be unrelated* to making stock payment deals. Thus, we hypothesize that energy prices would not relate to stock payments. Rather, at the same time, we hypothesize that market overvaluation is related to stock payments. This would distinguish commodity price driven acquisitions from stock market driven ones.

Table 7 presents the results of the logistic regression analyses of the determinants of stock payments in takeovers. The main variables of interest are market valuation and energy price changes in relation to whether firms make stock payments in a takeover. We use two definitions: market valuation and the top quartile rank of the market valuation of firms.

| **Table 7:** Logistic regression on determinants of stock payment in M&A | | |
|---|---|---|
| | Dependent Variable = Payment with Stock | |
| Independent variables | (1) | (2) |
| Top Quartile, Market to Book | | 1.69** (3.89) |
| Market to Book Value | .41 (1.66) | |
| Size (ln Sales) | -.04 (.02) | -.13 (.30) |
| Fixed asset ratio | 1.64 (.58) | 1.24 (.38) |
| Debt ratio | -1.65 (.88) | -1.16 (.44) |
| ROE | 1.41 (4.08) | 1.25* (3.07) |
| M&A type (merger/tender) | 2.50 (7.05) | 2.48*** (7.02) |
| Oil x Gas Price Change (P0-P2) | .27 (.00) | .31 (.00) |
| Control for years (19) | Yes | Yes |
| N | 85 | 85 |
| Nagelkerke R-Square | .54 | .40 |

This table presents results of logistic regression analysis of determinants of stock payment in United States oil and gas industry takeovers between 1990 and 2008. We report regression coefficients on top, and the Wald test statistics below in parentheses. We calculate Oil and Gas price changes by subtracting yearly spot prices for WTI crude and natural gas. We identify Top quartile of market to book ratio firms as a dummy variable. Significant levels are indicated by *,**,*** representing less than 10%, 5% and 1% levels respectively.

Model two results show overvaluation positively and significantly affects (p<.05) payment with stock as we would expect from a stock market driven motivation for takeovers. Moreover, the result for market-to-book (model 1) shows no relation to stock payment. Concurrently, and indeed, energy price changes show no relationship to stock payment takeovers in both models. Thus, these results suggest that when there is overvaluation of the oil and gas firms, firms do make stock payment in takeovers, and this is in line with the stock market driven acquisition hypothesis (Shleifer and Vishny, 2003). The type of acquisition, merger or tender offer, is positive and significantly related (p<.01) to stock payment. This is consistent with the stylized fact that acquirers make tender offers using stock payment. In sum, we further distinguish the commodity timing motivation for takeovers from the alternative explanation of stock overvaluation (Shleifer and Vishny, 2003; Dong et al., 2006; Rhodes-Kropf et al., 2005).

Energy prices affect commodity price-driven takeovers; in contrast, stock prices affect stock overvaluation takeovers.

## 6.0    Robustness

Our results on these motivations hold true in the presence of the traditional determinants of takeover performance such as synergy gains (negative acquirer performance and no operating performance gains), agency costs (free cash flow is not related), and elevated stock market prices (high valuation is not related). With respect to the estimation of M&A announcement return effects, we also find similar results, namely negative and significant CAARs for acquirers, using the Fama–French three-factor model estimation as shown in Table 7 below.

Using an alternative measure for oil prices, the energy price index results yield a similar conclusion using WTI crude oil prices. Further, we find that multi-collinearity is not an issue that affects our main findings on purchasing reserves and commodity market timing. We examine many other specifications of these regressions with or without White's correction for heteroscedasticity; these analyses yielded qualitatively similar results.

**Table 7:** United States acquirer Fama-French 3 factor model acquirer and target abnormal returns

| Event Windows | ACQUIRERS | | | TARGETS | | | |
|---|---|---|---|---|---|---|---|
| | Mean (%) | Pos:Neg % | z-statistic | Mean (%) | Pos:Neg % | Cross-sec Test | Rank Test |
| CAR(-30,30) | -4.21* | 40:60 | -2.33 | 20.43% | 82:19 | 7.05*** | 3.43*** |
| CAR(-20,20) | -3.60* | 39:61 | -2.19 | 18.97% | 84:17 | 8.59*** | 4.05*** |
| CAR(-10,10) | -2.59* | 42:58 | -1.88 | 16.58% | 82:19 | 8.53*** | 4.43*** |
| CAR (-5,5) | -1.11* | 41:59 | -1.67 | 13.26% | 84:17 | 8.01*** | 5.59*** |
| CAR (-3,3) | -0.47 | 45:55 | -1.00 | 13.09% | 84:17 | 8.18*** | 6.07*** |
| CAR (-1,1) | -1.10* | 40:60 | -2.33 | 11.48% | 83:18 | 7.81*** | 7.46*** |
| CAR (-30,2) | 1.85 | 59:41 | 1.60 | 8.50% | 72:29 | 4.89*** | 2.95** |
| CAR (2,30) | -4.96*** | 31:69 | -4.23 | | | | |
| | *n=148* | | | | | | *n = 101* |

The symbols *,**, and *** denote statistical significance at the 0.10, 0.05, 0.01 levels, respectively, using a generic one-tail test

Fama-French (1993) three-factor model:

$$R_{jt} = \alpha + \beta_j R_{mt} + s_j SMB_t + h_j HML_t + \varepsilon_{jt}$$

$R_{jt}$     = rate of return of the common share of the $j^{th}$ firm on day t

$R_{mt}$     = rate of return of the S&P 500 Composite index on day t

$SMB_t$    = average return on small market-capitalization portfolios minus the average return on three large market- capitalization portfolios

$HML_t$     = average return on two high market-to-book equity portfolios minus the average return on two low market-to-book equity portfolios.

## 7.0    Conclusions and policy implications

We examine merger and acquisition deals in the US oil and gas industry for a nineteen-year period from 1990. We demonstrate that energy reserves and prices affect takeover activity, value, and performance. That is, macroeconomic factors such as energy commodity prices influence corporations in making merger and acquisition decisions as opposed to traditional rationale of synergy gains, agency costs, overvalued equity, and positive net present value capital budgeting decisions. Managers do time the market with favorable energy prices to create takeover opportunities and enhancing reserves. As far as we know, these motivations to execute merger and acquisition deals are unique to the oil and gas industry.  It is possible that these motivations extend to other natural resource production industries, which produce globally traded commodities like forestry and mining.

We find US acquirers of oil and gas firms experience significantly negative returns at the acquisition announcement. Further, M & A values are negatively (positively) associated with oil (gas) reserves. More so, oil prices, but not gas prices, positively relate to the number of M & A deals.

The policy implications for potential target firms are divided into two takeover contexts: 1. those that want to repel takeovers and 2. those that want to sell out to the bidder. Firms wanting to prevent takeover need to put in place defenses and need to be ready when oil prices are high. Companies intending to sell can negotiate more strenuously for a higher price when oil (gas) reserves are low (high).

# References

Baker, W., Wurgler, J., (2002). Market timing and capital structure, Journal of Finance, 57(1): 1-32. http://dx.doi.org/10.1111/1540-6261.00414

Boyer, M. M., Filion, D., (2007). Common and fundamental factors in stock returns of Canadian oil and gas companies. Energy Economics, 29(3): 428-453. http://dx.doi.org/10.1016/j.eneco.2005.12.003

Brown, S. J., Warner, J. B., (1985). Using daily stock returns: the case of event studies. Journal of Financial Economics, 14(1): 3-31. http://dx.doi.org/10.1016/0304-405X(85)90042-X

Bruner, R. F., (2002). Does M & A pay? A survey of evidence for the decision maker. Journal of Applied Finance, 12(1): 48-69.

Dong, M., Hirshleifer, D., Richardson, S., Teoh, S. H., (2006). Does investor misevaluation drive the takeover market? Journal of Finance, 61(2): 725-762. http://dx.doi.org/10.1111/j.1540-6261.2006.00853.x

Fama, E. F., French, K. R., (1993). Common risk factors in the returns on stocks and bonds. Journal of Financial Economics, 33(1): 3-56. http://dx.doi.org/10.1016/0304-405X(93)90023-5

Fan, F., Lin, L., Officer, M. S., (2013). Journal of Financial Economics, 109(1): 24-29. http://dx.doi.org/10.1016/j.jfineco.2013.02.013

Ferguson, R., Popkin, P., (1982). Pulling rabbits out of hats in the oil business- and elsewhere. Financial Analysts Journal, 38(2): 24-27. http://dx.doi.org/10.2469/faj.v38.n2.24

Graham, J. R., Harvey, C. R., (2001). The theory and practice of corporate finance: evidence from the field. Journal of Financial Economics, 60(2/3): 187-243. http://dx.doi.org/10.1016/S0304-405X(01)00044-7

Granger, C. J., (1969). Investigating casual relationships by econometrics models and cross-spectral methods. Econometrica, 37(3): 425-435. http://dx.doi.org/10.2307/1912791

Jensen, M. C., Meckling, W. H., (1976). Theory of the firm: managerial behavior, agency costs and ownership structure. Journal of Financial Economics 3(4): 305-360. http://dx.doi.org/10.1016/S0022-5193(76)80085-9

Jensen, M. J., (1986). Agency costs of free cash flow, corporate finance and the market for takeovers. American Economic Review, 76(2): 323-329.

Jensen, M. C., (1993). The modern industrial revolution and the challenge to internal control systems. Journal of Finance, 48(3): 831-880. http://dx.doi.org/10.1111/j.1540-6261.1993.tb04022.x

Kretzschmar, G. L., Kirchner, A., (2009). Oil price and reserve location – effects on oil and gas sector returns. Global Finance Journal, 20(3): 260-272. http://dx.doi.org/10.1016/j.gfj.2009.08.001

Mitchell, M. L., Mulherin, J. H., (1996). The impact of industry shocks on takeover and restructuring activity. Journal of Financial Economics, 41(2): 193-229. http://dx.doi.org/10.1016/0304-405X(95)00860-H

Ng, A., Donker, H., (2013). Purchasing reserves and commodity market timing as takeover motives in the oil and gas industry. Energy Economics, 37(May): 167-181. http://dx.doi.org/10.1016/j.eneco.2013.01.010

Reid, S. R., (1973). Petroleum mergers, multinational investments, refining capacity and performance in the energy crisis. Financial Management, 2(4): 50-56. http://dx.doi.org/10.2307/3665424

Rhodes-Kropf, M., Robinson, D., Viswanathan, S., (2005). Valuation waves and merger activity: the empirical evidence. Journal of Financial Economics, 77(3): 561-603. http://dx.doi.org/10.1016/j.jfineco.2004.06.015

Ruback, R. S., (1983). The cities service takeover: a case study. Journal of Finance, 38(2): 319-330. http://dx.doi.org/10.1111/j.1540-6261.1983.tb02236.x

Shleifer, A., Vishny, R., (2003). Stock market drive acquisitions. Journal of Financial Economics, 70(3): 295-311. http://dx.doi.org/10.1016/S0304-405X(03)00211-3

Weston, J. F., Johnson, B. A., Siu, J. A., (1999). Mergers and restructuring in the world oil industry. Journal of Energy Finance and Development, 4(2): 149-183. http://dx.doi.org/10.1016/S1085-7443(99)00008-3

Weston, J. F., Kwang, S. C., Hoag, S. E., (1990). Mergers, Restructuring, and Corporate Control. Englewood Cliffs: Prentice Hall.

Wan, K. M., Wong, K. F., (2009). Economic impact of political barriers to cross-border acquisitions: an empirical study of CNOOC's unsuccessful takeover of Unocal. Journal of Corporate Finance, 15(4): 447-468. http://dx.doi.org/10.1016/j.jcorpfin.2009.03.004

**Appendix 1:** Variable Definitions Used in this Study

| Variables | Definition |
| --- | --- |
| Oil Price | Annual reported spot prices for Oil (WTI Crude) from the US Energy Administration |
| Gas Price | Annual reported spot prices for Gas (Henry Hub) |

| Reserves | Annual national proven reserves in US dollars of oil and gas obtained from the US Energy Administration |
| Takeover Deals | Annual number of takeover deals |
| Takeover Value | Average takeover deal value calculated as annual total deal value divided by total number of deals |
| Top Quartile, Market to Book | Dummy of 1, 0 for firms in the top quartile in market to book value |
| Market to Book Value | Market to book value of Equity |
| Size (ln Sales) | Natural log of firm Sales |
| Fixed asset ratio | Fixed assets divided by total assets |
| Debt ratio | Debt to equity ratio as total debt divided by the book value of equity |
| ROE | Return on Equity as Net Income divided by equity |
| M&A type (merger/tender) | Dummy of 1 for tender offers, 0 for merger deals |

# 12

# Religious holidays and analysts forecast optimism: Evidence from MENA countries

Harit Satt [a*]

[a] School of Business Administration, Al Akhawayn University in Ifrane, Morocco
*Corresponding author's email address: H.Satt@aui.ma

| ARTICLE INFO | ABSTRACT |
|---|---|
| Keywords:<br>Analyst Recommendations;<br>Holidays effect;<br>Optimism. | We investigate the effect of religious holidays on analyst recommendation on stock markets in MENA countries stock markets (Morocco, United Arab Emirates, Saudi Arabia, Jordan, Kuwait, Lebanon, Qatar, Algeria, Bahrain) for the period of 2004 to 2015. The result shows that on pre-holidays, analysts tend to issue pessimistic recommendations, and issue optimistic recommendations on post-holidays[1]. Prior literature on day-of –the week effect is consonant with our results which document an increase in stock prices during the week, and a decrease in stock prices over the weekend. We argue that analysts can benefit from the upward trend in stock prices during Post-Holidays by issuing an optimistic recommendation. Analysts may as well benefit from the downward trend in stock prices by issuing pessimistic recommendations on pre-holidays. We also exhibit that our results are more consistent among less experienced analysts and in firms with greater information uncertainty. |

## 1.0    Introduction

Religious values and practice have a significant effect on economic growth (Barro & McCleary 2003). We use Muslim holy days to study the latent mechanism of the effects of holidays. Muslim holy days are particularly useful to restraining the holy day effect. During Ramadan, the study reveals a positive change in stock returns.

Religion affects people in their daily life, in their decision-making, preferences, etc. Religion is a vital concern in people's lives. As religion affects people in such matters, this paper capitalizes on holy events to study the underlying mechanisms behind the holiday effect and to try to learn about how the stock market along with analysts' recommendations can be affected.

There are several Muslim holidays in the Arabic world, but in this paper, we will mainly focus on Eid al-Fitr and Eid al-Adha and Eid-al Mawlid. People in different countries celebrate those events in different ways, but the values and meaning are the same. These holidays are common in a family gathering and going to the mosque, and according to a study conducted in U.S on Health and Retirement, people who visit families and neighbors or go to church are more likely to invest in stocks (Hong et al. 2004). Same findings have been determined using a British panel survey. Following the same logic, we can claim that during these events, social interactions lead to a positive

---

[1] Post holidays are the period before Eid al-Fitr and Eid al-Adha and Eid-al Mawlid; three terms relating to Muslims holy-festival.

impact on the stock's market activities. Studies have been done on the Jewish events, and a study shows that after St. Patrick's and Rosh Hashanah there are positive returns, but returns turn negative after Yom Kippur, Solemn (Yatrakis and Williams, 2010). Other research conducted on lunar months such as Ramadan, Shawal, etc. and their effect on the Tehran stock market and the findings reveal a positive relationship (Ramezani, Pouraghajan and Mardani, 2013).

Several papers have investigated types of behavioral biases in analyst recommendations (Grossman and Stiglitz 1980; Hong, Kubik and Solomon 2000; Hong and Kubik 2003; Trueman 1994; Welch 2000). Some showed that analysts tend to issue more optimistic recommendations, mainly in emerging markets (Lin and McNichols, 1998). The same had been investigated by Satt (2015) addressing that average analyst recommendation is close to a Buy recommendation. Related studies show that analysts are hesitant about issuing negative recommendations since sell or underperform recommendation sum a total of less than 5 percent of all recommendations issued.

Another research shows that more than half of the recommendations issued are favorable and that unfavorable ones only make up less than 15 percent of all recommendations issued in G7 countries (Jegadeesh and Kim, 2006) and Satt (2016). Many regulators and financial economists claim that an analyst's career improvement has little to do with predicting accurately. They report that analysts' recommendations are optimistically biased (Brown, Foster, and Noreen 1985; Stickel 1990; Abarbanell 1991; Dreman and Berry 1995 and Chopra 1998).

There obviously are reasons for these inflated number of optimistic recommendations. These reasons are associated with the work environment, as shown in a study, analysts who are optimistic relative to the norms are less likely to experience unfavorable job separations, the study also revealed that brokerage houses reward analysts who are optimistic and who generate investment banking business and trading commissions (Harrison Hong, Jefrey D. Kubik, 2005). The same study shows that analysts who issue a large fraction of optimistic forecasts on the stocks that they follow are 90 percent more likely to move up the hierarchy. A survey was done by Michaely and Womack (1999) to understand whether the optimism bias is based on conflicts of interest or other justifications like cognitive bias, the answers favored the conflicts of interest explanation. This paper argues that interaction between the need to generate brokerage commissions and accuracy concerns may result in a situation where analysts are tempted to issue relatively more favorable (optimistic) recommendations on post-holidays and relatively less favorable (pessimistic) recommendations on pre-holidays. This situation is known as the Holidays Effect in analyst recommendations. We relied on prior literature on the day-of-the-week effect in return to the state that Holidays' effect can also exist in analyst recommendations (French, 1980; Lakonishok and Smidt, 1988; Solnik and Bousquet, 1990; Barone, 1990). According to it, stock returns tend to be relatively low on Post-Holidays, and relatively high on Pre-Holidays. The day-of-the-week effect in returns also suggests that stock returns are relatively high during the week and tend to decrease during weekends. We affirm that returns are the lowest on Post-Holidays and the highest during the Pre-Holidays. If the statement holds, analysts may be encouraged to issue more favorable recommendations on Post-Holidays because it will relief the pressures from employers concerning the issuance of optimistic recommendations. On the second hand, analysts may also benefit from the movement in stock prices based on their recommendations since it is proven in a study that analysts' recommendations influence stock prices (Loh, R. K., & Stulz, R. M. 2011) Since holiday's effect indicate an increase in stock prices during the week of holidays, analysts can issue pessimistic recommendations during Pre-Holidays to better optimize between pressure to generate brokerage commissions and their reputational concerns. Since there is a downward trend in stock prices over the week of holidays, according to the Holiday's Effect, if the pessimistic recommendation is issued on Post-Holidays their performance may improve.

This paper asserts that there is an impact of holiday's effect on analyst recommendations. Adopting analyst recommendation data from ten Mena stock markets (Morocco, United Arab Emirates, Saudi Arabia, Jordan, Kuwait, Lebanon, Qatar, Algeria, Bahrain and Yemen) during the period between 2004 and 2015, we could reveal that on Post-Holidays (two days after), analysts issue excessively optimistic recommendations, while on Pre-Holidays (two days before), analysts issue excessively pessimistic recommendation.

After controlling for several firm-specific characteristics, these findings are quite vigorous to alternate measure of optimism. We showed that the tendency of analysts issuing a Strong Buy or a Buy recommendation is higher on Pre-Holidays period, and again the tendency of analysts issuing an Underperform or Sell recommendation tend to be higher on Post-Holidays. Our results also show that firms with higher information uncertainty enhance the holiday's effect, we argue that whenever information uncertainty is high, reputational concerns for analysts gets lower. Following the same logic, it is somewhat easier for the analysts to issue optimistically biased recommendations for firms with increased level of information uncertainty. Throughout the paper, we also argue that holidays' effect is more prevalent among less experienced analysts. There is more pressure for these analysts from their employers; in consequence, there is a higher likelihood that they will issue optimistic recommendations. On the other hand, advanced analysts are less likely to issue optimistic recommendations as they are more skilled, they have wider networks and have more expertise. The effect of Muslim holidays on analyst recommendations is a theme that hasn't been much explored, so we would like to mention that to the best of our knowledge, this is the first evidence regarding the theme.

Following sections of this paper will be structured as follow: Section 2 summarizes the data. Section 3 presents an assessment of our arguments, and Section 4 document robustness of our analysis. Section 5 discusses some of the implications of our results and the paper ends with Section 6 where we present conclusions.

## 2.0    The Muslim holidays

The Islamic calendar is used in Muslim countries and by Muslims worldwide to date events and holy days. It is a lunar calendar composed of twelve lunar months a year (Lee and Hamzah 2010). The Gregorian calendar doesn't include Muslim events because they depend on the sighting of the moon, and therefore changes day and month in Gregorian calendar over years (Chowdhury and Mostari 2015).

The lunar Hijrah calendar begins with Muharram which is a holy month for Muslims, but only the 10th day named Ashura is the most sanctified among its days (Satt 2016). One of the most influential events in the Islamic calendar is Eid al-Adha, it is a sacrifice feast which falls on the 10th day of Dhu al-Hijjah. It is the second Eid celebrated worldwide, and is considered to be the holiest. It celebrates the readiness of Ibrahim (Abraham) to sacrifice his son as compliance to God's command before God intervened by sending his angel Jibrail (Gabriel) and communicate that the sacrifice was already accepted. During this period people tend to spend a great amount of money about other months, it is curious to study the behavior of trading activities in such situations (Chowdhury and Mostari 2015).

Ramadan is the 9th month of the Hijri calendar. The date is also revealed by monitoring the moon movements. It is one of the most celebrated worldwide among Muslims (Bialkowsiki, Etabari and Wisniewski 2010). The month of Ramadan is perceived by Muslims throughout the world as a month of fasting to honor the first revelation of the Quran to Muhamad based on Islamic belief. During this holy month of Ramadan people experience a series of emotion; although fasting promotes patience, devotion, and worship, it also intensifies emotions and senses. Theoretically, Ramadan can impact financial markets due to its effect on investors' reasoning.

Eid al-Fitr is an event that points the end of Ramadan. It falls on Shawwal which is the month that follows the month of Ramadan on the Islamic calendar. The event represents the breaking of the fasting month. It is well known for giving charity to needy people, family and friends gathering, and celebrating the accomplishment of the previous month (Al-Hajieh et al. 2011). Eid al-Mawlid an-Nabawī is the date that marks the birth of the Prophet Muhammad which is celebrated on Rabi al-awwal, the third month in the Islamic calendar, specifically the 12th day of that month.

## 3.0    Data

This study attempts to investigate holiday's effect on analyst recommendations. For our analysis, we will be using firms in the MENA region throughout the period between 2004 and 2015. The data will be more discussed in the following sub sections.

### 3.1    Analyst recommendations

I/B/E/S International history recommendation is a database from where investors can obtain different recommendations and estimations from different analysts. We also used this system to gather data about analyst recommendations. I/B/E/S has its 5-point rating system coded as follow: 1= Strong Buy, 2= Buy, 3= Hold, 4= Underperform, 5= Sell. The system converts the original text recommendations to one of the point listed above. The sample used in our study includes three events: Eid al-Fitr, Eid al-Adha, and Eid-al Mawlid. We gathered data for five trading days chosen as follow: 2 trading days before the event, the day of the event, and two days after the event. Table 1 shows the descriptive statistics for analyst recommendations. Our findings are consistent with prior literature showing that analysts issue fewer pessimistic recommendations (Jegadeesh and Kim, 2006).

In our sample, we observed that 20% of recommendations are Underperform or Sell and by far 45% of recommendations are Strong Buy or Buy. According to a study, downgrades lower analyst recommendations and their commissions; therefore, analysts tend to avoid issuing downgrade recommendations Satt (2015). Conflict of interests being the pressure that analysts face into generating brokerage commissions resulted in a significant disparity existing between the percentage of optimistic recommendations being the Strong Buy and Buy and the pessimistic recommendations being Underperform and Sell (Lin and McNichols, 1998; Barber et al., 2007).

**Table 1:** Descriptive statistics for analyst recommendations

| Country | Strong Buy | Buy | Hold | Under perform | Sell | TOTAL |
|---|---|---|---|---|---|---|
| Morocco | 686 | 1217 | 1639 | 681 | 169 | 4393 |
| | (15,63%) | (27,71%) | (37,30%) | (15,51%) | (3,86%) | (100,00%) |
| Saudi Arabia | 443 | 455 | 656 | 32 | 233 | 1820 |
| | (24,37%) | (25,02%) | (36,02%) | (1,77%) | (12,83%) | (100,00%) |
| Jordan | 675 | 1221 | 467 | 87 | 1126 | 3576 |
| Kuwait | 222 | 443 | 223 | 134 | 112 | 1134 |
| | (19,58%) | (39,07%) | (19,66%) | (11,82%) | (9,88%) | 100,00% |
| United Arab Emirates | 1233 | 1124 | 543 | 984 | 847 | 4731 |
| | (26,06%) | (23,76%) | (11,48%) | (20,80%) | (17,90%) | 100,00% |
| Qatar | 983 | 776 | 843 | 633 | 189 | 3424 |
| | (28,71%) | (22,66%) | (24,62%) | (18,49%) | (5,52%) | 100,00% |
| Lebanon | 198 | 244 | 212 | 190 | 113 | 957 |
| | (20,69%) | (25,50%) | (22,15%) | (19,85%) | (11,81%) | 100,00% |
| Algeria | 234 | 211 | 109 | 78 | 88 | 720 |
| | (32,50%) | (29,31%) | (15,14%) | (10,83%) | (12,22%) | 100,00% |
| Yemen | 89 | 142 | 98 | 78 | 26 | 433 |
| | (20,55%) | (32,79%) | (22,63%) | (18,01%) | (6,00%) | 100,00% |
| Bahrain | 234 | 115 | 178 | 89 | 19 | 635 |
| | (36,85%) | (18,11%) | (28,03%) | (14,02%) | (2,99%) | 100,00% |

This table documents the number and percentage of each type of recommendation. The sample period is between 2004 and 2015. The sample consists of firms listed in (Morocco, United Arab Emirates, Saudi Arabia, Jordan, Kuwait, Lebanon, Qatar, Algeria, Bahrain, and Yemen)

### 3.2    Recommendation optimism

Optimism is the tendency to expect the most favorable results and to focus on the most favorable side of an event. In our research optimism is defined as the divergence between the current analyst's recommendation and the previous' month consensus recommendation (Lai and Teo, 2008; Farooq and Taouss, 2012). Where the average of all outstanding recommendations is the consensus recommendation. The consensus recommendation is calculated for firms with a minimum of five outstanding recommendations. When measuring the optimism variable, the lower is the value the higher is the optimism. Table 2 represents the descriptive statistics that shows the recommendation optimism. As predicted, the findings reveal that on Post-Holidays, the recommendations issued have the highest optimism, while on Pre-Holidays, the recommendations issued has the least optimism. We note that on Post-Holidays, the mean and median values of optimism are the lowest; while we report the highest values on Pre-Holidays. The first illustration of day-of-the-week may be suggested in the Table 2.

**Table 2:** Descriptive statistics for optimism

| Statistics | J-2 | J-1 | Holiday | J+1 | J+2 |
|---|---|---|---|---|---|
| Mean | 0.1445 | 0.1357 | 0.1130 | 0.1315 | 0.1031 |
| Median | 0.1300 | 0.0999 | 0.100 | 0.1333 | 0.0833 |
| Standard Deviation | 1.3336 | 1.7693 | 1.5777 | 1.1900 | 1.1133 |
| Total Recommendations | 10331 | 7333 | 6333 | 5333 | 6333 |

This table documents the descriptive statistics for optimism during our sample period on each day. Optimism is the difference between analyst recommendation and last month's consensus recommendation. The sample period is between 2004 and 2015. The sample consists of firms listed in Morocco, Saudi Arabia, Jordan, Kuwait, United Arab Emirates, Qatar, Lebanon, Algeria, Yemen, and Bahrain.

### 3.3    Control variables

The control variables used in this paper are presented as following:
- **SIZE:** We use the log of market capitalization on the day of recommendation to illustrate SIZE. A study done by Lai and Teo (2008) shows that size has a moderate effect on recommendation optimism. Data for SIZE is gathered from the Datastream.

- **LEVERAGE:** is the total debt to total asset ratio. Firms are exposed to distress risk due to the high degree of leverage; therefore, it may have an effect on recommendation optimism. The data for LEVERAGE is gathered from the Worldscope.
- **EPS:** are the earnings per share. Higher earnings attract stock market participants. We argue that higher earnings may lead to higher optimism in recommendations. Data for EPS is obtained from the Worldscope.
- **GROWTH:** We define GROWTH as growth in firm's assets. We argue that firms with high growth attract investors. Greater visibility among investors may induce analysts to issue optimistic recommendations. Data for GROWTH is obtained from the Worldscope.
- **ANALYST:** We define ANALYST as the total number of analysts issuing recommendations for a firm during the year. Lai and Teo (2008) show that the extent of analyst coverage has a moderating effect on recommendation optimism. Data for ANALYST is obtained from the I/B/E/S.
- **EXPERIENCE:** This paper defines EXPERIENCE as the number of years since analyst first appeared in the I/B/E/S database. We argue that higher experience may make analysts more independent, thereby reducing recommendation optimism. Data for EXPERIENCE is obtained from the I/B/E/S.
- **STD:** We define STD as the dispersion in analyst recommendations. Higher dispersion is associated with higher information uncertainty. Ackert and Athanassakos (1997) argue that analysts tend to be more biased whenever information uncertainty is high. Data for STD is obtained from the I/B/E/S.

## 4.0    Methodology

### 4.1    Univariate analysis

This section will investigate the effect of the day-of-the-week on analyst recommendations; whether the relationship exists or not. To be more specific, we intend to exhibit whether analysts issue more or less optimistic recommendations on some specific days. Table 3 shows whether there is a difference in average recommendation optimism (Panel A) and median recommendation optimism (Panel B) using different days of the week. Our findings reveal that on PRE-HOLIDAY, average and median recommendation optimism are significantly less than recommendation optimism on other days. As an instance, we show that the difference between average (median) recommendation optimism on Post-holidays and average (median) recommendation optimism on Pre-holidays is 0.0440 (0.0550). We also report from table 3, panel A, that on Post-Holidays, average recommendation optimism is significantly more than average recommendation optimism on other days. As an instance, we show that the difference between average recommendation optimism on Post-holidays and average recommendation optimism on Thursdays is 0.0236. Our findings reveal that on other days – Tuesdays, Wednesdays, and Thursdays, there is no significant difference on average recommendation optimism.

**Table 3:** Difference between optimism

| Panel A: Difference between average optimism | | | | | |
| --- | --- | --- | --- | --- | --- |
| Days | J-2 | J-1 | Holiday | J+1 | J+2 |
| J-2 | - | | | | |
| J-1 | -0.024*** | - | | | |
| Holiday | -0.0122 | 0.0804 | - | | |
| J+1 | -0.044*** | -0.0022 | -0.0008 | - | |
| J+2 | -0.088*** | -0.0208** | -0.0022*** | -0.0442** | - |
| Panel B: Difference between median optimism | | | | | |
| Days | J-2 | J-1 | Holiday | J+1 | J+2 |
| J-2 | - | | | | |
| J-1 | -0.044*** | - | | | |
| Holiday | -0.040* | -0.0288** | - | | |
| J+1 | -0.0888 | -0.240 | -0.244 | - | |
| J+2 | -0.088*** | -0.020*** | -0.048*** | -0.088** | - |

This table documents the difference between optimism on different days. Optimism is the difference between analyst recommendation and last month's consensus recommendation. Panel A document differences in average optimism and Panel B documents differences in median optimism. The sample period is between 2004 and 2015. The sample consists of firms listed in Morocco, Saudi Arabia, Jordan, Kuwait, United Arab Emirates, Qatar, Lebanon, Algeria, Yemen, and Bahrain. 1% significance is represented by ***, 5% significance by **, and 10% significance by *.

### 4.2    Multivariate analysis

Our hypothesis indicates that day-of-the-effect exists in analyst recommendations. For us to test the theory, we assess a regression with (OPT) as the dependent variable being the optimism of analysts and four other dummy variables which will represent the different days of the week.

- If the recommendation is issued on Post-Holidays, POST-HOLIDAYS receives the value of 1. Otherwise, it is attributed the value of 0.
- If the recommendation is issued on Tuesday, TUESDAY receives the value of 1. Otherwise, it is attributed the value of 0.
- If the recommendation is issued on Thursday, THURSDAY receives the value of 1. Otherwise, it is attributed the value of 0.

If the recommendation is issued on Pre-Holidays, PRE-HOLIDAYS receives the value of 1. Otherwise it is attributed the value of 0. As mentioned above, SIZE, LEVERAGE, GROWTH, EPS, ANALYST, and EXPERIENCE are also included in the regression as control variables. To complete out regression equations, we also insert year dummies (YDUM), industry dummies (IDUM), and country dummies (CDUM). Our regression equations are presented as follow:

$$OPT = \alpha + \beta_1(MONDAY) + \beta_2(TUESDAY) + \beta_3(THURSDAY) + \beta_4(FRIDAY) +$$
$$\sum_{Year} \beta^{Year}(YDUM) + \sum_{Ind} \beta^{Ind}(IDUM) + \sum_{Ctry} \beta^{Ctry}(CDUM) + \varepsilon \tag{1}$$

$$OPT = \alpha + \beta_1(MONDAY) + \beta_2(TUESDAY) + \beta_3(THURSDAY) + \beta_4(FRIDAY) + \beta_5(SIZE)$$
$$+ \sum_{Year} \beta^{Year}(YDUM) + \sum_{Ind} \beta^{Ind}(IDUM) + \sum_{Ctry} \beta^{Ctry}(CDUM) + \varepsilon \tag{2}$$

And

$$OPT = \alpha + \beta_1(MONDAY) + \beta_2(TUESDAY) + \beta_3(THURSDAY) + \beta_4(FRIDAY) + \beta_5(SIZE)$$
$$+ \beta_6(LEVERAGE) + \beta_7(EPS) + \beta_8(GROWTH) + \beta_9(ANALYST) + \beta_{10}(EXPERIENCE) \tag{3}$$
$$+ \sum_{Year} \beta^{Year}(YDUM) + \sum_{Ind} \beta^{Ind}(IDUM) + \sum_{Ctry} \beta^{Ctry}(CDUM) + \varepsilon$$

Table 4 shows the results of our analysis. Our findings show the presence of a day-of-the-week effect in analyst recommendations; we assert that the most optimistic recommendations are issued on Post-Holidays period. For all equations, the coefficient of POST-HOLIDAYS is significantly negative. We suggest that the day-of-the-week effect in returns is the source of the day-of-the-week effect in analyst recommendations.

**Table 4:** Day-of-the-week effect and optimism in analyst recommendations

|                     | Equation (1) | Equation (2) | Equation (3) |
|---------------------|--------------|--------------|--------------|
| J-2                 | -0.0222**    | -0.0444**    | -0.0844**    |
| J-1                 | -0.0024      | -0.0044      | -0.0088      |
| J+1                 | 0.0222       | 0.0024       | -0.0002      |
| J+2                 | 0.0444***    | 0.0222***    | 0.0288**     |
| Size                |              | 0.0044***    | 0.00244*     |
| Leverage            |              |              | -0.0044**    |
| Eps                 |              |              | -0.0004      |
| Growth              |              |              | -0.0088***   |
| Analyst             |              |              | 0.0008       |
| Experience          |              |              | -0.0088***   |
| Std                 |              |              | -0.4888***   |
| Industry Dummies    | Yes          | Yes          | Yes          |
| Year Dummies        | Yes          | Yes          | Yes          |
| Country Dummies     | Yes          | Yes          | Yes          |
| No. of Observations | 2440         | 8888         | 4443         |
| F-value             | 18.44        | 24.22        | 34.00        |
| Adjusted R-square   | 0.04         | 0.04         | 0.022        |

This table uses Equation (1), Equation (2), and Equation (3) to document the relationship between recommendation optimism and two days before and after the holiday. The sample period is between 2004 and 2015. The sample consists of firms listed in Morocco, Saudi Arabia, Jordan, Kuwait, United Arab Emirates, Qatar, Lebanon, Algeria, Yemen, and Bahrain. 1% significance is represented by ***, 5% significance by **, and 10% significance by *.

For the analysts to amend between optimistic biases in their recommendations and their reputation as an unbiased investment advisor, Post-Holidays period is for analysts the most favorable period to issue the most optimistic recommendations. Analysts will be relieving pressure from employers to issue optimistic recommendations, at the same time assure that return would trend upwards in the short-term.

Our findings also indicate that recommendations issued on Pre-holidays are the most pessimistic. For all equations, the coefficient of PRE-HOLIDAYS is significantly negative. We suggest that by issuing bulk of unfavorable recommendations on Pre-Holidays, analysts expect the short-term returns would trend downwards.

## 4.3    Robustness checks

### 4.3.1    Day-of-the-week effect and optimism in analyst recommendations (alternate measure)

To check the robustness, we re-estimate Equation (1), Equation (2), and Equation (3) using an alternate measure of optimism being the difference between analyst's current recommendation and the median of last month's outstanding recommendations. The results are shown in Table 5 which are qualitatively similar to those shown in Table 4. We report higher optimism in recommendations issued on Post-holidays and lower optimism in recommendations issued on Pre-holidays. All equations reveal a negative coefficient of POST-HOLIDAYS and a positive coefficient of PRE-HOLIDAYS.

**Table 5:** Day-of-the-week effect and optimism in analyst recommendations (alternate measure)

| | Equation (1) | Equation (2) | Equation (3) |
|---|---|---|---|
| J-2 | -0.0022** | -0.0044** | -0.0022*** |
| J-0 | -0.0088 | -0.0044 | -0.0086 |
| J+1 | 0.0044 | 0.0024 | -0.0008 |
| J+2 | 0.0220*** | 0.0028*** | 0.0066* |
| Size | | 0.0022 | 0.0022*** |
| Leverage | | | -0.0000** |
| Eps | | | 0.0004 |
| Growth | | | -0.0000*** |
| Analyst | | | -0.0048*** |
| Experience | | | -0.0044*** |
| Std | | | -0.0668*** |
| Industry Dummies | Yes | Yes | Yes |
| Year Dummies | Yes | Yes | Yes |
| Country Dummies | Yes | Yes | Yes |
| No. of Observations | 2144 | 6022 | 4200 |
| F-value | 20.22 | 06.64 | 22.22 |
| Adjusted R-square | 0.04 | 0.01 | 0.04 |

This table uses Equation (1), Equation (2), and Equation (3) to document the relationship between recommendation optimism (using an alternate measure) and two days before and after the holiday. The sample period is between 2004 and 2015. The sample consists of firms listed in Morocco, Saudi Arabia, Jordan, Kuwait, United Arab Emirates, Qatar, Lebanon, Algeria, Yemen, and Bahrain. 1% significance is represented by ***, 5% significance by **, and 10% significance by *.

### 4.3.2    Day-of-the-week effect and optimism in analyst recommendations (quantile regression approach)

Our analysis entails that any analyzed point on the conditional distribution results in the same estimates of the relationship between optimism in an analyst recommendation and day-of-the-week effect. While testing particularly for linearity and the LINE assumptions, we conclude that the linearity assumption holds. We applied a quantile regression to test the empirical effectiveness of the assumption and to examine day-of-the-week at different points of conditional distribution of optimism in analyst recommendations; the quantile regression is implemented at five quantiles (0.10, 0.30, 0.50, 0.70, and 0.90).

Table 6 reports the results of our analysis, proving that the relationship between recommendations issued on Post-Holidays and optimism is accurate only in lower quantiles. POST-HOLIDAYS for the 10th, 30th, and 50th quantile report a negative coefficient. As for the two quantiles left, namely the 70th and 90th. We reveal insignificant coefficient of POST-HOLIDAYS. By comparing Table 4 and with our results, we report that at the 10th and 30th quantile, the relationship is underestimated. We also proved that the relationship between recommendations issued on Pre-Holidays and optimism is only valid in higher quantiles. PRE-HOLIDAYS for the 50th, 70th, and 90th quantile report a positive coefficient. As for the two quantiles left, namely the 10th and 30th. We reveal insignificant coefficient of PRE-HOLIDAYS. By comparing Table 4 and with our results, we report that at the 50th, 70th and 90th quantile, OLS regression underestimates the relationship.

**Table 6:** Day-of-the-week effect and optimism in analyst recommendations (quantile regression approach)

| | 0.10 | 0.30 | 0.50 | 0.70 | 0.90 |
|---|---|---|---|---|---|
| J-2 | -0.0684*** | -0.0242*** | -0.0222* | -0.0022 | -0.0044 |
| J-1 | -0.0222 | -0.0022 | 0.0022 | 0.0022 | -0.0028 |
| J+1 | -0.0024*** | -0.0022 | -0.0066 | 0.0222 | 0.0066 |
| J+2 | -0.0266 | 0.0066 | 0.0224** | 0.0222** | 0.0468*** |
| Size | 0.0448*** | 0.0486*** | -0.0004* | -0.0086** | -0.0868*** |
| Leverage | -0.0088 | -0.0044*** | -0.0008 | -0.0002** | 0.0022 |
| Eps | 0.0008 | -0.0008 | -0.0088* | -0.0028*** | -0.0048 |
| Growth | -0.0088*** | -0.0020*** | -0.0002*** | -0.00888*** | -0.0048*** |
| Analyst | -0.0044** | -0.0022 | 0.0002** | -0.00668 | 0.0066*** |
| Experience | -0.0024** | -0.0088** | -0.0044*** | -0.00444*** | -0.0088*** |
| Std | -0.4222*** | -0.4468** | -0.2220*** | -0.6886*** | -0.2224*** |
| Industry Dummies | Yes | Yes | Yes | Yes | Yes |
| Year Dummies | Yes | Yes | Yes | Yes | Yes |
| Country Dummies | Yes | Yes | Yes | Yes | Yes |
| No. of Observations | 2882 | 4862 | 4822 | 1882 | 2862 |
| F-value | | | | | |
| Adjusted R-square | 0.022 | 0.028 | 0.008 | 0.022 | 0.008 |

This table uses quantile regression and Equation (3) to document the relationship between recommendation optimism and two days before and after the holiday. The sample period is between 2004 and 2015. The sample consists of firms listed in Morocco, Saudi Arabia, Jordan, Kuwait, United Arab Emirates, Qatar, Lebanon, Algeria, Yemen, and Bahrain. 1% significance is represented by ***, 5% significance by **, and 10% significance by *.

### 4.3.3   Day-of-the-week effect and optimism in analyst recommendations (level of recommendations)

As a last robustness check, we substitute optimism measure with the level of recommendations. Given that level of recommendation is an ordinal variable, we use ordered probit regressions to estimate Equation (1), Equation (2), and Equation (3).[2] Table 7 reports the results of our analysis, showing that on Pre-holidays, analysts are more likely to issue pessimistic recommendations (Underperform and Sell). For all equations, we state a significantly positive coefficient of PRE-HOLIDAYS. Our findings from Equation (6) being the most comprehensive equation, shows that on Post-holidays, analysts are more likely to issue optimistic recommendations (Strong Buy and Buy)

**Table 7:** Day-of-the-week effect and optimism in analyst recommendations (level of recommendations)

| | Equation (4) | Equation (5) | Equation (6) |
|---|---|---|---|
| J-2 | -0.0044 | -0.0088 | -0.0224** |
| J-1 | 0.0006 | 0.0086 | -0.0026 |
| J+1 | -0.0006 | -0.0022 | -0.0088 |
| J+2 | 0.0660*** | 0.0224*** | 0.0888*** |
| Size | | -0.0444*** | -0.0444*** |
| Leverage | | | 0.0008*** |
| Eps | | | -0.0044*** |
| Growth | | | -0.0044*** |
| Analyst | | | 0.0088*** |
| Experience | | | -0.0066*** |
| Std | | | 0.2242*** |
| Industry Dummies | Yes | Yes | Yes |
| Year Dummies | Yes | Yes | Yes |
| Country Dummies | Yes | Yes | Yes |
| No. of Observations | 6620 | 1888 | 6822 |
| Wald Chi2 | 244.22 | 222.46 | 420.22 |
| Pseudo R-square | 0.02 | 0.02 | 0.08 |

This table uses Equation (1), Equation (2), and Equation (3) to document the relationship between the level of recommendations and two days before and after the holiday. The sample period is between 2004 and 2015. The sample consists of firms listed in Morocco, Saudi Arabia, Jordan, Kuwait, United Arab Emirates, Qatar, Lebanon, Algeria, Yemen, and Bahrain. 1% significance is represented by ***, 5% significance by **, and 10% significance by *.

---

[2] Level of recommendation is coded as follows: 1 for Strong Buy, 2 for Buy, 3 for Hold, 4 for Underperform, and 5 for Sell.

## 4.4    Discussion of results

### 4.4.1    Information uncertainty and day-of-the-week effect

Prior literature shows that stocks with higher uncertainty are more exposed to behavioral biases Ackert and Athanassakos (1997). They argue that the higher is the information uncertainty, the higher is the tendency for analysts to be biased. Once there is information uncertainty, reputation tends to be less of concern for analysts. As a result, certain information environment could be less exposed to day-of-the-week effect. To react to these possibilities. To react to these concerns, we break our sample into –first sub-sample formed by firms with above average dispersion in analyst recommendations and the second sub-sample is formed of firms with below average dispersion in analyst recommendations.

Equation (3) is re-estimated for both sub-samples. Table 8 reports the results of our analysis, showing that in firms with higher information uncertainty, the day-of-the-week effect is absent. For sub-sample with below average dispersion in analyst recommendations, we showed insignificant coefficients of both PRE-HOLIDAYS and POST-HOLIDAYS. Table 8 reveals that firms with higher information uncertainty are the ones exposed to day-of-the-week effect. For this sub-sample, we showed significant coefficients of both PRE-HOLIDAYS and POST-HOLIDAYS. Our argument that once information uncertainty is high, behavioral biases are more present, holds is consistent with Ackert and Athanassakos (1997).

| **Table 8:** Information uncertainty and day-of-the-week effect | | |
|---|---|---|
| | Low Information Uncertainty | High Information Uncertainty |
| J-2 | -0.0000** | -0.0224** |
| J-1 | -0.0224* | 0.0466** |
| J+1 | -0.0088** | 0.0022* |
| J+2 | 0.0044* | 0.0866*** |
| Size | 0.0082** | 0.0088* |
| Leverage | -0.0004** | -0.0022** |
| Eps | -0.0026 | -0.0004* |
| Growth | -0.0066*** | -0.0022*** |
| Analyst | 0.0044 | 0.0008* |
| Experience | -0.0088*** | -0.0066*** |
| Std | -0.4644*** | -0.4466*** |
| Industry Dummies | Yes | Yes |
| Year Dummies | Yes | Yes |
| Country Dummies | Yes | Yes |
| No. of Observations | 4464 | 2286 |
| F-value | 8.40 | 8.68 |
| Adjusted R-square | 0.066 | 0.080 |

This table uses Equation (3) to document the effect of information uncertainty on holidays' effect. The sample period is between 2004 and 2015. The sample consists of firms listed in Morocco, Saudi Arabia, Jordan, Kuwait, United Arab Emirates, Qatar, Lebanon, Algeria, Yemen, and Bahrain. 1% significance is represented by ***, 5% significance by **, and 10% significance by *.

### 4.4.2    Analyst experience and day-of-the-week effect

Our findings are restricted to analysts with less experience, which waken our concerns about the matter. Analysts with less experience may be more susceptible to pressures from their employers. Analysts with more experience, considering their skills and larger networks; in contrast, may be less susceptible to pressures from their employers. To react to these concerns, we break our sample into –first sub-sample formed by analysts with above average experience and the second sub-sample is formed of firms with below average experience. Equation (3) is re-estimated for both sub-samples. Table 9 shows the results of our analysis, showing that analysts with low experience tend to be more optimistic.

For the recommendations issued by less experienced analysts, we state a significantly negative coefficient of POST-HOLIDAYS. Our argument is stating that because of the pressures faced by employers, less experienced analysts are more likely to issue optimistic recommendations. We also argue that on PRE-HOLIDAYS, analysts with more experience tend to issue less optimistic recommendations. For the recommendations issue by more experienced analysts on PRE-HOLIDAYS, we report a significantly positive coefficient. We, therefore, argue that due to the skills and larger networks that analysts with high experience own, they can oppose the pressures from employers to issue optimistic recommendations.

| Table 9: Analyst experience and day-of-the-week effect | | |
|---|---|---|
| | Low Analyst Experience | High Analyst Experience |
| J-2 | -0.0447*** | 0.0024 |
| J-1 | -0.0444** | 0.0224 |
| J+1 | -0.0667** | 0.0944 |
| J+2 | 0.0046 | 0.0666*** |
| Size | 0.0066 | 0.0044* |
| Leverage | -0.0066 | -0.0046*** |
| Eps | -0.0006* | -0.0066 |
| Growth | -0.0066*** | -0.0044*** |
| Analyst | 0.0022 | 0.0044 |
| Experience | 0.0006*** | -0.0046*** |
| Std | -0.6666*** | -0.4664*** |
| Industry Dummies | Yes | Yes |
| Year Dummies | Yes | Yes |
| Country Dummies | Yes | Yes |
| No. of Observations | 1444 | 4667 |
| F-value | 14.44 | 34.26 |
| Adjusted R-square | 0.004 | 0.024 |

This table uses Equation (3) to document the effect of analyst experience on holidays' effect. The sample period is between 2004 and 2015. The sample consists of firms listed in Morocco, Saudi Arabia, Jordan, Kuwait, United Arab Emirates, Qatar, Lebanon, Algeria, Yemen, and Bahrain. 1% significance is represented by ***, 5% significance by **, and 10% significance by *.

## 5.0    Conclusions

This paper investigates the presence of religious holidays effect in analyst recommendations in MENA countries' stock markets (Morocco, United Arab Emirates, Saudi Arabia, Jordan, Kuwait, Lebanon, Qatar, Algeria, Bahrain) during the period between 2004 and 2015. Our findings reveal that on Pre-Holidays, analysts tend to issue pessimistic recommendations, and issue optimistic recommendations on Post-Holidays. Our results are robust to alternate measures of optimism and after controlling for various firm-specific characteristics. Prior literature on day-of –the week effect is consonant with our results which document an increase in stock prices during the week, and a slight decrease in stock prices over the weekend. We argue that analysts can benefit from the upward trend in stock prices during Post-Holidays by issuing an optimistic recommendation. Analysts may as well benefit from the downward trend in stock prices by issuing pessimistic recommendations on Pre-Holidays. Last but not least we also showed that our findings are more evident among analyst with less experience and in firms with higher information uncertainty. For eventual research, we suggest constructing buy-and-hold portfolios that are designed by relying on recommendations issued on each day of the week and computing their performance.

## References

Ajinkya, B. B., R. K. Atiase, and M. J. Gift, 1991, Volume of Trading and the Dispersion in Financial Analysts' Earnings Forecasts, Accounting Review 66, 389-401.

Al-Hajieh, H. Redhead, K. & Rodgers, T. (2011). Investor sentiment and calendar anomaly effects: A case study of the impact of Ramadan on Islamic Middle Eastern markets. Research in International Business and Finance, 25, 345– 356. http://dx.doi.org/10.1016/j.ribaf.2011.03.004

Barber, B., R. Lehavy, M. McNichols, and B. Trueman, 2001, Can Investors Profit from the Prophets? Security Analyst Recommendations and Stock Returns, Journal of Finance 56, 531-563. http://dx.doi.org/10.1111/0022-1082.00336

Barber, B., R. Lehavy, and B. Trueman, 2007, Comparing the Stock Recommendation Performance of Investment Banks and Independent Research Firms, Journal of Financial Economics 85, 490517. http://dx.doi.org/10.1016/j.jfineco.2005.09.004

Barro, R. J., & McCleary, R. (2003). Religion and economic growth (No. w9682). National Bureau of Economic Research. http://dx.doi.org/10.3386/w9682

Bialkowski, J., Etebari, A., & Wisniewski, T.P., (2010) Piety and Profits: stock market anomaly during the Muslim Holy month. Working paper No. 52/2010, University of Canterbury Christchurch, New Zealand.

Brown, Phillip, George Foster, and Eric Noreen, 1985, Security Analyst Multi-Year Earnings Forecasts and the Capital Market, American Accounting Association: Sarasota, FL.

Chan, L. K. C., J. Karceski, and J. Lakonishok, 2007, Analysts' Conflicts of Interest and Biases in Earnings Forecasts, Journal of Financial and Quantitative Analysis 42, 893-914 http://dx.doi.org/10.1017/S0022109000003434

Chowdhury, T. S. &Mostari, S. (2015). Impact of Eid-ul-Azha on Market Return in Dhaka Stock Exchange. Journal of Business and Management. Volume 17, Issue 2. PP 25-29.

Clement, M. B., and S. Y. Tse, 2005, Financial Analyst Characteristics and Herding Behavior in Forecasting, Journal of Finance 60, 307-341. http://dx.doi.org/10.1111/j.1540-6261.2005.00731.x

Francis, J., Philbrick, D., 1993. Analysts' decisions as product of multi-task environment. Journal of Accounting Research. 31, 216-230. http://dx.doi.org/10.2307/2491271

Hayes, R. M., 1998, The Impact of Trading Commission Incentives on Analysts' Stock Coverage Decisions and Earnings Forecasts, Journal of Accounting Research 36, 299-320. http://dx.doi.org/10.2307/2491479

Heflin, F., Subramanyam, K.R. and Zhang Y., 2003. Regulation FD and the financial information environment: early evidence. Accounting Review. 78, 1-37. http://dx.doi.org/10.2308/accr.2003.78.1.1

Hong, H. and Kubik, J., 2003. Analyzing the analysts: career concerns and biased earnings forecasts Journal of Finance. 58, 313-351. http://dx.doi.org/10.1111/1540-6261.00526

Hong, H., Kubik, J. D., Stein, J. C., Lins, K., Shleifer, A., & Wurgler, J. (2002). Thy Neighbor's Portfolio: Word-of-Mouth Effects. In Ohio State University.

Hong, H., Kubik, J. D., & Stein, J. C. (2004). Social interaction and stock-market participation. The journal of finance, 59(1), 137-163. http://dx.doi.org/10.1111/j.1540-6261.2004.00629.x

Jackson, A., 2005. Trade generation, reputation and sell-side analysis. Journal of Finance. 60, 673-717. http://dx.doi.org/10.1111/j.1540-6261.2005.00743.x

Jegadeesh, N., J. Kim, S. D. Krische, and C. M. C. Lee, 2004, Analyzing the Analysts: When do Recommendations Add Value? Journal of Finance 59, 1083-1124. http://dx.doi.org/10.1111/j.1540-6261.2004.00657.x

Jegadeesh, N., & Kim, W. (2010). Do analysts herd? An analysis of recommendations and market reactions. Review of Financial Studies, 23(2), 901-937. http://dx.doi.org/10.1093/rfs/hhp093

Lee, M. H. &Hamzah, N. A. (2010). Calendar variation model based on Time Series on Regression for sales forecasts: The Ramadhan effects. Proceedings of the Regional Conference Statistical Sciences (RCSS'10), 30-41 ISBN 978-967-363-157-5.

Lim, T., (2001). Rationality and analysts' forecast bias. Journal of Finance. 56, 369-385. http://dx.doi.org/10.1111/0022-1082.00329

Ljungqvist, A., F. Marston, and W. J. Wilhelm Jr., 2006, Competing for Securities Underwriting Mandates: Banking Relationships and Analyst Recommendations, Journal of Finance 61, 301-340. http://dx.doi.org/10.1111/j.1540-6261.2006.00837.x

Ljungqvist, A., F. Marston, and W. J. Wilhelm Jr., 2009, Scaling the Hierarchy: How and Why Investment Banks Compete for Syndicate Co-Management Appointments, Review of Financial Studies 22, 39774007 http://dx.doi.org/10.1093/rfs/hhn106

Loh, R. K., & Stulz, R. M. (2011). When are analyst recommendation changes influential? Review of Financial Studies, 24(2), 593-627. http://dx.doi.org/10.1093/rfs/hhq094

Malmendier, U., and D. Shanthikumar, 2007, Are Small Investors Naïve about Incentives? Journal of Financial Economics 85, 457-489. http://dx.doi.org/10.1016/j.jfineco.2007.02.001

Maremont, M., and C. Bray, 2004, In Latest Tyco Twist, Favored Analyst got Private Eye, Gratis, Wall Street Journal, 21 January, A1. Mehran, H., and R. Stulz, 2007, The Economics of Conflicts of Interest in Financial Institutions, Journal of Financial Economics 85, 267-296.

Michaely, R., and Womack K., 1999, Conflict of Interest and the Credibility of Underwriter Analyst Recommendations, Review of Financial Studies 12, 653-686. http://dx.doi.org/10.1093/rfs/12.4.653

Michaely, R., and Womack K., 1999, Conflict of interest and the credibility of underwriter analyst recommendations, Review of Financial Studies 12, 653-686. http://dx.doi.org/10.1093/rfs/12.4.653

Ramezani, A., A., H. (2013). "Studying Impact of Ramadanon Stock Exchange Index: Case of Iran", World of Sciences Journal, 1(12), 46-54.

Satt, H., (2016) "Holidays' effect and optimism in analyst recommendations: Evidence from Europe". Corporate Ownership and Control journal. Volume 13, issue 03.

Satt, H., (2016) "Do high levels of analyst following improve companies' credit ratings: Evidence from MENA region?" Forthcoming, Journal of Financial Studies & Research.

Satt, H., (2016) "The Impact of analysts' recommendations on the Cost of Debt: International Evidence." European Journal of Contemporary Economics and Management. May 2016 Edition Vol.3 No.1. ISSN: 2411-443X.

Satt, H., (2015) "The Impact of positive cash operating activities on bonds' pricing: International Evidence." Journal of Corporate and Ownership Control, 12.4, pp. 708-717.

Usmani, M.T. (2014) Muharram: The Start of the Islamic Calendar 10/24/2014 IC0303-1877. http://www.islamicity.com/articles/Articles.asp

Yaktrakis, P., & Williams, A. (2010). The Jewish Holiday Effect: Sell Rosh Hashanah, Buy Yom Kippur. Advances in Business Research, 1(1), 45-52.

# 13

# Still on board configuration: SEC recommendations and the efficiency of adhering firms in Nigeria

Bello Lawal[a]*

[a] Glasgow Caledonian University, Scotland, United Kingdom
* Corresponding author's email address: lawal.bello@nlng.com

| ARTICLE INFO | ABSTRACT |
|---|---|
| Keywords:<br>Board structure;<br>Corporate governance;<br>Firm performance;<br>Macroeconomic variables. | This paper scrutinizes the effects of adherence to an encoded board configuration on firm efficiency in terms operational and financial performances using an integrated research framework that combines four distinct theories including agency, stewardship, stakeholders and resource dependency models. The research explores three main aspects of compliance outcomes; benefits accrued to conforming firms in terms of enhanced efficiency and market value, board level drivers as well as the external moderators of these benefits using a sample of 127 listed companies on the Nigerian Stock Exchange covering for the period of 1999-2010. Result show that board independence, directors' cognitive competencies as measured in terms of their educational qualifications and professional experiences are positively associated with efficient management of assets (ROA) and firm stock marketability (Tobin's q). I find no substantive empirical evidence to suggest that either the adoption of specific leadership structure or directors' ethnic representation affects firm performance. Moreover, country-level macroeconomic variables, especially the degree of economic openness play a significant role in determining the strength of association between board structure variables and firm performance measures. |

## 1.0    Introduction

The spates of corporate scandals of the last twenty-five years had motivated significant drive towards institutional reforms particularly in numerous developed countries (e.g. Toshiba, Olympus, Enron, Lehman Brothers and WorldCom). One of the well cited examples of government response to these scandals is the passage into law of the famous Sarbanes-Oxley Act (2002) which is widely considered to be the most sweeping corporate governance regulation in the past 70 years (Bulent 2009). These waves of institutional reforms in the developed countries have motivated similar moves in the emerging markets. In Nigeria, where the quest for Direct Foreign Investments (FDIs) have heighten since the return to democratic governance in 1999, corporate governance has assumed a vital topic of public debate with significant focus on the internal mechanisms. The reason had been that comparable levels of corporate scandals were reported across key sectors. For instance, varying degrees of corporate malpractices led to the collapse of over fifty commercial banks between 1994 and 2011, whilst, an additional eight banks had to be rescued from impending bankruptcy (CBN 2011). The overstatement of the profit and balance sheets of Cadbury Nigeria Plc and the evidence of share price manipulation at the Fort Oil Plc (formerly African Petroleum) ensured that the two companies became the most famous cases of unethical practices in Nigeria (Egene 2009).

Regulatory responses to these corporate incidences were considerable as the institutional efforts saw the Nigeria Securities and Exchange Commission (SEC) issued the country's first ever Code of Corporate Governance in 2003 (hereafter, SEC Code). In order to enhance board effectiveness, the SEC Code recommended board structure characteristics covering size, composition and leadership. However, there has been lingering debate regarding the relevance of these features to corporate efficiency in Nigeria. Questions have been asked as to whether these suggestions which had mirrored developed economies styles of corporate governance can lead to efficiency in the management of firms operating in the emerging economies with completely different socio-cultural disposition.

Attempts have been made to empirically examine how important these board features are in firm governance but findings from previous studies set in Nigeria have been equivocal (see: Uadiale 2010). The majority of these studies took an agency approach, focusing mainly on the issue of managerial self-interested behaviour at the expense of other board role fundamentals such as resource co-optation, harmonisation of stakeholders' interests and executive stewardship (e.g. Kajola 2008). Most of these studies also suffered from methodological inadequacies ranging from the use of weak model, assumption of definite relationship and absence of control and moderating variables amongst others (Lawal 2011).

Relying on the SEC Code recommendations with reference to appropriate board structure, this paper is aimed at addressing three key fundamentals questions which include; whether adherence to the SEC Code in terms of board configuration, predict firm performance in Nigeria? If such is the case, then which of the specific board features have significant influence on measures of performance? And finally, are there any other explanatory variables outside the board factors that significantly drive these performance variations?

It is interesting to note that, the influence of corporate governance on firm performance has been a subject of intense discussion for over twenty years, but mainly in the US, Europe and Latin America, and most recently in the Asian business context (Finegold et al. 2007). In Sub-Saharan Africa, particularly Nigeria, a review of the literature points to insufficient evidence as, so far, very little research has been conducted in this vital field (Elsayed 2011, Ongore and K'Obonyo 2011). This paper aims to add an African perspective to this important research stream. The choice of Nigeria as a case study was based on the fact that it housed one of the four largest stock markets in Africa and above all the largest economy in the Continent.

The current study was equally motivated by the desire to verify whether, in line with suggestions from some quarters, countries with relatively frail corporate regulations see statistically significant effects of corporate governance variables on firms' performance (see: Klapper and Love, 2004; Cadbury 2000). Compared with the progress made in other emerging countries, the Nigerian corporate regulations still lag behind due to significant developments not yet appropriately allowed for in the country's company laws (see: Quadri 2010).

Board diversity has been hypothesised to enhance firm performance (Anderson et al. 2011). Specifically, Cadbury (2000) identified the issues of directors' educational qualifications, experience and continuous development programmes as being prerequisites for directors' ability to add value to board deliberations. However, the majority of previous studies on board diversity have tended to focus more on demographic variables (e.g. Kang et al. 2007; Campbell and Mínguez-Vera 2008). Issues related to directors' cognitive competencies, has not received the desired attention as only few studies have so far been conducted in this area (see: Lückerath-Rovers 2011). This study attempts to fill these gaps and contribute to the growing literature on board diversity.

Finally, Tian and Lau (2001) argued that the external environment within which a firm operates is critical to the effectiveness of the internal governance mechanism. However, it is interesting to note that the mainstream of previous empirical studies have ignored this simple fact, even in developing economies where these environmental factors are of the utmost importance (Rwegasira 2000; Krambia-Kapardis and Psaros 2006; Klapper and Love, 2004). This study is thus motivated by the need to take into account the effects of macroeconomic fundamentals as mediator of the relationship between corporate governance and firm performance in the context of emerging markets.

The remainder of this paper is structured as follows: the second section deals with the review of relevant literatures and development hypotheses. Third section covers the description of research methodology. The fourth section was dedicated to analyses, discussion of results and theoretical as well as the practical implications of the empirical findings. The fifth section, which is the final part, focuses on the conclusion drawn and offered some directions for future research.

## 2.0    Related literatures and hypotheses

Corporate governance is said to involve a set of nexus between parties to the firm operations (see: OECD 2004:11). In practical terms, it encompasses every aspect of running a corporate entity, which amongst other things includes the deployment of both internal and external mechanisms. Of these instruments, the use of internal mechanisms represented by the board of directors stands out and thus well documented in governance literature. Corporate board often regarded as the most significant constituency, plays varieties of intermediary roles that link firms and their owners with those who provide professional management and other ancillary support services (see: Chen et al. 2009; Bozec, 2005). From the *agency perspective*, the role of board is symbolised by effective monitoring of the executive management team in a way that curtails the perceived moral hazard and residual risk associated with the separation of ownership and control (Weir et al. 2002). Unlike the agency theory, the *stewardship theory* explores the intrinsic value orientation of the executive management. As corporate stewards, they are seen as individuals who are motivated by non-financial gains such as achievement, growth, self-actualisation and acknowledgment. Here, the role of board, *ceteris paribus*, is more of strategy formulation and ratification since information asymmetry issues are said to be limited under stewardship notion (Ahunwan 2002).

*Stakeholder theory* took a rather broader view of corporations as societal entities with arrays of interested parties. As well as the immediate owners, whose funds are being placed at risk, stakeholders include other groups that are at the receiving end of whatever course of action the firm, through the board, decides to pursue (Pfeffer 1994). The roles of corporate board therefore, include balancing proportionately, interests between the numerous stakeholders. Adam and Shavit (2009) had however, stressed the need for distributive justice that gives preference to the shareholders' interests. In addition to harmonisation of divergence interests, boards are expected to play a "resource-picking "roles which includes scouting for vital information that give the firm a competitive edge over its peers (see: Markarian and Parbonetti 2007). *Resource dependency theory* was first captured in the work of Pfeffer and Salancik (1978) where they argued that a firm's power in terms of competitiveness is dependent on the amount of resources at its disposal, and that most of this wealth comes from the outside environment. Consistent with the dependency hypothesis, a corporation is seen as an entity whose success and survival hinge on the developments in the environment within which it operates. Corporations thus look to the environment for the sourcing of key resources including human resources, capital and raw materials (see: Pfeffer and Salancik 1978).

Interestingly, each of these board roles highlighted under the respective theories offered some form of implication for effective firm governance especially from board structure perspective. Berghe and Levrau (2004) suggested that an investigation of board structure should focus on four dimensions: size, composition, international presence, and cognitive capabilities and diversity. The present study adopted a rather modified version of these dimensions by focusing on the key board features (i.e. size, composition, CEO duality and diversity) that are consistent with the Nigerian SEC Code recommendations regarding board structure.

## 2.01   Board size

The size of the Board is regarded as one of the critical elements of board effectiveness and a key determinant of the quality of deliberations that goes on in the so-called black box (Goodstein et al. 1994). Issues of appropriate board size has been a subject of intense discussion with varying degrees of opinions shared when it comes to determining the size of directors that engenders board performance. (Yermack 1996). However, prior discussions have majorly focused on the debate between the relative benefits or otherwise of keeping large and small board membership (Guest 2009; Coles et al. 2008).

Apart from the perceived inherent risk of CEO dominance and entrenchment, proponents of large board size have relied on the availability of pool of knowledge, directors' independence and external network connections which enhance firms' access to mobilisation of critical resources and vital industry information as some of the key benefits derived from large Board size (Larmou and Vafeas 2010; Kang et al. 2007). Jackling and Johl (2009) noted that due to the high degree of heterogeneity among the members, large board sizes are backed by the presence of directors with in-depth cognitive capabilities that enhances the quality of board decisions. Coles et al. (2008) observed that large boards composed of a higher proportion of non-executives are more vigilant and effective in carrying out the board counselling role.

Critics who favoured small Board size have centred their arguments on the agency implication of such a structure. Yawson (2006) observed that excessively large board membership posed monitoring challenges and the tendency to become more vulnerable to managerial entrenchment. Small boards are more effective at monitoring the CEO, and are more likely to invoke appropriate discipline when necessary, especially in the face of a run of poor firm performance (Yermack 1996; Lipton and Lorsch 1992). Proponents of moderate board sizes have advanced the problem of boardroom coordination and communication gap due to over crowdedness as part of the constraints associated with large boards for which small boards enjoy a relatively comparative advantage (Muth and Donaldson 1998). Pacini et al. (2008) argued that group think-tank syndrome and potential conflict resulting from the emergence of splinter groups within boards are likely to reduce the effectiveness of large board sizes. Similarly, Hermalin and Weisbach (2003) established that as the size of the board grows, its tendency to move from being an active organ to a passive element becomes even greater. The issue of social loafing has also surfaced in a large portion of the literature as a negative consequence of a relatively large board size. Bozec (2005) noted that there is a tendency for certain members to act as box tickers and not necessarily contributing anything of value to board discourse.

Several studies have been conducted to determine the empirical validity of the idea of an optimal board size and its effects on firm performance and market value. Significant numbers of these studies have yielded inconsistent outcomes ranging from positive findings (e.g. Tanna et al. 2011) to negative results (e.g. Bennedsen et al. 2008; Mak and Kusnadi 2005). However, unlike other board characteristics, significant numbers of previous studies on board size overwhelmingly pointed to a negative relationship with firm performance measures (Guest 2009). Consistent with the pattern of these previous empirical outcomes, this study hypothesises that;

H1:     Board size, irrespective of the measurement technique used is negatively associated with firm performance in Nigeria.

## 2.02    Board independence

Whenever it comes to gauging the level of board independence, the composition of directors is often used as a proxy (see: Chen et al. 2009). For the purpose of this study, board composition is defined in terms of the proportion of executives and non-executives directors who make up the board. Hermalin and Weisbach (1988) noted that the extent to which boards of directors are able to exercise legitimate power depends on their composition. Because insider directors are in possession of valuable corporate information and the non-executives bring to bear their expertise and objectivity, having an appropriate mixture of both categories of directors is strategic to firm governance (Byrd and Hickman 1992). Within the board composite however, the independent non-executive directors (NEDs) are seen as symbols of board freedom and sovereignty from CEO exuberant influences (Dalton et al. 1998).

The presence of these outside directors on corporate boards have been linked to different role plays, ranging from provision of independent judgement, expertise, resource co-optation and innovation, amongst others (John and Senbet 1998). Luan and Tang (2007) observed that NEDs are indication of good governance and strong external networks, which provide the management team with the strategic resources required to run the corporation successfully. Advocates of board independence have argued that, if the sole responsibility of the board of directors is to monitor the executives and the management team, then outside independent directors are more enthusiastic about instilling such control measures (Bhagat and Black 2000).

Despite the popularity that the case for increased non-executive representation has received, empirical evidence supporting claims that such an inclusion can engender improved firm value remains relatively unclear due mixed results that continued to dominate empirical findings (Finegold et al. 2007). In a study of panel data consisting of 672 UK listed firms, Mura (2007) found that the fraction of NEDs on a board was significantly and positively associated with market value. Positive results were equally reported in other similar empirical studies (e.g. Tanna et al. 2011; Shan and McIver 2011; Perry and Shivdasani 2005). However, Randøy and Jenssen (2004) conducted an empirical investigation into a selected number of firms facing strict product market competition and found that board independence was counterproductive to performance. Similarly, Bhagat and Black (2000) investigated the long-term effect of board independence using a sample of 934 largest US public companies and found no evidence to suggest that firms benefit financially from such an inclusion.

Conclusively, while the current study recognises the equivocality of previous empirical findings regarding the strategic relevance of independent NEDs (see: Jackling and Johl 2009; Kim 2007), the assumption that the presence of these outside directors enhances board monitoring and vigilance remains popular. Consistent with the above and the fact that the SEC Code had offered similar recommendations in Part b(4.3) that "...*the majority of Board members should be non-executive directors, at least one of whom should be independent director*", this study hypothesises as follows:

H2:     There is a statistically significant positive relationship between the presence of independent non-executive directors and firm performance in Nigeria, irrespective of the scenario and performance measures used.

## 2.03    CEO duality

Debate on the dual leadership structure is centred on whether the CEO should be allowed to hold the two top leadership positions within a corporation. Though many codes of corporate governance are structured in favour of the agency theory orientation, which encourages separation of power, advocates of CEO duality have emphasised the need for unity of command and control at the top management level (Dahya and Travlos 2000).

Proponents of duality have observed that the creation of the board chair position is more a conventional wisdom, which may not necessarily be effective in the actual governance of firms. Therefore, harmonisation of the positions, with the CEO at the helm, creates purposeful and clearly focused corporate leadership. Elsayed (2007) argued that the approach eliminates ambiguities and decreases the role conflicts that are usually associated with the separation of decision management and control functions. This enhances firm efficiency particularly the speed of corporate decision making (Boyd 1995).

The need for separation of power through non-duality has remained the most dominant school of thought. The reason for this shared sentiment is not farfetched. Series of reported corporate scandals have all pointed to the failure of leadership, especially the overbearing influence of CEOs on the Board of Directors (Jackling and Johl 2009). Therefore, a dual leadership structure in which corporate authority resides with the CEO is adjudged to be detrimental to shareholders' protection (Laing and Weir 1999).

Public debates have thus favoured an independent leadership structure that ensures decentralisation of power at the top corporate level. The situation in Nigeria's corporate environment is no exception to this bias. Critics have suggested that combining the two positions would impair objectivity and induced conflict of interest, as this could amount to being an arbitrator in one's own defence (Wan and Ong 2005). CEOs are said to be unable, by virtue of their position in the management team, to offer the kind of unbiased leadership that is required under contemporary institutional arrangements (Arslan et al. 2010). Laing and Weir (1999) argued that having too much power concentrated in the hands of an individual is likely to increase potential agency costs since it provides little or no room for checks and balances. This, according to Boyd (1995), will subdue board's usefulness in discharging its fiduciary obligations. Rechner and Dalton (1991) asserted that the quest for corporate probity, transparency and accountability might be compromised because of CEOs' overbearing tendencies resulting from the high concentration of power. In principle, the roles expected of the executives and the board of directors creates two separate constituents with very distinct functions. Therefore, handing so much power over these two different constituents to one person may amount to an aberration.

Ironically, the issue of corporate leadership structure has not commanded the same level of popularity and attention – in terms of volume of empirical evidence – as other board dynamics, such as size and composition (see: Rechner and Dalton 1991). Results from the few available studies are almost inconclusive as mixed evidences have been reported regarding how CEO duality impact firm performance (see: Elsayed 2007). In a study of 192 US firms drawn from twelve different industries, Boyd (1995) found CEO duality to be both positively and negatively associated with firm performance, depending on the prevailing environmental conditions facing the firm, mainly generosity, dynamism and complexity. Elsayed (2007) reported that the effect of CEO duality on firm performance varied significantly across industrial groupings and that both the agency and stewardship theories are crucial to understanding the association between the two variables (Elsayed 2007).

Despite not being absolutely supported empirically, the call for a separation of power has received tremendous citations (Faleye 2007). The Nigerian SEC Code had equally offered similar endorsement encouraging CEO non-duality. Consequently, this study adopted the following hypothesis:

H3:     There is a statistically significant negative link between the adoption of a dual CEO leadership structure and the performance of listed firms in Nigeria.

## 2.04    Board diversity

Globalisation has increasingly changed the dynamics of firm composition in terms of workforce. People of different diverse demographic and cognitive backgrounds are being co-opted into working together to achieve a common goal (see: Gomez-Mejia et al. 2005). At the board level, diversity entails having a board composition of directors not only from different cultural, ethnic, national, and other racial divides, but also of competent, qualified and experienced individuals from diverse background who bring to bear their versatility and external connections. Board diversity can be subdivided into demographic and cognitive characteristics. While board demographic features are easily recognisable, the cognitive characteristics are not obvious. To this end, significant numbers of previous studies have placed greater emphasis on demographic components such as gender, age, race, nationality and ethnicity because of its perceived empirical simplicity (Lückerath-Rovers 2011; Hagendorff and Keasey 2010; Campbell and Mínguez-Vera 2008). Only very few studies on board diversity can be found on cognitive-related issues such as directors' educational qualifications, professional memberships, industry experience and external network density (see: Anderson et al. 2011).

Early debates on the importance of board diversity are concerned with whether the directors' gender diversity; specifically the presence of female directors enhances the effectiveness of corporate boards. This aspect has resulted in two lines of arguments i.e. the corporate fair play built on "*equality*" and value maximisation which represents the "*business case*" for board diversity (see: Carter et al. 2003). Anchored in the stakeholder theory, advocates of corporate fairness argue in favour of the need to involve people of different races, sexes and cultures in the management and running of corporations, especially at the top level (Hagendorff and Keasey 2010). Regarding the business case, board diversity issues are entrenched in both the agency and resource dependency theories of corporate governance. Boards of directors composed of individuals from diverse demographic and cognitive backgrounds are seen as corporate assets whose synergistic effects are linked to increased firm performance (Hagendorff and Keasey 2010). Gender equality advocates have thus argued that women with excellent cognitive abilities need not be discriminated against, as they are just as capable of contributing meaningfully to board deliberations as their male counterparts (Carter et al. 2010). Kang et al. (2007) observed that female directors are much more independent as they are usually detached from the "*old boys*" syndrome, which allows them to offer an unbiased perspective during board meetings.

Interestingly, a new paradigm shift has emerged in the board diversity debate, with more focus on directors' cognitive characteristics, an aspect which had been under-studied in the past (see: Darmadi 2013). Issues related to academic qualifications have received most of the interest with predominant empirical works focusing on the effects of the directors' level of education on firm performance. Kim and Lim (2010) found that directors' fulfilment of their advisory role increases when they possess certain academic qualifications, especially in the areas of business and law. Advocates of cognitive board diversity strongly believe that the effectiveness of corporate board lies in the directors' aggregate competencies, which shape the quality of deliberation that goes on inside the boardroom. According to Lückerath-Rovers (2011) the cognitive heterogeneity among board members facilitates access to vital industry information that guides corporate strategic decisions. As a firm evolves from a single-country operator into a global player, understanding the unique characteristics of each market segment becomes more important for corporate strategic planning and firm competitiveness. Therefore, the composition of the board of directors that will ultimately make corporate strategy decisions needs to reflect the diversity in the marketplace. Eklund et al. (2009) noted that these diverse board memberships enhance a firm's ability to comprehend and keep track of changes in the external environment. Walt and Ingley (2003) argued that directors' cognitive characteristics are social capital that firms with a diversified board composition can tap into. The presence of well-connected directors, which usually accompanies diversity in the boardroom, makes it easier for firms to raise funds and attract other critical resources from the public. Nordberg (2011) contended that these included not only access to cheap capital, but also favourable regulatory treatment.

Remarkably, whereas, research evidence supporting demographic diversity remained inconclusive, findings from those that had investigated the effect of cognitive diversity were somewhat aligned (Nielsen and Huse, 2010; Randøy et al. 2006; Carter et al. 2003). Darmadi (2013) in a study consisting of 160 firms listed on the Indonesian Stock Exchange found that the directors' educational qualifications were instrumental to firm's improved performance. Fairchild and Li (2005) examined hostile takeovers as a predictor of directors' quality and reported that the quality of the board of directors, as measured in terms of their wealth creation propensity, played a crucial role, not only in the firm's governance, but in its continued existence as a going concern. These evidences were further affirmed by other similar research outcomes (e.g. Hsu 2010; Bhagat et al. 2010; Jalbert et al. 2002).

In line with the above empirical trends and the fact that the Nigerian SEC Code had in Part b(4.1) emphasised that the Board "*should be composed in such a way as to ensure diversity of experience without compromising independence, compatibility, integrity and availability of members to attend meetings*", this study adopted the following hypotheses:

H4:     The presence of directors with MBA is significantly associated with improved performance among companies quoted on the Nigerian Stock Exchange.

H5:     There is a statistically significant positive relationship between directors' experience and the performance of companies quoted on the Nigerian Stock Exchange.

H6:     The proportion of directors on a board that come from the three major ethnic groups is negatively associated with improved firm performance in Nigeria.

## 3.0     Methodology and model specification

### 3.01     Conceptual framework

Previous studies on the effect of board structure on firm performance has been characterised by inconsistent findings because of faulty research framework (see: Lawal 2011). The majority of these empirical studies had adopted the direct relationship approach whereby firm performance proxies are regressed against the relevant board variables of interest (e.g. Guest 2009; Yermack 1996). Various recommendations have been offered with respect to ways of addressing previous methodological flaws while simultaneously bringing robustness to future studies. Some of the new approaches suggested include the use of multiple theories, the deployment of multidimensional performance measures, and the inclusion of external environmental factors such as macroeconomic, societal and regulatory variables (see: Şener et al. 2011; El Sood 2008; Finegold et al. 2007; Nicholson and Kiel 2007; Ugur and Ararat 2006; Muth and Donaldson 1998).

Consistent with these suggestions, this study adopted an integrated approach and thus extended the constructs of the traditional econometric model commonly used in corporate governance studies from its simplistic form to one that includes variables capturing external environmental forces specifically the macroeconomic factors (see: Ugur and Ararat 2006). The underlying premise upon which this study was built is that firm performance in Nigeria is a function of adherence to SEC Code's recommended board structure and the overall macroeconomic situation facing the country at any given point. The sophistication of this framework is evident in the hypothesis advanced by Ugur and Ararat (2006) in support of an empirical shift towards the extended model in the study of the relationship between corporate governance and firm performance. They argued that past studies have ignored the effect of macroeconomic stability on firm performance. While good corporate governance might have the potential to improve a firm's performance, the presence of macroeconomic stability, or the lack of it, can equally promote or hinder performance (Ugur and Ararat 2006). They further contended that, in the hierarchy of determinants of firm performance, the first element in the pecking order is the rate of return, a variable linked to the macroeconomic factor. Consistent with previous investigations, the current study adopts two variables, the level of economic growth and the degree of economic openness, as proxies reflecting the general macroeconomic situation in Nigeria (see: Wanyama et al. 2009; El Sood 2008; Naceur et al. 2007; D'Souza et al. 2005; Boubakri et al. 2005).

**Figure 1:** Conceptual framework of corporate governance and influence of macroeconomic variables on the performance of firms in Nigeria

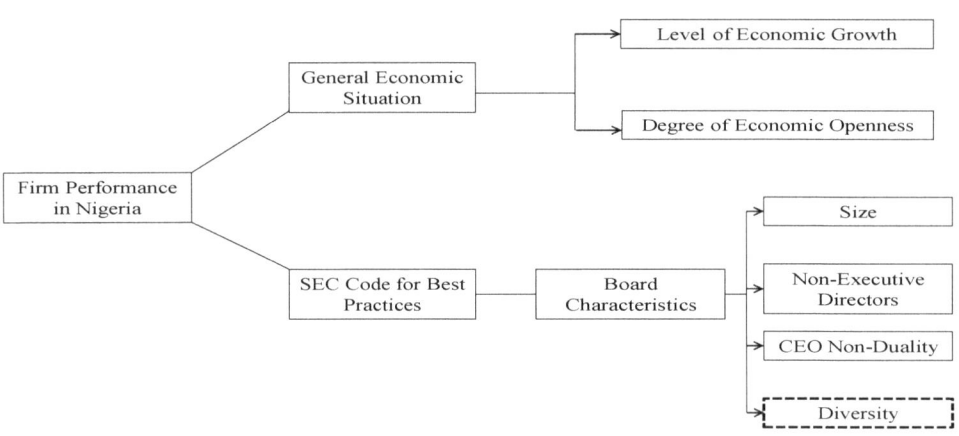

### 3.02　　Data and sample determination

This study is based on panel data from 177 firms listed on the Main Board of the NSE between 1st January 1999 and 31st December 2010. Qualitative data in respect of board characteristics were collected from the Nigerian SEC Database and the respective companies' annual reports. Macroeconomic data related to economic growth and the levels of economic openness were extracted from the 2011 CBN Annual Bulletin. Information on financial performance was composed from the respective companies' annual reports and the Nigeria Stock Exchange (NSE) Fact Books. Information on share prices for all of the companies considered were collected from the NSE Daily Price List, specifically on the last trading day of each of the financial years.

In order arrived at final sample that is reflective of the entire population and reduce the problematic nature of an unequal data sample, a filtering mechanism was developed. For a firm to be included in the final sample, therefore they had to be a listed company whose shares were traded on the floor of the NSE uninterruptedly for at least the twelve-year period between 1999 and 2010. The second consideration is the availability of audited annual financial reports for the period under consideration and finally the accessibility of detailed information on corporate governance disclosure, especially on the structure of the board of directors for 2003/2004 and

2009/2010 financial years. Whilst 2003/2004 represents the era prior to the introduction of SEC Code, the 2009/2010 financial year represents the post-2003 SEC Code era and the emergence of the 2009 reversed code.

Using the above parameters, the total number of eligible companies decreased from 177 to 127, and these companies formed the final sample size used throughout the various stages of the empirical analysis. The composite of firms that made final sample represents 72 per cent of the total number of quoted companies that had traded on the NSE platform as at the end of the 2010 financial year. The combined market capitalisation of these firms covers approximately 90 per cent of the market's all-share index. It is important to equally note that the final data sample used in this study is still the largest sample size ever used, so far, in a single empirical study in the context of Nigeria (e.g. Kajola 2008; Udiale 2010).

## 3.03 Definition and estimation of variables

The study adopted two sets of performance measures i.e. the accounting and market value-based techniques. Meyer (2002) noted that these measures focus on both the historical performance and future expectations. *Tobin's q,* a measurement of firm market value, provides the basis for statistical inferences regarding the investors' appetite for the firm's stock, whilst the use of accounting-based measures – return-on-assets (ROA) and net profit margin (NPM) enables the study to draw conclusions regarding the operational efficiency and profitability (see: Gentry and Shen 2010). *Tobin's q* is defined as the ratio of market capitalisation plus the book value of debt, to the total assets (e.g. Mak and Kusnadi 2005). ROA is taken as the ratio of net profit to total assets or net worth (see: Bennedsen et al. 2008). NPM, as a profitability ratio, is crucial to ascertaining the relative internal strength of a firm and the degree to which it can survive in turbulent times as a going concern. In this study, NPM is defined as the ratio of turnover to net profit. This definition is consistent with approaches adopted in Raithatha and Bapat (2012) and Gill et al. (2008).

*Board size (BS)* is used in this study as an independent variable and estimated in the model as the total number of directors on the board (e.g. Pacini et al. 2008; Yermack 1996). The definition of *board independence (BI)* offered in this study is an adaptation of the SEC Code's definition and it is taken as the proportion of independent NEDs, who are not current or former employees of the company and whose stake in the company is less than 0.1 per cent. Board independence is captured in the model as the total number of independent NEDs on the board during the relevant financial years (e.g. Mura 2007; Peng 2004; Weir et al. 2002). *CEO duality (CEODUAL)* is captured as a dummy variable and coded in binary which takes the value one (*1*) if CEO doubled as the Board Chair, signifying a dependent leadership structure and the value, zero (*0*) if the positions are separate suggesting an independent leadership configuration (e.g. Elsayed 2011; Chen et al. 2009). *Board cognitive diversity,* as employed in this study, is captured using two different proxies; the number of directors who hold MBA *(DMBA)* and the directors' average years of work experience-*AVGEXP* (e.g. Anderson et al. 2011; Hsu 2010). The *demographic diversity* is captured using ethnicity proxy and measured in two ways. The first approach measured board ethnic diversity *(ER)* on the basis of the absolute number of directors from the three major ethnic groups in Nigeria (i.e. Hausa, Yoruba and Igbo). The second approach uses the Blau index, a measure of heterogeneity and equilibrium: $1-\sum^{n}p_i^2$ where p is the proportion of directors from major ethnic groups (see: Darmadi 2013).

Relying on Ugur and Ararat's (2006) line of thought, as highlighted in the preceding section, two external variables that reflected Nigeria's macroeconomic situation are employed namely; the level of economic growth and degree of economic openness. The level of economic growth (LOGGDP) is defined as the rate of change in the real GDP year-on-year, while the degree of economic openness (LOGOPENNESS) is captured as the ratio of the balance of trade to GDP. Both definitions are consistent with methodologies used in previous studies (e.g. El Sood 2008; Nacuer et al. 2007; D'Souza et al. 2005).

## 3.04 Control variables

In the field of management sciences, endogeneity effect, resulting from simultaneity, omitted variables, measurement errors and other model specification errors has been identified as key impediment to reliability and robustness of empirical outcomes (see: Chenhall and Moers 2007). Most of the reported inconsistencies in the corporate governance research findings are thought to be linked to the inability of previous researchers to control the endogeneity effects in the estimated models (Wintoki, Linck, and Netter 2012). Bhagat and Black (2000) observed that the use of control variables can mitigate these potential errors and biases, thereby enhancing the credibility of statistical results. The study thus adapted two sets of control variables to moderate the potential effects of endogeneity on the proposed models. *Firm Leverage* (LEV) is introduced as a control variable and measured as the ratio of debt to assets (see: Chen et al. 2009; Pacini et al. 2008). The second control variable is *Firm Size* (FS) and it is measured as the logarithm of turnover (e.g. Yammeesri and Herath 2010; Nicholson and Kiel 2007).

## 3.05    Diagnostic tests and model specification

**Pre-diagnostic tests**

In order to ensure a fair and balance evaluation throughout the empirical process, a series of preliminary tests were conducted on the data sets and variables to be used in the regression model, to ascertain their reliability, level of usefulness and predictive power. *Chow breakpoint* test was conducted on pre- and post-SEC-Code board structure and the *CUSUM* (cumulative sum of squares residual) test was further carried out to validate the sustainability of the Chow breakpoint results. Both the board structure and the macroeconomic variables were subjected to *Stationarity* (Unit Root) and the *Normality* tests to ascertain the degree of data spread and the normality of data distribution. These preliminary assessments were consistent with the empirical works of Al-Haddad et al. (2011) and that of Lam and Lee (2008).

**Model specification**

The relationship between performance measures and the SEC Recommended board characteristics is tested using two clusters of multivariate regression models with each Cluster consisted of a base and sensitivity models. The first cluster, in equations (1) and (2) below, represents an intermediate analysis, designed to answer the first two of the three research questions. Using the base model, *Tobin's q*, a measure of firm performance (FP) was regressed against the board structure variables. Further sensitivity analyses are then conducted on the results from the base model, using equation (2) with net profit margin (NPM) as a proxy for FP. Sensitivity analyse was designed to evaluate the degree to which the base model results are sensitive to the performance measure (see: Darmadi 2013).

*Cluster 1: Intermediate Multivariate Analysis*
*Base Model*
$$FP_{it} = \alpha_1 + \beta_1 BS_{it} + \beta_2 BI_{it} + \beta_3 CEODUAL_{it} + \beta_4 DMBA_{it} + \beta_5 AAVGEXP_{it} + \beta_6 ER_{it} + \beta_7 LEV_{it} + \varepsilon_{it} \qquad (1)$$

*Sensitivity Model*
$$FP_{it} = \alpha_1 + \beta_1 BS_{it} + \beta_2 BI_{it} + \beta_3 CEODUAL_{it} + \beta_4 DMBA_{it} + \beta_5 AAVGEXP_{it} + \beta_6 ER_{it} + \beta_7 LEV_{it} + \varepsilon_{it} \qquad (2)$$

The second cluster models combine the features of Cluster 1 as well as the inclusion of external moderators (i.e. level of economic growth and degree of economic openness). Cluster 2 models were designed to affirm the robustness of Cluster 1 findings and offered empirical response to the final of the three fundamental questions that were raised at the beginning of the study. Equation (3) represents the base model and *Tobin's q* is regressed against the board and macroeconomic variables, with the outcome further exposed to a sensitivity test using ROA equation (4). The adopted models in this cluster are consistent with the previous empirical studies (e.g. El Sood 2008; Bozec 2005; D'Souza et al. 2005).

*Cluster 2: Extended Multivariate Analysis*

*Base Model*
$$FP_{it} = \alpha_1 + \beta_1 BS_{it} + \beta_2 BI_{it} + \beta_3 CEODUAL_{it} + \beta_4 DMBA_{it} + \beta_5 AAVGEXP_{it} + \beta_6 ER_{it} + \beta_7 LEV_{it} + \alpha_8 logGDP_{it} + \alpha_9 logOP_{it} + \varepsilon_{it} \qquad (3)$$

*Sensitivity Model*
$$FP_{it} = \alpha_1 + \beta_1 BS_{it} + \beta_2 BI_{it} + \beta_3 CEODUAL_{it} + \beta_4 DMBA_{it} + \beta_5 AAVGEXP_{it} + \beta_6 ER_{it} + \beta_7 FS_{it} + \alpha_8 logGDP_{it} + \alpha_9 logOP_{it} + \varepsilon_{it} \qquad (4)$$

**Post-diagnostic tests**

This study is designed, not only to investigate the variables that determine firm performance in Nigeria, as has been the case in most of the previous studies, but to likewise ascertain the relevance of these drivers of performance in the long run. Two sets of post-diagnostic examinations are conducted on the regression models using the *augmented Dickey–Fuller (ADF) co-integration* and *Theil inequality coefficient* forecast tests. The co-integration test covers every aspect of the entire model, both deterministic and non-deterministic variables. This extensiveness facilitates the spotting of any potential spuriousness in the regression results that were obtained across the two clusters (see: Marmol and Velasco 2004). The co-integration test was introduced to serves as a robustness check regarding the long-term sustainability of the model in explaining the causality between the board characteristics and performance measures as moderated by the macroeconomic variables. Interestingly, this approach was equally consistent with those adopted in previous studies (e.g. Rogers et al. 2008). The second post-diagnostic analysis, the Theil inequality coefficient forecast test was conducted to determine the reliability and predictive accuracy of the models across the three multidimensional performance measures (i.e. ROA, NPM and *Tobin's q*). The application of the Theil inequality coefficient is appropriate following the regression analysis to compare how far the actual model results are from the forecast. The coefficient is sub-divided into three measures: bias, variance and covariance. Whilst the forecast test is conducted for the three measures, statistical inferences regarding the precision and otherwise of the models is drawn using Theil's outcome of bias component, which measures the systematic error in the forecast model (see: Ocram and Biekpe 2007).

## 4.0    Empirical results and discussions

### 4.01    Description statistics

As highlighted in the preceding section, Nigeria operates a unitary board system, typical of most Anglo-Saxon countries. The board of directors comprises both executives and NEDs. The table 1 below shows the descriptive statistics of the board characteristics for the sample of firms covered in this study. An average board size (BS) in Nigeria, is approximately ten, which is above the minimum of five specified in the SEC Code. It is likewise within the band recommended in some previous empirical studies (e.g. Lipton and Lorsch 1992). Board independence (BI), which measures the monitoring role played by the corporate board, shows an average of three NEDs, representing almost 30 per cent of the average board size of the firms in the sample. This implies adequate representation of outside independent directors who held less than 0.1 per cent of the shares. The SEC Code had recommended the presence of at least one of such independent director on the boards of listed firms. Therefore, it might not be out of place to conclude that the board monitoring role is crucial to shareholders in Nigeria.

| **Table 1:** Descriptive of statistics of board structure and performance measures | | | | | | | | |
|---|---|---|---|---|---|---|---|---|
| Variables | BS | AVGEXP | BI | DMBA | ER | ROA | Tobin's q | NPM |
| Minimum | 5 | 5.38 | 0.00 | 1.00 | 2.00 | -2.15E4 | -150.27 | -3144 |
| Maximum | 20 | 40.4 | 9.00 | 9.00 | 20.00 | 3206.96 | 1206.22 | 373.13 |
| Mean | 9.57 | 20.32 | 2.78 | 2.57 | 7.78 | -4.23 | 8.97 | -1.77 |
| Std. Deviation | 3.07 | 7.37 | 1.81 | 1.71 | 3.54 | 1.2E3 | 7.1E1 | 2.2E2 |

The majority of companies in Nigeria have fully complied with the SEC recommendation regarding the separation of power at the top corporate level. Approximately 98 per cent of the companies covered in this study have adopted clear CEO non-duality with the positions of board chair and CEO occupied by two different individuals (see: Appendix 1). The directors in the study sample have an average of twenty years' experience, and a minimum of five years. At least three board members hold MBA, a cognitive qualification necessary for strategic business policy decision making (see: Hsu 2010; Bhagat et al. 2010). On average, eight directors on the boards of quoted companies in Nigeria are drawn from within the three major ethnic groups, namely Hausa/Fulani, Yoruba and Igbo.

Regarding the firm performance measures, the two accounting-based techniques, ROA and NPM, have negative average ratios of -4.23 and -1.77. These descriptive results imply that an average firm in the sample experienced negative financial performance over the period being investigated with regards to the management's efficiency at utilising the firms' assets and execution of marketing and distribution strategies. On the market value technique that measures the marketability of the firm in terms of investors' sentiment towards the company's stock, the *Tobin's q* is positive, with an average of 8.97 for the sample of 127 firms investigated.

### 4.02    Results of pre-diagnostic tests

Chow breakpoint test was conducted on the pre- and post-SEC-Code board structure data. The p-value of the F-test showed that the F-statistic (0.424) was not statistically significant at the 5 per cent level (see: Appendix 2). As a result, the null hypothesis that $H_0:\mu_1=\mu_2$ was not rejected. Consequently, this study accepts that there is no significant difference in board structure between the periods before and after the SEC Code's introduction, in the sample of listed companies investigated. This result is confirmed by the results of the CUSUM test on the breakpoint (shock), taken to be the 2004 financial year when the SEC Code became effective. The CUSUM graph shows that the trend stays within the acceptance region, which implies that the non-significant nature of the Chow breakpoint test result is sustainable over a long period (see: Appendix 3). Given the above result, the study is at liberty to use any of the partitioned data. Hence, the decision was made to adopt the post-Code data across the entire analysis (i.e. board structure data for the 2010 financial year). This approach is consistent with the methodology adopted in Tian and Lau, (2001), where the 1996 financial year was taken as the base year and some other similar studies (see: Chen et al. 2009).

The normality test found the SEC spread to be normally distributed around a zero mean and constant variance, except for the directors' average number of years of experience (AVGexp) (see: Appendix 4). This result shows that the data collected for the purpose of this study are well spread and cut across the entire population under investigation. The implication is that the outcome derived from this empirical investigation is most likely to be free from the inherent heteroskedasticity problem often associated with non-randomly distributed data. When data are normally distributed, it is easier to observe statistically the degree of spread within the sample. The absence of abnormality in data usually leads to more credible regression results and better statistical inferences (see: Razali and Wah 2011).

Granger (1969) observed that the use of non-stationary variables can lead to spurious regression results. Therefore, both the dependent and independent variables used in this study were further subjected to stationarity tests, as described in the previous section (using Levin, Lin and Chu; Pesaran and Shin; ADF-Fisher chi-square; Philip, Peron and Fisher chi-square). The stationarity test results show that the country-level macroeconomic variables (i.e. level of economic growth and degree of economic openness) and one of the accounting measures of firm performance (NPM) are stationary at the first difference. The proxies for board structure (i.e. board size, board independence, board experience, CEO duality, board professional qualifications and ethnic representation) and the control variables (i.e. leverage and firm size) are stationary at level (see: Appendix 5). The stationarity results validate the stability of the variables of interest used in the model, implying that the variables show no seasonality-driven behaviour but are rather stable over time.

## 4.03    Results of the regressions

Consistent with the proposed research methodology for the cluster one, performance measure was regressed against board variables without the inclusion of the macroeconomic variables (see: Table 2). The explanatory power of the resulting base model was high, with an $R^2$ of 0.645, which signifies that the model explains over 60 per cent of the variations in firm performance as measured by *Tobin's q*. The results of the base model regression show that the directors' years of experience (AVGEXP) and board independence (BI) are positive and significantly associated with *Tobin's q* a measure of market value at the 5 per cent level. Board size (BS), CEO duality (CEODUAL), directors' educational qualifications (DMBA) and ethnic representation were also positively related to the performance measure but statistically insignificant.

**Table 2:** Board features as determinants of firm performance

| Variable | Base Model (Tobin's *q*) | Sensitivity Model (NPM) |
|---|---|---|
| | *OLS Result* | *OLS Result* |
| Constant | 0.009 | -0.006 |
| | *(0.144)* | *(-0.104)* |
| BS | 0.077 | 0.076 |
| | *(0.728)* | *(0.728)* |
| AVGEXP | 0.129 [a] | -0.148 [a] |
| | *(1.863)* | *(-2.139)* |
| BI | 0.089 [a] | -0.088 [a] |
| | *(1.244)* | *(-1.243)* |
| CEODUAL | 0.036 | -0.034 |
| | *(0.582)* | *(-0.556)* |
| DMBA | 0.042 | -0.053 |
| | *(0.623)* | *(-0.788)* |
| ER | 0.000 | -0.003 |
| | *(0.003)* | *(-0.036)* |
| LEV | 0.081 [b] | -0.080 [a] |
| | *(1.214)* | *(-1.215)* |
| $R^2$ | 0.645 | 0.644 |
| Adjusted $R^2$ | 0.541 | 0.562 |
| *F*-statistics | 1.404 | 1.606 |
| *P-Value*(*F*-statistics) | 0.00 | 0.00 |

Notes: *a significant at 5% level; b significant at 10% level; t-statistics values captured in parentheses*

ROA is measured as the ratio of net profit to a firm's total assets. NPM is measured as the proportion of sales to net profit. Tobin's q is derived as the ratio of a firm's market capitalisation to total assets. Board size is estimated as the total number of directors on the board. Board Independence is captured as the total number of independent NEDs on the board. CEO Duality is captured as a dummy, which takes the value one if the same person holds the two positions and the value zero if the positions are separated. DMBA is captured as the number of directors with an MBA. AVGEXP is captured as the average number of years of work experience of the directors. ER is captured as the proportion of directors from the three major ethnic groups in Nigeria. Firm Leverage is measured as the ratio of firm debt to assets.

A follow-up sensitivity test was conducted on the preceding base model results to verify the robustness of the outcomes discussed above. Consistent with the previous operational procedure, the macroeconomic variables were dropped. In addition, a different measure of performance, NPM, was introduced to replace *Tobin's q*. The idea was to test whether the results obtained were sensitive to the performance measure employed. The performance of the sensitivity model, especially in terms of its explanatory power, was consistent with the base model. The $R^2$ and F-statistic of the model are 0.644 and 1.606 respectively. The p-value of 0.008 is much less than the 5 per cent (<0.05) critical threshold, which indicates that the entire model is statistically significant.

In the sensitivity model, three variables – directors' years of experience (AVGexp), board independence (BI) and firm leverage (LEV) – remained statistically significant although they exhibited an inverse relationship with the firm performance proxy NPM. On the other hand, board size (BS), CEO duality (CEODUAL), directors' educational qualifications (DMBA) and ethnic representation (ER) were found to be statistically insignificant in this model. It is interesting to note here that, while some variables maintained the same level of statistical significance, the effect of their relationship with the dependent variable, NPM, changed from that in the base model, where *Tobin's q* was used. For instance, the effect of board independence and directors' years of experience on firm performance, initially positive, became negative and statistically significant at the 5 per cent level. The proportion of directors with MBA and directors from major ethnic groups were found to be negatively and statistically insignificantly related to firm performance in this model. Board size was found to be positively associated with NPM but not statistically significant. While CEO duality also exhibited an inverse relationship with the dependent variable compared to the result obtained in the base model, the outcome still provided little support for the hypothesis: the sensitivity model shows CEO duality to be negatively associated with NPM but not significant statistically.

Table 3 presented the results of the second cluster. Board structure and macroeconomic variables were regressed against the firm performance proxy (*Tobin's q*). The results show the base model to be robust and offered high explanatory power, as reflected in the $R^2$ and F-statistic (0.871 and 14.274). The p-value, 0.000, which is less than the 0.05 level, also suggests that the base model is statistically significant. The $R^2$ value of 0.871 implies that the variables used in the model explain up to 87 per cent of the relationship between the independent variables and dependent variable.

**Table 3**: Board features and macroeconomic variables as determinants of firm performance (*Tobin's q*)

| Variable | Base Model (Tobin's q) | | Sensitivity Model (ROA) |
|---|---|---|---|
| | *OLS Result* | | *OLS Result* |
| Constant | 9.878 | | -0.805 |
| | *(-1.318)* | | *(-0.103)* |
| BS | 0.052 | | 0.135 |
| | *(0.454)* | | *(1.281)* |
| AVGEXP | 0.164 [a] | | 0.175 [a] |
| | *(2.154)* | | *(2.396)* |
| BI | 0.103 [a] | | -0.081 |
| | *(1.343)* | | *(-1.077)* |
| CEODUAL | 0.035 | | -0.062 |
| | *(0.544)* | | *(-0.920)* |
| DMBA | 0.272 [a] | | 0.022 |
| | *(3.694)* | | *(0.308)* |
| ER | 0.026 | | -0.058 |
| | *(0.236)* | | *(-0.577)* |
| LOGGDP(-1) | -1.156 | | -0.236 |
| | *(-1.474)* | | *(-0.289)* |
| LOGOPENNESS(-1) | 0.128 [a] | | 0.149 [a] |
| | *(1.635)* | | *(1.822)* |
| LEV | 0.023 [a] | FS | 1.128 [a] |
| | *(2.332)* | | *(1.933)* |
| $R^2$ | 0.871 | | 0.742 |
| Adjusted $R^2$ | 0.751 | | 0.675 |
| *F*-statistics | 14.273 | | 7.216 |
| *P-Value*(*F*-statistics) | 0.00 | | 0.00 |

Notes: *a significant at 5% level; b significant at 10% level; t-statistics values captured in parentheses*

ROA is measured as the ratio of net profit to a firm's total assets. NPM is measured as the proportion of sales to net profit. Tobin's q is derived as the ratio of a firm's market capitalisation to total assets. Board size is estimated as the total number of directors on the board. Board Independence is captured as the total number of independent NEDs on the board. CEO Duality is captured as a dummy, which takes the value one if the same person holds the two positions and the value zero if the positions are separated. DMBA is captured as the number of directors with an MBA. AVGEXP is captured as the average number of years of work experience of the directors. ER is captured as the proportion of directors from the three major ethnic groups in Nigeria. Economic growth is captured as the percentage change in the real GDP year-on-year. Economic Openness is measured as the ratio of the balance of trade to GDP. Firm Leverage is measured as the ratio of firm debt to assets.

With respect to the performance of the individual variables that made up the regressors, five variables were found to be statistically significant. These were directors' years of experience (AVGEXP), board independence (BI) and directors' qualifications (DMBA), leverage (LEV) and economic openness (LOGOPENNESS). Board size (BS), CEO duality (CEODUAL) and directors' ethnic representation, as well as the level of economic growth (LOGGGDP), were found to be statistically immaterial at the 5 per cent level of significance. The results regarding the effect of the relationships were equally significant. Board size was found to have a positive effect on *Tobin's q*, contrary to the prediction of Hypothesis 1, but the effect was statistically insignificant (coefficient =0.052; p-value = 0.650). Directors' years of experience was found to be positively and significantly associated with *Tobin's q* (coefficient =0.164; p-value = 0.032).

This result offers empirical support to the fifth hypothesis. Board independence was found to be strongly and significantly linked to firm performance. This outcome is consistent with the second hypothesis. Hypothesis 3's prediction of the effect of firm leadership structure (CEO duality) is not authenticated. CEO duality was found to be positively but insignificantly associated with the performance measure. Directors' educational qualifications (DMBA) were found to be significantly associated with *Tobin's q* (coefficient =0.272; p-value = 0.005) thus offering support for the fourth hypothesis. On the contrary, directors' ethnicity (ER) was found to be positively linked to firm performance as predicted in the sixth hypothesis, but the effect was statistically insignificant.

A further sensitivity analysis was conducted to verify whether the results obtained from the base model of Cluster 2 were sensitive to the performance measure employed, i.e. *Tobin's q* (see Table 3). The alternative model was regressed using a different performance measure (ROA) and with an additional control variable (firm size) to mitigate potential endogeneity. The overall outcome shows the model to have high explanatory power and robustness. The adjusted $R^2$ is 0.675, suggesting that nearly 68 per cent of the variation in the dependent variable (ROA) is explained by the estimated model. This is further corroborated by the $R^2$ (=74 per cent).

In terms of the relative effects of the explanatory variables on the dependent variable, directors' years of experience (AVGexp) was found to be statistically significant at the 5 per cent level. This result implies that, consistent with the fifth hypothesis, directors' years of experience are indeed positively associated with ROA. Board size (BS) and the proportion of directors with an MBA were found be positively associated with ROA, as expected, but statistically insignificant. The relationship between CEO duality (CEODUAL) and firm performance has the sign predicted in the third hypothesis but also not statistically significant (coefficient = -0.062; t-statistic = -0.920). Board independence is negatively associated with ROA but not significant (coefficient = -0.081; t-statistic = -1.077). Regression result of from sensitivity model offered no support for the strategic relevance of ethnic representation (ER) to firm performance.

## 4.04 Post-diagnostic results

The regression results obtained in the preceding models were further subjected to post-diagnostic evaluations to reaffirm their validity, reliability and long-term sustainability. A *co-integration test* result showed a high level of statistical significance. The reported p-value was 0.011 (coefficient = 0.018; t-statistic = 1.594). This result implies that all of the explanatory variables captured in the model, and the subsequent series of results obtained under various scenarios that examined their effects on firm performance are sustainable in the long term (see: Appendix 6). The second post-diagnostic test conducted was a static forecast experiment using the *Theil inequality coefficient* (see Table 4). The rationale behind this reliability test was to check the effectiveness of the model in reflecting future changes in the explained variables. Across the four dependent variables employed in this study, the Theil inequality coefficients were greater than zero but also less than one, which implies a relatively good fit.

**Table 4**: Static forecast tests of model reliability

| Variables | NPM | Tobin's q | ROA |
|---|---|---|---|
| Theil Inequality Coefficient | 0.636 | 0.663 | 0.707 |
| Bias Proportion | 0.000 | 0.000 | 0.000 |
| Variance Proportion | 0.405 | 0.440 | 0.500 |
| Covariance Proportion | 0.595 | 0.560 | 0.500 |

The Theil coefficient results are further divided into three proportions: bias, variance and covariance. The results from the division process show an absence of systematic bias (see: Table 4 above), which implies that the mean of the forecast and the mean of the actual series were not significantly far apart, but almost equal. Therefore, the estimated models used in this study are statistically valid. In addition, the overall residual variance proportion is relatively low, which suggests that the fluctuations seen in the estimated models had occurred by chance. Thus, the pattern of results observed and documented in terms of the effects of the independent variables on the dependent variables are sustainable (see: Theil 1966).

## 4.05    Discussion of results

The study has focused on establishing whether SEC Code-recommended board characteristics and macroeconomic variables are linked with improved firm performance in Nigeria. Several findings have emerged across the two clusters of the estimated models. Diverse results from a single study are not peculiar to this empirical investigation, but rather widely documented in corporate governance studies (e.g. Jackling and Johl 2009; Arslan et al. 2010; Anderson et al. 2011). Board size had maintained its positive but insignificant relationship with the firm performance measures *Tobin's q* and ROA respectively. This study thus concludes that the *Hypothesis 1* prediction of a negative association between board size and firm performance is invalid in the Nigerian context. This outcome is consistent with previous empirical evidences (e.g. Tanna et al. 2011; Larmou and Vafeas 2010).

Board independence was found to be positively associated with firm value and statistically significant at the 5 per cent level. Even when the sign of the relationship became negative during the sensitivity assessment, the resultant change was not statistically significant to invalidate the market value (*Tobin's q*) outcome. Therefore, this study has found credible evidence in support of *Hypothesis 2*, in that the presence of independent NEDs is vital to improving the performance of listed companies in Nigeria. This outcome is very much consistent with previous empirical studies examining the effects of board independence on firm performance (see: Jackling and Johl 2009; Rhoades et al. 2000). Regarding leadership structure, the study found neither significant support for *Hypothesis 3* or evidence to justify the presumption that CEO duality is a key determinant of firm performance in Nigeria. This finding is clearly consistent with previous empirical evidence in both developed and emerging economies (see: Arslan et al. 2010; Baliga et al. 1996; Boyd 1995).

The presence of directors with MBA was found to be positively and statistically significantly linked to firm market value (*Tobin's q*). In addition, the results obtained using the accounting-based measures (NPM and ROA) were both not significant enough to invalid the outcome from *Tobin's q* (see: Shan and McIver 2011). Therefore, the *Hypothesis 4* prediction, which suggested that MBA qualifications are significantly linked to improved firm performance in Nigeria, was sustained. However, the study acknowledges that the sign of this relationship tends to vary across performance measures. This finding is consistent with previous studies (e.g. Darmadi 2013; Anderson et al. 2011; Rakhmayil and Yuce 2008).

Directors' years of experience was found to be significantly linked to firm performance across the measures. Interestingly, this is the only board variable whose level of statistical significance was sustained across Clusters 1 and 2. The study found overwhelming evidence to suggest that board members' experience, one of the indicators of cognitive diversity, is relevant and a key determinant of firm performance in Nigeria. *Hypothesis 5* was thus supported empirically. This evidence is consistent with previous studies on cognitive diversity (e.g. Lai and Chen 2012; Anderson et al. 2011). The final board variable tested was the effect of directors' ethnicity (*Hypothesis 6*). The study found that the directors' ethnic representation was statistically insignificant to firm performance across the measures (i.e. both market and accounting-based). While the study acknowledges the importance of directors' demography on a firm's operations, the effect of such configuration seems to be immaterial when it comes to creating value for the firm. The finding on directors' ethnicity is consistent with the outcomes from previous studies on demographic diversity (e.g. Carter et al. 2010; Hagendorff and Keasey 2010; Randoy et al. 2006).

Whereas the level of economic growth was found to be statistically insignificant, the degree of economic openness was found to be strongly linked to firm performance. This result points to the effects of FDI on the performance of local companies in both small and emerging economies (see: Symeou 2009). Trade liberalisation is an important factor relating to the sustainable performance of firms in Nigeria, especially those quoted on the NSE. This finding is consistent with some previous studies that examined the combined effect of corporate governance and macroeconomic variables on firm performance (e.g. Naceur et al. 2007; Boubakri et al. 2005; D'Souza et al. 2005). This result further explains why the explanatory power of the models used in this study increased when the external variables relating to the state of the economy were introduced, as seen in Cluster 2.

Overall, the results from the estimated models were impressive in providing empirical answers to the fundamental research questions posed at the beginning of this study, and in laying a solid foundation that could guide future research on the nature of the relationship between the board and firm performance in the Nigerian context. In summary, the empirical answers to the key research questions are as follows:

*H1*: On whether adherence to the SEC Code in terms of board configuration, predict firm performance in Nigeria, the study found significant evidences of relationships between board independent, directors' academic qualification, professional experience and the measures of performance.

*H2*: Regarding which of the specific board features has the most significant influence on performance, the study found board independence in terms of the proportion of independent NEDs to be the most crucial element of board effectiveness in Nigeria.

*H3*: Relating to whether there any other explanatory variables outside the board factors that significantly drive these performance variations, the study found that the inclusion of macroeconomic variables in the estimated models increased their explanatory power from an average of 65 to 84 per cent. This study argued that, in the Nigerian context, external economic forces particularly, the degree of economic openness is a key determinant that needs to be taken into account in model estimation when investigating the relationship between board features and firm performance. The explanatory power of the models used in previous empirical studies in Nigeria is extremely weak and inadequate compared to the level achieved in this study (e.g. Kajola 2008).

## 5.0    Theoretical and practical implications of the findings

Findings from this study have three key implications that are rooted in the existing corporate governance theories. The first implication relates to the methodological approach used to study the board to firm performance relationship. Significant numbers of previous studies have relied on simplistic theoretical assumptions of linear relationships. However, the causality between the board characteristics and firm performance seems to be much more complicated than these theories have hypothesised (see: Nicholson and Kiel 2007). While the present study has found evidence suggesting that some specific board characteristics are linked to improved firm performance, the statistical levels of significance of these relationships are very weak in the absence of moderating variables, most of which are external to the firm. The explanatory power of the estimated models (i.e. $R^2$ and $R^2$ adjusted) used in this study, when macroeconomic variables were introduced as determinants of firm performance, ranged between 64 per cent and 87 per cent. The explanatory efficacy of these models is 30 to 50 per cent higher than those used in most previous studies that have assumed direct relationship between specific board features and measures of performance (e.g. Guest 2009; Kajola 2008; Mak and Kusnadi 2005). The assumption of *ceteris paribus*, corporate governance being the only determinant of firm performance, can be deceptive, especially in the context of emerging economies (see: Ugur and Ararat 2006; D'Souza et al. 2005; Boubakri et al. 2005). Researchers must begin to recognise, and capture in their estimation models, those variables that account for the interplay between firms' internal and external environments (see: Nicholson and Kiel 2007).

Second, the agency theory has received significant attention in corporate governance discourse, especially the issue of independent leadership structure. This study, however, found no empirical support for the separation of leadership as hypothesised in agency theory and recommended in the SEC Code. Ninety-eight per cent of firms in the data sample had adopted a non-dual leadership style with the positions of CEO and board chair held by two different individuals (see: Appendix 1). But, across the estimated models, no statistically significant results were recorded regarding the economic benefits associated with the adoption of such paradigm. This study's findings add to the growing empirical evidence suggesting that CEO duality or non-duality is contingent on firm-specific characteristics, as investors remain somewhat indifferent to the style of leadership firms adopt (see: Baliga et al. 1996; Dahya and Travlos 2000). It was observed, based on the pattern of data collected on CEO duality, that some firms have adopted a clear independent leadership structure in those industries that specifically require high technical expertise, such as construction, IT, health care and oil and gas. The bulk shareholders in these sub-sectors have assumed the position of board chair in their respective companies, whilst an independent person is appointed as CEO to run the affairs of the firm. Interestingly, the study found significant statistical evidence that the proportion of independent NEDs is linked to increased firm performance in Nigeria. While this result offers support to the agency theory, this study has attributed the relationship to firms' desire for resource co-optation, rather than for monitoring the CEO-led executives. This explains why similar results were obtained regarding the effects of the board cognitive diversity elements (i.e. directors' educational qualifications and experience) on firm performance. Peng (2004) argued that, in transition economies, NEDs play more of a resource dependency role than a role of monitoring the executives. Nigerian corporate boards may look well-configured and in line with the agency orientation but, in actual fact, the roles these directors are brought in to play differ significantly from the agency theory-based roles.

Third, the study findings also have implications for the board diversity debate, from both the resource dependency and stakeholder perspectives. In support of the resource dependency theory, the study offers significant evidence linking directors' competences with firm performance. The proportion of directors with MBA and their years of experience are both associated with increased market value (*Tobin's q*). However, no substantial evidence was recorded with regard to the relevance of ethnic diversity at the board level. This implies that, in the Nigerian context, the business case for board diversity, through the increased involvement of competent directors with appropriate educational qualifications and backgrounds/experience, takes precedence over ethnic considerations. The lack of empirical support for the importance of directors' ethnicity in this study does not undo the arguments put forward by board equality debaters but rather points to the fact that, in an emerging economy striving towards the attainment of developmental goals, demographic variables play a less significant role in determining who does what in the corporate environment.

## 6.0    Conclusion

This study has documented significant empirical evidence on the relevance of board independence and directors' competence in firm governance. The presence of independent NEDs and directors with specific educational qualifications (MBA) and professional experience were found to be vital instruments in improving a firm's market valuation and performance. While the contribution of this study in the area of board independence is more one of validating previous empirical findings, the evidence recorded here regarding directors' educational qualification and experience is crucial to the emerging debate on the strategic relevance of directors' competencies in firm governance. This study offers support for the business case for diversity, while rejecting the equality case for board heterogeneity. From the theoretical viewpoint, the agency and resource dependency theories of corporate governance were empirically supported in this study, with a high statistical level of significance achieved regarding the relevance of board independence and cognitive competence. The findings from these two key variables would provide corporate regulators in the emerging economies especially those in Nigeria, with an empirically proven lead that can help to guide future policy prescriptions in the area of corporate governance.

Finally, this study has added methodological originality to corporate governance research through the adoption of an integrated approach using three stages of analytical procedures (i.e. pre-diagnostic tests, regression analysis and post-diagnostic tests) to arrive at the final empirical results. The application of extensive econometric tools in single piece of corporate governance research is not a common phenomenon in this field of study, but rather an emerging trend with the approach mostly visible in those research works published over the last ten years (e.g. Peng 2007).

In terms of future study directions, the Nigerian corporate environment offers several untapped opportunities for the development of new research frameworks on the dichotomy of board dynamics and firm performance. This study thus calls for more corporate governance research with an emphasis on both internal and external mechanisms. Future studies are encouraged to pay equal attention to board structure and drilling down into the configuration of board committees (see: Pacini et al. 2008). Because of the constraints on holding board meetings as regularly as might be expected, much board business is being carried out at the committee level. It would be interesting to examine the composition of board committees and their relationship with firm performance. Board diversity originating from directors' demographic and cognitive features has been a subject of public debate in relation to corporate governance, mostly in developed economies. However, this study's findings of a significant relationship between cognitive variables (i.e. the directors' experience and educational qualifications) and firm performance opens up a new paradigm on board structure discourse in Nigeria. This study encourages further research in the two major areas of the diversity debate, but especially in that relating to directors' competencies. The literature on cognitive diversity remains very limited compared to that addressing the demographic elements.

## References

Adam, A. M., & Shavit, T. (2009). Roles and responsibilities of boards of directors revisited in reconciling conflicting stakeholders' interests while maintaining corporate responsibility. Journal of Management and Governance, 13(4), 281-302. http://dx.doi.org/10.1007/s10997-008-9076-3

Ahunwan, B. (2002). Corporate governance in Nigeria. Journal of Business Ethics, 37(3), 269-287. http://dx.doi.org/10.1023/A:1015212332653

Al-Haddad, W.M.Y., Alzurqan, S.T., & Al_Sufy F. J. (2011). The effect of corporate governance on the performance of Jordanian industrial companies: an empirical study on the Amman Stock Exchange. International Journal of Humanities and Social Science, 1(4), 56-69.

Anderson, R. C., Reeb, D. M., Upadhyay, A., & Zhao W. (2011). The economics of director heterogeneity. Financial Management, 40(1), 5-38. http://dx.doi.org/10.1111/j.1755-053X.2010.01133.x

Arslan, Ö., Karan, M. B., & Ekşi C. (2010). Board structure and corporate performance. Managing Global Transitions, 8(1), 3-22.

Baliga, B. R., Moyer R. C., & Rao, R. S. (1996). CEO duality and firm performance: what's the fuss? Strategic Management Journal, 17(1), 41-53. http://dx.doi.org/10.1002/(SICI)1097-0266(199601)17:1<41::AID-SMJ784>3.0.CO;2-#

Bennedsen, M., Kongsted, H. C., & Nielsen, K. M. (2008). The causal effect of board size in the performance of small- and medium-sized firms. Journal of Banking and Finance, 32(6), 1098-1109. http://dx.doi.org/10.1016/j.jbankfin.2007.09.016

Berghe, L. A., & Levrau, A. (2004). Evaluating boards of directors: what constitutes a good corporate board. Corporate Governance: An International Review, 12(4), 461-478. http://dx.doi.org/10.1111/j.1467-8683.2004.00387.x

Bhagat, S., Bolton, B. J., & Subramanian, A. (2010). CEO Education, CEO Turnover, and Firm Performance. http://papers.ssrn.com/sol3/papers.cfm?abstract_id=1670219. Accessed 5 October 2012.

Bhagat, S., & Black, B. (2000). Board Independence and Long-Term Firm Performance. Law and Economics Working Paper No. 143, New York: The Centre for Law and Economics Studies at CLS.

Boubakri, N., Cosset, J.C., & Guedhami, O. (2005). Liberalisation, corporate governance and the performance of privatised firms in developing countries. Journal of Corporate Finance, 11(5), 767-790. http://dx.doi.org/10.1016/j.jcorpfin.2004.05.001

Boyd, B. K. (1995). CEO duality and firm performance: A contingency model. Strategic Management Journal, 16(4), 301-312. http://dx.doi.org/10.1002/smj.4250160404

Bozec, R. (2005). Boards of directors, market discipline and firm performance. Journal of Business Finance and Accounting, 32(9 and 10), 1921-1960. http://dx.doi.org/10.1111/j.0306-686X.2005.00652.x

Bulent, G. (2009). The 2008 World Economic Crisis: Global Shifts and Fault Lines. http://www.globalresearch.ca/index.php?context=va&aid=12283. Accessed 7 June 2010.

Byrd, J. W., & Hickman, K. A. (1992). Do outside directors monitor managers? Journal of Financial Economics, 32(2), 195-221. http://dx.doi.org/10.1016/0304-405X(92)90018-S

Cadbury, S.A. (2000). The corporate governance agenda. Corporate Governance: An International Review, 8(1), 7-15. http://dx.doi.org/10.1111/1467-8683.00175

Campbell, K., & Mínguez-Vera, A. (2008). Gender diversity in the boardroom and firm financial performance. Journal of Business Ethics, 83(3), 435-451. http://dx.doi.org/10.1007/s10551-007-9630-y

Carter, D. A., D'Souza, F., Simkins, B. J. & Simpson, W. G. (2010). The gender and ethnic diversity of US boards and board committee and firm financial performance. Corporate Governance: An International Review, 18(5), 396-414. http://dx.doi.org/10.1111/j.1467-8683.2010.00809.x

Carter, D. A., Simkins, B. J. & Simpson, W. G. (2003). Corporate governance, board diversity, and firm value. The Financial Review, 38(1), 33-53. http://dx.doi.org/10.1111/1540-6288.00034

CBN, (2011). On capitalization of eight Nigerian banks. Abuja: Central Bank of Nigeria.

Chen, R, M., Dyball, C., & Wright, S. (2009). The link between board composition and corporate diversification in Australian corporations. Corporate Governance: An International Review, 17(2), 208-223. http://dx.doi.org/10.1111/j.1467-8683.2009.00734.x

Chenhall, R.H., & Moers, F. (2007). The issue of endogeneity within theory-based, quantitative management accounting research. European Accounting Review, 16(1), 173-195. http://dx.doi.org/10.1080/09638180701265937

Coles, J. L., Daniel, N. D., & Naveen, L. (2008). Boards: does one size fit all? Journal of Financial Economics, 87(2), 329-356. http://dx.doi.org/10.1016/j.jfineco.2006.08.008

Dahya, J., & Travlos, N.G. (2000). Does the one-man-show pay? Theory and evidence on the dual CEO revisited. European Financial Management, 6(1), 85-98. http://dx.doi.org/10.1111/1468-036X.00113

Dalton, D. R., Daily, C. M., & Ellstrand, A. E., & Johnson, J. L. (1998). Meta-analytic reviews of board composition, leadership structure, and financial performance. Strategic Management Journal, 19(3), 269-290. http://dx.doi.org/10.1002/(SICI)1097-0266(199803)19:3<269::AID-SMJ950>3.0.CO;2-K

Darmadi, S. (2013). Board members' education and firm performance: evidence from a developing economy. International Journal of Commerce and Management, 23(2), 113-135. http://dx.doi.org/10.1108/10569211311324911

D'Souza, J., Megginson, W., & Nash, R. (2005). Effect of institutional and firm-specific characteristics on post-privatisation performance: evidence from developed countries. Journal of Corporate Finance, 11(5), 747-766. http://dx.doi.org/10.1016/j.jcorpfin.2004.12.001

Egene, G. (2009). Nigeria: SEC Probes AP's Share Manipulation Allegation. THISDAY, 26 March, p. 10.

Eklund, J. E., Palmberg, J., & Wiberg, D. (2009). Ownership Structure, Board Composition and Investment. Working Paper No. 172, Stockholm: Centre of Excellence for Service and Innovation Studies (CESIS).

Elsayed, K. (2011). Board size and corporate performance: the missing role of board leadership. Journal of Management and Governance, 15(3), 415-446. http://dx.doi.org/10.1007/s10997-009-9110-0

Elsayed, K. (2007). Does CEO duality really affect corporate performance? Corporate Governance: An International Review, 15(6), 1203-1214. http://dx.doi.org/10.1111/j.1467-8683.2007.00641.x

El Sood, H.S.A. (2008). The usefulness of accounting information, economic variables and corporate governance measures to predict corporate failure. The Journal of Applied Business Research, 24(4), 1-10.

Fairchild, L., & Li, J. (2005). Director quality and firm performance. The Financial Review, 40(2), 257-279. http://dx.doi.org/10.1111/j.1540-6288.2005.00102.x

Faleye, O. (2007). Does one hat fit all? The case of corporate leadership structure. Journal of Management Governance, 11(3), 239-259. http://dx.doi.org/10.1007/s10997-007-9028-3

Finegold, D., Benson, G. S., & Hecht, D. (2007). Corporate boards and company performance: review of research in light of recent reforms. Corporate Governance: An International Review, 15(5), 865-878. http://dx.doi.org/10.1111/j.1467-8683.2007.00602.x

Gill, A., Biger, N., & Bhutani, S. (2008). Corporate performance and the chief executive officer's compensation in the service industry. The Open Business Journal, 1(1), 62-66. http://dx.doi.org/10.2174/1874915100801010062

Gomez-Mejia, L., Balkin, D. & Cardy, A. R. (2005). Management. New York: McGraw-Hill.

Goodstein, J., Gautam, K. & Boeker, W. (1994). The effects of board size and diversity on strategic change. Strategic Management Journal, 15(3), 241-250. http://dx.doi.org/10.1002/smj.4250150305

Granger, C. W. J. (1969). Investigating causal relations by econometric models and cross-spectral methods. Econometrica, 37(3), 424-438. http://dx.doi.org/10.2307/1912791

Guest, P. M. (2009). The impact of board size on firm performance: evidence from the UK. The European Journal of Finance, 15(4), 385-404. http://dx.doi.org/10.1080/13518470802466121

Hagendorff, J., & Keasey, K. (2010). The value of board diversity in banking: evidence from the market for corporate control. The European Journal of Finance, 18(1), 41-58. http://dx.doi.org/10.1080/1351847X.2010.481471

Hermalin, B. E., & Weisbach, M.S. (1988). The determinants of board composition. RAND Journal of Economics, 19(4), 589-606. http://dx.doi.org/10.2307/2555459

Hermalin, B., & Weisbach, M. (2003). Boards of directors as an endogenously determined institution: a survey of the economic literature. Federal Reserve Bank of New York Policy Review, 9(1), 7-26.

Hsu, H.E. (2010). The relationship between board characteristics and financial performance: an empirical study of United States initial public offerings. International Journal of Management, 27(2), 332-341.

Jackling, B., & Johl, S. (2009). Board structure and firm performance: evidence from India's top companies. Corporate Governance: An International Review, 17(4), 492-509. http://dx.doi.org/10.1111/j.1467-8683.2009.00760.x

Jalbert, T., Rao, R. & Jalbert, M. (2002). Does school matter? An empirical analysis of CEO education, compensation, and firm performance. International Business and Economics Research Journal, 1(1), 83-98.

John K., & Senbet, L.W. (1998). Corporate governance and board effectiveness. Journal of Banking and Finance, 22(4), 371- 403. http://dx.doi.org/10.1016/S0378-4266(98)00005-3

Kajola, S.O. (2008). Corporate governance and firm performance: the case of Nigerian listed firms. European Journal of Economics, Finance and Administrative Sciences, 14(4), 16-28.

Kang, H., Cheng, M. & Gray, S. J. (2007). Corporate governance and board composition: diversity and independence of Australian boards. Corporate Governance: An International Review, 15(2), 194-207. http://dx.doi.org/10.1111/j.1467-8683.2007.00554.x

Kim, H. & Lim, C. (2010). Diversity, outside directors and firm valuation: Korean evidence. Journal of Business Research, 63(3), 284-291. http://dx.doi.org/10.1016/j.jbusres.2009.01.013

Kim, Y. (2007). The proportion and social capital of outside directors and their impacts on firm value: evidence from Korea. Corporate Governance: An International Review, 15(6), 1168-1176. http://dx.doi.org/10.1111/j.1467-8683.2007.00638.x

Klapper, L.F., & Love, I. (2004). Corporate governance, investor protection, and performance in emerging markets. Journal of Corporate Finance, 10(5), 703-728. http://dx.doi.org/10.1016/S0929-1199(03)00046-4

Krambia-Kapardis, M., & Psaros, J. (2006). The implementation of corporate governance principles in an emerging economy: a critique of the situation in Cyprus. Corporate Governance: An International Review, 14 (2), 126-139. http://dx.doi.org/10.1111/j.1467-8683.2006.00492.x

Lai, J., & Chen, L. (2012). Does board experience matter? Evidence from foreign direct investment. Journal of Service Science and Management, 5(2), 140-150. http://dx.doi.org/10.4236/jssm.2012.52018

Laing, D., & Weir, C. M. (1999). Governance structures, size and corporate performance in UK firms. Management Decision, 37(5), 457-464. http://dx.doi.org/10.1108/00251749910274234

Lam, T.Y., & Lee, S.K. (2008). CEO duality and firm performance: evidence from Hong Kong. Corporate Governance, 8(3), 299-316. http://dx.doi.org/10.1108/14720700810879187

Larmou, S., & Vafeas, N. (2010). The relation between board size and firm performance in firms with a history of poor operating performance. Journal of Management and Governance, 14(1), 61-85. http://dx.doi.org/10.1007/s10997-009-9091-z

Lawal, B. (2012). Board dynamics and corporate performance: review of literature, and empirical challenges. International Journal of Economics and Finance, 4(1), 22-35.

Lipton, M., & Lorsch, J. W. (1992). A modest proposal for improved corporate governance. Business Lawyer, 48(1), 59-77.

Luan, C. J., & Tang, M.J. (2007). Where is independent director efficacy? Corporate Governance: An International Review, 15(4), 636-643. http://dx.doi.org/10.1111/j.1467-8683.2007.00593.x

Lückerath-Rovers, M. (2011). Women on boards and firm performance. Journal of Management and Governance, 17(2), 491-509. http://dx.doi.org/10.1007/s10997-011-9186-1

Mak, Y., & Kusnadi, Y. (2005). Size really matters: further evidence on the negative relationship between board size and firm value. Pacific-Basin Finance Journal, 13(3), 301-318. http://dx.doi.org/10.1016/j.pacfin.2004.09.002

Markarian, G., & Parbonetti, A. (2007). Firm complexity and board of director composition. Corporate Governance: An International Review, 15(6), 1224-1243. http://dx.doi.org/10.1111/j.1467-8683.2007.00643.x

Marmol, F., & Velasco, C. (2004). Consistent testing of co-integrating relationships. Econometrica, 72(6), 1809-1844. http://dx.doi.org/10.1111/j.1468-0262.2004.00554.x

Meyer, M. (2002). Rethinking Performance Measurement: Beyond the Balanced Scorecard. Cambridge: University Press.

Mura, R. (2007). Firm performance: do non-executive directors have minds of their own? Evidence from UK panel data. Financial Management, 36(3), 81-112. http://dx.doi.org/10.1111/j.1755-053X.2007.tb00082.x

Muth, M. M., & Donaldson, L. (1998). Stewardship theory and board structure: a contingency approach. Corporate Governance: An International Review, 6(1), 5-28. http://dx.doi.org/10.1111/1467-8683.00076

Naceur, S.B., Ghazouani, S. & Omran, M. (2007). The performance of newly privatised firms in selected MENA countries: the role of ownership structure, governance and liberalisation policies. International Review of Financial Analysis, 16(4), 332-353. http://dx.doi.org/10.1016/j.irfa.2006.09.006

Nicholson, G. J., & Kiel, G. C. (2007). Can directors impact performance? A case-based test of three theories of corporate governance. Corporate Governance: An International Review, 15(4), 585-608. http://dx.doi.org/10.1111/j.1467-8683.2007.00590.x

Nielsen, S., & Huse, M. (2010). The contribution of women on boards of directors: Going beyond the surface. Corporate Governance: An International Review, 18(2), 136-148. http://dx.doi.org/10.1111/j.1467-8683.2010.00784.x

Nordberg, D. (2011). Corporate Governance and the Board. In S. Idowu., & Louche, C. Theory and Practice of Corporate Social Responsibility. Verlag Berlin Heidelberg: Springer, pp. 39-53. http://dx.doi.org/10.1007/978-3-642-16461-3_3

Ocran, M.K., & Biekpe, N. (2007). Forecasting volatility in Sub-Saharan Africa's commodity markets. Investment Management and Financial Innovations, 4(2), 91-102.

OECD, (2004). Principle of Corporate Governance. France: OECD.

Ongore, V. O., & K'Obonyo, P.O. (2011). Effects of selected corporate governance characteristics on firm performance: empirical evidence from Kenya. International Journal of Economics and Financial Issues, 1(3), 99-122.

Pacini, C., Hillison, W., & Marlett D. (2008). Board size and firm performance in the property-liability insurance industry. Research in Finance, 24(1), 249-285. http://dx.doi.org/10.1016/S0196-3821(07)00210-9

Peng, M. W. (2004). Outside directors and firm performance during institutional transition. Strategic Management Journal, 25(5), 453-471. http://dx.doi.org/10.1002/smj.390

Peng, M.W., Zhang, S., & Li, X. (2007). CEO duality and firm performance during China's institutional transitions. Management and Organisation Review, 3(2), 205-225. http://dx.doi.org/10.1111/j.1740-8784.2007.00069.x

Perry, T., & Shivdasani, A. (2005). Do boards affect performance? Evidence from corporate restructuring. Journal of Business, 78(4), 1403-1431. http://dx.doi.org/10.1086/430864

Pfeffer, J. (1994). Competitive Advantage through People. Boston: Harvard Business School.

Pfeffer, J., & Salancik, G. (1978). The External Control of Organisations: A Resource-Dependency Perspective. New York: Harper and Row.

Quadri, H. (2010). Conceptual framework for corporate governance in Nigeria– Challenges and panaceas. PM World Today, 12(9), 1-8.

Raithatha, M., & Bapat, V. (2012). Corporate governance compliance practices of Indian companies. Research Journal of Finance and Accounting, 3(8), 19-26.

Rakhmayil, S., & Yuce, A. (2008). Effects of manager qualification on firm value. Journal of Business & Economics Research, 6(7), 129-138.

Randøy, T., Thomsen, S., & Oxelheim, L. (2006). A Nordic Perspective on Corporate Board Diversity. Oslo: Nordic Innovation Centre.

Randøy, T., & Jenssen, J. I. (2004). Board independence and product market competition in Swedish Firms. Corporate Governance: An International Review, 12(3), 281-289. http://dx.doi.org/10.1111/j.1467-8683.2004.00369.x

Razali, N.M., & Wah, Y.B. (2011). Power comparisons of Shapiro-Wilk, Kolmogorov-Smirnov, Lilliefors and Anderson-Darling tests. Journal of Statistical Modeling and Analytics, 2(1), 21-33.

Rechner, P. L., & Dalton, D. R. (1991). CEO duality and organisational performance: a longitudinal analysis. Strategic Management Journal, 12(2), 155-160. http://dx.doi.org/10.1002/smj.4250120206

Rhoades, D. L., Rechner, P. L., & Sundaramurthy, C. (2000). Board composition and financial performance: a meta-analysis of the influence of outside directors. Journal of Managerial Issues, 12(1), 76-91.

Rogers, P., Ribeiro, K.C.S., & Securato, J.R. (2008). Corporate governance, stock market and economic growth in Brazil. Corporate Ownership and Control, 6(2), 222-237.

Rwegasira, K. (2000). Corporate governance in emerging capital markets: whiter Africa? Corporate Governance: An International Review, 8(3), 258-267. http://dx.doi.org/10.1111/1467-8683.00203

SEC, (2009). Code of Corporate Governance. Abuja: Nigeria Securities and Exchange Commission.

SEC, (2003). Code of Corporate Governance. Abuja: Nigeria Securities and Exchange Commission.

Shan, Y. G., & McIver, R. P. (2011). Corporate governance in China: panel data evidence on listed non-financial companies. Asia Pacific Business Review, 17(3), 301-324. http://dx.doi.org/10.1080/13602380903522325

Symeou, P. (2009). The Effects of Economy Size on Firm Performance: Evidence from the Telecommunications Sector. Munich: Institute for Communication Economics.

Şener, İ., Varoğlu, A., & Aren, S. (2011). Board composition and organisational performance: Environmental characteristics matter. Procedia Social and Behavioural Sciences, 24(1), 1481-1493. http://dx.doi.org/10.1016/j.sbspro.2011.09.130

Tanna, S., Pasiouras, F., & Nnadi, M. (2011). The effect of board size and composition on the efficiency of UK banks. International Journal of the Economics of Business, 18(3), 441-462. http://dx.doi.org/10.1080/13571516.2011.618617

Theil, H. (1966). Applied Economic Forecasting. Amsterdam: North-Holland Publishing Co.

Tian, J. J., & Lau, C.M. (2001). Board composition, leadership structure and performance in Chinese shareholding companies. Asia Pacific Journal of Management, 18(2), 245-263. http://dx.doi.org/10.1023/A:1010628209918

Uadiale, O. M. (2010). The impact of board structure on corporate financial performance in Nigeria. International Journal of Business and Management, 5(10), 155-166.

Ugur, M., & Ararat, M. (2006). Does macroeconomic performance affect corporate governance? Evidence from Turkey. Corporate Governance: An International Review, 14(4), 325-348. http://dx.doi.org/10.1111/j.1467-8683.2006.00510.x

Walt, N. v., & Ingley, C. (2003). Board dynamics and the influence of professional background, gender and ethnic diversity of directors. Corporate Governance: An International Review, 11(3), 218-234. http://dx.doi.org/10.1111/1467-8683.00320

Wan, D., & Ong, C. (2005). Board structure, process and performance: evidence from public-listed companies in Singapore. Corporate Governance: An International Review, 13(2), 277-290. http://dx.doi.org/10.1111/j.1467-8683.2005.00422.x

Wanyama, S., Burton, B., & Helliar, C. (2009). Frameworks underpinning corporate governance: evidence on Ugandan perceptions. Corporate Governance: An International Review, 17(2), 159-175. http://dx.doi.org/10.1111/j.1467-8683.2009.00730.x

Weir, C., Laing, D., & McKnight, P. J. (2002). Internal and external governance mechanisms: their impact on the performance of large UK public companies. Journal of Business Finance & Accounting, 29(5 and 6), 579-611. http://dx.doi.org/10.1111/1468-5957.00444

Wintoki, M. B., Linck, J.S. & Netter, J. M. (2012). Endogeneity and the dynamics of internal corporate governance. Journal of Financial Economics, 105(3), 581-606. http://dx.doi.org/10.1016/j.jfineco.2012.03.005

Yammeesri, J., & Herath, S. K. (2010). Board characteristics and corporate value: evidence from Thailand. Corporate Governance, 10(3), 279-292. http://dx.doi.org/10.1108/14720701011051910

Yawson, A. (2006). Evaluating the characteristics of corporate boards associated with layoff decision. Corporate Governance: An International Review, 14(2), 75-84. http://dx.doi.org/10.1111/j.1467-8683.2006.00488.x

Yermack, D. (1996). Higher market valuation of companies with a small board of directors. Journal of Financial Economics, 40(2), 185-211. http://dx.doi.org/10.1016/0304-405X(95)00844-5

# APPENDICES

**Appendix 1:** Leadership structure and ethnic diversity

| Leadership Structure | No. of Company | Rate (%) |
|---|---|---|
| CEO Duality | 3 | 2 |
| CEO Non-duality | 124 | 98 |
| **Total** | **127** | **100%** |
| **Ethnic Diversity** | **Average Rep.** | **No. of Company** |
| Directors from Major Ethnic Groups | 8 | 127 |
| **Total** | | **127** |

**Appendix 2:** Chow breakpoint stability test of board dynamics (Pre and Post SEC Code)

Chow Breakpoint Test: 127
Null Hypothesis: No breaks at specified breakpoints
Varying Regressors: All equation variables
Equation Sample: 1180

| | | | |
|---|---|---|---|
| F-statistic | 0.424 | Prob. F(6,95) | 0.861 |
| Log likelihood ratio | 2.830 | Prob. Chi-Square(6) | 0.830 |
| Wald Statistic | 2.546 | Prob. Chi-Square(6) | 0.863 |

**Appendix 3:** Cumulative sum of squares residual (CUSUM) test on break point shock results (*Year 2004*)

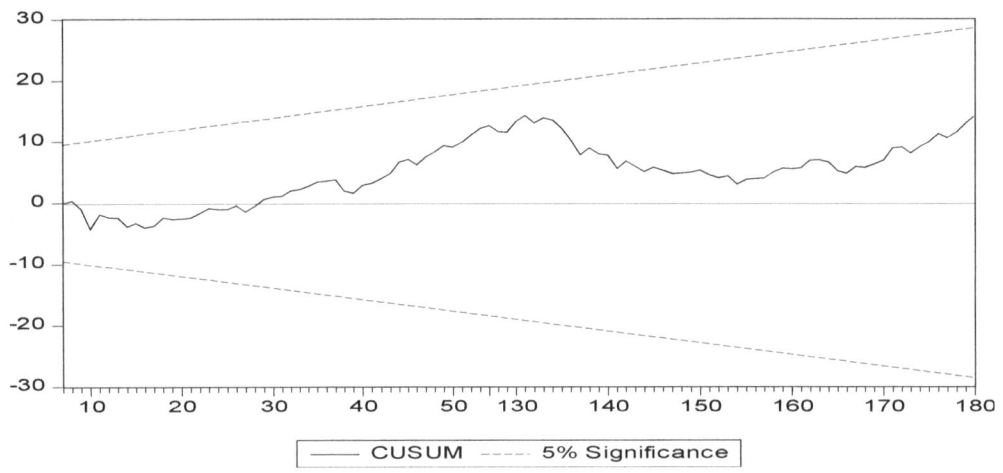

**Appendix 4:** Normality test of the board variables (*Z-standardized Values*)

| | BS | BI | CEOD | ER | AVGEXP | DMBA |
|---|---|---|---|---|---|---|
| Mean | -0.005 | -0.000 | -0.001 | -0.004 | -0.003 | -0.002 |
| Std. Dev. | 0.997 | 0.998 | 0.998 | 0.999 | 0.999 | 0.999 |
| Skewness | 0.952 | 0.684 | -3.994 | 1.005 | 0.075 | 1.485 |
| Kurtosis | 4.200 | 3.284 | 18.835 | 3.166 | 2.694 | 5.528 |
| | | | | | | |
| Jarque-Bera | 53.592 | 20.669 | 3329.218 | 43.079 | 0.585 | 67.833 |
| Probability | 0.000 | 0.000 | 0.000 | 0.000 | 0.746 | 0.000 |
| Sum | -1.269 | -0.056 | -0.157 | -1.010 | -0.387 | -0.247 |
| Sum Sq. Dev. | 251.686 | 252.045 | 251.919 | 252.644 | 119.849 | 105.938 |
| | | | | | | |
| Observations | 254 | 254 | 254 | 254 | 121 | 107 |

**Appendix 5:** Summary of Stationarity (Unit Root) Test Results

| Variables | | Levin & Chin | Pvalue | Pesran &Shin | Pvalue | ADF Fisher | Pvalue | Philip Peron & Fisher | Pvalue |
|---|---|---|---|---|---|---|---|---|---|
| BS | level | -4.564* | 0 | --3.389* | 0 | 94.54* | 0.001 | 180.72* | 0 |
| | 1st diff. | - | - | - | - | - | - | - | - |
| BI | level | -3.566* | 0 | -3.346* | 0 | 97.977* | 0.001 | 216.69* | 0 |
| | 1st diff. - | - | | - | - | - | - | - | - |
| logGDP | level | -3.819 | 0.999 | 8.508 | 1 | 1.783 | 1 | 0.037 | 1 |
| | 1st diff. | - 16.434* | 0 | -7.065* | 0 | 156.108* | 0 | 88.773* | 0 |
| logOpenness | level | -0.966 | 0.1595 | -0.259 | 0.602 | 34.886 | 0.98 | 184.24* | 0 |
| | 1st diff. | -6.379* | 0 | -6.3794* | 0 | 143.581* | 0 | 666.034* | 0 |
| AVGEXP | level | -8.360* | 0 | -6.056* | 0 | 121.492* | 0 | 218.204* | 0 |
| | 1st diff. | - | - | - | - | - | - | - | - |
| CEODual | level | -3.066* | 0.001 | -2.705* | 0 | 27.49* | 0.001 | 52.23* | 0 |
| | 1st diff. | - | - | - | - | - | - | - | - |
| DMBA | level | -6.622* | 0 | -5.113* | 0 | 116.93* | 0 | 246.36* | 0 |
| | 1st diff. | - | - | - | - | - | - | - | - |
| ER | level | -3.689* | 0 | -3.529* | 0 | 100.84* | 0 | 218.22* | 0 |
| | 1st diff. | - | - | - | - | - | - | - | - |
| LEV | level | -83.707* | 0 | -14.507* | 0 | 90.33* | 0.001 | 105.22* | 0 |
| | 1st diff. | - | - | - | - | - | - | - | - |
| FS | level | -90.289* | 0 | -17.34 | 0 | 68.73* | 0.085 | 105.86* | 0 |
| | 1st diff. | - | - | - | - | - | - | - | - |
| *Tobin's q* | level | -4.755* | 0 | -2.112* | 0.0174 | 74.12* | 0.036 | 115.34* | 0 |
| | 1st diff. | - | - | - | - | - | - | - | - |
| NPM | level | 5.367 | 1 | -1.489 | 0.068 | 68.32 | 0.091 | 117.24* | 0 |
| | 1st diff. | 7.879* | 0 | -6.167* | 0 | 141.93* | 0 | 283.26* | 0 |
| ROA | level | -55.587* | 0 | -9.395 | 0 | 87.993* | 0.002 | 153.611* | 0 |
| | 1st diff. | - | - | - | - | - | - | - | - |
| BIXFM | Level | -8.231* | 0 | -5.315* | 0 | -119.89* | 0 | 236.58* | 0 |
| | 1st diff | - | - | - | - | - | - | - | - |
| BIXETHC | Level | -8.231* | 0 | -5.315* | 0 | -119.89* | 0 | 236.58* | 0 |
| | 1st diff | - | - | - | - | - | - | - | - |
| BIXMBA | Level | -8.231* | 0 | -5.315* | 0 | -119.89* | 0 | 236.58* | 0 |
| | 1st diff | - | - | - | - | - | - | - | - |

**Note:** p values for Fisher tests are based on the Asymptotic Chi-square Distribution, hence others assume asymptotic normality.
*significant at 5% level.

**Appendix 6:** Co-integration test of the estimated regression equation-*test serial correlation of the residuals*

| Variable | Coefficient | Std. Error | t-Statistic | Prob. |
|---|---|---|---|---|
| C | 10.666 | 1.204 | 8.857 | 0.000 |
| RESID01(-1) | 0.018 | 0.011 | 1.595 | 0.011 |

Effects Specification

Cross-section fixed (dummy variables)

Weighted Statistics

| | | | |
|---|---|---|---|
| R-squared | 0.734 | Mean dependent var. | 43.792 |
| Adjusted R-squared | 0.706 | S.D. dependent var. | 241.061 |
| S.E. of regression | 132.191 | Sum squared resid. | 4019107. |
| F-statistic | 26.432 | Durbin-Watson stat | 1.477 |
| Prob.(F-statistic) | 0.000 | | |

Unweighted Statistics

| | | | |
|---|---|---|---|
| R-squared | 0.456 | Mean dependent var. | 10.699 |
| Sum squared resid. | 4023361 | Durbin-Watson stat | 1.632 |

# 14

# A Dynamic Scoring Simulation Analysis of How TEL Design Choices Impact Government Expansion

John D. Merrifield [a*], Barry W. Poulson [b]

[a] University of Texas at San Antonio College of Business.
[b] University of Colorado at Boulder, E-mail: barry.poulson@colorado.edu
[*] Corresponding author's email address: john.merrifield@utsa.edu

ARTICLE INFO

Keywords:
Budget stabilization;
Fiscal consolidation;
Fiscal rules;
State fiscal policy.
TEL.

ABSTRACT

A dynamic scoring simulation analysis compares the size-of-government effects of four state-government-level Tax and Expenditure Limit (TEL) and Budget Stabilization Fund (BSF) combinations. Two of the four TEL-BSF combinations have population-plus-inflation as the basis for the spending growth limit. The other two TEL-BSF combinations have personal-income-growth as the basis for the spending growth cap. A sensitivity analysis, including a regression analysis of Monte-Carlo-generated 'observations', measures the significance of the model parameter choices. The personal-income-growth TELs don't constrain spending growth at all in some states. In most states, a TEL based on a significant multiple of population plus inflation restrains fiscal expansion more than either version of our personal income growth TEL. The findings provide some important policy issues: there are significant differences in the fiscal and economic impacts of likely TEL design alternatives, and there is a likely trade-off between stringency and political durability.

## 1.0    Introduction

Early economic analysis of tax and expenditure limits (TELs) assessed the fiscal restraint effects of actual state and local fiscal rules. That perspective reflected the rapid growth in state government spending. It rose from 4% of GDP in the 1950s to 10% in the 1990s (Holcombe and Sobel 1997; Merrifield 2000). And it reflects attempts at push-back; for example, TEL referenda such as Howard Jarvis' Prop 13 in California that arose in the 1970s and continue to this day. Recent extraordinary economic and fiscal stress expanded interest in TELs to include budget stability and economic growth effects. But the "unprecedented"[1] aggregate state spending growth between the 2001 Recession and the Great Recession (Stansel and Mitchell 2008), and continued rapid growth thereafter, convinced us to focus, first, on how some possible second generation TELs would differ in terms of their effects on government size and growth. So, the purpose of our work is to compare our TEL simulation findings to the state spending record for 1998-2014. So, we assess how enforced TELs with specific features would have impacted fiscal expansion. That's a very different issue than how the first generation TELs actually impacted state

---

[1] A 1/26/09 Wall Street Journal editorial ("States of Fiscal Distress") said, "The state spending binge of the last five years has been unprecedented in American history." Thirty-seven states had FY 2005-08 general fund expenditure growth (NASBO.org data) that topped Calendar 2004-2007 personal income growth (BEA data). In those 37 states, FY 2005-08 general fund spending growth averaged five percentage points above personal income growth.

fiscal outcomes. Our perspective also sets aside the procedural rules issue (Kioko and Martell, 2012); that is, how TEL effectiveness varies with rules for changing a TEL's constraints on revenue or exclusions.

After the literature review and some background information, we describe our data, the 1999-2014 dynamic scoring simulation model that is our key exploratory tool, and the preferred parameter values of the four major TEL designs we examine. After we present the results that arise with our preferred parameter values, we use a sensitivity analysis that includes regression analysis of Monte Carlo-generated 'observations' to report the sensitivity of our findings to small changes in key parameters and assumptions. Policy recommendations and a summary complete the paper.

## 2.0    Background facts and literature review

The diverse fiscal stress policy responses to the Great Recession[2] included tax hikes that often ratchet up state revenue and spending over the business cycle. Some states felt obliged to raise taxes or borrow money to sustain spending financed with federal stimulus funds (Young and Sobel 2013). And there has been renewed interest in TELs, though, so far, none of the formal proposals to enact caps or strengthen existing limits have been enacted. Even without new caps on revenue or spending growth, nearly every state has some spending constraints. Only Vermont lacks a balanced budget requirement. Forty-seven states have reserve funds that can help them stabilize spending during recessions and for emergency response. A variety of other fiscal rules may constrain state fiscal policies, including TELs, line item veto and super-majority vote requirements to raise taxes or issue debt.[3] Probably because state legislators can easily suspend or circumvent most of the thirty-two TELs (Waisenen 2010; Zycher 2013), early studies found small and ambiguous impacts on state budgets (Abrams and Dougan, 1986; Bails, 1990; Bails and Tieslau, 2000; Howard, 1989; Joyce and Mullins, 1991; Mullins and Joyce, 1996; Poterba and Reuben, 1999; Poterba, 1994; Poulson and Kaplan, 1994). More recent research reveals that TEL effectiveness depends upon TEL design (Bails and Tieslau, 2000; Elder, 1992; Kousser et al., 2008; Merrifield 2000; Merrifield and Monson, 2011; Merrifield and Poulson, 2014b; Mitchell, 2010; Mitchell and Tusyznski, 2011; New, 2001, 2003; Poulson, 2004; Shadbegian, 1996; Stansel, 1994; Stansel and Mitchell 2008).

The most important design issues are spending category exemptions, the basis for the cap on the growth of state spending/revenues, and whether "re-basing (see below)" (Kioko, 2011) occurs if actual spending or revenue falls short of the cap amount. Seventeen states have TEL caps based on some measure of personal income, typically annual, or average annual, rate of growth in personal income. Six states link their TEL to spending as a share of personal income. When TEL caps linked to personal income are binding, the instability in personal income growth results in volatility in state spending over the business cycle (Crain, 2003; Holcombe and Sobel 1997; Kioko, 2011; Krol, 2007; Mitchell, 2010; Mullins and Wallin, 2004; Schunk and Woodward, 2005; Shadbegian, 1996; Wagner and Elder, 2005; Waisenen 2010). And the tax base of some states keeps personal income growth-based TELs from being binding very often.

The effectiveness of personal income-based TELs as state budget limits also depends upon the economic conditions and business cycle phase when they take effect (Mitchell, 2010). For example, they seem to be more binding in low income states. Florida introduced a TEL linked to personal income in the recession phase of the business cycle that was never binding. The spending cap rose more rapidly than the actual growth in state revenue. Inflation plus the rate of population growth is the basis of the most restrictive TELs. Arkansas, California, Colorado, Nevada, Ohio, Utah, and Washington have that type of TEL.

The impact of TELs on the size or growth in state budgets can depend upon what is referred to as 'rebasing' in the literature. When actual spending falls below the spending allowed by the TEL ceiling, re-basing creates a lower base against which the cap is applied in future years, a so-called 'ratchet down' effect. Ten states do such an annual 'rebasing' of their TEL (Kioko, 2011) cap. Five of those states use actual revenue or expenditures as the base for future budget caps: Connecticut, Montana, New Jersey, Texas, and Washington. The other five states set the limit as a percent of annually estimated revenues: Delaware, Iowa, Missouri, Oklahoma, and Rhode Island.

The 'ratchet down' effect of re-based TEL caps is controversial. For example, Colorado's original TEL (the Taxpayer Bill of Rights Amendment enacted in 1992) applied a stringent limit, inflation plus population growth, to actual revenue or allowable revenue, whichever was lower, and did not provide for a reserve fund to sustain spending growth above revenue growth when revenue grew more slowly than population plus inflation. So, after years of

---

[2] Demands for state government services tend to be countercyclical, whereas the revenue stream is pro cyclical (Holcombe and Sobel 1997).

[3]Similar issues arise in the discussions of state fiscal rules and fiscal consolidation and fiscal adjustment at the national level (Agenor and Yilmaz 2011, Fatas and Mihov 2006, Bird and Mandilaras 2013). Critics argue that state rules such as the balanced budget requirement are pro-cyclical and depress productive public investment and spending.

budget expansion at population plus inflation, plus surplus revenue rebates to taxpayers, Colorado experienced a spending 'ratchet down' effect when the 2001 Recession kept revenue growth well below population plus inflation. The spending limit fell more than it would have had the state kept some pre-recession surplus funds in a budget stabilization fund (BSF), or been allowed to catch up to the population plus inflation trend line once revenue growth recovered. So, the recession-driven shortfall below the cap amount set a lower limit on spending growth in the subsequent years of economic recovery. Dissatisfaction with that yielded narrow voter approval of Referendum C in 2005 which eliminated the annual rebasing feature of Colorado's TEL. The new TEL cap now bases allowable growth on the previous year's allowable spending, not actual expenditures. This is a good example of how TELs can change over time if voters become convinced that the TEL cap is overly stringent, and it signals a likely trade-off, at some level(s) of stringency between stringency and initial political feasibility and between stringency and political sustainability. A perception of excess stringency weakened Colorado's TABOR, while, arguably gradually leading to the now virtual irrelevance of California's TEL (the GANN spending limit that constrained California's spending growth in the 1980s).

The spending reduction achieved by a TEL also depends on the disposition of surplus revenue. Four states simply keep the surplus in the general fund (Arkansas, Hawaii, South Carolina, and Texas), leaving long-term spending unaffected. California, Colorado, Massachusetts, and Oregon rebate surplus revenue to taxpayers. Thirteen states allocate a portion of the surplus revenue to a budget stabilization fund (BSF). Surplus revenue may also be earmarked for emergency funds, capital funds, maintenance and repair, education, or debt relief (Merrifield and Monson, 2011; Primo 2006; Waisenen 2010; Zycher 2013).

## 3.0    Dynamic simulation analysis of TELs

Our dynamic scoring simulation model assesses two variations each of the two basic TEL basis options: 1a.) Population + Inflation; and 1b.) Because some legislators claim that pressures, such as pension liabilities and federal Medicaid mandates, can make a population growth plus inflation TEL too stringent, we explore (population growth plus inflation) x1.2 as a TEL basis; 2a.) The most recent annual growth in personal income; and 2b.) A seemingly less volatile personal income growth TEL basis is the average rate of increase for the previous ten years.

To focus on differences in TEL/BSF design, the model assumes effective enforcement of the model's caps. Except in some of the sensitivity analyses of our four TEL versions, each year's full BSF balance is available to bridge gaps between revenue and the TEL cap. So, in each period, General Fund spending is at the cap amount when revenue, or revenue plus BSF account balance, is equal to or greater than the cap amount. The BSF deposit-withdrawal rules allocate 100% of positive differences between revenue and the spending cap amount to the BSF, up to its account balance cap of ten percent of expected General Fund spending.

Our simulation model includes dynamic scoring to capture economic growth effects of the TEL impact on the size of government. Based on longstanding benefit-cost analysis practice the model uses a conservative estimate of six percent (Tietenberg and Lewis, 2012 [p 63]; OMB Circular A-94, 1992 mandates 7 percent; Randall, 1987 [p 240]) for the opportunity cost rate for moving resources from the private to the public sector. Consistent with Barro (1990), the model assumes that the opportunity cost rate applies to small private-to-public transfers of resources. When a surplus (Revenue > [Spending + BSF Deposit]) triggers a reduction in a state's Marginal Tax Rate, the model employs the conservative estimate in Poulson and Kaplan (2008) that a one percentage drop in a state's marginal tax rate increases that state's rate of economic growth 0.251 percent.

The state general fund revenue data, excluding Federal funds, come from the National Association of State Budget Officers (NASBO.org). Those data start in Fiscal Year 1998. Data gaps forced exclusion of Alaska and New Mexico. That eliminated the need to assess whether Alaska should be excluded, which is common, because of its unique revenue mix. Population data are from the Census Bureau. Personal income data are from the Bureau of Economic Analysis. The simulation analysis time period was 1998 to 2014 (economic growth years), which means the results are not biased by the choice of starting and ending years. After computing population plus inflation rates, and allowing for data availability lags,[4] the model calculates each state's revised General Fund spending for 1999 onward as follows:

$$RSPEND_t = (RSPEND_{t-1} \times (1 + TEL_t)) \tag{1a}$$
$$\text{When:} \quad RSPEND_t < RREV_t$$
$$\text{or } RSPEND_t < RREV_t + BSF_t$$
$$\text{Otherwise: } RSPEND_t = RREV_t + BSF_t \tag{1b}$$

---

[4] Fiscal year N budget-making must rely on the calendar year N-2 population estimate, and the May, N-1 CPI.

With:  $RSPEND_t$ = revised General Fund (GF) spending in fiscal year t
   $TEL_t$ = the spending growth rate cap for fiscal year t as a decimal
   $BSF_t$ = fiscal year t budget stabilization fund account balance
   $RREV_t$ = year t General Fund revenue revised via dynamic scoring

A cap 'shortfall' ($SHORTFALL_t$)occurs when:  $RSPEND_t < (RSPEND_{t-1} \times (1 + TEL_t))$.          (2)
Shortfalls occur only after depletion of the BSF.  The shortfall rate for year t is:
   $SHFALLRATE_t = SHORTFALL_t / RREV_t$          (3)

Shortfalls reduce the RSPEND base for subsequent years creating the so-called ratchet-down effect (Poulson, 2009; Kioko, 2011).  The year t ratchet-down effect is:  $1 - (RSPEND_t / RSPENDMAX_t)$.  $RSPENDMAX_t$ is the spending level in year t if there had been no shortfalls prior to year t, or in year t.  BSF outlays eliminate, reduce, or delay the ratchet-down effects of recessions.

Afirst Year (t=0=1998) BSF account balance results by applying the TEL cap to five previous years of spending data,[5] and allocating the net difference between actual and simulated spending to $BSF_0$.  When cap level spending tops revenue $\{(RSPEND_{t-1} \times (1 + TEL_t)) > RREV_t\}$, we debited the BSF as follows:
   $BSFDEBIT = (RSPEND_{t-1} \times (1 + TEL_t)) - RREV_t$, or $BSF_t$, whichever is less.          (4)

When cap level expenditure is less than revenue $\{(RSPEND_{t-1} \times (1 + TEL_t)) < RREV_t\}$, we deposited funds into the BSF as follows:
   $BSFDEPOSIT = (RREV_t - RPSEND_t)$ or $((RSPEND_t \times 0.1) - BSF_{t-1})$, whichever is less.          (5)
When $RREV_t > RSPEND_t$, surplus revenue may also be available for taxpayer rebates, and for deposit into other state accounts, such as for emergency preparedness and capital investment.
   $SURP_t = (RREV_t - RSPEND_t) - (BSF_t - BSF_{t-1})$          (6)

Surpluses trigger proportional marginal tax rate reductions.  So, a surplus that is ten percent of revised revenue, together with a parameter that mandates cutting taxes by half of the surpluses share of revised revenue ($NCYC = 0.5$), means a five percent MTR cut.  If the TEL growth rule is a target rather than a limit, shortfalls, as defined above, trigger MTR increases.  That yields personal income and tax revenue adjustments via dynamic scoring. When $SURP_{t-1} > 0$, the model increases economic growth ($GROWTH_t$ = the increase in growth) beyond the level that actually occurred:
   $GROWTH_t = (NCYC \times (SURP_{t-1}/RREV_{t-1}) \times MTR_{t-1} \times RMTR) + GROWTH_{t-1}$          (7)

   Where:  NCYC = 0.2 in our simulations.  Individual states would set NCYC at the
         perceived non-cyclical share of the surplus or shortfall.
   $MTR_t$ = average $MTR_t$ from Skidmore et al (2011) adjusted for MTR changes.
   RMTR = growth rate $\Delta$ per pct point drop in $MTR_t$ (Poulson and Kaplan 2008).

To limit the scope of the analysis, we examined the TEL growth rules as limits, not targets.  So, in our simulations, the extra $GROWTH_t = GROWTH_{t-1}$ in zero surplus or shortfall years.  That provides a basis for a revised personal income (RPI) estimate:
   $RPI_t = ((RPI_{t-1} \times (1 + ((API_t - API_{t-1})/API_{t-1})) \times (1 + GROWTH_t)) + (OCR \times SURP_t)$          (8)

   Where:  OCR= opportunity cost rate (0.06); $API_t$ = actual personal income in fiscal year t.

MTR change (lower tax rates) directly lowers tax revenue (STATIC), and then the personal income change that results from the MTR changes impacts tax revenue collection (DYNAMIC).
   $RREV_t = STATIC_t + DYNAMIC_t$          (9)
When $SURP_t \geq 0$:
   $DYNAMIC_t = (RPI_t - API_t) \times ((MTR_t/100) \times (1 - (NCYC \times (SURP_{t-1}/RREV_{t-1}))))$          (10)
   $STATIC_t = ((1 + ((AREV_t - AREV_{t-1})/AREV_{t-1})) \times RREV_{t-1}) \times$
                     $(1 - (NCYC \times (SURP_{t-1}/RREV_{t-1})))$          (11)
   Where:  $AREV_t$ = actual revenue for fiscal year t.

## 4.0  Empirical results

We present results for two growth years (FY 2008 and FY 2014) and two recession years: FY 2003, the bottom of the 2001 Recession, and for FY 2010, the bottom of the Great Recession.  More detailed simulation results are in an online technical appendix.

---

[5] NASBO's General Fund expenditure data series begins five years sooner than the revenue data series.

## Constrained state spending growth

The dynamic simulation analysis indicates that each of the TEL designs would have notably reduced state spending over the time period analyzed. Table 1 compares the ratio of simulated to actual spending. The 2008 and 2014 TEL impacts are not influenced by the effects of a recession.

**Table 1:** Ratio of simulated to actual spending

| TEL Cap Basis | FY1999 | FY2003 | FY2008 | FY2010 | FY2014 |
|---|---|---|---|---|---|
| Pop+Infl | 94.6% | 91.1% | 77.7% | 85.9% | 80.5% |
| (Pop+Infl)x1.2 | 95.5% | 93.2% | 82.0% | 88.7% | 84.1% |
| One-Yr ΔPI | 98.7% | 97.9% | 90.2% | 92.3% | 87.5% |
| Ten-YrAvg ΔPI | 98.2% | 98.1% | 89.4% | 93.6% | 90.0% |

After fifteen years, the basic population growth plus inflation basis constrains average state spending 7.5 to ten percentage points more than TELs based on personal income growth; about twice as much growth reduction as the growth at long-run personal income growth rates. The (Pop+Infl)x1.2 TEL ends the 15-year period roughly splitting the difference between the basic population growth plus inflation basis and the Personal Income TELs; without the volatility of the Personal Income TELs.[6]

The ratio of spending to personal income (Table 2) tells a similar story, again, as early as the first year, 1999; a year of rapid spending growth in most states. The TEL linked to population growth and inflation yields the sharpest drop (to 4.08%) in the ratio of simulated spending to dynamic scoring-revised personal income. Spending is half a percentage point larger at 4.57% with the least stringent Personal Income TEL.

**Table 2:** Ratio of simulated spending to personal income

| TEL Cap Basis | FY1999 | FY2003 | FY2008 | FY2010 | FY2014 |
|---|---|---|---|---|---|
| Pop+Infl | 5.28% | 4.89% | 4.29% | 4.39% | 4.08% |
| (Pop+Infl)x1.2 | 5.33% | 5.00% | 4.53% | 4.54% | 4.27% |
| One-Yr ΔPI | 5.50% | 5.27% | 4.99% | 4.74% | 4.46% |
| Ten-YrAvg ΔPI | 5.47% | 5.28% | 4.93% | 4.80% | 4.57% |

## Ratchet down' effects

The simulations set each year's cap amount as growth from the current year, so shortfalls lower future spending limits. Another study (Merrifield and Poulson, 2014a) explores the alternate approach wherein the TEL limit grows over time independent from actual revenue and spending. Table 3 indicates how much the size of government depends on ratchet-down effects of the different TELs. Years of economic growth and recovery, FY 2008 and FY 2014, are chosen to capture the cumulative average ratchet down effect. With the population plus inflation TELs, fewer states see ratchet-down effects, and where present, the ratchet-down effect is smaller. Part of the reason for the large differences between the population-plus-inflation and personal income TELs, and between the simulated 2008 and 2014spending with the personal income TELs and the no-shortfall level is that the personal income TELs are widely non-binding in the long-run; binding in some states in high economic growth years, but not over multiple years.

**Table 3:** Average ratchet-down effects of those ratcheted down

| TEL Cap Basis | FY 2008 | FY 2014 |
|---|---|---|
| POP+INFL | 10.1% / 17 | 14.2% / 30 |
| (POP+ INFL)x1.2 | 12.2% / 19 | 18.3% / 34 |
| One-YR PI | 13.6% / 33 | 23.9% / 46 |
| Ten-YR PI | 14.1% / 33 | 25.1% / 47 |

The personal income TEL ratchet-down effects are larger than the gap between simulated and actual spending. That is, most states would have spent more in 2008 and 2014 than they actually spent those years had they grown their General Fund spending every year by the personal income TEL cap rate. But with ratchet-down effects, even limiting spending growth over actual previous spending to personal income growth amounts to a long-run strategy to shrink the relative size of *most* state governments. That could be a legitimate strategy; to have periodic lean years to pressure legislators to assess spending priorities and eliminate marginal programs. For those who favor that, note from Table 7 that fifteen states (48 minus 33) were able to keep spending growing every year

---

[6] Other findings; beyond the scope of this article.

through 2008 by either personal income growth measure. It took the severity of the Great Recession to knock all but one or two of them off that path. With population plus inflation as the TEL cap basis, it does not take ratchet-down effects to shrink state governments, though for many states, the ratchet-down effects dominate the other grounds for reductions in spending growth.

## Sensitivity analysis

The Monte Carlo process for every combination of our parameter test values yielded 768 observations. The parameter test values included the preferred values described earlier, and at least one plausible alternative. For example, the BSF account limit parameter had three test values; 10% (preferred value), 15%, and 25% of General Fund spending. An ordinary least squares regression of the 768 observations generated by the Monte Carlo process yielded estimates of the average marginal effect of each parameter.

Because the personal income TEL basis is often not a limit, and possibly an un-attractive basis for a part-time limit, we focused our Monte Carlo-based, general sensitivity tests on the Population plus Inflation TEL basis. The OLS regressions yielded the 99% significant coefficients in Table 4. Noteworthy from the regressions is that the rate at which surplus revenue goes to the BSF (when BSFCRED $\geq$ 50%, the minimum test value) does not significantly affect any outcome. The average marginal effect of a change from Pop+Infl to (Pop+Infl)x1.2 is 1/5th of the first row's coefficients. Upping MULT from 1.0 to 1.2 (by 1/5th) raises the ratio of average 2014 general fund spending to personal income by nearly ¼ percentage point (1/5th of 0.0114).

| Table 4: OLS regression of Monte Carlo observations | | | |
|---|---|---|---|
| | 2014 GF/PI | GF Spend Sim/Act Ratio | Average Ratchet Down by 2014 |
| MULT | 0.0114 | 0.2115 | 0.1762 |
| BSFCRED | | | |
| BSFDEB | | | 0.0146 |
| BSFCAP | 0.0064 | 0.1249 | -0.0319 |
| OCR | | | |
| NCYC | -0.0080 | -0.1563 | 0.0227 |
| RMTR | 0.1499 | 3.5787 | -1.1851 |
| R-Squared | 0.924 | 0.926 | 0.89 |

The average effect of changing MULT from 1.0 to 1.2 is a 3.5% increase in the degree of ratchet down, including eight more states (not shown) with ratchet down by 2014. The BSFCAP coefficients indicate that a five percentage point increase in the allowed size of the budget stabilization fund (for example, from ten to fifteen percent of General Fund spending) would increase simulated spending's share of personal income by 0.032 percent (five times 0.0064), raising the ratio of simulated to actual spending by 0.625 percent, and decreasing ratchet down by 0.16 percent. A ten percentage point increase in the tax cut response to surplus revenue (NCYC = 0.2 vs. 0.1) cuts the average size of the state government's share of personal income by 0.08 percent, and it cuts the 2014 ratio of simulated to actual spending by 1.6 percent. NCYC = 0.2 vs 0.1 increases the average degree of ratchet down by 2014 by 0.23 percent. The large RMTR coefficients are deceptive. The RMTR changes – changes in dynamic scoring effects - are statistically significant explanatory variables, but the Monte Carlo tests only vary RMTR by about 1/10 of one percentage point. So, a change in RMTR from 0.00251 to 0.00374 would increase 2014 state spending's (more revenue to spend) share of personal income by 0.018 percent, increase the 2014 ratio of simulated to actual spending by 0.44 percent, and decrease the average ratchet-down effect by 0.15 percent.

## 5.0    Conclusion

The fiscal stress experienced by the states in recent recessions, and slow growth alongside rapid state government expansion in some states renewed interest in TELs; TELs with lower caps and less likely to be circumvented or gutted because of excessive stringency. Existing TELs have mostly done little to constrain state spending. A 48-state, 1998-2014 dynamic scoring simulation model adds to that literature by exploring differences in the impact of two population growth plus inflation TELs and two personal income growth TELs; designs that are representative of the TEL measure revisions introduced in most states. Each of those four TEL designs significantly reduced state spending relative to actual state spending. Our model measured the average differences between two population plus inflation TELs and two personal income TELs. Individual states can use the model to assess how the TEL alternatives would impact them.

A controversial issue in the TEL literature is the potential for cumulative 'ratchet down' effects over time. Our model identified likely significant 'ratchet down' effects of differences in TEL design. Periodic ratchet down effects can yield some desirable effects alongside the fiscal stress they create, and likely pressure to weaken the TEL.

The population growth plus inflation x1.2 TEL could be a good compromise in the tradeoff between tight limits with greater stability and faster economic growth, and accommodation of some of the spending pressures – some beyond the control of state-level policymakers - that could otherwise yield constitutional amendments that gut a TEL; that have an extensive history of doing so. For spending hawks, a slightly larger rate of state spending growth may be a price worth paying for increased political sustainability. Another likely political sustainability factor is a budget stabilization fund (BSF) with clear, stringent deposit/withdrawal rules. The tradeoff here is a somewhat higher rate of spending growth for fewer political support-eroding ratchet-down effects. Measurement of the likely BSF-generated improvement in budget stability – less fiscal stress – is another political durability factor that is beyond the scope of this article.

## References

Abrams, B., and A.Dougan."The Effects of Constitutional Restraints on Government Spending." Public Choice, 49(2), 1986,101-16. http://dx.doi.org/10.1007/BF00181033

Agenor, P. and D. Yilmaz."The Tyranny of Rules: Fiscal Discipline, Productive Spending, and Growth in a Perfect Foresight Model." Journal of Economic Policy Reform, 14(1), 2011, 69-99. http://dx.doi.org/10.1080/17487870.2010.503086

Amiel, L.,S. Deller, and J. Stallman. "Economic Growth and Tax Expenditure Limitations." Review of Regional Studies, 42, 2012, 185–206.

Bails, D. "The Effectiveness of Tax and Expenditure Limits: a Re-Evaluation." American Journal of Economics and Sociology, 49(2), 1990, 223-238. http://dx.doi.org/10.1111/j.1536-7150.1990.tb02274.x

Bails, D., and M. Tieslau."The Impact of Fiscal Constitutions on State and Local Expenditures." Cato Journal, 20(2), 2000,255-277.

Bania, N. and Stone, J.A. "Ranking State Fiscal Structures: Using Theory and Evidence," Journal of Policy Analysis and Management, 27(4), 2008, 751–770

Barro, R." Government Spending in a Simple Model of Endogenous Growth." Journal of Political Economy, 98(1), 1990, 103–117. http://dx.doi.org/10.1086/261726

Bennet, J.T., and T.DiLorenzo.1982. "Off-Budget Activities of Local Government." Public Choice, 39(3), 1982, 333-342.

Bergh, A. and M. Henrekson. "Government Size and Growth: A Survey and Interpretation of the Evidence." Journal of Economic Surveys,25, 2011, 872–97. http://dx.doi.org/10.1111/j.1467-6419.2011.00697.x

Bird, G., and A. Mandilaras. "Fiscal Imbalances and Output Cries in Europe: Will the Fiscal Compact Help or Hinder?" Journal of Economic Policy Reform, 16(1), 2013, 1-16. http://dx.doi.org/10.1080/17487870.2013.765081

Chapman, S. "A Hole They Dug for Themselves." Reasonline (July 30, 2009), http://www.reason.com/news/show/135123.html

Crain, M. Volatile States: Institutions, Policy, and the Performance of American State Economies. Ann Arbor, MI: University of Michigan Press, 2003. http://dx.doi.org/10.3998/mpub.16580

Dahlby, B. "Progressive Taxation and the Social Marginal Cost of Public Funds." Journal of Public Economics, 67(1), 1998, 105-122. http://dx.doi.org/10.1016/S0047-2727(97)00049-2

Deller, S., J. Stallman, and L. Amiel."The Impact of State and Local Tax and Expenditure Limits on State Economic Growth." Growth and Change,43, 2012, 56–84. http://dx.doi.org/10.1111/j.1468-2257.2011.00577.x

Douglas, J.W., and R.K. Gaddie."State Rainy Day Funds and Fiscal Crises: Rainy Day Funds and the 1990-1991 Recession Revisited." Public Budgeting & Finance, 22(1), 2002, 19-30. http://dx.doi.org/10.1111/1540-5850.00063

Elder, H. "Exploring the Tax Revolt: an Analysis of the Effectiveness of State Tax and Expenditure Limitation Laws. Public Finance Quarterly, 20(1), 1992, 47-63. http://dx.doi.org/10.1177/109114219202000103

Eliason, P., and Lutz, B. 2015. Can fiscal rules constrain the size of government? An analysis of the crown jewel of tax and expenditure limitations. Mimeo.

Fatas, A., and I. Mihov. "The Macroeconomic Effect of Fiscal Rules in the U.S. States." Journal of Public Economics, 90, 2006, 101-117. http://dx.doi.org/10.1016/j.jpubeco.2005.02.005

Gold, S.D. Preparing for the Next Recession: Rainy Day Funds and Other Tools for the States. Legislative Finance Paper No. 41, National Conference of State Legislatures, 1983.

Holcombe, R. and R. Sobel. Growth and Variability in State Tax Revenue. London: Greenwood Press, 1997.

Howard, M. Tax and expenditure limitations: there is no story. Public Budgeting and Finance 9, 1989, 83-90. http://dx.doi.org/10.1111/1540-5850.00820

Joyce, P., and Mullins, D. "The changing fiscal structure of the state and local public sector: the impact of tax and expenditure limits. Public Administration Review 51, 1991, 240-53. http://dx.doi.org/10.2307/976948

Kalita, M. "Governors Try to Convince Voters that Budget Woes are Theirs, Too." Wall Street Journal, October19, 2009, A2.

Kioko, S., and Martell, C. "Impact of state level tax and expenditure limits (TELs) on government revenues and aid to local governments." Public Finance Review 40(6), 2012, 736-766. http://dx.doi.org/10.1177/1091142112438460

Kioko, S.N. "Structure of State-Level Tax and Expenditure Limits." Public Budgeting & Finance,31(2), 2011, 43-79. http://dx.doi.org/10.1111/j.1540-5850.2011.00979.x

Kousser, T., M. McCubbins, and E. Moule. "For Whom the TEL Tolls: Can State Tax and Expenditure Limits Effectively Reduce Spending?" State Politics and Policy Quarterly, 8, 2008, 331-361. http://dx.doi.org/10.1177/153244000800800401

Knight, B., and A. Levinson, A. "Rainy Day Funds and State Government Savings." National Tax Journal, 52(3), 1999, 459-72.

Krol, R. "The Role of Fiscal and Political Institutions in Limiting the Size of State Government." Cato Journal, 27(3), 2007, 431-445.

Ladner, M., and B. Schlomach. Government Growth or Poverty Reduction? Lessons from the States. Austin, TX: Texas Public Policy Foundation, 2007, RR 01–2007 Available at www.texaspolicy.com/pdf/ 2007-01-RR01-poverty-ladner-bs.pdf

Lav, I. J. TABOR Has Hampered Economic Growth and Reduced the Quality of Life in Colorado. Washington, DC: Center on Budget and Policy Priorities (October, 2009).

Lav, I. J., and E. Williams. Tax and Spending Limits. Washington, DC: Center on Budget and Policy Priorities (March, 2010).

Lyons, K., and N. Johnson. Education Investment, Not TABOR, Fueled Colorado's Economic Growth in the 1990s. Washington, DC: Center on Budget and Policy Priorities (March, 2006).

Makin, A.J. "Expansionary Versus Contractionary Government Spending." Contemporary Economic Policy, 33(1), 2015, 56-65. http://dx.doi.org/10.1111/coep.12051

McBride, W. What Is the Evidence on Taxes and Growth? Washington: Tax Foundation, Special Report No. 207, 2012. Available at http://taxfoundation.org/article/what-evidence-taxes-and-growth.

McGuire, T., and K. S. Reuben. The Colorado Revenue Limit: The Economic Effects of TABOR. Washington, DC: Economic Policy Institute, (March, 2006).

Merrifield, J. "Factors That Influence the Level of Underground Government." Public Finance Quarterly,22(4), 1994, 462–82. http://dx.doi.org/10.1177/109114219402200404

Merrifield, J. and D. Monson. "Simulation of a Constitutional Spending Limit for a Conservative State: with Dynamic Adjustment and Sensitivity Analysis." Public Budgeting & Finance, 31(3), 2011, 1-25. http://dx.doi.org/10.1111/j.1540-5850.2011.00984.x

Merrifield, J. "State Government Expenditure Determinants and Tax Revenue Determinants Revisited." Public Choice, 102(1-2), 2000, 25-50. http://dx.doi.org/10.1023/A:1005036918713

Merrifield J., and B. Poulson. "Ratchet-Down Effects of Spending Caps: A Dynamic Scoring Simulation Analysis." Denver: Western Economic Association International, 2014a.

Merrifield J. and B. Poulson."State Fiscal Policies for Budget Stabilization and Economic Growth: a Dynamic Scoring Analysis." Cato Journal, 34(1), 2014b, 47-81.

Merrifield J., and B. Poulson. Can the Debt be Stopped?: Rules Based Policy Options for Addressing the Federal Fiscal Crisis. (forthcoming) Lexington, MA: Lexington Books, 2016.

Mitchell, M. TEL It Like It Is: Do State Tax and Expenditure Limits Actually Limit Spending? George Mason University: Mercatus Center, Working Paper No. 10–71, 2010.

Mitchell, M., and N. Tuszynski. Institutions and State Spending: An Overview. George Mason University: Mercatus Center, Working Paper No. 11–39 (October, 2011).

Mullins, D., and Joyce, P. "Tax and expenditure limitations and state and local fiscal structure: an empirical assessment." Public Budgeting and Finance 16, 1996, 75-101. http://dx.doi.org/10.1111/1540-5850.01061

Mullins, D., and B. Wallin. "Tax and Expenditure Limitations: Introduction and Overview." Public Budgeting & Finance,24(4), 2004, 2–15. http://dx.doi.org/10.1111/j.0275-1100.2004.00344.x

New, M. Limiting Government through Direct Democracy: The Case of Tax and Expenditure Limitations. Washington, DC: Cato Institute Policy Analysis No. 420, 2001.

Office of Management and Budget. Circular A-94, 1992.

Padquit, K. (2011) State Business Tax Climate Index, 8th ed. Washington, DC: Tax Foundation.

Peterson, W. "Over-Investment in Public Sector Capital." Cato Journal,14(1), 1994, 2011, 1–6.

Poterba, J., and Reuben, K. 1999. Fiscal rules and state borrowing costs: evidence from California and other states. San Francisco, CA: Public Policy Institute of California.

Poterba, J. "Budget Institutions and Fiscal Policy in the States." American Economic Review, 86(2), 1996, 395-400.

Poterba, J. "State Responses to Fiscal Crises: the Effects of Budgetary Institutions and Politics. The Journal of Political Economy, 102(4), 1994, 799–821. http://dx.doi.org/10.1086/261955

Poulson, B. Tax and Spending Limits: Theory, Analysis, and Policy. Denver: Independence Institute Issue Paper IP–2–2004, 2004.

Poulson, B., and J. Kaplan. (1994) "A Rentseeking Model of TELs." Public Choice, 79(1-2), 117-134 http://dx.doi.org/10.1007/BF01047922

Poulson, B., and J. Kaplan. (2008) "State Income Taxes and Economic Growth." Cato Journal, 28(1), 53-71.

Primo, D.M. "Stop Us Before We Spend Again: Institutional Constraints On Government Spending." Economics & Politics, 18(3), 2006, 269–312. http://dx.doi.org/10.1111/j.1468-0343.2006.00171.x

Randall, A. Resource Economics (2nd Ed). NY: John Wiley & Son, 1987.

Rueben, K. and C. Rosenberg. (2009) "State and Local Tax Policy: What Are Rainy Day Funds and How Do They Work," in: The Tax Policy Briefing Book. Washington, DC: Tax Policy Center.

Reed, R.W.,C.L. Rogers, and M. Skidmore. "On Estimating Marginal Tax Rates for U.S. States." National Tax Journal,64(1), 2011, 59–84. http://dx.doi.org/10.17310/ntj.2011.1.03

Reuben, K., and C. Rosenberg. "State and Local Tax Policy: What Are Rainy Day Funds and How Do They Work?" in: Tax Policy Briefing Book, Washington, DC: Tax Policy Center (August 2009).

Schunk, D., and D. Woodward. "Spending Stabilization Rules: a Solution to Recurring State Budget Crises." Public Budgeting & Finance, 25(4), 2005, 105-124. http://dx.doi.org/10.1111/j.1540-5850.2005.00376.x

Shadbegian, R. "Do Tax and Expenditure Limitations Affect the Size and Growth of State Government?" Contemporary Economic Policy, 14(1), 1996, 22-35. http://dx.doi.org/10.1111/j.1465-7287.1996.tb00600.x

Sobel, R.S. "The Political Costs of Tax Increases and Expenditure Reductions: Evidence from State Legislative Turnover." Public Choice, 96(1-2), 1998, 61-79. http://dx.doi.org/10.1023/A:1004953215739

Spencer, R.W., and W.P. Yohe. "The Crowding Out of Private Expenditures by Fiscal Policy Actions." Federal Reserve Bank of St. Louis Review (October, 1970), 12–24.

Stallman J. "State Tax and Expenditure Limitations and Economic Performance." Public Budgeting & Finance, 31(4), 2011, 109–35. http://dx.doi.org/10.1111/j.1540-5850.2011.00995.x

Stallman J., and S. Deller. "Impact of State and Local Tax and Expenditure Limits on Economic Growth." Applied Economic Letters,17, 2010, 645–48. http://dx.doi.org/10.1080/13504850802297954

Stansel, D. Taming Leviathan: Are Tax and Spending Limits the Answer? Washington, DC: Cato Institute Policy Analysis No. 213, 1994.

Stansel, D., and D. Mitchell. "State Fiscal Crises: are Rapid Spending Increases to Blame?" Cato Journal, 28(3), 2008, 435-448.

Taylor, J.B. "Why Permanent Tax Cuts Are the Best Stimulus." Wall Street Journal, November 25, 2008.

Tietenberg, T., and A. Lewis. Environmental and Natural Resource Economics (9th Ed.). Boston, MA: Pearson, 2012.

Vock, D., P. Prah,S. Fehr, M. Stephen, M. Maynard, J. Gramlich, and K. Leonard. Beyond California: States in Fiscal Peril. Washington, DC: Pew Center on the States, 2009.

Wagner, G.A. "Are State Budget Stabilization Funds Only the Illusion of Savings: Evidence From Stationary Panel Data." Quarterly Review of Economic and Finance,43(2), 2003, 2213-38. http://dx.doi.org/10.1016/S1062-9769(01)00132-6

Wagner, G.A. "The Bond Market and Fiscal Institutions: Have Budget Stabilization Funds Reduced State Borrowing Costs?" National Tax Review, 57(4), 2004, 75-804. http://dx.doi.org/10.17310/ntj.2004.4.01

Wagner, G., and E. Elder. "The Role of Budget Stabilization Funds in Smoothing Government Expenditures over the Business Cycle." Public Finance Review, 33(4), 2005, 439-465. http://dx.doi.org/10.1177/1091142105276442

Wagner, G., and E. Elder. "Revenue Cycles and the Distribution of Shortfalls in U.S. States: Implications for an Optimal Rainy Day Fund." National Tax Journal, 60(4), 2007, 727-742. http://dx.doi.org/10.17310/ntj.2007.4.03

Wagner, G., and R. Sobel. "State Budget Stabilization Fund Adoption: Preparing for the Next Recession or Circumventing Fiscal Constraints?" Public Choice, 126(1-2), 2006, 177-199. http://dx.doi.org/10.1007/s11127-006-7752-x

Waisanen, B. State Tax and Expenditure Limits-2010. Washington, DC: National Conference of State Legislatures, 2010.

Young A., and R. Sobel."Recovery and Reinvestment Act Spending at the State Level: Keynesian Stimulus or Distributive Politics." Public Choice, 155(3-4), 2013, 449-468. http://dx.doi.org/10.1007/s11127-011-9876-x

Zycher B. (May, 2013) State and Local Spending: Do Tax and Expenditure Limits Work? Washington, DC: American Enterprise Institute.

# 15

# Fiscal policy, employment, and output in South Africa: An open economy analysis

Mthokozisi Mlilo [a*], Umakrishnan Kollamparambi [b]

[a] Lecturer, University of the Witwatersrand; Faculty of Commerce, Law and Management. Tel: +27 11 717 8099.
[b] Associate Professor, University of the Witwatersrand; Faculty of Commerce, Law and Management. Email: uma.kollamparambil@wits.ac.za. Tel: +27 11 717 8113.
*Corresponding author's email address: mthokozisi.mlilo@wits.ac.za.

| ARTICLE INFO | ABSTRACT |
|---|---|
| Keywords:<br>Employment;<br>Fiscal policy shocks,<br>South Africa;<br>VAR. | We provide strong evidence of a positive shock to government spending on increase in employment (public and private), an appreciation of the real effective exchange rate and deterioration in the trade balance; but it has no effect on output for South Africa during the period 1994:1-2008:4. We also document that positive shocks to net taxes generate an increase in output, private employment and have no effect on public employment; it also leads to a depreciation of the real effective exchange rate and an improvement in the trade balance. An important finding in this study is that the transmission channel between government expenditures and output is not as direct as suggested in the Keynesian doctrine, but is indirectly shown by public employment's effects on output. We conclude that classical effects are predominant in the South African economy, i.e., only improvements in the supply-side components can be linked to increases in output. |

## 1.0    Introduction

There is a renewed interest amongst economists on the role of fiscal policy in fostering economic development (Benetrix & Lane, 2007; Fatas & Mihov, 2009). Fiscal policy works through both aggregate demand and aggregate supply channels. Changes in total taxes and public expenditure affect the level of aggregate demand in the economy, whereas, the structure of taxation and public expenditure affect, among others, the incentives to save, work and invest, export and import goods and services (Jha, 2007).

The most notable quest for explaining the effects of fiscal policy shocks in an open economy, arguably, began with Kim and Roubini (2005). Nonetheless, there is no universally agreed upon transmission channel both in the closed and open economy scenarios (Giordano, Momigliano, Neri, & Perotti, 2007; Perotti, 2002, 2007). The empirical evidence matches this theoretical ambiguity, with some studies finding a positive association between government spending and output (Blanchard & Perotti, 2002; Fatas & Mihov, 2009), others a negative association (Baxter & King, 1993).

Despite numerous studies being done on the subject and the lack of consensus among different theoretical models, there is scant empirical evidence on the effects of fiscal policy shocks on private and public sector employment.

Most of the debate in the literature on the transmission channel of fiscal policy has concentrated on non-African economies with the exception of a few authors (see, M'Amanja, Morrissey, & Lloyd, (2006) for Kenya and; Perkins, Fedderke, and Luiz (2005) for South Africa). To the best of our knowledge there is no study done for the South African economy that links the impact of fiscal shocks on employment whilst controlling for the external sector. This study aims to fill this gap.

To understand the workings of the macroeconomy, economists have often found it useful to think of the economy as a dynamic, stochastic system, which responds to both present and past random shocks. It is from this perspective that we employ the vector autoregressive (VAR) model in this study to analyse the effects of fiscal policy shocks[1] on output and employment in South Africa.

The results reveal that in the short run, a positive shock to government spending results in an increase in employment (public and private), an appreciation of the real effective exchange rate and deterioration in the trade balance; but it has no effect on output. Positive shocks to net taxes generate an increase in output, private employment and have no effect on public employment; it also leads to a depreciation of the real effective exchange rate and an improvement in the trade balance. An important finding in this study is that the transmission channel between government expenditures and output is not as direct as suggested in the Keynesian doctrine, but is indirectly shown by public employment's effects on output.

This study is organised as follows; literature review is discussed in section 2; section 3 delivers the methodology and in section 4 we talk about the empirical estimation and results whilst section 5 provides the conclusion and recommendations.

## 2.0    Literature review

### 2.1    Fiscal policy effects on output and employment

The impact of fiscal policy on output and employment is inconclusive both in the theoretical and empirical literature. In the body of theoretical literature, according to the Keynesian (old and new) doctrine and the real business cycle (RBC) theory, expansionary fiscal policy has a positive effect on output and employment whilst in the classical and neo-classical theory, fiscal policy is considered to be ineffective in the long run.

The distinguishing feature in these theories is the nature of household behaviour. Classical theory bases its argument on the presence of Ricardian equivalence and consumption smoothing, wherefore households are rational and quickly notice that an expansionary fiscal policy in the form of an increase in government spending will eventually be met by a future tax rise, hence they adjust their consumption patterns (i.e., decrease) in an attempt to save for the future when wealth is diminished from a tax increase. In doing so, the decrease in consumption reduces output through aggregate demand and eventually lowering the equilibrium level of output and employment. In RBC models on the other hand, households seek to maximise their lifetime utility through intertemporal and intratemporal substitution effects of leisure. Faced with a rise in government spending, these households in their bid to maximise utility would cut consumption and leisure through intertemporal substitution. This would result in an increase in labour supply and output.

The New Keynesian and Keynesian theories to fiscal policy transmission differ markedly from the classical theories by claiming the presence of non-Ricardian type of households and 'crowding-in' effects which ultimately lead to a positive correlation between government spending, consumption, output and employment.

Keynesian economics differs markedly from laissez-faire economics in that; it believes public expenditures can be the key engine for higher output or economic growth. The Keynesians argue that, public expenditures have a positive impact on output through the multiplier effect. This rests on its assumption of price rigidity and the existence of excess capacity. Traditional Keynesian IS-LM model explains that an increase in government spending directly boosts aggregate demand and leads to an increase in employment levels. This channel is through the consumption - multiplier effect on output. The New-Keynesian (NK) school is borne out of disequilibria and price-wage stickiness in the economy. From this perspective, involuntary unemployment is seen as the outcome of quantity constraints generated by trading at non-market-clearing prices. In the NK world, price rigidities and non-Ricardian consumers form the major assumptions. If the two assumptions hold then increases in government expenditures will result in increases in private consumption. The rise in labour income triggers an increase in consumption of 'rule of thumb' households implying a rise in aggregate demand, leading to a further expansion in output and employment.

---

[1] Fiscal policy shocks in this context comprise government spending and revenue shocks. Different fiscal policies such as balanced budget expansions can then be described as different linear combinations of these two basic shocks.

A central conclusion of Keynesian economics is that there is no strong automatic tendency for output and employment to move towards the full employment level. This conclusion conflicts with the tenets of classical economics, and other schools, such as supply-side economics or the Austrian school, which assume a general tendency towards equilibrium. Policy conclusions derived from the new-classical school is for governments not to rely on fiscal policy or monetary policy to stabilize the economy but rather rely on the self-correcting mechanisms of the market. If new classical view holds, fiscal policy is completely ineffective in the long run.

According to RBC theorists, there is no need for policy to affect the level of output in the economy as fluctuations in output are real and they do not represent a failure of markets to clear, but rather reflect the most efficient possible operation of the economy. However, recently RBC models of government spending have reaffirmed the role of the government expenditure in output and employment generation. RBC studies argue that government expenditure shocks are more important in explaining labour market movements along a cycle (Finn, 1998).

## 2.2    Empirical evidence

Using a VAR model on U.S. data, Koray and McMillin (2007) obtain results that support the NOEM framework, where positive shocks to government expenditure leads to a transitory positive effect on output and long-lived positive effect on the price level. There is a depreciation of the real exchange rate and the trade balance improves. This finding is similar to the result obtained by Kim and Roubini (2005); they find that government deficits are associated with a currency depreciation and an improvement in the current account. Afonso and Sousa (2009) also report similar findings for Spain.

Fatas & Mihov (2009) investigates the effects of fiscal policy shocks on the USA economy. In their study, they show that positive innovations to public expenditures had a positive and significant impact on GDP, employment and private consumption. Their empirical findings are at odds with a number of versions of real business cycle models, while they fit in with the predictions of the Investment Savings and Liquidity Monetary (IS-LM) model.

On the other hand, Rezk, Avramovich, and Basso (2006) and found that the effects of fiscal shocks on a set of macroeconomic variables notably unemployment and gross domestic product had relatively low statistical significance and the impact of the innovations was short lived thus casting doubt on the Keynesian doctrine of fiscal transmission mechanism.

Kneller, Bleaney, and Gemmell (1999) uses panel data on OECD countries and finds that productive expenditures, other (unclassified) expenditures and the budget surplus have a significant positive coefficient in explaining GDP per capita. However they note that these positive coefficients are only significant in the short run period and insignificant in the long run. These findings support the classical framework, that fiscal policy has no long run effects on output.

Studies on the issue are limited in the South African context. In one of the earliest studies on fiscal policy impact, Perkins et al. (2005) investigate the effects of public infrastructure investments on economic growth and find a bidirectional relationship between the variables. Ocran (2011), investigates the impact of fiscal policy on output and interest rate. While he finds the impact on output to be modest but persistent, the impact on interest rate is found to be substantial but temporary. Jooste, Liu, and Naraidoo (2013) analysed the impact of government expenditure and taxes on short and long-run GDP growth. The findings point to a positive and negative impact in the short run respectively but no significant impact is found in the long run. The surveyed studies do not look into the impact of fiscal policy on private and public employment.

## 2.3    Variables and expected signs

There are diverse and differing explanations when it comes to the transmission channel of fiscal policy shocks, hence this study seeks to trace out these relationships for the South African economy. The time chosen is before the financial crisis of 2009 which could distort the transmission of fiscal shocks.

Total government expenditure ($g$) and Net taxes ($nt$) are used as measures of fiscal policy in this study. It is assumed in this model that $g$ is exogenous since the government determines the values of $g$ prior to the fiscal period. Net taxes is used as a measure of government revenue. There is a need to control for the budget constraint, failure to do so leads to non-robust and inefficient estimates, hence the need to include net taxes (Deverajan, Swaroop, & Zou, 1996; Levine & Renelt, 1992; Su, Yucel, & Taylor, 2003). The aim of this study is to capture how employment responds to fiscal policy shocks. To capture these responses we would use the private ($pe$) and public ($ple$) employment indices taken from the South African reserve bank database. One transmission channel for this could be through output growth, where fiscal shock impacts output growth which in turn impacts employment levels as enunciated under Okun's law (Attfield & Silverstone, 1998). The study follows on previous studies on fiscal policy shocks that adopted real GDP ($y$) as a measure of real output in the transmission channel of fiscal policy shock (see Blanchard & Perotti, 2002; De Castro & Hernandez de Cos, 2006; Perotti, 2002). However fiscal policy shocks can impact on employment more directly through public works programme which may or may not result in output growth in the short run (Koohi-Kamali, 2010).

During the period under study the South African economy has become progressively more open to the world, hence we need to control for external influences by including the effects of international trade and we also exclude the time period after the financial crisis of 2009. Trade openness leads to lower volatility through a number of channels. Firstly, openness reduces the effectiveness of monetary policy as the prices of more goods become linked to the exchange rate, thus reducing the incentives to pursue inflationary policies (see, Rogoff, 1985; Romer, 1993). Secondly, it allows for a quicker recovery from external shocks (Calvo & Mishkin, 2003). Finally, it is expected that the role of fiscal policy is less emphasised in an open economy. It has become common in SVAR analysis to include the trade balance ($tb$) (for example see, Koray & McMillin, 2007; Monacelli & Perotti, 2006) and the real effective exchange rate ($reer$) in favour of their counterparts (for example see, Beetsma, Giuliodori, & Klaassen, 2007), i.e., current account and the real exchange rate, hence we follow suit. The exchange rate variable is used as a proxy for international influence by including the real effective exchange[2] rate for South Africa's 15 trading partners while the trade balance is constructed from the ratio of exports to imports.

The study makes use of quarterly data for South Africa spanning 1994q1 to 2008q4. The data employed in this study are obtained from the South African reserve bank database, and the International Monetary Fund's International Financial Statistics database (see, Table A.1 for a list of variables and summary statistics). Government expenditure is measured by gross government expenditure and net taxes are measured by tax revenue less transfers. Gross domestic product (GDP) is used as a proxy for output. Public and private employment figures are expressed as indices. Due to unavailability of quarterly data for the real effective exchange rate index, monthly indices are used to compute quarterly figures (see, MacDonald & Ricci, 2002). All level variables have been logged and deflated using the GDP deflator with year 2005 as the base year. Further the data is seasonally adjusted by making use of the Census X12 procedure. Following on Koray & McMillin, (2007), the trade balance is derived from the ratio of real exports to real imports. We note that there is a structural break in private and public employment series at about 2002q3 (see, figure A.1), we follow the procedure done in Blanchard and Quah (1989) to demean the series.

## 3.0    Methodology

In an attempt to trace the short run relationship we utilize the innovation accounting technique and variance decomposition in the vector autoregression (VAR) modelling framework. This has the ability to capture the dynamic interaction of fiscal policy variables and macroeconomic variables endogenously.

## 3.1    VAR Model

In a VAR model, all variables are treated as endogenous hence a VAR is a system of n-equations and n-variables put in a linear representation where each variable is explained by its own past, the past values of the other variables in the system and an error term. The equations in the system can be estimated using ordinary least squares (OLS) with each error term capturing 'surprise movements' or 'shocks'.
The VAR model is derived from the following structural model:

$$Y_t = \sum_{k=0}^{n} A_k \ Y_{t-k} + \varepsilon_t \qquad\qquad\qquad \text{Eq. (01)}$$

$Y_t$ is a 7x1 matrix of endogenous variables. This vector comprises of real gross domestic product ($y$) in logarithms, net taxes ($nt$) in logarithms, public expenditure ($g$) in logarithms, trade balance ratio ($tb$), real effective exchange rate ($reer$), total public employment index ($ple$) and total private employment index ($pe$), $A_0$ is a 7x7 matrix of coefficients specifying contemporaneous relations among variables in the model and $A_k$, $k=1,...n$, are coefficient matrices on $k$ lagged values of $Y$, and $\varepsilon_t$ is a vector of structural shocks which are independent and identically distributed ($iid$). The reduced form of the structural model yields the VAR model:

$$Y_t = B \ (L) Y_{t-1} + u_t \qquad\qquad\qquad \text{Eq. (02)}$$

Where $B = (1-A_0)^{-1}A_k$ and $U_t = (1-A_0)^{-1}\varepsilon_t$. $U_t = [u_t^y, u_t^g, u_t^r, u_t^{reer}, u_t^{tb}, u_t^{ple}, u_t^{pe}]'$, (L) is the lag operator, hence $B(L)$ is a matrix of autoregressive coefficients. The relationship between structural shocks and the reduced form residuals is given by this representation:

$$\mathcal{C}\varepsilon_t = Bu_t \qquad\qquad\qquad \text{Eq. (03)}$$

---

[2] We use monthly real effective exchange rate to construct the average quarterly real effective exchange rate.

where $\varepsilon_t \sim$ WN $(0, \Omega)$ and B and C are 7x7 matrices. Structural shocks are assumed to be contemporaneously uncorrelated; hence $\Omega$ is a diagonal matrix with the variances of the structural shocks on the diagonal. $U_t \sim$ WN $(0, \Sigma)$ are reduced form innovations, they are a linear combination of the structural shocks and reduced form innovations of the other variables (see, for example, Enders (2004) and Hamilton (1994)) with $\Sigma$ being a matrix of covariance. For one to analyse the effects of shocks, identifying restrictions should be imposed on the contemporaneous relations in the model by constraining some elements of matrix $A_0$ to equal zero.

## 3.2    Identification of fiscal shocks

Fiscal policy shocks are unanticipated changes to fiscal variables. However, such a definition is not only utopian but unrealistic (Mountford & Uhlig, 2002; Perotti, 2002) in a world where information dissemination is ever improving. In an attempt to recover these shocks, we employ the Choleski factorisation and the non-recursive decomposition would be used as an alternative identification scheme for sensitivity analysis.

In this study we are interested in estimating structural shocks of the fiscal variables ($g_t$ and $nt_t$) and in studying the responses of macro-economic variables; ($y_t$; $reer_t$; $tb_t$; $pe_t$; $ple_t$). The relationship in Equation (03) can be decomposed into the following equations;

$$u_t^g = \alpha_y^g u_t^y + \alpha_{reer}^g u_t^{reer} + \alpha_{tb}^g u_t^{tb} + \alpha_{ple}^g u_t^{ple} + \alpha_{pe}^g \alpha_t^{pe} + \beta_{nt}^g \varepsilon_t^{nt} + \varepsilon_t^g \qquad \text{Eq. (04)}$$

$$u_t^{nt} = \alpha_y^{nt} u_t^y + \alpha_{reer}^{nt} u_t^{reer} + \alpha_{tb}^{nt} u_t^{tb} + \alpha_{ple}^{nt} u_t^{ple} + \alpha_{pe}^{nt} \alpha_t^{pe} + \beta_g^{nt} \varepsilon_t^g + \varepsilon_t^{nt} \qquad \text{Eq. (05)}$$

$$u_t^y = \partial_g^y u_t^g + \partial_{nt}^y u_t^{nt} + \varepsilon_t^y \qquad \text{Eq. (06)}$$

$$u_t^{reer} = \partial_y^{reer} u_t^y + \partial_g^{reer} u_t^g + \partial_{nt}^{reer} u_t^{nt} + \varepsilon_t^{reer} \qquad \text{Eq. (07)}$$

$$u_t^{tb} = \partial_y^{tb} u_t^y + \partial_E^{tb} u_t^E + \partial_{reer}^{tb} u_t^{reer} + \partial_g^{tb} u_t^g + \partial_T^{tb} u_t^r + \varepsilon_t^{tb} \qquad \text{Eq. (08)}$$

$$u_t^{ple} = \partial_y^{ple} u_t^y + \partial_{tb}^{ple} u_t^{tb} + \partial_{reer}^{ple} u_t^{reer} + \partial_g^{ple} u_t^g + \partial_{nt}^{ple} u_t^{nt} + \varepsilon_t^{ple} \qquad \text{Eq. (09)}$$

$$u_t^{pe} = \partial_y^{pe} u_t^y + \partial_{tr}^{pe} u_t^{tr} + \partial_{reer}^{pe} u_t^{reer} + \partial_{ple}^{pe} u_t^{ple} + \partial_g^{pe} u_t^g + \partial_{nt}^{pe} u_t^{nt} + \varepsilon_t^{pe} \qquad \text{Eq. (10)}$$

Where : $\alpha_j^i$ capture both the automatic elasticity of fiscal variable $i$ to the macroeconomic variables $j$ ($y$; $reer$; $tb$; $ple$; $pe$) and the discretionary change in variable $i$ by the policymaker in response to an innovation in these macro variables.

$\beta_j^i$, measures how structural shocks to the fiscal variables affect each other contemporaneously and $\partial_j^i$ measures the contemporaneous effects of shocks from one variable $j$ to another $i$ within the system. As a result the innovation accounting technique can be reduced into equation (03) and represented by these matrices:

$$
\begin{bmatrix}
1 & \beta_g^{nt} & 0 & 0 & 0 & 0 & 0 \\
\beta_{nt}^g & 1 & 0 & 0 & 0 & 0 & 0 \\
0 & 0 & 1 & 0 & 0 & 0 & 0 \\
0 & 0 & 0 & 1 & 0 & 0 & 0 \\
0 & 0 & 0 & 0 & 1 & 0 & 0 \\
0 & 0 & 0 & 0 & 0 & 1 & 0 \\
0 & 0 & 0 & 0 & 0 & 0 & 1
\end{bmatrix}
*
\begin{bmatrix}
\varepsilon_t^g \\
\varepsilon_t^{nt} \\
\varepsilon_t^y \\
\varepsilon_t^{reer} \\
\varepsilon_t^{tb} \\
\varepsilon_t^{ple} \\
\varepsilon_t^{pe}
\end{bmatrix}
=
\begin{bmatrix}
1 & 0 & -\alpha_y^g & -\alpha_{reer}^g & -\alpha_{tb}^g & -\alpha_{ple}^g & -\alpha_{pe}^g \\
0 & 1 & -\alpha_y^{nt} & -\alpha_{reer}^{nt} & \alpha_{tb}^{nt} & \alpha_{ple}^{nt} & -\alpha_{pe}^{nt} \\
-\partial_g^y & -\partial_{nt}^y & 1 & 0 & 0 & 0 & 0 \\
-\partial_g^{reer} & -\partial_{nt}^{reer} & -\partial_y^{reer} & 1 & 0 & 0 & 0 \\
-\partial_g^{tb} & -\partial_{nt}^{tb} & -\partial_y^{tb} & -\partial_{reer}^{tb} & 1 & 0 & 0 \\
-\partial_g^{ple} & -\partial_{nt}^{ple} & -\partial_y^{ple} & -\partial_{reer}^{ple} & -\partial_{tb}^{ple} & 1 & 0 \\
-\partial_g^{pe} & -\partial_{nt}^{pe} & -\partial_y^{pe} & -\partial_{reer}^{pe} & -\partial_{tb}^{pe} & \partial_{ple}^{pe} & 1
\end{bmatrix}
*
\begin{bmatrix}
u_t^g \\
u_t^{nt} \\
u_t^y \\
u_t^{reer} \\
u_t^{tb} \\
u_t^{ple} \\
u_t^{pe}
\end{bmatrix}
$$

From the above system, it is difficult to extract coefficients from the above system of equations, we need to impose some restrictions; following on Blanchard & Perotti (2002) who cite the existence of decision lags in fiscal policy which render automatic response to macroeconomic variables impossible within a short period of time, i.e., in a quarter. Blanchard & Perotti (2002) further identify these parameters based on institutional information about automatic elasticity of fiscal variables to macro variables. It takes more than a quarter for policymakers to adjust and respond to a fiscal policy shock, hence $\alpha_j^i = 0$. Blanchard & Perotti (2002) suggest the need to independently derive estimates of the automatic elasticities; however, in this study we utilise the *Eviews* structural factorisation procedure in estimating such elasticities.

We proceed to derive the reduced form residuals for the fiscal variables;

$$u_t^g = \beta_{nt}^g \varepsilon_t^{nt} + \varepsilon_t^g \qquad \text{Eq. (11)}$$

$$u_t^{nt} = \beta_g^{nt} \varepsilon_t^{nt} + \varepsilon_t^{nt} \qquad \text{Eq. (12)}$$

Based on the above system, we cannot solve for the coefficients yet. For identification purposes, we impose restrictions so as to ascertain the order of exogeneity. We do this by making these assumptions:

- Assume that government spending is totally exogenous and 'comes first' irrespective of other budget components, i.e., expenditures are set before the start of the fiscal year, therefore $\beta_{nt}^{g} = 0$
- Government revenue\net taxes are ordered second, revenue targets are set after the budget has been announced for the forthcoming fiscal year. Equation (13) and (14) reduce to;

$$u_t^g = \varepsilon_t^g \qquad\qquad\qquad \text{Eq. (13)}$$

$$u_t^{nt} = \beta_g^{nt} \varepsilon_t^g + \varepsilon_t^{nt} \qquad\qquad\qquad \text{Eq. (14)}$$

The ordering of the other variables in the system is not important since we want to investigate the effects of fiscal policy shocks (Koray & McMillin, 2007).

## 4.0    Estimation and discussion of results

### 4.1    Benchmark model estimation

We pre-test for the presence of unit roots and cointegration. However, its relevance for VAR analysis is not emphasized because firstly, the variables are integrated of differing orders. Secondly, the data may be quasi-nonstationary as the presence of unit roots in the time series cannot be tested with high power (Enders 2004).

Neglecting of cointegration constraints is further motivated by the following considerations. The analysis is generally focused on short-run constraints and the short-run dynamic response of the system. When cointegration constraints are excluded, this only implies that the long-run responses of some variables are not constrained and might follow a divergent path. However, the short-run analysis is still valid (Breuting, Bruggemann, & Lutkepohl, 2004; Hamilton, 1994, Chapter 18; Koray & McMillin, 2007; Rezk et al., 2006). Additionally, Sims et al. (1990) prove that standard asymptotic inference is not affected even when the variables included in a VAR in levels are cointegrated see for example, Breuting et al. (2004, p. 175 and 185). Nonetheless, we find that the Johansen test fails to reject the null hypothesis of no-cointegrating relationship at 1% level of significance. Above all, the goal of this study is to determine the short run dynamics, interrelationships among variables and not the interpretation of parameter estimates.

We also decided to use variables in levels despite some of them being non-stationary (see, results in Table A.2); this is motivated by Sims (1980) and Sims et al. (1990) who advise against differencing even if variables have unit roots (Kamps, 2005, p. 537; Koray & McMillin, 2007, p. 4; Phillips, 1998; Rezk et al., 2006, p. 6). Sims cites the danger of 'differencing away' important information on the relationship and co-movements contained in the data. Enders (2004, p. 270) also notes that variables in a VAR system should mimic the real data generating properties, hence one should be careful not to difference.

The optimal lag length for the VAR was chosen by using the Schwarz Bayesian Information Criteria (SBIC) as this method has been found to have desirable properties if the sample size employed is small (Perotti, 2002). Accordingly the VAR estimate with the lowest SBIC is the most efficient and will be chosen.

| Table 01: Lag length selection | | | | | | |
|---|---|---|---|---|---|---|
| lag | LL | LR | df | AIC | HQIC | SBIC |
| 0 | -2292.06 | | | 82.1 | 82.2 | 82.36 |
| 1 | -1971.83 | 640.48 | 49 | 72.49 | 73.2* | 74.44* |
| 2 | -1928.9 | 85.853 | 49 | 72.63 | 74.11 | 76.44 |
| 3 | -1843.79 | 170.32 | 49 | 71.34 | 73.5 | 76.92 |
| 4 | -1772.3 | 142.85* | 49 | 70.54* | 73.39 | 77.89 |

*, 1% significance level
Source: Author's calculations

After weighing the pros and cons of choosing between parsimony over efficiency we decided to use a single lag (see, Table 01). This was motivated by the fact that the HQIC also chose a single lag and VAR estimates produce stable characteristic roots, shown in Figure 01.

### 4.2    Impulse response for benchmark model

With the aid of impulse response functions (IRFs) we trace out the dynamic interaction between fiscal variables and other variables of interest.

**Figure 01:** Inverse roots

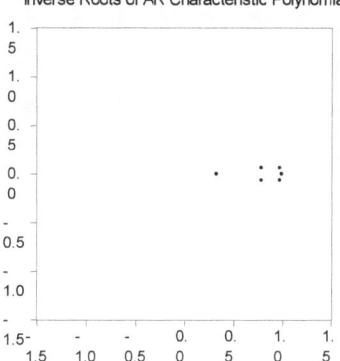

Inverse Roots of AR Characteristic Polynomial

Source: Author's calculations

### 4.2.1 Impact of government expenditure shock

In Figure A.2 the first row shows the responses following an increase of government expenditure. The response of output is statistically insignificant throughout the time horizon; this is in sharp contrast with the Keynesian doctrine, and in line with the classical theory which negates any demand induced output growth. This could be linked to the limited and less emphasised role of fiscal policy in spurring economic growth in South Africa for the period 1994-2008, for example the privatisation of most services by the government as spelt in GEAR (Hoskins, 1999).

The impulse response of public employment to a fiscal policy shock in the form of a positive increase to government expenditure is positive and statistically significant. The impact of expenditure shock on public employment is long lived, reaching its maximum at the second quarter. Private employment responses are significant and positive for a period of six quarters. This implies a responsive private sector employment to government efforts. This could be due to the nature of expenditures that were carried out during the period under review; in the last decade and a half the government has been pursuing poverty mitigation policies that had a main thrust on basic education, infrastructure building and health for the majority (Gordhan, 2009). While at first instance the impact of government expenditure on output and employment seem against expectations, it must be remembered that the period under study saw the government of South Africa pursue policies that were meant to reduce government deficits, redress inequality and reduce unemployment and poverty among the black population through the PWPs. The likely effect of such a fiscal mix coupled with low and falling labor productivity (Ferreira, 2013), is an increase in employment with no direct link to output. This finding is in line with that of Giordano et al. (2007, p. 720) who notes that the response of output to government wages/employment is unresponsive and statistically insignificant.

The response of the trade balance and exchange rate are statistically insignificant. This finding is in line with Baxter and King (1993) where she finds that a shock to government expenditure in a small open economy with incomplete asset markets among other rigidities had no effect on the current account (trade balance). This could be due to the low influence that fiscal policy had in shaping the South African economy for the period under study. The South African economy has over the years been steered from the monetary side, since mid-nineties, when the central bank adopted the inflation targeting policies while the treasury aimed at reducing its deficit and achieving balanced budgets (Manuel, 2007).

### 4.2.2 Impact of net taxes shock

The second row in figure A.2 shows the responses following an increase in net taxes. The response of output is positive and statistically significant; this defies the Keynesian doctrine, and coincides with classical theory where we have Ricardian agents who increase their labour supply following an increase in taxation. With an increase in labour supply, we expect an increase in production hence output too.

A positive shock to net taxes has no effect on public employment; impulse responses are statistically insignificant throughout the time horizon. Having looked at the South African budget deficit/surplus time series, one can argue that a government bent on reducing its budget deficit would be expected to have an inelastic 'public sector employment-tax elasticity', i.e., unresponsive public sector employment to an increase in net taxes (Weeks, 1999). This result perhaps resides in the flow of causality between the two variables, it is expected that a rising public sector wage-bill will lead to a need to increase the tax base and not the other way around. Taxes are not raised with the hope of increasing the public sector workforce.

However, private employment responses are positive and significant for a period of three quarters. This could imply the presence of Ricardian effects in the South African economy, an increase in taxes and the associated reduction in wealth, raises the marginal utility of wealth, inducing workers to devote a large fraction of their time to work, thereby increasing the long-run output growth and employment levels (Turnovsky, 2000). Perhaps an increase in net taxes makes consumers substitute away from consumption of leisure in favour of labour in the South African context, this finding is at odds with RBC models.

The response of the exchange rate is negative as expected; a positive net tax shock leads to an exchange rate depreciation with a one period lag response. The response is short lived with a span of three quarters and thereafter becoming insignificant. The impulse response reaches its peak after three quarters from impact and then steadily subsides for the next quarter. This is consistent with findings of Bartolini and Lahir (2006). It also matches the portfolio balance approach to balance of payments which stipulates that, following an increase in taxation the local unit depreciates due to a fall in spending. A fall in spending leads to an increase in overall savings and a decrease in interest rates if we assume Ricadian equivalence does not hold, possibly due to uncertainty. This result is at odds with the findings of Koray and McMillin (2007), Rebei (2004) and Burnside, Eichenbaum, and Fischer (2004) support the standard Mundell-Fleming models (Dornbusch, 1976; Fleming, 1962; Mundell, 1963) that postulate an exchange rate depreciation after an increase in taxation.

Trade balance's response is negative and ephemeral, lasting for a single quarter before it becomes insignificant. Interestingly the trade balance moves into a positive position after the first quarter despite the IRFs being insignificant. Net tax shock on the external economy can be reconciled with the J-curve phenomenon to current account adjustment following an exchange rate depreciation; it can be seen that the trade balance deteriorated on impact following an exchange rate depreciation before it started trending upwards. However, caution must be taken before making definite conclusions; this is in light of the noticeably low impact and the lack of statistical significance along the time horizon. Nonetheless, this could be linked to the nature of South Africa's current account position (2004-2008), i.e., being a net-importer and most of those imports commanding an inelastic demand (e.g., capital goods and petroleum products); hence the effect of an increase in taxes will not significantly reduce the volume of imports entering the economy. This is further supported by the negatively trending trade balance series for the period under study (see, Figure A.1). The South African economy has over the years been moving from a net-exporter position to being a heavily importing country of consumer and capital goods.

## 4.3    Variance decomposition

With variance decomposition we are able to analyse the proportion of movements in one variable that are due to errors in own and other variables' shocks in the system.

Variance decompositions to a government shock are shown in table 03. Government expenditure deviations barely explain output variation; it reaches a maximum of 2% at the second quarter and then declines gradually throughout the forecast period. This could be due to the strong presence of neo-classical characteristics in the economy's production function, where output growth is attributable to supply-side components and not demand-side components like government consumption of final goods. Table 3 also shows that deviations in public employment (PLE) are mostly explained by the government expenditure with the impact rising over the forecast period, starting from a low of 12.8% in the first period before reaching a peak of 35.3% in the 12th quarter. The proportion of deviations in private employment (PE) due to government expenditure (G) shock is also significant, averaging 28% over the forecast period. Government expenditure explains the greater part of the deviations in private employment in the forecast period than any other variable but private employment itself. This suggests that the type of expenditures carried out by the government were labour augmenting and hence 'crowded-in' private employment (SARB, 2002) . The impact of G on REER is too insignificant to draw any conclusions. The impact of government expenditure on trade balance starts off at very insignificant levels but grows to 5.9% over the forecast period.

Variance decompositions for Net taxes are shown in table 04. Net taxes' variation explains about 11% of the variation in output at the 5th period before it starts decreasing steadily to 7% by the 12th period. Although an average of 7% is a small figure, the results suggest a weak support for Ricardian type of agents in the South African economy, where an increase in taxation leads to a reduction in wealth and a subsequent increase in output. The proportion of deviations in private employment (PE) due to net taxes (NT) averages 16% over the forecast period. Although modest; it highlights the possibility of Ricardian effects in the manner with which agents make their decisions, i.e., increasing labour supply when faced with high taxes.

**Table 03:** Impact of G on the variance decomposition of Y, NT, PLE, PE, TB & REER

| Period | Y | NT | TB | REER | PLE | PE |
|---|---|---|---|---|---|---|
| 1 | 1.792799 | 9.880458 | 0.314922 | 0.189499 | 17.81057 | 13.27593 |
| 2 | 2.017832 | 9.983101 | 0.34362 | 0.424056 | 19.1404 | 17.10915 |
| 3 | 1.994196 | 9.796975 | 0.686089 | 0.348407 | 20.97606 | 20.53444 |
| 4 | 1.864319 | 9.490302 | 1.282115 | 0.307983 | 23.11299 | 23.70924 |
| 5 | 1.694445 | 9.135598 | 2.041058 | 0.358005 | 25.36014 | 26.58849 |
| 6 | 1.512798 | 8.757696 | 2.861208 | 0.458645 | 27.56648 | 29.08646 |
| 7 | 1.332404 | 8.362961 | 3.656805 | 0.568256 | 29.61553 | 31.12989 |
| 8 | 1.161116 | 7.95363 | 4.369285 | 0.662454 | 31.42029 | 32.67933 |
| 9 | 1.005451 | 7.533215 | 4.966042 | 0.731501 | 32.92057 | 33.73375 |
| 10 | 0.871807 | 7.107698 | 5.434449 | 0.774663 | 34.08126 | 34.32473 |
| 11 | 0.766662 | 6.685117 | 5.775587 | 0.795873 | 34.89013 | 34.50611 |
| 12 | 0.696432 | 6.274708 | 5.999183 | 0.801017 | 35.35464 | 34.34322 |

Net taxes' contribution to REER variation is seen to increase with time until it reaches a maximum of 31.7% at the 12th quarter supporting the standard Mundell-Fleming models that postulate an exchange rate depreciation after an increase in taxation. Net taxes explain on average 8% of the variation in the trade balance (TB).

**Table 04:** Impact of NT on the variance decomposition of Y, PLE, PE, TB & REER

| Period | Y | TB | REER | PLE | PE |
|---|---|---|---|---|---|
| 1 | 2.4742 | 8.4216 | 0.16393 | 0.386855 | 8.550918 |
| 2 | 6.709422 | 7.353828 | 6.666825 | 0.228326 | 16.51045 |
| 3 | 9.442033 | 6.974635 | 13.65691 | 0.18178 | 19.63844 |
| 4 | 10.77905 | 7.173633 | 19.04143 | 0.14879 | 20.2035 |
| 5 | 11.1734 | 7.542348 | 22.91125 | 0.129249 | 19.52213 |
| 6 | 10.99992 | 7.883697 | 25.64513 | 0.11729 | 18.2867 |
| 7 | 10.51233 | 8.141401 | 27.58008 | 0.106525 | 16.87225 |
| 8 | 9.871513 | 8.314771 | 28.96402 | 0.09692 | 15.48435 |
| 9 | 9.176052 | 8.419196 | 29.9679 | 0.094432 | 14.23004 |
| 10 | 8.484285 | 8.47172 | 30.70696 | 0.107743 | 13.15603 |
| 11 | 7.828914 | 8.486727 | 31.25856 | 0.145071 | 12.27219 |
| 12 | 7.226506 | 8.475203 | 31.67492 | 0.212119 | 11.56726 |

## 4.4    Robustness checks

The robustness of the results reported in the benchmark model was checked by employing a different identification criterion, and graphs for the IRFs for robustness checks are available on request.

In the Choleski decomposition we assumed that net tax decisions are made before output has been realized. We checked whether allowing net tax decisions to be made concurrently with output realization (i.e., case 1, $\partial_{nt}^{y} = 0$, $\alpha_{y}^{nt} \neq 0$) had any effect on our results. $A_0$ was specified as follows for case 1:

$$
A_0 = \begin{bmatrix}
1 & 0 & 0 & 0 & 0 & 0 & 0 \\
0 & 1 & -\alpha_{y}^{nt} & 0 & 0 & 0 & 0 \\
-\partial_{g}^{y} & 0 & 1 & 0 & 0 & 0 & 0 \\
-\partial_{g}^{reer} & -\partial_{nt}^{reer} & -\partial_{y}^{reer} & 1 & 0 & 0 & 0 \\
-\partial_{g}^{tb} & -\partial_{nt}^{tb} & -\partial_{y}^{tb} & -\partial_{reer}^{tb} & 1 & 0 & 0 \\
-\partial_{g}^{ple} & -\partial_{nt}^{ple} & -\partial_{y}^{ple} & -\partial_{reer}^{ple} & -\partial_{tb}^{ple} & 1 & 0 \\
-\partial_{g}^{pe} & -\partial_{nt}^{pe} & -\partial_{y}^{pe} & -\partial_{reer}^{pe} & -\partial_{tb}^{pe} & \partial_{ple}^{pe} & 1
\end{bmatrix}
$$

We found that the IRFs (not shown) computed using the above structural decomposition behave the same way as those of the Choleski decomposition. The contemporaneous effect of output on net taxes is positive; this is expected considering that indirect taxes and income tax move in tandem with output. We note that net tax revenue responds positively to a positive shock in output. Thus the previous results are robust to allowing contemporaneous correlation between $nt$ and $y$.

A second structural model was estimated. By allowing a dual contemporaneous correlation between the amount of realized output and net tax revenue (i.e., case 2, $\partial_{nt}^{y} = 0$, $\alpha_{y}^{nt} \neq 0$); and also $\partial_{nt}^{ple} = 0$ was restricted, i.e., contemporaneous effect of tax revenue on public employment was set to 0. In the benchmark model, this coefficient ($\partial_{nt}^{ple}$) is not significantly different from 0. The same ordering of variables was maintained as before, the contemporaneous relationships among the model variables ($A_0$) was specified to be the following for case 2:

$$
A_0 = \begin{bmatrix}
1 & 0 & 0 & 0 & 0 & 0 & 0 \\
0 & 1 & -\alpha_y^{nt} & 0 & 0 & 0 & 0 \\
-\partial_g^y & 0 & 1 & 0 & 0 & 0 & 0 \\
-\partial_g^{reer} & -\partial_{nt}^{reer} & -\partial_y^{reer} & 1 & 0 & 0 & 0 \\
-\partial_g^{tb} & -\partial_{nt}^{tb} & -\partial_y^{tb} & -\partial_{reer}^{tb} & 1 & 0 & 0 \\
-\partial_g^{ple} & 0 & -\partial_y^{ple} & -\partial_{reer}^{ple} & -\partial_{tb}^{ple} & 1 & 0 \\
-\partial_g^{pe} & -\partial_{nt}^{pe} & -\partial_y^{pe} & -\partial_{reer}^{pe} & -\partial_{tb}^{pe} & \partial_{ple}^{pe} & 1
\end{bmatrix}
$$

We found that our results are robust and similar to those of the benchmark model. Also we note that the restriction on employment is binding and valid (i.e., results of the Chi-square are not shown). We further check for robustness by employing a different sample starting in 1990:1-2008:4 and find that the results (not shown) are qualitatively similar to those of the benchmark model.

## 5.0   Conclusion

Drawing on the extant literature, this study investigates the effects of fiscal policy shocks on the South African economy. We examined the effects of fiscal policy shocks in a small open economy within a seven-variable VAR model. We find that the response of output to a shock in government expenditure variable is insignificant whilst output's response to a revenue (net tax) shock is positive.

The empirical findings indicate that there is a positive link between government spending and employment (private and public) and contrary to common belief, there seems to be a positive relationship between net taxes and private employment. Our findings also indicate that there is no link between government expenditure and output. This is surprising but reconcilable with classical doctrine; we also note that the effect of net taxes weakly increase output and this signals the presence of Ricardian effects in the economy.

The analysis suggests that employment levels can be boosted through government initiatives, mainly government expenditures seem to 'crowd-in' private sector employment and inflate public employment. An important finding in this study is that the transmission channel between government expenditures and output is not so direct as suggested in the Keynesian doctrine, but is indirectly shown by public employment's effects on output, hence we can conclude that classical effects are predominant in the South African economy, i.e., only improvements in the supply-side components can be linked to increases in output.

## References

Afonso, A., & Sousa, R. (2009). The Macroeconomic Effects of Fiscal Policy. ECB Working Paper Series, No. 991.
Attfield, C., & Silverstone, B. (1998). Okun's Law, Cointegration and Gap Variables. Journal of Macroeconomics, 20(3), 625-637. http://dx.doi.org/10.1016/S0164-0704(98)00076-7
Bartolini, L., & Lahir, A. (2006). Twin Deficits, Twenty Years Later. Current issues in economics and finance, 12(7).
Baxter, M., & King, R. (1993). Fiscal Policy in General Equilibrium. American Economic Review, Vol.83(3).
Beetsma, R., Giuliodori, M., & Klaassen, F. (2007). The Effects of Public Spending Shocks on Trade balances in the European Union. CEPR Discussion Paper.
Benetrix, A., & Lane, P. (2007). The Impact of Fiscal Shocks on the Irish Economy. IIIS Discussion paper No.287.
Blanchard, & Perotti. (2002). An Empirical Characterization of the Dynamic Effects of Changes in Government Spending and Taxes on Output. Quarterly Journal of Economics, Vol.4, 1329-1368. http://dx.doi.org/10.1162/003355302320935043
Blanchard, & Quah. (1989). The Dynamic Effects of Aggregate Demand and Supply Disturbances. American Economic Review, 79(September), 655-673.
Breuting, Bruggemann, & Lutkepohl. (2004). Stuctural Vector Autoregressions and Impulse Response Functions. In H. Lutkepohl & M. Kratzig (Eds.), Applied Times Series Econometrics (pp. 186-196). New York: Cambridge University Press.

Burnside, C., Eichenbaum, M., & Fischer, J. (2004). Fiscal Shocks and Their Consequences. Journal of Economic Theory, 115(1), 89-117. http://dx.doi.org/10.1016/S0022-0531(03)00252-7

Calvo, G., & Mishkin, F. (2003). The Mirage of Exchange Rate Regimes for Emerging Market Countries The Journal of Economic Persperctives, 17(4), 99-118.

De Castro, F., & Hernandez de Cos, P. (2006). The Effects of Exogenous Fiscal Policy in Spain.A SVAR Approach. European Central Bank Working Paper Series No. 647.

Deverajan, S., Swaroop, V., & Zou, H. (1996). The composition of public expenditure and economic output. Journal of Monetary Economics, 313-344. http://dx.doi.org/10.1016/S0304-3932(96)90039-2

Dornbusch, R. (1976). Expectations and Exchange rate dynamics. Journal of Political Economy, 84, 1161-1176. http://dx.doi.org/10.1086/260506

Enders, W. (2004). Applied Econometrics Time Series. New York: John Wiley and Sons.

Fatas, A., & Mihov, I. (2009). Why fiscal stimulus is likely to work. Journal of Finance, 12(1), 57-73. http://dx.doi.org/10.1111/j.1468-2362.2009.01235.x

Ferreira, E. (2013). Perspectives Of Administrative Employees On Service Delivery In The Public Sector. Retrieved 27 August, 2015, from http://uir.unisa.ac.za/bitstream/handle/10500/18690/ ferreira_ej_inaugural %20lecture.pdf?sequence=1&isAllowed=y

Finn, M., G. (1998). Cyclical effects of Government's employment and goods purchases. International Economic Review,Vol.39(3), 635-657. http://dx.doi.org/10.2307/2527394

Fleming, M. (1962). Domestic Financial Policies under Fixed and under Floating Exchange Rates. International Monetary Fund Staff Paper, 9, 369-79. Washington. http://dx.doi.org/10.2307/3866091

Giordano, Momigliano, Neri, & Perotti. (2007). The effects of fiscal policy in Italy: Evidence from a VAR model. European Journal of Political Economy, Vol.23(3), 707-733. http://dx.doi.org/10.1016/j.ejpoleco.2006.10.005

Gordhan, P. (2009). Annual Report (2008/09). Pretoria: Government of South Africa.

Hamilton, J. D. (1994). Time Series Analysis. Princeton, New Jersey: Princeton University Press.

Hoskins, S. (1999). The experience with trade liberalisation of selected industries in the Port Elizabeth-Utinehage Metropolitan Area. Paper presented at the TIPS 1999 Annual Forum, 19-22 September 1999, Muldersdrift.

Jha, R. (2007). Fiscal Policy in Developing Countries: A Synoptic View. Australia South Asia Research Centre, ASARC Working Paper 2007/01. http://dx.doi.org/10.2139/ssrn.978101

Jooste, D., Liu, G., & Naraidoo, C. (2013). Analysing the effects of Fiscal policy in the South African econmy. ERSA Working Paper No. 351.

Kamps, C. (2005). The Dynamic Effects of Public Capital: VAR Evidence for 22 OECD Countries. International Tax and Public Finance, Vol.12(4), 533-558. http://dx.doi.org/10.1007/s10797-005-1780-1

Kim, S., & Roubini, N. (2005). "Twin Deficits or Twin Divergence? Fiscal Policy, Current Account, and the Real Exchange Rate in the U.S.". mimeo.

Kneller, Bleaney, & Gemmell. (1999). Fiscal Policy and Growth: Evidence from OECD Countries. Journal of Public Economics, Vol.74, 171-190. http://dx.doi.org/10.1016/S0047-2727(99)00022-5

Koohi-Kamali, F. (2010). Public Works and Social Protection. European Union Report on Development.

Koray, F., & McMillin, D., W. (2007). Fiscal Shocks, the Trade Balance, and the Exchange Rate. Louisianna State University, Department of Economics Working paper Series 2007-05.

Levine, R., & Renelt, D., 1992. (1992). A sensitivity analysis of cross country growth regressions. American Economic Review 82, 942-963.

M'Amanja, D., Morrissey, O., & Lloyd, T. (2006). Chapter 16; Aid and Growth in Kenya: A Time Series Approach. In H. Beladi & E. Kwan Choi (Eds.), Theory and Practice of Foreign Aid (Frontiers of Economics and Globalization, Volume 1 (pp. 313-332): Emerald Group Publishing Limited.

MacDonald, R., & Ricci, L. (2002). Estimation of the equilibrium exchange rate for South Africa. IDEAS.

Manuel, T. (2007). Economic Policy And South Africa's Growth Strategy. Ministry of Finance.

Monacelli, T., & Perotti, R. (2006). Fiscal Policy,the Trade Balance, and the Real Exchange Rate:Implications for International Risk Sharing. CEPR Discussion papers.

Mountford, A., & Uhlig, H. (2002). What are the effects of fiscal policy shocks? CEPR, Working Paper 3338.

Mundell, R. (1963). Capital Mobility and Stabilization Policy under Fixed and Flexible Exchange Rates. Canadian Journal of Economics and Political Science, 29(November), 475-485. http://dx.doi.org/10.2307/139336

Ocran, M. (2011). Fiscal policy and economic growth in South Africa. Journal of Economic Studies, 38(5), 604-618. http://dx.doi.org/10.1108/01443581111161841

Perkins, P., Fedderke, J., & Luiz, J. (2005). An Analysis Of Economic Infrastructure Investment In South Africa. South African Journal of Economics, 73(2). http://dx.doi.org/10.1111/j.1813-6982.2005.00014.x

Perotti, R. (2002). Estimating the Effects of Fiscal Policy in OECD Countries. European Central Bank Working Paper No. 168.

Perotti, R. (2007). Fiscal Policy in Developing Countries: A Framework and Some Questions. World Bank Policy Research Working Paper, (WPS4365). http://dx.doi.org/10.1596/1813-9450-4365

Phillips, P. (1998). Impulse response and forecast error variance asymptotics in nonstationary VARs. Journal of Econometrics, 83, 21-56. http://dx.doi.org/10.1016/S0304-4076(97)00064-X

Rebei, N. (2004). Characterization of the Dynamic Effects of Fiscal Shocks in a Small Open Economy. Bank of Canada Working Paper 2004-41.

Rezk, E., Avramovich, M., & Basso, M. (2006). Dynamic Effects of Fiscal Shocks upon diverse Macroeconomic Variables: A Structural VAR Analysis for Argentina. Paper presented at the Presented at the XLI Annual Reunion of the Argentine Association of Political Economy, 15-17 November 2006. http://dx.doi.org/10.2139/ssrn.2005159

Rogoff, K. (1985). The Optimal Degree of Commitment to an Intermediate Monetary Target. Quarterly Journal of Economics,100(4), 1169-1190. http://dx.doi.org/10.2307/1885679

Romer, D. (1993). Openness and Inflation: Theory and Evidence. Quarterly Journal of Economics CVII, 869-904. http://dx.doi.org/10.2307/2118453

SARB. (2002, December). Quarterly Bulletin. South African Reserve Bank, (December). Pretoria.

Sims, C. A. (1980). Macroeconomics and reality. Econometrica, 48, 1-48. http://dx.doi.org/10.2307/1912017

Sims, C. A., Stock, & Watson. (1990). Inference in linear time series models with some unit roots. Econometrica, 58, 113-144. http://dx.doi.org/10.2307/2938337

Su, D., Yucel, M., & Taylor, L. (2003). Fiscal Policy and Output. Federal Reserve Bank of Dallas. Working Paper 0301.

Turnovsky, S. (2000). Fiscal Policy, elastic labour supply, and endogenous growth models. Journal of Monetary Economics, 45(1), 185-210. http://dx.doi.org/10.1016/S0304-3932(99)00047-1

Weeks, J. (1999). Commentary: Stuck in low GEAR? Macroeconomic policy in South Africa, 1996-98. Cambridge Journal of Economics, 23(6), 795-811. http://dx.doi.org/10.1093/cje/23.6.795

## Appendix

| Table A.1: Summary Statistics | | | | | | | |
|---|---|---|---|---|---|---|---|
|  | $G$ | $NT$ | $Y$ | $TB$ | $REER$ | $PLE$ | $PE$ |
| Mean | 269156.1 | 71480.38 | 348338.6 | 1.04 | 105.28 | 103.89 | 139.97 |
| Standard Error | 5311.04 | 4962.57 | 7209.51 | 0.01 | 1.47 | 0.78 | 5.49 |
| Standard Dev | 41139.21 | 38439.93 | 55844.68 | 0.08 | 11.38 | 6.05 | 42.57 |
| Kurtosis | -0.79 | -0.38 | -0.89 | -0.97 | -0.34 | -1.37 | -1.20 |
| Skewness | 0.78 | 0.83 | 0.53 | -0.19 | -0.47 | -0.03 | 0.63 |
| Range | 136780 | 139091 | 199480.1 | 0.33 | 45.45 | 21.7 | 115.5 |
| Minimum | 221487 | 22645 | 264654 | 0.88 | 76.65 | 93.9 | 98.2 |
| Maximum | 358267 | 161736 | 464134 | 1.21 | 122.10 | 115.6 | 213.7 |
| Count | 60 | 60 | 60 | 60 | 60 | 60 | 60 |

| Table A.2: ADF test results in levels | | | |
|---|---|---|---|
| Variable | ADF statistic | Critical 10% | Conclusion |
| g* | -5.199 | -2.593 | Stationary |
| nt | 0.814 | -2.593 | Non-stationary |
| y | 1.1 | -2.593 | Non-stationary |
| reer | -2.035 | -2.593 | Non-stationary |
| tb | -2.436 | -2.593 | Non-stationary |
| ple | -0.541 | -2.593 | Non -Stationary |
| pe | -1.82 | -3.172 | Non -Stationary |

**Figure A.1:** Graphs for all variables (In Levels)

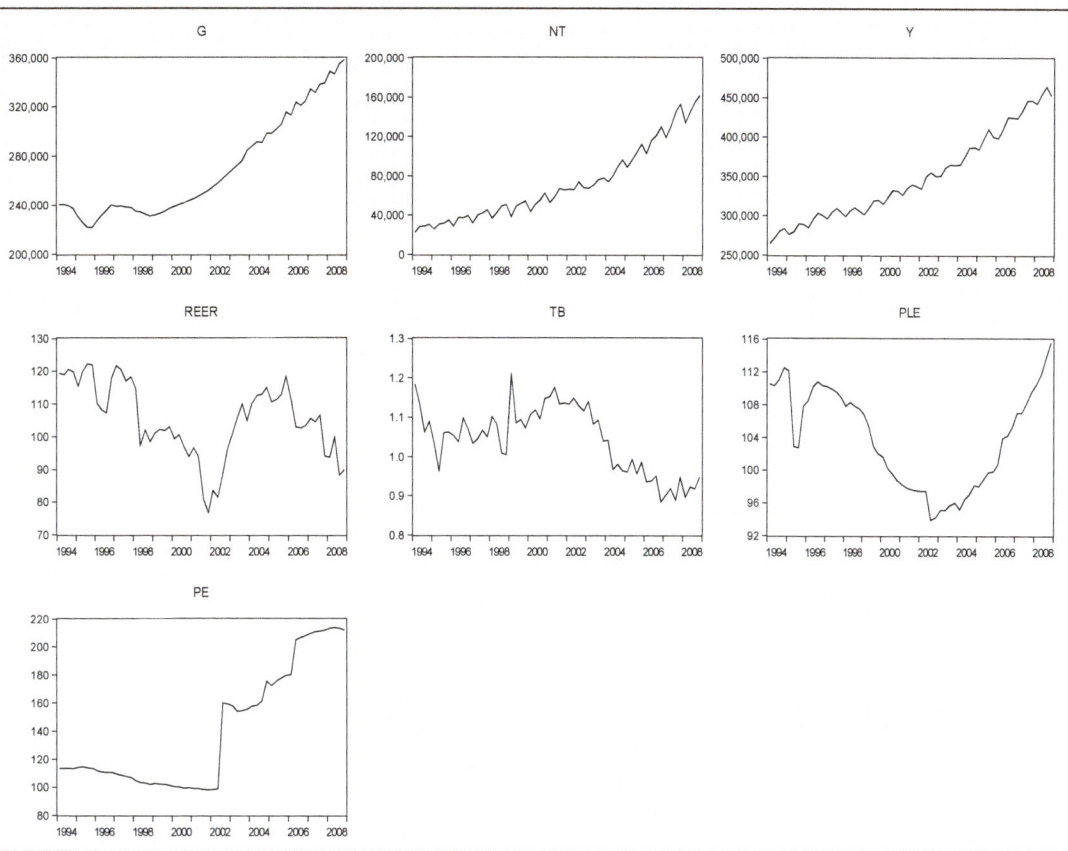

**Figure A.2:** Impulse response functions to a shock in government spending (g), Net Taxes (NT) and Public Employment (PLE)

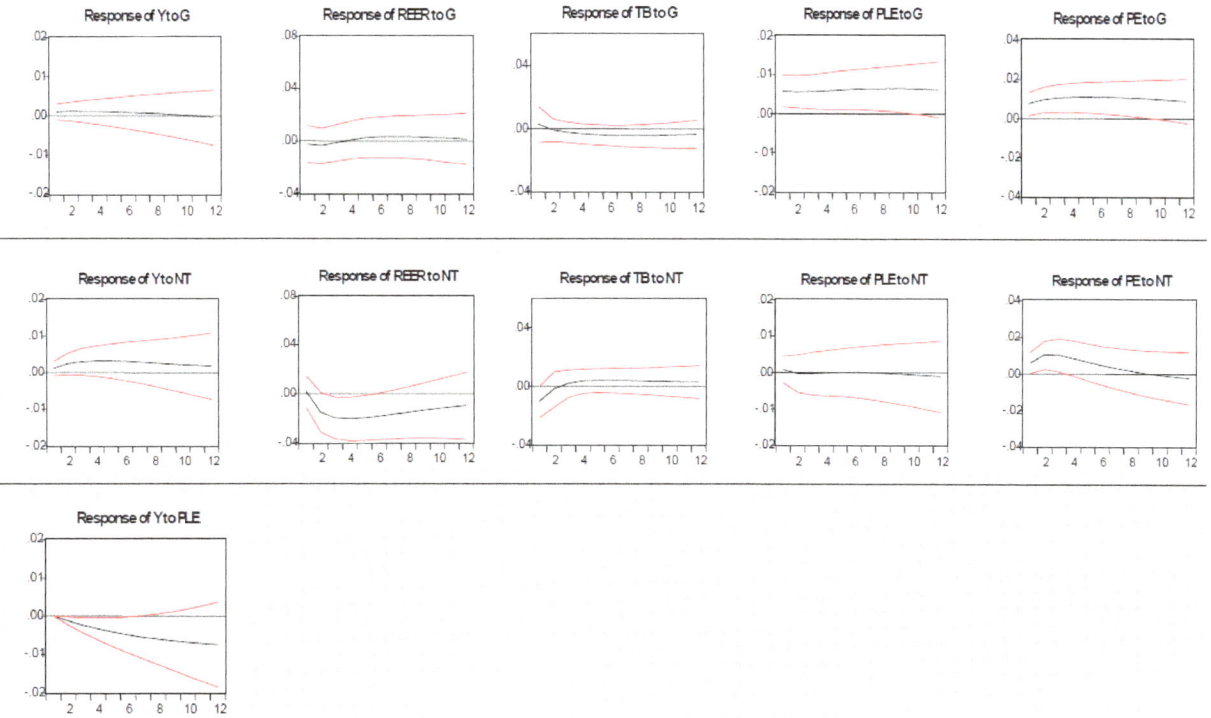

# 16

# Relation between ISE 30 index and ISE 30 index futures markets: Evidence from recursive and rolling cointegration

Aysegul Ates [a*]

[a] Akdeniz University, Department of Economics, Antalya, Turkey.
[*] Corresponding author's email address: aates@akdeniz.edu.tr

ARTICLE INFO

ABSTRACT

Keywords:
Emerging Markets;
Index Futures;
ISE 30;
Rolling Cointegration.

Turkey is one of the most dynamic emerging markets in the world and its futures market has developed significantly since the introduction of futures contracts by Turkish Derivatives Exchange in 2005. Istanbul Stock Index 30 (ISE 30) futures was one of the first contracts introduced and its trading increased rapidly over time. This study specifically focuses on the evolution and stability of cointegration relationship between the futures and spot prices of ISE 30 index during the sample period from February 4, 2005 through October 19, 2012. We test whether changing market conditions have an impact on the long-run relationship between spot index and index futures markets by employing recursive and rolling cointegration techniques. The findings reveal that the cointegration relationship weakens significantly during the global financial crisis and eurozone debt crisis periods but holds mostly over the estimation period.

## 1.0    Introduction

Turkey is one of the most dynamic emerging markets in the world and its futures market has developed significantly since 2005.[1] The development of the organized derivatives market in Turkey was a result of the growth of Turkish capital markets and economy in general. Turkish Derivatives Exchange (TurkDEX) was established in 2003 and formal trading of futures contracts started in February 2005. ISE 30 index futures contract was one of the first contracts introduced in 2005 and its trading volume has experienced tremendous growth since its introduction and it is currently the most liquid futures contract in Turkey.

Futures market has two important functions: Risk transfer and price discovery. The first of these functions pertains to hedging. Successful trading in equity index futures contracts would provide risk management solutions for hedgers and fund managers by shifting the price risk to others. Besides the traditional role of risk sharing, futures markets play an important role in the aggregation of information (Subrahmanyam 1991). Specifically, price discovery is defined as the search of equilibrium price by Harris et al. (1995) and as the dynamic process by which market impounds new information and market participants' expectations into asset prices by Hasbrouck (1995). Due to liquidity, relatively low transaction costs and low margin requirements new information about

---

[1] In 2006 TurkDEX was ranked the world's fastest growing derivatives exchange with a 273 percent increase to 6,848,087 contracts and in 2012 its trading volume reached to 62,474,464 contracts. (FIA, 2007, 2012).

asset prices are generally reflected in futures markets first. In sum, futures markets meet an important economic need by facilitating risk management and enabling price discovery.

The extent to which futures markets perform risk transfer and price discovery functions depends on a close relationship between cash and futures prices (Garbade and Silber, 1983). In other words, market linkage is essential for successful futures market. Theoretically prices in futures and cash markets are linked by an arbitrage relationship (cost-of-carry model) in the long run and the possibility of arbitrage prevents spot and futures prices of same asset from drifting apart over time. According to the cost-of-carry model theoretical price of index futures should be equal to underlying index price adjusted for the cost-of-carry. Specifically, arbitrage should ensure the difference between the current asset price and the futures price, which is the cost of carrying the asset, which involves transaction costs, dividend yields, interest rates and other factors (Stoll and Whaley 1990). The cost-of-carry formula can be presented as;

$$F_{t,T} = S_t e^{(r_t - d_t)(T-t)} \tag{1}$$

where $S_t$ is the index price at time t, $F_{t,T}$ is the index futures price at time t with maturity T, $r_t$ is the risk free interest rate, $d_t$ is the dividend yields and (T-t) is the time to maturity of the futures contracts. The literature which examines this arbitrage relationship uses error correction models (ECM) where error correction coefficient indicates the relative magnitude of adjustments in each market toward long run equilibrium price.[2] Market efficiency is related to no arbitrage and rapid elimination of arbitrage opportunities suggests that the market operates efficiently. The existence of the long run relationship indicates that the markets are efficient in the long run.[3] Another strand of this literature explains the relation between spot and futures markets in the context of price discovery hypothesis. This literature indicates that futures market and underlying spot market should share a common stochastic trend since both markets trading same underlying asset (Hasbrouck, 1995). Thus, spot and futures prices form a cointegration system. The cointegration system will have one cointegrating vector and one common stochastic trend. Hasbrouck (1995) employs the common trends representation of a set of variables to measure each market's contribution to the efficient price innovation. Futures and cash markets contribute to the discovery of a unique and common unobservable price that is the efficient price. In conclusion, the theoretical literature suggests that spot and futures price dynamics are based on a cointegrated system and this market linkage is essential to a successful futures market.

There is a large body of work dedicated to investigating the long-run relationship between spot index and index futures prices (i.e. market linkage), explicitly whether spot and futures prices are cointegrated has been tested extensively in literature (See Ghosh, 1993, Wang and Yau, 1994, Harris et al. 1995, Pizzi et al. 1998, Brooks et al., 2001, Lien et al.,2003, Pattarin and Ferretti, 2004, Floras and Vougas, 2008 etc.). Most of the literature in this area focuses on index futures market in developed countries. For example, Wahap and Lashgari (1993) examine the linkages between S&P 500 and FTSE 100 index spot and futures markets using daily data and find that futures and spot prices are cointegrated and conclude that the results are consistent with market efficiency. Arshanapalli and Doukas (1997) examine the S&P 500 spot and futures market linkages during the October 1987 market crash and using error correction model and find a cointegration relationship between these markets before and after the market crash with the exception of October 16 and 19 by using intraday data. More recently, Pattarin and Ferretti (2004) examine Mib30 index and index futures relationship in Italian derivatives market employing daily data from 1994 to 2002 and find that there is a long-run relationship between these markets and Italian stock index futures plays an vital role in price discovery process. On the other hand, the literature on equity index futures in emerging market setting is limited. This limited literature mostly focuses on the spot index and index futures relationship in the framework of price discovery hypothesis. Among them Lin et al. (2002), Zhong et al. (2004), Hou and Li (2013) can be counted. These studies focus on testing the long-run relationship between spot index and index futures market and find there is cointegration between these markets. However, time varying characteristics of cointegration are largely neglected in the literature.

Investigating the relationship between futures and spot index prices and the nature of the cointegration relationship is important in interrelated markets and time varying characteristics of cointegration between futures and cash prices should have implications for market efficiency, price discovery and hedging. A vital shortcoming of limited empirical research on Turkish index futures markets is that they do not examine time variation in data generating process linking these two markets. This paper addresses and examines the time variation in long-run relationship between ISE 30 index and index futures markets in Turkey. Recursive and rolling cointegration techniques allow us to examine how cointegration relationship changes over time due to new

---

[2] See Brenner and Kroner (1995) for an analysis of the link between arbitrage and cointegration.
[3] This is no-arbitrage definition of efficiency which is characterized by the absence of arbitrage opportunities in the market. Note that this definition is different from Fama's (1970) definition of efficient market in which prices always fully reflect available information.

information. It is relevant to focus on the Turkish index futures market developments during the recent crises (2008 global financial crisis and eurozone debt crisis) since market turmoil in the financial markets might affect the underlying data generating process. Previous studies that examine cointegration between Turkish index and futures markets conclude that there is a long run relationship between ISE 30 index and index futures markets. Kasman and Kasman (2008) test cointegration relationship between ISE 30 index and index futures using both Engle Granger two-step procedure and Johansen cointegration test and conclude that two markets are related in long-run for the period February 2005 to October 2007. Cagli and Mandaci (2013) also find spot and futures prices of underlying ISE 30 index are cointegrated by employing weekly data from February 2005 to October 2012 after accounting structural breaks. However, all of these analyses are static in nature. Neither of these studies explicitly accounts for time variation in long run relationship between index and index futures due to new information in Turkish derivatives market.[4] In order to examine how the process evolves over time techniques such as recursive and rolling methods that allow for the investigation of gradual change in the data generating process should be employed.

Thus, the first contribution of this paper is to assess the statistical significance of the cointegration relationship over time from the start of index futures trading on February 4th, 2005 to October 19th, 2012 by employing the recursive and rolling cointegration techniques in Turkish index futures markets. These procedures allow for the time-variation in the data generating process. Secondly, our data period covers an extensive range of economic conditions including, a period of robust economic growth and price stability in Turkish economy, global financial crisis, Eurozone debt crisis and increased sophistication in asset markets in general. This gives us a chance to examine whether recent global financial and Eurozone crises hampered the cointegration relationship between spot and futures markets, hence market efficiency in Turkish index futures markets. Thirdly, previous studies on stock index futures mainly examine developed markets and studies on emerging markets are relatively scarce and this paper focuses on Turkish index futures market (i.e. ISE 30 index spot and futures prices) which is one of the most dynamic emerging markets in the world. The results of this study have implications for hedgers, traders as well as regulators.

The paper is organized as follows: Section 2 introduces data and methodology Section 3 presents and discusses the empirical results and Section 4 concludes the paper.

## 2.0    Data and methodology

The data employed in this study comprise daily observations on ISE 30 stock index futures and underling ISE 30 index from February 4th, 2005 to October 19th, 2012.[5] Data is obtained from TurkDEX. Futures prices are the prices of nearby futures contracts. The choice of data period is motivated by the fact that data period covers extensive range of economic conditions including, a period of robust economic growth and price stability in Turkish economy, 2008 global financial crisis as well as Eurozone debt crisis of 2009-2010. Moreover, data period includes the introduction period of futures markets which is defined with low trading volumes as well as mature period where trading volumes increased noticeably. Focusing on this data period allows us to test whether the cointegration relationship changes with changing market conditions.

If the price series are individually non-stationary but there exists a linear combination of prices that is stationary then these series are cointegrated. Such cointegrated variables cannot drift far apart and they tend to move together in the long run. However, the extent of cointegration may change over time or cointegration relationship may break down as the underlying data generating process changes due to policy changes, financial crises and other exogenous factors. Therefore, appropriate examination of this relationship requires a time varying procedure such as recursive or rolling cointegration methods.

The empirical analysis is based on a vector autoregression (VAR) system. $x_t$ denotes a vector which includes the log of futures and spot index price series and the error correction representation is:

$$\Delta x_t = \Pi x_{t-1} + \sum_{i=1}^{k-1} \Gamma_i \Delta x_{t-i} + \mu + e_t \tag{2}$$

[4] Rangvid and Sorensen (2002) argue that econometric techniques that include structural breaks are not suitable for inspecting gradual change in the data generating process since structural changes is well defined points in time. Thus, following Rangvid and Sorensen (2002) rolling and recursive techniques employed in this paper.

[5] The underlying asset of ISE 30 index futures is ISE 30 index, which is composite index of 30 actively traded stocks listed on the Istanbul Stock Exchange (i.e. Borsa Istanbul). Contracts' months for the ISE 30 futures are February, April, June, August, October and December. Contracts with three different expiration months nearest to current period are traded.

where $x_t$ is a price vector, $\mu$ is a (2x1) vector of constants. The parameter matrix, $\prod$, contains information about the long-run relationship between two prices $\Gamma_i$ are short run parameter matrices, $e_t$ is normally distributed error term.   If the prices are non-stationary, then one can examine the cointegration relationship between these two series by determining the number of cointegrating vectors, r, as follows:

$$\text{H(r):} \quad \prod \; = \; \alpha\beta'  \qquad\qquad\qquad (3)$$

where $\alpha$ is weighting elements for the cointegration relationship, $\beta$ is vector of cointegration relationship.

In order to determine the number of cointegrating vectors (r), the Johansen (1991) trace test is conducted.  The null hypothesis for the trace test is that there are at most r number of cointegrating vectors. For system of two non-stationary variables (futures and spot prices) the rejection of null hypothesis of no cointegration indicates that there is a common stochastic trend driving the movements of the futures and spot prices. To examine the stability of the identified cointegration relationship over each data point, both the recursive cointegration and the rolling cointegration methods based on Hansen and Johansen (1999) and Rangvid and Sorensen (2002) are applied in this paper. This is accomplished by testing constancy of cointegration rank. This approach involves the estimation of the Johansen (1991) over various intervals of the sample period. Two different windowing strategies -recursive and  rolling- are applied.

In recursive approach, first $\lambda_{trace}$ statistic is estimated over the chosen period $t_0$ to $t_n$. Then the initial sample is kept fixed and sample length is increased by adding an additional observation at each recursive estimation.  The relevant statistics ($\lambda_{trace}$ statistics) obtained from these estimations are plotted over time. This plot is called global plot by Aggarwal et al. (2004). The plotted trace test statistics are also normalized by the 5% critical value. If the normalized values are above 1, then the null hypothesis of no cointegration is rejected at 5 % significance level. An upward slope is interpreted as rising comovements. In sum, by applying this recursive approach one can see the evolution of the $\lambda_{trace}$ statistics and long-run relationship over time. One advantage of recursive method is that it takes into account all historic information.

Pascual (2003) argues that this method might be misleading because the expansion of the sample size by adding observations recursively increases the path of the $\lambda_{trace}$ statistics. Since recursive tests gradually add more observation into the sample, this method does not allow us to differentiate whether the calculated test statistics are due to increasing power of the tests arising from the additional observation or result of a change in the extent of cointegration relationship.  In order to avoid this problem, we also calculated the $\lambda_{trace}$ statistics by keeping the time interval constant as rolling over the next time interval. This method is rolling estimation approach.  In this method, the tested sample size (i.e. number of observations) is maintained fixed. Therefore, the test statistic is estimated over a time interval of a constant length. In other words, the $\lambda_{trace}$ statistic is estimated over an i period interval from, for example, $t_0$ to $t_{0+i}$ and estimation period is then moved $k$ data points and $\lambda_{trace}$ is reestimated from $t_{0+k}$ to $t_{0+i+k}$. In sum, in the rolling approach, the data are divided into a number of overlapping samples and then the Johansen (1991) methodology is applied to obtain each $\lambda_{trace}$ statistics.  This approach has been employed by Kutan and Zhu (2003) to examine the link between spot and forward exchange rates.  The obtained $\lambda_{trace}$ statistics are normalized again by the 5% critical value and plotted over time. This plot is called Local Plot (Aggarwal et al. 2004). In sum, in the rolling tests the sample size is maintained, but the sample period allowed to change. In this method when the sample period changes with each estimation the observed trace test statistics reflects the variation in the degree of cointegration due to new information.

## 3.0    Empirical results

In this section, we report the results of our analysis. Daily log prices of futures and spot markets are plotted in Figure 1 which shows that both series appear to move closely. Both series presents upward trend until the end of 2007. During the financial crisis period both series show a declining trend as a result of the ongoing financial crisis until the beginning of 2009. Price series started to move upwards again in mid-2009. Table 1 presents summary statistics, namely first and second moments for log price series in first differences. Mean and standard deviation are almost same for two series. However, kurtosis and skewness (absolute) measures of the cash return series are greater than that of futures return series suggesting that the cash market may be more volatile than futures market and Jarqua-Bera test rejects normality at 1 percent level. Augmented- Dickey Fuller (ADF) test results are also given in Table 1 for both in levels and in first differences. It is generally accepted in the literature that spot and futures prices are non stationary and ADF test results confirm the presence of unit root for both price series at 1 percent level. Both futures and spot prices are integrated order of one (i.e. I(1)). Preliminary analysis confirms that ISE 30 index and index futures series present the empirical characteristics of most financial returns sampled at daily intervals. Given the non-stationary nature of prices we proceed to test for cointegration relationship between spot and futures prices.

### Figure 1

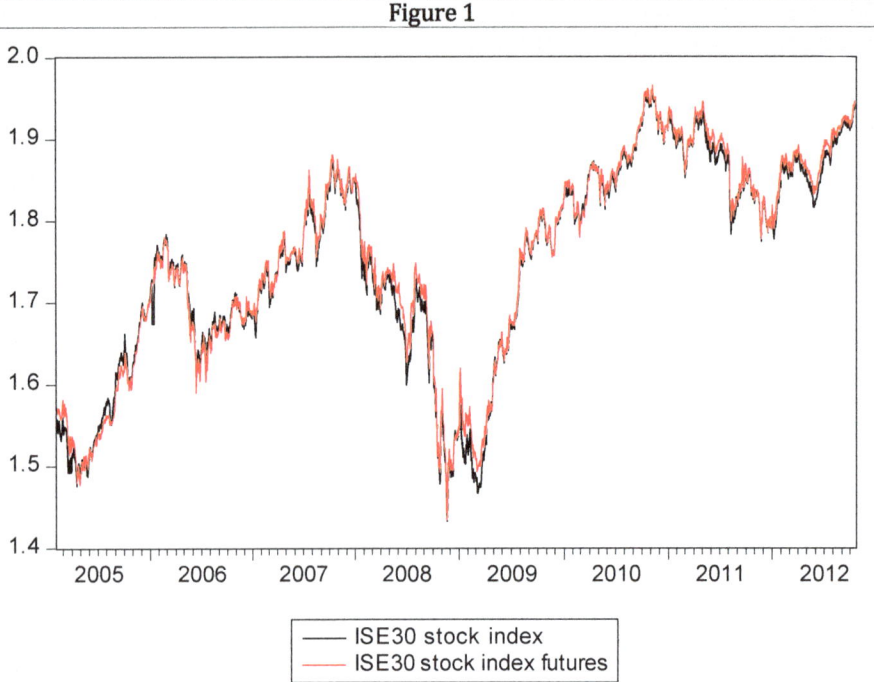

— ISE30 stock index
— ISE30 stock index futures

### Table 1: Descriptive statistics

|  | $\left(\Delta P_F\right)$ | $\left(\Delta P_C\right)$ |
|---|---|---|
| Mean | 0.0002 | 0.0002 |
| Maximum | 0.0494 | 0.0761 |
| Minimum | -0.0436 | -0.0544 |
| Std. Dev. | 0.0085 | 0.0086 |
| Skewness | -0.0927 | 0.1485 |
| Kurtosis | 6.4048 | 9.1439 |
| Normality[a] | 973.74* | 3168.76* |
| ADF Test[b] $\left(P_t\right)$ | -1.4819 | -1.5484 |
| ADF Test[b] $\left(\Delta P_t\right)$ | -23.3201* | -21.3106* |

Note: $\Delta\Pi_\Phi$ ανδ $\Delta P_C$ are changes in log price series of futures and cash markets respectively. * denotes significance at 1 % level. a. Jarqua-Bera test for normality b.$H_0$: Unit root. The lag orders are determined by Schwartz criterion. Only intercepts are included in the level series. Critical value for ADF test is 3.4336 (2.8629) for 1 % (5 %) significance level.

Table 2 presents Johansen trace test results for the full sample. The static examination of cointegration relationship indicates that there is one cointegration relationship between the series of ISE 30 index futures and the underlying spot index, i.e. in the long-run there is a stable relation between these two series over the full sample period. This result provides information about full sample, including both normal and crisis periods and is in line with findings of previous studies. However, studies such as Longin and Solnik (2001) suggest that market behavior is different in extreme periods such as crisis. Kledon and Whaley (1992) claim that in normal trading conditions the stock market and futures market comprise virtually one market but their results indicates that there was a delinkage during the October 1987 market crash. In order to examine whether market conditions have an impact on cointegration relationship we employ recursive and rolling cointegration techniques which allow us to observe the evolution and stability of long-run relationship over time.

### Table 2: Johansen trace test

| Hypothesized Number of Cointegrating equations | Trace Statistics | 5 % critical value |
|---|---|---|
| None | 54.6217* | 15.4947 |
| At most 1 | 2.8001 | 3.8415 |

Note: * denotes rejection of the hypothesis at 5% level. Trace test indicates one cointegrating equation at the 5% level for the period February 4th 2005 to October 19th 2012.

In the recursive approach, the Johansen (1991) methodology is applied to an initial subset of the data. In this case, the sub-period (February 4, 2005 – December 29, 2006) is employed as the base period.[6] Then an additional data point is added to the system and $\lambda_{trace}$ statistic reestimated. This process continues until we exhaust all the observations and in the final stage we perform cointegration analysis for the full sample and calculate the $\lambda_{trace}$ statistic. Thus this allows us to examine evolution of $\lambda_{trace}$ statistics and thereby the change in the cointegrating relationship between ISE 30 index and index futures prices over the sample period. As mentioned all statistics are normalized by the 5% critical value. The rescaled $\lambda_{trace}$ statistics suggests the rejection of null hypothesis of no cointegration if it is above one. The plot of estimated $\lambda_{trace}$ statistics is presented in Figure 2 which indicates a robust cointegration relationship between spot and futures markets since all the normalized trace statistics are above one. Recursive estimations suggest that although the cointegration relationship weakened starting mid 2008s, which coincides with global financial crisis period, has not broken down and overall a stable relationship prevails.

**Figure 2:** Recursive $\lambda_{trace}$ statistics

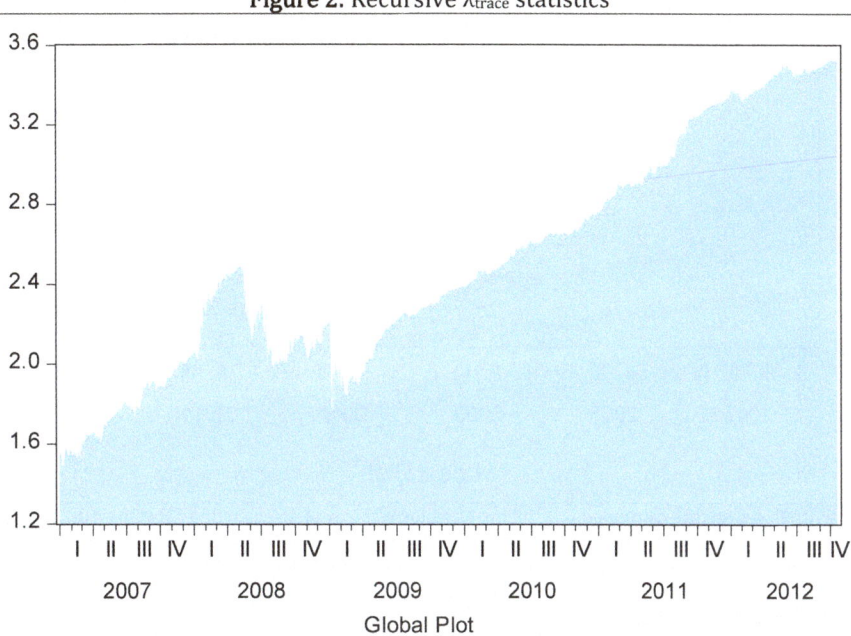

Global Plot

Note: This figure presents $\lambda_{trace}$ statistics calculated on a recursive basis, starting February 4th, 2005 and initially ending December 31th 2006. Thereafter $\lambda_{trace}$ statistics are recalculated by adding one observation each period successively. Values greater than one in the plot indicate the rejection of no cointegration at 5 percent level.

However, in order to take into account of Pascual's (1993) critique, $\lambda_{trace}$ statistics are recalculated by using rolling window as well. In this case, again the sub-period from February 4, 2005 to December 29, 2006 is employed as the base period.[7] Then the $\lambda_{trace}$ statistics are estimated moving sample by one data point (i.e. $k = 1$) in each estimation. The plot of normalized the $\lambda_{trace}$ statistics is presented in Figure 3. The overall results indicate a stable cointegration relationship between futures and spot prices with the exception of global financial crisis and Eurozone debt crisis periods. It can be seen from Figure 3 that the strength of cointegration relationship increased until mid 2007. This suggests that during the early stages of TurkDEX (started its official operation on 4 February 2005) there was a relatively weak cointegration relationship between futures and spot markets as futures markets matured (i.e. trading volume and liquidity increased in the futures market) the strength of cointegration relationship increased as well. However, there was a significant drop in the strength of the cointegration relationship between futures and spot prices starting from 2008 and weakened relationship continued until the mid-2010. There are also periods where the cointegration relationship was broken as financial crisis amplified and pricing in financial markets became seriously disturbed and series started drifting apart from each other.[8] The co-movement pattern of futures and spot prices seems to have been re-established in the mid-2010. Rolling estimation results indicate that recent global financial crisis and Eurozone debt crisis weakened and at times

---

[6] This subperiod can be considered as the introduction period (i.e. early stage of market development) of Turkish futures markets since the trading volume of futures contracts relatively low compared to the following periods.

[7] In this method fixed sample size (February 4, 2005 – December 29, 2006) contains 496 observations. To obtain plot of $\lambda_{trace}$ statistics 1514 regression estimated.

[8] Lehman Brothers' bankruptcy on September 15, 2008 triggered the global financial crisis and the real impact of crisis in emerging markets started to be seen after November 2008. The Eurozone sovereign debt crisis started with Greek government debt crisis in late 2009 and it was intensified in early 2010. Examination of those periods where $\lambda_{trace}$ statistics does fall below the 5 percent critical value reveal that our results of broken cointegration relationship between spot and futures coincide with these events. (See Figure 3)

broke the long-run relationship between cash and futures prices. In times of crisis, strained liquidity, increased transaction costs, and amplified volatility in the financial markets may hamper the cointegration relationship between futures and cash markets. An important lesson is that future studies need to take into account the potential changes in the nature of the long run relationship due to extreme market events driving the data generating process in order to obtain more reliable results when conducting research based on cointegration relationship between futures and cash markets.

**Figure 3:** Rolling $\lambda_{trace}$ statistics

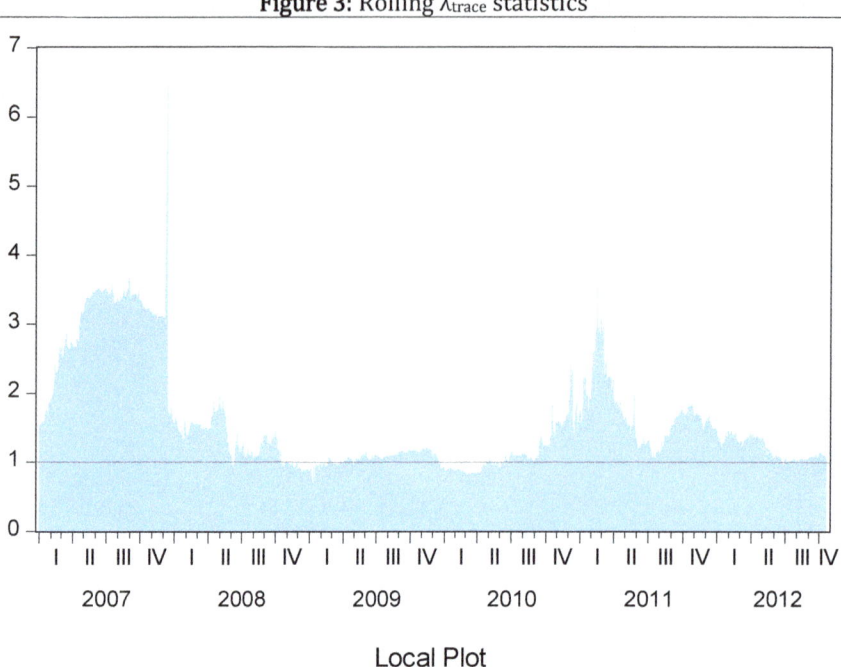

Local Plot

Note: This figure presents $\lambda_{trace}$ statistics calculated on a rolling basis for window of 469, starting February 4th, 2005 and initially ending December 29th 2006. The sample length is maintained the same but the sample is allowed to change one observation at a time. Values greater than one in the plot indicate the rejection of no cointegration at 5 percent level.

## 4.0    Conclusion

This paper contributes to the literature by using two techniques namely time varying recursive and rolling cointegration tests to reexamine the dynamics of the spot index and index futures prices in Turkey. The results of cointegration tests provide evidence of a long run relationship between spot and futures markets which displays time variation in Turkish equity index market. We find that the cointegration relationship noticeably weakened and even broke down at times during the financial crisis and Eurozone crisis periods however, overall a stable relationship prevails. Our findings suggest that the weakened relationship is related to market turmoil and changing market sentiment. Since investor sentiment has a positive impact on price volatility and trading costs on both spot and futures markets this might explain the changing cointegration relationship between spot and futures prices during the recent crises. Our findings have policy implications for traders, hedgers and portfolio managers. When traders and hedgers determine their trading and hedging strategies and exchange regulators set rules to provide efficiency and liquidity in the markets, they have to take into account that economic functions of futures might be severely hampered during the distressed markets.

### References

Aggarwal, R., Lucey, B., Muckley, C. (2004). Dynamics of equity market integration in Europe: Evidence of changes over time and with events. IIIS Discussion Paper No.19.

Arshanpalli, B. and Doukas, C. (1997). The linkages of S&P 500 stock index and and S&P 500 stock index futures prices during October 1987. Journal of Economics and Business. 49: 253-266. http://dx.doi.org/10.1016/S0148-6195(97)00003-9

Brenner, R. J., Kroner, K. F. (1995). Arbitrage, cointegration and testing the unbiasedness hypothesis in financial markets. Journal of Financial and Quantitative Analysis. 30(1):22-42. http://dx.doi.org/10.2307/2331251

Brooks, C., Rew, A. G., & Ritson, S. (2001). A trading strategy based on the lead–lag relationship between the spot index and futures contract for the FTSE 100 International Journal of Forecasting, 17(1):31–44. http://dx.doi.org/10.1016/S0169-2070(00)00062-5

Cagli, E. C., Mandaci, P. E. (2013). The long run relationship between the spot and futures markets under multiple regime shifts: Evidence from Turkish derivatives exchange. Expert Systems with Applications. 40(10):4206-4212. http://dx.doi.org/10.1016 /j.eswa. 2013.01.026

FIA Volume Growth Accelerates (2007). Futures Industry Association. Retrieved from: https://fia.org/articles/11859266610-volume-growth-accelerates (accessed 28 June 2015).

FIA Annual Volume Survey (2013). Futures Industry Association. Retrieved from: https://secure.fia.org/downloads/FI-2012_Volume_Survey.pdf (accessed 28 June 2015).

Floros, C., Vougas, D. V. (2008). The Efficiency of Greek stock index futures market. Managerial Finance. 34(7):498-519. http://dx.doi.org/10.1108/03074350810874451

Garbade, K. D. and Silber, W. L. (1983). Price movements and price discovery in futures and cash markets. Review of Economics and Statistics, 65(2): 289-297. http://dx.doi.org/10.2307/1924495

Ghosh, A. (1993). Cointegration and error correction models: Intertemporal causality between index and futures prices. Journal of Futures Markets .13(2):193-8. http://dx.doi.org/10.1002/ fut.3990130206

Hansen, H., Johansen, S. (1999). Some tests for parameter constancy in cointegrated-VAR models. Econometric Journal. 2: 306-333. http://dx.doi.org/10.1111/1368-423X.00035

Harris, F. T., McInish, T. H., Shoesmith, G. L., Wood, R. A. (1995). Cointegration, error correction and price discovery on informationally linked security markets. Journal of Financial and Qualitative Analysis. 30:563-579. http://dx.doi.org/10.2307/2331277

Hasbrouck, J. (1995). One security, many markets: Determining the contributions to price discovery. Journal of Finance. 50(4):1175-1199. http://dx.doi.org/10.2307/2329348

Hou, Y. and Li, S. (2013). Price discovery in Chinese stock index futures market: New evidence based on intraday data.Asia-Pacific Financial Markets. 20(1): 49-70.

Johansen, S. (1991). Estimation and hypothesis testing of cointegrating vectors in Gaussian vector autoregressive models. Econometrica, 59(6):1551-80. http://dx.doi.org/ 10.2307/2938278

Kasman, A. and Kasman, S. (2008) The impact of futures trading on volatility of the underlying asset in the Turkish stock market. Physica A: Statistical Mechanics and its Applications, 387(12):2837-2845. http://dx.doi.org/10.1016/j.physa.2008.01.084

Kledion, A.W. and Whaley, R. E. (1992) One market? Stocks, futures, and options during October 1987.The Journal of Finance. 47(3):851-77.h ttp://dx.doi.org/10.2307/2328969

Kutan, A. M., Zhu, S. (2003). Has the link between the spot and forward exchange rates broken down? Evidence from rolling cointegration tests. Open Economies Review, 14(4): 369-379.

Lien, D., Tse, Y. K., & Zhang, X. (2003). Structural change and lead–lag relationship between the Nikkei spot index and futures price. A genetic programming approach. Quantitative Finance, 3(2), 136–144. http://dx.doi.org/10.1088/1469-7688/3/2/307

Lin, C. C., Chen, S. Y., Hwang, D. Y. and Lin, C. F. (2002). Does index futures dominate index spot? Evidence from Taiwan market. Review of Pacific Basin Financial Markets and Policies. 5(2):255-275. http://dx.doi.org/10.1142/S021909150200078X

Longin, F. and Solnik, B. (2001). Extreme correlation of international equity markets. The Journal of Finance.56(2): 649-676. http://dx.doi.org/10.1111/0022-1082.00340

Pascual, A. G. (2003). Assessing European stock market cointegration. Economics Letters, 78: 197-203. http://dx.doi.org/10.1016/S0165-1765(02)00245-8

Pattarin, F. and Ferretti, R. (2004). The Mib30 index and futures relationship: Econometric analysis and implications for hedging. Applied Financial Economics, 14(18):1281–1289. http://dx.doi.org/10.1080/0960310041233131578

Pizzi, M.A., Economopous, A.J. and O'Neill, H.M. (1994) An examination of the relationship between stock index cash and futures markets: A cointegration approach. Journal of Futures Markets. 18:23-35. http://dx.doi.org/10.1002/(SICI)1096-9934(199805)18:3<297::AID-FUT4>3.0.CO;2-3

Rangvid, J., and Sørensen, C. (2002). Convergence in the ERM and declining numbers of common stochastic trends. Journal of Emerging Markets Finance, 1(2):183-213. http://dx.doi.org/10.1177/097265270200100203

Stoll, H. R. and Whaley, E. R. (1990). The dynamics of stock index and stock index futures returns. Journal of Financial and Quantitative Analysis, 25, 4:441-468. http://dx.doi.org/ 10.2307/2331010

Subrahmanyam, R. (1991). A Theory of trading in stock index futures. Review of Financial Studies. 4:17-51. http://dx.doi.org/ 10.1093/rfs/4.1.17

Wahap, M. and Lashgari, M. (1993). Price dynamics and error correction in stock index futures markets: a cointegration approach. Journal of Futures Markets. 13: 711-742. http://dx.doi.org/10.1002/fut.3990130702

Wang, G. H. K. and Yau, J. (1994). A time series approach to testing for market linkage: unit root and cointegration tests. Journal of Futures Markets. 4(4): 457-474. http://dx.doi.org/ 10.1002/fut.3990140407

Zhong, M., Darrat, A. F. and Otero, R. (2004). Price discovery and volatility in index futures markets: Some evidence from Mexico. Journal of Banking and Finance. 28(12):3037-3057. http://dx.doi.org/10.1016/j.jbankfin.2004.05.001

# 17

# Bilateral trade agreements and the rise of global supply chains[×]

Zdzisław W. Puślecki[a*]

[a] Adam Mickiewicz University, Poznań, Faculty of Political Science and Journalism, 61-614 Poznań, Poland
[*]Corresponding author's email address: zdzislaw.puslecki@amu.edu.pl

| ARTICLE INFO | ABSTRACT |
|---|---|
| Keywords:<br>Bilateral trade policy;<br>Foreign trade;<br>Global supply chains;<br>Multilateral trade negotiations. | This paper investigates the influence of the rise global supply chains on bilateral trade agreements. Given that a few multinational firms are responsible for a major share of world trade, our findings suggest that these firms may support regulatory harmonization across different Preferential Trade Agreements (PTAs) to lower trade costs or resist harmonization – and encourage certain non-tariff measures – to prevent new competitors from entering markets. The finding partly explains the persistence of regulatory divergence. Building on institutional and comparative trade hypothesis, the findings of the paper present new tendencies in the foreign trade policy: the impact of the rise global supply chains on the political economy of trade, motivations for countries in cooperating on trade policies, and the increasing importance of bilateral agreements in the foreign trade policy. Additionally, the findings suggest that the political economy of regulatory convergence may be more complex than is sometimes suggested in the prior literature. |

## 1.0    Introduction

Trade interfaces with many other policy areas, such as macroeconomic policy, intellectual property, environmental protection, health, and employment. In some of these policy areas, there are well-developed multilateral regimes, while in other areas multilateral cooperation is more incipient and institutional frameworks are less developed. The fragmented, decentralized and non-hierarchical nature of the international trade system makes the pursuit of coherence particularly challenging; fragmentation has the advantage of allowing for experimentation as different policies can be tested at the bilateral, regional and multilateral levels. Several institutions and policy processes are in place to enforce better surveillance of exchange rates and reduce global imbalances. However, the question arises as to whether these will be used to set up a more cooperative system of exchange rates at the international level, and what role the World Trade Organisation (WTO) will play in this system.

There are a growing number of WTO disputes involving measures relating to environmental goods or policies. The challenge of securing agreement is made acuter by the need to resolve difficult questions about the effectiveness of different policies and their impact on trading partners, the answers to which depend on several factors, such as the technology involved, the characteristics of the sector and the markets at issue. Under a model of multilateral level governance, which was originally developed in the context of European integration, policy-making can take place at many different levels (international, national and various sub-national levels) and involve diverse actors (including non-state actors). While these additional layers of governance – and the

[×] Paper prepared in the framework of the Grant OPUS, National Centre of Science – (NCS), UMO – 2013/11/B/HS5/03572

resulting policy dispersion – can better target policies and encourage policy experimentation, they can also make coordination more difficult. This policy will also have an impact on international trade. Without some level of agreement at the multilateral level, the trade impact of these national or domestic measures is likely to lead to frictions between WTO members and may eventually result in formal disputes being brought to the WTO.

Since the early 2000s, the development of various firm models has made it possible to explore the effects of differences in firms on the political economy of trade. Trade opening has two opposing effects on domestic firms within the same industry. First, the cost of exporting decreases, which allows more firms to export and increases the sales of established exporters. Secondly, competition increases, which harms domestic firms. Which of these channels dominates for an individual firm depends on firm characteristics, such as size. Thus, lobbying competition arises not only between sectors but also within sectors in which some firms benefit, and some lose due to trade. This effect might especially arise in the context of fixed costs because they raise entry costs and thereby shield existing producers or exporters from competition.

The least and most productive firms oppose more open trade when it comes to a reduction of NTMs because the competition effect outweighs the sales effect. It is the firms close to the export cut-off, i.e. those that just break even considering the costs of exporting, which benefit from trade opening and support it. This results we can use to explain a persistent feature of trade policy, namely the reluctance to accept opening trade in homogeneous goods. The emergence of supply chains exacerbates the issue and might weaken reciprocity in trade negotiations. It must be underline that as the largest firms are engaged in global production networks, they support NTMs to protect their foreign affiliates. The mechanism is like the one described above: multinational affiliates have fewer problems to overcome fixed exporting costs compared with less productive competitors.

Large firms promote NTMs not only to reduce domestic competition but also to shield their foreign affiliates from the export competition. One implication of the argument is that market access based rules of reciprocity might be insufficient to address the distributional effects of NTMs because reciprocal tariff concessions cannot account for them. Overall, these theoretical studies suggest that while the largest firms benefit from tariff reductions, they may not support the reduction of NTMs that influence fixed costs. Large firms can more easily pay the sunk costs of adapting products to different specifications and benefit afterward from less competition.

Methodologically inclusive account breaks new ground in the new political economy models on contemporary foreign trade policy. In paper presents new tendencies in the international business, the impact of the rise global supply chains on the political economy of trade and countries motivations for cooperating on trade policies and the increasing importance of bilateral agreements in the foreign trade policy. The general theoretical approach will be of broad interest to economists interested in international and institutional questions as well as to political scientists.

The rest of the paper is structured as follows. Section 2 presents new tendencies in the foreign trade policy. Section 3 present the impact of the rise of global supply chains on the political economy of trade and motivations for countries to cooperate. Section 4 presents the increasing importance bilateral agreements in the foreign trade policy. Section 5 concludes the paper outlining several policy implications of this study.

## 2.0    New tendencies in the foreign trade policy

Countries and producers increasingly specialize in certain stages of production depending on their comparative advantage (Krist, 2013; Jackson, 2013). It is importance and magnitude of this development for foreign trade policy.  It is also important to underline that transport and energy costs, for instance, are reasons why supply chains remain more regional than global. Krugman (1991) brings increasing returns together with capital and labor migration and transport costs into one model. Krugman's (1991) model has become a workhorse of economic geography and international trade.  The model is too complex to explain here, but the reasons for that complexity are clear to see – when everything becomes "endogenous" small initial differences can make for big effects. To minimize transport costs, for example, firms want to locate near consumers, but consumers want to locate near work.  Thus, there are multiple equilibria, and at a tipping point, the location decisions of a single firm or consumer can snowball into big effects. A related trend also is the new form of regionalism that is sometimes referred as integration process development (Baldwin, 2012).

The differences among firms involved in the trade are also important for the future development. The picture that arises from the trade literature and the data is that even if many firms are indirectly involved in trade-related activities, only relatively few are exporting or importing and these firms tend to be larger and more productive than others (Figure 1). Such firms also have a role in technology advancement and the diffusion of know-how through supply chains. Trends in the composition of trade show that trade in services has grown faster than trade in goods over the last two decades (Krist, 2013). In this context, important is how advances in information and communication technology have enabled a rapid expansion of services trade (Jackson, 2013). This trend might in the future be spurred by rising energy costs. Moreover, the share of services in both manufacturing firms' inputs and outputs has increased. Digitalization and 3D printing are examples of the increasing gray zone between goods and services. Whether they are classified as one or the other is significant as different regulatory regimes might apply. Regarding natural resources, it shows that their price has increased and that the price of food products has become more volatile. The open question is how higher and more volatile agricultural commodity prices raise concerns regarding food security in developing countries (Eagleton-Pierce, 2013).

**Figure 1:** Contributions to year-on-year growth in world merchandise exports, 2010Q1 - 2013Q1
(Percentage change in US$ values)

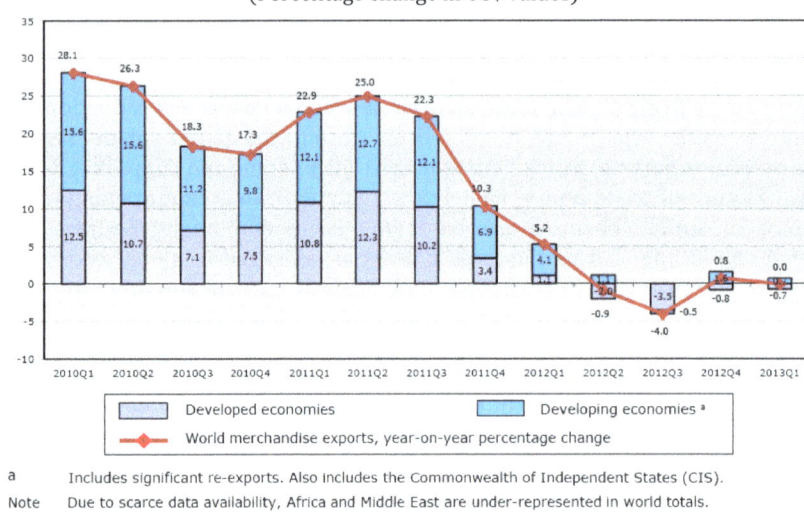

a       Includes significant re-exports. Also Includes the Commonwealth of Independent States (CIS).
Note    Due to scarce data availability, Africa and Middle East are under-represented in world totals.

Source: WTO Secretariat estimates, based on data compiled from IMF International Financial Statistics; Eurostat Comext Database; Global Trade Atlas; and national statistics. WTO Secretariat, 2013
Developed economies, Developing economies [a]

Another major trend in international trade is the rise of several emerging economies and the associated increase in their shares in world trade (Jackson, 2013). Especially China but also India and Brazil have transformed the balance of power in the multilateral trading system (Jackson, 2013). Between 1980 and 2011, for example, China's share of world merchandise exports and imports increased tenfold, making the country the largest exporter of the world (Jackson, 2013; Kupchan, 2014).

It can observe that comparable development has occurred in foreign direct investment. Inflows into developing countries and outflows from these countries now represent a major share of total foreign direct investment (FDI) (Jackson, 2013), and FDI between developing countries is rapidly expanding. Related to this development are the industrialization of developing countries and de-industrialization of developed countries which, once again, is closely interconnected with global supply chains. However, this growth is limited to only a few economies. It has caused greater differences among developing countries, with growing emerging economies and struggling least-developed countries (LDCs).

Distributional effects of trade play an important role in the broader socioeconomic context. It is important examines the extent to which the recent sharp increase in the unemployment rates of developed countries may be linked to trade and what this could mean for attitudes towards trade. While there is no conclusive evidence that trade contributes significantly to changes in long-run unemployment or income inequality, public concerns about current levels of unemployment and income distribution in several countries are likely to have a bearing on trade policy-making. Another ongoing trend is the increasing importance of consumer concerns (regarding the environment or food safety, for example) which has led to a proliferation of public policy measures that affect trade (WTO, 2011b). Global supply chains might exacerbate the issue when large firms impose private standards throughout their respective supply chains. A further trend is fierce competition for scarce natural.

## 3.0    Global supply chains, the political economy of trade, and motivations for cooperation

The industrialization and spectacular growth of emerging economies, together with the fast expansion of services trade and FDI, are inextricably related to the next intensive growth of production. The focus here will be on how the rise of global supply chains has had an impact on the political economy of trade and countries motivations for cooperating on trade policies (Jones, 2015). There is both theory and evidence suggesting that participation in global supply chains tends to strengthen anti-protectionist forces (Jones, 2015). These forces have helped to drive some multilateral trade opening in the WTO (Jackson, 2013), both in specific sectoral as well as in broader accession-related negotiations (with 32 governments joining the WTO since its creation on April 15, 1995, in Marrakesh) (Jackson, 2013). The main impact, however, has been on unilateral tariff reductions (mostly among developing countries) and the proliferation of preferential trade agreements (PTAs) and bilateral investment treaties (WTO, 2011; Krist, 2013; Jones, 2015; Deudney, 2014). A considerable amount of trade opening has thus taken place outside the WTO.

The internationalization of supply chains was very important for fast economic development and industrialization of developing countries. Before the emergence of supply chains – and the information and communication technology (ICT) revolution that underpinned it – industrialization involved building a strong industrial base often behind the protection of tariffs and other NTMs (Jupill, Mattli, Snidal, 2013). The unbundling of global production made it possible for countries to industrialize by joining international supply chains (Jones, 2015).

There are three mechanisms through which production unbundling can lead to unilateral tariff reductions. First, the offshoring of production is likely to alter lobbying over trade policy in the host country. The relocation of production transforms importers of the products concerned into exporters. Thus, lobbying in favor of import tariffs on these goods decreases and pressure to reduce upstream tariffs increases. This effect, however, is more limited in cases where governments set up export processing zones to exploit the growing industrialization opportunities offered by supply chains (Jones, 2015). Secondly, a fall in coordination and communication costs may also have an impact on lobbying. With high trade costs, producers of final products may support infant industry protection of intermediate products if they believe that it could lower the price of domestically produced intermediate goods compared with imports. However, a fall in coordination and communication costs can break the coalition of interests behind high trade barriers, and lead downstream producers to lobby against tariffs on intermediate goods. Thirdly, offshoring improves the competitiveness of developed countries' products by reducing their costs, thus undermining import substitution strategies in developing countries (Jackson, 2013). Developing country governments may either respond by lowering the tariffs on final goods, or, alternatively, by lowering upstream tariffs to improve the competitiveness of final domestic goods.

Empirical evidence seems to confirm that lobbying is indeed an important determinant of trade policy. There is evidence suggesting that supply chains can explain why the recent financial crisis did not lead to significant protectionism even though many countries had prudence in their applied tariffs, meaning they could raise them without violating their WTO commitments (Jones, 2015).

While unilateral tariff reductions have clearly been a positive step in the direction of more open trade, they may also have complicated multilateral, reciprocity based tariff reductions in the WTO. It must be underline that developing countries have already significantly reduced their applied tariffs, giving developed country exporters less to fight for in multilateral negotiations (Jackson, 2013). Developed country exporters also see less value in asking developing countries to commit to lower tariffs because they do not believe that developing country governments have strong incentives to raise them (Jones, 2015).

It is interesting to underline that foreign investment may lead governments to unilaterally reduce tariffs, thereby lowering the incentive to exchange tariff reductions in the WTO. Existing theoretical work suggests that a government's optimal tariff decreases when its constituents hold an ownership stake in a foreign market, leaving it with less incentive to manipulate the terms of trade (Krist 2013). Extending terms of trade model of trade agreements to account for international ownership shows that by eroding large countries' motives to improve terms of trade by raising tariffs, international ownership can also reduce their incentive to sign trade agreements. It must be emphasizing that calculations of reciprocity in tariff negotiations should consider patterns of international ownership as well as trade flows.

Unilateral tariff reductions, in as much as they were not bound in the WTO, have tended to increase the level of prudence in developing countries' tariffs – i.e. the difference between the level at which tariffs are bound and the level at which they are applied – which has in turn complicated the Doha Development Agenda (DDA) non-agricultural market access negotiations (Jones, 2015).

In the DDA's early days, the discussion focused on the question of whether and how credit should be granted for autonomous trade opening (Mattoo & Olarreaga, 2001). Even when WTO members gave one's consent to negotiate reductions of their bound, rather than applied, tariff rates, the underlying problem did not disappear but merely reappeared under a different guise. Members started arguing about the value of reductions in bound rates that do not imply equivalent reductions of the corresponding applied rate.

The changing dynamics of trade policy brought about by the internationalization of supply chains have not only resulted in unilateral tariff reductions but also in negotiated tariff reductions in the WTO (e.g. the Information Technology Agreement) and, even more significantly, in fast-proliferating PTAs (WTO, 2011; Jones, 2015). While in many cases, particularly in Asia, these PTAs are aimed at mutual integration and rule-making, they typically also include a traditional tariff component. In other cases, such as PTAs in Africa, tariffs are central to the agreements. Preferential tariffs raise several challenges for the multilateral trading system. One concern, extensively discussed in the economic literature, on the systemic effects of preferential tariff reductions, relates to the linkages between discriminatory and nondiscriminatory tariff reductions.

Several different mechanisms have been identified through which PTAs either foster or hinder multilateral trade opening. While the evidence on the relative size of these effects is inconclusive, there is a shared sense among observers that the coherence between PTAs and the WTO needs to be improved (WTO, 2011; Krist, 2013; Jones, 2015).

## 4.0    Increasing importance bilateral agreements in the foreign trade policy

Theoretical approaches that provide a rationale for trade agreements (Krist, 2013; Jones, 2015) offer interesting insights into the impact of emerging new trading powers (Jackson, 2013). An early contribution in this area was made by Krasner (1976). He analyses the linkage between distributions of potential economic power, defined by the size and level of development of individual states, and the structure of the international trading system, defined regarding openness. He argues that while a hegemonic system (in which one dominant player holds sway of smaller states) is likely to lead to an open trading system, a system composed of a few very large but unequally developed states is likely to lead to a closed structure (Kirshner, 2013). Since Krasner, however, the open economy politics literature has been largely silent on how the rise of emerging powers in the 21st century is affecting international economic relations.

 The fact that governments respond to the internationalization of supply chains by signing deep integration agreements at the regional level is broadly consistent with the limited amount of theory available on this topic (WTO, 2011b; Jones, 2015). It is important to underline that, deep rather than shallow integration agreements and more individualized rules are needed to address the policy problems associated with the internationalization of supply chains (Antràs & Staiger, 2012). Countries intensively involved in supply chain trade may find it increasingly difficult to rely on broad GATT/WTO principles alone to address their trade-related problems and may turn to more narrowly focused PTAs to achieve the deep and customized bargains they need (Jones, 2015).

An important result of the terms of trade theory (Krist, 2013) is that shallow integration, i.e. tariff commitments, can achieve internationally efficient policies (Bagwell & Staiger, 1999). However, Antràs & Staiger (2012) find that this result does not hold in the presence of offshoring and, more generally, when international prices are determined through bargaining. If producers are locked into trade relationships with foreign firms – and prices are set via bargaining – there are incentives to manipulate the markets of both the intermediate and the final product to shift the bargaining surplus. Governments might also try to pursue redistributive goals via a trading partner's policies.

Deep integration agreements are needed to resist these pressures. However, this, in turn, means that negotiations must cover a wider array of internal/domestic measures than are typically covered trade agreements (Krist, 2013). Thus, the rise of offshoring raises both a direct and an indirect challenge for the WTO (Jackson, 2013). It puts direct pressure on the WTO to evolve towards deeper integration and more individualized agreements. It also puts indirect pressure on the WTO to evolve in this direction, as member governments increasingly turn to PTAs to solve their trade-related problems.

It is interesting to explore the effect of proliferating deep regional agreements on coherence in international trade governance (Jackson, 2013). The WTO suggested that new international trade rules are being negotiated and decided outside the WTO where power differences are greater and where the principles of non-discrimination and reciprocity are absent. It also argued that PTAs be here to stay. Governments will need to ensure that regional agreements and the multilateral trading system are complementary and that multilateral disciplines minimize any negative effects from PTAs (Krist, 2013). While the available literature suggests that deep integration rules are often non-discriminatory – for instance, provisions in the services or competition policy areas are often extended to non-members - certain provisions in regional agreements can contain discriminatory aspects that clash with the multilateral trading system. It has been shown that PTAs which make it more difficult to apply contingency measures to PTA partners may divert protectionist measures towards non-members (Prusa & Teh, 2010).

Deep provisions can also have several adverse systemic effects. For example, the important effects of regional regulatory harmonization can make it more difficult to multilateral rules. PTAs may not include third-party most-favoured nation (MFN) clauses, thus effectively discriminating against other countries. Developed country exporters may view bilateral and regional rather than multilateral agreements as faster and easier routes for achieving their objectives, further weakening the principle of non-discrimination.

Regarding services supply chains, some argue that their growth creates an additional need to re-examine and modernize current rules for services trade, as these rules were designed for the world where services were exported as final products from national firms, not the world where multiple firms supply stages of services production from multiple locations. Recent research on how differences in firms have an impact on trade policies reveals a related concern. Ciuriak et al. (2011) point at another difference between deep integration at the regional and the multilateral level (Ciuriak et al., 2011). If a trade is perceived by most voters as causing unemployment and increasing inequality, governments could refrain from pursuing further trade opening and may even be tempted by protectionism. Regarding increased pressure for protectionism, there is some evidence that the WTO has played a significant role in recent years in preventing protectionist barriers. WTO rules and governments commitments, together with reinforced monitoring mechanisms, may account at least in part for the limited protectionist reactions to the crisis. One problem that may arise in the future is if governments turn to measures that are currently undisciplined or untested by WTO rules. Pressure on the WTO to impose or apply disciplines in new areas would increase, as is the case now regarding exchange rate misalignments. Another possibility would be for governments to use more intensively public policies for protectionist purposes.

Regarding trade negotiations, focusing exclusively on the efficiency effect of trade opening may no longer be possible. Distribution and labour-market effects will also need to be considered, and accompanying measures may need to be proposed to win the support of most voters for open trade. Although most accompanying measures fall outside the remit of the WTO, mechanisms available under the WTO to facilitate adjustments, such as implementation periods and flexibilities, may have a role to play.

Now it is time to consider the concept of a new WTO model development. Under this approach, countries willing to strengthen the trade rules regarding currency manipulation, state-owned enterprises, and other loopholes in the current rules, and to develop rules for the new issues such as digital commerce and regulatory coherence would negotiate an PTA among themselves that would supplement the current WTO system. The negotiations for the bilateral PTA could provide the basis for developing new WTO Plus system.

Negotiations for the bilateral PTA could be vehicles for establishing a WTO Plus system. These agreements establish effective rules regarding neomercantilism practices and eschew special interest provisions. Such a WTO Plus system would both open markets for countries willing to accept strengthened trade rules and put pressure on nonparticipating countries to further open their markets and adopt similar rules in a future multilateral trade round in the framework of the WTO.

## 5.0    Conclusion and policy implications

The economic incentives for multilateral trade liberalization remain strong, and the new international economy of more broadly shared economic power represents a major victory for its success in the framework of the WTO multilateral trade system, but the power in the WTO has a symbolic character. The rise of global supply chains and the symbolic character of the WTO has had an impact on the political economy of trade and countries motivations for cooperating on trade policies. Participation in global supply chains tends to strengthen anti-protectionist forces. The internationalization of supply chains is very important for fast economic development. This process also changed the political economy of trade policy, creating in many countries a strong incentive to undertake unilateral tariff reductions. The changing dynamics of trade policy brought about by the internationalization of supply chains have not only resulted in unilateral tariff reductions but also in negotiated tariff cuts in the WTO and, even more significantly, in fast-proliferating PTAs.

The preferential agreement raises several challenges for the multilateral trading system. It is important to underline that; deep rather than shallow preferential bilateral agreements and more individualized rules are needed to address the policy problems associated with the internationalization of supply chains. Countries intensively involved in supply chain trade may find it increasingly difficult to rely on broad WTO principles alone to address their trade-related problems and may turn to more narrowly focused PTAs to achieve the deep and customized bargains they need.

Governments will need to ensure that regional agreements and the multilateral trading system are complementary and that multilateral disciplines minimize any negative effects from PTAs. Differences in firms have an impact on trade policies reveals a related concern. While heterogeneous firms trade models suggest that more importance should be granted to extensive than to intensive margin responses to trade opening, there is evidence suggesting that PTAs have positive effects at the intensive margin and negative effects at the extensive margin, whereas the opposite is true of opening in the multilateral context. It is important to underline also that there are differences between deep integration at the regional and the multilateral level.

A few multinational firms are responsible for a major share of world trade. On the one hand, these firms should support regulatory harmonization across different Preferential Trade Agreements (PTAs) to lower trade costs. On the other hand, they might also resist harmonization – and encourage certain non-tariff measures – to prevent new competitors from entering markets. This may partly explain the persistence of regulatory divergence, and suggests that the political economy of regulatory convergence may be more complex than is sometimes suggested.

The bilateral and regional trade agreements have emerged as the alternative to multilateral WTO agreements. In this situation, institutional reforms will be necessary to restore the WTO's ability to complete multilateral trade agreements, including a more flexible application of the consensus rule. Aid for trade may also play an instrumental role in bringing more developing countries into WTO disciplines. It must be emphasizing that WTO members must develop new ways especially with developing countries, by financial, economic and trade aid for them also because of the importance of agriculture. It is important also to find common ground to negotiate for mutual gains from foreign trade and first of all from new models of foreign trade policy with the importance of the rise global supply chains and new forms of cooperation between developed, developing, and emerging countries like China, India, Brazil, Mexico, South Africa regarding also regulatory protectionism between USA and European Union.

## References

Antràs, P.&Staiger, R.W. (2012). Trade agreements and the nature of price determination, American Economic Review Papers and Proceedings 102 (3), 470-476.

Bagwell K.,& Staiger, R.W. (1999).Domestic policies, national sovereignty and international economic institutions, NBER Working Papers, 7293. National Bureau of Economic Research, Inc.Baldwin, R. (2012). WTO 2.0. Global governance of supply chain trade, Policy Insight, 64. Centre for Economic Policy Research.

Ciuriak D., B. Lapham, &Wolfe, R. with Collins-Williams, T. & Curtis, J.M. (2011). Firms in International Trade: Towards a New Trade Policy.

Deudney D. (2014). Hegemony, nuclear weapons, and liberal hegemony, In G. J. Ikenberry (Ed.), Power, order, and change in world politics, Cambridge, Cambridge University Press.

Eagleton-Pierce, M. (2013). Symbolic power in the World Trade Organization, Oxford. Oxford University Press.

Jackson R. J. (2013). Global politics in the 21st century, New York, Cambridge University Press.

Jones, K. (2015). Reconstructing the World Trade Organization for 21st century, an institutional approach, Oxford, New York, Oxford University Press.

Jupill, W.M. & Snidal, D. (2013). Institutional choice and global commerce, New York, Cambridge University Press.

Kirshner, O. (2013). American trade politics and the triumph of globalism, New York &London, Routledge Taylore & Francis Group.

Krasner, S. D. (1976). State power and the structure of international trade. World Politics 28, 317-347.

Krist, W. (2013). Globalization and America's trade agreements, Baltimore, John Hopkins UniversityPress.

Krugman, P. (1991). Increasing returns and economic geography, Massachusetts Institute of Technology.

Kupchan, Ch. A. (2014). Unpacking hegemony: the social foundations of hierarchical order, In: G. J. Ikenberry (Ed.), Power, order, and change in world politics, Cambridge, Cambridge UniversityPress.

Mattoo A. & Olarreaga M. (2001). Should credit be given for autonomous liberalization in multilateral trade negotiation, CEPR Discussion Papers 2821.

Prusa, T.J. & Teh, R. (2010). Protection reduction and diversion: PTAs and the incidence of antidumping disputes", NBER Working Papers 16276, National Bureau of Economic Research, Inc.

WTO, (2011) The2011WorldTrade Report,

# 18

# Entrepreneurial orientation in Mexican family businesses

José Luis Esparza-Aguilar [a*], Argentina Soto-Maciel [b], Ma. Isabel De la Garza-Ramos [c]

[a] Universidad de Quintana Roo. Mexico.
[b] Universidad Anahuac, Argentina. Email: argentina.soto@anahuac.mx
[c] Universidad Autónoma de Tamaulipas. Mexico. Email: igarza@uat.edu.mx
*Corresponding author's email address: jlesparza@uqroo.edu.mx

| ARTICLE INFO | ABSTRACT |
|---|---|
| Keywords:<br>Family business;<br>Entrepreneurial orientation;<br>Innovation;<br>Risk taking. | We examine factors affecting entrepreneurial orientation in Mexican family businesses. We aim to shed light on the relevance and value of such factors by analyzing five widely recognized dimensions: proactivity, innovation, risk taking, aggressiveness and autonomy. Results from a sample of 542 family businesses extracted from the INEGI-ENAFIN 2010 database and the first entrepreneurial stage of the Global Entrepreneurship Monitor (GEM) show a marked conservative tendency in the family businesses' entrepreneurial orientation. |

## 1.0    Introduction

The literature on family-owned enterprises has traditionally been concerned with deepening our understanding of the succession stage (Bird et al., 2002; Benavides et al., 2011; Yu et al., 2012). This has been confirmed by Benavides et al. (2011), who analyzed 684 research papers and identified that succession is the most widely studied topic, with 123 of them. This situation can mainly be explained by the recognition that the succession stage is one of the most critical issues in the continuity of the family business. Nonetheless, the study of succession has focused on the characteristics of its process, the influence of succession plans, some of the transitions tool, the relevance of management training and development or the impact of compensation schemes (Yu et al., 2012). However, little attention has been given to issues related to viables options to perennate the family business. Examples of such options include corporate entrepreneurship (Schöllhammer, 1982; Burgelman, 1984; Kanter, 1982; Guth and Ginsberg, 1990; Zahra, 1991), or the influence of the family dynamics on these businesses' entrepreneurship process (Aldrich and Cliff, 2003).

Benavides et al. (2011) found that as little as 4% of the analyzed research addressed the topic of entrepreneurship and innovation, and their focus was strategic management. The literature on entrepreneurship and innovation is predominantly descriptive. Therefore, they suggest the need for more empirical research on this topic and identify two new research perspectives: continuity and the capacity to take advantage of new opportunities.

The paper is made up of four major sections. First, the research literature on family businesses and entrepreneurial orientation is reviewed. Then the research methodology used is described. After that, the research findings are presented and discussed. Finally, the paper concludes with a discussion of the theoretical and practical contributions of the study, as well as its limitations and implications for future research.

## 2.0    Literature review

### 2.1    Family businesses

The notion of family business does not have an agreed-upon definition (Wortman, 1994: Cabrera and García, 1998; Poza, 2005; Sharma, 2012). However, there are three recurrent conditions when trying to understand this construct. First, the participation of family members in *i)* ownership of the business (Barnes and Hershon, 1976; Rosenblatt et *al.*, 1985); *ii)* management (Beckhard and Dyer, 1983; Handler, 1989); and *iii)* the intention to become the successor (Miller and Rice, 1967; Churchill and Hatten, 1987). When looking back to its origins, it can be observed that for some authors the notion is necessarily dichotomous. Therefore, some definitions include both the ownership and management as part of the members' participation in the business (Bork, 1986; Davis, 1983; Gallo and Sveen, 1991); for some other authors, the notion entails ownership and continuity (Donelly, 1964). However, for some others, the definition of it is trichotomous; that is to say, the members necessarily participate in its ownership, management and continuity (Handler, 1989; Aragonés, 1992). In fact, all these positions are still polarized and no consensus has been reached at the international level to be able to compare and contrast them. The literature on family businesses has gradually made evident their differentiated behavior as a result of the interconnection and respective logics of the subsystems that make them up.

### 2.2    Entrepreneurial orientation

The corporate entrepreneurship is the result of two perspectives. On the one hand, there is an interest in reducing the risk capital. On the other hand, there is a need to generate a strategic alternative (Morris et al., 2010). In the first case, entrepreneurship gives origin to a new enterprise by choosing to enter a new market. In the latter, entrepreneurship seeks to create a competitive advantage (Kuratko, 2010) through the exploration of opportunities (Ireland et *al.*, 2003) and is closely related to the organizational performance (Arzubiaga et al., 2012). The entrepreneurial behavior can become critical for family businesses (Astrachan, 2003), particularly for their capability of innovation and flexibility (Naman y Slevin, 1993), which constitute two differential characteristics of their entrepreneurial trait.

From this perspective, the entrepreneurial orientation (EO) notion emerges and different models aimed at facilitating their measurement have been proposed. Miller (1983), one of the pioneers, proposes three sub-dimensions: innovation, risk taking and proactivity and endorses their positive covariation. In this sense, the EO is the exent to which the top management is willing to take risks related to the business (risk taking dimension) in order to bring about change and innovation with the aim of gaining a competitive advantage for it (innovation dimension), and to be able to aggressively compete with others firms (proactivity dimension) (Arzubiaga et al., 2012). While various authors have been associated with this perspective (Covin and Slevin, 1989), some others have incorporated two more dimensions into the model, competitive aggressiveness and autonomy (Lumpkin and Dess, 1996). In this context, the EO is referred to as the processes, the decision-making practices and activities leading to a new entrance (to the market). The construct evolution presents two alternatives. While the first one makes reference to the capitalization of a series of interconnected internal processes, the second one appears to be focused on the opening of new market entry points.

Recently, Martin and Lumpkin (2003) introduce the notion of *family orientation* which is in sharp contrast with the entrepreneurial orientation conception that is more closely associated with an organizational level. In this sense, Cruz and Nordqvist (2007) and Kellermanns and Eddelston (2006) in agreement with Martin and Lumpkin (2003) suggest that the EO increases during the founder period and lowers as new generations are integrated into the business. For their part, Zellweger et al. (2012) propose the *family entrepreneurial orientation* (FEO) notion to refer to family's attitudes and mentalities to engage in entrepreneurial activities.

Arzubiaga *et al.,* (2012) have significantly contributed to the understanding of the family business entrepreneurial orientation notion trough identifying some dimensions based on the literature review. Among the results obtained, they acknowledge that two main interests are privileged in the related literature. The first emphasizes the relationship between EO and the business performance and constitutes the most widely studied perspective (Rauch *et al.,* 2001) recently incorporating external factors into the models (Kellermanns and Eddleston, 2006; Wang, 2008; Moreno and Casillas, 2008). The second identifies factors that influence the business' EO (Covin and Slevin, 1991; Borch, Huse and Senneseth, 1999; Baum, Locke and Smith, 2001; Wiklud and Shepherd, 2005). However, other studies have sought to understand the influence of certain organizational variables on it (Wiklud,

1999; Zahra and Garvin, 2000; Lumpkin and Dess, 2001; Wiklud and Shepherd, 2005). It seems to suggest that there is a general agreement that the businesses' EO is a multidimensional construct.

## 2.3    Research model

This study seeks to identify some of the Mexican family businesses' main behavioral characteristics during their entrepreneurial stage. It focuses on the proactivity, innovation, risk taking, competitive aggressiveness and autonomy dimensions. For the entrepreneurial activity classification, we have considered the *Global Entrepreneurship Monitor* (GEM, 2014) document, which states that the emerging enterprise is that whose existence in the market ranges from 3 to 42 months and generates the payment of wages and salaries. Such an enterprise has also gone through the initial stage of its development.

Hughes and Morgan's (2007) study uses five dimensions as independent variables. One of such variables is proactivity, which is related to the constant search for new markets and the introduction of new products or services that can help them gain a competitive advantage. The family business genesis and the superposition of its sub-systems strongly influence its performance and strategic approach due to the fact that a defensive strategy usually prevails in this type of enterprises (Arzubiaga et al., 2012), and, are, therefore, less proactive.

H1:    *The Mexican family firms tend to be less proactive during their entrepreneurial stage in terms of expansion or growth.*

For Lumpkin and Dess (1996), innovation is considered as the willingness that an enterprise has to engage in and support new ideas, novelty, experimentation and the creative processes that give rise to new products, services or processes. Innovations can be either internal or external to the business. Internal innovation is inherent in the enterprise's organizational culture and is related to its capability to generate added value. External innovation gradually transforms products, services or processes. In this perspective, Schumpeter (1934) endorsed its importance by making reference to the "new combinations" that promoted the economy's dynamic evolution. In spite of the difficulty to avoid tautological traps between process and product innovation, the role played by innovation as an important component in EO has been recognized. The value of innovation has entailed, for example, the financial measurement devoted to I&D (Miller, 1987); the enterprise's predisposition to acquire, develop or display technology (Zahra and Covin, 1993); or its capability to adapt itself to new processes (Miller, 1983). In the case of family businesses, Zellweger and Sieger (2010) claim that these processes favor the tendency to maintain a medium or lower level of external innovation and a medium or higher level of internal innovation. Nonetheless, there is the recognition that family firms are able to activate both internal and external innovation. In this article, external innovation is assessed, particularly, that related to the processes.

H2:    *The Mexican family businesses tend to be more innovative with respect to ICT use during their entrepreneurial stage.*

H3:    *The Mexican family businesses tend to be less innovative with respect to their use of financial products as payment methods during their entrepreneurial stage.*

About risk taking, it is related to the actions as a result of decision making in a context of a high level of uncertainty. For Lumpkin and Dess (1996), risk taking represents the management's level of willingness to compromise organizational resources when the decision has a considerable probability of failure. The literature review recognize that family businesses suffer from strategic inertia and risk taking aversion (Meyer and Zucker, 1989). Sometimes, these behaviors are associated with property concentration (Chandler, 1990); government structure (Fama and Jensen, 1983); or the grounds that the family's wealth assumes completely the eventual financial losses (Naldi *et al.*, 2007). As result of such aversion, some strategic decisions such as the international expansion, the launching of a new product or the allocation of resources to I&D are postponed (Schulze, Lubatkin and Dino, 2002). For the purposes of this study, risk taking is focused on the financial dimension and is understood as the business propensity for debt, which implies greater responsibilities with important stakeholders such as banks and suppliers.

H4:    *The Mexican family businesses tend to take fewer risks when obtaining credit from financial institutions during their entrepreneurial stage.*

H5:    *The Mexican family businesses tend to take more risks when obtaining credit from suppliers during their entrepreneurial stage.*

Competitive aggressiveness is understood as the business' tendency to directly and intensively challenge its competitors with the aim of surpassing its rivals within the sector (Lumpkin and Dess, 1996). The objective is to gain a greater level of participation in the market (Hughes and Morgan, 2007). In relation to the family business behavior, there are contrasting opinions regarding the organizational stage, the role of image and the generational level it is in. However, the tendency is for businesses to engage in defensive, rather than offensive, competitive aggressiveness (Arzubiaga et al., 2012). The interaction between the business and the family plays an important role in the development of an appropriate internationalization process, which is managed with a lower level of intensity; and therefore, it starts later than that in other businesses (Gallo et al., 2008). In this study, competitive aggressiveness is seen as the family business' participation in international markets.

H6:     *The Mexican family businesses tend to be less aggressive to compete in and explore new markets abroad.*

Autonomy can be considered as an independent action undertaken by an individual or a team to start up an idea or a vision and to realize it (Lumpkin and Dess, 1996). Scholars such as Mintzberg (1973) and Mintzberg and Waters (1985) have argued that this trait is closely related to a strong leadership. Shrivastava and Grant (1985), for their part, state that this is an autocratic exercise, which is common in small businesses where the action of an individualized vision prevails (Mintzberg and Waters, 1985). Zellweger and Sieger (2010) claim that a greater degree of autonomy exists in family businesses due to their conservative approach (Zellweger and Sieger, 2010). Other perspectives suggest that autonomy is dependent on business size, leadership style or ownership characteristics. Nordqvist et al. (2008) state that internal autonomy is inherent in the management practices within the organization (for example, in relation to shareholders) and external autonomy is related to different agents such as banks, suppliers, customers or financial markets. For Burgelman (1984), autonomy reinforces innovation, promotes the beginning of business projects and enhances competitiveness and internal effectiveness (Arzubiaga *et al.,* 2012). This study focuses on the kind of autonomy related to business management and control.

H7:     *The Mexican family businesses tend to exert greater levels of autonomy for business management and c ontrol during the entrepreneurial stage.*

## 3.0    Method

This study analyzes data from the "Encuesta Nacional de Competitividad, Fuentes de Financiamiento y Uso de Servicios Financieros de las Empresas" (ENAFIN, 2010), conducted by the "Banco Interamericano de Desarrollo" (BID), the "Comisión Nacional Bancaria y de Valores" (CNBV), and the "Instituto Nacional de Estadística y Geografía" (INEGI). The survey was conducted during the last trimester of 2010, using a sample of 986 enterprises, which represents a sampling frame of 281,545 due to the expansion factor included. For the purposes of this study, the total data about each type of business is first presented; after that, the family business sample used is provided.

Table 1: Total sample and sampling frame composition

| Stratum | Sample | | Sampling Frame | |
|---|---|---|---|---|
| | Number | % | Number | % |
| Micro | 367 | 37 | 137,585 | 49 |
| Small | 328 | 33 | 114,262 | 41 |
| Medium | 148 | 15 | 23,545 | 8 |
| Large | 143 | 15 | 6,152 | 2 |
| Total | 986 | 100 | 281,545 | 100 |

Source: own design based on ENAFIN (2010).

According to the ENAFIN (2010) report, the data from the 986 businesses enable us to make inferences regarding business size for a considerable number of variables at the national level (the numerical variables estimates presented a wide variance, though). The sampling method employed was stratified and multi-staged. The stratification considered previous results obtained from Economic Censuses and the business categories developed by the Mexican Ministry of Economy according to the number of employees. The sample included businesses belonging to the construction, commercial and the private non-financial services sectors (including transportation) with more than 5 employees (Table 2). The study had national coverage taking into consideration localities with a population of 50,000 or more inhabitants.

Table 2: Employee number ranges by economic sector

| Stratum | Commercial | Service | Industry |
|---|---|---|---|
| Micro | 6 a 10 | 6 a 10 | 6 a 10 |
| Small | 11 a 30 | 11 a 50 | 11 a 50 |
| Medium | 31 a 100 | 51 a 100 | 51 a 250 |
| Large | 101 y más | 101 y más | 251 y más |

Source: Official Gazette of the Mexican Federation dated June 30, 2009, with the exception of the micro stratum.

Based on data presented above and for the purposes of this study, the following Table shows the sample of 542 family businesses used and the sampling frame (157,136), which was segmented from the entire database in order to be able to conduct the respective analysis.

Table 3: Sample and sampling frame composition of family businesses

| Stratum | Sample | | Sampling Frame | |
| | Number | % | Number | % |
| --- | --- | --- | --- | --- |
| Micro | 244 | 45 | 89,247 | 57 |
| Small | 172 | 32 | 56,520 | 36 |
| Medium | 74 | 14 | 9,123 | 6 |
| Large | 52 | 9 | 2,246 | 1 |
| Total | 542 | 100 | 157,136 | 100 |

Source: Author's design based on ENAFIN (2010).

## 3.1    Variables

For the purposes of this study and based on the literature review, the following variables have been established. They include the dependent, independent and control variables that are part of the research model used.

### 3.1.1    Dependent variable

*Entrepreneurship:*
This variable has been obtained based on the last two stages of the entrepreneurial activity process established by the *Global Entrepreneurship Monitor* (GEM, 2014): (a) owner or manager of a new business (Emerging enterprises). It refers to the entrepreneur whose activity generates the payment of wages and salaries and has overcome the initial stage. This type of entrepreneurs already has been exercising their entrepreneurial practice between 3 and 42 months; (b) owner or manager of an established business (Well-established enterprises). It refers to the entrepreneur whose businesses have been in existence for more than 3.5 years (42 months).

To achieve this, a *dummy* variable was constructed. Such variable has a value of 1 when the business finds itself in the entrepreneurial stage, with up to 3.5 years in the market, and a value of 0 when the business is already established, with more than 3.5 years of existence.

### 3.1.2    Independent variables

Among the independent variables that have been established taking into consideration factors related to the family businesses' entrepreneurial activity are:

*Proactivity:*
Proactivity has been considered as part of the expansion or widening of new establishments or businesses that entail the incorporation of new or greater variety of products or services that the enterprise has to offer in the market in order to gain competitive advantage. To do so, a categorical variable has been constructed. Such variable has a value of 1 if the business owns more than one establishment or branch, and 0 otherwise.

*Innovation in ICT:*
External innovation performed in product, process or service, is a key factor in corporate entrepreneurship. Therefore, a variable has been established. This variable has a value of 1 if the business has incorporated information and communication technology as an important element in the productive or service process, and 0 otherwise.

*Innovation in financial products:*
As part of innovation that the business has incorporated into its management processes is the use of different financial products as payment methods. This includes the way the business pays its customers, suppliers and employees. To do so, a *dummy* variable has been constructed. Such variable has a value of 1 if the business has used electronic payment options such as electronic and bank transfers, and 0 otherwise.

*Risk taking:*
As part of the business' risk taking approach towards different financial and non-financial resources, it is important to assess its relation to entrepreneurship. To achieve that, a variable has been established. This variable has a value of 1 if the business has acquired debt using resources from suppliers or short term credit lines from financial institutions, and 0 otherwise.

*Competitive aggressiveness:*
As part of a competitive strategy, the business entrepreneurial activity has been incorporated. In doing so, a *dummy* variable has been created. It has a value of 1 if the business has sold products or services in foreign markets, and 0 otherwise.

*Internal autonomy:*
This variable has been measured through the control the business's main owner has within it. The variable has a value of 1 if the business manager is also its main owner or partner, and 0 otherwise.

*External autonomy:*
This variable has been measured through the control on the part of another business or economic group. The variable has a value of 1 if the business or economic group is the owner of 50% or more of the company.

### 3.1.3   Control variables

*Gender:*
Gender has become an important factor in the business world nowadays, with more women engaged in business managerial roles every day. Therefore, this variables has been measured through a dichotomic question, which has a value of 1 if the manager or main owner is male, and 0 if female.

*Size:*
The business size has been measured through the number of both temporal and permanent employees the business has hired during the study period. The businesses were grouped into micro, small, medium or large categories.

*Sector:*
The economic activity sector to which the business belongs has been considered too. The businesses were categorized into the two sectors where they mostly participate. It has a value of 1 the business belongs to the tertiary sector (commerce, services, transportation), and 0 if they belong to the secondary one (construction, manufacturing industry).

## 4.0   Results

The main results obtained from the data analysis are presented in this section. The results, which are shown in the following crossed tables, are presented using the Chi square test given that measurable data are used in category scales.

Table 4 shows that family enterprises are more conservative, rather than proactive, during their entrepreneurial stage regarding business expansion to aggressively compete with other businesses within their markets (Arzubiaga et al., 2012). This situation is common in this type of enterprises due to their cautious approach to promoting the business' permanence in the market. These findings are consistent with those of Zellweger and Sieger (2010); and therefore, hypothesis H1 may be accepted.

Table 4: Entrepreneurship and proactivity

| Business expansion | Entrepreneurship | Well-established businesses | Sig. |
|---|---|---|---|
| One single establishment or branch | 91.3 % | 75.0 % | *** |
| More than one establishment or branch | 8.7 % | 25.0 % | |

Note: Pearson's $\chi 2$ test and Yates correction for continuity; (*): $p < 0.1$; (**): $p < 0.05$; (***): $p < 0.01$;
(NS) Statistically non-significant.
Source: author's design.

The next Table shows that the majority of family businesses are more likely to implement and use Information and Communication Technologies during their entrepreneurial stage. Such innovation is part of the resilience process that these businesses must adopt to be able to face the changes in the context in which they operate. Innovation in family businesses has been studied by Craig and Moores (2006), who have found a relationship between innovation and the family business' life cycle as this type of enterprises showed significantly greater levels of innovation during the initial stages of their development. As a result of that, and the Zellweger's and Sieger's (2010) findings, hypothesis H2 may be accepted.

Based on the aforementioned, it is important to point out that the family business has specific characteristics due to the influence that the family or family group has on the business and their relationship with the other members.

This sometimes hinders innovation due to the obstacles or inertias that exist within the family. In the following Table, it can be observed that innovation in financial products as payment methods is not incorporated by entrepreneurial family businesses as part of their processes. This is mainly due to their fear of change due to the lack of ideas for new proposals (Webb, Ketchen and Ireland, 2010) which in turn leads to lower levels of innovation (Zellweger and Sieger, 2010). Considering these arguments, hypothesis H3 may be accepted.

Table 5: Entrepreneurship and innovation in ICT

| Innovation in ICT | Entrepreneurship | Well-established businesses | Sig. |
| --- | --- | --- | --- |
| Incorporate ICT into the business | 86.0 % | 89.1 % | *** |
| Do not incorporate ICT into the business | 14.0 % | 10.9 % | |

Note: Person's $\chi 2$ test and Yates correction for continuity; (*): $p < 0.1$; (**): $p < 0.05$; (***): $p < 0.01$; (NS) Statistically non-significant.
Source: author's design.

As part of entrepreneurship and risk taking, the following Table shows that the majority of the family businesses to a low extent obtain credit lines from financial institutions, mainly due to their risk aversion (Meyer and Zucker, 1989), to the high financial costs and to their fear of losing control of the business (Zellweger and Sieger, 2010). In agreement with these findings, hypothesis H4 may be accepted.

Table 6: Entrepreneurship and innovation in financial products

| Innovation in financial products | Entrepreneurship | Well-establsihed businesses | Sig. |
| --- | --- | --- | --- |
| Incorporate electronic payment systems | 30.3 % | 48.5 % | *** |
| Do not incorpórate electronic payment systems | 69.7 % | 51.5 % | |

Note: Person's $\chi 2$ test and Yates correction for continuity; (*): $p < 0.1$; (**): $p < 0.05$; (***): $p < 0.01$; (NS) Statistically non-significant.
Source: author's design.

However, risk taking becomes lower when the family businesses obtain most credits from their suppliers. This can be explained by the fact that suppliers offer greater flexibility of payment without a required contract or high financial costs involved. With these arguments, hypothesis H5 is accepted.

Table 7: Entrepreneurship and risk taking

| Risk taking | Entrepreneurship | Well-established businesses | Sig. |
| --- | --- | --- | --- |
| Yes credit from financial institutions | 19.4 % | 27.1 % | *** |
| No credit from financial institutions | 80.6 % | 72.9 % | |
| Yes credit from suppliers | 70.8 % | 39.8 % | *** |
| No credit from suppliers | 29.2 % | 60.2 % | |

Note: Person's $\chi 2$ test and Yates correction for continuity; (*): $p < 0.1$; (**): $p < 0.05$; (***): $p < 0.01$; (NS) Statistically non-significant.
Source: author's design.

Competitive aggressiveness is a characteristic of entrepreneurial family businesses. This situation is mainly influenced by the conservative nature of this type of enterprises to explore new foreign markets or by their resistance to internationalization (Schulze, Lubatkin and Dino, 2002). The next Table shows that the majority of family businesses do not undertake activities that involve participation in international markets during their entrepreneurial stage. Based on Gallo et al.'s. (2008) findings, hypothesis H6 is accepted.

Table 8: Entrepreneurship and competitive aggressiveness

| Competitive aggressiveness | Entrepreneurship | Well-established enterprises | Sig. |
| --- | --- | --- | --- |
| Engage in export activities | 1.4 % | 6.0 % | *** |
| Do not engage in export activities | 92.4 % | 92.4 % | |

Note: Person's $\chi 2$ test and Yates correction for continuity; (*): $p < 0.1$; (**): $p < 0.05$; (***): $p < 0.01$; (NS) Statistically non-significant.
Source: author's design.

Regarding the degree of autonomy that family businesses have both internally and externally, it can be observed in the following Table that the majority of family businesses tend to be more autonomous in terms of direction and control during their entrepreneurial stage. This can be accounted for the fact that the majority of them have the main owner or partner as the business manager also, which will provide them with greater stability for future generations. Similarly, it can also be observed that the majority of family firms exert a higher degree of autonomy regarding the participation of other external companies or economic groups in the business. These findings are in line with those of Zellweger and Sieger (2010), and therefore, hypothesis H8 can be accepted.

Table 9: Entrepreneurship and autonomy

| Internal and external autonomy | Entrepreneurship | Well established businesses | Sig. |
|---|---|---|---|
| Business manager is the main owner or partner | 77.6 % | 93.2 % | *** |
| Business manager is not the main owner or partner | 22.4 % | 6.8 % | |
| Another company or economic group is the owner of 50% or more of the business | 10.4 % | 12.9 % | *** |
| Another company or economic group is not the owner of 50% or more of the business | 89.6 % | 87.1 % | |

Note: Person's $\chi 2$ test and Yates correction for continuity; (*): $p < 0.1$; (**): $p < 0.05$; (***): $p < 0.01$; (NS) Statistically non-significant.
Source: author's design.

Additionally and with the purpose of confirming the results obtained through the *Chi-squared test*, a logistics regression model that includes all the variables established in previous analyses has been utilized. First, an analysis through the automatic step adjustment Wald method was conducted. This method uses the Veracity test REASON to verify the co-variables to be included in or excluded from the established model. The results indicated that the external autonomy variable was eliminated as it has the greatest *Odds Ratio* (OR) closer to zero, the OR's confidence interval is greater than 1; in other words, it does not have any effect on the dependent variable. Once the variables to be included in the model were obtained, an analysis through the introduction method was conducted. The following Table shows the results with their respective probabilities.

Table 10: Binary logistics regression

| Independent Variables | B | S.E. | Wald | Sig. | Exp (B) |
|---|---|---|---|---|---|
| Proactivity (business expansion) | -1.364 | .038 | 1312.577 | .000 | .256 |
| Innovation in ICT | .241 | .034 | 49.346 | .000 | 1.273 |
| Innovation in financial products | -.530 | .024 | 471.902 | .000 | .589 |
| Credit from financial institutions | .409 | .028 | 208.206 | .000 | 1.505 |
| Credit from suppliers | -1.168 | .024 | 2367.877 | .000 | .311 |
| Competitive aggressiveness | -2.032 | .031 | 4331.846 | .000 | .131 |
| Internal autonomy | .019 | .000 | 2037.386 | .000 | 1.019 |
| Gender | .349 | .026 | 184.868 | .000 | 1.417 |
| Size | -.105 | .018 | 35.027 | .000 | .900 |
| Sector | .398 | .027 | 213.781 | .000 | 1.488 |
| *Constant* | *-.255* | *.054* | *22.603* | *.000* | *.775* |

Dependent variable Entrepreneurship: 1, up to 3.5 years; and 0 otherwise.
Notes: B: Logistics coefficients are used to measure changes in the probability ratios, called odds ratio. A positive coefficient increases the forecasted probability, while a negative value lowers it. S.E.: standard error. Wald: Wald test. Sig.: level of significance. Exp(B): exponential coefficient. The model's statistical significance has been determined using the globally adjusted Hosmer Lemeshow test, which obtains a statistical contrast that indicates the existence of a statistically significant difference between the observed and the forecasted classifications, as the Chi square value is significant (Chi-square: 2885.35, sig.: 0.000). As a quality adjustment measure, we obtain a global right percentage of 92.2 % if we use a classification function model. Model summary: -2 log likelihood: 62931.98; Cox-Snell R2: 0.088; Nagelkerke R2: 0.191.
Source: Author's design.

## 5.0    Discussions

Based on the results presented above, it can be observed that the Mexican family businesses tend to be less proactive, or more conservative, during their entrepreneurial stage in terms of their expansion or growth to gain a greater competitive advantage; they tend to be more innovative in the use of ICT, but also less innovative in the use of financial products as payment methods; they obtain, to a greater extent, credits from Banks (which is in sharp contrast with the findings in the risk taking crossed tables); they also tend to obtain, to a lesser extent, credits from suppliers, to be less aggressive to compete or explore new foreign markets, and to have greater degrees of internal autonomy for business' direction and control.

With respect to gender, it can be argued that the tendency is for males to hold management positions. This situation can be understood by the division of labor that has traditionally prevailed in the Mexican family business culture. According to Ward and Sorenson's (1989), males have historically been in charge of the family business and females have taken up the roles of wifes, housewifes and childcare givers. However, in Mexico, a gradual change has been observed, with females starting to participate more actively in business management activities. Likewise, it was found that most of the entrepreneurial family businesses tend to belong to the tertiary sector of the Mexican economy and are usually smaller in size.

## 6.0    Conclusions

Mexican family businesses' entrepreneurship and particularly their entrepreneurial orientation are topics that have received little attention in the literature. Therefore, the lack of clear definitions and limitations continue to be a challenge for researchers to engage in comparative studies which can help understand different organizational behaviors related to the interaction among the family, the business and the management.

This study aims to explore the Mexican businesses' entrepreneurial orientation during their entrepreneurial stage through their five key dimensions: proactivity, innovation, risk taking, aggressiveness and autonomy. The findings enabled us to confirm the initially proposed hypotheses. This confirms the used variables and their respective results previously obtained by different studies in other contexts such as those of (Meyer and Zucker, 1989; Schulze, Lubatkin and Dino, 2002; Gallo et al., 2008; Zellweger and Sieger, 2010). However, it is acknowledged that Mexican family businesses experience conservative behavior regarding their orientation during their entrepreneurial stage. Once again, marked tendencies are present within them. These include the prevalence of passivity or reactivity and risk aversion. It is important to recall that 90% of the sample is made up of businesses whose size ranges from micro to small; that is, they have between 6 and 50 employees mainly if we consider the tertiary sector. In this context, it seems relevant and perhaps necessary to include in both the decision making process and the management of family businesses the participation of competent external actors who can counteract such inertia.

We suggest that future studies explore the Mexican family businesses' entrepreneurial orientation taking into consideration the use of constructs developed by international scholars as benchmarks in order to be able to make comparisons. Future studies could also consider the influence of other factors such as the business sector or life cycle's stage of development (Arzubiaga et al., 2012). Such studies could help explain why businesses focus more on some aspects than others, without losing their entrepreneurial orientation.

## References

Aldrich, S. & Cliff, J. (2003). The pervasive effects of family on entrepreneurship: Toward a family embeddedness perspective. Journal of Business Venturing, 18, 576-596. https://doi.org/10.1016/S0883-9026(03)00011-9

Aragonés, J. (1992). La sucesión en las empresas familiares. Revista Alta Dirección, 162, 37-46.

Arzubiaga, U., Iturralde, T. & Maseda, A. (2012). La medición de la Orientación Emprendedora en las empresas familiares: una revisión crítica de la literatura. Revista de Empresa Familiar, 2(2), 57-71.

Astrachan, J. (2003). Commentary on the special issue: The emergence of a field. Journal of Business Venturing, 28, 567-572. https://doi.org/10.1016/S0883-9026(03)00010-7

Barnes, L. & Hershon, S. (1976). Transferring power in the family business. Harvard Business Review, 54, p. 105-114.

Baum, J., Locke, E. & Smith, K. (2001). A multidimensional model of venture growth. Academy of Management Journal, 44, 292-303. https://doi.org/10.2307/3069456

Beckhard, R. & Dyer, W. (1983). Managing continuity in the family-owned business. Organizational Dynamics, 12(1), p. 5-12. https://doi.org/10.1016/0090-2616(83)90022-0

Benavides, C. A., Guzmán, V. F., & Quintana, C. Q. (2011). Evolución de la literatura sobre empresa familiar como disciplina científica. Cuadernos de Economía y Dirección de la Empresa, 14(2), 78-90. https://doi.org/10.1016/j.cede.2011.02.004

Bird, B., Welsch, H., Astrachan, J. H. & Pistrui, D. (2002). Family business research: The evolution of an academic field. Family Business Review, 15(4), 337-350. https://doi.org/10.1111/j.1741-6248.2002.00337.x

Borch, O. Huse, M. & Senneseth, K. (1999). Resource configuration, competitive strategies and corporate entrepreneurship: An empirical examination of small firms. Entrepreurship Theory and Practice, 24(1), 49-70.

Bork, D. (1986). Family Business. Risky Business, New York, NY, USA: Amacom.

Burgelman, R. (1984). Designs for corporate entrepreneurship in established firms. California Management Review, 26(3), 154-166. https://doi.org/10.2307/41165086

Cabrera, K. & García, J. (1998). Cambios en la cultura y estructura de las empresas frente a las tecnologías de la información empírica. VIII Congreso Nacional sobre Empresa Familiar de la Asociación Científica de Economía y Dirección de la Empresa (ACEDE), Universidad de las Palmas de la Gran Canaria, Espa-a.

Chandler, A. (1990). Scale and scope: The dynamics of industrial capitalism. Boston, MA: Harvard University Press.

Churchill, N. & Hatten, K. (1987). Non-market-based transfer of wealth and power: A research framework for family business. American Journal of Small Business, 12, p 53-66.

Covin, J. & Slevin, D. (1989). Strategic management of small firms in hostile and benign environments. Strategic Management Journal, 10, 75-87. https://doi.org/10.1002/smj.4250100107

Covin, J. & Slevin, D. (1991). A conceptual model of entrepreneurship as firm behavior. Entrepreneurship Theory and Practice, 16(1), 7-24.

Craig, J. B. & Moores, K. (2006). A 10-Year Longitudinal Investigation of Strategy, Systems, and Environment on Innovation in Family Firms. Family Business Review, 19 (1), 1-10. https://doi.org/10.1111/j.1741-6248.2006.00056.x

Cruz, C. & Nordqvist, M. (2007). Environmental factors and entrepreneurial orientation in family business: A generational perspective. Paper presented at 3rd Workshop on Family Firms Management Research, Jonkoping, Sweden.

Davis, P. (1983). Realizing the potential of the family business. Organizational Dynamics, 12(1), p. 47-56. https://doi.org/10.1016/0090-2616(83)90026-8

Donnelly, R. (1964). The family business. Harvard Business Review, 42 (4), 93-105.

ENAFIN (2010). Encuesta Nacional de Competitividad, Fuentes de Financiamiento y Uso de Servicios Financieros de las Empresas. From http://www.cnbv.gob.mx/CNBV/Estudios-de-la-CNBV/Paginas/Encuesta.aspx

Fama, E. & Jensen, M. (1983). Separation of ownership and control. Journal of Law and Economics, 26, 301-325. https://doi.org/10.1086/467037

Gallo, M. & Sveen, J. (1991). Internationalizing the family business: facilitating and restraining factors. Family Business Review, 2(IV), p.181-190. https://doi.org/10.1111/j.1741-6248.1991.00181.x

Gallo, M. A., Ari-o, A., Má-ez, I. & Cappuyns, K. (2008). "Internacionalización vía alianzas estratégicas en la empresa familiar", en Transformarse o desaparecer. Estrategias de la empresa familiar para competir en el siglo XXI, Ediciones Deusto, Barcelona, p. 138.

GEM     (2014).     Global     Entrepreneurship     Monitor,     Global     Report     2014.     From http://www.babson.edu/Academics/centers/blank-center/global-research/gem/Documents/GEM%202014%20Global%20Report.pdf

Guth, W. & Ginsberg, A. (1990). Guest Editor's Introduction: "Corporate Entrepreneurship". Strategic Management Journal, 11: 5-15.

Handler, W. (1989). Methodological Issues and Considerations in Studying Family Business. Journal of the Family Firm Institute, 2 (3), 257-276.

Hughes, M. & Morgan, R.E. (2007). Deconstructing the relationship between entrepreneurial orientation and business performance at the embryonic stage of firm growth. Industrial Marketing Management, 36, 651–661. https://doi.org/10.1016/j.indmarman.2006.04.003

Ireland, R., Hitt, M. & Sirmon, D. (2003). A model of strategic entrepreneurship: The construct and its dimensions. Journal of Management, 29(6), 963-989. https://doi.org/10.1016/S0149-2063_03_00086-2

Kanter, R. (1982). The middle manager as innovator. Harvard Business Review, 60(4), 95-106.

Kellermanns, F. & Eddleston, K. (2006). Corporate venturing in family firms: Does the family matter? Entrepreneurship Theory and Practice, 30(6), 837-854. https://doi.org/10.1111/j.1540-6520.2006.00153.x

Kuratko, D. (2010). Corporate entrepreneurship: An introduction and research review. Handbook of Entrepreneurship Research, 129-163. https://doi.org/10.1007/978-1-4419-1191-9_6

Lumpkin, G. & Dess, G. (1996). Clarifying the entrepreneurial orientation construct and kinking it to performance. Academy of Management Review, 21-81), 135-172. https://doi.org/10.5465/AMR.1996.9602161568

Lumpkin, G. & Dess, G. (2001). Linking two dimensions of entrepreneurial orientation to firm performance: The moderating role of environement industry life cycle. Journal of Business Venturing, 16, 429-451. https://doi.org/10.1016/S0883-9026(00)00048-3

Martin, W. & Lumpkin, G. (2003). From entrepreneurial orientation to family orientation: Generational differences in the management of family business. Paper presented at the Babson College Entrepreneurship Research Conference, Babson College, Wellesley, MA, USA.

Meyer, M. & Zucker, L. (1989). Permanently failing organizations. Newbury Park, CA: Sage Publications.

Miller, D. (1983). The correlates of entrepreneurship in three types of firms. Management Science, 29, 770-792. https://doi.org/10.1287/mnsc.29.7.770

Miller, D. (1987); Strategic making and structure: Analysis and implications for performance. Academy of Management Journal, 30: 7-32. https://doi.org/10.2307/255893

Miller, E. & Rice, A. (1967). System of Organization, Tavistock, London.

Mintzberg, H. (1973). Strategy making in thee modes. California Management Review, 16(2): 44-53. https://doi.org/10.2307/41164491

Mintzberg, H. & Waters, J. (1985). Of strategies, deliberate and emergent. Strategic Management Journal, 6: 257-272. https://doi.org/10.1002/smj.4250060306

Moreno, A. & Casillas, J. (2008). Entrepreneurial orientation and growth os SMEs: A causal model. Entrepreneurship Theory and Practice, 32(3), 507-528. https://doi.org/10.1111/j.1540-6520.2008.00238.x

Morris, M., Kuratko, D. & Covin, J. (2010). Corporate entrepreneurship & innovation South-Western Pub.

Naldi, L., Nordqvist, M., Sjöberg, K. & Wiklund, J. (2007). Entrepreneurial orientation, risk taking, and performance in family firms. Family Business Review, 20(1), 33-47. https://doi.org/10.1111/j.1741-6248.2007.00082.x

Naman, J. & Slevin, D. (1993). Entrepreneurship and the concept of fit: A model and empirical test. Strategic Management Journal, 14(2), 137-153. https://doi.org/10.1002/smj.4250140205

Nordquvist, M., Habbershon, T. & Melin, L. (2008). Transgenerational entrepreneurship: Exploring entrepreneurial orientation in family firms. In H. Landström, D. Smallbone, H. https://doi.org/10.4337/9781848443952.00014

Poza, E. (2005). Empresas Familiares. México: Editorial Thomson.

Rauch, A., Wiklund, J., Frese, M. & Lumpkin, G. (2001). Entrepreneurial orientation and business performance: An assessment of past research and suggestions for the future. Entrepreneurship Theory and Practice.

Rosenblatt, P., de Mik, L., Anderson, R. & Johnson, P. (1985). The family in business. San Francisco: Jossey-Bass.

Schöllhammer, H. (1982). Internal corporate entrepreneurship. In C. A. Kent, D. L. Sexton, and K. H. Vesper (Eds.), Encyclopedia of entrepreneurship, pp. 209-233. Englewood Cliffs, NJ: Prentice Hall.

Schulze, W., Lubatkin, M. & Dino, R. (2002). Altruism, agency and the competitiveness of family firms. Managerial and Decision Economics, 23, 247-259. https://doi.org/10.1002/mde.1064

Schumpeter, J. (1934). The theory of economic development. Cambridge, MA: Harvard University Press.

Sharma, P. (2012). 25 years of Family Business Review: reflections on the past and perspectives for the future. Family Business Review, 25, 5-15. https://doi.org/10.1177/0894486512437626

Shrivastava, P. & Grant, J. (1985). Empirically derived models of strategic decision-making processes. Strategic Management Journal, 6: 97-113. https://doi.org/10.1002/smj.4250060202

Wang, C. (2008). Entrepreneurial orientation, learning orientation, and firm performance. Entrepreneurship Theory and Practice, 32(4), 635-657. https://doi.org/10.1111/j.1540-6520.2008.00246.x

Ward, J. L. & Sorenson, L. S. (1989). The role of mom. Nation's Business, vol. 11, nº 77, pp. 40-41.

Wiklud, J. & Shepherd, D. (2005). Entrepreneurial orientation and small business performance: A configurational approach. Journal of Business Venturing, 20, 71-91. https://doi.org/10.1016/j.jbusvent.2004.01.001

Wiklud, J. (1999). The sustainability of the entrepreneurial orientation – performance relationship. Entrepreneurship Theory and Practice, 24(1), 37-48.

Webb, J., Ketchen, D. & Ireland, R. D. (2010). Strategic entrepreneurship within family-controlled firms: Opportunities and challenges. Journal of Family Business Strategy, 1(2), 67-77. https://doi.org/10.1016/j.jfbs.2010.04.002

Wortman, M.S. Jr. (1994). Theoretical foundations for family-owned business: a conceptual and research –based paradigm, Family Business Review, Journal of the Family Firm Institute, USA, 7 (1), 3-27.

Yu, A., Lumpkin, G. T., Sorenson, R. L. & Brigham, K. H. (2012). The landscape of family business outcomes a summary and numerical taxonomy of dependent variables. Family Business Review, 25(1), 33-57. https://doi.org/10.1177/0894486511430329

Zahra, S. (1991). Predictors and financial outcomes of corporate entrepreneurship: An exploratory study. Journal of Business Venturing, 6, 259-285. https://doi.org/10.1016/0883-9026(91)90019-A

Zahra, S. & Covin, J. (1993). Business strategy, technology policy and firm performance. Strategic Management Journal, 14: 451-478. https://doi.org/10.1002/smj.4250140605

Zahra, S. & Garvin, D. (2000). International corporate entrepreneurship and firm performance: The moderating effects of international environment hostility. Entrepreneurship Theory and Practice, 15(4), 469-492. https://doi.org/10.1016/s0883-9026(99)00036-1

Zellweger, T., Nason, R. S. & Nordqvist, M. (2012). From longevity of firms to transgenerational entrepreneurship of families introducing family entrepreneurial orientation. Family Business Review, 25(2), 136-155. https://doi.org/10.1177/0894486511423531

Zellweger, T. & Sieger, P. (2010). Entrepreneurial orientation in long-lived family firms, Small Business Economics, DOI10.1007/s11187-010-9267-6. https://doi.org/10.1007/s11187-010-9267-6

# 19

# When a mature technology company pivots: A case study of Logitech

Anderson Darrell [a]*, Daniel K.N. Johnson [b]

[a] Product Manager, FSharp, 140 E 30th Street, New York City, NY.
[b] Schlessman Professor of Economics, Colorado College, CO, 80903. E-mail: djohnson@ColoradoCollege.edu.
*Corresponding author's email address: abdarrell@gmail.com.

| ARTICLE INFO | ABSTRACT |
|---|---|
| Keywords:<br>Life cycle theory;<br>Logitech; pivot; stock price. | Life cycle theory has been shown to be an important explanation of the relationship between sales and stock prices. This study explores how the technology company Logitech attempted a transition from a mature life-cycle company in computer peripherals to a growth company in the music, tablet, and gaming industries. We show that stock price correlates with accounting performance differently across the company's life cycle. |

## 1.0    Motivation

There is a deep literature documenting life-cycle paths for firms, and an equally deep literature correlating stock prices with accounting fundamentals (Anthony and Ramesh, 1992). However, to our knowledge, there are no studies of how this underlying pattern of accounting fundamentals might reflect a mature technology company attempting to pivot to trending markets far outside the scope of its pre-established business. In a nimble economy, it seems unremarkable that such cases will occur; indeed, we analyze here the case of Logitech, an established technology company with a significant global presence that decided to redirect its future from computer peripherals into quite unrelated (yet still technological) markets: the music, tablet and gaming sectors.

Logitech started in 1976 as a computer peripheral company, incorporating in 1981 and marketing their first computer mouse in 1982 (Logitech, 2007). They expanded internationally (to Ireland and then to China) to produce more efficiently, expanding to scanners and digital cameras by 1992. Web cameras and cordless devices followed in the early 2000s. The company made a much-publicized pivot in 2012 under a new Chief Executive Officer to focus on gaming and music. The authors chose this company as a sample of convenience; personal contacts within the company made it possible to obtain financial data for a case study of this nature.

To communicate clearly with the existing literature, we analyze the recent history of Logitech using the standard model of the business life cycle, empirically testing how the relationships between accounting fundamentals and stock price respond during the pivot period, and reflect on how redirection might affect standard life cycle theory. The remainder of the paper is organized in standard fashion: section 2 is a literature review, section 3 outlines the model, section 4 describes our data, section 5 reports our results, and section 6 reflects on the implications of the analysis for theory and empirical study in the future.

## 2.0 Literature review

Building on the seminal work of Modigliani (1966) who asserted that households followed a life cycle of savings, Ball and Brown (1968) argued that investor sentiment must expect the same behavior of firms. They found that the accounting fundamentals of firms also regularly showed departures from market efficiency, displaying rampant examples of seemingly irrational behavior around announcement dates where annual reports resulted in abnormally large changes in stock prices. By sampling announcement data, Beaver (1968) created an earnings response model that classified a company's stock price according to risk and volatility, confirming and extending Ball and Brown's (1968) results; not only prices, but price volatility and market volume responded disproportionately upon the arrival of news. Benston (1972) argued that previous studies missed the important 'utility' of news to investors, since risk-aversion obviously played a role in investor responses.

Boston Consulting Group (1972) introduced the idea of an "experience curve", that the accounting costs of a firm decline with the experience of a firm, other things held equal. In short, depending on the maturity of a firm, the same accounting values might mean very different results for profits (and therefore, for investors). Atiase (1985) and Freeman (1987) added to this insight by empirically showing that a firm's size and input magnitudes change the relationship between accounting fundamentals and stock price. Freeman (1987) showed that stock prices for large firms are anticipated earlier than those of small firms and that smaller firms tend to exhibit higher levels of "unexpected" results. Reversing the tests, Beaver (1968), Collins et al. (1987) and Collins and Kothari (1989) asked whether stock prices could in turn re-predict accounting values but found disconcertingly weak results, suggesting a unidirectional causality (if indeed, even that one direction worked consistently).

Upon this historical literature, Anthony and Ramesh (1992) proposed a working model of how life cycle theory applies to the relationship between a company's stock price and its accounting performance measures. Using data on over 3,000 firms, they assigned life stages to each firm based on three key variables: dividends paid, sales growth, capital expenditures. Unexpected stock price changes were modeled as a linear function of these variables, with the function varying by the period of the firm's life cycle.

Recent work on Life Cycle Theory has slowed for firm-base analysis, focusing instead on whether the same models might hold true for individuals. Deaton (2005) and Mankiw (2009) tested whether predictions about consumption and saving behavior depend on the Life Stage label of a person.

## 3.0 Model

We build our work on the baseline model of Anthony and Ramesh (1992), where abnormal stock returns (AR) for any firm are influenced by changes in earnings (IBED, or income before extraordinary or discontinued items), changes in capital expenditures (CE), changes in sales growth (SG) and the firm's life cycle stage (as indicated by a dummy variable) here:

$$AR = D_i \left( \Delta IBED + \Delta CE + \Delta SG \right) + u \qquad (1)$$

However, this simple model assumes away much of the interesting complexity in considering a mature company that pivots into a different economic sector. For example, sales might remain constant but represent enormous growth in a new sector simultaneous with withdrawal from an old sector. Thus, in the case of Logitech we distinguish between "old sector sales" (in their case, personal computer peripheral equipment, SG1) and "new sector sales" (in their case, music, gaming and tablet equipment, SG2):

$$AR = D_i \left( \Delta IBED + \Delta CE + \Delta SG1 + \Delta SG2 \right) + u \qquad (2)$$

To test the fit of this model, we follow the accounting data for Logitech before and after their pivot year (2012). That year was chosen as the pivot year after personal conversation with administrators in the company, after comparison of trends in each key variable for points of inflection, and in accordance with significant news at the firm: the election of a new Chief Executive Officer with a mandate to change course. In contrast, we identified the 2000-2004 period as a period of stagnancy for Logitech, where its core business never showed strong growth. After that period, accounting values seemed to be more in line with a growth or mature life cycle stage. Our results tested for robustness around the precise date of movement from growth to mature life cycle stage.

## 4.0 Data

We were privileged to obtain accounting data from Logitech for the 54 financial quarters of our study through personal contacts within the company. However, due to the proprietary nature of the data, we may only describe their definitions here.

The independent variables of our analysis (IBED, CE, SG1, and SG2) are taken as changes between their annual averages before their pivot (2012) and after their pivot (post-2012). All are measured in millions of real dollars, so the dependent variable AR is also in those units. Stock price is public information from the NASDAQ exchange.

## 5.0    Results

Primary results as presented in Table 1 use standard definitions of the life cycle stages, matching the approach of Anthony and Ramesh (1992). Each fiscal quarter of each year is therefore categorized according to their definitional breakpoints. However, alternative breaks for each life cycle offer extremely similar results, both qualitatively and quantitatively. Standard tests on the errors (tests for heteroskedasticity, first-order autocorrelation, multicollinearity and normality) show predictable but modest problems; Prais-Winston corrections change little in the flavor of the results, and we report robust standard errors here with an acknowledgement of potential biases due to high correlations between explanatory variables. We elect to report the results as they accord with theory, recognizing that unavoidable multicollinearity predisposes our coefficients toward statistical insignificance.

| Table 1: Estimation results | | | |
|---|---|---|---|
| Life Cycle Stage | Variable | Coefficient | t-statistic |
| Stagnant | Earnings (IBED) | -0.013 | (0.89) |
| | Capital expend. (CE) | 6.719 | (1.04) |
| | Sales growth (SG1, old) | 0.129 | (1.34) |
| | Sales growth (SG2, new) | -0.005 | (0.13) |
| Growth | Earnings (IBED) | $3.720 \times 10^{-7}$ | (0.47) |
| | Capital expend. (CE) | -4.268 | (0.54) |
| | Sales growth (SG1, old) | -0.072 | (1.89)* |
| | Sales growth (SG2, new) | 0.100 | (4.68)*** |
| Mature | Earnings (IBED) | -0.002 | (0.22) |
| | Capital expend. (CE) | -12.135 | (1.49) |
| | Sales growth (SG1, old) | 0.010 | (0.27) |
| | Sales growth (SG2, new) | -0.006 | (0.24) |
| Constant | | 16.057 | (15.14)*** |
| Observations | | | 54 |
| Adjusted $R^2$ | | | 0.398 |

Notice that the prominent pattern is a simple one: the linear constant is by far the most important factor in determining stock price.

Interestingly though, the only other statistically significant variable is sales growth, which pivots demonstrably not only in size but actually in sign, as the company moves from an old business line to a new business line. In other words, increased sales in their old market niche are actually interpreted by investors as a negative, a detriment to stock price appreciation, while sales growth in the new market niche is understandably seen as a factor that favors stock price rises.

Perhaps even more significantly, this pivot is only seen when the company is in its growth phase; while the firm is either stagnant or mature, the impact of sales growth in either market niche (old or new) is statistically irrelevant to stock prices. Naturally, this could be due to multicollinearity concerns over the subsamples in those life cycle periods. However, it might suggest that investors watch sales composition more carefully during growth periods than they do during more stable periods.

## 6.0    Conclusion

The goal of this paper was to explore the applicability of Anthony and Ramesh (1992) model relating accounting performance measures to stock price over the life cycle of a firm, to explore its usefulness specifically for a seasoned technology-based firm engaged in a market pivot from computer peripherals to a focus in other electronics. We appear to have found that while the model has limited explanatory power, investors may be keying on precisely the issue that concerns us the most: sales growth in the old market niche versus sales growth in the new market niche. In fact, investors may actually be seeing sales growth as a detrimental factor if it occurs in the old market. If replicable with other firms in similar circumstances, there are implications of this result for investors, for business leaders and for policymakers alike.

The implications are important not only for investors but for business leaders and for policymakers. Investors should be particularly careful in reading sales reports for growth-stage firms engaged in a pivot, as a decomposition of sales by sector appears to be warranted. There appears to be value in a careful reading of how quickly and thoroughly the pivoting growth-stage company is earning sales in the new sector instead of the old sector; even if that does not matter to the firm's accounting fundamentals, it matters to other investors who are contributing to the stock's price.

As a business leader, the timing of the announcement of a potential pivot and the speed of execution of that pivot appear to be important. Investors appear to favor the quick pivot rather than the slow transition, at least for a growth-stage company, so a strategic timing of the pivot announcement seems wise.

Finally, policymakers should be aware that growth-stage firms are sensitive to this investor phenomenon. In regions or time periods where many growth-stage firms are pivoting, we may see stock market declines regardless of the underlying accounting fundamentals. Assistance that can be offered to speed the transition, to reduce structural tensions as firms adjust and adapt, alongside patience with the ambiguity during the pivot, would seem to be warranted.

Clearly, there are limitations to the current study, most notably that we investigate only one company for which data were available to us. For example, we cannot comment on whether the effects we see are unique to this firm, unique to this economic sector, or unique to this particular pivot at this point in time. We look forward to exploring and comparing the phenomenon of the pivot among other established technology firms as examples and data become available.

## Bibliography

Anthony, J.H. and K. Ramesh (1992). "Association between Accounting Performance Measures and Stock Prices." Journal of Accounting and Economics 15(2-3):203-27. http://dx.doi.org/10.1016/0165-4101(92)90018-W

Atiase, K. (1985). "Predisclosure Information, Firm Capitalization, and Security Price Behavior around Earnings Announcements". Journal of Accounting Research 23(1): 21-36. http://dx.doi.org/10.2307/2490905

Ball, R. and P. Brown (1968). "An Empirical Evaluation of Accounting Income Numbers." Journal of Accounting Research 6(2): 159-160. http://dx.doi.org/10.2307/2490232

Beaver, W.H. (1968). "The Information Content of Annual Earnings Announcements." Journal of Accounting Research 6: 67-68. http://dx.doi.org/10.2307/2490070

Benston, G.J. (1972). "Economies of Scale of Financial Institutions." Journal of Money, Credit and Banking 4(2): 312-314. http://dx.doi.org/10.2307/1991041

Boston Consulting Group (1972). Perspectives on Experience. Boston.

Collins, D.W. and S.P. Kothari (1989). "An Analysis of Intertemporal and Cross-sectional Determinants of Earnings Response Coefficients." Journal of Accounting and Economics 11(2-3): 143-81. http://dx.doi.org/10.1016/0165-4101(89)90004-9

Collins, D.W., S.P. Kothari and J.D. Rayburn (1987). "Firm Size and the Information Content of Prices with Respect to Earnings." Journal of Accounting and Economics 9(2): 111-38. http://dx.doi.org/10.1016/0165-4101(87)90002-4

Deaton, A. S. (2005). Franco Modigliani and the Life Cycle Theory of Consumption. SSRN Electronic Journal SSRN Journal. doi:10.2139/ssrn.686475

Freeman, R.N. (1987). "The Association between Accounting Earnings and Security Returns for Large and Small Firms." Journal of Accounting and Economics 9(2): 195-228. http://dx.doi.org/10.1016/0165-4101(87)90005-X

Hagerman, R.L. (1984). "The Association between the Magnitude of Quarterly Earnings Forecast Errors and Risk-Adjusted Stock Returns." Journal of Accounting Research 22(2): 526-40. http://dx.doi.org/10.2307/2490662

Logitech (2007). Logitech History. Downloaded from http://www.logitech.com/lang/pdf/logitech_history_2007 03.pdf on October 4, 2016.

Mankiw, N. Gregory (2009). Macroeconomics (Seventh ed.). New York: Worth. pp. 509–513. ISBN 978-1-4292-1887-0

Modigliani, F. (1966). The Life Cycle Hypothesis of Saving, the Demand for Wealth and the Supply of Capital, 1966.

# 20

# Real wages, inflation, and labor productivity: Evidences from Bulgaria and Romania

Chaido Dritsaki [a*]

[a] Associate Professor, Department of Accounting and Finance, Western Macedonia University of Applied Sciences, Kozani, Greece.
*Corresponding author's email address: dritsaki@yahoo.com

| ARTICLE INFO | ABSTRACT |
|---|---|
| Keywords:<br>Bulgaria; inflation;<br>labor productivity;<br>real Wages; Romania. | This study examines the effect of inflation and real wages on labor productivity for two European Union(EU) countries: Bulgaria and Romania using cointegration Autoregressive Distributed Lag (ARDL) test and causality test of Toda and Yamamoto (1995). Results suggest that inflation reduces labor productivity. Moreover, the impact of wages on labor productivity is far greater the impact of inflation. Additionally, there exists unidirectional relation between inflation and real wages for Bulgaria, and real wages and labor productivity for Romania. |

## 1.0    Introduction

*"Productivity isn't everything, but in the long run it is almost everything. A country's ability to improve its standard of living over time depends almost entirely on its ability to raise its output per worker"*

*(Paul Krugman 1994).*

Productivity is usually defined as a ratio between production size and input size. It is the fundamental element in distinguishing the standard of living for each country. It is usually measured as GDP per capita in most countries and in all regions within a country. For a long time, productivity growth was the only way to sustain improvements in the standard of living or quality of life. (Krugman, 1994). It provided the basis for investments, environment's improvement and poverty reduction. Furthermore, it was a vital factor of international competitiveness. Given its importance, the improvement of productivity has been a substantial national issue for many countries. This led to give emphasis on the comprehension of factors that lead to a higher increase of productivity both for research and politics. (Tang and Wang, 2004).

The increase of productivity in all countries has played an important role on the preservation of competitiveness and the long-run economic growth. Therefore, the role of central banks and governments is to keep low the levels of interest rates and stable the levels of inflation aiming at the improvement of competitiveness. From a macroeconomic point of view, labor productivity has been related with real wages and inflation both in theoretical and empirical literature. Thus, the analysis of the relationship between labor productivity, real wages and inflation is of vital importance for governments that make plans for structural breaks for the strengthening of productivity and for inflation control.

Inflation is the increase on average level of the prices of goods and services in an economy during a time period. When the price level is increasing, we buy less goods and services. Thus, inflation reflects the reduction of purchasing power for each currency unit. A measure of inflation is the consumer price index. Inflation affects economies positively and negatively. The negative consequences of inflation consists the increase of opportunity cost of holding money whereas uncertainty over future inflation discourages investments and savings. The positive results of inflation are the reduction of real burden of public and private debt keeping the nominal interest rates above zero, so that central banks can adjust the interest rates for the stabilization of economy and the reduction of unemployment due to nominal wage rigidity (Mankiw 2002).

Wages is regarded as the compensation that an employer gives to the employee as a return for his labor. Yet, economists separate wages in nominal and real. Nominal wages is measured in money. Real wages is the one adjusted on inflation. Real wages are received by the deflator of nominal wages index based on the consumer price index. Real wages is a guide for how the cost of living has changed.

Information related to wages' level is essential in evaluating the standard of living, labor conditions and life of employees. Given that nominal wages fail to explain the purchasing power of employees, real wages is considered an important index of purchasing power and can be used as proxy for income level. Fluctuations on the real wages rate have significant consequences on poverty and income distribution. When used in relation to other economic variables, for instance employment or output, it is a valuable measure in the analysis of business cycles. (Malik and Ahmed 2000).

Literature supports that wages' rise positively affects labor productivity with the reduction on labor positions. Furthermore, the empirical literature claims that wage increase influences labor productivity positively by reducing the number of jobs. Moreover, the empirical literature shows the direction of causality that variables can have between them. For example, the theory of wage efficiency claims that causality runs from wages to productivity from wages to productivity whereas marginal productivity theory argues that causality runs from productivity to wages. There are also two more theoretical views for the causal relationship between productivity and inflation. The first argues that causality runs from productivity towards inflation and the second that causality runs from inflation to productivity.

Bulgaria and Romania have similar routes on the transition and integration of EU structures. However, they differ on the economy size, on some features connected with industrialization and on different macroeconomic evolution due to different options on monetary policy. The differences on monetary policies applied on Bulgaria and Romania respectively, have impact on the economic and political system on these countries. (Nenovsky et al. 2013). The monetary and fiscal policies that Bulgaria applied, led the economic activity to the private sector. The policy applied by the Central Bank of Romania was the accumulation of public deficit.

Despite the differences in monetary and fiscal policies, the accession of Bulgaria and Romania in EU had the same positive impact on the realization of economic growth, which is driven by private consumption, investment activities, exports' growth and unemployment reduction. This fiscal discipline allows for tax cuts aiming at investments' attraction and the reduction of taxes on the population. The average rate of economic growth for Bulgaria and Romania is 6% on average each year. The favorable economic situation on EU affects positively the development of Romania and Bulgaria from 2006 until 2008. Investments which are an integral part of the strategy of economic development, were 20-30% of GDP for Bulgaria for 2005-2008 and almost 10% of GDP for Romania for the years 2004-2008. Economic crisis stops the trend of economic development on the two countries.

Despite the crisis, Bulgaria's GDP was 1.28% on 2013, 1.55% on 2014 and 2.97% on 2015. For Romania, GDP increased by 3.5% on 2013 thanks to exports of industrial production while this increase was 2.96% on 2014 and 3.74% on 2015. The main sources of the Romanian economic growth were industrial activity, agriculture and construction. The purchasing power of Bulgaria has increased in combination with low inflation. Inflation on Bulgaria was 0.9% for 2013, -1.4% for 2014 and -0.1% for 2015 while for Romania was 4% for 2013, 1.08% for 2014 and -0.6% for 2015. Moreover, the decline of interest rate improves credit conditions. On the contrary, in Romania wages on public sector have frozen for several years.

In empirical literature there are many studies that analyze the relationship between labor productivity and wages, and also between labor productivity and inflation. However, there are few studies that examine the relationship among labor productivity, real wages and inflation and fewer that are focused on less developed countries.

This paper examines the interconnections among labor productivity, real wages and inflation on two countries of European Union, Bulgaria and Romania for the period 1991 until 2014 using the ARDL technique for cointegration of variables and Toda and Yamamoto technique for causality testing. This paper is important for two reasons. No other study has been conducted with reference to the relationship of the examined variables for the two countries. Secondly, there is no other study that examines these variables using the above methodology for developing countries.

The results of the paper show a long-run relationship between real wages and labor productivity on both countries, as well as between inflation and productivity. Moreover, real wages have larger effect on productivity rather than inflation on both examined countries. There is a unidirectional causal relationship between inflation and wages for Bulgaria and unidirectional causal relationship between wages and productivity for Romania. The results of this paper provide some policy implications. Central Banks on both countries can considerably contribute to productivity, hence to long run development controlling inflation and keeping interest rates in low levels. Moreover, the attraction of foreign direct investment and rapid absorption of European funds will help in the increase of productivity and development.

This paper is structured as follows. Section 2 is a brief overview of the empirical literature. Section 3 describes data and methodology. Section 4 presents the empirical results. Finally, Section 5 provides conclusions and policy implications.

## 2.0    Literature review

The relationship between labor productivity and wages and also labor productivity and inflation has drawn the attention of many researchers. The literature is being surrounded by a number of empirical tests on a data group corresponding to the above variables.

### 2.1    Inflation and productivity

During the last decades, there are many studies that examined the relationship between inflation and productivity. The findings from these studies are mixed. Some have found out a negative relationship between inflation and productivity (see Buck and Fitzroy 1988, De Gregorio 1992, Christopoulos and Tsionas, 2005, Barsden et al. 2007, Narayan and Smyth 2009). According to Barsden et al. (2007), inflation reduced the motives for labor and leads companies to insufficient investment plans, influences capital amortization coefficients and causes changes in the preferences of production techniques. Christopoulos and Tsionas (2005) support that inflation shrinks tax reductions for amortization resulting in price increase of capital leasing, cutting down productivity growth.

However, other papers have established that there is no important relationship between inflation and productivity (see Cameron et al.1996, Hondroyiannis and Papapetrou, 1998, Freeman and Yerger 2000). These studies that have been conducted, as far as the causal relationship between inflation and productivity is concerned, show ambiguous results. For example, Freeman and Yerger (2000) claim that there is a unidirectional causal relationship running from exogenous productivity to inflation. Many authors have claimed that the correlation between inflation and productivity is false due to cyclical movements between two variables. (see Hondroyiannis and Papapetrou, 1998, Freeman and Yerger 1998).

Recent studies examine the long-run relationship between productivity and inflation using unit root and cointegration techniques (see Mehra, 2000, Christopoulos and Tsionas 2005). For example, the study of Mehra (2000) concluded that the relationship between inflation and productivity is bidirectional in a long run basis. Finally, there is a number of studies claiming that a rise in inflation rate could adversely affect productivity.

### 2.2    Real wages and productivity

The positive relationship between real wages and labor productivity is well anchored in economic theory. According to the efficiency of economic theory, a rise on real wages can cause higher labor productivity with a higher opportunity cost of job loss. In a macroeconomic level, a rise of real wages will raise the unit of labor cost, thus causing substitution from labor to capital. The labor substitution from capital could increase the marginal labor productivity (see Wakeford, 2004). On the other hand, we can say that a positive relationship between real wages and labor productivity show that higher real wages increase the opportunity cost of job loss and strengthens the labor effort in order to avoid dismissal. Finally, the relationship between real wages and labor productivity is based on the fact that larger capital stocks will raise demand, thus raising real wages and stimulating labor productivity. Several studies have established the positive relationship between real wages and labor productivity (see Erenburg 1998, Hsu, 2005, Mora et al. 2005, Klein 2012).

## 2.3    Inflation, real wages and productivity

All the above relationships have been merged aiming at empirical results on several studies. Mehra (1991) examined the relationship between inflation, productivity and adjusted wage and found out that long run inflation has a positive effect per unit labor costs. Hondroyiannis and Papapetrou (1997) examined the relationship among inflation, productivity and wages in Greece for the period 1975-1992. On their results, they found that inflation has a negative influence on productivity while there is no clear impact for wages on productivity. Strauss and Wohar (2004) examine the long-run relationship between price wages and productivity in a group of 459 manufacturing industries of USA for the period 1956-1996. Using cointegration technique on panel data they found out that long run relationship among variables is valid for many industries not for all of them. However, Granger causality showed a bilateral relationship between real wages and productivity.

Narayan and Smyth (2009) employ cointegration techniques on panel data in order to examine the relationships between inflation, real wages and productivity of G7 countries during the period 1960-2004. The results of their paper showed a positive relationship between real wages and productivity but there is no important relationship between productivity and inflation. Kumar et al. (2009) analyzed the relationship between real wages, inflation and labor productivity for Australian data for the period 1965-2007 using cointegration technique and Granger causality. The results of this paper confirmed that a 1% increase of wages has driven to an increase of productivity between 0.5% and 0.8% with the presence of a structural break on 1985. The relationship between inflation and productivity showed a restricted statistical significance. Finally, Yildirim (2015) examined the relationships between productivity, real wages and inflation for a Turkish manufacturing industry using quarterly data for the period 1988-2012. Using cointegration technique and Granger causality he presented that inflation has larger influence on labor productivity rather than real wages. Moreover, Granger causality test showed that there is a strong bilateral relationship between labor productivity and inflation.

Other related studies are those of Hall (1986) and Alexander (1993) that proved inflation, real wages and productivity have a cointegrating relationship for United Kingdom, with an implication that higher wage rates stimulate labor productivity via the efficiency wage argument. Gunay et al. (2005) examined the relationship among inflation, real wages and profit margins over twenty-nine Turkish manufacturing sub-sectors during 1980-1996. They ascertained that profit margins are influenced by real wage costs and price inflation positively and in a significant level. Wakeford (2004) examining the relationship among labor productivity, unemployment and wages for South Africa, found a long- term equilibrium between real wages and productivity.

Mahadevan and Asafu- Adjaye (2006) study the relationship between inflation, productivity and money supply in nine Asian countries showing a bi-directional relationship between inflation and productivity. Sonmez- Atesoglu and Smithin (2006) examined the relationship among productivity, real wages and economic growth of G7 countries from 1960-2002. On their findings, they argue that an explicit inflation-targeting policy is not likely to be a desirable monetary policy rule.

## 3.0    Data and methodology

### 3.1    Data

According to theoretical and empirical literature, labor productivity depends on real wages and inflation. This paper uses annual data from 1991 until 2014 from labor productivity (proxied by real values added per worker). Productivity represents average labor productivity (production index/employment index). Real wages (proxied by real salaries and wages paid for the manufacturing sector) are obtained by deflating the nominal wage index with the CPI deflator. Inflation rate (proxied by the growth of the consumer price index) represents the growth of the CPI deflator. Data were obtained from the International Financial Statistics (IFS). All data used in the study are in logarithmic form. This transformation was made to minimize heteroscedasticity problems (see Gujarati 2004).

### 3.2    Unit root tests

Our first aim is to investigate the order of integration on series data. The test of series order will lead us to use the most suitable test for series cointegration. In order to find the integration order of series, we use the Dickey-Fuller (ADF) (1979, 1981) and Phillips-Perron (PP) (1988) tests.

### 3.3    Cointegration tests

Following Kumar et al. (2012), we specify the production function as follows:

$$PR_t = \beta_0 + \beta_1 W_t + \beta_2 CPI_t + e_t \tag{1}$$

where $PR_t$ is the labor productivity, $W_t$ is the real wages, $CPI_t$ is the price levels and $e_t$ is white noise. The coefficient of $\beta_1$ of real wages shows the labor's productivity elasticity in relation to real wages and is expected to be positive. The coefficient $\beta_2$ of inflation shows labor's productivity elasticity and is expected to be negative. Logarithmic transformation of the above equation would leave the basic equation as follows:

$$\ln PR_t = \beta_0 + \beta_1 \ln W_t + \beta_2 \ln CPI_t + e_t \tag{2}$$

For the long run relationship between the series on equation (2) there is a number of tests. The most popular tests of an equation for the cointegration of a group of series integrated order I(1) are the tests of Engle-Granger (1987) and Phillips-Ouliaris (1990) named as residuals tests. Also, there is Johansen methodology (1988, 1991) which is referred to a system's equations of the series and uses the method of maximum likelihood.

Recently, in most empirical studies we find the Autoregressive Distributed Lag ARDL cointegration test, developed by Pesaran et al (2001). The basic advantages of ARDL test in relation to other tests are the following:
1. It has more power when the size of the sample is small (see Pesaran et al. 2001).
2. It can be used on series which are not integrated same order as long as there are no series second order I(2). (see Pesaran et al. 2001).
3. It allows series to have different optimal lags.
4. It uses just one single equation.

ARDL (p,$q_1$,$q_2$) test presupposes the estimation on the following unrestricted error correction model:

$$\Delta y_t = \beta_0 + \sum_{i=1}^{p} \beta_i \Delta y_{t-i} + \sum_{j=0}^{q_1} \gamma_j \Delta x_{1t-j} + \sum_{k=0}^{q_2} \delta_k \Delta x_{2t-k} + \varphi_0 y_{t-1} + \varphi_1 x_{1t-1} + \varphi_2 x_{2t-1} + e_t \tag{3}$$

where p,$q_1$,$q_2$ is the order of lags on the variables $y_{t-i}$, $x_{1t-j}$ and $x_{2t-k}$ respectively.

ARDL (p,$q_1$,$q_2$) procedure consists the following steps:

This test uses F distribution and the null of non-cointegration of series as follows:
$$H_0 : \varphi_0 = \varphi_1 = \varphi_2 = 0 \text{ (No cointegration of series).}$$

against the alternative of cointegration of series.
$$H_1 : \varphi_0 \neq \varphi_1 \neq \varphi_2 \neq 0 \text{ (series cointegration).}$$

The asymptotic critical values are provided by Pesaran et al. (2001). An important issue in applying the bounds testing procedure is the selection of the lags (p,$q_1$,$q_2$). The maximum lag length is selected based on the minimum value of Akaike (AIC), Schwarz (SBC), Hannan-Quinn (HQC) criteria.

If bounds test lead us to series cointegration, we can estimate the long run relationship of series from equation (4) as well as the restricted error correction model from equation (5).

$$y_t = \alpha_0 + \alpha_1 x_{1t} + \alpha_2 x_{2t} + u_t \tag{4}$$

$$\Delta y_t = \beta_0 + \sum_{i=1}^{p} \beta_i \Delta y_{t-i} + \sum_{j=0}^{q_1} \gamma_j \Delta x_{1t-j} + \sum_{k=0}^{q_2} \delta_k \Delta x_{2t-k} + \vartheta z_{t-1} + e_t \tag{5}$$

where p,$q_1$,$q_2$ is the order of lags on the variables $y_{t-i}$, $x_{1t-j}$, and $x_{2t-k}$ respectively, the term $z_t$ is the error term created by the cointegrating regression (equation 4).

## 3.4    Causality analysis

On this section we examine the causal relationship between labor productivity, real wages and inflation using the seemingly unrelated regression model with three variables. Toda and Yamamoto (1995), in order to investigate the causality they developed a method based on the estimation of an augmented VAR model ($k+d_{max}$). VAR causality model of Toda and Yamamoto is being formed as follows:

$$y_t = \mu_0 + \left( \sum_{i=1}^{k} \alpha_{1t} y_{t-i} + \sum_{i=k+1}^{d_{max}} \alpha_{2t} y_{t-i} \right) + \left( \sum_{i=1}^{k} \beta_{1t} x_{t-i} + \sum_{i=k+1}^{d_{max}} \beta_{2t} x_{t-i} \right) + \varepsilon_{1t} \tag{6}$$

$$x_t = \varphi_0 + \left( \sum_{i=1}^{k} \gamma_{1t} x_{t-i} + \sum_{i=k+1}^{d_{max}} \gamma_{2t} x_{t-i} \right) + \left( \sum_{i=1}^{k} \delta_{1t} y_{t-i} + \sum_{i=k+1}^{d_{max}} \delta_{2t} y_{t-i} \right) + \varepsilon_{2t} \tag{7}$$

where k is the optimal time lag on the initial VAR model and $d_{max}$ is the maximum integration order on VAR model variables.

The null hypothesis of no causality is defined for every equation on VAR model. For example, variable $x_t$ will cause variable $y_t$ ($x_t => y_t$) when $\beta_{1t} \neq 0, \forall i$. Toda and Yamamoto test for the no Granger causality can be performed for every integration order of the variables either they are cointegrated or not, given that the inverse roots of autoregressive (AR) characteristic polynomial should be inside of the unit circle, in order the above test to be valid.

## 4.0 Empirical results

In the empirical analysis, we use annual data for the period 1991-2014 related to labor productivity, real wages and inflation for both countries. We start with series stationarity on both countries.

## 4.1 Unit root tests

The results of Dickey-Fuller (ADF) (1979, 1981) and Phillips-Perron (PP) (1988) test are presented on table 1.

| Table 1: Unit root tests | | | | |
|---|---|---|---|---|
| Variable | ADF | | | P-P |
| | C | C,T | C | C,T |
| Bulgaria | | | | |
| lnPRB | -0.796(0) | -1.771(0) | -0.859[2] | -1.738[1] |
| ΔlnPRB | -5.496(0)* | -5.415(0)* | -5.494[1]* | -5.414[1]* |
| lnWB | -2.953(2)*** | -1.483(1) | -5.554[5]* | -1.285[4] |
| ΔlnWB | -3.134(1)** | -4.344(1)* | -3.158[4]** | -4.186[8]* |
| lnCPIB | -14.911(5)* | -1.492(0) | -3.197[1]** | -1.495[2] |
| ΔlnCPIB | -3.138(0)** | -3.215(1)*** | -3.138[0]** | -3.913[2]** |
| Romania | | | | |
| lnPRR | 0.050(0) | -2.385(4) | -0.093[2] | -1.931[2] |
| ΔlnPRR | -3.557(0)* | -3.434(0)*** | -3.591[2]* | -3.474[2]*** |
| lnWR | -1.470(0) | -2.131(2) | -1.670[2] | -2.618[2] |
| ΔlnWR | -4.981(0)* | -4.967(0)* | -4.919[2]* | -4.924[2]* |
| lnCPIR | -5.303(2)* | -2.308(4) | -37.562[22]* | -15.406[22]* |
| ΔlnCPIR | -2.046(4) | -8.091(5)* | -2.448[11] | -3.017[21] |

Notes:
1. *, ** and *** show significant at 1%, 5% and 10% levels respectively.
2. The numbers within parentheses followed by ADF statistics represent the lag length of the dependent variable used to obtain white noise residuals.
3. The lag lengths for ADF equation were selected using Schwarz Information Criterion (SIC).
4. Mackinnon (1996) critical value for rejection of hypothesis of unit root applied.
5. The numbers within brackets followed by PP statistics represent the bandwidth selected based on Newey West (1994) method using Bartlett Kernel.
6. C=Constant, T=Trend, Δ=First Differences.

The results of table 1 show that other series are integrated order null I(0) and other first order I(1) for both countries. Therefore, the methodology we can use for cointegration test is that of ARDL (Autoregressive Distributed Lags).

## 4.2    ARDL bounds testing approach

From model (3) we find the maximum values for lags p, $q_1$ and $q_2$, using Final Prediction Error (FPE), Akaike Information Criterion (AIC), Schwarz Information Criterion (SIC), Hannan-Quinn Criterion (HQC), and Likelihood Ratio (LR) criteria. The results of these criteria are presented on table 2.

**Table 2:** VAR lag order selection criteria

| Lag | LogL | LR | FPE | AIC | SBC | HQC |
|---|---|---|---|---|---|---|
| Bulgaria | | | | | | |
| 0 | 48.034 | NA* | 0.0007 | -4.424 | -4.126* | -4.374 |
| 1 | 49.173 | 1.439 | 0.0007* | -0.439* | -4.091 | -4.380* |
| 2 | 49.174 | 0.001 | 0.0008 | -4.334 | -3.936 | -4.266 |
| 3 | 49.185 | 0.011 | 0.0009 | -4.230 | -3.782 | -4.154 |
| 4 | 49.186 | 0.000 | 0.0010 | -4.124 | -3.627 | -4.040 |
| Romania | | | | | | |
| 0 | 44.876 | NA* | 0.0011 | -3.909 | -3.644 | -3.914 |
| 1 | 44.927 | 0.063 | 0.0010* | -4.092* | -3.794* | -4.041* |
| 2 | 45.085 | 0.183 | 0.0012 | -3.903 | -3.506 | -3.836 |
| 3 | 46.751 | 1.753 | 0.0011 | -3.973 | -3.526 | -3.898 |
| 4 | 46.769 | 0.017 | 0.0013 | -3.870 | -3.373 | -3.786 |

Notes: *denotes the optimal lag selection

Most of the criteria show that the maximum number of lags for series 1 on both countries. The order of optimal lag length on equation (3) is chosen from the smallest value of AIC, SBC and HQC criteria. On table 3 we present the results on these criteria.

**Table 3:** Order of optimal lags ARDL($p,q_1,q_2$)

| ARDL($p,q_1,q_2$) | AIC | SBC | HQC |
|---|---|---|---|
| Bulgaria | | | |
| (p=1, $q_1$=0, $q_2$=0)* | **-4.65** | **-4.31** | **-4.57** |
| (p=1. $q_1$=1, $q_2$=0) | -4.54 | -4.19 | -4.46 |
| (p=1, $q_1$=0, $q_2$=1) | -4.63 | -4.28 | -4.55 |
| (p=1, $q_1$=1, $q_2$=1) | -4.54 | -4.19 | -4.46 |
| Romania | | | |
| (p=1, $q_1$=0, $q_2$=0)* | **-3.98** | **-3.64** | **-3.90** |
| (p=1. $q_1$=1, $q_2$=0) | -3.21 | -2.87 | -3.13 |
| (p=1, $q_1$=0, $q_2$=1) | -3.92 | -3.57 | -3.84 |
| (p=1, $q_1$=1, $q_2$=1) | -3.04 | -2.69 | -2.96 |

Notes: *denotes the optimal lag selection, Statistics in bold denote the value of the minimized AIC, SBC and HQC.

Results on table 3 show that ARDL model ($p,q_1,q_2$) with lags p=1 $q_1$=0 and $q_2$=0 is the best for both countries. Afterward, we conduct independence test of the errors (LM test) until first order (maximum number of lags). The following table presents the above test.

**Table 4:** Errors independence test (LM Test)

| Bulgaria | |
|---|---|
| F-stat =0.086 | Prob. F(1,14)=0.773 |
| N*R²=0.134 | Prob. X²(1)=0.134 |
| Romania | |
| F-stat =0.060 | Prob. F(1,14)=0.809 |
| N*R²=0.094 | Prob. X²(1)=0.758 |

Notes: N=observations.

The results on table 4 introduce that errors are not autocorrelated. We continue testing for dynamic stability of ARDL (1,0,0) test for both countries. This test is conducting with the unit cycle. If inverse roots of equation (3) are inside the cycle, then the model is characterized as dynamically stable.

The results of diagram 1 show that there is a dynamic stability of the models on both countries. Before continuing with the bounds test we introduce the actual and fitted residuals from ARDL (1,0,0) on both countries which is the unrestricted error correction model.

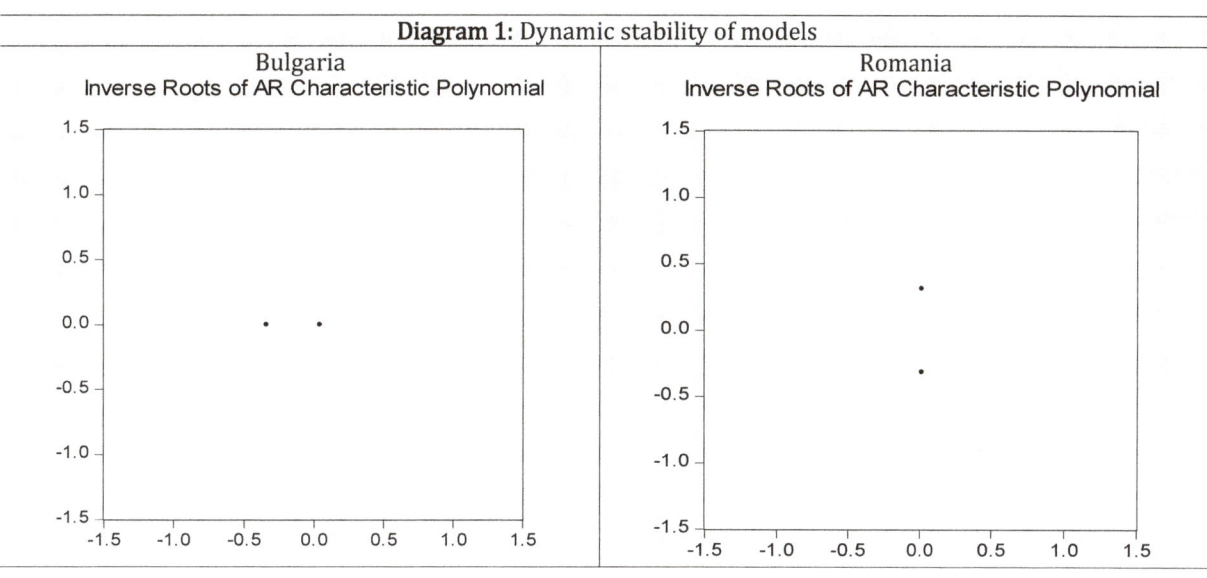

**Diagram 1:** Dynamic stability of models

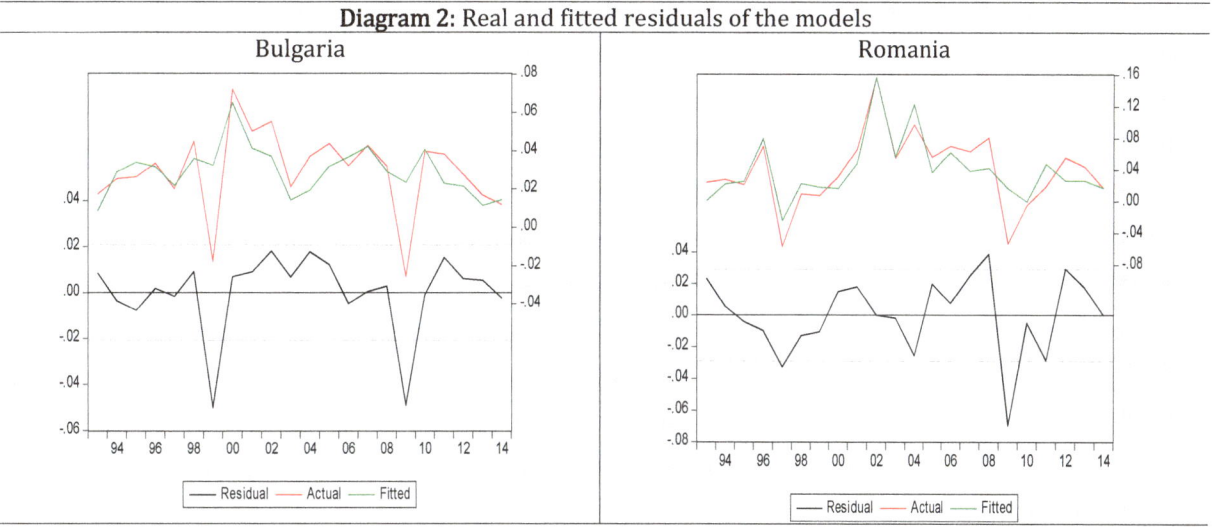

**Diagram 2:** Real and fitted residuals of the models

Afterwards, we continue with cointegration test of the bounds on autoregressive distributed lag. In other words, we test if coefficients $\varphi_0$, $\varphi_1$ and $\varphi_2$ of the model (3) are zero on the estimated models.

| Test Statistic | Value | df | Probability |
|---|---|---|---|
| **Table 5:** Bounds test (wald test) | | | |
| Bulgaria | | | |
| F-statistic | 4.415* | (2,15) | 0.094 |
| Chi-square | 4.830 | (2) | 0.089 |
| Romania | | | |
| F-statistic | 4.590* | (2,15) | 0.091 |
| Chi-square | 5.180 | (2) | 0.087 |

Notes: Table CI (iii) on page 300 of Pesaran et al. 2001 give lower and upper bounds for 10%, 5% and 1% levels of significance [3.17, 4.14], [3.79, 4.85] and [5.15, 6.36] respectively. *, ** and *** show significant at 1%, 5% and 10% levels respectively.

The results of the above table show that the value of F-statistic for both countries is larger from the upper bound of Pesaran et al. (2001) table, for 10% level of significance (see Pesaran et al. 2001, p.300) for (k+1)=3 variables. So, we can say that there is cointegrated relationship between examined series on both countries for 10% level of significance.

On the following table the results from the estimation of unrestricted error correction model (equation 3) are presented for both countries.

**Table 6:** Estimation of unrestricted error correction model

Dependent variable = $\Delta \ln PR_t$

Short run analysis

Bulgaria                                                    Romania

| Variables | Coeffic. | t-statistic | Variables | Coeffic. | t-statistic |
|---|---|---|---|---|---|
| Constant | -4.417 | -1.586 | Constant | -0.127 | -0.127 |
| $\Delta \ln PRB_{t-1}$ | -0.272 | -1.874 | $\Delta \ln PRR_{t-1}$ | 0.021 | 2.147 |
| $\Delta \ln WB_t$ | 1.205 | 1.948 | $\Delta \ln WR_t$ | 0.995 | 4.192 |
| $\Delta \ln CPIB_t$ | -0.006 | -1.610 | $\Delta \ln CPIR_t$ | -0.049 | -2.051 |
| $\ln PRB_{t-1}$ | -0.235 | -2.029 | $\ln PRR_{t-1}$ | -0.144 | -2.041 |
| $\ln WB_{t-1}$ | 0.340 | 1.973 | $\ln WR_{t-1}$ | 0.185 | 1.509 |
| $\ln CPIB_{t-1}$ | -0.003 | -2.508 | $\ln CPIR_{t-1}$ | -0.009 | 2.481 |
| $R^2$ | 0.346 | | $R^2$ | 0.727 | |
| F-stat | 1.326 | | F-stat | 6.667 | |
| D-W | 2.050 | | D-W | 2.045 | |
| Diagnostic Test | $X^2$ | Prob. | Diagnostic Test | $X^2$ | Prob. |
| Normalily | 5.217 (2) | 0.102 | Normality | 4.217 (2) | 0.121 |
| Serial Corr. | 0.094 (1) | 0.758 | Serial Corr. | 0.094 (1) | 0.758 |
| ARCH | 0.302 (1) | 0.582 | ARCH | 0.302 (1) | 0.582 |

Notes. ***, ** and * show significant at 1%, 5% and 10% levels respectively. $\Delta$ denotes the first difference operator, $X^2$ Normal is for normality test, $X^2$ Serial for LM serial correlation test, $X^2$ ARCH for autoregressive conditional heteroskedasticity, () is the order of diagnostic tests.

The results on table 6 show that both statistic and diagnostic tests are quite satisfying. Before move on to the next step, we find the long-run results from the unrestricted error correction model equation (3).
For Bulgaria we get:

$$-\left(\frac{LWB}{LPRB}\right) = -\left(\frac{0.340}{-0.235}\right) = 1.45 \qquad -\left(\frac{LCPIB}{LPRB}\right) = -\left(\frac{-0.003}{-0.235}\right) = -0.013$$

For Romania we get:

$$-\left(\frac{LWR}{LPRR}\right) = -\left(\frac{0.185}{-0.144}\right) = 1.28 \qquad -\left(\frac{LCPIR}{LPRR}\right) = -\left(\frac{-0.009}{-0.144}\right) = -0.062$$

Thus, we can say that an increase of 1% on wages, will bring an increase on labor productivity by 1.45% in Bulgaria and by 1.28% in Romania. Furthermore, an increase in inflation by 1% will reduce labor productivity by 0.013% in Bulgaria and by 0.062% in Romania.

We estimate the long and short run relationship of the series on equations (4) and (5).

**Table 7:** Estimation of the long and short run relationship

Dependent variable = $\ln PR_t$

Long run analysis

Bulgaria                                                    Romania

| Variables | Coeffic. | t-statistic | Variables | Coeffic. | t-statistic |
|---|---|---|---|---|---|
| Constant | -21.832 | -10.521 | Constant | -6.169 | -8.658 |
| $\ln WB_t$ | 5.954 | 12.483 | $\ln WR_t$ | 2.437 | 14.156 |
| $\ln CPIB_t$ | -0.040 | -3.620 | $\ln CPIR_t$ | 0.117 | 19.406 |
| $R^2$ | 0.961 | | $R^2$ | 0.967 | |
| F-stat | 262.251 | | F-stat | 308.224 | |
| D-W | 0.903 | | D-W | 1.263 | |
| Diagnostic Test | $X^2$ | Prob. | Diagnostic Test | $X^2$ | Prob. |
| Normality | 1.456 (2) | 0.482 | Normality | 0.348 (2) | 0.839 |
| Serial Corr. | 5.757 (1) | 0.016 | Serial Corr. | 2.915(1) | 0.087 |
| ARCH | 0.613 (1) | 0.433 | ARCH | 1.287(1) | 0.256 |
| White | 1.968 (5) | 0.853 | White | 3.049(5) | 0.692 |

| Dependent variable = $\Delta \ln PR_t$ | | | | | |
|---|---|---|---|---|---|
| Short run analysis | | | | | |
| Bulgaria | | | Romania | | |
| Variables | Coeffic. | t-statistic | Variables | Coeffic. | t-statistic |
| Constant | 0.031 | 3.704 | Constant | 0.043 | 3.704 |
| $\Delta \ln PRB_{t-1}$ | -0.257 | -1.237 | $\Delta \ln PRR_{t-1}$ | -0.165 | -1.024 |
| $\Delta \ln WB_t$ | 1.215 | 1.835 | $\Delta \ln WR_t$ | 1.249 | 5.142 |
| $\Delta \ln CPIB_t$ | -0.011 | -1.621 | $\Delta \ln CPIR_t$ | -0.019 | -1.674 |
| $ECM_{t-1}$ | -0.227 | -2.024 | $ECM_{t-1}$ | -0.306 | -1.923 |
| $R^2$ | 0.293 | | $R^2$ | 0.684 | |
| F-stat | 1.764 | | F-stat | 8.665 | |
| D-W | 1.964 | | D-W | 1.892 | |
| Diagnostic Test | $X^2$ | Prob. | Diagnostic Test | $X^2$ | Prob. |
| Normalily | 11.35 (2) | 0.03 | Normality | 2.568 (2) | 0.276 |
| Serial Corr. | 0.047 (1) | 0.827 | Serial Corr. | 0.095 (1) | 0.757 |
| ARCH | 0.352 (1) | 0.552 | ARCH | 0.009 (1) | 0.922 |
| White | 6.012 (14) | 0.966 | White | 10.99 (14) | 0.686 |

Notes: ***, ** and * show significant at 1%, 5% and 10% levels respectively. $\Delta$ denotes the first difference operator, $X^2$ Normal is for normality test, $X^2$ Serial for LM serial correlation test, $X^2$ ARCH for autoregressive conditional heteroskedasticity, and $X^2$ White for white heteroskedasticity . ( ) is the order of diagnostic tests.

The results on table 7 show that both statistic and diagnostic tests are quite satisfying. The unrestricted dynamic error correction model derived from ARDL bounds test within a simple linear transformation, incorporates the short run dynamic with long run equilibrium. The negative and statistically significant estimation of the coefficients on error correction model $ECM_{t-1}$ on equation (5) show a long run relationship between variables on the examined model.

On the following figures (3) and (4) we examine the dynamic stability of the unrestricted error correction model with Brown et al. tests (1975).

**Figure 3:** Plot of cumulative sum of recursive residuals

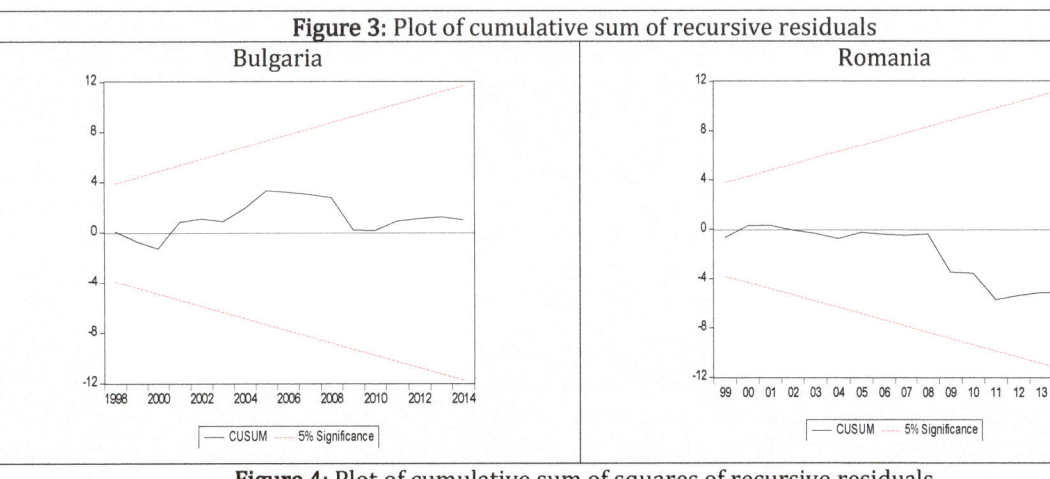

**Figure 4:** Plot of cumulative sum of squares of recursive residuals

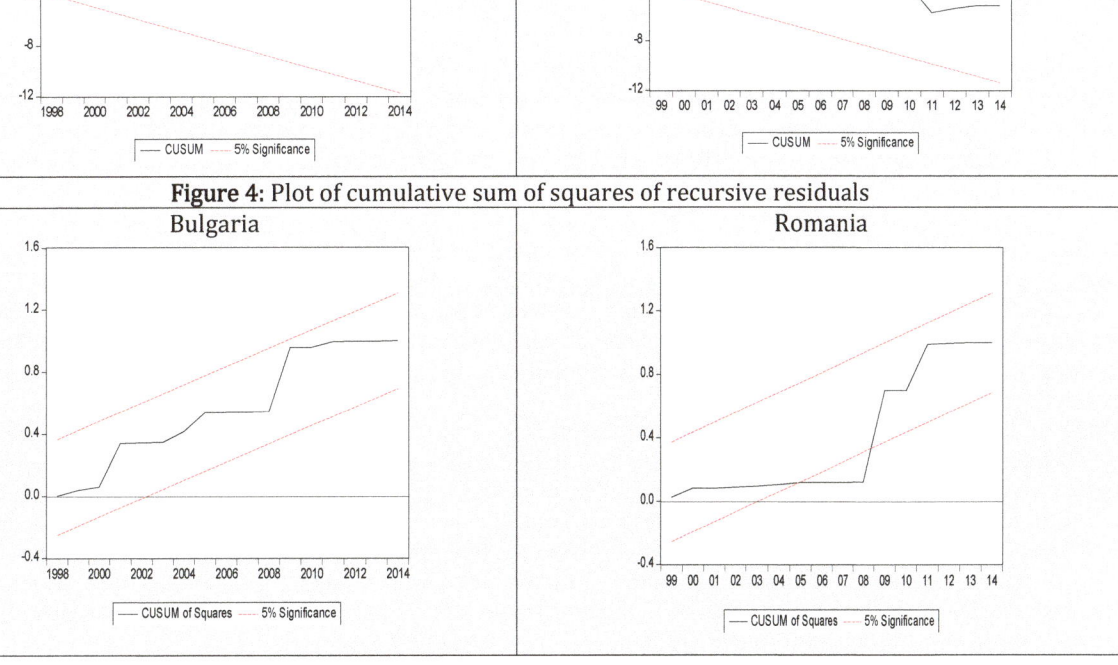

From the above figures we can see that Bulgaria has stable coefficients intertemporal on the examined model, contrary to Romania whose coefficients are unstable (figure 4).

## 4.3    Toda –Yamamoto causality test

Table 8 presents the results of causality test of Toda and Yamamoto according to equations 6 and 7.

| Table 8: Toda and Yamamoto no-causality test | | | | | |
|---|---|---|---|---|---|
| Excluded | Lag(k) | Lag(k+dmax) | Chi-sq | Prob. | Direction of Causality |
| **Bulgaria** | | | | | |
| Dependent variable: LPRB | | | | | |
| LWB | 1 | 1+1 | 1.629 | 0.442 | LWB # LPRB |
| LCPIB | 1 | 1+1 | 0.297 | 0.861 | LCPIB # LPRB |
| Dependent variable: LWB | | | | | |
| LPRB | 1 | 1+1 | 4.373 | 0.112 | LPRB # LWB |
| LCPIB | 1 | 1+1 | 5.024* | 0.081 | LCPIB => LWB |
| Dependent variable: LCPIB | | | | | |
| LPRB | 1 | 1+1 | 2.090 | 0.351 | LPRB # LCPIB |
| LWB | 1 | 1+1 | 2.716 | 0.257 | LWB # LCPIB |
| **Romania** | | | | | |
| Dependent variable: LPRR | | | | | |
| LWR | 1 | 1+1 | 1.961 | 0.375 | LWR =>LPRR |
| LCPIR | 1 | 1+1 | 0.116 | 0.943 | LCPIR # LPRR |
| Dependent variable: LWR | | | | | |
| LPRR | 1 | 1+1 | 5.770** | 0.055 | LPRR # LWR |
| LCPIR | 1 | 1+1 | 1.424 | 0.490 | LCPIR # LWR |
| Dependent variable: LCPIR | | | | | |
| LPRR | 1 | 1+1 | 1.580 | 0.453 | LPRR # LCPIR |
| LWR | 1 | 1+1 | 1.663 | 0.435 | LWR # LCPIR |

Notes: The (k+dmax ) denotes VAR order. The lag length selection was based on LR: sequential modified LR test statistic (each test at 5% level), FPE: Final prediction error, AIC: Akaike information criterion, SC: Schwarz information criterion, HQ: Hannan-Quinn information criterion. ***, ** and * denotes 1% and 5%, 10% significance level, respectively.  => denotes one - way causality, # denotes not causality.  EViews 9.0 was used for all computations.

The results on table 8 show that there is a unidirectional causal relationship between inflation and real wages for Bulgaria with direction from inflation to real wages. For Romania there is a unidirectional causal relationship between real wages and labor productivity with direction from real wages to labor productivity.

## 5.0    Conclusion and policy implications

This paper expands the literature as far as the relationship between productivity, inflation and real wages in concerned in two countries of EU, Bulgaria and Romania. The aim is to improve the knowledge of these variables due to their complexity and interrelation between them. According to Kumar et al (2012), the analysis of this mutual connection can provide policy directions for productivity improvement, inflation testing and consumption strengthening.

In this paper for the relationship among labor productivity, real wages and inflation in two countries of EU, we use Pesaran et al (2001) cointegration as well as the Toda and Yamamoto (1995) methodology for the causal relationship of the examined variables. Cointegration results show a weak relationship for both countries among the three variables that we examine when labor productivity is dealing as the endogenous variable. Moreover, cointegration results showed that real wages and inflation cause productivity in a long run basis. Also, causality results showed that there is a unidirectional causal relationship from inflation to wages for Bulgaria and from wages to labor productivity for Romania (this result is in accordance with various studies such as Kumar et al (2009) and Yildirim (2015). Thus, the theory of wage efficiency in Romania is confirmed. The lack of causality among real wages and labor productivity for Bulgaria can be explained not only by macroeconomic but also by institutional factors. These factors tend to create a wedge between two variables in the short or long run (Bentolila and Saint-Paul, 2003). Inflation's influence on real wages in Bulgaria has been documented both in theoretical and empirical literature. It is well known that, in the short run, inflation's reduction increase real income and can also increase real wages temporarily. However, in the long run, real wages are not influenced by inflation because real wages depend upon productivity's increase and employees negotiating power.

From a macroeconomic perspective, the most serious risk for economic development in Bulgaria is low consumption. However, in periods of weak domestic demand the Bulgarian economy has been able to partly compensate this low consumption with higher net exports. The decline of FDI entries in Bulgaria can be stimulated by the improvement of EU Structural Funds absorption rate. The continuation of the reform process, in Romania, is necessary particularly on the fiscal consolidation process, based on the preventive financing agreement contracted with EU and IMF. This agreement can bring coherence to the macroeconomic and financial policies, thus adding to the consolidation of investors' confidence and preserving the macroeconomic and fiscal stability.

Finally, if Bulgaria and Romania achieve a higher level of utilization of EU funds, they will be able to reduce the economic gap with the Central European EU states. In the long run, Bulgaria and Romania have a long road ahead in terms of improving their still low absorption capacity. To achieve that, they need to significantly reduce bureaucracy and introduce more transparent processes of project selection.

# References

Alexander, C. O. (1993). The changing relationship between productivity, wages and unemployment in the UK, *Oxford Bulletin of Economics and Statistics,* 55, 87-102. http://EconPapers.repec.org/RePEc:bla:obuest:v:55:y:1993:i:1:p:87-102.

Bardsen, G., Hurn, S. and Mchugh, Z. (2007). Modeling wages and prices in Australia. *The Economic Record,* 83, 143-158. doi: 10.1111/j.1475-4932.2007. 00390.x.

Bentolila, S. and Saint-Paul, G.(2003). Explaining movements in the labor share, *The B.E. Journal of Macroeconomics*, 3(1), 1103-1103.

Buck, A. J. and Fitzroy, F. (1988) Inflation and productivity growth in the federal republic of Germany, *Journal of Post Keynesian Economics*, 10(3), 428–444. http://www.jstor.org/stable/4538085?origin=pubexport (text/html).

Brown, R.L., Durbin, J., Ewans, J.M., (1975). Techniques for testing the constance of regression relations overtime. *Journal of the Royal Statistical Society.* 37(2), 149–172. http://www.jstor.org/stable/2984889.

Cameron, N., Hum, D. and Simpson, W. (1996). Stylized facts and stylized illusions: inflation and productivity revisited, *Canadian Journal of Economics*, 29(1), 152–162. doi: 10.2307/136156

Christopolous, D. K., and Tsionas, E. G. (2005). Productivity growth and inflation in Europe: Evidence from panel cointegration tests. *Empirical Economics*, 30(1), 137–150. doi: 10.1007/s00181-004-0227-3.

De Gregorio, J. (1992) The effects of inflation on economic growth: lessons from Latin America, *European Economic Review*, 36(2-3), 417–425. doi:10.1016/ 0014-2921(92)90098-H.

Dickey, D., and Fuller, W.A. (1979). Distribution of the estimates for autoregressive time series with a unit root. *Journal of the American Statistical Association* 74(366), 427-431.doi: 10.2307/2286348.

Dickey, D., and Fuller, W.A. (1981). Likelihood ratio statistics for autoregressive time series with a unit root. *Econometrica,* 49(4), 1057-1072. doi: 10.2307/ 1912517.

Engle, R.F., and Granger, C.W.J. (1987). Co-integration and error-correction: representation, estimation and testing. *Econometrica,* 55(2): 251-276. http://links.jstor.org/sici?sici=00129682%28198703%2955%3A2% 3C251%3ACAECRE%3E2.0.CO%3B2-T.

Erenburg, S. J. (1998). Productivity, private and public capital and real wage in the US, *Applied Economics Letters*, 5(8), 491–495. http://www.informaworld.com/ openurl?genre=article& ... 40C6AD35DC6213A474B5 (text/html).

Freeman, D. G. and Yerger, D. B. (1998). Inflation and multifactor productivity growth in Germany: a response to Smyth, *Applied Economics Letters*, 5(5), 271–274.http://www.informaworld.com/openurl?genre=article& 40C6AD35DC6213A474B5 (text/html).

Freeman, D. G. and Yerger, D. B. (2000). Does inflation lower productivity? Time series evidence on the impact of inflation on labour productivity in 12 OECD nations, *Atlanta Economic Journal*, 28(3), 315–332. doi: 10.1007/BF02298324.

Gujarati, D.N. (2004). (Fourth Edition). Basic econometric, New York: The McGraw-Hill companies Inc.

Gunay, A., Metin-Ozcan, K. and Yeldan, E. (2005) Real wages, profit margins and inflation in Turkish manufacturing under post liberalization, *Applied Economics*, 37(16), 1899–1905. http://www.tandfonline.com/doi/abs/ 10.1080/00036840500217903 (text/html).

Hall S. G. (1986) An application of the Granger and Engle two-step estimation procedure to United Kingdom aggregate wage data, *Oxford Bulletin of Economics and Statistics,* 48(3), 229-239. http://EconPapers.repec.org/ RePEc: bla:obuest:v:48:y:1986:i:3:p:229-39.

Hondroyiannis, G. and Papapetrou, E. (1997). Seasonality cointegration and the inflation, productivity and wage growth relationship in Greece, *Social Science Journal*, 34(2), 235–247.doi:10.1016/S0362-3319(97)90053-7.

Hondroyiannis, G. and Papapetrou, E. (1998). Temporal causality and the inflation-productivity relationship: evidence from eight low inflation OECD countries, *International Review of Economics and Finance*, 7(1), 117–135. http:// EconPapers.repec.org/RePEc:eee:reveco:v:7:y:1998:i:1:p:117-135.

Hsu, P. F. (2005) Inter-industry wage premiums and industry-specific productivity in Taiwan, *Applied Economics*, 37(13), 1523–33. doi: https:// doi.org/ 10.1080/ 00036840500118861.

Johansen, S. (1988). Statistical analysis of cointegration vectors. *Journal of Economic Dynamics and Control*, 12(2-3), 231–254. doi:10.1016/0165-1889(88)90041-3.

Johansen, S. (1991). Estimation and hypothesis testing of cointegration vectors in Gaussian vector autoregressive models, *Econometrica*, 59(6), 1551 -1580.doi: 10.2307/2938278.

Klein, N. (2012). Real wage, labor productivity, and employment trends in South Africa: A closer look, IMF Working Paper, WP/12/92.

Kumar, S. (2009) Structural breaks and exports in Philippines, *Global Economy Journal*, 9(2), 1-9. http://www.degruyter.com/view/j/gej.2009.9.2/gej.2 ... .1504.xml?format =INT (text/html).

Kumar, S., Webber, D. J., and Perry, G. (2012). Real wages, inflation and labor productivity in Australia. *Applied Economics*, 44(23), 2945–2954. http://dx.doi.org/ 10.1080/00036846.2011.568405.

Krugman, P.R.(1994). The age of diminished expectations (Cambridge: MIT Press, 1994).

MacKinnon, J.G. (1996). Numerical distribution functions for unit root and cointegration tests. *Journal of Applied Econometrics*, 11(6), 601-618. doi: 10.1002/(SICI)1099-1255(199611)11:6<601::AID-JAE417>3.0.CO;2-T.

Mahadevan, R. and Asafu-Adjaye, J. (2006) Is there a case for low inflation-induced productivity growth in selected Asian economies?, *Contemporary Economic Policy*, 24(2), 249–261. doi: 10.1093/cep/byj018.

Mankiw, N. G. (2002). *"Macroeconomics" (5th ed.). Worth.* measurement of inflation is discussed in chapter 2, 22–32, Money growth and Inflation in chapter 4, 81–107, Keynesian business cycles and inflation in chapter 9, 238–255.

Malik, A., and Ahmed, A. M. (2000). The relationship between real wages and output:Evidence from Pakistan, *The Pakistan Development Review*, 39(4), 1111-1126.

Mehra, Y. P. (1991). Wage growth and the inflation process: An empirical note, *American Economic Review*, 81(4), 931-937. http://links.jstor.org/sici?sici =0002-8282%2819910 0%3B2-U&origin=repec full text (application/pdf).

Mehra, Y. P. (2000). Wage-price dynamics: are they consistent with cost-push?, *Federal Reserve Bank of Richmond Economic Quarterly*, 86(3), 27–43.

Mora, T., Lopez-Tamayo, J. and Surinach, J. (2005). Are wages and productivity converging simultaneously in euro-area countries?, *Applied Economics*, 37(17), 2001–2008.http://dx.doi.org/10.1080/000368405002 17655.

Narayan, P. K., and R. Smyth (2009). The effect of inflation and real wages on productivity: New evidence from a panel of G7 countries. *Applied Economics* 41 (10), 1285–1291.http://dx.doi.org/10.1080/000368407015 37810.

Nenovsky, N., Tochkov K, C.Turcu, (2013). Politiques monétaires et integration européenne. Le cas de deux pays des Balkans, *Revue d'études comparatives Est-Ouest*, 44(2), 141-162.

Newey, W.K. and K.D.West (1994). Automatic lag selection in covariance matrix estimation, *Review of Economic Studies*, 61(4), 631-653.http://hdl.handle.net/ 10.2307/2297912 (application/pdf).

Pesaran, M. H., Shin, Y., and Smith, R. J. (2001). Bounds testing approaches to the analysis of level relationships. *Journal of Applied Econometrics*, 16(3), 289–326. doi: 10.1002/jae.616.

Phillips, P.C., and Perron, P. (1988). Testing for a unit root in time series regression. *Biometrika*, 75(2), 335-346. doi: 10.1093/biomet/75.2.335.

Phillips, P. C., and Ouliaris, S. (1990). Asymptotic properties of residual base tests for cointegration, *Econometrica*, 58(1), 165-193. http://www.jstor.org/stable/ 2938339.

Sonmez, H, Atesoglu and J. Smithin (2006). Inflation targeting in a simple macroeconomic model, *Journal of Post Keynesian Economics*, 28(4), 673-688. http://mesharpe. metapress.com/link.asp?target=contribution& id=ARK3DEPE0EVYDF5W.

Strauss, J., and Wohar, M. (2004). The linkage between prices, wages and labour productivity: A panel study of manufacturing industries. *Southern Economic Journal*, 70(4), 920–941. doi: 10.2307/4135280.

Tang, C. F. (2014). The effect of real wages and inflation on labour productivity in Malaysia. *International Review of Applied Economics*, 28(3), 311-322.http://hdl.handle.net /10.1080/02692171.2013.872084.

Tang, J. and W. Wang (2004). Sources of aggregate labour productivity growth in Canada and the United States, *The Canadian Journal of Economics* 37(2), 421-444. doi: 10.1111/j.0008-4085.2004.00009.x.

Toda, H.Y. and Yamamoto (1995). Statistical inference in vector autoregressions with possibly integrated processes. *Journal of Econometrics*, 66(1-2), 225-250. http://dx.doi. org /10.1016/0304-4076(94)01616-8.

Wakeford, J. (2004). The productivity-wage relationship in South Africa: An empirical investigation. *Development Southern Africa*, 21(1), 109–132. http://www.tandfonline.com/doi/abs/10.1080/037683 5042000181444.

Yildirim, Z. (2015). Relationships among labour productivity, real wages and inflation in Turkey. *Economic Research-Ekonomska Istraživanja*,28(1), 85–103.http://dx.doi.org /10.1080/1331677X.2015.1022401.

# 21

# Chinese born global firms and international entrepreneurial mechanism[x]

Junjie Zhang [ab*], Rongyao Cheng [a], Weibin Wang [b]

[a] Xuri Business School, Donghua University, 200051, Shanghai, China.
[b] Business School, Jiaxing University, Jiaxing 314001, China.
*Corresponding author's email address: junjiezhanguk@163.com

| ARTICLE INFO | ABSTRACT |
|---|---|
| Keywords:<br>Global firms;<br>International entrepreneurship;<br>Overseas market opportunity. | This paper explores Chinese-born global firms' entrepreneurial mechanism and development mode from multi-theoretical perspectives using company case studies. The findings suggest that for Chinese born global firms, overseas market opportunity's recognition and exploitation is the starting point and catalyst for their establishment and growth, while global resources integration is growing mode for their continuous development. Results suggest that overseas market knowledge and organization learning are the bases for Chinese born global firms to cultivate and maintain sustainable competitive advantages after they have entered international markets. |

## 1.0    Introduction

China's growing international integration into the world economy and its outward foreign direct investment especially in astounding cross-border M&A activities such as TCL's acquisition of French Thomson in 2003, Lenovo's acquisition of IBM PC business unit in 2005 and Geely a obscure Chinese private-owned automobile company's acquisition of world famous car brand Volvo in 2010 have attracted many international business scholars' great attention, while beneath that high-visibility media coverage about M&A activities undertaken by Chinese giant corporations with long histories, a large number of Chinese small and medium enterprises have also emerged to embark on international expansion journey, some even targeted international markets as a primary source of sales from their inception or very shortly after company's foundation, which are termed as "Born Global or International new venture" in academic field which belong to cross discipline of international business and entrepreneurship research put forwarded by Oviatt and McDougall in their milestone paper named *toward theories of international new ventures.* (Oviatt and McDougall, 1994)

In that paper, they have used two companies in United States (LASA Industries, Inc and IXI Limited) as case studies to indicate that new venture's internationalization phenomenon which was neglected in past research. They described: "LASA Industries, Inc., which sold an unusually efficient microprocessor prototyping technology, is representative of these international new ventures formed within the past decade. Its founders were American, Swiss and French. Its funding was European. The operational headquarters and R&D were in the United States,

---

[x] The paper is co-supported by Zhejiang provincial soft science project (2016C25012) and grants of philosophy and social sciences planning projects of Zhejiang province (17NDJC093YB) and (13NDJC052YB).

while marketing was managed from France and finance from Switzerland. Manufacturing was centered in Scotland, and initial sales were in France and the United States". "IXI Limited, a British venture that became a leading supplier of desktop windowing computer software for UNIX operating systems, violated the usual expectation that firms begin with sales in their home country and later sell to foreign countries. When Anderson (a British company founder) started IXI, his strategy was to target the United States first, Japan second, and then move back into the United Kingdom." (Oviatt and McDougall, 1994).

Although lots of research on this new breed of enterprises can be found in extant literature, most of them are conducted under western developed countries' context. The paper tries to assess the validity of western born global theories by applying them to Chinese context since in practice; there is also a large amount of small and medium Chinese firms internationalize very rapidly at the inception or very shortly after company's foundation. For example, Chinese ZhanXun Telecommunication Company specializing in wireless telecommunication and multi-media end core CPU, customized software and reference design platform's development was founded in the year 2001. From its initial inception, company's founding team immediately took advantages of global talents, favored governmental policies and technological superiority in different locations of the world to boost ZhanXun Company's internationalization development. The company has set up R&D centers and subsidiaries in Silicon Valley, Austin, and Chinese Taibei. In 2007, the company was listed on NASDAQ stock exchange, in 2008, ZhanXun Company acquired American Quorum Company to further its international expansion. Another Chinese case company was Sun-Tec Corporation which is specialized in solar energy generating products manufacturing and research. In 2001, the company's founder Dr. Zhengrong Shi returned China to set up Sun-Tech Corporation with his accumulated rich knowledge and experiences in photovoltaic industry studied in Australia. At the beginning of company's development, Sun-Tech succeeds in expanding into the European market by focusing on German market rather than following gradual domestic market to overseas market process. Currently, Sun-Tech takes important sales percentage in European and North American, Middle Eastern, and South eastern Asian market, while single European market has occupied 90% of sales in Sun-Tech Corporation.

Therefore, two intertwined and step-up questions should be seriously taken account into: How can Chinese born-global firms involve international activities in their early stages? How do Chinese born-global firms utilize global resources they can access to evolve and compete with formidable established MNCs?

Traditional international business theories reckoned that enterprises tend to expand into international markets after they have gradually developed well in domestic markets. Among traditional theories, Johanson and Vahlne (1977)'s Uppsala mode seems the most persuasive one. However, as economic globalization and information technologies' fast development; the global business environment has undergone fundamental changes. Since the 1990s, lots of small firms had successfully implemented international expansion just after firms' foundation or in a very short period of inception; those firms are featured with clear globalization mindset at the beginning, innovative, customized, flexible technology and product design which can rapidly make an adjustment to meet niche customer needs. (Madsen, Servais, 1997) That phenomenon is not constrained to only some western developed countries but is also widely existed in other parts of the world such as Middle East, Asia, and South Pacific regions. In China, as the pace of firms' internationalization quickens, a bundle of high-technology firms targeted international markets when they were just established, and they have successfully realized a high degree of internationalization of capital, technology, human resources and markets in a very short time. Although those firms are very small, they have successfully survived and competed in international markets, and they also constitute important drivers for China's industry structure upgrading and innovative country's construction, and they are also playing increasingly important role in realizing mass entrepreneurship and innovation strategy advocated by the Chinese government in 2014.

The paper tries to explore Chinese-born global firms' international entrepreneurial mechanism and development modes through several representative case studies analyses.

## 2.0    Characteristics and motives of born global companies

### 2.1    Definition of born global company

In 1994, Oviatt and McDougall published their seminal paper named *toward theories of international new ventures,* that paper is widely cited by researchers in the field, they defined international new venture as "a business organization that, from inception, seeks to derive significant competitive advantage from the use of resources and the sale of outputs in multiple countries" (Oviatt and McDougall, 1994). In the paper, the authors also classify those firms into export/import start-up, multinational trader, geographically focused start-up, and global start-up types. Then Knight and Madsen & Servais reckoned that born global is "firms less than 20 years old that internationalized on average within three years of founding and generate at least 25 percent of total sales from abroad." (Knight, Madsen & Servais, 2004). Loustarinen & Gabrielsson (2006) defined global ventures as the firms that "have usually first started to internationalize their operations and, on top of that, have entered global markets, deriving most of their income (over 50%) from non-domestic continents." (Luostarinen & Gabrielsson, 2006)

## 2.2 Some distinctive features of born global firms

Lots of scholars have summarized distinctive features of born global firms, they believe that majority of born global firms are highly technology oriented, lots of cases from western countries support that born global firms are always firms that own some specific leading edge technology, some of them originate from universities' technical departments and incubators, they are the outcomes of some technological inventions being transferred into commercial usage.

Studies in the field also indicate that more born global firms engage in B2B markets (Business to Business) than in B2C markets (Business to Customer), since number of customers in B2B markets are much smaller than B2C markets, which make it easier for born global firms to serve their business customers with relatively lower cost of marketing and distribution.

Born global firms tend to focus on niche markets rather than commodity markets, due to their limitations in resources and capabilities, it is impossible for them to serve a wide range of customers in industries, some specific kind of customers with specific needs seem more viable for them. Gassmann & Keupp even proposed "the extent, to which the firm can take a specialized position in international value chains, to be one of the factors that enable an early and rapid internationalization of SMEs" (Gassmann & Keupp, 2007).

Mort & Weerawardena (2006), Freeman et al. (2006), Bell et al. (2003) deemed that networking is playing very important role in born global firms' survival and growth in international markets. As mentioned above, born global firms are constrained by resources and capabilities' limitation, thus, networking become viable channels for born global firms to integrate and leverage resources and capabilities externally, they use "vertical and horizontal network relations to rapidly gain access to international markets, to the partners' marketing infrastructure and capabilities" (Coviello & Munro, 1995), and "to overcome resource limitations related to product development" (Coviello & Munro, 1997).

Autio believed that absent of embedded organizational routines is the source of born global firms' competitive advantages over some long-established big companies. (Autio et al., 2000) Embedded organization routines sometimes play negative roles in renewing companies' old structure and obsolete business model, thanks to deficiency of those embedded organization routines, born global firms can cultivate innovative and entrepreneurial corporate culture faced with fewer impediments than long-established companies, which is crucial for firms' accelerated internationalization.

Thus, born global firms are featured with inherent entrepreneurial and innovative elements from the beginning, Knight & Cavusgil argued "international entrepreneurial orientation reflects the firm's overall innovativeness and proactiveness in the pursuit of international markets. It is associated with innovativeness, managerial vision, and proactive competitive posture. A posture that is innovative, visionary, and proactive may be necessary amongst a class of firms that, in the face of relatively limited resources, takes the initiative to pursue new opportunities in complex markets, typically fraught with uncertainty and risk." (Knight, Madsen & Servais, 2004)

The researchers have not only explored the features of born global firms as complete organization, they have also shed their research attention on the characteristics of born global firms founders, they state that most of the founders have strong entrepreneurial drive, international mindset, and good networking capabilities, some of them also have high level of education, experiences of working for international business in MNCs.

## 2.3 Motives of born-global firms

A very important question must be asked is that why born global firms can embark on internationalization journey in the strikingly short period after inception although they do not own substantial resources and advantages comparing with long-established MNCs. According to prior research, the motives behind can be probed into from three perspectives.

### 2.3.1 Entrepreneur is individual perspective

The entrepreneur's individual perspective attempts to seek the forming and growth factors of born global firms from individual entrepreneur aspect, they stressed entrepreneur's overseas experience and knowledge, international aptitude and categories' influences on the growth of born global firms. Oviatt and McDougall analyzed the different characteristics between born global firms and domestic new firms in the foundation, they found that entrepreneur's global mindset and overseas experience are key driving forces to determine the international entrepreneurship. Harveston et al. deemed that managers of born global firms are featured with higher global orientation, risk tolerance and richer international experience comparing with managers in traditional firms which tend to follow gradual stage mode in international expansion.

### 2.3.2    Enterprise-level perspective

Enterprise-level perspective analyzes the born global firms' distinctive features which differentiate from other enterprises. Autio, et al.'s research indicate that most of the born global firms are knowledge-intensive firms because knowledge intensity has amplifying effects on internationalization: in new environment, firms which rely on knowledge's creation and exploitation to cultivate competitive advantages are doing better in adaptive learning than firms which are mainly dependent on physical resources; knowledge, especially explicit knowledge is transferable resource, knowledge's internal fluidity enable it to combine with firms' fixed costs such as manufacturing resources and distribution channels at lower cost. Thus, knowledgeable new ventures are more flexibly in taking advantages of international markets opportunities than firms dependent on physical resources. Knight and Cavusgil (1996) have paid more attention to the innovative culture of born global firms; they considered that born global firms are more international market-oriented in strategy; they focus on developing capabilities needed for internationalization from inception.

### 2.3.3    External environment perspective

Research in that perspective boils down to the emergence and growth of born global firms into the changes of external environment. Madsen and Servais (1997) thought that comparing with countries endowed with large domestic markets, countries with narrow domestic markets will push new ventures to actively expand into overseas markets. McDougall and Oviatt (1994) pointed out that international trade's liberalization, technology advancement of IT, especially the advent of the internet make firms more viable to connect with customers, distributors, and suppliers worldwide, which become the catalyst of born global firms. Other scholars sum the born global firms' Advent up to the results of multi-factors' combination effects: the function of a niche market; development of processing and communication technology; inherent advantages such as flexibility of SMEs; availability of international tools and formation of global networks.

### 3.0    Chinese-born global companies case studies

Since China's open door policy are still relatively short in time comparing with Western developed countries, the quantity of Chinese-born global firms may be smaller than their counterparts, which determine that large quantity research approach may be not very viable due to its requirement for a large amount of research samples. Thus, the paper selects case studies as a research approach, which is in accord with most research approaches in the field. Because the research aim of case studies is to induce relevant theory rather than frequency calculation, so the selection of case studies does not need to follow sampling rule but ensure case studies are special and typical enough. Of course, under the correct circumstances, multiple case studies approach will be more effective to extract theories and form a better structure for research.

### 3.1    Individual case study

The paper selects three Chinese new established small and medium firms with international sales as case studies. The reasons for choosing those three companies are based on following consideration: firstly, internationalization activities should be occurred within three years after firms' foundation. Anderson and Wictor (2003) defined born global firm as "percentage of overseas sales exceed 25% in the first three years after company's foundation." Above all three firms actively enter international markets within three years after their foundation, they just skip and accelerate traditional internationalization development path which evolves according to "local markets-regional market-national market–international markets." Second issue is about company's internationalization mode, although Andersson, etc. applies quantitative criteria, their definition doesn't take entry mode into consideration, we argue that a firm can not be regarded as truly international company if it relies on export as only overseas market entry mode although its overseas sales take high proportion among whole sales revenues. The case companies the paper has selected all undertake a higher level of entry modes such as cross-border merger and acquisition, establishing wholly owned subsidiaries in foreign markets besides export. Through applying higher commitment of entry modes, those companies seek location advantages and acquire efficiencies from business operating worldwide. The third issue is that those companies realize their fast growth thanks to internationalization activities. Theories on born global firms need to not only answer the question of how newly established firms go global but also to explore how newly established firms expand into overseas markets under complicated international business environment.

## Case study one: Company A

Company A was established in 1993 in Tsingtao city, Shandong province of China; the company developed its patent glass product in 1994, and it expanded into American market very rapidly in 1995. During company's 20 years development history, its overseas markets expanded very quickly, its products and brand are recognized by a large number of foreign customers. In 2005, company's total sales revenue reached about RMB 1600 million, among them, 95% of sales revenue come from the overseas market. The company's products are widely sold and distributed among world's 110 countries and districts, directly serve more than 1500 clients globally. Especially in European and American markets, one in four families use company's products, after the success of overseas markets expansion, Company turns back to develop domestic markets, which immeasurably contrast with traditional firms' internationalization process.

The founder of Company A recognized the invaluable business opportunity of candle consumption which is prevalent due to western cultural influence when he studied in the United States. According to statistics, glass products like glass candleholder yield not less than $3000 million volume of trade globally. Company A's founder believed that glass products are the last industrial factors China lacks, the company would realize its supernormal development based on glass products. By recognizing and exploiting that business opportunity, company rapidly develop in very short period, till now, company has established business alliances with lots of Fortune 500 companies such as Wal-Mart, Metro, Carrefour, etc. At the same time, Company further its go-global strategy to meet local customers' needs through localized R&D, design, production, and sales. To avoid international trade and technological barriers, Company has set up its subsidiaries, R&D centers, outbound processing plants in many countries of Europe, North America, and Southeast Asia. By that way, Company A's R&D, manufacturing and sales activities are effectively integrated into the global value chain.

## Case study two: Company B

Company B was founded in 2001 by Dr. Zhengrong Shi who has been committed to photovoltaic industry for a long time, In 1999, He got his Ph.D. Degree in photovoltaic products research in Australia, then he chose to return China to set up his own company in 2001, thanks to his Ph.D. supervisor's reputation in the field, company B entered German markets in 2002, then the company gradually expanded its business into other countries in Western European countries. Due to European countries environmental protection bill's compulsory implementation, solar energy photovoltaic industry gradually develops into a seller's market, which makes supplying of company products' is not adequate for the market demand. Under that environment, Company B further strengthen its international marketing networks, the company formulates its marketing strategy of extending to other countries in Europe, Australia, United States and Asia Southeastern countries through centering on the German market. Company B has become a recognizable brand in the international photovoltaic industry, according to international authoritative photovoltaic industry magazine Photon international's statistics, the solar energy cell production capabilities of company B was ranked No. 8 in 2005 and Top 3 in 2006.

On 14th Dec 2005, company B was listed in American New York Stock Exchange, which made the company the first non-state-owned high technology firm which was listed in New York Stock Exchange. Till 2007, the NYSE value of company B reached $5000 million, which was the highest among Chinese private firms, while Dr. Zhengrong Shi's personal wealth also reached $2340 million. Transforming from an unknown overseas scientist to one of richest guys in China, Zhengrong Shi only takes six years, which become the most rapidly growth case among China's entrepreneurial histories.

## Case study three: Company C

Company C was founded by several returned Chinese Silicon Valley scientists in 1999 under the proposition and support from national information industry ministry, the company headquartered in Beijing Zhongguan Village which aspires to become China's Silicon Valley. Contrast to traditional company's domestic market-overseas market internationalization path, company targets overseas market at the beginning of its foundation. In 2000, company C set up a subsidiary in American Silicon Valley, in 2002, company C set up a subsidiary in Hong Kong to strengthen its overseas marketing efforts.

Company C has dedicated to developing advanced digital multi-media technology, going through two years painstaking efforts; the company launched its Chips with whole independent intellectual property rights in international markets in Sep. 2001, which demonstrated that a private company only took two years to expand into intensely competitive international markets, its internationalization pace has surprised lots of its competitors. Company's chips are widely adopted by international reputable electronics companies such as Samsung, Philips, and HP, etc. It occupies about 60% market share in computer image input chips at the moment.

## 3.2    Cross case studies analysis

### 3.2.1    International entrepreneurship opportunity is recognition and exploitation

According to different entrepreneurial motives, entrepreneurial activities can be divided into opportunity-pull and poverty-push entrepreneurial activities. Under Opportunity-pull perspective, entrepreneurs are mainly attracted by markets opportunities in contrast to compelling due to poverty in poverty-push perspective. As a new entrepreneurial mode of globalization epoch, born global firms' foundation and growth are featured with distinct opportunity-pull entrepreneurial activities characteristics, they focus more on utilizing various resources to exploit unknown business opportunities rather than compelled by poverty. In above three case studies, all founders of Company A, Company B and Company C and the founding team have a higher level of education, they all had enviable jobs before setting up their own business, why did they give up those stable and enviable job and choose to set up their company with risks? The main reason is that they all have discovered and recognized business opportunities from international markets.

When Company A's founder studied in the United States, he just noticed that candle related glass products have great business potential in Western countries, while all production factors related to glass products are prevalent and inexpensive in China, by connecting inexpensive China's manufacturing capabilities with customized R&D and marketing capabilities in western countries, company succeed in achieving rapid international expansion in just very short time.

In Company B's case, due to the cost of photovoltaic electricity generating system is much higher than market's mainstream electricity generating system, so its market expansion is closely related to host countries' government policies, since the year 2003, European countries had forcefully implemented environmental protection bills, which made low carbon solar energy an ideal government supported electricity generating alternative, by that reason, company B ushered in a rare opportunity, and the solar energy photovoltaic industry gradually evolved into a seller's market.

In Company C's case, the company is proactively involved in the cutting edge technological transferring trend from western developed countries to Asian countries especially China, which endows Chinese domestic high-tech companies invaluable opportunity to develop their innovative core technology and commercialize those technologies. Although western countries are advantageous in leading technologies and mature fund raising system, China is also endowed with growing market economic environment, large increasing domestic demand, comparatively lower cost of human capital and innovative technologies which are greatly valued and supported by Chinese government, all of which provide domestic firms with fantastic development opportunity and environment.

### 3.2.2    Global resources and knowledge is integration

To newly established ventures with very constrained resources, the crucial question of internationalization activities not lie in how to fully elaborate and exploit their extant resources and capabilities, but how to acquire, accumulate external resources from external environment for further growth with a better, faster, and more effective approach. In the foundation and development process of Company A, not only domestic industrial resources and low-cost production capabilities were fully exploited, but external networking opportunities such as distribution channels of international giant supermarkets such as Wal-Mart, Carrefour are leveraged. In Company B's case, its founder utilized every network resource in the solar photovoltaic industry he was able to access at the beginning of firm's foundation. To enter developed countries market, company B's founder asked his Ph.D. supervisor Martin Green to help him in product introduction, his colleagues in Australia Pacific solar energy research center were invited to do market research. In start-up capital aspect, the company was also substantially supported by China's local municipal government's state-owned enterprises funds. In target market aspect, company B was fundamentally European markets oriented. Thus, company B's entrepreneurial path and resource integration approach can be summed up into "Overseas returnee + Overseas advanced technology + International markets + Listed in Overseas stock exchange" mode. At the beginning of Company C's start-up, it established subsidiaries in American Silicon Valley and Austin, the purpose was not only to obtain latest scientific breakthrough information but also demonstrate and distribute company C's cutting edge technological products. Developed technologies, expertise, mature business management and venture capital running industrial factors are widely existed in Silicon Valley, while large markets with great potential, numerous clients, and qualified engineers are available in China. By connecting Silicon Valley's high technology, innovative corporate governance with Chinese markets and manufacturing capabilities, company C grows rapidly, and the overseas market could be expanded in an accelerated way.

### 3.2.3    Entrepreneurial team with rich overseas market experiences

One crucial reason for born global firms to realize their global resources and knowledge integration, successfully recognize and exploit opportunities in overseas market lies in that born global firms are endowed with the entrepreneurial team which has rich overseas market experiences.

The founder of above case companies all once studied or worked in foreign countries. Company A's founder once studied in America and obtained master degree in economics there, he also worked four years in a local American company; Company B's founder once studied in Australian University of New South Wales, and was supervised by "Father of solar energy", 2002 Nobel Environmental Prize winner Professor Martin Green, when he completed his Ph.D. studies in Australia UNSW, he worked as senior manager and Scientist in Australian Pacific solar energy electricity company, Ltd. In Company C's case, the entrepreneurial team was formed up of about 45 overseas returnees, most of them once studied in top universities in western developed countries and worked for reputable companies in Silicon Valley.

Thus, those entrepreneurs with overseas education background, overseas working and living experiences have demonstrated intensified global mindset and internationalization tendency, international experiences and overseas knowledge which they have obtained before setting up their companies enabled them to reduce risks and exploring costs in international markets expansion effectively, and by that reason, those newly established Chinese companies managed to conduct their internationalization activities very shortly after foundation.

### 3.2.4    Born global firms are more advantageous than traditional firms in learning

Comparing with large Multinational Corporation with a long history, newly established firms which are less constrained by routine and traditions are more advantageous in learning especially under new international business environment. Born global firms are much simpler in corporate organization structure, managers and employees from company's different departments have more opportunities to communicate and discuss with each other, and those intimate interactions would enable tacit knowledge to be shared throughout the company. The reason why Company C manage to realize series of technological heavy weight innovation and breakthrough lies in that the company benefits a lot from knowledge sharing platform which was set up by those entrepreneurial returnees from Silicon Valley, most of them had rich work experiences in computer chips design when they worked for international famous IT companies in Silicon Valley, they didn't take their experiences and knowledge as top secrets which must be kept carefully but are willing to communicate with each other and encourage employees to learn from the sharing knowledge. Company founder and technological gurus do scientific experiments with employees, they just transfer their cutting edge technologies to those employees who have just graduated from universities in a generous way, that mentoring knowledge sharing method enabled lots of employees who have just graduated from universities to get access to world's most advanced technologies.

Company C also encourages its employees to learn related technologies in other departments apart from their departments, to undertake more challenging technological projects. That mentoring organization learning platform promotes company C to cultivate a technological research and development team which can compete with foreign computer chip design giants; the company combines every excellent resource it can access to produce world's leading technologies and products.

### 4.0    Conclusion

As a new form of internationalized companies, one fundamental question must be asked is that how born global firms are set up. A further question follows is that how those born global firms realize their fast development when they are not endowed with resources advantages and competencies that are widely available in mature multinational corporations? Through above Chinese-born global companies case studies analysis, we found that International entrepreneurship enables Chinese entrepreneurs to perceive and exploit oversea opportunities by taking risks, which become the prerequisite for Chinese born global firms' emergence; international social capital and network relationships serve as intermediaries to make Chinese-born global firms' further growth viable; Chinese-born global firms' ongoing process of internalization also provides firms with newly international knowledge and organizational learning opportunities which are absorbed, assimilated and leveraged by Chinese firms to constitute sustainable competitive advantages.

## References

Andersson S, Wictor I. (2003). Innovative internationalization in new firms: Born globals—The Swedish case. *Journal of International Entrepreneurship,* 1 (3), 249—276. http://dx.doi.org/10.1023/A:1024110806241

Autio E. (2005). Creative tension: The significance of Ben Oviatt and Patricia McDougalls article"toward a theory of international new ventures". *Journal of International Business Studies,* 36(1), 9—19.

Autio E, Sapienza H J, Almeida J G. (2000). Effects of age at entry, knowledge intensity, and imitability on international growth. *Academy of Management Journal,* 43(5), 909—924. http://www.jstor.org/stable/1556419

Dimitratosa P, Jonesh M V. (2005). Future directions for international entrepreneurship research. *International Business Review,* 14 (2), 119—128.

Eisenhardt K. (1989). Building theories from case study research. *Academy of Management Review,* 14 (4), 532—550. http://dx.doi.org/10.5465/AMR.1989.4308385

Gabrielsson, M. and Pelkonen, T. (2008). Born internationals: Market expansion and business operation mode strategies in the digital media field. *Journal of International Entrepreneurship,* 6(2), 49-71. http://dx.doi.org/10.1007/s10843-008-0020-z

Harveston P D, Kedia B L, Davis P S. (2000). Internationalization of born global and gradual globalizing firms: The impact of the manager. *Advances in Competitiveness Research,* 8 (1), 92—99.

Johanson, J., & Vahlne, J.-E. (1977). the internationalization process of the firm: A model of knowledge development and increasing foreign market commitments. *Journal of International Business Studies,* 8(1), 23–32. http://dx.doi.org/10.1057/palgrave.jibs.8490676

Knight G A, Cavusgil S T. (2004). Innovation, organizational capabilities, and the born global firm. *Journal of International Business Studies,* (35), 124—141. http://dx.doi.org/10.1057/palgrave.jibs.8400071

Knight G G, Cavusgil S T. (1996). The born global firm: A challenge to traditional internationalization theory. *Advances in International Marketing,* 8 (1), 11—26.

Kuemmerle W. (1997). Building effective R&D capabilities abroad. *Harvard Business Review,* 75 (Mar/Apr), 61—70.

Madsen T K, Servais P., (1997). The internationalization of born globals: An evolutionary process? International Business Review, 6 (6), 561—583. http://dx.doi.org/10.1016/S0969-593(97)00032-2

McDougall P P, Oviatt B M. (2000). International entrepreneurship: The intersection of two research paths. *Academy of Management Journal,* 43(5), 902—908. http://dx.doi.org/10.2307/1556418

Oviatt B M, McDougall P P. (1994). Toward a theory of international new ventures. *Journal of International Business Studies,* 25 (1), 45—64. http://dx.doi.org/10.1057/palgrave.jibs.8490193

Oviatt B M, McDougall P P. (1995). Global start-ups: Entrepreneurs on a worldwide stage. *Academy of Management Executive,* 9 (2), 30—44. http://www.jstor.org/stable/4165256

Stevenson H H, Jarillo C J., (1990). A paradigm of entrepreneurship: Entrepreneurial management. *Strategic Management Journal,* 11 (5), 17—27. http://dx.doi.org/10.1007/978-3-540-48543-8_7

Weerawardena J, Sullivan GM, Liesch PW, et al. (2007). Conceptualizing accelerated internationalization in the born global firm: A dynamic capabilities perspective. *Journal of World Business,* 42 (3), 294—306. http://dx.doi.org/10.1016/j.jwb.2007.04.004

Yamakawa Y, Peng MW, Deeds D L. (2008). What drives new ventures to internationalize from emerging to developed economies? *Entrepreneurship Theory and Practice,* 32 (1), 59—82. http://dx.doi.org/10.1111/j.1540-6520.2007.00216.x

Zahra S A, Ireland R D, Hitt M A. (2000). International expansion by new venture firms: International diversity, mode of market entry, technological learning, and performance. *Academy of Management Journal,* 43 (5), 925—950. http://dx.doi.org/doi: 10.2307/1556420

# Permissions

All chapters in this book were first published in JEFS, by LAR Center Press; hereby published with permission under the Creative Commons Attribution License or equivalent. Every chapter published in this book has been scrutinized by our experts. Their significance has been extensively debated. The topics covered herein carry significant findings which will fuel the growth of the discipline. They may even be implemented as practical applications or may be referred to as a beginning point for another development.

The contributors of this book come from diverse backgrounds, making this book a truly international effort. This book will bring forth new frontiers with its revolutionizing research information and detailed analysis of the nascent developments around the world.

We would like to thank all the contributing authors for lending their expertise to make the book truly unique. They have played a crucial role in the development of this book. Without their invaluable contributions this book wouldn't have been possible. They have made vital efforts to compile up to date information on the varied aspects of this subject to make this book a valuable addition to the collection of many professionals and students.

This book was conceptualized with the vision of imparting up-to-date information and advanced data in this field. To ensure the same, a matchless editorial board was set up. Every individual on the board went through rigorous rounds of assessment to prove their worth. After which they invested a large part of their time researching and compiling the most relevant data for our readers.

The editorial board has been involved in producing this book since its inception. They have spent rigorous hours researching and exploring the diverse topics which have resulted in the successful publishing of this book. They have passed on their knowledge of decades through this book. To expedite this challenging task, the publisher supported the team at every step. A small team of assistant editors was also appointed to further simplify the editing procedure and attain best results for the readers.

Apart from the editorial board, the designing team has also invested a significant amount of their time in understanding the subject and creating the most relevant covers. They scrutinized every image to scout for the most suitable representation of the subject and create an appropriate cover for the book.

The publishing team has been an ardent support to the editorial, designing and production team. Their endless efforts to recruit the best for this project, has resulted in the accomplishment of this book. They are a veteran in the field of academics and their pool of knowledge is as vast as their experience in printing. Their expertise and guidance has proved useful at every step. Their uncompromising quality standards have made this book an exceptional effort. Their encouragement from time to time has been an inspiration for everyone.

The publisher and the editorial board hope that this book will prove to be a valuable piece of knowledge for researchers, students, practitioners and scholars across the globe.

# List of Contributors

**Azwifaneli Innocentia (Mulaudzi) Nemushungwa**
Department of Economics, University of Venda, South Africa

**Augustine C. Osigwe**
Department of Economics and Development Studies, Federal University, Ikwo, Nigeria

**Kenneth O. Ahamba**
Department of Economics and Development Studies, Federal University, Ikwo, Nigeria

**Onur Sunal**
Başkent University, Department of Banking and Finance, Bağlıca Kampüsü, Ankara-Turkey

**Özge Sezgin Alp**
Başkent University, Department of Accounting and Financial Management, Bağlıca Kampüsü, Ankara-Turkey

**Muhammad Shariat Ullah**
Associate Professor, Department of Management, University of Dhaka, Dhaka 1000, Bangladesh

**Mohammad Thoufiqul Islam**
Associate Professor, Department of Management, University of Dhaka, Dhaka 1000, Bangladesh

**Mohammad Anisur Rahman**
Department of Logistics Management and e-Commerce, Glorious Sun School of Business and Management Donghua University, Shanghai, China
Department of Management Information Systems, University of Dhaka, Bangladesh

**Xu Qib and Md. Tariqul Islam**
Department of Logistics Management and e-Commerce, Glorious Sun School of Business and Management, Donghua University, Shanghai, China

**Yaya Keho**
Ecole Nationale Supérieure de Statistique et d'Economie Appliquée (ENSEA) Abidjan

**Talla M Aldeehani**
Department of Finance & Financial Institutions, College of Business Administration, Kuwait University, Safat 13055, Kuwait

**Slimani Salma , El Abbassi Idriss and Tounsi Said**
Department of Economics, Mohammed V Rabat – Agdal University, Faculty of Juridical, Economic and Social Sciences, Morocco

**Yutaka Kurihara**
Professor, Department of Economics, Aichi University, Japan

**Paul J. Bolster**
CFA, Professor of Finance, D'Amore-McKim School of Business, Northeastern University, Boston, MA 02115

**Emery A. Trahan**
CFA, Senior Associate Dean, D'Amore-McKim School of Business, Northeastern University, Boston, MA 02115

**Pinshuo Wang**
Ph.D. Candidate, Department of Economics, College of Social Studies and Humanities, Northeastern University

**Alex Ng**
Thompson Rivers University, Associate Professor of Finance, British Columbia, Canada

**Raymond A. K. Cox**
Thompson Rivers University, Chair and Professor of Finance, Department of Accounting & Finance, British Columbia, Canada

**Harit Satt**
School of Business Administration, Al Akhawayn University in Ifrane, Morocco

**Bello Lawal**
Glasgow Caledonian University, Scotland, United Kingdom

**John D. Merrifield**
University of Texas at San Antonio College of Business

**Barry W. Poulson**
University of Colorado at Boulder

**Mthokozisi Mlilo**
Lecturer, University of the Witwatersrand; Faculty of Commerce, Law and Management

**Umakrishnan Kollamparambi**
Associate Professor, University of the Witwatersrand; Faculty of Commerce, Law and Management

**Aysegul Ates**
Akdeniz University, Department of Economics, Antalya, Turkey

**Zdzisław W. Puślecki**
Adam Mickiewicz University, Poznań, Faculty of Political Science and Journalism, 61-614 Poznań, Poland

**José Luis Esparza-Aguilar**
Universidad de Quintana Roo. Mexico

**Argentina Soto-Maciel**
Universidad Anahuac, Argentina

**Ma. Isabel De la Garza-Ramos**
Universidad Autónoma de Tamaulipas. Mexico

**Anderson Darrell**
Product Manager, FSharp, 140 E 30th Street, New York City, NY

**Daniel K.N. Johnson**
Schlessman Professor of Economics, Colorado College, CO, 80903

**Chaido Dritsaki**
Associate Professor, Department of Accounting and Finance, Western Macedonia University of Applied Sciences, Kozani, Greece

**Junjie Zhang**
Xuri Business School, Donghua University, 200051, Shanghai, China Business School, Jiaxing University, Jiaxing 314001, China

**Rongyao Cheng**
Xuri Business School, Donghua University, 200051, Shanghai, China

**Weibin Wang**
Business School, Jiaxing University, Jiaxing 314001, China

# Index

Lightning Source UK Ltd.
Milton Keynes UK
UKHW05n0722210518
322900UK00002B/31/P

9 781632 406880